THE ROUTLEDGE COMPANION TO THOUGHT EXPERIMENTS

Thought experiments are a means of imaginative reasoning that lie at the heart of philosophy, from the pre-Socratics to the modern era, and they also play central roles in a range of fields, from physics to politics. *The Routledge Companion to Thought Experiments* is an invaluable guide and reference source to this multifaceted subject. Comprising over 30 chapters by a team of international contributors, the companion covers the following important areas:

- the history of thought experiments, from antiquity up to the trolley problem and quantum non-locality;
- thought experiments in the humanities, arts, and sciences, including ethics, physics, theology, biology, mathematics, economics, and politics;
- theories about the nature of thought experiments;
- new discussions concerning the impact of experimental philosophy, cross-cultural comparison studies, metaphilosophy, computer simulations, idealization, dialectics, cognitive science, the artistic nature of thought experiments, and metaphysical issues.

This broad ranging companion goes backwards through history and sideways across disciplines. It also engages with philosophical perspectives from empiricism, rationalism, naturalism, skepticism, pluralism, contextualism, and neo-Kantianism to phenomenology. This volume will be valuable for anyone studying the methods of philosophy or any discipline that employs thought experiments, as well as anyone interested in the power and limits of the mind.

Michael T. Stuart is a fellow of the Centre for Philosophy of Natural and Social Science, London School of Economics, UK.

Yiftach Fehige is Associate Professor at the Institute for the History and Philosophy of Science and Technology, University of Toronto, Canada.

James Robert Brown is Professor of Philosophy at the University of Toronto, Canada.

ROUTLEDGE PHILOSOPHY COMPANIONS

Routledge Philosophy Companions offer thorough, high quality surveys and assessments of the major topics and periods in philosophy. Covering key problems, themes and thinkers, all entries are specially commissioned for each volume and written by leading scholars in the field. Clear, accessible and carefully edited and organised, *Routledge Philosophy Companions* are indispensable for anyone coming to a major topic or period in philosophy, as well as for the more advanced reader.

Recently published:

The Routledge Companion to Philosophy of Medicine
Edited by Miriam Solomon, Jeremy R. Simon, and Harold Kincaid

The Routledge Companion to Philosophy of Literature
Edited by Noël Carroll and John Gibson

The Routledge Companion to Islamic Philosophy
Edited by Richard C. Taylor and Luis Xavier López-Farjeat

The Routledge Companion to Virtue Ethics
Edited by Lorraine Besser-Jones and Michael Slote

The Routledge Companion to Bioethics
Edited by John Arras, Rebecca Kukla, and Elizabeth Fenton

The Routledge Companion to Hermeneutics
Edited by Jeff Malpas and Hans-Helmuth Gander

The Routledge Companion to Eighteenth Century Philosophy
Edited by Aaron Garrett

The Routledge Companion to Ancient Philosophy
Edited by Frisbee Sheffield and James Warren

The Routledge Companion to Social and Political Philosophy
Edited by Gerald Gaus and Fred D'Agostino

For a full list of published *Routledge Philosophy Companions*, please visit https://www.routledge.com/series/PHILCOMP

THE ROUTLEDGE COMPANION TO THOUGHT EXPERIMENTS

Edited by
Michael T. Stuart, Yiftach Fehige
and James Robert Brown

LONDON AND NEW YORK

First published in 2018
by Routledge
4 Park Square, Milton Park, Abingdon, Oxon OX14 4RN
605 Third Avenue, New York, NY 10017

First issued in paperback 2023

Routledge is an imprint of the Taylor & Francis Group, an informa business

© 2018 selection and editorial matter, Michael T. Stuart, Yiftach Fehige and James Robert Brown; individual chapters, the contributors

The right of Michael T. Stuart, Yiftach Fehige and James Robert Brown to be identified the authors of the editorial material, and of the authors for their individual chapters, has been asserted by them in accordance with sections 77 and 78 of the Copyright, Designs and Patents Act 1988.

All rights reserved. No part of this book may be reprinted or reproduced or utilised in any form or by any electronic, mechanical, or other means, now known or hereafter invented, including photocopying and recording, or in any information storage or retrieval system, without permission in writing from the publishers.

Trademark notice: Product or corporate names may be trademarks or registered trademarks, and are used only for identification and explanation without intent to infringe.

British Library Cataloguing-in-Publication Data
A catalogue record for this book is available from the British Library

Library of Congress Cataloging-in-Publication Data
A catalog record for this book has been requested

ISBN: 978-1-03-256971-0 (pbk)
ISBN: 978-0-415-73508-7 (hbk)
ISBN: 978-1-315-17502-7 (ebk)

DOI: 10.4324/9781315175027

Typeset in Goudy
by Book Now Ltd, London

Publisher's Note
The publisher has gone to great lengths to ensure the quality of this reprint but points out that some imperfections in the original copies may be apparent.

CONTENTS

List of contributors   viii

Thought experiments: state of the art   1
MICHAEL T. STUART, YIFTACH FEHIGE
AND JAMES ROBERT BROWN

PART I
Selected history of thought experiments   29

1. The triple life of ancient thought experiments   31
   KATERINA IERODIAKONOU

2. Thought experiments in Plato   44
   ALEXANDER BECKER

3. Aristotle and thought experiments   57
   KLAUS CORCILIUS

4. Experimental thoughts on thought experiments in medieval Islam   77
   JON McGINNIS

5. Galileo's thought experiments: projective participation
   and the integration of paradoxes   92
   PAOLO PALMIERI

6. Thought experiments in Newton and Leibniz   111
   RICHARD T. W. ARTHUR

7. Thought experiments, epistemology and our cognitive (in)capacities   128
   KENNETH R. WESTPHAL

PART II
Thought experiments and their fields — 151

8 Thought experiments in political philosophy — 153
   NENAD MIŠČEVIĆ

9 Thought experiments in economics — 171
   MARGARET SCHABAS

10 Theology and thought experiments — 183
    YIFTACH FEHIGE

11 Thought experiments in ethics — 195
    GEORG BRUN

12 Happiest thoughts: great thought experiments of modern physics — 211
    KENT A. PEACOCK

13 Thought experiments in biology — 243
    GUILLAUME SCHLAEPFER AND MARCEL WEBER

14 Thought experiments in mathematics — 257
    IRINA STARIKOVA AND MARCUS GIAQUINTO

PART III
Contemporary philosophical approaches to thought experiments — 279

15 The argument view: are thought experiments
    mere picturesque arguments? — 281
    ELKE BRENDEL

16 Platonism and the a priori in thought experiments — 293
    THOMAS GRUNDMANN

17 Cognitive science, mental modeling, and thought experiments — 309
    NANCY J. NERSESSIAN

18 Kantian accounts of thought experiments — 327
    MARCO BUZZONI

19 Phenomenology and thought experiments: thought
    experiments as anticipation pumps — 342
    HARALD A. WILTSCHE

PART IV
Issues, challenges and interactions   367

20 Intuition and its critics   369
STEPHEN STICH AND KEVIN TOBIA

21 Thought experiments and experimental philosophy   385
KIRK LUDWIG

22 Thought experiments in current metaphilosophical debates   406
DANIEL COHNITZ AND SÖREN HÄGGQVIST

23 Historicism and cross-culture comparison   425
JAMES W. McALLISTER

24 A dialectical account of thought experiments   439
JEAN-YVES GOFFI AND SOPHIE ROUX

25 The worst thought experiment   454
JOHN D. NORTON

26 Thought experiments and idealizations   469
JULIAN REISS

27 Thought experiments and simulation experiments: exploring hypothetical worlds   484
JOHANNES LENHARD

28 Images and imagination in thought experiments   498
LETITIA MEYNELL

29 Art and thought experiments   512
DAVID DAVIES

30 How thought experiments increase understanding   526
MICHAEL T. STUART

31 On the identity of thought experiments: thought experiments rethought   545
ALISA BOKULICH AND MÉLANIE FRAPPIER

Index of thought experiments discussed, mentioned or invented in this companion   558
Author–subject index   561

CONTRIBUTORS

Richard T. W. Arthur is a professor of Philosophy at McMaster University. He specializes in early-modern natural philosophy and mathematics, with special attention to Leibniz, Newton and Descartes. His research interests also include the theory of time, the infinite and the epistemology of science, especially thought experiments. He has a book manuscript on Leibniz's theory of substance on the verge of publication and he is currently finishing a book defending the reality of becoming in modern physics. Books include *G. W. Leibniz: The Labyrinth of the Continuum* (2001), *Leibniz* (2014) and *Introduction to Logic* (2017).

Alexander Becker is Professor of Philosophy at the University of Marburg. His interests include philosophy of language, metaphysics, ancient philosophy and aesthetics. On Plato, he has published an introduction to the *Theaetetus* (2008). An introduction to the *Republic* is forthcoming (2017).

Alisa Bokulich is Professor of Philosophy at Boston University and Director of the Center for Philosophy and History of Science, where she organizes the Boston Colloquium for Philosophy of Science. She is an associate member of Harvard University's History of Science Department and a Series Editor for *Boston Studies in the Philosophy and History of Science*. She is author of *Reexamining the Quantum-Classical Relation: Beyond Reductionism and Pluralism*, and her research focuses on scientific models and explanations in the physical sciences, including, more recently, the geosciences.

Elke Brendel is a professor of Philosophy at the University of Bonn, Germany. She has published numerous books and articles on topics in logic, epistemology, philosophy of language, and meta-philosophy. Besides her interest in thought experiments, she has mainly worked on logical and semantic paradoxes, theories of truth and knowledge, epistemic contextualism and relativism, and the semantics of disagreement.

James Robert Brown is a professor of Philosophy at the University of Toronto. His interests include thought experiments, foundational issues in mathematics and physics, visual reasoning, and issues involving science and society, such as the role of commercialization in medical research. His books include *The Rational and the Social* (1989), *The Laboratory of the Mind: Thought Experiments in the Natural Sciences* (1991/2010), *Smoke and Mirrors: How Science Reflects Reality* (1994), *Philosophy of Mathematics: An Introduction to the World of Proofs and Pictures* (1999/2008), *Who Rules in Science: A Guide to the Wars* (2001), *Platonism, Naturalism and Mathematical Knowledge* (2012) and others.

Georg Brun is a research fellow in philosophy at the University of Bern. He has a special interest in methodological issues, particularly in epistemology, argumentation theory, philosophy of logic and metaethics. He is the author of *The Right Formula: Problems of Logical Formalization* (2004 in German) and co-editor of *Epistemology and Emotions* (2008).

Marco Buzzoni is Professor of Philosophy of Science at the University of Macerata and Co-editor of "Epistemologia," a special issue of *Axiomathes*. His main fields of research include Popper's and Kuhn's philosophy of science, science and technology, epistemology and methodology of human and social sciences, thought experiment in the natural sciences, and philosophy of biology. He is the author of *Thought Experiment in the Natural Sciences* (2008).

Daniel Cohnitz is Professor of Theoretical Philosophy at Utrecht University. He is the author of *Gedankenexperimente in der Philosophie* (2006) and numerous articles on thought experiments and other topics in theoretical philosophy. His current research focuses on metaphilosophy, philosophy of language and logic, and epistemology.

Klaus Corcilius is Associate Professor of Philosophy at the University of California, Berkeley. His primary interest is ancient philosophy, theoretical and practical, and especially Aristotle. Currently, he is working on Aristotle's scientific conception of the soul and human and animal agency. He is co-editor of *Partitioning of the Soul in Ancient, Medieval and Early Modern Philosophy* (2014).

David Davies is Professor of Philosophy at McGill University. He is the author of *Art as Performance* (2004), *Aesthetics and Literature* (2007) and *Philosophy of the Performing Arts* (Wiley-Blackwell 2011), and editor/co-editor of *The Thin Red Line* (2008) and *Blade Runner* (2015). He has published widely on philosophical issues relating to film, photography, performance, music, literature, and visual art and also on issues in metaphysics, philosophy of mind and philosophy of language.

Yiftach Fehige is Associate Professor of Philosophy at the University of Toronto. His appointment is for the interdisciplinary field of Christianity and science. The Institute for the History and Philosophy of Science and Technology is his academic home. He has published widely in the major journals in his field. Among the most recent publications is an edited volume on science and religion as it relates to the encounter between East and West (Routledge 2016).

Mélanie Frappier is Assistant Professor of Humanities at the University of King's College, Halifax, Canada. She works on the role of thought experiments in physics and has co-edited *Thought Experiments in Science, Philosophy, and the Arts* with Letitia Meynell and James R. Brown.

Marcus Giaquinto is Emeritus Professor of Philosophy at University College London. His research falls mostly in philosophy of mathematics. He is the author of two books, *The Search for Certainty: A Philosophical Account of Foundations of Mathematics* (2002) and *Visual Thinking in Mathematics: An Epistemological Study* (2007). He is currently working on the philosophy of number with attention to relevant findings in the cognitive sciences.

Jean-Yves Goffi is Professor Emeritus at the Université Grenoble-Alpes. He has published in applied ethics, philosophy of technology and history of philosophy. He is currently working on the transhumanist movement and its relation to utopian thought.

Thomas Grundmann is Professor of Philosophy at the University of Cologne, Germany. He has widely published on epistemology, metaphilosophy, and philosophy of mind. His specific interests include thought experiments and intuitions, experimental philosophy, a priori knowledge, the concept of justification, skepticism, themes from social epistemology, and epistemology of disagreement. His more recent books include *Experimental Philosophy and Its Critics* (co-edited with Joachim Horvath, 2012) and *Analytische Einführung in die Erkenntnistheorie* (2008).

Sören Häggqvist is Associate Professor of Philosophy at Stockholm University. He works mostly on thought experiments and philosophical methodology and partly on the semantics of natural kind terms and the metaphysics of natural kinds. A philosophical dilettante, however, he has strong side interests in the philosophy of biology, general philosophy of science and philosophy of mind (among other things).

Katerina Ierodiakonou is Professor of Ancient Philosophy at the University of Athens and at the University of Geneva. She has published extensively on ancient and Byzantine philosophy, especially in the areas of epistemology and logic. She currently works on a monograph about ancient theories of colour, as well as on an edition, translation and commentary of Theophrastus' *De sensibus* and of Michael Psellos' paraphrase of Aristotle's *De interpretatione*.

Johannes Lenhard works in philosophy of science with a particular focus on the history and philosophy of mathematics and statistics. Over the last years, his research concentrated on various aspects of computer modeling, culminating in his monograph *Calculated Surprises* (in German). Currently, he is senior researcher at the philosophy department of Bielefeld University, Germany.

Kirk Ludwig is a professor of Philosophy and Cognitive Science at Indiana University, Bloomington. He works in the philosophy of mind and action, philosophy of language, epistemology and metaphysics. He is co-author with Ernie Lepore of *Donald Davidson: Meaning, Truth, Language and Reality* (2005) and *Donald Davidson's Truth-theoretic Semantics* (2007). He is the author of *From Individual to Plural Agency: Collective Action I* (2016) and *From Plural to Institutional Agency: Collective Action II* (2017). He is the editor of *Donald Davidson* (2003), co-editor with Ernie Lepore of *Routledge Companion to Donald Davidson* (2013) and co-editor with Marija Jankovic of *Routledge Handbook of Collective Intentionality* (2017).

James W. McAllister is University Senior Lecturer in Philosophy at Leiden University. He is the author of *Beauty and Revolution in Science* (1996) and the editor of *International Studies in the Philosophy of Science*. His current research involves two themes within philosophy of science: the influence of emotions on the decisions of scientists and the relation between the patterns in empirical data and the structure of the world.

Jon McGinnis is a professor of classical and medieval philosophy at the University of Missouri, St. Louis. In addition to numerous articles, he is the author of *Avicenna* in the Oxford University Press' *Great Medieval Thinkers* series (2010), translator and editor of Avicenna's *Physics* from his encyclopedic work, *The Healing* (2009), and was co-translator with David C. Reisman of *Classical Arabic Philosophy: An Anthology of Sources* (2007).

Letitia Meynell is an associate professor of philosophy (cross-appointed with gender and women's studies), specializing in philosophy of science, epistemology, aesthetics and feminist philosophy. Her research, which has been published in various collections and journals such as *Synthese*, *Hypatia* and *International Studies in Philosophy of Science*, addresses two main areas – the use of pictures and thought experiments in the production of science and technology and feminist critiques of biology, especially the animal sciences. She has two co-edited collections, *Thought Experiments in Science, Philosophy, and the Arts*, with Mélanie Frappier and James R. Brown, and *Embodiment and Agency*, with Sue Campbell and Susan Sherwin.

Nenad Miščević is a professor of philosophy at the University of Maribor, Slovenia, and Central European University, Budapest. His interests include epistemology, philosophy of language, philosophy of politics, and he is also working on history of continental philosophy. In philosophy of politics, he has published a book in English and one in his native Croatian, and edited a volume in English, all on the nationalism–cosmopolitaism divide. He is now preparing a volume on thought experiments in general, and one on political thought experiments in particular.

Nancy J. Nersessian is Regents' Professor (Emerita), Georgia Institute of Technology. She currently is Research Associate, Department of Psychology, Harvard University. Her research focuses on the creative research practices of scientists and engineers, especially how modeling practices lead to fundamentally new ways of understanding the world. This research has been funded by NSF and NEH. She is a fellow of AAAS, the Cognitive Science Society, and a Foreign Member of the Royal Netherlands Academy of Arts and Sciences. Her numerous publications include *Creating Scientific Concepts* (2008, Patrick Suppes Prize in Philosophy of Science, 2011) and *Science as Psychology: Sense-making and Identity in Science Practice* (with L. Osbeck, K. Malone, W. Newstetter, 2011, William James Book Prize, 2012).

John D. Norton is Distinguished Professor in the Department of History and Philosophy of Science at the University of Pittsburgh. He works in history and philosophy of physics, with a special interest in the work of Albert Einstein, and on topics in general philosophy of science, including inductive inference and thought experiments.

Paolo Palmieri teaches at the University of Pittsburgh. His interests include early modern history, the Montessori method, pragmatism and phenomenology. His latest monograph, *Hermes and the Telescope: In the Crucible of Galileo's Life-World* (2016), explores the life of Galileo Galilei utilizing a hermeneutic perspective that places his work in the wider context of hermeticism, religious heresy and libertinism.

Kent A. Peacock is a professor of philosophy at the University of Lethbridge. He has published on the history and philosophy of physics and the philosophy of ecology, and he is completing a text on symbolic logic. He currently devotes much attention to the ethical and policy implications of global warming.

Julian Reiss is a professor of philosophy at Durham University and Co-Director of the Centre for Humanities Engaging Science and Society. He is the author of *Error in Economics* (2008), *Philosophy of Economics* (2013), *Causation, Evidence, and Inference* (2015), and over 50 journal articles and book chapters on topics in the philosophy of the biomedical and social sciences.

Sophie Roux is Professor of the History and Philosophy of Science at the École Normale Supérieure, Paris. She works mainly on natural philosophy in the early modern period.

Margaret Schabas is a professor of philosophy at the University of British Columbia. She works primarily in the history and philosophy of economics and has published over 40 articles or book chapters. She is the author of two monographs, *A World Ruled by Number* (1990) and *The Natural Origins of Economics* (2005), both of which are in paperback. She is the recipient of a UBC Killam Research Prize (2015) and has given many keynote addresses to the Hume Society, HOPOS, CPA, and as President of the HES (2013–14).

Guillaume Schlaepfer is a graduate student at the Department of Philosophy at the University of Geneva. He works on the relations between thought experiments and scientific models with a focus on models in evolutionary biology. He is particularly interested in using formal methods to develop the understanding of methodological issues in the sciences.

Irina Starikova is a postdoctoral researcher at the University of São Paulo. Her research areas are the philosophy of mathematical practice, epistemic and cognitive aspects of geometrical thinking, epistemic roles of visualisations in mathematics, thought experiments and mathematical aesthetics. Her work focuses on examples from current advanced mathematics such as Gromov's geometric approach to group theory and Thurston's geometrization of topology. She studied mathematics at Novosibirsk Phys-Maths College and the University at Akademgorodok Scientific Center and completed her PhD in philosophy of mathematics at Bristol.

Stephen Stich is Board of Governors Professor of Philosophy and Cognitive Science at Rutgers University and Director of the Research Group on Evolution and Cognition. He is also Honorary Professor of Philosophy at the University of Sheffield. Prior to joining the Rutgers faculty in 1989, he taught at the University of Michigan, the University of Maryland and the University of California, San Diego. He has lectured in more than 30 countries around the world and has been visiting professor at a number of leading universities in the United States, United Kingdom, Australia, New Zealand and South Korea. His publications include six books, a dozen anthologies and over 150 articles. He is a fellow of the American Academy of Arts and Sciences, a recipient of the Jean Nicod Prize awarded by the French Centre National de la Recherche Scientifique, the first recipient of the Gittler Award for Outstanding Scholarly Contribution in the Philosophy of the Social Sciences, and the 2016 recipient of the Lebowitz Prize for Philosophical Achievement and Contribution awarded by the Phi Beta Kappa Society in conjunction with the American Philosophical Association.

Michael T. Stuart is a postdoctoral researcher at the Centre for Philosophy of Natural and Social Science at the London School of Economics. He is funded by the Social Sciences and Humanities Research Council of Canada. He works on scientific imagination and understanding.

Kevin Tobia is a graduate student in philosophy at Yale University.

Marcel Weber is Professor of Philosophy of Science at the Department of Philosophy at the University of Geneva. He is the author of *Philosophy of Experimental Biology* (2005) and of numerous articles on various problems in the philosophy of biology. He is also editor of the journal *Dialectica* and a member of the German National Academy of Sciences Leopoldina.

Kenneth R. Westphal is Professor of Philosophy, Boğaziçi Üniversitesi (İstanbul). His research focuses on the character and scope of rational justification in non-formal, substantive domains, both theoretical (epistemology, history and philosophy of science) and moral (ethics, justice, history and philosophy of law, philosophy of education). His most recent book, *How Hume and Kant Reconstruct Natural Law: Justifying Strict Objectivity without Debating Moral Realism*, was published in 2016.

Harald A. Wiltsche is currently Assistant Professor at the Department for Philosophy at the University of Graz, Austria. His research interests include philosophy of science and phenomenology.

THOUGHT EXPERIMENTS
State of the art

*Michael T. Stuart, Yiftach Fehige
and James Robert Brown*

Introduction

Hans-Christian Ørsted introduced the term "thought experiment" to philosophy in 1811, although it did not get much philosophical attention until the 1980s. This is therefore a relatively young topic of discussion (in philosophical timescales), still concerned with the most fundamental questions of what thought experiments are, what they do, and how they do it. This introduction will trace some of the work that has been done already. The chapters that follow will take us further.

An enumeration of some classic examples will display how diverse the category of thought experiments can be.[1] In philosophy, there is Searle's Chinese room, Putnam's twin Earth (and brain in a vat), Nozick's experience machine, Rawls' original position, Jackson/Dennett's colour scientist, Thomson's violinist, Chalmers's zombies, Wittgenstein's beetle, Plato's cave (and ring of Gyges), Quine's *gavagai*, Davidson's Swampman, Poincaré's diskworld, Foot's trolley problem and many more.[2] These thought experiments in large part define the history of philosophy and are woven into its pedagogy. Indeed, there is a textbook (now in its fifth edition) that aims to introduce students to philosophy entirely through thought experiments (Schick and Vaughn 2012). And their power to engage minds often extends beyond philosophy classrooms: there are several collections of thought experiments aimed at wider public audiences (e.g., Tittle 2004; Cohen 2004), and they appear frequently in educational contexts online.

Thought experiments are equally common in science. Some famous examples include Lucretius' throwing a spear at the edge of the universe, Maxwell's demon, Einstein's elevator (and train), Schrödinger's cat, Newton's bucket (and cannonball), Heisenberg's microscope, Galileo's falling bodies (and pendulums, inclined planes and ship), the Prisoner's Dilemma, and Stevin's chain draped over a prism. They are found also in pure and applied mathematics, where they play important roles from geometry to infinity.[3]

While philosophical and scientific thought experiments have stolen most of the scholarly spotlight, the scope of thought experiments grows substantially when we recognize the many works of art that we can fruitfully characterize as thought experiments. These might include paintings such as Jackson Pollock's "Number One"; novels such as Mark Twain's *Huckleberry Finn*, Harper Lee's *To Kill a Mockingbird*, Sophocles' *Oedipus Rex*, Charles Dickens' *A Tale of Two Cities*, Vladimir Nabokov's *Lolita*, George Eliot's *Middlemarch*, William Shakespeare's *Henry V*, *King Lear* and *Hamlet*, George Orwell's *Animal Farm*, Harriet Beecher Stowe's *Uncle Tom's Cabin* and E. M. Forster's *Howards End*; and films including *The Matrix* and *2001: A Space Odyssey* (see Carroll 2002; Wartenberg 2007; Camp 2009; Davies 2012, this volume; Elgin 1993, 2014). It might also be useful to discuss the creation and appreciation of art as a kind of thought experiment.

Besides humanistic, scientific and artistic pursuits, thought experiments are deeply important for ordinary life (Nersessian 2007). On an inclusive conception of "thought experiment," simply planning out a busy day might require several; figuring out how best to get from one place to another, deciding what to eat, etc. Thought experiments and repeated visualizations may also be used in therapy, for example, to overcome phobias (Gendler 2004).

Thought experiments thus form an extremely diverse set of mental activities. Since there is no conventional definition, we should resolve to begin our inquiry with as broad a notion as possible. That is, we should be aware of and minimize our pre-theoretical definitional criteria until we have exposed ourselves to the full diversity of cognitive activities that might warrant the label "thought experiment." Only when it comes time to develop historical, sociological and philosophical accounts of thought experiments should we narrow our focus to the subsets and properties of thought experiments that interest us.

We therefore invite the reader to treat this book as a companion, not in the sense of an expert guide who can navigate unfamiliar terrain to a predetermined destination, but in the sense of an enthusiastic fellow explorer. Our first step (to be taken in Part I) exposes us to many of the different types and aims of thought experiments.

Thought experiments in their historical contexts

One important approach to thought experiments is historical, the value of which far outstrips any use philosophers make of it. We want to know what role Ibn Sīnā's (Avicenna's) thought experiments played in his epistemology and how they were received by his contemporaries independently of what such an inquiry might tell us about thought experiments in general. Focusing on thought experiments merely provides historians with another useful lens through which to study thinkers and periods that are already worth studying. And in Part I we look through this lens.

Still, it would be wrong to underplay the close connection between the history and philosophy of thought experiments. Generally speaking, historians will not be able to catalogue and analyze historical thought experiments without making philosophical assumptions about the nature of inference, evidence, imagination and their mutual relations. Conversely, philosophers have no hope of producing a general account of thought experiments without the examples and insights of historians. In particular, historical studies such as Gellard (2011), Ierodiakonou (2005, 2011), Knuuttila and Kukkonen (2011), Kühne (2005), Lautner (2011) and Palmerino (2011) have raised important philosophical issues that might otherwise have gone unnoticed. For instance, the history of thought experiments shows that many have acquired lives of their own, despite Ian Hacking's (1992) claim to the contrary. This is an important datum for developing ontologies and taxonomies of thought experiments (see Bokulich and Frappier, this volume). The interdependence of the history and philosophy of thought experiments is clearly reflected in the chapters of Part I, which may also serve as an extended introduction to thought experiments and (with Part II) a source of evidence against which to test the philosophical claims made in Parts III and IV.

Given the ubiquity of thought experiments, we could not attempt to provide comprehensive historical coverage. In the literature to date, there has been a focus on thought experiments in Western traditions, mostly following Galileo and the birth of what is called modern science. James McAllister (this volume) argues that this focus is appropriate since thought experiments are a tool introduced by Galileo with a specific sort of evidential significance linked to the Western notion of scientific experiment. For the reasons given above, we have sought chapters that go beyond this conception. Plato might be using his imagination in a way that is not the same as Galileo's, but similar enough that we might learn something new about thought experiments or thought experiment–like inferences by considering them. So in Part I, we tentatively expand our notion of thought experiment, while still covering the cases that are most discussed in the literature. We hope this provides a balance between historical scholarship on well-known thought experiments and those that are less well-known. In the first category we have thought experiments in the presocratics, Plato, Galileo, Newton and Leibniz. In the second we have Aristotle, Islamic/Arabic thinkers, Kant, Wittgenstein and Hegel. This selection should provide readers who are new to the topic of thought experiments the historical background necessary to appreciate the rest of the companion, while readers already comfortable with the history of thought experiments will find new scholarship that opens original directions for research. In terms of expanding the literature, we have only gone a small fraction of the way. Thinkers from feminist philosophy, African, Asian, Latin American traditions and others should also be represented in the discussion, as well as disciplines that have not traditionally received the attention of philosophers, including architecture, engineering, law and advertising, which are all likely to have a great deal to contribute.

Before moving on, we would like to provide a brief summary of the chapters of Part I. Katerina Ierodiakonou in her chapter on the ancients argues that thought experiments were used for three main purposes: to support, to attack and to induce suspension of judgment on philosophical claims. She considers three illustrative episodes: Archytas of Tarentum's throwing a spear at the edge of the universe, the myth of Gyges in Plato's *Republic*, and Sextus Empiricus' "partless places." Rather than discussing these episodes as thought experiments, Ierodiakonou helpfully refers to them as *paradeigmata*, or "examples." To illustrate how such examples were marshalled, Ierodiakonou considers a few more cases, including the ship of Theseus, Chrysippus' Dion and Theon, and the skepticism-inducing arguments of the stoics and Skeptics.

In his chapter on Plato, Alexander Becker draws attention to Plato's many literary devices and styles in order to ask how Plato's fictional creations compare to thought experiments and how we are supposed to learn from them. Becker focuses on the *Republic*, which includes not only what we might classify as thought experiments but also a discussion of what we can learn from fiction. He identifies three main fictional styles in Plato – myth, simile and dialogue – and relates these to the myth of Gyges, the myth of Er, the allegory of the cave, the myth told to the citizens of the model city, the construction of the model city, and the *Republic* itself as a dialogue.

Klaus Corcilius begins his chapter on Aristotle as Ierodiakonou and Becker do: by admitting there is no simple way to read into Aristotle our notion of thought experiment. And this is no accident, argues Corcilius, since Aristotle regarded plain-sight observation as superior to the "artificial extraction of hidden facts" (this volume, 58). However, "there can be no doubt," Corcilius argues, that Aristotle did use what *we* call thought experiments. Their principle function seems to be to "compensate for a lack of data in epistemically difficult terrain" (60). To illustrate what this means and how Aristotle achieves it, Corcilius considers examples from both Aristotle's esoteric writings (dense philosophical notes) and his exoteric (literary) writings. The latter include a cave allegory similar to Plato's and a frightening analogy of the soul's relation to the body in terms of a living person chained to a dead one. The former include "the striptease argument," which analyzes substance itself, imagining if there were a second sun, a consideration of "if all things were colours" (or if everything were only one colour), why flesh is not the organ of touch, and finally what moves the universe and how.

Jon McGinnis discusses medieval Arabic/Islamic thought experiments by discussing fictions, idealizations and "ingenious machines," primarily in the work of Ibn Sīnā, but also in Ibn al-Haytham, Abū Ḥamid al-Ghazālī and others. These philosophical tools were put to a variety of uses, including supporting modal claims and illustrating ideas. McGinnis shows that the use of hypothetical conditionals, a tradition going back to Aristotle, was beginning to be recognized as philosophically problematic, especially in connection to its dependence on the imagination. McGinnis follows this with a fascinating discussion of an internal sensory faculty introduced by Ibn Sīnā to avoid objections about hypothetical counterfactuals called *wahm*, which is a faculty separate from imagination and intellect that enables us to perceive non-sensible features or intentions in sensible particular things (as when a sheep perceives the ferocity of a wolf, or I "see how you feel"). This faculty was crucial for explaining our ability to grasp mathematical objects, work with idealizations and employ thought experiments. McGinnis goes through Ibn Sīnā's famous "flying man" thought experiment and many others to show the creativity and subtlety with which thought experiments were used and criticized during this period.

In striking contrast to the usual way Galileo is presented, Paolo Palmieri rejects the distinction between real and thought experiments for Galileo. Instead, Galileo's "experiential engagements" are recast as "projective participations." One way to put the point is that recent recreations of Galileo's experiments reveal that his experiments, if material, could not have shown what Galileo concluded from them. Therefore, the experiments must have been conceived and completed always (at least partially) projectively in thought. Palmieri's second main point is that Galileo was not trying to dissolve paradoxes with his experiments. He was celebrating them. To show this, he displays some of Galileo's most beautiful struggles with falling (and floating bodies).

Richard T. W. Arthur fruitfully groups together some deservedly famous thought experiments of Isaac Newton and Gottfried Leibniz. These include Newton's bucket and the Leibniz shifts, wherein God creates the universe in a different place, in the same place but rotated, or at a different time. The unifying theme of all these thought experiments is the use of indistinguishability to show something about the nature of motion and matter. Arthur discusses the context and motivations of these thought experiments in relation to the work of other philosophers like Descartes, Hobbes and Locke, and shows how historically important theses such as Leibniz's identity of indiscernibles were originally grounded in indistinguishability thought experiments about matter and motion. The discussion branches out to other indistinguishability thought experiments concerning God's abilities, the nature of perception and the nature of mind, one of which anticipates Searle's Chinese room thought experiment.

In Chapter 7, Kenneth R. Westphal charts the development of transcendental thought experiments found in Kant, Hegel, Wittgenstein and others. Westphal prefaces this with a historical-philosophical discussion of the nature of philosophy and its limits, especially with respect to the possibility of global perceptual skepticism and massive reference failure. Through this preface, Westphal breathes life and immediacy into his discussion of these thought experiments which are transcendental in the sense that they try to grasp some of our key cognitive capacities and their limits. Examples include Kant's thought experiments that ask us to conceive of a complete absence of space or time; Kant's thought experiment in which there is no regularity in the sensory manifold; and Wittgenstein's thought experiments in *On Certainty* which ask us to violate in imagination some of the most fundamental regularities we know to obtain, such as conservation of mass. Despite their apparently external subject matter, these are thought experiments about what we can and cannot think. Our failures or difficulties become crucial data for the construction of philosophical theory.

The glimpse provided by Part I into historical uses and examples of thought experiments naturally leads to certain philosophical and sociological questions such as: What are the features common to (sets of) thought experiments? Do different communities draw different divisions between thought experiments, fictions, models and arguments? How contextual are the success criteria for thought experiments, and what causes a community to change them? Answering these questions requires a somewhat broader perspective, and a natural thing to do is to look at *fields* of inquiry rather than periods and thinkers. For example, what are the sorts of thought experiments used in politics, economics, theology, ethics, physics, biology and mathematics? What unites them, how are they used and how have they changed? This is the goal of Part II, which collects domain-specific observations and presents accounts of the characteristics and practices of thought experimentation in the fields just mentioned. This part of the collection is organized like the first, to include chapters that summarize and expand on previous work (e.g., in physics, mathematics and ethics) with some relatively new areas ripe for cultivation (economics, biology, theology and politics). As with the previous section, further expansion is desirable, for example, to thought experiments in metaphysics, chemistry, geology, sociology, engineering, law, architecture, etc. A brief summary of these chapters follows.

Thought experiments in their disciplinary contexts

Nenad Miščević (co-originator of the mental models account discussed by Nancy Nersessian in Chapter 17) discusses thought experiments in political philosophy. These typically present some social arrangement, ask us to judge it, and then use that judgement as evidence for a political or philosophical claim. From the model city (also discussed by Becker, this volume), we learn about justice itself. From behind Rawls' veil of ignorance, we judge different arrangements of "the basic structure" of society and reason about which is best. Similar thought experiments are found in Rousseau, Dworkin, Cohen and Kukathas, and many more are collected in Tetlock and Belkin's (1996) *Counterfactual Thought Experiments in World Politics*, which helped to spur recent literature on the topic. Miščević considers the characteristics and stages of such thought experiments, analyzes historical and contemporary examples, and argues even for the indispensability of such thought experiments in political thought by canvassing the possible sources of evidence available to political philosophy. Finally, Miščević outlines some general desiderata for successful political thought experiments and asks what this discussion can tell us about ongoing philosophical issues, such as the status of ideal theories in political reasoning.

Some authors claim or imply that economics proceeds primarily by thought experiment. Taking up a contrary position, Margaret Schabas argues that not only are thought experiments rare in economics, but when we do find something that looks like one, it usually isn't. Her position relies on a conception of thought experiments according to which at least some experimental manipulation is necessary (which in turn relies on a particular notion of experiment). According to this conception, a mathematical model that operates by derivation, no matter how hypothetical its content is, cannot be a thought experiment. Schabas also rejects the view that modelling (and mental modelling) is experimental. Schabas does identify a few genuine thought experiments in economics, such as Hume's, in which everyone in a society wakes up with an extra five units of currency in their pocket. And she is happy to admit that economics is increasingly experimental. However, the "thought" and "experiment" portions of economics are not very often combined in the way that we see, for example, in physics. Some of these claims are taken up by Julian Reiss (this volume), who attempts to explain why there are less thought experiments in economics than elsewhere.

Thought experiments have long been part of the method of theology, but the features of such thought experiments and what their involvement says about theology are open questions. Yiftach Fehige considers six ways thought experiments and theology have or might come together in philosophical discourse. First, there are some who dismiss the use of thought experiments in ethics for theological reasons. Second, their appearance in theological contexts has been taken as evidence against the reliability of thought experiments in general. Third, the presence of thought experiments in both science and theology has been used to argue that there are comparable standards of rationality in these two disciplines. Fourth, theological thought experiments have an intriguing literary nature that might be helpful in advancing the investigation of thought experiments through aesthetics (as in, for example, Davies, this volume; Elgin 2014; and Meynell, this volume). Fifth, the claim that philosophy would be impossible (or at least severely impoverished) without thought experiments also appears to be true of philosophical theology. Finally, what is called revealed theology has its own thought experiments, which are fundamentally different from those we find elsewhere.

This brings us to ethical thought experiments, which are among the most well-known in any discipline. Like philosophers of politics (if Miščević is correct), ethicists seem *required* to appeal to thought experiments because normative claims are not amenable to the same sources of evidence as less normative disciplines. In his chapter, Georg Brun provides a general characterization of ethical thought experiments, including the infamous trolley problem, Thomson's violinist, Singer's drowning child, Shue's ticking time bomb diffused by torturing a terrorist, and Rawls' original position. Brun produces a typology and considers objections (including moral objections) to the use of thought experiments in ethics.

Kent A. Peacock turns us to physics, which is the only discipline that could rival philosophy in terms of the quantity and historical significance of thought experiments. Though it is an open matter whether thought experiments in ethics, epistemology or metaphysics achieve their goals, the question in physics is not if, but how. Peacock is more liberal in his characterization of thought experiments than Schabas, including even textbook problems that deal with simplified scenarios like blocks sliding down inclined planes. Peacock notes that there are thought experiments that illustrate or draw attention to certain ideas, but he chooses to focus on those that have left indelible marks on physical theory and practice well beyond the intentions of their creators. These include Maxwell's demon, the Einstein-Podolsky-Rosen thought experiment, Einstein's riding a light wave, Einstein's elevator (and its progenitor – an observer falling off a roof), Einstein's "hole" argument, Plank's oscillators, Einstein's mirror, Heisenberg's microscope, Schrödinger's cat and even quantum computation. In all of these cases, theoretical solutions to the problems raised by thought experiments, and problems with the theoretical solutions suggested by those thought experiments, make up important parts of the history of physics. Peacock concludes with a discussion of the future of thought experimentation in physics.

Unlike physics, biology is not brimming with famous thought experiments. Guillaume Schlaepfer and Marcel Weber begin their chapter by considering why this might be. For instance, the theoretical portion of biology seems to play a "more marginal" role in biology compared to the role played by theoretical physics in physics. And biology, unlike physics, has more direct experimental access to its systems. This does not mean that there are no interesting thought experiments in biology, however. For example, Darwin's work contains many. Schlaepfer and Weber consider Jim Lennox's (1991) account of these thought experiments and raise some interesting questions. For example, if thought experiments should involve the imagination, *how much* imagination do we require for something to count as a thought experiment? This is especially poignant in the case of Darwin, whose thought experiments are characteristically full of references to empirical evidence. Does this make them less imaginative (and therefore less thought experimental)? At this point the chapter turns to the work of mathematically focused population geneticists. In this literature we find R. A. Fisher's sexually reproducing community with three (or more) sexes, and other candidates for biological thought experiments.

Finally, Irina Starikova and Marcus Giaquinto tackle the question of thought experiments in mathematics, where, as they point out, it is not at all strange to see our stock of knowledge increase from thought alone. A more interesting issue, they claim, is the use of sensory imagination in mathematical thought experiments. They provide several examples of such thought experiments from knot theory, graph theory and geometric group theory. Many of these are justified because the visualizable manipulations of mathematical objects (like knots) are tied directly to formal manipulations. "For foundational purposes there needs to be some way of fixing the subject matter in mathematical terms, so that the correctness of basic assumptions and methods can be proven. But once that job has been done, we may proceed without adverting to our foundational definitions" (this volume, 262).

In their exploration of graph theory, they find visual imaginings that proceed "in a truly experimental way" (272). They go on:

> The utility of visual imagination depends on confining our efforts to images and image transformations which are simple enough for us to manipulate reliably in imagination. But the variety of images and image transformations that we can handle reliably suffices to make visual imagination a potent instrument of mental experimentation in mathematics.
>
> (272)

In sum, there are thought experiments in mathematics that involve "active use of visual imagination" and go "beyond the application of mathematically prescribed rules, as a way of answering questions or overcoming obstacles" (275). Intriguingly, the epistemic support provided by these thought experiments is deemed *empirical*. This might seem counterintuitive, but "empirical evidence has a much larger role in the epistemology of actual mathematical belief acquisition than is often thought" (276).

With some understanding of the history and disciplinary context of thought experiments, we turn to Part III, which presents and reappraises the main existing philosophical accounts of thought experiments. Our contributors develop, defend and criticize epistemological accounts that attempt to explain when and how a thought experiment succeeds. There is a deflationary empiricist account that treats thought experiments as a mere subset of arguments (Chapter 15), a rationalist account that treats thought experiments as possible stimulants of rational insight (Chapter 16), a naturalist account that portrays thought experiments as the manipulation of what cognitive scientists call "mental models" (Chapter 17), a transcendental account that portrays thought experiments both as continuous with real experiments and also as conditions for the possibility of real experiments (Chapter 18), and a phenomenological account that takes as fundamental the first-person experience of performing a thought experiment (Chapter 19).

To introduce this section, we think it might be helpful to have a quick look at the history of these accounts.

Some history of the philosophy of thought experiments

Unfortunately, there are only a few resources concerning the history of the philosophy of thought experiments (e.g., Kühne 2005; Moue, Masavetas, and Karayianni 2006; Fehige and Stuart 2014), and those sources focus mostly on philosophy of science. This can perhaps be forgiven, since the earliest notion of a *Tankeexperiment* relied for its meaning on the scientific experiment. This is equally true for Ørsted as it was for Georg Christoph Lichtenberg, Novalis, and Immanuel Kant, who were writing just before Ørsted using similar notions (see Schildknecht 1990; Daiber 2001; Fehige and Stuart 2014). The philosophers who followed Ørsted, including Ernst Mach, Alexius Meinong, Pierre Duhem, Thomas Kuhn, and Imre Lakatos, continued to focus on the experimental nature of thought experiments.

Mainstream philosophers picked up the moniker in the mid-1980s. Jonathan Dancy considered the use of thought experiments in ethics, and Daniel Dennett considered them in epistemology and metaphysics under the name of "intuition pumps." Dancy and

Dennett weren't convinced by thought experiments that purported to establish certain philosophical conclusions. Skepticism intensified with the introduction of experimental philosophy.[4] But whether the discussion takes place in metaphilosophy or philosophy of science, the main epistemological worry is the same: can these thought experiments really be doing what they seem to be doing? This question takes its present form in the chapters of Part III through a dialogue that we think started with Kuhn.

Unlike Mach and those before him, Kuhn wrote about thought experiments mainly as a tool for motivating or justifying scientific revolutions. For Kuhn,

> A crisis induced by the failure of expectation and followed by revolution is at the heart of the thought-experimental situations we have been examining. Conversely, thought experiment is one of the essential analytic tools which are deployed during crisis and which then help to promote basic conceptual reform.
> (Kuhn 1977, 263)

Kuhn cites Einstein's train, Heisenberg's microscope, and several fragments from Galileo as examples of thought experiments that play this role in theory change. He calls these "an important class of thought experiments" (260–61), and he concludes that "from thought experiments most people learn about their concepts and the world together" (253).

For Kuhn, revolutionary thought experiments were not used to generate new facts, but to ease scientists through the arational period of crisis that exists between scientific paradigms, back to the rational progress of what Kuhn calls "normal science." In a period of crisis, we must weigh the competing claims, methods and potentials of rival paradigms. And it seems that thought experiments can and have helped us partially to transcend the confines of our paradigms, which is necessary if we are to be convinced of a new world-view. Kuhn argues that by changing and exploring our world-views by means of thought experiments, we learn indirectly about the world as well.

Kuhn's answer to the question of how thought experiments fuel scientific progress did not win widespread acceptance, although there is still some sympathy (for example, Sorensen 1992; Gendler 1998; Van Dyck 2003). What is important in the present context is Kuhn's idea that thought experiments play a justificatory role in science, and especially in scientific revolutions. This idea was central for those who organized the first conference on thought experiments in 1986, and it has been a point of contention ever since. The proceedings of that conference were published in Horowitz and Massey (1991), and on the first page of their introduction the editors point out that what is at stake is a "paradox" inspired by Kuhn's paper. The paradox of thought experiments consists in the "puzzling fact that thought experiments often have novel empirical import even though they are conducted entirely inside one's head."[5]

Kuhn's "puzzling fact" only became a "paradox" via the ensuing debate between James Robert Brown and John D. Norton, which presented two clear but conflicting solutions: one with "epistemic magic," and one without. Brown and Norton assumed with Kuhn that thought experiments could play a justificatory role in scientific revolutions, and they both took the scientific record as their main source of information. However, they disagreed about what thought experiments were and what they could do. Brown presented a Platonic theory of thought experiments and Norton developed an empiricist account that characterized thought experiments as arguments. Brown claimed that thought experiments could provide direct access to truths about laws of nature, which is something Norton derided as magical. Each was attempting to resolve Kuhn's puzzle.

Brown began with Galileo's falling bodies thought experiment (see Palmieri, this volume) in which

> we have a transition from one theory to another which is quite remarkable. There has been *no* new empirical evidence. The old theory was rationally believed before the thought experiment, but was shown to be absurd by it. The thought experiment established rational belief in a new theory.
>
> (Brown 1986, 10)

It does this independently of experience because "there has been no new observational data" (11), the conclusion does not follow deductively from the premises (11–2), and because "it is not a case of seeing old empirical data in a new way" (which is, Brown writes: "essentially Kuhn's thesis" 1986, 11). So Brown accepted that at least some thought experiments perform the role that Kuhn envisaged, "a crucial role in paradigm change" (2). They play this role by providing reasons to reject one theory and adopt another, and those reasons are not strictly logical, nor do they rely solely on previous sense-experience.

Norton also focused on revolutionary thought experiments, and he agreed with Brown concerning the problem: "Thought experiments in physics provide or purport to provide us information about the physical world. Since they are *thought* experiments rather than *physical* experiments, this information does not come from the reporting of new empirical data." But he drew a very different conclusion:

> There is only one non-controversial source from which this information can come: it is elicited from information we already have by an identifiable argument ... The alternative to this view is to suppose that thought experiments provide some new and even mysterious route to knowledge of the physical world.
>
> (1991, 129)

Norton thus presented Kuhn's puzzle in the form of a dichotomy, bringing us to the paradox: if thought experiments provide new information about the physical world, yet do not require new information about the physical world, either the new information is a rearrangement of old data, or else it comes from rational insight.

A great deal of papers and books published on thought experiments since 1991 in philosophy of science have mentioned or focused on this paradox.[6] Most of them present Kuhn's problem in slightly different terms, or call it by a different name. Given that the paradox is rarely presented in the same words, some writers have begun to question whether there is actually more than one paradox.

For instance, Horowitz and Massey characterized the paradox in terms of the "fact that thought experiments often have novel empirical import even though they are conducted entirely inside one's head." Depending on how we interpret "novel," "empirical import," and "entirely inside one's head," we get different versions of the paradox. There are many ways for something to be novel, for example, by being surprising, non-derivable, or by presenting us with a previously non-existing belief, experience, ability, pattern, property, or relation. Likewise, there are many ways of having empirical import, for example, by prompting a change in our existing set of empirical beliefs, knowledge, evidence, understanding, information, etc. Finally, to be "inside one's head" might require that the *elements* manipulated in a thought experiment be in the head, that the thought experimental *process* be in the head, or that the *evidence* that justifies the output of a thought experiment be in the head (for an extended discussion of these and other options, see Stuart 2015, ch. 1 §§3–5).

For Brown and Norton, empirical import meant empirical knowledge. Brown and Norton disagreed, however, concerning the relevant sense of novelty and also concerning the sources of evidence in the heads of thought experimenters.

Before considering where other philosophers in the literature stand with respect to novelty, empirical import and independence of experience, we'd like to summarize the two chapters in this volume dedicated to the views of Brown and Norton. In her chapter, Elke Brendel helpfully distinguishes five main sub-claims of Norton's position. Using this framework, she explains the various attacks and defenses that have been made, and others that could be made, against each of them. She identifies one of these claims as impossible to reject without begging the question against Norton, and presents several powerful arguments against three others. One of the claims, the *Reconstruction thesis*, is argued to be defensible. Brendel concludes by showing that if we reject what she regards as the weaker of Norton's claims, this will not commit us to Brown's position.[7]

In his chapter, Thomas Grundmann focuses on the two main arguments Brown gives for his position: 1) an inference to the best explanation, according to which Platonism is the best explanation for the practice of scientific thought experimentation, and 2) an argument from analogy that ties Platonism in mathematics to Platonism in science. Both of Brown's arguments rely on a particular account of the laws of nature, namely, the Dretske-Tooley-Armstrong account. According to this account, laws of nature are relations between universals. If it is correct, perhaps Brown is right that empiricism cannot explain our mental access to such universals and their relations. And since the rational access to the mathematical realm is *also* a matter of access to universals, we gain support for the analogy between mathematical and scientific thought experiments. Grundmann forcefully attacks both of the two main arguments, in addition to the account of laws of nature that Brown relies on. He then considers the ways in which Brown's account could be revised, and closes by asking whether and how a Platonic account of thought experiments could deal with philosophical thought experiments.

Faced with the extremes of rationalism and empiricism, many who contributed to the debate after 1991 sought a middle ground. Sören Häggqvist (1996, 2009) agreed with Norton that insofar as thought experiments are to play an evidential role in science or philosophy, they must participate in arguments. That is, thought experiments are used to contest or bolster theoretical claims by providing (usually modal) evidence that counts for or against a claim (see Williamson 2005, 2016 for a similar view). For Häggqvist, a thought experiment thus plays a justificatory role in the same way a real experiment does: by contradicting or supporting a claim made by the theory through participation in an argument. This makes (thought) experiments *parts of* arguments. However, Häggqvist denies Norton's claim that the performance of a thought experiment just is the performance of an argument, because an experiment cannot be formally valid or invalid.[8] Häggqvist's insight is taken up by Tim De Mey (2003), who argues that we should investigate the epistemic impact of the thought experiment's conclusion in one way, and how it produces that conclusion in another.

In other words, there is the conclusion of the thought experiment, which is a product of psychological mechanisms including imagination, memory and intuition. And there is the use of that conclusion in an argument for or against the truth of a claim, which might be justified in the standard ways identified by logicians. It is therefore important to be clear which of these two very different characterizations of the paradox we are addressing in any epistemological account of thought experiments: the reliability of the processes that bring us to the conclusion of the thought experiment, or the reliability of the inferences we use to make that conclusion bear on a theory or theoretical claim.

There are also naturalists in the debate who claim that we can and should use science to discover how thought experiments work. This idea was already present in Mach (1905) and Wolfgang Yourgrau (1962, 1967). But Roy Sorensen was the first to give an in-depth naturalist account of thought experiments (1992).

Like Häggqvist and Williamson, Sorensen portrayed thought experiments as a type of modal reasoning. And like Mach (1905), he placed thought experiments on a continuum with real experiments. Along with several others (including Richard Arthur, Alisa Bokulich, Tamar Gendler, Kuhn and Lichtenberg), Sorensen argued that thought experiments mostly eliminate irrationalities in our thought. And again following Mach, he claimed that thought experiments function by drawing upon the stores of empirical knowledge that we accumulate in our lifetimes, combined with the innate ideas and structures that have been programmed into our minds by evolution. This is what makes Sorensen a naturalist in particular: his use of evolutionary psychology to justify the reliability of thought experiments.

Sorensen agreed with Norton that thought experiments "repackage" old information to make it "more informative" (1992, 4). In this sense, he adopted Norton's notion of novelty. But his interpretation of empirical import is quite different. Instead of empirical knowledge, he took the goals of thought experiments to include the creation and stabilization of phenomena, atheoretical exploration, and the definition of concepts. Achieving these goals does not usually amount to creating new empirical knowledge in the sense of providing new justified beliefs. One important point to learn from Sorensen about the paradox is that empirical import can mean much more than empirical knowledge. Catharine Elgin (1993, 2000, 2002, 2004, 2006 and 2014) has been focusing on thought experiments with respect to understanding instead of knowledge for some time. Mike Stuart (2016a, 2017, this volume) develops this idea as well.

Since Sorensen, more naturalists have emerged, many of whom rely to some extent on the argument from evolution. An important subset of these characterize thought experiments as "mental models," a technical term from cognitive science first applied to thought experiments independently and simultaneously by Nenad Miščević (1992, 2004 and 2007) and Nancy Nersessian (1992a, 1992b, 2007, 2008, this volume), and later by Tamar Gendler (2004) and others. Miščević and Nersessian agreed that "thought experiment descriptions" guide us in the creation of dynamic mental models which "mobilize" cognitive skills that render the outcome of the model manipulation epistemically efficacious. For example, we can make mental models that help us to produce reliable guesses about how and when water will spill out of variously shaped containers whose openings are tilted increasingly towards the ground. Such models draw on our everyday experience with containers and liquids and pouring. It is easy to see why many problems are easier and faster to solve when represented in a mental model as opposed to verbally or formally: we get to use the same abilities and knowledge we use in everyday real-life situations (like moving in a gravitational field), and this is (supposed to be) very different from working out a solution using logical inferences, as Norton would have it.

In more detail, Nersessian argues that the narrative presentation of a thought experiment triggers the creation of a mental model, which is "a structural, behavioral, or functional analog to a real-world phenomenon" (this volume, 311). The mental model is analogous in the sense that it preserves something of the constraints operating on the objects and events of the imagined phenomenon (311). Such mental models are often visual or tactile in nature, are manipulated in real time, draw on embodied wisdom (1992, 294), and embed a specific and personal point of view into the model (1992, 295). With respect to the paradox, Nersessian made a telling remark early on:

> The constructed situation, itself, is apprehended as pertinent to the real world in several ways. It can reveal something in our experience that we did not see the import of before ... It can generate new data from the limiting case ... [and] it can make us see the empirical consequences of something in our existing conceptions.
>
> (1992, 296)

In other words, like Sorensen, Nersessian recognized many of the different ways empirical import could be interpreted. Instead of producing new knowledge, a thought experiment can highlight old data that did not initially seem important, it can separate phenomena that seem necessarily connected, it can generate new data from limiting cases, and it can clarify the consequences of previous conceptual commitments.

In her chapter in this volume, Nancy J. Nersessian begins with a presentation of the varied advancements in the literature on mental models from psychology, cognitive science, philosophy and neuroimaging studies. After all, if we're going to take seriously the suggestion that thought experiments are mental models in the scientist's sense, we must understand what the scientists are saying. And once we do, there are many remarkable details concerning how we reason using models that can inform the discussion, or pose new problems. Nersessian closes by considering how the account relates to or subsumes other accounts already mentioned in this introduction.

There are many important insights to gain from the naturalists. In terms of novelty, Gendler, Nersessian and Miščević all agree with Norton that existing knowledge can be manipulated, transformed or rearranged in a thought experiment to draw our attention to something we didn't notice before. However, these philosophers also identify additional sources of novelty, including truly novel mental presentations, which could take the form of new experiences, concepts or beliefs. But unlike Brown, these would not be interactions with real, mind-independent abstract entities. Gendler, Nersessian and Miščević also agree that rearrangement can help us to "possess" our beliefs by giving us the power to act on them, as when a thought experiment helps us to overcome a fear of flying that we know is irrational. Statistical knowledge that flying is safe is not enough to prevent fear in some people, yet thought experiments in the form of repeated positive visualizations can help agents to make their statistical knowledge about the safety of airline travel useful

(Gendler 2004, 1160). This sense of novelty concerns our abilities, and the relationships between our beliefs.

One final point concerns the distinction between propositional and non-propositional cognitive processes. Norton claims that "The actual conduct of a thought experiment consists of the execution of an argument, although this may not be obvious, since the argument may appear only in abbreviated form and with suppressed premises" (2004b, 50). Norton could be correct that the best way to explain the epistemological efficacy of thought experiments is to reconstruct them as arguments, which are manipulations of propositions, without being correct about the additional claim that the actual conduct of a thought experiment is the execution of an argument. Nevertheless, for Norton to be correct about this additional claim, we need to know if non-propositional cognitive processes are necessary for "the actual conduct" of a thought experiment. Mental modellers typically claim that such processes are necessary, or they reject the distinction altogether. (On this issue see Peijnenburg and Atkinson 2003, 121–5, and Goffi and Roux, this volume). Others have sided with Norton, arguing that we need only make reference to manipulations of propositions for a descriptively accurate epistemological account of thought experiments (e.g., Salis and Frigg forthcoming). This issue remains open.

In addition to empiricism, rationalism and naturalism, there is a Kantian account of thought experiments that has been developed in detail by Marco Buzzoni (2008, 2010, 2011, 2013a, 2013b, 2015, 2016 and this volume). According to Buzzoni, thought experiments should be considered from two philosophical levels of analysis. According to the first, thought experiments are a condition for the possibility of real experiments. That is, without thought experiments, we could not see objects and events as answers to questions that we put to nature. In order to question nature, we have to imagine different ways the world could be (2008, 116–20). Without our ability to distance ourselves cognitively from the actual situations in which we find ourselves, we would not be able to think of how things *might* be, and so we could not generate questions or hypotheses about what *is*. Therefore, not until we are in a position to entertain different hypotheses about what the world is really like (as opposed to how it merely appears) does experimental practice become possible. In this sense, thought experiments and real experiments are *not* the same; thought experiments are more fundamental. According to the second level of analysis, however, we note that thought experiments are given their content by experience: they put questions to nature, anticipate answers using induction and deduction, and must ultimately be justified by appeal to experience. In this sense, thought experiments are on a par with real experiments. To put it in a slogan: real experiments without thought experiments are blind, and thought experiments without real experiments are empty.

One insight that results from this view is that we must be careful to differentiate between thought experiments as cognitive actions necessary for the scientific enterprise in general, and on the other hand as mental variations of variables that anticipate how nature will answer our questions. Failing to do this, Buzzoni argues, will force us to dismiss what is common to thought and laboratory experiments (as Norton must), or to misidentify thought experiments as epistemologically indistinguishable from laboratory experiments (as Brown's account seems to allow).[9] Buzzoni's account can accommodate both views. In his chapter in this collection, Buzzoni updates his account, first by responding to objections made by Yiftach Fehige (2012 and 2013), and then by mapping the terrain of possible Kantian approaches to thought experiments based on different interpretations of the Kantian a priori.

Another option is to produce a phenomenological account of thought experiments (see e.g., Mohanty 1991; Kujundzic 1995; Froese and Gallagher 2010; Fehige and Wiltsche 2013; Wiltsche 2013, this volume; Hopp 2014). Phenomenology takes as fundamental the "phenomena," that is, how things appear in conscious experience. One major insight of phenomenology is that what appears to us always outstrips our given sensory experience of it. Perceiving an object is not just receiving certain patterns of light on the retina; it requires recognizing the object as something with various properties and a certain history, which would appear different from different perspectives or under different conditions, and so on. Given this, our experience of any object (material or otherwise) consists also of our expectations, background knowledge, and abilities. Edmund Husserl called this expanded notion of experience when applied to an object, "horizontal givenness." Harald A. Wiltsche (this volume) applies this phenomenological framework to thought experiments, first by providing an excellent introduction to phenomenology in terms that anyone can understand, and second by pointing out that it is not only material objects that have horizontal givenness, but imaginings as well. Drawing on imagined cases from *The Simpsons* as well as special relativity, Wiltsche presents a general but careful consideration of how the action of performing a thought experiment can shed light on the different ways that objects and events appear in the imagination, how our background knowledge figures into the action of thought experimentation, and how we can learn from the process.

Besides rationalism, empiricism, naturalism, Kantianism and phenomenology, there are still other positions that are possible to take, for example, pluralism, contextualism and skepticism.[10] And there can be combinations of existing approaches. Walter Hopp is a phenomenologist who treats thought experiments as fictions that give us rational access to universals (Hopp 2014), and one could be a Kantian who, when it comes to assessing individual thought experiments, is an empiricist. But we want to stress that despite the form of the above narrative, the philosophy of thought experiments is not a game of philosophical bingo in which we wait for all the philosophical -isms to be filled in and then go home. Thought experiments represent a rare four-way intersection of history, philosophy, cognitive science, and social science, and the opportunity for mutual information is precious. Here, knowledge from each of these disciplines (and others) can come together to enhance our understanding about the powers and limits of the mind. Each of the philosophical -isms can therefore be expected to inform but also *be informed* by historical discoveries, and cognitive and social scientific research.

The chapters in Part III represent much of the current state of affairs in the philosophy of thought experiments. Naturally, however, these chapters do not (aim to) exhaust all the possibilities. Addressing the questions they raise and also those that they don't is the purpose of Part IV.

Future directions

One lacuna in the above discussion is the lack of engagement between mainstream philosophy and philosophy of science. The first several chapters of Part IV help to address this. In the first, Stephen Stich and Kevin Tobia discuss the role of intuition in philosophical thought experiments and the impact of experimental philosophy. They begin by differentiating intuitions stimulated by thought experiments that are used as evidence for claims about "in-the-head mental entities" (like the content or extension of concepts, or the warrant for implicit or tacit theories) versus "outside-the-head non-psychological entities" (like universals, modal or moral truths, or natural kinds). Their primary question echoes the paradox/puzzle mentioned above: how can intuitions about philosophical thought experiments be evidence for claims about extra-mental entities? While we lack a good story for why such intuitions might be thought to be reliable sources of evidence for extra-mental entities, experimental philosophy provides a set of powerful reasons to be skeptical about those intuitions. Stich and Tobia introduce and summarize what they take to be the major relevant insights of experimental philosophy, and then turn to some criticisms. They consider and reject the "expertise" defense, according to which the intuitions of professional philosophers are less vulnerable to irrelevant factors, and another defense that restricts what we mean by "intuition" in a way that would enable us to avoid the charges of experimental philosophy. This latter defense is one taken up by Kirk Ludwig, author of the second chapter of Part IV.

Kirk Ludwig asks what experimental philosophy would have to be like if it were to justify the skeptical conclusions of Stich and Tobia and others. Ludwig breaks experimental philosophy down into several sub-kinds, presents the main contemporary criticisms of experimental philosophy, and argues that experimental philosophy as it stands cannot cast serious doubt on the use of thought experiments in philosophy. It can display variation in intuitions, but this does not demonstrate the further claim that philosophical intuitions are mistaken, or that folk intuitions are correct. According to Ludwig, these further claims cannot be addressed using survey-based methods. Of course, this does not mean that experimental philosophy is not useful for philosophy; on the contrary, it can alert us to important cognitive biases and defects, it can help us design better thought experiments, and be better teachers to our students. Ludwig closes with a five-point reply to the criticisms of Stich and Tobia.

Sticking with thought experiments in philosophy, Sören Häggqvist and Daniel Cohnitz discuss a specific and very common *kind* of philosophical thought experiment, namely, the counterexample. For these thought experiments to succeed, they typically require the evaluation of at least one modal claim, usually a counterfactual, which raises the following question (another echo of the paradox): what reason(s) do we have to think that thought experiments can be reliable guides to modal claims?[11] To address the problem, several formal reconstructions of the use of thought experiments as modal defeaters are considered, as well as the possibility of skepticism raised by experimental philosophy, and insights from the literature on the inference from conceivability to possibility (e.g., Gendler and Hawthorne 2002). Like Stich and Tobia, Häggqvist and Cohnitz vote for pluralism: different subfields of philosophy might require different things from thought experimental intuitions, and different epistemological accounts might be necessary. They finish by urging a closer connection between the discussion of thought experiments in metaphilosophy and philosophy of science. In both subfields, they argue, the dialectical context of a thought experiment appears necessary for a full epistemological account. This is an idea also championed by Goffi and Roux in Chapter 24.

In the next chapter, James W. McAllister considers cross-cultural and historical comparisons of thought experiments to "problematize the category of thought experiment and its application in different historical and cultural contexts" (425). He does this by asking *where* different communities draw the line between thought experiments and other kinds of reasoning, *when* they use thought experiments, and under *which* conditions thought experiments are taken to have evidential significance. These issues are closely connected to the metaphilosophical issues of the previous three chapters, to the metaphysical concerns of the final chapter, but also to the entire first two parts of the collection, in which we find displayed exactly the sorts of differences McAllister examines. Based on these observations, McAllister argues against using the term "thought experiment" for any inference occurring before Galileo. In so doing, McAllister takes the contextual nature of thought experimental justification even further than Cohnitz and Häggqvist and Stich and Tobia. He employs a fully historicized view of evidential significance, according to which something counts as evidence *only* in a given socio-historical context. Because of this, ancient Greeks, for example, would not have accepted thought experiments as a method with evidential significance since they would not have accepted experiment in general as such a method. McAllister considers the use of thought experiments in the discipline of history as well as in the philosophical traditions of India and China to provide additional reasons against imperialistically labelling various imaginative activities as thought experiments.

Taking seriously the contextual and dialectical nature of thought experiments suggested by the previous chapters, Jean-Yves Goffi and Sophie Roux present a dialectical account of the logic of thought experiments. They argue that all thought experiments require the entertainment of a scenario, the mental manipulation of which requires non-propositional knowledge (knowledge-how, tacit knowledge, etc.). Meanwhile, for thought experiments to produce propositional knowledge, they must also trade in propositions. However, no propositional reconstruction could ever be completely filled in, and this renders thought experiments irreducibly "opaque." According to them, a more complete account must admit the importance of propositional reasoning while accounting for this irreducible opacity. They argue that dialectical accounts of reasoning were created to deal with exactly this sort of opacity, since in the dialectical exchanges of natural conversation we operate without agreed upon rules or definite background assumptions. They examine three different ways dialectic argumentation theory has been developed in the twentieth century, and argue in favour of Nicholas Rescher's account (1977), which they apply to thought experiments.

When we want to circumscribe the epistemological power of thought experiments, we often focus on successful instances. But an equally fruitful way of proceeding is to concentrate on those that fail. One very helpful example is given by John D. Norton in Chapter 25, "The Worst Thought Experiment." This is a thought experiment proposed by Leo Szilard in 1929, which was presented as a development of Maxwell's demon. Through a characteristically clear historical account, Norton identifies two important features of our interaction with thought experiments. First, we allow "extensive latitude" to the creator of a thought experiment in introducing idealizations, which are necessary to focus the narrative. Second, we typically presume with the creator of the thought experiment that the case considered is a typical one, from which an inductive generalization can follow. Norton explains the failure of Szilard's thought experiment in terms of its (mis)use of both of these features.

Following Norton's discussion of idealization in Szilard's thought experiment, Julian Reiss analyzes the role of idealizations in thought experiments in general. First, he distinguishes several kinds of idealizations, and argues that only one is relevant to this discussion: what Ernan McMullin called "Galilean idealizations." Of the subtypes of Galilean idealization, Reiss concentrates on causal idealizations, or in other words, those that "isolate a single causal line." Reiss asks how and under which conditions such idealizations can be justified. He identifies two conditions, one epistemic and another empirical. To satisfy the epistemic condition, there must be some way to know what would happen in the idealized single causal line. One way is to look at an asymptotic series of material idealizations and infer to the extreme case, like experimenting with increasingly smooth objects to infer to the behaviour of frictionless ones. To satisfy the empirical condition, the idealization must be informative concerning the behaviour of the same causal line when in the non-idealized context of the real world. Reiss argues that these two conditions explain why we see more thought experiments in some domains than others.

Reliance on idealizations is one of many features thought experiments share with computer simulations. Their similarity has inspired strong claims, such as the prediction that in some domains, computer simulations will replace thought experiments altogether (Chandrasekharan, Nersessian, and Subramanian 2013). In Chapter 27, Johannes Lenhard reviews and tackles various comparisons between thought experiments and computer simulations. Despite the similarities, Lenhard argues that the production of intuitions is importantly different from the automated iterations of formal algorithms, and that this has epistemological ramifications. Most notably, computer simulations can be opaque in the sense that they are not completely accessible to epistemic assessment, and this is because there is a type of iteration they employ that would be impossible in a thought experiment. This sort of iteration is displayed in Schelling's model of social segregation, the Ising model, complex systems models like dynamic meteorological models, and models that approximate the Schrödinger equation for systems of molecules too complicated to solve directly. Because of the differences in iteration-type, different epistemological accounts will be needed to explain the different strengths and weaknesses of computer simulations and thought experiments.

Lenhard concludes by discussing the common historical roots of thought experiments and computer simulations. For one thing, both emerge from a natural need and ability to explore hypothetical possibilities. Whatever we call this ability in the silicone domain, in humans we tend to call it imagination. In Letitia Meynell's "Images and Imagination in Thought Experiments" (Chapter 28), we get an in-depth look at the imaginative core of human thought experiments. Part of Meynell's project is to bring together insights from the literature on imagination in philosophy of mind and aesthetics. Through a discussion of how we interact imaginatively with images, Meynell considers the strengths and weaknesses of images in the context of thought experimentation. For instance, Einstein's train is accompanied by an image in the original text that might not be necessary to justify the conclusion of the thought experiment, but which serves as an extra "prop" (in the sense of Walton 1990) that directs us to imagine scenarios in certain ways, reassures novices that they are imagining the right things, and foregrounds certain aspects of the imaginary scenarios as well as certain skills and subsets of background knowledge. And because there aren't any norms dictating how we must approach a given image, for example, from right to left or top to bottom, we are encouraged to work through it ourselves, which compliments the experimental nature of thought experiments. Meynell closes with some epistemological considerations about how to justify uses of the imagination in thought experiments.

There are other ways to bring aesthetics to bear on the topic of thought experiments. For example, Ichikawa and Jarvis (2009) argue that it is not just background assumptions that we rely on in a thought experiment, but our ability to interact with *stories*. Perhaps the human brain has evolved some reliable way of forming modal inferences from imagining what would be true in a fictional world, and thought experiments take advantage of this. Such an account would work nicely with the mental models account, since fictionalism about scientific models has also been a popular topic in philosophy of science for some time, and if thought experiments are used as models are, then insights from that literature can be brought to bear.

David Davies presents just such a combination. An on-going question in philosophy of art concerns how we learn from fiction. One might think that all literary and cinematic fiction could do in order to increase our stock of knowledge would be to *suggest* hypotheses for empirical study. That is, we might think that works of artistic fiction are (at best) confined to the context of discovery. On the other hand, we don't (always) make this same claim for the thought experiments found in science and philosophy. A number of issues are pertinent to a defense of the possibility of learning through fiction by comparison with thought experiments. For one, in science we make explicit claims about the world, and there are (at least conventional) epistemic standards by which we can judge whether those claims are true or warranted. This does not seem to be the case in fiction, as fictions typically do not make explicit claims about the world and there are typically no standards by which to judge the epistemic value of their content. These are the "no-argument" and "no-evidence" problems, respectively. That is, fictions make no arguments that the world is a certain way, and they provide no evidence independent of what the reader herself brings to the fiction. After arguing against several influential accounts of learning through fiction, Davies presents his account of what it means to be a fictional narrative, and argues that thought experiments in science and philosophy satisfy it. He then provides a helpful taxonomy of epistemological views on the issue of learning from fiction ranging from extreme deflationism to extreme inflationism, and selects "moderate inflationism" as the best option. This view is meant to cohere with the mental models account of thought experiments, according to which thought experiments mobilize unarticulated cognitive resources to learn something new about the world from fiction. Davies argues that this survives the "no-evidence" objection because through such mobilization, a fiction can make us aware of patterns that "underlie the complexity of prior and present actual experience" (this volume, 521). And it survives the "no-argument" objection because we test the fiction's claims *through* our engagement with it, so we need not appeal to anything external to the fiction. Several interesting questions remain, however. For instance, how do we apply this moderate inflationist account to thought experiments in film, which are not "verbally mediated" as most thought experiments are?

Like Meynell and Davies, Michael T. Stuart also seeks to connect the discussion of thought experiments to insights in another philosophical subdomain. In this case, we are directed to the literature on understanding. Stuart argues that the epistemological challenge of thought experiments is equally interesting when phrased in terms of understanding as when phrased in terms of knowledge. He proposes three ways that thought experiments can increase understanding of x: by explaining x, making x more meaningful, and making x more fruitful. He argues that these different ways of enhancing understanding can yield the different types of understanding identified in the epistemological literature.

To address the question of how thought experiments produce understanding, Stuart draws on new work in epistemology and aesthetics by Elizabeth Camp and Alison Hills.

In the final chapter, Alisa Bokulich and Mélanie Frappier critically appraise various definitions of thought experiments to see if anything definite can be said. Bokulich and Frappier must deal with several related challenges: First, what makes two thought experiments similar enough to be counted as repetitions of the same experiment? Second, how do we accommodate the insight that *what counts as equal* will itself be relative to the purposes of classification? That is, for some purposes historical continuity is what matters, for others it is propositional content or structural form. Third, and closely related: do thought experiments change over time, and if so, how? To answer these questions, Bokulich and Frappier take up a pluralist stance. They argue that what counts as identical depends on what we think thought experiments are. If they are intuition pumps, identical thought experiments should produce the same intuitions. Given the variability of intuitions mentioned by Stich and Tobia and Cohnitz and Häggqvist, perfect identify between two thought experiments might be rare. If thought experiments are sets of premises and a conclusion, thought experiments cannot change or be modified (except in the order or presentation of the premises, or in the irrelevant but picturesque details of the narrative). If thought experiments are mental models, then the thought experiment outstrips its linguistic presentation. While there are worries about what might count as equal for the (essentially private) mental models, there might be enough to give thought experiments identities which can be modified over time. If thought experiments are props for the imagination (Salis and Frigg forthcoming; Meynell 2014, this volume) then for each thought experiment there are two sets of fictional truths, one that is objective and socially shared, and one that is created in the subjective imagination of each participant using their own principles of generation (see Meynell, this volume). Since these sets differ, we can explain why two different conclusions can be drawn from the same thought experiment: the principles that generated the intersubjective sets of fictional truths were different, or improperly applied by one party, or the same but insufficiently clear. This will not describe all cases, however, since in many it is not just the principles of generation that are different or variously applied, but the narrative itself that is changed, sometimes drastically. Finally, if thought experiments are experiments, they will be replicated just like other kinds of experiments. Again, however, there are different aspects of experiments that can be replicated. This brings us again to the "dual-structure view" of thought experiments (originally inspired by Hans Radder's dual view of laboratory experiments (1996) which was developed by Häggqvist and De Mey. However Bokulich and Frappier point out that this account might still be insufficient to capture certain important cases.

Concluding thoughts

We hope Part IV of the collection furthers the existing debates about thought experiments, and creates conceptual space for new competing accounts and issues. As a whole, we hope the companion invites discussion, criticism and comparison in as many new directions as possible.

Before concluding, we want to emphasize again that the distinctions between the parts of this companion are not, and could not be, strict. The chapters in Parts I and II present new research, much of which pertains directly to the soundness of the arguments in Parts III and IV. For example, if Paolo Palmieri is correct in his re-telling of the history of Galileo's falling bodies thought experiment, this might impact those philosophical accounts that rely heavily on the features of this thought experiment as evidence (perhaps including McAllister 1996, this volume; Norton 1996; Gendler 1998 and Brown 2011). And the accounts presented in Parts III and IV will inspire new ways to interpret the examples considered in Parts I and II. To this end, we have encouraged as much interaction between the chapters of the different parts of this book as possible, and we hope this has improved the collection.

Of course, fruitful interaction between history, philosophy and social and cognitive science has been present in the literature on thought experiments since its beginning. Accordingly, most chapters in this companion present historical arguments with epistemological and metaphysical assumptions in mind, or philosophical arguments that depend on specific readings of history, cognitive science, or social psychology. Thus, while the parts of this book are separated in a way that we hope will make them easy to access and pleasant to read, the distinctions between the parts are always more or less artificial. For instance, Kenneth Westphal's chapter (Part I) could easily have been in Part IV, and James McAllister's chapter (Part IV) could easily have been in Part I.

One final point: this collection draws together many different sorts of first and second order knowledge, including: (1) expertise in the history and methods of the disciplines discussed in the chapters (theology, history, philosophy, physics, biology, etc.), and (2) expertise in the fields from which the analyses are carried out, that is: history, sociology, cognitive science and philosophy as they are currently practiced. No one of the three editors of this companion pretends to possess such comprehensive knowledge. But rather than cater the chapters to what an average reader could digest, we've chosen to include a wide range of chapters all of which rely to some degree on different background knowledge, in order to maximize breadth. For example, Lenhard assumes familiarity with Monte Carlo simulations and Markov chains, while Palmieri assumes some Husserl. We hope the reader finds this exciting rather than discouraging.

The topic of thought experiments – perhaps because it draws together so many disciplines – appears boundless. Though much has been covered, there is very much more to be done. As at least one of us is inclined to say: Welcome to Plato's heaven.

Notes

1 Please see also our special index cataloguing the thought experiments discussed in this Companion (page 558).
2 For Searle's Chinese room, see Arthur (this volume). For Rawls' original position, see Miščević (this volume), and Brun (this volume). For Plato's thought experiments, see Becker (this volume). For the trolley problem, see Brun (this volume). For more philosophical thought experiments, see Dennett (2013).
3 For Lucretius' thought experiment, see Brown (2011), Ierodiakonou (2011), Brown and Stuart (2013); Meynell (this volume). For Maxwell's demon, see Brown (2011), Buzzoni (2008, 97–100), Krimsky (1973), Myrvold (2011), Norton (this volume), Peacocke (this volume), Schlesinger (1996, 473–76), Stuart (2016a). For Einstein's thought experiments, see Norton (1991) Peacocke (this volume), Meynell (this volume). For Schrödinger's cat, see Peacocke (this volume). For Newton's thought experiments, see Arthur (this volume), Norton (1996); Peijnenburg and Atkinson (2003); Brown (2011). For Heisenberg's microscope, see Popper (1959), Stuart (2016a), Van Dyck (2003), and Camilleri (2007). For Galileo's thought experiments, see Brown (2011),

Norton (1996), Gendler (1998, 2000), Buzzoni (2008, 106–7), Palmieri (2003, this volume), McAllister (1996, this volume). For Stevin's chain, see Brown (2011), Norton (1996, 349–51), and Mach (1905). For thought experiments in mathematics, see Buzzoni (2011), Witt-Hansen (1976), Müller (1969), Brown (1999, 2007a/b), Glas (1999), Van Bendegem (2003), Sherry (2006), Starikova (2007), Starikova and Giaquinto (this volume) and Cohnitz (2008). For thought experiments in geometry, see Lakatos (1976). In infinity, see Galilei (1638, 32), and Hilbert (2013).

4 See Antsey and Vanzo (2016) for a look at the relationship between experimental philosophy and thought experiments going back to the seventeenth century. See also Systema and Buckwalter (2016), Stich and Tobia (this volume), Ludwig (this volume) and Cohnitz and Häggqvist (this volume).

5 This wording is pretty close to the way Kuhn framed the problem, although not exactly. In Kuhn's words the problem is: "How, then, relying exclusively upon familiar data, can a thought experiment lead to new knowledge or to a new understanding of nature?" (1977, 241).

6 E.g., Aligica and Evans (2009), Arthur (1999), Bishop (1998, 1999), Bokulich (2001), Brendel (2004), Brown (1991a, 1992, 2004, 2007a), Butkovic (2007), Buzzoni (2008), Camilleri (2014), Chandrasekharan, Nersessian and Subramanian (2013), Clatterbuck (2013), Cooper (2005), Davies (2007), De Baere (2003), De Mey (2003, 2005, 2006a, 2006b), Ducheyne (2006), Fehige (2012, 2013), Gendler (1998, 2000, 2004), Georgiou (2007), Gooding (1992, 1994), Häggqvist (1996, 2007, 2009), Hopp (2014), Horowitz and Massey (1991), Humphreys (1993), Irvine (1991), Kujundzic (1998), Laymon (1991), Machery (2011), McAllister (1996), McComb (2013), Moue, Masavetas, and Karayianni (2006), Nersessian (1992, 2007). Norton (1991, 1996, 2004a), Pitcha (2011), Roberts (1993), Schlesinger (1996), Shepard (2008). Sorensen (1992), Urbaniak (2012) and Wilson (1991).

7 For other criticisms of Norton's view, see e.g., Gendler (1998) and Stuart (2016b).

8 See Brendel (this volume) for criticism of Häggqvist's use of this argument against Norton.

9 More needs to be said here: Brown does portray the intuitive aspect of a thought experiment as something akin to sense experience, though he does not agree that he is committed to there being only one kind of epistemological account for both sense experience and rational insight.

10 Examples of pluralists might be Bokulich and Frappier (this volume), Cohnitz and Häggqvist (this volume) and Stich and Tobia (this volume), while Rachel Cooper (2005) argues against pluralism. An example of a contextualist might be McAllister (this volume). Norton (2004a and 2004b) argues against this approach, since for him the mark of a good thought experiment "cannot be something external to the thought experiment; that is, something about the person who authors the thought experiment or about the context in which it is proposed" (2004b, 54). Almost all who write on thought experiments are skeptical concerning at least some of their uses, but it is difficult to find anyone who is skeptical about thought experiments tout court. For example, Pierre Duhem is often quoted as a skeptic, but Buzzoni argues convincingly that he was only drawing attention to some of the dangers we face when putting too much weight on them (Buzzoni forthcoming). Daniel Dennett has been cited as a skeptic by many, and perhaps for good reason: he calls thought experiments "intuitions pumps," and admits that his first use of this term "was derogatory" (1996, 182). But again, his skepticism was only directed toward the over-confident use of thought experiments. In later work, he writes,

> If you look at the history of philosophy, you see that all the great and influential stuff has been technically full of holes but utterly memorable and vivid. They are what I call 'intuition pumps' – lovely thought experiments. Like Plato's cave, and Descartes's evil demon, and Hobbes' vision of the state of nature and the social contract, and even Kant's idea of the categorical imperative. I don't know of any philosopher who thinks any one of those is a logically sound argument for anything. But they're wonderful imagination grabbers, jungle gyms for the imagination. They structure the way you think about a problem. These are the real legacy of the history of philosophy. A lot of philosophers have forgotten that, but I like to make intuition pumps.
>
> (Dennett 1996, 182)

Paul Thagard is another candidate for a skeptic. He argues that "the made-up thought experiments favored by many philosophers are not evidence at all" (2010, 209). Rather, "philosophical attempts to establish truths by a priori reasoning, thought experiments, or conceptual analysis have been no more successful than faith-based thinking has been. All these methods serve merely to reinforce existing prejudices" (2010, 41). Still, Thagard allows thought experiments a function in science, and his naturalism about philosophy implies that the same methods should be used there as in science, which a fortiori grants a role for thought experiments in philosophy (see Stuart 2014. See also Buzzoni 2016; and Fehige, this volume). The best candidate for a true skeptic might be Alexius Meinong, who argues against Mach that "an experiment that in fact does not exist at all, can neither prove nor teach anything" (1907, 276–77).

11 This question can also be thought of as an instantiation of Stich and Tobia's main question, given that modal claims are one of the extra-mental entities they discuss.

References

Aligica, P. D. and Evans, A. J. (2009) "Thought experiments, counterfactuals and comparative analysis," *The Review of Austrian Economics* 22: 225–239.

Antsey, P. and Vanzo, A. (2016) "Early modern experimental philosophy," in *A Companion to Experimental Philosophy*, edited by J. Systema and W. Buckwalter, Somerset, UK: Wiley-Blackwell.

Arthur, R. (1999) "On thought experiments as a priori science," *International Studies in the Philosophy of Science* 13: 215–229.

Bishop, M. (1998) "An epistemological role for thought experiments," in *Idealization IX: Idealization in Contemporary Physics*, edited by N. Shanks, Amsterdam: Rodopoi.

Bishop, M. (1999) "Why thought experiments are not arguments," *Philosophy of Science* 66: 534–541.

Bokulich, A. (2001) "Rethinking thought experiments," *Perspectives on Science* 9: 285–307.

Brendel, E. (2004) "Intuition pumps and the proper use of thought experiments," *Dialectica* 58: 89–108.

Brown, J. R. (1986) "Thought experiments since the scientific revolution," *International Studies in the Philosophy of Science* 1: 1–15.

Brown, J. R. (1991a [2011]) *The Laboratory of the Mind: Thought Experiments in the Natural Sciences*, London: Routledge.

Brown, J. R. (1991b) "Thought experiments: A Platonic account," in *Thought Experiments in Science and Philosophy*, edited by T. Horowitz and G. Massey, Lanham: Rowman and Littlefield.

Brown, J. R. (1992) "Why empiricism won't work," *Proceedings of the Philosophy of Science Association* 2: 271–279.

Brown, J. R. (1999) *Philosophy of Mathematics: An Introduction to the World of Proofs and Pictures*, London: Routledge.

Brown, J. R. (2004) "Why thought experiments do transcend empiricism," in *Contemporary Debates in the Philosophy of Science*, edited by C. Hitchcock, Malden: Blackwell.

Brown J. R. (2007a) "Thought experiments in science, philosophy, and mathematics," *Croatian Journal of Philosophy* 7: 3–27.

Brown J. R. (2007b) "Comments and replies," *Croatian Journal of Philosophy* 7: 249–268.

Brown, J. R. and Stuart, M. T. (2013) "Review: Ierodiakonou, K. and Roux, S. (eds), *Thought Experiments in Methodological and Historical Contexts*," *HOPOS: The Journal of the International Society for the History of Philosophy of Science* 3: 154–157.

Butkovic, A. (2007) "What is the function of thought experiments: Kuhn vs. Brown," *Croatian Journal of Philosophy* VII: 63–67.

Buzzoni, M. (2008) *Thought Experiment in the Natural Sciences*, Würzburg: Königshausen and Neumann.

Buzzoni, M. (2010) "Empirical thought experiments: A transcendental-operational view," *Epistemologia* XXXIII: 5–26.

Buzzoni, M. (2011) "On mathematical thought experiments," *Epistemologia* XXXIV: 61–88.

Buzzoni, M. (2013a) "Thought experiments from a Kantian point of view," in *Thought Experiments in Science, Philosophy, and the Arts*, edited by M. Frappier, L. Meynell, and J. R. Brown, London: Routledge.

Buzzoni, M. (2013b) "On thought experiments and the Kantian a priori in the natural sciences: A reply to Yiftach J. H. Fehige," *Epistemologia* 2: 277–293.
Buzzoni, M. (2015) "Causality, teleology, and thought experiments in biology," *Journal for General Philosophy of Science* 46: 279–299. DOI: 10.1007/s10838-015-9293-9.
Buzzoni, M. (2016) "Thought experiments in philosophy: A neo-Kantian and experimentalist point of view," *Topoi*. DOI: 10.1007/s11245-016-9436-6.
Buzzoni, M. (forthcoming) "Duhem and Mach on thought experiments. Or: Did Duhem really reject Mach's thought experiments?", in *Vienna Circle Institute Yearbook*, Dordrecht: Springer.
Camilleri, K. (2007) "Indeterminacy and the limits of classical concepts: The transformation of Heisenberg's thought," *Perspectives on Science* 15: 178–201.
Camilleri, K. (2014) "Toward a constructivist epistemology of thought experiments in science," *Synthese* 191: 1697–1716.
Camp, E. (2009) "Two varieties of literary imagination: Metaphor, fiction, and thought experiments," *Midwest Studies in Philosophy* XXXIII: 107–130.
Carroll, N. (2002) "The wheel of virtue: Art, literature, and moral knowledge," *Journal of Aesthetics and Art Criticism* 60: 3–26.
Chandrasekharan, S., Nersessian, N. and Subramanian, V. (2013) "Computational modeling: Is this the end of thought experiments in science?", in *Thought Experiments in Science, Philosophy, and the Arts*, edited by M. Frappier, L. Meynell, and J. R. Brown, London: Routledge.
Clatterbuck, H. (2013) "The epistemology of thought experiments: A non-eliminativist, non-Platonic account," *European Journal for Philosophy of Science* 3: 309–329.
Cohen, M. (2004) *Wittgenstein's Beetle and Other Thought Experiments*, Somerset: Wiley-Blackwell.
Cohnitz, D. (2008) "Ørsteds 'Gedankenexperiment': Eine Kantianische Fundierung der Infinitesimalrechnung? Ein Beitrag zur Begriffsgeschichte von 'Gedankenexperiment' und zur Mathematikgeschichte des frühen 19. Jahrhunderts," *Kant-Studien* 99: 407–433.
Cooper, R. (2005) "Thought experiments," *Metaphilosophy* 36: 328–347.
Daiber, J. (2001) *Experimentalphysik des Geistes: Novalis und das romantische Experiment*, Göttingen: Vadenhoeck and Ruprecht.
Davies, D. (2007) "Thought experiments and fictional narratives," *Croatian Journal of Philosophy* VII: 29–45.
Davies, D. (2012) "Can philosophical thought experiments be 'screened'?", in *Thought Experiments in Science, Philosophy, and the Arts*, edited by M. Frappier, L. Meynell, and J. R. Brown, London: Routledge.
De Baere, B. (2003) "Thought experiments, rhetoric, and possible worlds," *Philosophica* 72: 105–130.
De Mey, T. (2003) "The dual nature view of thought experiments," *Philosophica* 72: 61–78.
De Mey, T. (2005) "Remodeling the past," *Foundations of Science* 10: 47–66.
De Mey, T. (2006a) "Kuhn's paradox of thought experiments resolved," *The Baltic International Yearbook of Cognition, Logic and Communication* 1: 111–125.
De Mey, T. (2006b) "Imagination's grip on science," *Metaphilosophy* 37: 222–239.
Dennett, D. (1996) "Intuition pumps," in *Third Culture: Beyond the Scientific Revolution*, edited by J. Brockman, New York: Simon and Schuster.
Dennett, D. (2013) *Intuition Pumps and Other Tools for Thinking*, New York: W. W. Norton and Company.
Ducheyne, S. (2006) "The argument(s) for universal gravitation," *Foundations of Science* 11: 419–447.
Elgin, C. Z. (1993) "Understanding art and science," *Synthese* 95: 13–28.
Elgin, C. Z. (2000) "Interpretation and understanding," *Erkenntnis* 52: 175–183.
Elgin, C. Z. (2002) "Creation as reconfiguration," *International Studies in the Philosophy of Science* 16: 13–25.
Elgin, C. Z. (2004) "True enough," *Philosophical Issues* 14: 113–121.
Elgin, C. Z. (2006) "From knowledge to understanding," in *Epistemology Futures*, edited by S. Hetherington, Oxford: Clarendon Press.
Elgin, C. Z. (2014) "Fiction as thought experiment," *Perspectives on Science* 22: 221–241.
Fehige, Y. (2012) "'Experiments of pure reason': Kantianism and thought experiments in science," *Epistemologia* XXXV: 141–160.
Fehige, Y. (2013) "The relativized a priori and the laboratory of the mind: Towards a neo-Kantian account of thought experiments in science," *Epistemologia* XXXVI: 55–73.
Fehige, Y. and Stuart, M. T. (2014) "On the origins of the philosophy of thought experiments: The forerun," *Perspectives on Science* 22: 179–220.

Fehige, Y. and Wiltsche, H. A. (2013): "The body, thought experiments, and phenomenology," in *Thought Experiments in Science, Philosophy, and the Arts*, edited by M. Frappier, L. Meynell, and J. R. Brown, London: Routledge.
Froese, T. and Gallagher, S. (2010) "Phenomenology and artificial life: Toward a technological supplementation of phenomenological methodology," *Husserl Studies* 26: 83–106.
Galilei, G. (1638 [1954]) *Dialogues Concerning Two New Sciences*, translated by H. Crew and A. de Salvio, New York: Dover.
Gellard, C. (2011) "Thought experiments in late Medieval debates on atomism," in *Thought Experiments in Methodological and Historical Contexts*, edited by K. Ierodiakonou and S. Roux, Leiden: Brill.
Gendler, T. S. (1998) "Galileo and the indispensability of scientific thought experiment," *British Journal for the Philosophy of Science* 49: 397–424.
Gendler, T. S. (2000) *Thought Experiment: On the Powers and Limits of Imaginary Cases*, London: Routledge.
Gendler, T. S. (2004) "Thought experiments rethought—and reperceived," *Philosophy of Science* 71: 1152–1163.
Gendler, T. S. and Hawthorne, J. (2002) *Conceivability and Possibility*, Oxford: Oxford University Press.
Georgiou, A. (2007) "An embodied cognition view of imagery-based reasoning in science: Lessons from thought experiments," *Croatian Journal of Philosophy* VII: 29–45.
Glas, E. (1999) "Thought-experimentation and mathematical innovation," *Studies in History and Philosophy of Science* 30: 1–19.
Gooding, D. (1992) "What is experimental about thought experiments?," *PSA: Proceedings of the Biennial Meeting of the Philosophy of Science Association* 2: 280–290.
Gooding, D. (1994) "Imaginary science," *The British Journal for the Philosophy of Science* 45: 1029–1045.
Hacking, I. (1992) "Do thought experiments have a life of their own? Comments on James Brown, Nancy Nersessian and David Gooding," *PSA: Proceedings of the Biennial Meeting of the Philosophy of Science Association* 2: 302–308.
Häggqvist, S. (1996) *Thought Experiments in Philosophy*, Stockholm: Almqvist and Wiksell International.
Häggqvist, S. (2007) "The a priori thesis: A critical assessment," *Croatian Journal of Philosophy* VII: 47–61.
Häggqvist, S. (2009) "A model for thought experiments," *Canadian Journal of Philosophy* 39: 55–76.
Hilbert, D. (2013) *David Hilbert's Lectures on the Foundations of Arithmetics and Logic 1917–1933*, edited by W. Ewald and W. Sieg, Heidelberg: Springer-Verlag.
Hopp, W. (2014) "Experiments in thought," *Perspectives on Science* 22: 76–97.
Horowitz, T. and Massey, G. (eds) (1991) *Thought Experiments in Science and Philosophy*, Lanham: Rowman and Littlefield.
Humphreys, P. (1993) "Seven theses on thought experiments," in *Philosophical Problems on the Internal and External Worlds: Essays on the Philosophy of Adolf Grunbaum*, edited by J. Earman, A. I. Janis, G. J. Massey, and N. Rescher, Pittsburgh: University of Pittsburgh Press.
Ichikawa, J. and Jarvis, B. (2009) "Thought-experiment intuitions and truth in fiction," *Philosophical Studies* 142: 221–246.
Ierodiakonou, K. (2005) "Ancient thought experiments: A first approach," *Ancient Philosophy* 25: 125–140.
Ierodiakonou, K. (2011) "Remarks on the history of an ancient thought experiment," in *Thought Experiments in Methodological and Historical Contexts*, edited by K. Ierodiakonou and S. Roux, Leiden: Brill.
Irvine, A. D. (1991) "Thought experiments in scientific reasoning," in *Thought Experiments in Science and Philosophy*, edited by T. Horowitz and G. Massey, Lanham: Rowman and Littlefield.
Knuuttila, S. and Kukkonen, T. (2011) "Thought experiments and indirect proofs in Averroes, Aquinas, and Buridan," in *Thought Experiments in Methodological and Historical Contexts*, edited by K. Ierodiakonou and S. Roux, Leiden: Brill.
Krimsky, S. (1973) "The use and misuse of critical Gedankenexperimente," *Zeitschrift für allgemeine Wissenschaftstheorie* 4: 323–334.
Kuhn, T. S. (1977) "A function for thought experiments," in *The Essential Tension*, Chicago: University of Chicago Press.

Kühne, U. (2005) *Die Methode des Gedankenexperiments*, Frankfurt: Suhrkamp.
Kujundzic, N. (1995) "Thought experiments: Architecture and economy of thought," *Journal of the British Society of Phenomenology* 26: 86–93.
Kujundzic, N. (1998) "The role of variation in thought experiments," *International Studies in the Philosophy of Science* 12: 239–243.
Lakatos, I. (1976) *Proofs and Refutations*, Cambridge: Cambridge University Press.
Lautner, P. (2011) "Thought experiments in the De Anima commentaries," in *Thought Experiments in Methodological and Historical Contexts*, edited by K. Ierodiakonou and S. Roux, Leiden: Brill.
Laymon, R. (1991) "Thought experiments by Stevin, Mach and Gouy: Thought experiments as ideal limits and as semantic domains," in *Thought Experiments in Science and Philosophy*, edited by T. Horowitz and G. Massey, Lanham: Rowman and Littlefield.
Lennox, J. G. (1991) "Darwinian thought experiments: A function for just-so stories," in *Thought Experiments in Science and Philosophy*, edited by T. Horowitz and G. Massey, Lanham: Rowman and Littlefield.
Mach, E. (1905) "On thought experiments," in *Knowledge and Error: Sketches on the Psychology of Enquiry*, translated by T. J. McCormack, Dordrecht: D. Reidel Publishing Company.
Machery, E. (2011) "Thought experiments and philosophical knowledge," *Metaphilosophy* 42: 191–214.
McAllister, J. (1996) "The evidential significance of thought experiment in science," *Studies in the History of the Philosophy of Science* 27: 233–250.
McComb, G. (2013) "Thought experiment, definition, and literary fiction," in *Thought Experiments in Science, Philosophy, and the Arts*, edited by M. Frappier, L. Meynell, and J. R. Brown, London: Routledge.
Meinong, A. (1907 [1973]) "Das Gedankenexperiment," in *Über die Stellung der Gegenstandstheorie im System der Wissenschaften*, edited by R. Haller and R. Kindinger, Graz-Austria: Akademische Druck und Verlagsanstalt.
Meynell, L. (2014) "Imagination and insight: A new account of the content of thought experiments," *Synthese* 191: 4149–4168.
Miščević, N. (1992) "Mental models and thought experiments," *International Studies in the Philosophy of Science* 6: 215–226.
Miščević, N. (2004) "The explainability of intuitions," *Dialectica* 58: 43–70.
Miščević, N. (2007) "Modelling intuitions and thought experiments," *Croatian Journal of Philosophy* VII: 181–214.
Mohanty, J. N. (1991) "The method of imaginative variation in phenomenology," in *Thought Experiments in Science and Philosophy*, edited by T. Horowitz and G. Massey, Lanham: Rowman and Littlefield.
Moue, A., Masavetas, K. and Karayianni, H. (2006) "Tracing the development of thought experiments in the philosophy of the natural sciences," *Journal for General Philosophy of Science* 37: 61–75.
Müller, I. (1969) "Euclid's Elements and the axiomatic method," *The British Journal for the Philosophy of Science* 20: 289–309.
Myrvold, W. (2011) "Statistical mechanics and thermodynamics: A Maxwellian view," *Studies in History and Philosophy of Science Part B* 42: 237–243.
Nersessian, N. J. (1992a) "How do scientists think? Capturing the dynamics of conceptual change in science," in *Cognitive Models of Science*, edited by R. N. Giere, Minneapolis: University of Minnesota Press.
Nersessian, N. J. (1992b) "In the theoretician's laboratory: Thought experimenting as mental modeling," *Proceedings of the Philosophy of Science Association* 2: 291–301.
Nersessian, N. J. (2007) "Thought experiments as mental modelling: Empiricism without logic," *Croatian Journal of Philosophy* VII: 125–161.
Nersessian, N. J. (2008) *Creating Scientific Concepts*, Cambridge: MIT Press.
Norton, J. D. (1991) "Thought experiments in Einstein's work," in *Thought Experiments in Science and Philosophy*, edited by T. Horowitz and G. Massey, Lanham: Rowman and Littlefield.
Norton, J. D. (1996) "Are thought experiments just what you thought?," *Canadian Journal of Philosophy* 26: 333–366.
Norton, J. D. (2004a) "On thought experiments: Is there more to the argument?," *Philosophy of Science* 71: 1139–1151.
Norton, J. D. (2004b) "Why thought experiments do not transcend empiricism," in *Contemporary Debates in the Philosophy of Science*, edited by C. Hitchcock, Malden: Blackwell.

Ørsted, H. C. (1811 [1920]) "Første Indledning til den almindelige Naturlaere," in *Hans Christian Ørsted: Naturvidenskabelige Skrifter: Samlet Udgave me to Afhandlinger om Hans Virke*, vol. 3, edited by K. Meier, Kopenhagen: Andr. Fred. Høst and Søn.
Palmerino, C. R. (2011) "Galileo's use of Medieval thought experiments," in *Thought Experiments in Methodological and Historical Contexts*, edited by K. Ierodiakonou and S. Roux, Leiden: Brill.
Palmieri, P. (2003) "Mental models in Galileo's early mathematization of nature," *Studies in History and Philosophy of Science* 34: 229–264.
Peijnenburg, J. and Atkinson, D. (2003) "When are thought experiments poor ones?," *Journal for General Philosophy of Science* 34: 305–322.
Pitcha, M. (2011) "How to reconstruct a thought experiment," *Organon F* 18: 154–188.
Popper, K. (1959) "On the use and misuse of imaginary experiments, especially in quantum theory," in *The Logic of Scientific Discovery*, London: Hutchinson.
Radder, H. (1996) *In and About the World: Philosophical Studies of Science and Technology*, Albany: State University of New York Press.
Rescher, N. (1977) *Dialectics: A Controversy-Oriented Approach to the Theory of Knowledge*, Albany: SUNY Press.
Roberts, F. (1993) "Thought experiments and social transformation," *Journal for the Theory of Social Behaviour* 23: 399–421.
Salis, F. and Frigg, R. (forthcoming) "Capturing the scientific imagination," in *The Scientific Imagination*, edited by P. Godfrey-Smith and A. Levy, New York: Oxford University Press.
Schick, T. and Vaughn, L. (2012) *Doing Philosophy: An Introduction through Thought Experiments*, 5th ed., New York: McGraw-Hill.
Schildknecht, C. (1990) *Philosophische Masken: Literarische Formen der Philosophie bei Platon, Descartes, Wolff und Lichtenberg*, Stuttgart: Metzler.
Schlesinger, G. (1996) "The power of thought experiments," *Foundations of Physics* 26: 467–482.
Shepard, R. N. (2008) "The step to rationality: The efficacy of thought experiments in science, ethics, and free will," *Cognitive Science* 32: 3–35.
Sherry D. (2006) "Mathematical reasoning: Induction, deduction and beyond," *Studies in History and Philosophy of Science* 37: 489–504.
Sorensen, R. (1992) *Thought Experiments*, Oxford: Oxford University Press.
Starikova, I. (2007) "Picture-proofs and Platonism," *Croatian Journal of Philosophy* 7: 81–92.
Stuart, M. T. (2014) "Cognitive science and thought experiments: A refutation of Paul Thagard," *Perspectives on Science* 22: 98–121.
Stuart, M. T. (2015) *Thought Experiments in Science*, Ph.D. thesis, University of Toronto, Canada.
Stuart, M. T. (2016a) "Taming theory with thought experiments: Understanding and scientific progress," *Studies in the History and Philosophy of Science* 58: 24–33.
Stuart, M. T. (2016b) "Norton and the logic of thought experiments," *Axiomathes* 26: 451–466.
Stuart, M. T. (2017) "Imagination: A sine qua non of science," *Croatian Journal of Philosophy* Vol. XVII, No. 49.
Systema, J. and Buckwalter, W. (eds) (2016) *A Companion to Experimental Philosophy*, Somerset: Wiley-Blackwell.
Tetlock, P. E. and Belkin, A. (eds) (1996) *Counterfactual Thought Experiments in World Politics*, Princeton: Princeton University Press.
Thagard, P. (2010) *The Brain and the Meaning of Life*, Princeton: Princeton University Press.
Tittle, P. (2004) *What If … : Collected Thought Experiments in Philosophy*, Essex: Pearson.
Urbaniak, R. (2012) "'Platonic' thought experiments: How on earth?," *Synthese* 187: 731–752.
Van Bendegem, J. P. (2003) "Thought experiments in mathematics: Anything but proof," *Philosophica* 72: 9–33.
Van Dyck, M. (2003) "The roles of one thought experiment in interpreting quantum mechanics: Werner Heisenberg meets Thomas Kuhn," *Philosophica* 72: 79–103.
Walton, K. (1990) *Mimesis as Make-Believe: On the Foundations of the Representational Arts*, Cambridge: Harvard University Press.
Wartenberg, T. E. (2007) *Thinking on Screen: Film as Philosophy*, London: Routledge.
Williamson, T. (2005) "Armchair philosophy, metaphysical modality and counterfactual thinking," *Proceedings of the Aristotelian Society* 105: 1–23.

Williamson, T. (2016) "Knowing by imagining," in *Knowledge through Imagination*, edited by A. Kind and P. Kung, Oxford: Oxford University Press.

Wilson, M. (1991) "Reflections on strings," in *Thought Experiments in Science and Philosophy*, edited by T. Horowitz and G. Massey, Lanham: Rowman and Littlefield.

Wiltsche, H. A. (2013) "How essential are essential laws? A thought experiment on physical things and their givenness in adumbrations," in *Wahrnehmen, Fühlen, Handeln. Phänomenologie im Wettstreit der Methoden*, edited by I. Günzler and K. Mertens, Münster: Mentis.

Witt-Hansen, J. (1976) "H.C. Ørsted, Immanuel Kant, and the thought experiment," *Danish Yearbook of Philosophy* 13: 48–65.

Yourgrau, W. (1962) "On the logical status of so-called thought experiments," in *Proceedings of the Tenth International Conference of the History of Science*, Paris: Hermann.

Yourgrau, W. (1967) "On models and thought experiments in quantum theory," *Monatsberichte der Deutschen Akademie der Wissenschaften zu Berlin* 9: 886–874.

Part I
SELECTED HISTORY OF THOUGHT EXPERIMENTS

Part I

SELECTED HISTORY OF THOUGHT EXPERIMENTS

1
THE TRIPLE LIFE OF ANCIENT THOUGHT EXPERIMENTS

Katerina Ierodiakonou

There is no ancient Greek term corresponding to what we nowadays refer to as a thought experiment, and presumably ancient philosophers did not have our modern notion of a thought experiment. But there is no doubt that they did use thought experiments. In fact, they often employed them in ways similar to those of contemporary philosophers, that is, both for defending their own theories as well as for refuting the theories of their opponents. What seems to be particularly intriguing, though, is a third way in which thought experiments were used in antiquity, and particularly in Hellenistic philosophy, namely in order to induce suspension of judgement. The ancient Sceptics, who wanted to avoid being saddled with dogmatic opinions, made abundant use of thought experiments not in order to settle philosophical controversies but to formulate arguments of the same strength in support of contradictory beliefs. Indeed, in some cases the hypothetical scenario of one and the same thought experiment was evoked on both sides of a philosophical dispute. Thus, thought experiments were used by ancient philosophers: first, to support philosophical theories; second, to rebut philosophical theories; and third, to induce suspension of judgement. This is what I call the triple life of ancient thought experiments.

Let me start by presenting three thought experiments from different periods of antiquity and from different areas of ancient philosophical thought: The first thought experiment, which is in fact the first recorded thought experiment ever, is to be found in Simplicius' commentary on Aristotle's *Physics* (467.26–35)[1] and is the thought experiment of the man who stands at the edge of the universe trying to extend his hand or his staff. It is attributed to the Pythagorean Archytas of Tarentum in the first half of the fourth century B.C.E., who first constructed it in order to prove the infinity of the universe, but it subsequently had an illustrious history: It was appropriated by the Epicureans and the Stoics during the Hellenistic period; in late antiquity, the Aristotelian commentators discussed its uses in detail; in the Middle Ages, Thomas Aquinas, followed by a number of fourteenth-century scholars such as John Buridan, Nicholas Oresme and Richard of Middleton, used its Stoic version and at the same time elaborated on it in the light of their Christian beliefs; finally, in early modern times, Pierre Gassendi, Otto von Guericke, John Locke and Isaac Newton also referred to it, each for one's own reasons. The general structure of Archytas' thought experiment is the following: Imagine, Archytas says, that the universe is finite, that there is a man at its outermost edge and that he tries to extend his hand or his staff. There are two possibilities: either he can or he cannot extend it. But it is absurd to think that he cannot extend it. And if he can extend it, it means he is not at the edge of the universe; so, the same question will be raised when he moves further out, and this question will continue to be raised *ad infinitum*. Hence, if we assume that the universe is finite, we either reach an absurdity or conclude that the universe is infinite. Therefore, the universe is infinite.[2]

The second thought experiment is an equally famous thought experiment from Plato's *Republic* (360b3–c8),[3] in which Socrates' interlocutor Glaukon uses a myth, namely the myth of Gyges, to show that people who practice justice do so unwillingly: Imagine, Glaukon says, what would happen if both a just and an unjust man were given a ring, like Gyges' ring, which has the power to make them invisible and thus allows them to do with impunity what they really want to do. Glaukon suggests that both the just and the unjust man would behave unjustly, which proves his point that just people behave justly unwillingly. However, this seems to go against Socrates' notion of justice, and Plato devotes the whole of his *Republic* in order to prove what he stresses at the very end of the dialogue (612a8–b5), namely that the just person would not change his behaviour, but he will continue to behave justly whether or not he has Gyges' ring.[4]

The third thought experiment, which is admittedly less renowned, comes from a passage in Sextus Empiricus' *Against the Physicists* (2.144–147),[5] in which he attacks the basic Epicurean doctrine of the existence of atoms while discussing the possibility of motion: Imagine, Sextus says, a distance composed of nine partless places with two partless bodies moving through it from each of its end-points at equal speed. Each partless body, i.e., each atom, will evidently go through its first four places in the same time. But what happens next? There are three alternatives: (1) Both stop after occupying four places, but this is implausible since there is nothing to stop them. (2) One stops while the other occupies the remaining place, but this runs counter to the hypothesis that they are travelling at equal speed. (3) They both occupy the halves of the remaining place, but if the places are partless, according to the initial hypothesis, there is no middle for the bodies to meet in, and if the bodies are also partless, it cannot be the case that they occupy a part of the remaining place with a part of themselves. Hence, if motion is possible there are no partless bodies, i.e., atoms do not exist.

So, here are three cases which are meant to either defend or refute an ancient philosophical theory in ethics and in natural philosophy and which would nowadays unreservedly be regarded as thought experiments. But did the ancients themselves think of such cases as thought experiments? There are good reasons to doubt it. As I have argued elsewhere (Ierodiakonou 2005, 125–40), the ancients did not have a technical term for thought experiments; more importantly, it is also questionable whether they had the notion of a thought experiment. For when we currently talk about thought experiments, we rely on some notion of an experiment that we ourselves construct in thought in order to test a theory. However, it is not at all clear whether the ancients had the notion of an experiment, since they did not seem to use a special term to denote the manipulation of experience, or even some artfully planned observations, with the view to test a scientific hypothesis construed as an answer to a problem under study. So, even if we accept that in certain branches of ancient science, for instance medicine, the ancients did perform experiments that could have met the contemporary criteria of scientific experiments,[6] they seem not to have considered what we now treat as experiments, or for that matter as thought experiments, as belonging to a category of their own.

How, then, did the ancients characterize the three mentioned cases regarded by us as thought experiments? There are ancient texts that refer to typical cases of thought experiments as *"paradeigmata,"* i.e., as "examples."[7] For instance, there is a passage from Plutarch's *Parallel Lives*, and in particular from his *Life of Theseus*, in which he preserves the earliest occurrence of the well-known example of Theseus' ship and refers to it as a *"paradeigma"*:

> The ship on which he [i.e. Theseus] sailed with the youths and returned in safety, the thirty-oared galley, was preserved by the Athenians down to the time of Demetrius Phalereus. They would take away the old planks, and put new ones in their place and thus make it solid again, so that the ship also has become a controversial example (*amphidoxoumenon paradeigma*) for the philosophers in the context of the Growing Argument, some declaring that it [i.e. the ship] remains the same, others that it does not.
>
> (Plutarch, *Life of Theseus* 23.1)

Leaving aside for the moment the intricacies of this thought experiment, let us focus on the term *"paradeigma"* itself: the preposition *"para"* indicates that something is being put, placed, thrown beside something else for comparison or juxtaposition, while *"deigma"* means "sample," "pattern," "plan," "model," "sketch"; and so *"paradeigma"* must be understood, in its literal sense, to mean "the sample, pattern, plan, model, sketch that is placed beside something else for comparison or juxtaposition." Interestingly enough, it seems that the term *"paradeigma"* was first used to refer to the builder's plan or model of a building or of a ship (Herodotus 5.62), as well as to the sculptor's model or the painter's rough sketches and drawings (Plato, *Timaeus* 28c6; *Republic* 500e3). And it is exactly from this sense of the term that we come to get its meaning as an example that serves as a standard by which one can judge something. But if such cases as the above were treated as examples, did the ancients classify them as a particular category of examples? Did they group them in a class of their own?

In our third example of an ancient thought experiment, namely the attack on the Epicurean thesis that atoms exist, Sextus refers to the case which he constructs as hypothetical (*ex hupotheseōs/para tēn hupothesin*). And it is true that in this case, just as in all such cases, we start from an imaginary or invented assumption, that is, a hypothetical scenario: Imagine a distance composed of nine partless places, with two partless bodies moving through it from each of its end-points at equal speed. Or again, imagine that over a certain period of time every single plank of Theseus' ship has rotted and has been replaced. Besides, the language used in such examples leaves little doubt: They often start by the phrase "let it be the case that" (*estō, hupokeisthō*), or they use conditional sentences of the form "if this were the case, then it would make sense to think that." Also, phrases such as "for the sake of the argument" (*theorias heneka*, e.g., Philo, *De aeternitate mundi* 48), "in theory" (*logō*, e.g., Philoponus, *in Phys.* 575.6), "in thought" (*kat" epinoian*, e.g., Philoponus, *in Phys.* 574.14, 575.8, 575.10, 575.18), and "if we were to conceive" (*ei noēsaimen*, e.g., Sextus Empiricus M. 3.78, 8.456, 9.431, 11.52), which are sometimes used by our ancient sources in order to introduce or characterize such examples, are clearly indicative of their hypothetical status.

More specifically, the hypothetical state of affairs in such cases could be:

(i) impossible and counterfactual, for instance in Archytas' or in Sextus' thought experiments, or
(ii) possible; when possible, it means that either

    (ii.a) human beings can bring it about, though there may be no evidence that anyone ever did due perhaps to practical difficulties or moral obstacles, for instance in Plutarch's thought experiment about Theseus' ship, or
    (ii.b) human beings cannot bring it about due to our lack of the relevant power, though it may be brought about through the action of some other agent, typically a divine being, for instance in Plato's thought experiment about Gyges' ring.

But although ancient philosophers recognized the distinctive role of the hypothetical scenarios in these and similar thought experiments, there is no evidence that they classified examples based on imaginary or invented assumptions in a special category. It is thus reasonable to think that they conceived of thought experiments as examples, though they had no notion of them as a distinct class.

This should not make us suspicious, however, about applying the notion of a thought experiment to certain ancient examples. For it seems that the ancients employed a kind of argumentation that fits in perfectly with the contemporary customary usage of the notion of thought experiments. Besides, although elementary textbooks on thought experiments often begin with, or at least include, a catalogue of Albert Einstein's famous thought experiments, for instance Einstein's train, Einstein's lift, Einstein's chase after a beam of light, Einstein himself chose as a rule not to use the term "thought experiment" (*Gedankenexperiment*), which had already been coined by Hans Christian Ørsted in the early nineteenth-century and used extensively by Ernst Mach; he spoke instead of "examples," "arguments," "analogies," "illustrations," "idealized experiments." Nevertheless, since Einstein employed specific methods of argumentation that we nowadays designate as thought experiments, we generally have no qualms to make use of the notion of a thought experiment when analysing his works (cf. Roux 2011, esp. 4–19). And we should follow, I think, the same practice concerning the use of the term "thought experiments" in the case of certain ancient examples.

So, assuming that many ancient philosophers used thought experiments and regarded them as examples based on hypothetical scenarios, that is, as some kind of imaginary or invented examples, it is time now to investigate what sort of function they attributed to them. But first, let us briefly consider how contemporary philosophers understand the cognitive function of thought experiments; for instance, how Anna-Sara Malmgren presents in brief outline the standard model of the procedure and function of thought experiments, as currently used in philosophy:

> the hypothesis or theory that is under evaluation states or entails some modal claim (typically a necessary bi-conditional or one-way implication) and in a thought experiment we check that modal claim against our intuitive verdict on

an imaginary problem case. If the claim conflicts with our intuitive verdict, this is treated as strong evidence against the theory—indeed the theory may be abandoned as a result. We say that we found a counterexample to it. If not, this is treated as at least some evidence in support of the theory. We say that it accommodates our intuitions about the case.

(Malmgren 2011, 264)

In addition, contemporary philosophers may also resort to a thought experiment, especially in popular writings, simply as a striking illustration of a theory that is otherwise well founded, without thus attempting to establish the theory on the basis of this thought experiment. But even if thought experiments may have such an illustrative and didactic function, their main cognitive intention seems to be what Malmgren describes, namely to prove or to disprove a philosophical theory.

Ancient thought experiments, too, were formulated with the same purpose in mind, that is, to prove or to disprove philosophical theories and, in other words, to function as evidence for or as counterexamples against philosophical theories. In such cases, the aim may be achieved by a *reductio ad absurdum* argument; that is, we start by imagining the contrary of what the thought experiment is supposed to show, and since this assumption leads to an absurdity, the point at issue is proved. For instance, Archytas' thought experiment, which was meant to prove the infinity of the universe, starts with the assumption that the universe is finite and, since this proves to be absurd, it shows that the universe is infinite. Nevertheless, it is not invariably the case that thought experiments have the form of a *reductio ad absurdum* argument. For instance, Plato's thought experiment simply assumes that both the just and the unjust man are offered Gyges' ring, and then investigates whether the just man will behave justly or unjustly, without involving any *reductio ad absurdum* argument. Still, what this thought experiment has in common with all the others is the fact that its hypothetical scenario leaves open at least two different alternatives that we need to investigate and, most importantly, it is by no means clear from the beginning which alternative we should accept as the most plausible. This, I content, constitutes the required condition for an ancient thought experiment; that is to say, the imaginary assumption initiates a process of thinking without a previously settled or determined conclusion, namely a series of arguments that should be clearly spelt out, compelling us to make up our mind on a particular subject. So, Archytas' thought experiment investigates whether the man at the edge of the universe could extend his hand or not, Plato's thought experiment investigates whether the just man will behave justly or unjustly when given Gyges' ring, and Plutarch's thought experiment investigates whether Theseus' ship is the same or not if all its planks were to be replaced. All these ancient thought experiments are characterized both by their hypothetical scenarios as well as by their openness to generating different responses.

Now, although the hypothetical scenarios at the basis of ancient thought experiments are meant to be accepted as somehow imaginable both by those who use the thought experiments in favour of their theories and by their opponents, it is not necessary that there be agreement as to the responses induced by the situations imagined. In other words, it is not necessary that there be agreement as to which alternative is the most reasonable, and thus the conclusions drawn from the hypothetical scenarios are particularly open to criticism and disagreement. For instance, two of the thought experiments mentioned already could be used, and were actually used, to defend both the position in support of which they were initially introduced as well as the contrary position. The thought experiment about Gyges' ring was first presented in Plato's *Republic* by Glaukon with the aim to prove that the just man behaves unjustly when there is no chance that his unjust actions can be discovered, while the same imaginary situation is used later in the dialogue also by Socrates in order to show that the just man acts justly in all circumstances, irrespectively of whether or not he enjoys impunity. Moreover, the thought experiment about Theseus' ship is said by Plutarch to have been used both by those who thought that the ship does not remain the same as well as by those who thought that it does; and it is presumably in this sense that Plutarch characterizes this example as "controversial" (*amphidoxoumenon*). Therefore, the most intriguing aspect of such thought experiments is the fact that they cannot immediately settle the controversy at issue; for they evoke in some people the originally expected intuitions, but at the same time they also evoke in others rather different if not contradictory intuitions.

To understand better the controversial character of thought experiments, let us discuss in more detail the thought experiment about Theseus' ship; and in particular, let us examine how this thought experiment was used in Hellenistic period both by the Stoics and by their opponents, the Academic Sceptics. According to the passage from Plutarch's *Life of Theseus*, this thought experiment was discussed by ancient philosophers in connection with the Growing Argument. Plutarch (*On Common Conceptions* 1083A–4A)[8] also reports that the Growing Argument goes back to the early fifth-century comic poet Epicharmus, who argued that just as a number or measure when added to, or subtracted from, becomes a different number or measure – for instance, if we add 1 to 2 we get a different number, i.e. 3 – so too a person who grows or diminishes in size becomes a different person.[9] The Sceptics exploited this argument in putting together oppositions on whether there is growth and diminution, with the aim to question the very concepts of growth and diminution, and consequently the notion of identity. They invoked the dogmatic position that when we say, for instance, that something grows, this only makes sense if one and the same thing persists throughout the process; but if the person in growing becomes a different person, there is no one thing there which has grown. Similarly, in the case of the thought experiment about Theseus' ship, the Sceptics employed this line of argument as nicely suited to generating suspension of judgement; with this in mind, they defended the position that here we have a clear case of something, namely Theseus' ship, which does not remain the same, since it obviously has been subtracted from and added to over time. On the other hand, the Stoics insisted that, even if all the planks were to be replaced, the ship would remain the same, since its peculiar quality, i.e. the original plan of the ship, has not changed.[10]

Furthermore, the Stoic Chrysippus is said to have used a rather sophisticated example, in fact another thought experiment, in order to refute the Growing Argument and defend the possibility of growth and diminution. According to Philo of Alexandria (*On the Indestructibility of the World* 48), Chrysippus in his treatise *On the Growing Argument* created a freak, as he says, of the following kind:

> Chrysippus, the most distinguished member of their school, in his work *On the Growing [Argument]*, creates a freak of the following kind. Having first established that it is impossible for two peculiarly qualified individuals to occupy the same

substance jointly, he says: 'For the sake of argument, let one individual be thought of as whole-limbed, the other as minus one foot. Let the whole-limbed one be called Dion, the defective one Theon. Then let one of Dion's feet be amputated.'
(Long and Sedley 1987, 171)

So, Chrysippus' thought experiment asks us to imagine two individuals – let us call them "Dion" and "Theon." Theon seems to be thought of as being a part of Dion, in the sense that Dion is the whole-limbed human being, while Theon is defined as the same human being minus a leg; then, we are supposed to imagine what happens if Dion loses the leg which Theon is lacking. One would intuitively expect, Philo says in what immediately follows the text just quoted, that Dion perishes and Theon survives, since it is Dion's leg that has been amputated whereas Theon has had no part of his chopped off.[11] This, indeed, is what one would be saying, if one accepted the Growing Argument, as the Sceptics employed it in their oppositions; having his leg amputated, i.e. having suffered some diminution, Dion does not remain the same. Chrysippus, however, was of a different view. He defended the thesis that, if Dion loses a leg, it is Dion who survives, even though he has suffered some diminution, whereas Theon cannot be said to exist anymore. For Theon, by definition, was a genuine part of Dion with its own peculiar quality, namely Dion minus the leg that was then amputated; and this peculiar quality that made him a distinct individual has gone out of existence, once Dion's leg was amputated. Hence, Chrysippus presented this thought experiment as a clear case in which it is what diminishes, namely Dion, which survives, whereas the undiminished Theon perishes; and it is in this way that this thought experiment was meant to defend the notions of growth and diminution against the Growing Argument endorsed by the Sceptics.[12]

In both these thought experiments, therefore, that is, both in the thought experiment of Theseus' ship and in that of Dion and Theon, the Stoics and the Sceptics made use of the same hypothetical scenario in order to defend or, in the case of the Sceptics, in order to arrive at contrary claims of an opposition; in this sense, both thought experiments would rightly be regarded as controversial cases. And there are other such cases in Hellenistic philosophy. For instance, according to Cicero (*On Duties* 3.90[13]; cf. also: *De re publica* 3.30 = Lactantius, *Inst. Div.* 5.6.10), the Sceptics argued against the Stoic notion of justice, by asking us to imagine what would happen if after a shipwreck there were two survivors with just one plank that could only carry one person. The Stoics replied that, if the two men were really wise, and hence just, they would have decided to leave the plank to the one whose life most mattered for his own and for his city. The Sceptics, on the other hand, suggested that there are good reasons to believe that any person, not excluding the wise man, would naturally have tried to get hold of the plank for himself. Thus, once again both the Stoics and the Sceptics were willing to imagine the same imaginary situation of two survivors after a shipwreck with just a single plank, but they disagreed as to how the survivors would behave in such a hypothetical state of affairs.

In yet another controversial thought experiment, the Sceptics tried to argue against the Stoic thesis that there are certain true impressions, the so-called "cognitive impressions" (*katalēptikai phantasiai*), which are guaranteed to be true, and thus may serve as our criteria of truth and the foundations of our knowledge; in fact, this thought experiment was presented by the Sceptics in the following two versions:

> For instance, if there are two eggs exactly alike, and I give them to the Stoic one after the other, will the wise person after fastening upon them, have the capacity to say infallibly whether the egg he is being shown is a single one, or the one and then the other? The same argument also applies in the case of twins. For the superior person will grasp a false appearance, even though he has the appearance as from a real thing and stamped and impressed in accordance with just *that* real thing, if he gets an appearance of Castor as if from Polydeuces.
>
> (Sextus Empiricus 2005, 81)

That is to say, the Sceptics' thought experiment asked the Stoics to imagine what would happen, if they were first shown one egg and then another identical one, or one man and then his identical twin brother; would they be able to distinguish them as two different eggs or two different brothers? The Sceptics suggested that it would not be possible to distinguish them, and thus the Stoic wise man may have false impressions though he considers them as true; for instance, it may be the case that he thinks he has a cognitive impression of Polydeuces, when in reality he looks at Castor. The Stoics, however, replied that, on the basis of their doctrine of indiscernibility, according to which there are no two things which are exactly alike, it is always possible for the wise man, at least in principle, to distinguish between two eggs or between twin brothers.

Finally, according to Cicero (*On Academic Scepticism* 2.47)[14] and Plutarch (*On Stoic Self-contradictions* 1057A),[15] the Sceptics tried once more to question the Stoic doctrine of cognitive impressions, by asking them to imagine what would happen if a god, given his enormous powers, made them have certain false impressions that were just like the cognitive ones. To this thought experiment, which reminds us of Descartes' evil demon, the Stoics responded by claiming that it is still up to the wise man not to give assent to such false impressions. The Sceptics, on the other hand, claimed that, since we are not able to distinguish the false impressions from the cognitive ones, we are thus prone to wrongly accept them as cognitive, and consequently the distinction between cognitive and non-cognitive impressions fades away.

All these Hellenistic thought experiments, constructed in most cases by the Sceptics, are clearly representative cases of what Plutarch calls "controversial examples"; as such, they did not lead decisively to the verification or the falsification of a philosophical theory. For both the Stoics and the Sceptics were willing to argue on the basis of the same hypothetical scenario, but the conclusions which they reached were diametrically different; the Stoics used a thought experiment in order to defend one position, whereas the Sceptics used the same thought experiment in order to arrive at the contrary position and induce suspension of judgement. Indeed, the Sceptics seem to have used, or even to have invented, such thought experiments, not in order to defend a theory which they themselves endorsed, but in order to show that the reasons in favour of the theory contrary to that of the Stoics could be as good enough, or as strong, as those that the Stoics presented. For the Sceptics did not adhere to any theory whatsoever; their ultimate goal was simply to make clear that the dogmatic theories of the Stoics were not well founded, since the contrary ones could also be supported by equally strong arguments. To this end, they introduced certain techniques, the so-called "sceptical modes" (*skeptikoi tropoi*), which offered them ways to counter any given claim, by formulating arguments of the same strength as those of their dogmatic opponents. They managed in this manner to show that, at the present state of philosophical research, no dogmatic position could be accepted as true. Therefore, the use of thought experiments should be viewed, I think, as another particularly effective way of reaching the Sceptics' aim of equipollence between arguments. For thought experiments serve perfectly the sceptical strategy; the same hypothetical scenario invokes contrary responses, and this leads to an impasse that brings about what the Sceptics prescribed, namely suspension of judgement.

In which cases, though, do thought experiments lead us to suspension of judgement, instead of constituting evidence for the corroboration or the refutation of a theory? In other words, what is it exactly that permits contrary responses to the hypothetical scenarios of certain thought experiments, so that they can be used to induce suspension of judgement? Some ancient thought experiments, like for instance Archytas' thought experiment, are formulated in such a way that there is no hesitation as to how one may respond to them. Everyone finds it absurd to think that it is not possible to extend one's hand, everyone agrees that, if it is possible to extend one's hand, one is not at the edge of the universe. On the other hand, there are ancient thought experiments, like for instance Plato's thought experiment about Gyges' ring and all the Hellenistic thought experiments previously discussed, which may provoke diametrically different responses. Glaukon thinks that the just man who has Gyges' ring will behave unjustly, whereas Socrates claims that the just man will always behave justly whether he has Gyges' ring or not. Hence, there are thought experiments that invoke in all of us common intuitions that nobody would question, while there are others that result in different responses prompted by different intuitive judgements. Of course, the thought experiments of the first category are generally considered as more successful, in the sense that they can effectively be used in order to prove or to disprove a theory. So, if one wants to use a thought experiment for this purpose, it is crucial to make sure that the intuitions invoked by its hypothetical scenario are shared by everyone.

But, here, I want to briefly focus on the second category of thought experiments. The fact that in such cases our intuitions may differ greatly raises intriguing questions concerning their epistemic status and the kind of knowledge they are supposed to provide. For what, if anything, makes such intuitive judgements justified and what, if anything, makes them reliable? More specifically, are the intuitive judgements invoked by our thought experiments empirically justified or are they reasoned intuitions? In the current debate on this subject the received opinion among its participants seems to be that intuitive judgements are justified a priori, i.e. independently of experience, to the extent that they are justified at all. But, of course, there are also modern philosophers who hold that intuitive judgements are empirically justified.[16] I do not intend to enter the contemporary debate and its sophisticated intricacies. Rather, I want to explore, even in broad strokes, what kind of intuitive judgements the ancient philosophers employed in connection with the thought experiments discussed at the time. Can they be said to be empirically justified or reasoned intuitions?

Glaukon's intuition that the just man who has Gyges' ring will behave unjustly, or Socrates' intuition that the just man will behave justly whether he has or does not have Gyges' ring, are not empirically supported in Plato's *Republic*; both Glaukon and Socrates seem to rely on their respective notions of what it means for a man to be just. In fact, the whole of the *Republic* aims at developing the Socratic notion of justice in contrast to Glaukon's notion. So, even if Socrates often makes use of particular examples taken from everyday life, there is no doubt that what mostly matters to him is to reason extensively in order to justify his notion of justice. Thus, his intuitive response to the thought experiment about Gyges' ring cannot be said to derive directly from experience. What about the intuitive judgements of the Stoics and of the Sceptics as recorded in the Hellenistic thought experiments? For instance, what about the Stoics' statement that after the shipwreck one of the wise men may have good reasons to leave the plank to the other wise man whose life most mattered for his own and for his city? Or again, the Stoics' statement that the wise man can distinguish the two eggs and the twin brothers, or that he can avoid giving assent to false impressions even if a god makes them just like the cognitive ones. In all these cases, it becomes clear, I think, that the Stoics do not rely on empirical evidence, but on their notion of a wise man or on their philosophical principles such as the principle of indiscernibility.

On the other hand, it seems that the Sceptics' responses to such thought experiments depend more on their own empirical observations or on those reported by dogmatic philosophers, medical writers, historians, and poets.[17] The Sceptics often refer to the testimony of the *phainomena*, i.e. of the appearances, and their intuitive judgements seem to be guided by the experience of specific cases. For instance, most people will not be able to distinguish the two eggs or the twin brothers, most people will not be able to resist the false impressions given to them by an omnipotent god, even if they are wise. It thus seems plausible to suggest that the Sceptics favoured empirically justified intuitions than those founded on elaborate theoretical systems. However, it is also worth noting that the way thought experiments are constructed does not allow immediate access to the empirical reality. For thought experiments differ in an important sense from ordinary examples: Although examples refer to particular cases from everyday life, and hence their familiarity and simplicity is conducive to the verification or the falsification of a theory, thought experiments are mental constructions which often introduce situations that are not part of our human experience; so, our reactions to them cannot simply be regarded as self-evident, but require the use of our ability to abstract from the direct appearances and to reason.

To conclude: I have discussed the way philosophical thought experiments were used in antiquity, and in particular the way thought experiments were used by Hellenistic philosophers. Of course, I do not expect ancient thought experiments to be helpful to those constructing thought experiments in contemporary philosophy, or for that matter in the sciences. I do hope, though, that they might be illuminating; not so much the particular thought experiments but their different functions, and especially their third function to induce suspension of judgement. For the ancient philosophers, and in particular the ancient Sceptics, seem to have used thought experiments in order to destabilize us from our dogmatic positions and to show that, since we have not yet reached true knowledge, our theoretical quest needs to be continued. Admittedly, neither a philosopher nor a scientist would nowadays be principally interested in constructing a thought experiment in order to suspend judgement; it is certainly more reasonable to assume that they use thought experiments in order to verify or to falsify a proposed theory. Being conscious, though, of the third function of thought experiments and reflecting on it could protect the philosopher as well as the scientist from hasty conclusions. For they could better recognize the dangers of adhering to a theory on the basis of evidence provided by a thought experiment, evidence that could turn out to also support its contrary.

Acknowledgements

I would like to thank my colleagues Jim Hankinson, Jaap Mansfeld, Teun Tieleman, Katja Vogt, and Jan Willem Wieland for their helpful comments and suggestions.

Notes

1 "But Archytas," as Eudemus says,

> used to propound the argument in this way: 'If I arrived at the outermost edge of the heaven [that is to say at the fixed heaven], could I extend my hand or staff into what is outside or not?' It would be paradoxical not to be able to extend it. But if I extend it, what is outside will be either body or place. It doesn't matter which, as we will learn. So then he will always go forward in the same fashion to the limit that is supposed in each case and will ask the same question, and if there will always be something else to which his staff [extends], it is clear that it is also unlimited. And if it is body, what was proposed has been demonstrated. If it is place, place is that in which body is or could be, but what is potential must be regarded as really existing in the case of eternal things, and thus there would be unlimited body and space.
> (Huffman 2005, 541)

2 On Archytas' thought experiment, cf. Ierodiakonou 2011, 37–50.
3 Let's suppose, then that there were two such rings, one worn by a just and the other by an unjust person. Now, no one, it seems, would be so incorruptible that he would stay on the path of justice or stay away from other people's property, when he could take whatever he wanted from the marketplace with impunity, go into people's houses and have sex with anyone he wished, kill or release from prison anyone he wished, and do all other things that would make him like a god among humans. Rather his actions would be in no way different from those of an unjust person, and both would follow the same path. Thus, some would say, is a great proof that one is never just willingly but only when compelled to be. No one believes justice to be a good when it is kept private, since, wherever either person thinks he can do injustice with impunity, he does it (Plato 1992, 36).
4 For an analysis of this thought experiment, see also Becker (this volume).
5 But even apart from this kind of impasse, it is possible to discredit the Epicureans' position using this scenario (*ex hupotheseōs*). Imagine a distance consisting of nine partless places lined up in a row, and two partless bodies in motion over this distance from each of its end-points – in motion at equal speed. Then since the motion is at equal speed, each of these bodies will have to go through four partless places. And when they have arrived at the fifth place, which is in the middle between the four and the four, either they will stop, or one of them will be faster, so that this one has gone through five partless places and the remaining other only four, or they will not stop nor will one be faster, but they will run together and will both occupy the fifth partless place at once, half and half. Well, their both stopping is very implausible; for when a place is there, and nothing resists their motion, they will not stop. But for one of them to be faster than the other is against what we were supposing (*para tēn hupothesin*); each of them was imagined moving at equal speed. It remains, therefore, to say that they will run together to the same spot and will both occupy the halves of the remaining place. But if this one occupies its own half, and that one its own half, the place will not be partless, but separated into two halves. So too will the bodies; for since they take up their part of the place with a part of themselves, they will not be partless (Sextus Empiricus 2012).
6 On the use of experimentation in antiquity and, more specifically, in medicine, cf. Lloyd (1964), von Staden (1975) and Tieleman (2002).
7 There are also ancient sources that alternatively refer to thought experiments as "*hupodeigmata*"; e.g. Sextus Empiricus, *Against the Mathematicians* 9.431, 10.55, 10.101, 10.156, 10.347.
8 The argument about growth is an old one, for, as Chrysippus says, it is propounded by Epicharmus. Yet when the Academics hold that the puzzle is not altogether easy or straightforward, these people [sc. the Stoics] have laid many charges against them and denounced them as destroying our

preconceptions and contravening our conceptions. Yet they themselves not only fail to save our conceptions but also pervert sense-perception. For the argument is a simple one and these people grant its premises: (a) all particular substances are in flux and motion, releasing some things from themselves and receiving others which reach them from elsewhere; (b) the numbers or quantities which these are added to or subtracted from do not remain the same but become different as the aforementioned arrivals and departures cause the substance to be transformed; (c) the prevailing convention is wrong to call these processes of growth and decay: rather they should be called generation and destruction, since they transform the thing from what it is into something else, whereas growing and diminishing are affections of a body which serves as substrate and persists (Long and Sedley 1987, 166).

9 It so happens that we have a fragment attributed to Epicharmus (DK 23 B2) which puts forth just this argument (cf. also: Plutarch, *De sera numinis vindicta* 559A–B; Anonymus, *in Plat. Theaet.* 70.5–26, 1.12–40).

10 For a more detailed analysis of the Stoic response to the Growing Argument, cf. Ierodiakonou (2005, 126–9).

11 The question arises which one of them has perished, and his claim is that Theon is the strongest candidate. These are the words of a paradox-monger rather than of a speaker of truth. For how can it be that Theon, who has had no part chopped off, has been snatched away, while Dion, whose foot has been amputated, has not perished? "Necessarily," says Chrysippus. "For Dion, the one whose foot has been cut off, has collapsed into the defective substance of Theon. And two peculiarly qualified individuals cannot occupy the same substance. Therefore it is necessary that Dion remains while Theon has perished" (Long and Sedley 1987, 171–2).

12 Sedley (1982, 269) offers a different explanation as to why Chrysippus thinks that Dion rather than Theon survives. According to him, Dion survives because it is after all he who loses a leg, as Theon cannot lose a leg which has never been part of him in the first place. But, as Sedley himself says, our sources do not make Chrysippus' reason entirely clear, and in any case this issue of interpretation does not affect the point I want to make here.

13

"Well, suppose there is one plank and two sailors, both of them wise men. Would each of them grab it for himself, or would one give in to the other?"

"One should give in to the other, that is, to the one whose life most matters for his own or the republic's sake."

"And what if such considerations are equal for both?"

"There will be no contest, but one will give in to the other as if losing by lot, or by playing odds and evens."

(Cicero 1991, 134–5)

14 Since the Academics have a methodical approach, I will set out their argument systematically. The first type tries to show that there are often "persuasive" impressions of things that don't exist at all, since our minds are moved vacuously by what is not the case in exactly the same way as by what is the case. *After all, they say, you claim that some impressions are sent by god, for instance in dreams and revelations from oracles, auspices, or entrails.* (They report that these are accepted by their Stoic opponents). *Well, they ask, how is it that god can make persuasive impressions that are false, but can't make persuasive impressions that approximate the truth very closely? Or, if he can also do that, why not persuasive impressions that can only just be discriminated "from true impressions" though with considerable difficulty? And if that, why "not false but persuasive impressions" that don't differ at all "from true impressions"?* (Cicero 2006, 29).

15 Furthermore, Chrysippus says that both god and the wise man implant false impressions, not asking us to assent or yield but merely to act and be impelled towards appearance, but that we inferior persons out of weakness assent to such impressions (Long and Sedley 1987, 256).

16 For recent bibliography on this issue, cf. Malmgren 2011, 263–327.

17 On the Sceptics' use of material from other sources, cf. Vogt 2008, 49.

References

Cicero, M. T. (1991) *On Duties*, translated by M. T. Griffin and E. M. Atkins, Cambridge: Cambridge University Press.
Cicero, M. T. (2006) *On Academic Scepticism*, translated by C. Brittain, Indianapolis: Hackett.
Huffman, C. A. (2005) *Archytas of Tarentum. Pythagorean, Philosopher and Mathematician King*, Cambridge: Cambridge University Press.
Ierodiakonou, K. (2005) "Ancient thought experiments: A first approach," *Ancient Philosophy* 25: 125–140.
Ierodiakonou, K. (2011) "Remarks on the history of an ancient thought experiment," in *Thought Experiments in Methodological and Historical contexts*, edited by K. Ierodiakonou and S. Roux, Boston: Brill.
Lloyd, G. E. R. (1964) "Experiment in early Greek philosophy and medicine," *Proceedings of the Cambridge Philological Society*, N.S 10: 50–72.
Long, A. A. and Sedley, D. N. (1987) *The Hellenistic philosophers*, vol. 1, Cambridge: Cambridge University Press.
Malmgren, A-S. (2011) "Rationalism and the content of intuitive judgements," *Mind* 120: 263–327.
Plato. (1992) *Republic*, translated by G. M. A. Grube and rev. C. D. C. Reeve, Indianapolis: Hackett.
Roux, S. (2011) "Introduction: The emergence of the notion of thought experiments," in *Thought Experiments in Methodological and Historical contexts*, edited by K. Ierodiakonou and S. Roux, Boston: Brill.
Sedley, D. N. (1982) "The Stoic criterion of identity," *Phronesis* 27: 255–275.
Sextus Empiricus (2005) *Against the Logicians*, translated by R. Bett, Cambridge: Cambridge University Press.
Sextus Empiricus. (2012) *Against the Physicists*, translated by R. Bett, Cambridge: Cambridge University Press.
von Staden, H. (1975) "Experiment and experience in Hellenistic medicine," *Bulletin of the Institute of Classical Studies* 22: 178–199.
Tieleman, T. (2002) "Galen on the seat of the intellect: Anatomical experiment and philosophical tradition," in *Science and Mathematics in Ancient Greek Culture*, edited by C. J. Tuplin and T. E. Rihll, Oxford: Oxford University Press.
Vogt, K. (2008) *Law, Reason, and the Cosmic City: Political Philosophy in the Early Stoa*, Oxford: Oxford University Press.

2
THOUGHT EXPERIMENTS IN PLATO

Alexander Becker

1 Introduction

In the history of thought experiments, Plato plays a major part not only because we find in his writings one of the earliest documented uses of thought experiments[1] but also because one of the most influential thought experiments ever concocted is due to him. For the systematic study of thought experiments he is interesting also in two other respects. Usually, a thought experiment is a piece of fictional writing, but not every piece of fiction is a thought experiment. Plato's writings are full of different kinds of fiction so that the question poses itself what distinguishes thought experiments from those other kinds of fiction he employs. Further, every thought experiment is an invitation by the author to imagine something, usually addressed to the reader. Plato's texts are dialogues where one interlocutor proposes something to another interlocutor. This is true, of course, also for thought experiments which appear in the dialogues. Therefore, Plato not only presents thought experiments but he presents their audience and the reaction of the audience as well. This does not imply, of course, that the reader is not addressed. But she is addressed in more than one way – directly, as far as she might put herself in the place of a dialogue interlocutor; indirectly, as far as she is witness to the presentation and reception of a thought experiment like the spectator of a drama who is able to observe both sides and to take a look at the use of thought experiments from the outside.

In order to present Plato's use of thought experiments as well as the peculiar setting they undergo in Plato's writings, I will focus on one text, the *Republic*. I will do so for three reasons:

1. The *Republic* contains the clearest as well as the most influential examples of thought experiments to be found in Plato's texts.
2. The *Republic* offers sufficiently various material for fictitious writing and uses of the dialogue form in order to investigate the peculiarities of Plato's employment of thought experiments.

3 In the *Republic*, the use of fiction is, more than in most other texts, explicitly addressed as a topic of discussion, so that we find here more hints than elsewhere at Plato's own stance towards the use of fiction, and possibly also at his stance towards thought experiments.

A thoroughgoing as well as comprehensive collection and presentation of all material potentially relevant to the discussion of thought experiments in Plato is not possible within the limits of a handbook article. As will soon become clear, it would mean to collect all instances of fictional writing to be found in Plato's texts, which are far too numerous. My approach, therefore, will be by way of presenting and discussing a small selection of carefully chosen examples.

2 Kinds and levels of fictional writing in Plato

Before turning to my examples, it might be helpful to give an overview of the uses of fiction in Plato's texts. As already mentioned, I proceed from the assumption that thought experiments include something fictional. If they did not, they would appeal only to factual or at least obtainable experience and would cease to be *thought* experiments. This assumption suggests a closer look at Plato's uses of fiction in general, in order to prepare for the answer to what will be my guiding question: how thought experiments stick out among these different kinds of fiction, and which of them might count as thought experiments at all.

(i) The most noticeable kind of fiction in Plato's dialogues are myths. They are usually told by the interlocutor who guides the conversation (in the *Republic* as well as the majority of other dialogues, this is Socrates). Since he does so normally by asking questions, myths stand out insofar as they present a longer narrative instead of a quick exchange of questions and answers. They are not intended to be approved step by step but to be listened to as a whole. The myths we can find in Plato's texts are, as far as we can tell, composed by Plato himself. Although he draws on material which is known from other sources and mostly part of the tradition well known to his contemporaries, the particular shape and narrative they receive is peculiar to Plato. Therefore, myths belong to the genuine accomplishments of Plato as a writer, just as much as the dialogical passages in which arguments are brought forward. Recently, this fact has become generally acknowledged in the research on Plato, and the myths have, therefore, received growing scholarly attention (e.g., Brisson 1998; Janka and Schäfer 2002; Partenie 2009; Collobert, Destrée and Gonzales 2012). In the text which will be my main focus here, the *Republic*, there are four larger myths: the story of Gyges (359d–360b); the myth to be told to the inhabitants of the model city that they are all born from the earth and differently composed of gold, silver and bronze (414c–415d); the myth about the geometrical number ruling the celestial periods, presented as the Muse's tale (546a–547a); and finally the Myth of Er, a soldier only apparently dead whose soul travels through the otherworld and who tells after reviving about what he has seen and heard there (614a–621d). Most of these myths I will present and discuss later in more detail.[2]

The word "myth" (gr. *mythos*) is used by Plato himself in order to characterize a particular use of language. At the beginning of their investigation into the best education for the guardians of the model state, Socrates and Adeimantus talk about the use of myths in the education (traditionally, myths played a major role in Greek education). Myths are generally classified as "false speech," albeit with truths in it (377a). This is at first glace a self-contradictory qualification, yet it elucidates two important points about Plato's stance towards myths: firstly, he regards them as truth-apt in principle; and secondly, there is no clear-cut opposition between a non-mythical true speech and a mythical false speech. The seeming contradiction in Plato's remark can be resolved if one takes into account that myths talk about things that transcend the limits of human verifiability, being about matters too far away in time and space, or about things like gods which are beyond the reach of human experience (cf. 382d). Telling a myth means putting forward statements which claim to be true, and could be so in principle (they are "truth-apt," so to speak), yet which cannot answer to this claim, at least within the limits of human life. Hence, they may contain true statements, but the risk is high that they are mostly false. Telling myths, therefore, is not generally illegitimate within a discourse aimed at truth; in fact, with some topics it is the only means available. But it is dangerous and requires heightened attention by the audience – in particular, they should know when they are told a myth. There is a puzzling passage on lies in the *Republic*, which fits in well with this way of looking at myths. Talking about the questions whether Gods may be represented as lying in a myth, Socrates distinguishes a "true lie" from a "lie in words." The true lie is a lie which is committed because the lying person herself is deceived about the truth. The lie is merely in words if the lying person herself knows the truth but decides to tell falsehoods to others. The distinction is plausible enough, yet according to Socrates the true lie is much worse than the lie in words (382b–c). What might seem to the modern reader to be a perversion of moral standards is for Socrates a purely epistemic evaluation: Who tells a lie – or for that matter, a myth – without knowing what she is doing is indeed worse off than someone who tells a lie (a myth) fully conscious about what she is doing. Among the latter cases may also count a situation when somebody tells a myth because he is aware that nothing epistemically better is available. This, I think, applies to many myths which are told by Socrates in Plato's dialogues – and in this sense we can understand that even the elaboration of the model state is introduced as a "myth" (376d; more on this below).

Often Platonic myths can also be characterized by way of their content. Gods and heroes appear; the events they relate take place in a distant and indeterminate past and in remote or even subterranean realms. Such myths share with their non-philosophical fellows a narrative structure which requires a continuous storyline and a suitable decoration with details. In this sense, what Plato calls a myth is in line with the common usage of the term. Such a content-related characterization of myths does not contradict the epistemic one given before. What those myths are about is in principle hidden from human experience, yet presented in a way as if it were accessible to human experience. We are made witness to the deeds of Gods and heroes, or to otherworldly events, as if we could verify the tales with our own eyes and ears. In fact, however, we do not even know whether Gods are visible and audible at all. Myths extrapolate our ways of verifying statements to realms where it is not even clear whether our ways of examination are applicable at all. Therefore, mythical statements are located in a kind of truth-evaluative limbo.[3]

(ii) The Platonic similes are another famous instance of fictional writing. They feature prominently not least in the *Republic*. The most famous of them, the simile of the Cave, tells a fictional story about people sitting in a cave and held by bonds, and about one of them who is released from the bonds and guided upstairs in order to become acquainted with the world outside the cave (514a–517d). Similes are surrounded by a strongly visual language: The first word by which Socrates starts the simile of the Cave is "look!" (*ide*), and Glaucon, who is the interlocutor at this time, answers with "I see" (*horô*) (514ab). Afterwards, Socrates calls the whole simile a "picture" (*eikon*) (517a8). The same word is used for two other similes in the *Republic*, the simile of the State ship (488a–489a; *eikon* is used at the beginning as well as in the end), and the simile in which the soul is compared to a composite of a many-headed beast, a lion and a human being (588b–e; *eikon* is used in the introductory remarks at 588b10). Similes are often accompanied by explicit or at least suggested explanations. In the case of the simile of the Cave, Socrates begins to expound a full-fledged interpretation in which he correlates elements of the simile to elements of what he wanted to explain by the simile (517a–c). Although this interpretation is not carried through to the end and leaves out many details of the simile, it provides a model how to understand the simile. In the case of the simile of the State ship, it is also obvious how to relate simile and explanandum. Although Socrates does not give an interpretation, he states clearly that this is the way to comprehend it by remarking that "it is not necessary to see the picture explained" (489a9). The terminology and the explicit or implicit presence of interpretations make obvious that a simile does not invite the audience to hold the picture itself to be true. Its intended use is a different one: it is to be related to an explanandum in a way that illustrates the latter, or makes it more easily comprehensible. Fiction is helpful in fulfilling this task because a fictional story is often more easily accessible than a possibly abstract explanandum. But it is not required, as other famous similes – the simile of the Sun and the Line – show which both do not employ fictional pictures.[4]

(iii) Finally, the Platonic dialogues themselves are fictional. Although they are set in realistic sceneries and employ real-life figures, it is most likely that none of the dialogues written down by Plato has ever occurred at least not in the way Plato seemingly records them. Due to a lack of independent historical evidence, the question of how much fiction there is in Plato's dialogues cannot be settled conclusively, yet there are strong hints provided by Plato himself that point towards a fictional character. In the *Phaedo*, he has Phaedo, who recounts the last day of Socrates, remark that Plato was not present because he felt ill (59b). In the case of the *Republic*, it is the sheer length of the conversation which makes it unlikely that we are confronted with the notes of a conversation which Socrates actually held. Moreover, there are clear indications of literary techniques which are directed towards a reader who is able to browse back and forth through the text (on this, see below, page 52). In the end of this chapter, I will turn to question whether the fictional character of the dialogues as a whole might be related to the topic of thought experiments.

3 Thought experiments in the *Republic*

3.1 Among this variety of fictional writing, are there pieces which might qualify as thought experiments? This is the question I will now turn to. Before doing so, some preliminary remarks are helpful.

Firstly, as Katerina Ierodiakonou has shown (2005), there is neither a word nor even a concept in Plato as well as in the major part of ancient philosophy that might come close to the modern expression of "thought experiments." In trying to answer our question, therefore, we cannot avoid applying *our* terminology and *our* criteria to texts which are, at the surface, devoid of them. Hence, I will proceed by discussing some cases in point and confronting them with each other in order to find out in what way they might be regarded as thought experiments.

Secondly, since the task of this chapter is not to define thought experiments, I will restrain from attempting to give a full-fledged definition of the term. Yet, in order to make the concept workable, some restraints in form of necessary conditions are indispensable. Anything that is to pass muster as a thought experiment has to comply with them. The following three constraints seem to me to be suitable for this task:

1. Thought experiments are tools intended to establish a claim which in itself doesn't belong to any fictional world. Their point is not just to build a fictional world. Instead, their epistemic function is directed towards the actual world. If this constraint were dropped, any kind of fiction (myth, novel, or whatever) would be a thought experiment.
2. Thought experiments are not merely illustrations of something that could as well be established without them.[5] If this requirement were lifted, any fictional example used in a philosophical text would count as a thought experiment. Of course, this constraint is context relative: the thought experiment has to be irreplaceable only within a given context.
3. Thought experiments must somehow be decidable. At least, they must invoke some means by which the acceptability of the claim they are to support can be decided, even if in fact the decision might not be feasible. Without this constraint, thought experiments would merely be more or less entertaining stories, but they would lack an epistemic payoff.

I hope these conditions are uncontroversial. They are far from giving a complete answer to what thought experiments are, and therefore they do not restrict the scope of the notion in advance – which is important if one is to approach an author who offers such a great variety of candidates for the title of a thought experiment as Plato does.

3.2 I will start with what seems to me an obvious case in point. It is the myth of Gyges in Book II of the *Republic*. Glaucon, who is here the active interlocutor, has confronted Socrates with three possible motives why people act justly: they do so either because justice is a good which is desirable in itself, or because it has desirable consequences, or because it is desirable in both ways (357b–d). Socrates opts for the third answer, the combination of the first two. Glaucon, too, would like to become convinced that justice is desirable also in itself, yet he is aware of the common view (which he probably shares at this moment, albeit unwillingly) that justice is desirable not in itself but only for its consequences. He asks Socrates to demonstrate to him that justice is good in itself. Yet, in order to make the task more difficult for Socrates, he sets out to argue for the common view. He does so by presenting at first a contractual definition of justice (358e–359b). By their nature, people want to get as much as possible and therefore don't mind getting more than others, or taking things away from others. They understand, however, that they can do so only as long as they are stronger, and that there is no guarantee that they will always be stronger than the others. Therefore, they agree to some rules of distribution and property ownership which henceforth determine what is just. These rules are provided with sanctions so that violating them has unpleasant consequences.

Thus, people stick to the rules because they understand that, all things considered, the consequences of being just are better than those of being unjust. In order to support this definition, Glaucon next tells the story of Gyges. Gyges was a shepherd in the service of the king of Lydia. One day, he found in a subterranean cave a ring which could make him invisible. By doing so, this ring allowed him to do and to get whatever he wanted without being discovered. What he wanted was, firstly, the king's wife, and then, the king's position. With the help of the ring, he obtained both easily. Now consider, Glaucon continues, two people, one just, one unjust, both given such a ring: how would they behave? In the end not so differently, says Glaucon. Even the just man could not resist the chance to take whatever he wants if he had no longer to fear any consequences. This is, so Glaucon's conclusion, a sure sign or proof (*mega tekmêrion*) that nobody acts justly if not for the consequences of acting justly.

It is obvious that this story is intended to establish a thesis which is supposed to apply generally. It is the claim that justice is desirable only for its consequences. So, the first one of the constraints listed above is fulfilled. Further, the story invites us to imagine a situation – the details of the myth are merely an embellishment of the situation we are to imagine – and asks us to decide, on the basis of what we are imagining, whether somebody who acts justly under normal conditions would do so also under circumstances which allow him to avoid the sanctions connected with violating the rules of justice. Glaucon himself suggests the answer, and calls this decision a "proof" or "sure sign" (the Greek word *tekmêrion* is not used in a terminologically strict way by Plato[6]). What Glaucon here does can, I think without hesitation, be called an appeal to the intuitions of whoever is addressed by the story. That he anticipates the addressee's decision would be not very significant in an ordinary philosophical text; in the dialogical situation constructed by Plato it is not a matter of course that Socrates is not given the chance to utter his own decision. It might be taken as a sign that what Glaucon is doing here might have presuppositions which are questionable – for example the assumption that people always want to have as much as they can get, and that they have no equally strong altruistic impulses. Yet, Glaucon's "proof" seems not so bad if it is taken as a reminder of how one acts under circumstances in which one can be sure that some little cheating will pass unnoticed. Maybe more than one reader has succumbed to the temptation in such a case, and will therefore agree to Glaucon's decision. Therefore, also the third one of my requirements is fulfilled. The second one can be taken as satisfied as well since in the context of the conversation there is no alternative at hand. Moreover, what Glaucon is doing here shares an important feature with modern-day scientific experiments. Glaucon proposes that there are two possible motivations for acting justly: because justice is desirable in itself, and because it has desirable consequences. In actual situations, the second motivation is always in play so that we have no chance to decide whether the first motivation in itself might be sufficient. The situation Glaucon imagines locks the second motivation out so that we can observe how human behaviour varies with the first motivation. The result, as anticipated by Glaucon, tells us that the first motivation in itself doesn't influence human behaviour. Therefore, Glaucon creates – if only in imagination – a classical experimental setting.

Taking all these points together, I think my claim is vindicated that the story of Gyges is a clear example of a thought experiment.[7]

3.3 My next case seems to me to be equally clear, yet as an example of a fictional story which does not count as a thought experiment. It is the great myth of Er's travel through the otherworld which concludes the *Republic*. This myth, too, serves to support a claim of general relevance. Throughout books II-IX of the *Republic*, Socrates tried to show that being just is desirable in itself. This long argument ends with three proofs that the life of the just is happier than the life of the unjust in Book IX. Yet, in Book II Socrates claimed that justice is desirable in itself *and* because of its consequences. That justice has good consequences might seem obvious, but the point still has to be dealt with, and Socrates does so by telling a myth in which we learn about the rewards which are bestowed on the souls of the just after death. The myth is narrated as the recounting of what Er's soul experienced when it traveled through the otherworld. It traveled together with the souls of the deceased to the under-worldly judgement place. There, it becomes witness of how some souls are sent downwards, others upwards, and it listens to the reports of those who return from these places. Then it follows those who have finished their time of punishment or reward and who are ready for another round of reincarnation; on this way, it also catches a glimpse of the structure which holds the world together.

Again, we are invited to imagine something – actually, a whole world. Plato might even invite us to hold true what is recounted in the myth. But we are not asked to make any decision based on what we imagine. The myth does not summon our intuitions in order to corroborate or doubt what is told, he simply asks us to believe that just souls are rewarded after the death, and that unjust souls are punished, and that the rewards and punishments are a multiple of the just or unjust deeds in this life.[8] Certainly, there is no replacement for the myth so that the condition 2) is met. Fulfilment of condition 1) is doubtful; on the one hand, the claim that justice has desirable consequences goes beyond the fictional sphere of the myth, on the other hand, the more specific claim that justice has desirable consequences after death remains within the mythical realm which is inaccessible to our methods of verification and falsification. Certainly violated is condition 3): of course, we have the option to believe in what the story suggests, or not to believe in it; but this choice would be equal to accept or not to accept the use of thought experiments in the first place.

3.4 Equally briefly can be settled the case of similes. My example will the simile of the Cave. Again, the point at issue is a thesis which reaches beyond the fictional story; the nature of a simile in itself ensures this. The simile of the Cave is not about what happens to some unspecified people in some unspecified cave. It is about our way of education, learning and understanding if we want to pursue the road of philosophy. The elucidation the simile promises critically depends on whether we find the picture it offers plausible. Can we accept that being removed from a bounded and epistemically limited, yet familiar situation needs force and effort? Is it comprehensible that one has to get accustomed slowly to new epistemic situations, that the change of epistemic circumstances can even bring about temporary blindness? These are some of the questions the addressee of the simile is confronted with, and they obviously appeal to her intuitions, inviting her to decide the plausibility of the simile on the basis of these intuitions. So, we can take conditions

1) and 3) to be met. Condition 2), however, is violated, due to the simple fact that similes are open to an interpretation which replaces the simile by an account which deals directly with the explanandum. As mentioned above, Socrates himself enters upon such an interpretation of the simile of the Cave. Therefore, similes are useful tools, but they are certainly not indispensable, so that I would suggest not to regard them as thought experiments.

3.5 My next example will prove to be more complicated and less easy to classify as thought experiment or not. It is the myth which is to be told to the inhabitants of the model city, telling them that they are all born from the earth and differently composed of gold, silver, and bronze. The model state is almost established; we know that besides the ordinary citizens who work as farmers, craftsmen or merchants, a special group of guardians is required; we have learnt a lot about how to educate these guardians, and what makes a guardian a good guardian. What is still missing is the answer to one question: who rules in this city? The best of the guardians, is Socrates' first answer; the best of the guardians are those who are most skillful at guarding the city (412c). This is not only not a very substantial explanation; it is also tainted with a serious difficulty since the difference between the best guardians and the others is a gradual one whereas the difference between guardians and rulers is a principled one. Even when the best guardians are successfully selected it might not be easy to convince the other guardians that from now on they are reduced to the rank of mere auxiliaries to the ruling ones.[9] It is probably in order to overcome this difficulty that Socrates suggests to tell the inhabitants of the model state a myth – a myth which he presents from the very beginning as a "noble lie," as one of those lies "in words" which are not necessarily bad but might serve some good purpose (414b). The myth itself has two parts. The first part describes how the citizens are born in fully developed adult state, from the earth as their mother (414d–e); the second part describes that all citizens have some metal in their soul: those who are competent to rule have gold, the auxiliaries have silver, and the rest of the citizens have bronze in their soul. This difference in composition explains why they are assigned different roles in the city (415a–c).

This myth clearly is supposed to fulfil two functions towards the inhabitants: firstly, to convince them that they are all brothers because they are born from the same mother; secondly, to establish the principled distinction between three ranks within the city which is now based not upon excelling over the others by degree but upon a difference in substance.

It is not obvious in what way this myth might work as a thought experiment, but they are some features in the way it is presented that bring it at least in the proximity of thought experiments. After expounding the myth, Socrates asks Glaucon whether the inhabitants of the city might be inclined to believe it. Glaucon is most doubtful (415c–d). Yet it is exactly this question which reminds of a thought experiment: The initial problem is, how can we establish the distribution of the citizens into three ranks among the city's inhabitants? Socrates invites us to imagine that a myth is told to the citizens which, if it were believed, would perform this task. Glaucon accepts the invitation but his intuition tells him that telling such a myth would not work because the myth is too incredible. Seen this way, the three requirements on thought experiments listed above are met.

Of course, Glaucon's intuitions are somewhat biased since the whole myth is introduced by Socrates as a lie. One might think that Glaucon would not have needed such a hint; hardly anybody would believe such a story, would they? Yet, the telling of the myth has further ramifications in the sequel of the *Republic*. It is not only the citizens of the model state who are in need of an explanation why rulers and guardians are distinct by rank. Glaucon hasn't got an explanation himself, and also the reader hasn't got one (at least at that stage of his reading the *Republic*). A few pages later, however, when Glaucon is asked where to locate wisdom, and where to locate courage in the city, he answers quite naturally that wisdom is the property peculiar to the rulers (428d–e), and courage the property peculiar to the guardians (429a–c). That is, he now distinguishes rulers and guardians not because they exemplify the same property in different degrees, but because they exemplify substantially different properties. Socrates comments on this surprising move by remarking that "we have found – I don't know how – this one [viz. wisdom] in the city" (429a). Socrates is right: if Glaucon were asked how he came to believe that rulers have a property that qualifies them as rulers and that distinguishes them from the guardians in principle, he would be at a loss. So, how did he come to believe? One explanation is: it is the myth that influenced Glaucon subliminally – although he was well aware of its being a lie.[10]

How does this relate to thought experiments? If my reading of the presentation of the myth as part of a thought experiment is correct, then Glaucon invoked his intuitions about the credibility of myths in order to decide that Socrates' proposal would not work. After that, Plato used the setting of an ongoing conversation to show that one's behaviour might belie one's intuitions: even if a myth is incredible it might be effective. Glaucon is not given the chance to notice this; the reader however – who at first might agree to Glaucon's judgement about the credibility of the myth, and who might even agree with Glaucon's later account of rulers and guardians – has the chance to notice that, in spite of her intuition, the myth was not as ineffective as it was supposed to be. Consequently, she has the chance to reconsider her intuitions. She might learn that intuitions have to be revised from time to time, that a close look at her own behaviour is a good touchstone for doing so, and hence that intuitions are not the kind of solid bedrock they are supposed to be, not least in the context of thought experiments.

3.6 After this rather complex example it is time to turn to the most famous and influential use of fiction in the *Republic*: the construction of the model state which covers the larger parts of books II-V as well as books VIII and IX. Although it is not unusual to classify it as a thought experiment[11], it is not obvious at first glance in which way the draft of a model state might count as a thought experiment.

One important section – the development of an educational program for the future guardians – is presented by Socrates as a "myth" in which the guardians are educated "in words" (376d9f.).[12] Probably the best way to take these remarks is as a indication that what follows is not to be intended as a true story – true in the sense that it can be checked against some piece of reality –, and that it is done not actually, but – and here it seems appropriate to say: "in thoughts."

The purpose of the construction of the model state is to define justice (368b–369a). Although justice is usually regarded as a property of social structures, at this point of the conversation it is already settled that justice is first and foremost a property of individuals, in line with the task to show that a just life is desirable in itself. In order to accomplish this task it is necessary to define justice. Socrates suggests to study justice by a larger case in point, viz. a state; therefore some kind of model state has to be developed. This move has some puzzling aspects. Firstly, it presupposes that a state and an individual can be just in the same way. Otherwise, it would be impossible to transfer the results from the state to the individual. Actually, Socrates seems to be aware of this problem. In his introductory remarks, he says that he wants first to turn to a larger object and to study justice there, and then to investigate whether the same can be found in the smaller object (that is, the individual) (368d6). Before proceeding to the definition of individual justice in book IV, Socrates dedicates a long argument to show that the presuppositions for the transfer of the definition from state to individual are indeed fulfilled (435b–441c).

Secondly, it is a moot issue of the interpretation of the *Republic* as a whole whether the drafting of the model state is relevant on its own, or whether it is merely a helpful device on the way to define individual justice. The textual evidence throughout the dialogue points both ways. Sometimes, the description of the model state seems clearly oriented towards the requirements of defining individual justice[13], sometimes the description develops a life of its own.[14]

If we now turn to the topic of thought experiments, it is important to clarify which claim could possibly be under consideration. One option is the possibility of a just state. Given that in reality there is no just state, can we imagine a state or city which is just? – this would then be the question to be decided on the basis of a thought experiment. What would be the intuitions which such a thought experiment appealed to? On the one hand, it would be intuitions about the structure of a state. Indeed, we can find such intuitions in the initial stage of the construction of the model state: Socrates presupposes that a state is based upon division of labour (369b–c), and further that we have to take into account the presence of desires which are not limited by themselves (372c–373d). The main subsequent step in the construction of the model state is the outline of an educational program for future guardians (376c–412b); later Socrates introduces the equal position of women and the dissolution of traditional family structures (451c–471d), and finally the rule of the philosophers (471e–502c) as further components of the model state. Glaucon, Adeimantos, and we as the readers, might learn in this way about what a just state requires, according to Socrates; and we can decide on the basis of further intuitions of ours whether, e.g., the educational program or the community of property, women (or men, respectively), and children is feasible.

Taken this way, reading the construction of the model state as a thought experiment seems to be plausible indeed. Yet, on the other hand this way of reading requires intuitions about justice as well; actually, it requires knowing what justice is. And this seems to contradict the clearly stated aim of the whole argument, namely to find a definition of justice. That there is a contradiction is not so clear, however. When the definition of justice finally is reached, it is staged by Socrates in a rather strange way: he talks in an almost childish manner as if he were finding something that was there from the very beginning and has just been overlooked all the time (432b–e). Indeed, the definition of justice – doing one's own (433a) – is very close to the principle of the division of labour which was presupposed from the beginning. The way Plato makes Socrates introduce this definition could be a hint that intuitions about justice were in play from the start. And then, the model state might be taken as a thought experiment intended to test the feasibility of a just state.

Is it possible to read the model state as a thought experiment which aims at finding a definition of justice? Again, the crucial question is: which intuitions might be invoked to decide about which claim? If, once again, they were taken to be intuitions about justice which were used to decide whether the state just outlined is just or not, the claim at issue would once more be about the state. Taking the model state as a thought experiment aiming at the definition of justice means that we need a proposed definition of justice at the outset which is then put to test by the thought experiment. But there is no such definition. Instead, the thought experiment would have to be taken as a heuristic device which helps to transform intuitions into a definition, or rather, to discover that some intuitions are already very close to a definition of justice.

On any of these readings, conditions 1) and 2) are clearly met. Whatever might be the purpose of the model state as a thought experiment, it is a purpose which extends beyond the fictional world of the model state. And in the dialogue setting, there is no shortcut way to the definition of justice at hand which would make the development of the model state dispensable. As to condition 3), the situation is not so obvious. Taking the development of the model state as thought experiment in order to investigate whether a just state is possible promotes the topic of a just state to a matter of self-contained interest. It is possible to read the *Republic* this way, yet it does not square perfectly with the textual evidence. Taking it as a thought experiment in order to find out what justice is turns the thought experiment into a heuristic device rather than a tool by which we can decide whether a claim is plausible or not.

4 Conclusion: Platonic dialogues as thought experiments?

By way of conclusion, I would like to take a brief look at the idea that Platonic dialogues on the whole, being fictional, might count as thought experiments. Doing so requires, in the first place, that the reader step back from the conversation that unfolds before her. It is a natural approach to a Platonic dialogue to identify with the interlocutor who is inquired by Socrates, and to take Socrates' questions as being posed to the reader herself. This approach can be overcome as soon as the reader feels puzzled by the course of the conversation, and starts to look for their own answers to Socrates' questions. If she does so, she enters into a kind of conversation with Socrates himself which could end up in rewriting the dialogue. It might be well the case that Plato intended such an effect by opting for the dialogue form, and by shaping it as he did, with unsatisfying aporetic ends, unsound arguments, equivocations, and even tricks played at Socrates' interlocutor.

Such a way of reading Plato's dialogue does not yet mean to read them as thought experiments. Taking them this way would come down to reading them as constructions of laboratory settings in which we imagine how a certain group of people would behave if they were given some topic to discuss and some ideas or theories to work with. There might be dialogues which can be seen in this way.[15] But in general, it seems to me to demand too much distance between the reader and the dialogue. To use once again the *Republic* as an example: of course, the whole dialogue might be read as a thought experiment as to how a philosopher like Socrates could convince two young men, Glaucon and Adeimantus, that a just life is the best life. The reader could consult her own intuitions in order to decide whether such an attempt would succeed or fail. But it seems to me to be more natural to take the dialogue as an appeal to the reader herself to lead a just life. In other words, the dialogue seems to me to ask the reader to get personally involved in what would be mere fiction if taken as a thought experiment.

Notes

1 As to the order of invention, the honour of primacy probably goes to Archytas; on him, see Ierodiakonou (this volume). As to the order of traceable transmission, the first is Plato's.
2 In order to provide some material from other Platonic texts to the reader, I will list a few other famous Platonic myths and briefly mark how they are placed within the spectrum of truth and falsity:

   i *Timaeus*. The whole cosmological story of the *Timaeus* is presented as a "myth," albeit as a "eikos mythos," a "probable myth". On the reading of this formula, see Burnyeat (2009, 167–86). In the end, Burnyeat calls the whole cosmological account a thought experiment (186).

   ii The myth of Atlantis and old Athens which is told twice in the *Critias* (passim) and the *Timaeus* (21e–26d). In the *Critias*, the whole story is put under the tutelary of the muses and therefore placed in the realm of poetry. In the *Timaeus*, the story is rather presented as a kind of historical narrative, attested by Egyptian sources (and accompanied by an explanation why the historical records of the Egyptians reach further back than those of the Greek). Moreover, against what is contained in the Greek myths about the early history of mankind, the tales of the Egyptians are implicitly contrasted as the true account (22c–d) (on this, see Gill 1979).

   iii The myth in which the soul is described as a charioteer and two winged horses in the *Phaedrus* (246a–256e) is recited by Socrates in the context of a speech in which he praises love as a kind of inspired madness, and Socrates himself presents the myth in a hymnical tone which gets more and more inspired itself. Yet, the myth is not without well thought out elements (on this, see the commentary ad loc. by Heitsch 1997 and Ferrari 2010).

   iv The myth of Theuth in the *Phaedrus* 274c–275b about the invention of writing. In this myth, a (human) king criticizes the divine invention of writing because of its effects on memory. The criticism contained in the myth is taken as a prophecy fulfilled later (after humans adopted the practice of writing), and hence taken as literally true (see the commentaries just mentioned).

   v The myth of metempsychosis in the *Meno* (81a–d). Socrates claims to have learned this myth from some priests and priestesses. At first he characterizes the myth as "true and divine speech"; in the end, however, he makes clear that in the first place the myth has to serve a certain function: viz., to refute the eristic thesis that nothing can be learned, and to encourage people to learn.

   vi The eschatological myth in the *Phaedo* (107d–115a) is clearly set off against the preceding dialogical passages in which Socrates faced some opposition against his conviction that the soul is immortal. According to the interpretation of Ebert (2004, 421ff.), Socrates is here referring to Pythagorean sources when he draws a picture of the otherworld. Interestingly, however, even in this myth there is a passage (108d–110a) which Socrates explicitly marks as his own conviction (the passage is about the true nature of the earth).

3 For this analysis of Platonic myths, see Brisson (1998).
4 Well-known similes in other Platonic dialogues are the similes of the wax block and the bird cage in the *Theaetetus* (191c–e and 197d–198d), the simile of the magnetic stone in the *Ion* (533d–536b), and the simile of the soul as vessel and cask in the *Gorgias* (492e–493c).
5 Nenad Miščević (2012) has put this requirement under the title "inferentialist objection": "Can one arrive at the same judgement just by using observation of actual behaviour and arguing from it?" (160).
6 Since he often adds *mega* ("big"), *tekmêrion* appears as something that comes in degrees; therefore, "evidence" might be a good translation, provided it is not taken to mean sensory evidence (apart from the passage quoted here, see also e.g. *Republic* 405b, *Symposium* 196a, *Gorgias* 456b).
7 Such is also the conclusion of Miščević (2012) and of Shields (2006).
8 It is significant in this respect that Plato omits any report of Glaucon's or Adeimantos' reaction to the myth. Socrates' report of Er's tale is the final word of the *Republic*.
9 Since the guardians are characterized by a competitive spirit, they might continue to compete with each other for being the best guardian. Such a competition has to be prevented by installing a principled distinction by rank.

10 On this reading, see Becker (2009–11).
11 Cf. e.g. Höffe (2005, 71), Sedley (2007, 273), Halliwell (2007, 452), and the extended defense of the classification as thought experiment in Miščević (2012).
12 The formula "in words" is also used in the introductory remarks of the whole construction (369a5).
13 For example, the kind of unjust cities which are discussed in books VIII and IX is clearly aligned to the nature of the individual soul (on this, cf. Blösner 1997, 62ff.).
14 For example when the position of women or the organization of family life are discussed (which have no parallel in the individual), or when the idea of philosopher-rulers is introduced by way of the question whether the model state can become real at all.
15 For instance, Rowe (2010, 97), mentions in passing the possibility that the whole *Phaedo* is a thought experiment – maybe in order to investigate how a philosopher as Socrates, equipped with theories like the idea of anamnesis and the theory of forms, could argue and behave when facing death.

References

Becker, A. (2009–2011) "Platons Gesprächsdramaturgie und der Leser. Zwei Beispiele aus der Politeia," *Bochumer Philosophisches Jahrbuch für Antike und Mittelalter* 14: 84–102.
Blösner, N. (1997) *Dialogform und Argument: Studien zu Platons "Politeia,"* Stuttgart: Steiner.
Brisson, L. (1998) *Plato the Myth Maker*, translated and edited by G. Naddaf, Chicago: University of Chicago Press.
Burnyeat, M. (2009) "Eikos mythos," in *Plato's Myths*, edited by C. Partenie, Cambridge: Cambridge University Press.
Collobert, C., Destrée, P. and Gonzales, F. J. (eds) (2012) *Plato and Myth. Studies on the Use and Status of Platonic Myths (Mnemosyne Supplements 337)*, Leiden: Brill.
Ebert, T. (2004) *Platon: Phaidon, Übersetzung und Kommentar*. Göttingen: Vandenhoek & Ruprecht.
Ferrari, G. R. F. (2010) *Listening to the Cicadas: A Study of Plato's Phaedrus*, Cambridge: Cambridge University Press.
Gill, C. (1979) "Plato's Atlantis story and the birth of fiction," *Philosophy and Literature* 3: 64–78.
Halliwell, S. (2007) "The life-and-death journey of the soul: Interpreting the myth of Er," in *The Cambridge Companion to Plato's Republic*, edited by G. R. F. Ferrari, Cambridge: Cambridge Univeristy Press.
Heitsch, E. (1997) "Phaidros. Übersetzung und Kommentar," in *Platon, Phaidros: Übersetzung und Kommentar*, Göttingen: Vandenhoek and Ruprecht.
Höffe, O. (2005) "Zur Analogie von Individuum und Polis," in *Platon: Politeia* (Klassiker auslegen Bd. 7), edited by O. Höffe, Berlin: Akademie-Verlag.
Ierodiakonou, K. (2005) "Ancient thought experiments: A first approach," *Ancient Philosophy* 25: 125–140.
Janka, M. and Schäfer, C. (eds) (2002) *Platon als Mythologe: Neue Interpretationen zu den Mythen in Platons Dialogen*, Darmstadt: Wissenschaftliche Buchgesellschaft.
Miščević, N. (2012) "Plato's Republic as a thought experiment," *Croatian Journal of Philosophy* 12: 153–166.
Partenie, C. (ed.) (2009) *Plato's Myths*, Cambridge: Cambridge University Press.
Rowe, C. (2010) *Plato and the Art of Philosophical Writing*, Cambridge: Cambridge University Press.
Sedley, D. (2007) "Philosophy, forms, and the art of ruling," in *The Cambridge Companion to Plato's Republic*, edited by G. R. F. Ferrari, Cambridge: Cambridge University Press.
Shields, C. (2006) "Plato's challenge: The case against justice in Republic II," in *The Blackwell Guide to Plato's Republic*, edited by G. Santas, Oxford: Blackwell.

3
ARISTOTLE AND THOUGHT EXPERIMENTS

Klaus Corcilius

Aristotle, as far as we know, has no conception of thought experiments. He does not discuss them in his works, and his writings do not show signs that he has identified a distinctive mode of pointing out something, philosophically or otherwise, that could plausibly be described in terms of what we call thought experiments. Aristotle does not even have a *word* for "thought experiment." And it is not difficult to see why this is so. To start with, for our conception of "thought experiment" to make the specific sense it has (however vague it might be), it requires a context in which the concept of "experimentation" has some currency among a relevant community of thinkers. But in Aristotle's time, there is no scientific community to which the conception of "thought experiment" could, as it were, speak: the notion relies on a specifically post-Aristotelian conception of experimentation, according to which experimenters contrive repeatable physical events, by means of which they demonstrate some correlation between physical states or events that are usually not available to immediate experience. An important aspect of this is that the experimenter produces her demonstration through exerting control over the relevant parameters (typically, with the aid of technical instruments) so as to isolate the occurrence of the phenomenon about which she wishes to demonstrate her point. The basic idea is that she, by wilfully manipulating the parameters, makes available to repeatable experience a regularity in nature that was previously not evident to her scientific community. According to this conception, experimentation is an artificial means to make available to repeatable experience hitherto unobservable facts about nature or, shorter still, a means to provide such data in otherwise unobservable natural terrain. Our notion of thought experiment depends on some such ideas of empirical experimentation. The difference is of course that thought experiments are not confined to *physical* facts, which is also why they do not require artificial production of physical events; what makes them experiments of *thought* is that repeatable imagined scenarios are used instead.[1] But, notwithstanding this difference, our notion of thought experiments seems to preserve what is basic for the early modern idea of empirical experimentation: they are imagined scenarios, wilfully contrived through manipulations of relevant parameters and with the purpose of isolating, and thus disclosing to experience, some previously non-evident fact; only that thought experiments, instead of providing us with experiences in an unqualified sense, provide us with what Ernst Mach calls a *Gedankenerfahrung*, an *experience in thought* (Mach 1905, 186).

There is of course no trace of this in Aristotle. But *could* there have been? It seems to me that the absence of a conception of thought experimentation in Aristotle's works is not a matter of mere contingency. Aristotle, unlike early modern experimenters, does not attach much methodological weight to empirical experimentation as a means to the discovery of facts. Notoriously, his natural science relies much more on the observation of what is there and plain to see for the philosophically acute, yet instrumentally unaided, observer rather than on artificial extraction of hidden facts. Indeed, his views on the status of scientific data in empirical sciences seem to be at odds with our more engineer-like attitude towards nature.[2] According to Aristotle's conception, empirical science divides labour between the collection of the relevant facts, on the one hand, and the scientific explanation of these facts, on the other. The former he calls by the name of "the that (*to hoti*)," or the "the phenomena (*ta phainomena*)," or sometimes simply "experience (*empeiria*)" of a science, whereas he refers to the latter as the "on account of which" or "the because of which (*to dihoti*)" these facts obtain. Zoological science, for instance, is a twofold enterprise, consisting of the collection of relevant facts about animals and the statement of reasons for these facts. On that picture, engaging in the explanatory task of stating the reasons requires the collection of facts to be more or less completed.[3] Aristotelian sciences are in this sense holistic: their explanations are meant to exhaustively capture the relevant explanatory order that structures their respective domains as a whole. To us, by contrast, the thought that the empirical observation of facts in a given domain is completed would not occur too easily. We tend to think of natural inquiry as an open-ended task. And it looks as if the reason for why we think that way has to do precisely with the incredible success of the post-Aristotelian method of extracting data from nature by the way of technical artifice. For that success story strongly suggests both that our ability to collect data and thus to extend the ambit of our experience beyond what is plain to see is more or less a function of our technical abilities, and that there is no obvious limit to these abilities. From a historicizing and progress-oriented standpoint such as ours, then, it is not without irony when Aristotle calls the collections of "the" observable data of a given scientific domain "experience."[4] But however that may be, a philosopher who thinks about natural science in the way Aristotle does is not likely to regard the discovery of new data as the scientist's main occupation. Rather, he will be inclined to think of it as a very important and necessary, yet manageable, prerequisite for the proper business of scientific investigation, which is the explanation of the facts. And as there is little reason for such a philosopher to attach great methodological weight to experimentation as a means to the discovery of facts, there is even less reason for him to do so for *thought* experimentation.

This, to be sure, is not to say that there is no place for empirical experimentation in Aristotle's conception of science. There is no particular reason why he should have regarded experimentation as in any way problematic or illegitimate: experimentation just does not form a vital part of his understanding of what empirical science is all about. This, it seems to me, is certainly – and perhaps also trivially – true of Aristotle.[5] In this regard our engineer-like manner of doing science is simply very different.[6] But there is also another element in our very concept of thought experiment that probably would have struck Aristotle as alien. For talk of experiments "in thought" somehow trades on the idea that the results of mere thoughts and the results of "genuine" experiments conducted by natural scientists can have similar epistemic value. What makes this parallel potentially alien to Aristotle is that it often comes with the additional idea that having an equal or similar epistemic value as empirical science somehow legitimates, or perhaps even rehabilitates, mere thoughts as a method of scientific discovery. That, however, would be a strange line of thought for a philosopher who precedes the modern divide between science and philosophy and who, apart from firmly believing in the dignity and purpose of the human capacity of reason, is ignorant of the discredit into which the (largely Aristotelian) "philosophy-schooles" fell in early modern times.[7] There is reason, therefore, to doubt that Aristotle would have regarded appeal to empirical experimentation as a selling point.

**

In spite of this absence of a positive conception of thought experimentation in his thinking, Aristotle undoubtedly makes abundant use of what we call thought experiments. His works, especially the ones on natural philosophy, virtually bristle with them.[8] And it is not difficult to see why this is so either. Aristotle is, after all, a philosopher. What I mean by this is that, even on our by comparison very narrow conception of philosophy, he is concerned with questions that we would classify as philosophical questions, as, e.g., on the nature of value, meaning, modality, life, god, and so on. If we are to believe Aristotle's own line of reasoning, these philosophical topics are superbly difficult precisely in virtue of the fact that they concern unobservable matters.[9] And since thought experimentation, according to the minimal characterization just given, is a means of providing data in otherwise unobservable terrain, it seems to have a natural affinity with the treatment of these philosophical questions. *Qua* being a philosopher who is concerned with unobservable and otherwise epistemically difficult matters, this seems true of Aristotle as well. He too uses imagined hypothetical scenarios when he has reasons to do so. So the same functional account seems to apply: Aristotle uses thought experiments in order to compensate for a lack of available data in epistemically difficult terrain. However, I should add here that his conception of philosophy extends further than ours. For Aristotle, as is well known, *all* knowledge that we pursue for its own sake counts as philosophical knowledge, including natural science. I should also add that Aristotle's usage of thought experiments in "epistemically difficult terrain" should be understood broadly as well. He uses thought experiments not only in cases where it would be impossible or exceedingly difficult to carry out physical experiments, but also, as we will see, in cases where it would be relatively easy to perform the corresponding physical experiments. This holds in particular for a number of thought experiments in his philosophical psychology. But this is not to say that these experiments occur in readily accessible epistemic terrain. Rather, in these cases the epistemic difficulty is located on the receiver's end: they typically concern claims that in one way or another conflict with widespread or otherwise deeply ingrained intuitions. One such claim is the widespread view that flesh is the organ of touch (see 4.1 below). Aristotle attacks this view by way a thought experiment that could easily be performed as an actual experiment.

But in such a case we may still regard the thought experiment as a device for providing data in epistemically difficult terrain, because the data that it does provide us with are counterintuitive, i.e. they contradict common views and would not occur easily in ordinary thought. Finally, a clarification. For the purposes of this chapter, I would like to distinguish thought experiments from imagined scenarios that merely exemplify or illustrate a point, such as the following illustration of the thesis that the constitution of a living body is best preserved in an environment akin to it:

> For example, if nature were to constitute a thing of wax or of ice, she would not preserve it by putting it in a hot place, for the opposing quality would quickly destroy it, seeing that heat dissolves that which cold congeals. Again, a thing composed of salt or nitre would not be taken and placed in water, for fluid dissolves that of which the consistency is due to the dry.
> (*De Juv.* 477^{b}18–23, transl. G.R.T. Ross)

I would not classify this as a thought experiment because in this case Aristotle is not *doing* anything with the imagined scenario. He is not generating evidence on the basis of which he going to make a point, but merely illustrates a general point he made previously in the text.[10] The scenarios I will discuss as thought experiments in what follows, by contrast, somehow *generate* data by having these data in one way or the other *follow* from the imagined parameters, so that we can experience them as happening. On the minimalistic functional perspective I am suggesting on Aristotle's behalf, then, thought experiments are a means to compensate for a lack of data in epistemically difficult terrain, by somehow generating data from imagined scenarios. This, at any rate, is the somewhat pedestrian perspective under which I shall present a small number of examples of thought experiments. My guiding principle in choosing the examples is to illustrate some of the *variety* in the ways he uses them. But I should warn the reader that I make no claim towards a representative selection of examples, and let alone towards an exhaustive typology.[11] I end this chapter with a brief discussion of what Aristotle might himself have thought about his own usages of thought experimentation.

Note on the examples

Aristotle is known to most of us as an author of densely written philosophical treatises. These are his so-called esoteric writings, which were intended to be read only by a small elite of technically skilled philosophical insiders. He is less known for his published philosophical works. These works, the so-called exoteric writings, were intended for a wider audience of philosophically interested non-experts. Today, unfortunately, we possess these writings only in a comparatively small number of fragments. Many of these writings were philosophical dialogues. As far as we know, they very much resembled the dialogues of Aristotle's teacher Plato, not only in literary style but apparently also – and astoundingly – in their philosophical doctrine. There is, for instance, a cave analogy also in Aristotle (see below), and even arguments for the immortality of the soul, a doctrine that Aristotle appears to contradict in his esoteric works. Naturally, in the literally setting of a Platonic dialogue, the style of reasoning will be more colourful than that in the mostly terse esoteric writings. In order to illustrate this aspect of Aristotle's usage of thought experiments, I shall briefly present one example from his exoteric writings. All other examples are taken from his esoteric works.

1 Dialogues

1.1 *The cave*

We know of this thought experiment from a report by Cicero. He says:

> Thus Aristotle brilliantly remarks:
> Suppose there were men who had always lived underground, in good and well-lighted dwellings, adorned with statues and pictures, and furnished with everything in which those who are thought happy abound. Suppose, however, that they had never gone above ground, but had learned by report and hearsay that there was a divine spirit and power. Suppose that then, at some time, the jaws of the earth opened, and they were able to escape and make their way from those hidden dwellings into these regions which we inhabit. When they suddenly saw earth and seas and skies, when they learned the grandeur of clouds and the power of winds, when they saw the sun and realized not only its grandeur and beauty but also its power, by which it fills the sky with light and makes the day; when, again, night darkened the lands and they saw the whole sky picked out and adorned with stars, and the varying light of the moon as it waxes and wanes, and the risings and settings of all these bodies, and their courses settled and immutable to all eternity; when they saw those things, most certainly would they have judged both that there are gods and that these great works are the works of gods.
> Thus far Aristotle.
>
> (Cicero, *De natura deorum* II, xxxvii 95, Fragment 12 Rose[3]: transl. Barnes/Lawrence)

Aristotle invites us to imagine people who, apart from living in underground dwellings without knowledge of the existence of outside world, live in circumstances similar to ours; they have everything they need, as well as some vague stories from hearsay about the existence of a divine power. Next he invites us to imagine that "the jaws of the earth opened" so as to expose the cave-dwellers to the sight of the stars and their regular motions. On that basis, he argues that the cave-dwellers, overwhelmed by the sight, would "most certainly" come to believe there to be gods, who, as only gods could, have created this marvelous universe. We do not know in which context Aristotle originally made use of this thought experiment, but it certainly is remarkable for its poetic force. Aristotle tries to, as it were, alienate us from our own macroscopic environment, so as to allow us to take a fresh, and presumably also *philosophically* more adequate, perspective on it: he uses the cave - scenario to detach us from our habit of taking for granted the existence of the outside world, and seeks thereupon to establish a causal link between the overwhelming beauty of the firmament, and the existence of divine creators. Here, I take it, the thought experiment provides otherwise unavailable data, not by disclosing hitherto hidden facts, but by providing a new perspective on data that are all too obvious to everyone.

2 Metaphysics

2.1 The "stripping argument"

This is the perhaps most famous thought experiment in Aristotle, and certainly the most famous in his *Metaphysics*. It is a part of his investigation into the question: "what is substance?" Unlike in the previous example, Aristotle here uses the experiment for a critical purpose, namely to refute a particular thesis about what substance is. According to that thesis what makes substances being what they are is that they are underlying subjects of predication. Aristotle puts that thesis to a test. He asks us to imagine an uncontroversial instance of a substance, namely a three-dimensional natural body, and then to strip it of its predicates. The idea is straightforward enough: if the nature of substances really consists in their being the underlying subjects of predication, then stripping away all the predicates from an underlying subject of predication (a natural body) should leave us with its pure substance. That, however, is not what happens:

> We have now outlined the nature of substance, showing that it is that which is not predicated of a subject, but of which all else is predicated. But we must not merely state the matter thus; for this is not enough. The statement itself is obscure, and further, on this view, matter becomes substance. For if this [i.e. matter] is not substance, it is beyond us to say what else is. When all else is taken away evidently nothing but matter remains: For the [predicates] other [than substance] are either active doings, and passive affections, and capacities of the bodies, while their length, breadth, and depth are quantities and not substances. For a quantity is not a substance; the substance is rather that to which these primarily belong. But when length and breadth and depth are taken away we see nothing left except that which is bounded by these, whatever it be; so that to those who consider the question thus matter alone must seem to be substance. By matter I mean that which in itself is neither a particular thing nor of a certain quantity nor assigned to any other of the categories by which being is determined. For there is something of which each of these is predicated, so that its being is different from that of each of the predicates; for the predicates other than substance are predicated of substance, while substance is predicated of matter. Therefore the ultimate subject is of itself neither a particular thing nor of a particular quantity nor otherwise positively characterized; nor yet negatively, for negations also will belong to it only by accident.
> (*Metaphysics* 7.3, 1029^{a}6–1029^{a}26, transl. Ross, slightly modified)

Aristotle distinguishes two kinds of predicates: predicates that denote what bodies actively do or passively undergo along with their corresponding capacities (powers), and predicates that denote their dimensional extensions (length, breadth, and depth). Stripping away in thought the first group of predicates leaves us with the bodies' bare spatial extension; stripping away these extensions, however, does not result in the isolation of the *substance* of these bodies; rather, what we then "see" is only what was bounded by their extensions "length," "breadth," and "depth," which for Aristotle is completely indeterminate physical matter (*hulê*). But as physical matter does not meet two other fundamentally important criteria for being a substance, namely having independent ("separate") existence and being a determinate "certain this" (1029^{a}27–29), something must be wrong with the criterion the application of which led us to the assumption that matter is substance. The conclusion is that being an underlying subject of predication is not a sufficient criterion for substance.

2.2 A second sun

The passage exhibits two cases of usage of thought experimentation, one of which seems particularly close to some thought experiments in recent philosophy. They occur in Book 7 of his *Metaphysics*, where Aristotle critically confronts the Platonic doctrine of Ideas with difficulties. In the first case, his argument relies on the practice, already common at his time, of defining things by way of proximate genus and specific difference. Previously in the text, it has been established that such definitions are *general*: they apply to whatever "falls under" them. This, however, has the consequence that definitions cannot isolate individuals *as such*, but merely their universal characterizations (their "being" as Aristotle says). This presents a difficulty for the theory of Ideas because by that theory, Ideas would be both universal objects of definition and unique undefinable individuals. To make his point, Aristotle considers a particular and well-known case of a particular and (according to him and many of his contemporaries) also eternal individual: the sun.

> As has been said, then, the impossibility of defining individuals escapes notice in the case of eternal things, especially those which are unique, like the sun or the moon. (a) For people err not only by adding attributes whose removal the sun would survive, e.g. 'going round the earth' or 'night-hidden,' for from their view it follows that if it stands still or is visible, it will no longer be the sun; but it is strange if this is so; for 'the sun' means a certain substance; (b) but also by the mention of attributes which can belong to another subject; e.g. if another thing with the stated attributes comes into existence, clearly it will be a *sun*; the defining formula therefore is general. But the sun was supposed to be an individual, like Cleon or Socrates. After all, why does not one of the supporters of the Ideas produce a definition of an Idea? It would become clear, if they tried, that what has now been said is true.
>
> (*Metaphysics* 7.15, 1040^{a}27–^{b}4, transl. Ross, slightly modified)

If definitions by proximate genus and specific difference do not isolate individuals, but only their general characteristics, then there can be no definition that isolates a unique Platonic Idea either – there can only be a general characterization under which the Idea would "fall." Section (b) shows that the terms we use in defining the sun all denote general attributes, each one of which could apply to a plurality of objects, even if it should happen that there actually exists only one of them: hence, if another individual that shares the same characteristics as the sun came into existence, that individual clearly would have to be thought of as a *sun*. Considering the scenario of a second sun shows that defining formulas are general by their very nature and, therefore, cannot capture individual entities. The other experiment in (a) introduces a different scenario for a different purpose, the refutation of certain definitions of the sun current at his time. What Aristotle doesn't like about them is that they try to capture the nature of the sun by reference to non-essential attributes, such as that it "goes around the earth" and is "hidden at night." To make us see why this kind of definition must fail, Aristotle imagines a scenario in which these purportedly definitional attributes are removed: it turns out that even if we counterfactually suppose that the sun stands still or be visible at night, it would still be true that we would think of it as the *sun*.[12] Hence, defining the sun by way of such and other "attributes whose removal the sun would survive" fails to capture what the sun most fundamentally is (a thing or a substance).

2.3 *If all things were colours*

Here, Aristotle argues against a certain class of mathematically minded philosophers. These philosophers posit unity ("the one") and numbers to be fundamental items of their ontologies and explain what things other than numbers are in terms of such metaphysical numbers. His aim is to demolish that thesis by showing how number and unity are too thin as concepts to be able to account for what things other than numbers are. The structure of the argument is a *reductio*. Aristotle starts by considering a case of metaphysical analysis of things by way of unity and numbers, namely the at his time widely accepted analysis of colours as numerical proportion of white and black.

> But in colors the one is a color, e.g. white – the other colors are observed to be produced out of this and black, and black is the privation of white, as darkness of light.

In this instance, the colour white takes the place of "the one," i.e. the first metaphysical principle, in its domain (colours) because the other colours are generated by way of numerical proportions of white and of black, where black is conceived as the complete absence (or privation, lack) of white on the colour-scale. Aristotle agrees with this theory. He agrees that all other colours are defined as values in-between the extreme values on the colour spectrum white and black, and that therefore all intermediate colours are products of (numerical) proportions of white and black. The colour "green," for instance, consists in a mixture of a certain portion of white plus a certain portion of black. But since black is just the complete lack of white on the colour spectrum, white is "the one" in the domain of colours: all intermediate colours can be reduced to a combination of it and the lack thereof. Now, Aristotle dramatically expands the scenario:

> Therefore if all existent things were colors, existent things would have been a number, indeed, but of what? Clearly of *colors*; and the one would have to be *something* one, e.g. white.
>
> (Meta. 1. 2, 1053^{b}29–34, transl. Ross)

Aristotle uses the absurd scenario that all existent things are colours to bring out a fundamental flaw in the theory of the mathematically minded philosophers. These thinkers assume that unity and numbers are somehow self-subsisting entities, to which all other things can be metaphysically reduced. However, while this may work in the case of numerical quantities, it does not work in the case of other categories, not even in the relatively uncontroversial case of the numerical analysis of colours: for even if Aristotle agrees that colours are to be analyzed in terms of numerical proportions of white and black, they still remain numerical proportions *of colours*. The numbers of colours are relative to what they are the numbers *of*, namely colours. So if there is a reduction of colours to numbers, this is so in virtue of the fact that the numbers are numbers of colours. What we learn from this is that the reduction of colours to numerical proportions of other colours, even when possible, does not amount to the reduction of colours to numbers. The mathematically minded theory fails because it ignores this basic conceptual fact. The experiment brings that out by imagining a very simple qualitative world: even if all things were colours, and therefore reducible to numerical proportions of white and black, this would not give us a reduction of *colour* to unity and number. Unity and number are too thin as concepts to account for anything outside of quantities.[13]

3 Philosophical psychology

3.1 *Why flesh is not the organ of touch: the membrane and the air envelope*

Again a thought experiment with a critical purpose. The thesis put to test this time is that flesh is the organ of touch. The experiment comes in two stages. In the first stage, Aristotle tries to defuse what others count as good evidence for thinking that flesh is the organ of touch, namely that we perceive the affections of our flesh immediately:

> To the question whether the organ of touch lies inward or not (i.e. whether we need look any farther than the flesh), no indication can be drawn from the fact that if the object comes into contact with the flesh it is at once perceived. For even under present conditions if we stretched a membrane tight over the flesh, as soon as this is touched the sensation is reported in the same manner as before, yet it is clear that the organ is not in this membrane. And if the membrane could even be grown on to the flesh, the report would travel still quicker.
>
> (*DA* 2. 11, 422^{b}34–423^{a}6, transl. Smith)

Here, Aristotle casts doubt on the idea that our immediate perception of touch upon our flesh shows that flesh is the organ of touch: for if we imagine that an external membrane be stretched tightly over our flesh, it would feel the very same. Why think, then, that our flesh is any different from such a membrane? And if we further imagine that this membrane be grown together with our body (as is the case with our flesh), it follows from the scenario that we would perceive contact upon the membrane with the same immediacy as contact with our flesh. In this case, the justification with which we would think that this outer membrane is the organ of touch is just about the same as the justification with which we now think that the flesh is that organ. In the next step, Aristotle extends the scenario in order to bring out one of the positive roles our flesh plays in perception. If we imagine our bodies to be surrounded by an envelope of air growing around our bodies – in a way similar to how our flesh grows out of our bodies – we would be naturally lead towards believing that the distal senses of hearing, seeing, and smelling all belonged to one and the same sense modality. But, as it is, we do not believe this *because* the bodies and organs through which these different sense-objects are channeled to us are different in each case, which is Aristotle's point:

> That is why that part of the body which is of that quality [i.e. the flesh] relates to us in a way very similar to an air-envelope that grows round our body; had we such an envelope we should have supposed that it was by a single organ that we perceived sounds, colours, and smells, and we should have taken sight, hearing, and smell to be a single sense. But as it is, because that through which the different movements are transmitted is not naturally attached to our bodies, the difference of the various sense-organs is evident. But this is now unclear in the case of touch.
> (DA 422^{b}34–432^{a}12, transl. Smith, slightly modified)

What about the proximal senses? In what follows in the text, Aristotle argues that nature had, as it were, no choice but to construe the bodies through which we receive the input of touch, taste, and smell with one and the same kind of body, flesh.

3.2 *If white would be the only perceptible*

This thought experiment is used to suggest that nature has equipped us with a plurality of senses so that we can distinguish, and isolate in thought, the perceptual features common to a plurality of our senses, such as extension, numbers, and movement, from what he calls "special sensibles." Special sensibles are those perceptible objects that are exclusive to each sense modality (colour for sight, sound for hearing, scent for the sense of smell and so on). Aristotle seeks to establish this point by imagining an extreme scenario of monomodal perception, in which we possess only one single sense modality, namely sight, with one single perceptible object, namely the colour "white." In that scenario, we would be unlikely to distinguish number, movement, extension and the like from the whiteness we perceive. And this in turn suggests that we possess more than one sense modality – perhaps among other things – in order to be able to distinguish the content specific to each sense modality from the perceptible features common to a plurality of them:

> It might be asked why we have more senses than one. Is it to prevent a failure to apprehend the common sensibles, e.g. movement, magnitude, and number, which go along with the special sensibles? Had we no sense but sight, and that sense no object but white, they would have tended to escape our notice and everything would have merged for us into an indistinguishable identity because of the concomitance of colour and magnitude. As it is, the fact that the common sensibles are given in the objects of more than one sense reveals their distinction from each and all of the special sensibles.
> (DA 425^{b}5–11)

4 Cosmology

4.1 Refutation of the Atlas-theory

This is a particularly interesting thought experiment. Aristotle engages in a continuous discussion of what for him is a manifestly false theory of the movement of the universe. His motive in doing so is to bring across a general limitation of the *type* of theory as represented by the Atlas-theory. To see the extent of how Aristotle exploits counterfactual scenarios for his philosophical purposes, we must follow the course of his argument along a larger part of a whole chapter of *On the Movement of Animals*. The context is the discussion of a mechanical principle of animal self-locomotion that Aristotle has introduced and defended in the previous chapters of the treatise. According to this principle, locomotive agents, in order to move their bodies from place to place, necessarily require an external and unmoved resting point, so as to be able to support themselves against it.

EXTERNAL SUPPORTING POINT PRINCIPLE: Self-locomotive agents, in order to move their bodies from one place to the other, necessarily require an external resting point which is unmoved in relation to them.

In the previous chapter, three examples were given to illustrate the impossibility of self-locomotive change without some such external and unmoved prop. 1. Mice whose feet are stuck in a pitch won't move forward because they cannot *separate* their own movement from the movement of the ground on which they stand. They take, so to speak, their ground with them. 2. Walkers who walk on sand won't move forward because the sand fails to provide a support that remains *unmoved* in relation to their own movement. 3. A sailor on a boat cannot move the boat by supporting himself from within the boat. This last example illustrates very clearly the necessity that the supporting point be *external* to the self-moving body: the supporting point must be no part of the self-moving body, which in the case of the third example is not the sailor but the boat on which the sailor stands. Without such an external supporting point, says Aristotle, not even the mythical giant Tityus, nor the wind-god Boreas as he blows into the sail, would move the boat. At this point, once the principle is established, Aristotle broadens the scope of discussion to cosmological scale, asking whether the motion of the universe as a whole would require such an external supporting point as well.[14]

> Someone might pose this problem: if something moves the whole heavens, must there, too, be something unmoved which is neither any part of the heavens, nor in the heavens?
>
> (699ᵃ12–14)

In response, Aristotle distinguishes two different scenarios in which the universe ("the whole heavens") is moved by a mover, and answers affirmatively in both cases:

> For if it [i.e. the mover of the universe] is moved itself and also moves the heavens, it must touch something that is unmoved in order to impart the movement, and

this must be no part of the mover; and if the mover is unmoved from the first, it must, equally, be no part of what is moved.

(699ª14–17)

In the first scenario, the universe is moved by a moved mover, i.e. a self-mover, which on its part will require an external and unmoved resting point; in the second scenario, the universe is moved by a mover in which the two functions of resting point and mover coincide: an unmoved mover. In the former and more familiar scenario, the mover must support itself against an unmoved and external resting point as in the case of animals; in the latter scenario, by contrast, the mover itself will have to be located outside of the universe. Hence both scenarios confirm that the External Supporting Point Principle applies across the board: all motions, including the motion of the universe as a whole, require an external unmoved supporting point.

The cosmological application of the Supporting Point Principle leads to a paradoxical result. How can there be anything outside of the *universe*? And how can that something be strong enough to serve as a platform for the universe's movement?[15] Now, we know that for Aristotle this outcome is all but absurd, as he teaches in his *Metaphysics* the doctrine of a first and entirely unmoved mover outside of the universe. But Aristotle also believes in the methodological independence of physics from other branches of philosophy. So he is careful to avoid explicit reference to his metaphysical doctrine here, and therefore has left out his high-minded and contentious claim of a first and entirely unmoved mover outside of the universe. All we "officially" know at this point is that the application of the External Supporting Point Principle on a cosmological scale requires an external platform also for the motion of the universe. Still, as we will see, what drives him here in further pursuing the cosmological dimension of the External Supporting Point Principle is clearly that it provides him with an independent confirmation of his metaphysical doctrine.

So much for the context. Now, Aristotle proceeds to discuss rival *theories* concerning the origin of the motion of the universe. He starts with a theory that has been suggested by previous thinkers. What makes this theory interesting for him is that these thinkers seemed to have been aware of the problem that the External Supporting Point Principle poses for theories that postulate internal movers of the universe; what is more, they also seemed to have suggested a solution to the problem that avoids the principle's paradoxical consequence of the existence of a supporting platform outside of the universe. This potential rival to Aristotle's doctrine of a first unmoved mover of the universe is the so-called Pole-theory.

And on this point, at least, they are quite right who say that when the sphere is borne in a circle no part at all remains still; for it would be necessary either that the whole of it remain still, or that its continuity be torn asunder. But they are not right to ascribe power to the poles, which have no size and are termini and points. For besides the fact that nothing of this kind has any substance, it is impossible for a simple motion to be imparted by what is two; and they make the poles two. From considerations such as these one might doubt that there is something that bears the same relation to the whole of nature that the earth does to animals and the things moved by them.

(699ª17–27[16])

Aristotle praises the holders of the Pole-theory for having identified a problem that seems to be very close to what he himself had just described in terms of the External Supporting Point Principle: a rotating universe has *all* of its parts moving, which is to say that no part remains still; however, if mover and moved need to be separate from one another, as the proponents of the Pole-theory seem to agree, *none* of the parts of the universe can serve as the mover (on pain of either bringing the whole universe to a standstill or disrupting its physical cohesion by making one part of it rest and the other move). This seems to be the fundamental insight on which the Pole-theory rests. And Aristotle agrees. However, the theory suggests a way out of the predicament that he doesn't agree with: if the *poles* of its rotational axis are the movers of the universe, the movers will be unmoved (geometrical entities are not subject to motion) and neither physical parts, nor outside, of the universe. So, on the face of it, the Pole-theory fulfills all the demands of the External Supporting Point Principle, while it manages to avoid the counterintuitive consequence Aristotle drew from its application to the motion of the universe, namely that there must be an unmoved platform outside of the universe.

Aristotle's main move in demolishing the Pole-theory is simply to insist on the causal inertia of poles: poles are geometrical entities. As such they lack physical powers ("have no size" and "substance"): there is nothing they could possibly set into motion. In this regard, poles are no different from other non-physical entities such as lines, points, termini, and so on.[17] With this Aristotle takes himself to have refuted the Pole-theory. Accordingly, he concludes the section, on a somewhat triumphant note, by saying that objections of that kind (i.e. of the kind of the Pole-theory) can be raised against his thesis that there must be an external unmoved supporting point of the movement of the heaven. This clearly implies that theories that seek to circumvent the External Supporting Point Principle on the basis of the assumption of internal movers of the universe must fail.

However, Aristotle continues to discuss a yet *further* theory that proposes the already refuted hypothesis of an internal mover of the universe, and a particularly crude one at that. This is the Atlas-theory, which is moreover a theory of Aristotle's own artifice. He extrapolates it from mythically inspired artistic depictions of the Titan Atlas:

> Now those who, in a mythical manner, represent Atlas with his feet on the earth would seem to have told their fable with the intention to describe him as a kind of axis, whirling the heavens around the poles. Now this would be quite reasonable, since the earth remains still.
>
> (699ª27–31)

Aristotle does not discuss the Atlas-theory as a viable alternative. Quite obviously the theory falls prey to the same lethal objection against all theories of internal movers of the universe that Aristotle has just leveled against the Pole-theorists: since in a rotating universe no part of the universe stands still, the External Supporting Point Principle will necessitate an external resting point also for Atlas. He either will have to stand on a platform outside of the universe, which by hypothesis he doesn't, or there will be an unmoved platform for him to stand on inside of the universe, namely the earth. However, as the Pole-theorists already saw, that would tear asunder its physical continuity, as the External Supporting Point Principle requires the platform to be no part of the universe.[18] Why, then, does Aristotle bother to discuss the Atlas-theory? What he is interested in is not the theory as such, but the fact that discussion of the theory will bring out a common feature of all physical theories of internal movers of the universe. This is that all such theories, as we will see, by virtue of proposing physical entities as movers viz. platforms, lack the explanatory power to account for the *absolute necessity* with which Aristotle believes that the movements of the heavens occur: physical entities are *contingent*, i.e. they allow for the possibility of being otherwise than they actually are. That modal feature of physical movers makes them unfit to account for the order of the large-scale movements of the universe in Aristotle's eyes, which he believes cannot be otherwise. To bring out this principled lack in explanatory power of physical theories of the movements of the heavens – and to thereby hint at the virtue of his own theory of a non-physical first unmoved mover – is what drives him in discussing the at this point manifestly false Atlas-theory.

He starts by teasing out some of the consequences and explanatory duties of the Atlas-theory. If Atlas is to function as an axis extending between the earth and the outermost heaven, the External Supporting Point Principle requires not only that the earth remains unmoved, but also that the earth be no part of the universe. This is a first absurd consequence of the Atlas-theory. But Aristotle continues to discuss the Atlas-scenario. His next blow to the theory consists in pointing out just how much physical force Atlas's supporting platform – the earth – will have to resist. This will not only, as one might perhaps think, have to be the kinetic force with which Atlas whirls the heavens around himself, but also the static forces of the heavens and of Atlas himself:

> But if they give such an account they must concede that the earth is no part of the universe. Further, the forces of that which causes movement (i.e. Atlas) and of that which remains still (i.e. the earth) must be made equal. For there is a certain amount of force and power in virtue of which what remains remains, just as there is of force in virtue of which the mover imparts motion. And there is a necessary proportion, just as of opposite motions, so also of states of rest. And equal forces are unaffected by one another, but they are overcome by a superiority of force. So Atlas, or anything similar that imparts movement from within, must exert a pressure no greater than the fixedness with which the earth remains stable, or the earth will be moved away from the center, out of its proper place. For just as the pusher pushes, so the pushed is pushed—i.e., with similar force. But that which imparts the motion starts out by being at rest, so that its force must be greater than, rather than similar and equal to, its own stability, and, similarly, greater than the stability of that which is moved but does not impart movement. Then the earth's power of stability will have to be as great as that of the whole heavens and that which moves them.
>
> (699^{a}32–^{b}10)

If Atlas stands on the earth, the earth will have to resist the entire weight of both Atlas and the heavens, and, on top of that, also of the moving force with which Atlas revolves the heavens around himself. Given the immense disproportion between the sizes of the earth and the heavens, Aristotle insinuates that attributing such resisting force to the earth amounts to nothing less than a physical impossibility:

And if this is impossible, it is also impossible that the heavens be moved by anything of this kind within them.

(699^{b}10–11)

Aristotle here clearly uses the Atlas-theory to make a general point against *all* theories of internal movers of the heavens:[19] for the sheer disproportion of the sizes of the mover and the moved, *no* such theory will succeed in making plausible the claim that there is some resting platform within the universe strong enough to resist both the resting and the moving forces of everything else in it. But, notwithstanding the foregoing, discussion continues. Aristotle further dwells on the scenario to isolate an additional feature of the Atlas-theory and its likes, that he is particularly interested in. This is the principled limitation in the *modality* with which it, and any such theory, can account for the motions of the heavens. Now the discussion takes the form of a problem (*aporia*):

There is a problem about the motions of the parts of the universe that we might consider, as being closely connected to what we have just said. For if someone could overcome by power of motion the stability of the earth, it is clear that he would move it away from the center. And it is obvious that the force from which this power would derive is not infinite. For the earth is not infinite, so its weight is not either.

(699^{b}12–17)

Aristotle confronts the Atlas–theory with the following imagined scenario: if we suppose a further mover who moves the earth away from its center position, then this movement would require only a finite amount of force, since the size (and resting force) of the earth is finite as well. This means that the order of the movements of the universe could be dissolved by a finite force, which is to say that, in the scenario suggested by the Atlas theory, and all theories that postulate internal movers of the universe, it would be *possible* to dissolve the order of the universe. The physical character of their hypotheses imply that the resting force of the supporting point for the universe's movement will be of a physically determinate, and therefore finite, quantity. It is this *possibility* of a disruption of the order of the physical world, as it is implied by the physical character of theories like the Atlas-theory, that Aristotle takes issue with:

Now "impossible" has several senses: for when we say it is impossible to see a sound and for us to see the men in the moon, we use two different senses of the word. The former is invisible of necessity; the latter, though of such a nature as to be visible, will not actually be seen. Now we believe that the universe is imperishable and indestructible of necessity.

(699^{b}18–21)

Mere physical impossibility, according to which something that possibly could happen will actually never happen, is not enough for Aristotle when it comes to the physical order of the universe; that order must be impossible to dissolve in the same way in which it is impossible to see a sound, i.e. necessary in the sense of "impossible of being otherwise." This kind of necessity is something the Atlas-theory (and with it the whole class of theories it here represents) *cannot* deliver: these theories explain the order of the universe by way of a physical event. Physical events are finite and contingent. So, regardless whether such theories can account for the movement of the heavens (and Aristotle has given us ample grounds for believing that they cannot), they are incapable to account for the necessity with which Aristotle believes the physical order of the universe exists:

> But the result of this argument [of a physical mover of the universe] is that it is not so of necessity. For it is natural and possible for there to be a motion greater than that in virtue of which the earth remains stable, and in virtue of which fire and the body above are moved. If, then, there are overwhelming motions, these bodies will be parted asunder one from another.[20] And if there are not, but might possibly be (since there could not possibly be an infinite motion, because it is not even possible for a body to be infinite), it would be possible for the heavens to be dissolved. For what prevents this from happening, if it is not impossible? And it is not impossible unless the opposite is necessary. Let us, however, discuss this problem further another time.
>
> (699^{b}23–31)

With the concluding statement that the truth of the Atlas-theory is compatible with the possibility of the dissolution of the order of the universe, Aristotle has reached his goal. The discussion of a counterfactual and, for Aristotle at least, also manifestly false and even impossible theoretical scenario served him to isolate a modal feature that all theories of internal physical movers share, and to thus bring out their principled explanatory limitation. Now, Aristotle returns to the question raised at the beginning of the section:

> But must there be something unmoved and at rest outside what is moved, and which is no part of it, or not? And must this necessarily hold true of the universe as well? For it looks as if it would be paradoxical if the origin of motion were inside. That is why, to those who see it this way, Homer's words would appear to be well spoken:
> *But you could not draw from the heavens to the ground*
> *Zeus, loftiest of all, no, not even if you should struggle exceedingly, till you were weary.*
> *Lay hold of the rope, all you gods and goddesses.*
>
> For what is wholly unmoved cannot possibly be moved by anything. Herein lies the solution of the problem we mentioned above, namely whether it is possible or impossible to dissolve of the composition of the heaven, if it depends on an unmoved origin.
>
> (699^{b}32–700^{a}6[21])

By bringing out the limitations of the Atlas-theory, and with it of all other theories that postulate internal movers of the universe, Aristotle points to what he believes is an important virtue of his own theory (indicated by his triumphant quotation of Homer): only a non-physical ("wholly unmoved") mover outside of the universe, as claimed in Aristotle's *Metaphysics*, is able to account for the absolute indestructability of the order of the universe.

5 Conclusion: how would Aristotle have thought about thought experiments?

Aristotle employs thought experiments, on the minimal conception I have here adopted, in order to generate data in epistemically difficult terrain. As far as we can gather from the few examples I here presented, the contexts of usage vary: some serve to positively establish a point, while others (most of them) are used for critical purposes, i.e. they serve to demolish a given thesis. We may say, therefore, that Aristotle uses thought experiments for argumentative persuasion and in places where, due to the obscure nature of the subject matter or the counterintuitive nature of the thesis they are meant to support, insight cannot be readily communicated by appeal to observational facts.[22] And, as we have seen in the case of the Atlas theory, his target may even be a whole class of theories instead of a particular claim. This, however, is not to say that thought experiments are *indispensable* for Aristotle. I cannot think of an example whose point he could not have communicated in other, even if perhaps significantly less striking, ways. So much for the different contexts of usage of thought experiments in Aristotle.

How would he himself have categorized thought experiments? This is a difficult question. My best guess is that he would have wanted to distinguish between thought experiments as a method of generating data from imagined scenarios on the one hand and *forms of reasoning* on the other. The identity of forms of reasoning should be independent from whether their contents involve imagined scenarios or not. Also, the forms of reasoning acknowledged by Aristotle that bear most similarities to thought experiments, namely hypothetical syllogisms, *reductio ad absurdum*, and (Aristotelian) examples, do not seem to give us what we want: none of them are defined in terms of the quality of the scenarios or assumptions they involve. The features of hypothetical arguments (Aristotelian hypothetical syllogisms) certainly relate importantly, if not crucially, to the argumentative contexts in which he uses thought experiments (I cannot go into this here[23]), but to identify them with hypothetical syllogisms would implausibly broaden the conception of thought experimentation so as to cover perfectly abstract cases as well, such as an argument starting with "assume that not-p." And as Aristotle's thought experiments occur both in *reductio ad absurdum* and in constructive arguments, we can safely rule out *reductio* as well.[24] Finally, examples, at least in the Aristotle's distinctive understanding of them as a *form of inference* (not to be confused with examples as the items that are used in such inferences), do not fit the bill either. An Aristotelian example (*paradeigma*) is the inference from a particular as falling under some given universal to another and lesser known particular *as falling under that same universal* (*Anal. Pr.* II. 24[25]). That, however, seems to be at odds with the spirit of thought experiments as we understand – and as we found Aristotle to use – them here, since it seems vital for this kind of inference that the particular example it uses be a *familiar* case of falling under the relevant universal.[26]

It seems more promising to me to look at thought experiments from the perspective of their *conditions of usage*. We may want to consider thought experiments to be something much weaker than forms of reasoning, namely "strategies of reasoning" (although nothing hangs on that name): as I understand it, a strategy of reasoning is a domain-specific argumentative strategy a reasoner might employ in areas where the standard argumentative repertoire does not lead to satisfying results. An example is Aristotle's maxim "nature does nothing in vain," which serves as a specific heuristic device for the identification of explanatory features in some of the more difficult terrains of his natural philosophy.[27] Another example is Aristotle's adoption, in his astrophysical work *On the Heavens*, of the thesis that the heavenly bodies are animated and somehow partake in intentional action. The adoption of this thesis seems to amount to some kind of inference to the best explanation.[28] Aristotle's motivation in doing so seems clearly strategic: roughly, he argues that given the sparsity of empirical data in astrophysics, due to the remoteness of the heavenly bodies from sense perception, we can best answer otherwise insoluble astrophysical questions by postulating that stars are intentional agents.[29] In terms of methodological self-awareness, this is a remarkable statement. Aristotle here consciously compensates for the lack of empirical data in astrophysics with a (bold) hypothesis that will allow him to account for what for him otherwise would be completely intractable problems. It is tempting to generalize here and infer from such statements a general methodological maxim to the effect that our usage of more inventive ways of reasoning ought to positively co-vary with the empirical inaccessibility of relevant empirical data. This, it seems to me, would be a plausible candidate for a general attitude that Aristotle might have taken towards the employment of more inventive argumentative strategies, including the consideration of hypothetical scenarios in thought experiments. After all, thought experiments, the typical ones at least, serve to make us experience something in thought that we otherwise could not experience.

Notes

1. Which is why the term "scenario" seems more apt that "event": what thought experiments show may go beyond events.
2. Kant's classical formulation of the nature of empirical experimentation describes a procedure that seems not only entirely absent in Aristotle but also alien to the spirit of his natural philosophy: "[Reason] compels nature to answer its questions rather than letting nature guide its movements by keeping reason, as it were, in leading strings" (Kant 1998, B xiii).
3. Cf. *Anal. Pr.* I 30. His treatise on zoological facts *Historia Animalium* is meant to provide such a collection, see HA 1. 6, 491a7 ff.
4. This conception of *empeiria* should be distinguished from his epistemological conception of *empeiria* as a psychological state (*Metaphysics* 1. 1., *Anal. Post.* 2.19).
5. This is something the famous Greek physician Galen of Pergamon (Second-century CE) will later take him to task for. He says that Aristotle, while engaging in anatomical speculation, lacked the patience to concern himself with the actual work of anatomical inquiry. (*De placitis* I 10, 7–8, 96–99, De Lacy). See also Lloyd (1996), who argues that Aristotle had only very limited interest in experimentation.
6. The question why this is so may have to do with the low social status of manual labor in Ancient Greek societies, see, e.g., (Störig 1965, 56f).
7. See, for instance, Hobbes (1994, ch. 1).
8. Ernst Mach goes so far as to claim that "the physical investigations of Aristotle for the most part are thought experiments" (1905, 187).
9. In his *Metaphysics* where he says that the inquiry into what is farthest removed from sense perception is the most difficult (*Meta.* 1.2, 982^{a}23–25).
10. In the text, the imagined scenario above occurs in the immediate sequel of the following statement: "Excess in a bodily state is cured by a situation or season of opposite character, but the constitution is best maintained by an environment akin to it. There is a difference between the material of which any animal is constituted and the states and dispositions of that material" (*De Juv.* 477^{b}16–18).

11 A much fuller – though still far from complete – collection of thought experiments in Aristotle can be found in Mulligan (2008).
12 In Aristotle's own cosmology, this is an impossible scenario.
13 Aristotle continues with a series of similar scenarios: suppose that all existent things were tunes, the quarter tone would be "the one," in spoken sounds "the one" would be the vowel, in plane geometrical figures the triangle, concluding that the same holds for the other genera of being (categories) as well (up to 1054^{a}19).
14 Translations from *De Motu Animalium* are from Nussbaum (1985), modified according to Primavesi (2017).
15 There are, to be sure, more questions.
16 In 699^{a}26–27 I read ἀπορήσειεν instead of Nussbaum's διαπορήσειεν, both of which have good support in the manuscript tradition.
17 Note that the Pole-theory can in some ways be seen as a precursor of Aristotle's own theory of unmoved movers. Aristotle certainly seems indebted to the basic idea of the theory that there are *unmoved movers* of the universe, i.e. entities in which, due to their immaterial nature, the two functions of providing a supporting platform and imparting motion coincide, even if he disagrees with the Pole-theory's contention that these unmoved movers are *mathematical* entities. Aristotle thinks of mathematical entities as largely fictional, while he conceives of his own unmoved movers as real substances. The author of the Pole-theory has been believed to be Speusippus, who allegedly (and unlike Aristotle) conceived of points as substances. For a recent brief summary of the discussion, see Menn (2012, 441, 457 n. 28), who also mentions Eudoxus as another possible candidate. Aristotle's other argument against the pole theory, at first blush at least, seems less convincing. It seems intended as a refutation of the specific thesis that the *poles* of the axis of the universe are the causes (movers) of its rotation. He argues that the poles of the axis are two in number, yet since rotational motion is a simple motion, the cause of that motion ought to be simple as well. Aristotle here operates on assumptions about the structural similarity of cause and effect that I cannot go into here. In any case, it seems the main weight of his rejoinder to the Pole-theory lies on the first argument, which can easily be applied to other abstract entities as well, as e.g. the axis of the universe (cf. Plato *Timaeus*, 40b8f.).
18 One may object here that Aristotle's own cosmology locates the resting earth at the center of the rotating universe. That, however, does not conflict with the External Supporting Point Principle, as Aristotle doesn't make the earth the mover/platform of the universe's motion. I thank Yue Lu for bringing this point to my attention.
19 See the above "by *anything* of this kind within them" in ^{b}11 (*hypo tinos toioutou tôn entos*).
20 Reading with ms. (Parisinus Graecus 1853) E διαλυθήσεται ταῦτα ἀπ' ἀλλήλων in 699^{b}26 (instead of ὑπ' ἀλλήλων).
21 Aristotle's formulation in 700^{a}6 that the order to the heavens "depends (êrtêtai) on an unmoved origin" is a direct verbal echo of his statement about the first unmoved mover in his *Metaphysics* ("on such origin the heaven and nature depend (êrtêtai)," 12. 7,1072^{b}14).
22 One may find this characterization to lack breadth, as it seems to neglect the heuristic function of thought experiments when we use them to actually find out what happens if something is the case. That, it seems to me, would be a fair objection. The only grounds I have for not including thought experiments as a tool in the service of actual and open-ended intellectual experimentation in Aristotle is the fact that his writings do not seem to wrestle with their subject matter so as to genuinely lead him to the discovery of new facts. That, however, should not be understood as implying that Aristotle did not actually use thought experiments in that way. He might very well have done that. We just lack evidence for this.
23 For hypothetical syllogisms in Aristotle see Crivell (2011).
24 For a discussion of the distinction between indirect argumentation and thought experiments, see Kukkonen (2002).
25 Aristotle thinks of this kind of inference by example as a sort of inductive inference (see *Anal. Post.* I 1, 71^{a}9–10, *Anal. Pr.* II. 24, 69^{a}16–19). See Ierodiakonou (2005).
26 There is also a perhaps lesser-known method Aristotle uses in establishing his syllogistic theory that might be judged to be a possible candidate. This is what he calls the "setting-out" (*ecthesis*) of a term. Basically, the method consists in testing a general rule by going through an imagined

particular case so as to either confirm or disconfirm it (*Anal. Pr.* 28ª23–26). Apart from presupposing a general rule (which does not seem to be the case in thought experiments), *ecthesis* seems too abstract.

27 There is discussion as to whether the principle is part of the actual explanation of phenomena or merely a heuristic device for the identification of explanations (cf. Lennox 1997).

28 See next footnote.

29 *Cael.* 287ᵇ28ff., 291ᵇ24ff., especially 292ª14: "On these questions it is well that we should seek to increase our understanding, though we have but little to go upon, and are placed at so great a distance from the facts in question. Nevertheless if we base our consideration on things such as the following, we shall not find this difficulty by any means insoluble. We think of the stars as mere bodies, and as units with an order indeed but entirely inanimate; but we should rather conceive them as enjoying life and action. On this view the facts cease to appear surprising" (transl. Stocks 1922, slightly modified). Cf. PA 1.5, 644ᵇ22ff, see Burnyeat (2004, 15f.), and Leunissen (2010, 152–174).

References

Burnyeat, M. (2004) "Introduction: Aristotle on the foundations of sublunary physics," in *Aristotle's On Generation and Corruption*, edited by F. de Haas and J. Maansfeld, Oxford: Oxford University Press.

Crivell, P. (2011) "Aristotle on syllogisms from a hypothesis," in *Arguments from Hypothesis in Ancient Philosophy*, edited by E. Longo and D. Del Forno, Naples: Bibliopolis.

Galen (1978) *De Placitis Hippocratis et Platonis*, edited, translated and with commentary by P. De Lacy. Berlin: Akademie Verlag.

Hobbes, T. (1994 [1651]) *Leviathan or The Matter, Forme and Power of a Common Wealth Ecclesiasticall and Civil*, Indianapolis: Hackett.

Ierodiakonou, K. (2005) "Ancient thought experiments: A first approach," *Ancient Philosophy* 25: 125–140.

Kant, I. (1998 [1781]) *Critique of Pure Reason*. Cambridge: Cambridge University Press.

Kukkonen, T. (2002) "Alternatives to alternatives: Approaches to Aristotle's arguments per impossibile," *Vivarium* 40: 137–173.

Lennox, J. (1997) "Nature does nothing in vain," in *Beiträge zur antiken Philosophie: Festschrift für Wolfgang Kullmann*, edited by H.-C. Günther and A. Rengakos, Stuttgart: Franz Steiner.

Leunissen, M. (2010) *Explanation and Teleology in Aristotle's Science of Nature*, Cambridge: Cambridge University Press.

Lloyd, G. E. R. (1996) *Aristotelian Explorations*, Cambridge: Cambridge University Press.

Mach, E. (1905) *Erkenntnis und Irrtum*, translated as *Knowledge and Error: Sketches on the Psychology of Enquiry*, by Thomas J. McCormack. Dordrecht: D. Reidel Publishing.

Menn, S. (2012) "Aristotle's theology," in *The Oxford Handbook of Aristotle*, edited by C. Shields, Oxford: Oxford University Press.

Mulligan, S. D. (2008) *If Fishes Were Made of Iron*, Ph.D. dissertation, Library and Archives Canada, Bibliothèque et Archives Canada.

Nussbaum, M. C. (1985) *Aristotle's De Motu Animalium*, Princeton: Princeton University Press.

Primavesi, O. (2017) *Aristoteles, De Motu Animalium: Ein Neues Bild der Überlieferung und ein Neuer Text*, Berlin: De Gruyter.

Stocks, J. L. (1922) *The Works of Aristotle Translated into English*, Oxford: Clarendon Press.

Störig, H. J. (1965) *Kleine Weltgeschichte der Wissenschaft*, Stuttgart: Kohlhammer.

4
EXPERIMENTAL THOUGHTS ON THOUGHT EXPERIMENTS IN MEDIEVAL ISLAM

Jon McGinnis

1 Introduction

There is no (medieval) Arabic term or phrase for "thought experiment." Be that as it may, medieval philosophers and scientists working in Arabic both concretely employed thought experiments in their philosophies and discussed their merits and demerits abstractly. Indeed, it would seem that thought experiments truly captured the imagination of medieval thinkers in the Muslim world, who left behind a significant body of examples and analyses of such experiments. What follows makes no pretense to being a complete history of that body of work. Instead, this study focuses primarily, although by no means exclusively, on thought experiments as they are used and discussed in Ibn Sīnā (980–1037), the Avicenna of Latin fame. Along the way, however, this study also touches on other notable figures and their uses and thoughts about thought experiments. These figures include the famed medieval Arabic optician Ibn al-Haytham (965–1040, Lt. Alhazen) and the renowned Muslim theologian Abū Ḥamid al-Ghazālī (1058–1111).

As a first pass, one can divide thought experiments in the medieval Arabic world into two classes: those that are in principle impossible to carry out and those that at least appear to be possible to carry out even if in practice they cannot. Examples from contemporary philosophy of the first class include zombie worlds and persons splitting and recombining, etc. In the medieval period just as now such thought experiments functioned primarily as intuition pumps intended to give someone a sense of what is at least possible. I refer to this class of thought experiments as "fictional thought experiments." Contemporary examples of the second class of thought experiments abound in the works of Einstein, as, for instance, riding a light beam or his use of moving trains and lightning flashes in relation to simultaneity or one's expected experience in a free-falling elevator to explain gravity. Since within the medieval period thought experiments of this sort frequently describe idealized accounts of otherwise realizable situations, I refer to this class as "idealized thought experiments." The class of idealized thought experiments further divides into those that appeal to some form of mechanical apparatus, to which the name "mechanical thought experiments" is appropriate, and those that do not.

Continuing this first pass, medieval thinkers in the Muslim world also had different aims for thought experiments. In some cases, the aim was simply to help one envision or vividly grasp some abstract conclusion of a demonstration. As such, the thought experiments are not integral to the actual proof(s) for the desired conclusion. In other cases, a thought experiment is integral to the proof in that it either constitutes the whole of the argument or is intended to establish a necessary premise for the argument. Additionally, in those cases where the thought experiment intends to prove a premise, it might show that some state of affairs is at least possible or more significantly that some scenario is factive.

Towards developing these sketchy remarks, I begin with a brief discussion about the language and psychology of imagination, particularly as it occurs in the works of Avicenna. That Avicenna in fact embedded thought experiments within an overall psychology seems to set him apart from the thinkers that preceded him. Following the comments on psychology, the remainder of the study is a taxonomy of various sorts of thought experiments used among thinkers in the medieval Islamic world: first, instances of fictional ones and second idealized ones. When possible, I also discuss the philosophical attitudes and responses to the various thought experiments. What I hope emerges is a sketch of the place of thought experiments among medieval Arabic-speaking philosophers and scientists that others may use to fill in the whole picture.

2 The language and psychology of thought experiments in the medieval Muslim world[1]

While there is little doubt that ancient Greek philosophers crafted and employed what we now call "thought experiments" (see Ierodiakonou and Becker, this volume), Katerina Ierodiakonou has also noted, "there is no evidence that [the ancients] classified examples based on imaginary or invented assumptions in a special category" (see Ierodiakonou, this volume, p. 34). By the time of Avicenna, however, the premises driving thought experiments were seen to form a special category or at the very least to present a special problem. To appreciate the problem one must begin with the language that Aristotle and his commentators used for thought experiments, for it is that terminology that medieval Arabic-speaking philosophers primarily inherited and used when constructing or discussing thought experiments.

Perhaps most frequently Aristotle introduces thought experiments with a conditional statement (See Kukkonen 2002 and 2014, esp. §I; and Ierodiakonou 2005, esp. §IV). The conditional's antecedent then functions as an initial supposition that governs the thought experiment. In some places—like *Physics*, 7.1, 242a9–10, where Aristotle argues against the possibility of self-motion—he explicitly introduces a thought experiment as a hypothesis or supposition (*hupekeito*). In medieval Arabic, or at least in Avicenna's philosophical vocabulary, the notion of a hypothesis or supposition, particularly as used in thought experiments, is usually rendered by *farḍ*.

Additionally, Aristotle and his commentators sometimes refer to thought experiments using terms derived from *noein*, "to think." One example in Aristotle is at *Physics*, 3.8, 208a14–16, where he criticizes certain thought experiments involving infinity. Aristotle's late Neoplatonic commentator, John Philoponus (490–570), in his commentary on the

Physics (Philoponus, *In Physicorum*, 574.14, 575.8, 575.10, 575.18) has a more approving appraisal of experiments "in thought" (*kat' epinoian*) when defending the idea of an immaterial extension. The Greek term *noein* and its cognates were frequently rendered into Arabic with some form of *'aql*, "to intellect." The objects of intellect (*ma'qūlāt*) indicate the universal essences of things abstracted from their material conditions. As such the objects of intellect hardly seem suitable in cases where particulars are being imagined or where counterfactual premises are needed.

What is needed in these cases are more fantastical imaginations, in Greek *phantasia*. The transliteration *fanṭāsīyā* or the native term *khayāl* was frequently used in Arabic to capture the notion of *phantasia*. Among medieval Arabic Peripatetics both *fanṭāsīyā* and *khayāl* were used to indicate either a particular psychological faculty, namely, imagination, or the product of some internal psychological faculty. The recognized difficulty with using mere imaginations or fantasies in thoughts experiments is that there seems to be no check on the imaginative faculty to ensure that its objects tell us something informative about the world. It is just such a concern that prompted the late Hellenistic Neoplatonist, Simplicius (c. 490–c. 560), to complain about putting one's faith in such fantasies (Simplicius, *In De caelo*, 418.30).

One is now in a position to see the special problem that Avicenna seems to recognize about the premises used in thought experiments. If these premises are products of the faculty of intellect, then, as Taneli Kukkonen acutely observes, they "only idealize material circumstances in the framework of a well-defined set of assumed natural laws and invariance" (Kukkonen 2014, 446). In other words, premises produced by the intellect do not lend themselves to the counterfactual scenarios that frequently are at the core of thought experiments. Alternatively, if the premises of thought experiments are nothing more than unbridled compositions of the imagination, then there is no assurance that their content connects up with anything in the world so as to give one a deeper insight into the world. For Avicenna the question at stake is a psychological one: what faculty of the soul produces the premises employed in (legitimate) thought experiments as opposed to wild ravings? Intellect seems too restricted and imagination seems too unrestrained.

Avicenna's solution to this dilemma was to introduce a new internal sensory faculty, *wahm*, which for lack of any exact English translation is usually termed the estimative faculty. (For discussions of Avicenna's theory of *wahm* see Black 1993; Hasse 2000, esp. II.2; Hall 2006; Kukkonen 2014, esp. §3.) Avicenna identifies the estimative faculty among the five internal perceptive faculties, which are common to humans and (higher) non-human animals alike (Avicenna, *De anima*, 4.3). These faculties include common sense, memory, the retentive and compositive imaginations, and finally the estimative faculty. According to Avicenna, the estimative faculty perceives non-sensible features or intentions (sing. *ma'ná*) within sensible particular things. The classic example is the sheep's recognition of the particular ferocity in a given wolf, for while ferocity is not itself something sensible it is manifested in the sensible features of the wolf, like its sharp fangs and claws and the carnivorous odor that it exudes. In non-human animals the estimative faculty is the highest functioning psychological power, less than intellect but also more than mere imagination. It allows these animals to interact with the world around them in a fairly accurate way. Even in humans, according to Avicenna, it is the estimative faculty that allows us to navigate many of our day-to-day interactions.

Additionally, Avicenna appeals to the estimative faculty to explain the objects and premises of the mathematical sciences. The objects of mathematics, Avicenna tells us, are certain formal features of material objects but they can be considered in the estimative faculty as abstracted from their material conditions, like, for example, squareness (Avicenna, *Madkhal*, 1.2, 12–13). In this respect, the estimative faculty is what allows the mathematician to consider perfect geometrical figures or numbers in the abstract even though these are never instantiated physically; it is the power that allows the physicists to imagine perfectly frictionless planes or a sphere touching a two-dimensional surface at a single point, even though again in the nitty-gritty world around us none of these exists. These mathematical abstracta, Avicenna says, exist by supposition (*bi-l-farḍ*), usually a supposition imagined by the estimative faculty. That is to say, while mathematical abstracta exist in a mental act of conceptualization (*taṣawwur*), they do not exist, at least not in the exact way that the mathematician investigates them, in the concrete material particulars that populate the world. It is the estimative faculty, then, that provides mathematicians and (theoretical) physicists with an idealized picture of the world. In this respect, the estimative faculty offers up a rough and ready guide to real physical possibilities. Still, one must be careful to distinguish between what exists as such in the estimative faculty and what actually exist as separate in the world. For Avicenna, if one is to move from the possibilities imagined in the estimative faculty to what actually exists, one must also have a demonstration or provide some actual instance in the world of what the estimative faculty posits.

To sum up, Avicenna developed the notion of an estimative faculty in order to explain a number of disparate, albeit related, phenomena. Among these phenomena are the semi-rational thoughts and cognitive processes of those higher animals that lack an intellect. Another was to show how idealizations used in mathematics, which do not actually exist separately in the world, can be informative about the world. Finally, the estimative faculty provides Avicenna with a psychological underpinning for thought experiments, which does justice to their frequently counterfactual nature while also explaining how they can have import about the world as it actually is.

3 Fictional thought experiments in the medieval Islamic world

In this section I consider two sorts of fictional thought experiments with very different aims. In one case, the thought experiment functions as a subsidiary aid to help one better grasp the conclusion of some argument that is independent of the thought experiment. In the other case, the thought experiment is integral to the overall argument. Again fictional thought experiments proceed from an initial supposition that is physically impossible in principle to carry out, although presumably an all-powerful agent, like God, could realize the scenario. Arguably, the best known fictional thought experiment coming from the medieval Islamic world is Avicenna's famous "flying man" (see Marmura 1986; Druart 1988; Hasse 2000, esp. II.1). Here is that thought experiment in Avicenna's own words:

> One should imagine through an act of the estimative faculty (*yatawahhama*) as if one of us were created complete and perfect all at once but his sight is veiled from directly observing the things of the external world. He is created as though floating

in air or in a void but without the air supporting him such that he would feel it, and the limbs of his body are stretched out and away from one another, so they do not come into contact or touch. Then he considers whether he can assert the existence of his self. He has no doubts about asserting his self as something that exists without also [having to] assert the existence of any of his exterior or interior parts, his heart, his brain, or anything external.

(Avicenna, *De anima*, 1.1, 16)

Avicenna presents this thought experiment no fewer than five times throughout his oeuvre.[2] The purpose of the thought experiment is to get one to think of one's self (*dhāt*) as perhaps distinct from one's body or sensible apprehensions. For it certainly seems possible, even if only by an act of God, that an individual could come into existence all at once devoid of any sensory input, sensations or sensible memories. Yet even in this deprived state the individual, one imagines, would be aware or conscious of his or her self (*shuʿūr bi-dhāt*), or so Avicenna imagines. (For a detailed study of self-awareness (or consciousness) in the thought of Avicenna see Jari Kaukua 2015.)

What is important to note is that Avicenna does not claim here that this thought experiment demonstrates that the human soul or self is immaterial. What is needed truly to establish that conclusion is a proper demonstration, which Avicenna provides in addition to the thought experiment (see Avicenna, *De anima*, 5.2). Instead, the thought experiment, Avicenna tells us, is only a way of arousing (*tanbīh*) in us some consideration of what an immaterial existence might be like (Avicenna, *De anima*, 1.1, 15).

Interestingly, Avicenna also uses a close etymological cousin of *tanbīh*, namely, *tanabbuh*, again "arousing," in association with the aim of induction (*istiqrāʾ*) (Avicenna, *Burhān*, 3.5, 158). Induction, Avicenna informs us, cannot establish some universally true claim, but at best can only show that something is probable (Avicenna, *Burhān*, 1.9, 48). While the link is admittedly tenuous it does suggest that Avicenna may have viewed thought experiments as at least on par with induction in scientific practice.

Avicenna, however, does not use fictional thought experiments solely as incitements, which play no substantive role in demonstrations. In some cases, they form an integral part of a demonstration as in indirect proofs. In fact, Avicenna relies on thought experiments and the use of the estimative faculty in just this way scores of times throughout his *Physics*. Examples include *Physics*, 2.1 when discussing self-motion (discussed in depth in Kukkonen 2014); numerously throughout *Physics*, 2.7–9 and 4.11, when discussing place, void, and space (McGinnis 2007a; Lammer 2016); thought experiments also frequently appear in his criticism of the infinitely small, i.e., atomism at *Physics*, 3.4–5 (Lettinck 1999; McGinnis 2015); and the infinitely large at *Physics*, 3.7–9 (McGinnis 2010). These are just to mention some of the more prominent appearances of thought experiments within the works of Avicenna. Let me consider briefly some of Avicenna's comments concerning the void and how one thought experiment features prominently in his refutation of it.

Avicenna introduces the notion of a void (*khalāʾ*), by claiming that its proponents appealed to a certain thought experiment to motivate their position (Avicenna, *Physics*, 2.6 [5]). In the thought experiment, the proponents of the void consider some contained body, whether the water in a jug or what lies between the moon's orbit around the earth. Here the contained body exists within certain limits of the containing body. They, then, through an act of the estimative faculty, Avicenna continues, imagine that the contained body is eliminated; however, the elimination of the contained body does not eliminate the interval or dimension (*buʿd*) between the limits of the containing body. What is eliminated and what is not eliminated, however, are distinct things. Thus, the thought experiment concludes, the interval or dimension is distinct from the body existing in it, albeit, that interval is something existing together with the body when the body exists in it.

Avicenna's criticism of this argument is precisely to appeal to the limits of the estimative faculty's abilities (Avicenna, *Physics*, 2.9 [11]). To begin, Avicenna happily endorses the general method of analysis (*taḥlīl*) that the thought experiment employs: one uses the estimative faculty to isolate some formal feature within a body for closer scrutiny. In fact, Avicenna maintains that it is just this method that allows one conceptually to distinguish the form of a body from its matter. The problem in the present case comes from thinking that what is separable in thought must also be separable in reality. He clarifies by appealing to the form-matter case: Were one able to remove all forms from some matter, the matter, Avicenna observes, would simply cease to exist, for the form is the principle of actualization. As for the case of the imagined void interval, he writes:

> Let us grant that this interval is assumed in the estimative faculty, when a certain body or bodies are eliminated. How does one know that this act of the estimative faculty is not false [when applied to something existing separate from the estimative faculty], such that what follows upon it is absurd, and whether this assumption is, in fact, even possible, such that what follows upon it is necessary?
> (Avicenna, *Physics*, 2.9 [11])

Avicenna's complaint is twofold. First, if the thought experiment is to show the extramental existence of a void interval, one must show that a separate void interval can exist separate from an act of the estimative faculty. In other words, one must demonstrate that the separate existence of a void does not lead to some absurdity, as in the form-matter case, where the actual elimination of form would entail the actualization of matter without its having any principle of actualization, i.e., any form. Second, even assuming that one can show that the separate existence of a void is *possible*, the thought experiment has not shown that a void's existence is *necessary*. A hallmark of scientific knowledge, however, which goes back at least as far as Plato and Aristotle (cf. Plato, *Theaetetus*, 152C[3] and Aristotle, *Posterior Analytics*, A.2, 71b9–12), is that scientific knowledge (Gk., *epistēmē*, Ar. *ʿilm*) is necessary and explanatory of what is. Avicenna accepts these criteria for knowledge. Thus he complains that the thought experiment alone has failed to meet one of the conditions for knowledge; what is additionally needed to show that a void's existence is necessary is a demonstration.

None of this is to say that a thought experiment for Avicenna cannot be an integral part of a demonstration. His own refutation of the void provides one with just such an example. At *Physics*, 2.8, Avicenna aims to show that the existence of a void would make motion impossible. He identifies three general sorts of motion: natural circular motion (such as that of the heavens), natural rectilinear motion (such as that of the elements, earth, water, air and fire) and finally forced motion (such as a projectile like an arrow or a thrown ball). Thought experiments in the form of indirect proofs for the impossibility of a void appear in Avicenna's treatment of all three classes of motion. I shall consider just one: his refutation of the possibility of forced motion in a void (Avicenna, *Physics*, 2.8 [18]).

The argument begins by imagining along with the proponents of the void that an infinite void exists in which objects move. Now in the case of forced motion, for example, my shooting an arrow, I, by means of the bow, impart a certain motive power to the arrow. Given this scenario, either the arrow will continue in its motion unabated infinitely or it will come to a stop. The arrow cannot continue on infinitely, Avicenna believes, for a finite agent, and I am finite, can only ever produce a finite effect, but should the arrow continue moving without ever stopping, I would have produced an infinite effect. If the arrow ceases to move, then the privation or absence (*'adam*) of motion must belong to the arrow either essentially or owing to some external cause. If not moving, that is, the absence of motion, belonged to the arrow essentially, then its motion would be impossible from the start, for its essence would preclude its moving. As for an external thing bringing the arrow to rest, we have been asked to imagine a void, and so something literally devoid of any causes that might arrest the arrow's motion. Of course, Avicenna develops each of these moments in the argument in greater detail, but almost every moment has one imagining how the projectile would move or come to rest in a void.

In this case and the others where thoughts experiments are integral to the demonstration Avicenna is not restricted to limiting his conclusion to a mere possibility existing in the estimative faculty. That is because these arguments are intended precisely to show that the separate existence of the subject of the thought experiment is impossible. Thus, if the initial supposition plus a set of auxiliary premises, all of which are taken to be true or even necessary, lead to an absurdity or impossibility, the initial supposition must be jettisoned. None of this is new to Avicenna. Still, it does suggest that Avicenna was principled with respect to his use of fictional thought experiments: either they must be accompanied by an independent demonstration or they are conceded because one's opponent actually accepts them as true depictions of reality.

4 Idealized thought experiments in the medieval Islamic world

What distinguishes idealized thoughts experiments from fictional thought experiments is that the former at least give the appearance that they are physically possible and so could actually be realized without necessarily appealing to the action of an all-powerful agent. I consider two broad classes of idealized thought experiments used in the medieval Islamic world: mechanical thought experiments and non-mechanical ones. Mechanical thought experiments appeal to some ingenuous machine or apparatus and at the very least give the impression that one could actually carry out the experiment or build the apparatus. Before turning to these mechanical thought experiments, let me begin with a classic example of a non-mechanical idealized thought experiment.

In his *Incoherence of the Philosophers* (2000), al-Ghazālī (1058–1111) challenges the philosophers' insistence that a principle of sufficient reason must govern all actions. He denies that the principle necessarily applies when it comes to the choices of volitional agents. More specifically al-Ghazālī wants to show that even if presented with two completely indiscernible options, God and even humans can, unlike Buridan's ass, choose one over the other. His argument for this conclusion relies solely on the following idealized thought experiment:

Let us suppose (*nafriḍu*) two indiscernible dates immediately before someone who looks on them hungrily, but is incapable of taking both. He will take one of them necessarily through an attribute whose character is to specify one thing from its like. Everything you mentioned concerning specifications of superiority, proximity or facility of access, we determine, by supposition (*'alá farḍ*), to be absent, but the possibility of taking remains. You have two options: either (1) to say that the indiscernibility in relation to his desires is wholly inconceivable, which is fatuous given that the supposition [of the date's indiscernibility] is possible, or (2) to say that when the indiscernibility is supposed, the hungrily longing man would always remain undecided, staring at the two [dates], but not taking either of them simply by willing, but choosing to stand aloof from the desire, which is also absurd, whose falsity is known necessarily.

(al-Ghazālī, *Incoherence*, Disc. 1 [46])

The argument is straightforward. We are asked to imagine an idealized situation where every conceivable factor for preferring one desired option over another has been eliminated. Al-Ghazālī takes it as patently possible that the imagined scenario could exist in the world and not merely in the estimative faculty. If the situation is possible, then it is certainly possible that the hungry man will choose one piece of fruit over another without any reason weighing in for his preference for that particular piece. Indeed, al-Ghazālī thinks that choosing in this situation is not merely possible but necessary. He thus concludes that even in humans there must be some psychological faculty that chooses between indiscernible things, called "will" or "volition" (*irāda*).

I know of no philosopher working within an Avicennan psychological framework who addresses this thought experiment. Presumably, if confronted with it, Avicenna would have required some proof that the imagined scenario could exist in the world and not merely in the estimative faculty.

Perhaps a more interesting response comes from the Andalusian Peripatetic, Ibn Rushd (1126–98), that is, Averroes. Although Averroes' comments say little about the nature of idealized thought experiments as a class of arguments, they are informative about the present example (Averroes, *The Incoherence of the Incoherence*, Disc. 1, [39–41]). Averroes complains that al-Ghazālī's thought experiment does not set out one unique set of preferences, for example, to prefer to eat $date_1$ or $date_2$. Instead, observes Averroes, there are two distinct sets of preferences: (1) to eat or not to eat and (2) to eat $date_1$ or $date_2$. Of course with respect to set (1), the hungry man has every reason to prefer to eat over not eating, and so indeed wills to eat on the basis of that reason. That action is achieved regardless of whether he eats $date_1$ or $date_2$. As for case (2), if the man were subsequently asked why he preferred, for example, $date_1$ over $date_2$, he would say that he did *not* prefer the one date over the other; he simply preferred to eat rather than not to eat. Thus, while there is no reason for preferring one date over another, neither is there any preference for one date over another that needs a reason. Again, however, there seems little to glean from Averroes' discussion here about the nature of thought experiments or idealization (although see Knuuttila and Kukkonen 2011, esp. §2).

Turning now to the mechanical variety of idealized thought experiments, for obvious reasons they were almost exclusively applied to issues and problems in the natural sciences. That is because this class involves describing a machine or apparatus that can, at least in principle, be constructed and as such must be constrained by the laws of physics and principles of mechanics. One such physical issue, in which there was a proliferation of mechanical thought experiments, was the problem of the *quies media*, that is, medial rest.

The issue at stake is whether a body that undergoes contrary changes must come to some rest between one change and then the contrary change. For example, must a ball thrown upward come to a slight rest, be it ever so short, before it moves downward or can the ball change from moving upward to moving downward instantaneously? Aristotle in his *Physics*, 8.8, had argued for a medial rest. His general argument assumed something like the following form. Let a body move from A to C. At every moment in its motion from A to C, the body is in a process of arriving at C, whereas at every moment in its motion from C back to A the body is in a process of arriving at A. A is not C, and so during the body's motion back to A, it is *not* in a process of arriving at C. Now to-be-in-a-process-of-arriving-at-C and *not*-to-be-in-a-process-of-arriving-at-C are contradictory predicates, and nothing can simultaneously have contradictory predicates. Hence, reasons Aristotle, there must be some instant at which the body arrives at C and some other instant at which it departs C. Finally, since time is continuous and between any two points (or in this case instants, i.e., temporal points) on a continuum there is some magnitude, there must be some temporal magnitude, and so some time, between the instant of the body arriving at C and of its departing from C when it is at rest at C.

Aristotle's word on this subject was far from the last. Indeed, the issue was still very much alive in Avicenna's time (see Rashed 1999, esp. §2, Morrison 2005, 58–9 and 91–2, and Langermann 2008). In fact, the issue had generated so much unrest that Avicenna dedicated an entire chapter of his *Physics*, 4.8, to the problem. Avicenna himself even confesses that he did not find the arguments on either side particularly impressive (Avicenna, *Physics*, 4.8 [9]). The issue is particularly pressing for Avicenna since he provided an analysis of motion that allowed for motion at an instant in such a way to avoid Aristotle's conclusion (see Hasnawi 2001; McGinnis 2006; Ahmed 2016). As for the arguments' pros and cons, Avicenna notes that the main premise in arguments for there being a rest between contrary motions involves identifying some purported impossibility in the situation, like the contradiction that Aristotle mentioned in the above case. He further notes that the counter-arguments simply need to show that the instantaneous change from one type of motion to its contrary is not impossible. Those who opposed Aristotle's conclusion appealed to this last point, and an easy enough way to show that possibility is simply to describe a machine that produces just such a motion.

Avicenna himself mentions one such contraption proposed by the detractors of a medial rest (Avicenna, *Physics*, 4.8 [4]). We are to imagine a sphere mounted upon a wheel and the wheel makes a continuous rotation. Next imagine a two-dimensional plane above the apparatus that is situated such that, when the sphere is at its apex during the wheel's rotation, the sphere encounters that plane at some single point, C. Since the wheel that is carrying the sphere is moving continuously, the sphere will touch C for only an instant. Thus, during the sphere's ascent it will have been in a process of arriving at C, while during its descent it will be in process of departing from, i.e., not arriving at, C, just as Aristotle describes, and yet contrary to Aristotle, the sphere will be at C for only an instant. While the example takes advantage of circular motion, it does suggest that a body can *actually* be at a point for an instant and at that instant change from one sort of motion to its contrary.

As already noted, Avicenna was not impressed with any of the available arguments concerning this issue, pro or con.[4] His objection to the present one involves a digression about the nature of mechanical thought experiments more generally (Avicenna, *Physics*, 4.8 [12]). His concerns are much like those registered about fictional thought experiments. The difference is that, while in the case of fictional thought experiments one must provide a demonstration that what the thought experiment describes can exist separate from the estimative faculty, in a mechanical thought experiments one must first ask if the proposed machine can in fact actually work. Can it be constructed in principle? If it cannot, then the thought experiment must be treated as if it is a fictional one.

Today we might think that the proposed thought experiment immediately fails the can-it-work test since it appeals to perfect spheres and planes, i.e., mathematically idealized ones, rather than to physical ones. In fact, Avicenna mentioned that some complained about this thought experiment in just this way. Avicenna dismisses the objection as inadequate, since in his cosmology there actually were perfectly instantiated spheres, namely, the celestial spheres that carry the planets along their orbits. Consequently, at least part of the imagined apparatus can, by Avicenna's lights, be physically instantiated.

Avicenna's complaint comes when considering whether these rotating spheres can come in contact with a flat surface at a single point. The perfect spheres that Avicenna permits are embedded within one another. Thus, while a sphere may be in contact with the surface of another sphere, on Avicenna's view, it would not contact it at a single point but in its entirety, either containing or being contained. He in fact argues that one can demonstrate the physical impossibility of a sphere actually touching a flat plane at a single point, even if one grants the physical existence of both a perfect sphere and a two-dimensional surface. He reasons thusly: between the flat surface and the sphere there must be a void or not. At *Physics*, 2.8, Avicenna spilt much ink to show that a void is not only physically impossible but also conceptually impossible (McGinnis 2007b, esp. §IV and Lammer 2016, §5.3). Thus, if the proposed apparatus entails a void, then it entails an impossibility, and so must itself be a vacuous product of the imagination.

If there is no void, Avicenna's argument continues, then there must be a plenum whose surface contacts the flat two-dimensional plane and the convex surface of the sphere. Now, according to the continuous theory of physical bodies, which Avicenna adopts, points have no determinate existence in a continuous surface, save as endpoints of lines. Consequently, Avicenna goes on, points exist in the continuum only if there is a physical separation of the continuous surface, in which case the point exists as an endpoint; otherwise it exists merely as a product of the estimative faculty which posits the point. Thus, Avicenna continues, it is impossible that the single point of the sphere should have some separate, determinate position in the surface of the plenum that touches the flat two-dimensional plane given the very nature of continua.

He concludes his critique of this thought experiment thus:

> This [argument] makes the laws of nature dependent upon certain mathematical abstractions of the estimative faculty, which is not right. In fact, beyond going outside the discipline [of physics], that [argument] doesn't even entail what [they] wanted it to prove, but only requires that the continuity of the two designated motions be in the estimative faculty. We, however, don't deny that that continuity

is in the estimative faculty. We deny [the continuity] only of the natural things that deviate from the abstractions of the estimative faculty.

(Avicenna, *Physics*, 4.8 [12])

As a curious historical addendum, the post-Avicennan polymath, Quṭb al-Dīn Shīrāzī (1236–1311), showed how a model used in astronomy could produce a continuous motion between a body that ascends and then descends, which is perhaps immune to Avicenna's criticism (Morrison 2005, 58–9 and 91). Shīrāzī took advantage of a mathematical devise—the eponymous Ṭūsī couple—that Naṣīr al-Dīn al-Ṭūsī (1201–74) had constructed to bring about a better match between astronomical observations and the predictions of the geocentric model of the universe adopted by ancient and medieval astronomers. The Ṭūsī couple assumes two continuous and uniformly rotating circles (but the device could also be constructed using spheres). One circle is inside the other with the contained circle having half of the diameter of the containing circle and rotating twice as fast as and in the opposite direction as the containing circle. The overall effect, Ṭūsī observed, is that a certain point on the circumference of the smaller circle oscillates up and down the diameter of the larger circle. This oscillating "point" was subsequently identified with some planet.[5] Shīrāzī's contribution to the debate about medial rest was to note that since solely continuous rotations produce the oscillation, the point/planet will come to one endpoint of the diameter and then without rest (for the rotations do not stop) instantaneously move back toward the other endpoint. Consequently, to the extent that one believed that the astronomical model used in Ptolemaic systems described the actual workings of the heavens, the Ṭūsī couple would pass Avicenna's can-it-work test.

Let me conclude with one final set of possible mechanical idealized thought experiments, now drawn from the great medieval Muslim optician, Ibn al-Haytham.[6] (I say, "possible" because for some the examples that I give are seen as instances of *actual* experiments rather than *thought* experiments; I let the reader decide). Throughout his *Book of Optics* (*Kitāb al-Manāẓir*, Lt. *De aspectibus*) Ibn al-Haytham takes what by all appearances is a staunch empirical approach to the study of optics, suggesting numerous experiments and apparatus to verify empirically various principles used in optics. In numerous cases, he suggests a set of experiments that require the construction of highly precise apparatuses, which he describes with meticulous care, indeed such care that they appear to be more idealizations than devices actually used by him. Unfortunately, the exacting details of his descriptions and the length it would take to describe them preclude presenting even one of them here in full detail, although one example might help make my point.

When considering refraction, Ibn al-Haytham describes an apparatus for testing the refractive properties of different media which requires, as one of its parts, a relatively large quarter sphere of glass (like, for example, ABCD in Figure 4.1). Rays of light are allowed to pass through the quarter sphere before passing through a different medium like air or water. The technological state of glass working, particularly at a time before machine-produced glassware, makes it difficult to assume that any quarter sphere produced in Ibn al-Haytham's time would have been free of the various flaws that typify handmade glass items, such as the tiny bubbles or various stretch, mold, shear or pontil marks. These imperfections, however, would have distorted the observed results of the experiments. Similarly, for the device to give the mathematically exact results, which Ibn al-Haytham claims, the two flat surfaces of

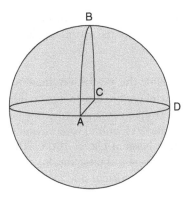

Figure 4.1

the quarter sphere would need to be exactly perpendicular and the curved surface perfectly convex, again features that seem all but impossible given the technology of the time.

Ibn al-Haytham makes similar exacting demands on the specifications for another apparatus, now used in validating the equal-angles law found in discussions of reflection. Noted historian of science, A. Mark Smith, has this to say about the level of precision required of that apparatus in order to get the purported results:

> Indeed, given [the apparatus'] obvious unfeasibility as actually described—with all planes perfectly aligned and all measurements perfectly reproduced—the test appears to have been an elaborate thought experiment designed to confirm what [Ibn al-Haytham] already took for granted, that is, that light reflects at equal angles.
> (Smith 2015, 199)

It is not my intention to diminish the significance of Ibn al-Haytham's contribution to optics—it is impressive indeed—rather, I merely want to suggest that some of his experiments might best be classified as instances of what I have been calling idealized thought experiments.

5 Conclusion

There can be little doubt that thinkers in the medieval Islamic world appreciated the role and significance of thoughts experiments for philosophy and the sciences. Indeed the prevalence of thoughts experiments in these areas seems to have lead Avicenna to explore the psychology behind them and present rules for determining acceptable and unacceptable use of premises relying on them.

He lauded and even employed thought experiments himself when used as intuition pumps primarily to arouse in us a better understanding of some independently proven points. When thought experiments were integral parts of a proof, however, he was more hesitant. If thought experiments were used in indirect proofs, they needed to be part of a conditional premise, ideally functioning as the consequence of some hypotheses whose very possibility was being questioned. In any other use, Avicenna stresses that one must prove that the situation imagined in the thought experiments can actually occur in the real world, and so does not have its existence merely as a product of the mind, or particularly, of the estimative faculty. In other words, when thought experiments were to play some integral role in a proof, Avicenna requires that the assumed scenario be executable at least in principle.

A scenario could be shown to be executable in principle, at least in some cases, if it relies on a mechanical apparatus that did not violate any physical principles. Indeed there appears to have been a proliferation of idealized mechanical thoughts experiments within natural philosophy, whether physics proper, optics, astronomy, or the like. Such a proliferation at least suggests that physics within the medieval Islamic world was beginning to show the first tendencies of an experimental approach to the sciences, although this tendency is better described in terms of "methodological experience" (see McGinnis 2003 and Janssens 2004). Whatever the case, the use of thought experiments would have been part of an empiricism that went hand in hand with a marked rationalist leaning.

As for evidence of this last point, we have seen Avicenna's demand that thought experiments really need to be accompanied by a demonstration (*burhān*). A demonstration in this context would have meant a logically valid syllogism proceeding from necessary first principles, where first principles are products of the intellect (*'aql*) not the estimative faculty. This same tendency also seems to be present in the experiments of Ibn al-Haytham. The punctilious precision with which he described the apparatus that his experiments employed all but necessitates that the demands of an idealized mathematical demonstration directed his detailed instructions. Finally, the medieval Jewish philosopher, Abū l-Barakāt (1080–1165), after cataloging various arguments against a *quies media*, notes that those who favor there being a medial rest would only be satisfied by a demonstration proceeding from the intellect (Abū l-Barakāt, *al-Mu'tabar*, 2.14, 97). By implication mechanical arguments, whether of the thought experiment variety or otherwise, would have taken a back seat to a proper intellectual demonstration.

To conclude, thought experiments in the medieval Islamic milieu seemed to function as a halfway house between empiricism and rationalism, allowing the idealization that rationalism demands while also appealing to sensible intuitions favored by an empiricist approach to the sciences.

Notes

1 The most detailed discussion to date about the relation of thought experiments to theories of psychology developed in the medieval Arabic world is Tanelli Kukkonen's landmark 2014 article, to which this section is heavily indebted.
2 These are in *De anima* 1.1 (translated here) and 5.7, the *Mashriqīyūn*, *Ishārāt wa-l-tanbīhāt* and *al-Risāla al-Aḍḥawīya fī l-ma'ād*. See Hasse (2000, 80–7) for a discussion of the differences among the various presentations.
3 Admittedly Plato is speaking about perception here, but the suggestion is that perception just is knowledge because it has the hallmarks of knowledge: it is about what is and is infallible (*apseudēs*).
4 While Avicenna ultimately will agree with Aristotle that there must be a rest between contrary motions, his own unique argument for this thesis appeals to the forces producing the motions rather than the sorts of motion involved.
5 A graphic representation can be found on Wikipedia under "Tusi Couple": https://en.wikipedia.org/wiki/Tusi_couple
6 The position I present here draws heavily upon Smith (2015, ch. 5).

References

Abū l-Barakāt. (1938–1939) *Kitāb al-Mu'tabar fī l-ḥikma*, 3 vols, Hyderabad: Jam'īya Dā'irat al-Ma'ārif al-Uthmānīya; repr. Beirut: Dār wa Maktaba Biblion, (2012).
Ahmed, A. (2016) "The reception of Avicenna's theory of motion in the twelfth century," *Arabic Science and Philosophy* 26: 215–243.
Averroes. (1992) *The Incoherence of The Incoherence*, 3rd ed., edited by M. Bouyges, Beirut: Dar al-Machreq sarl; trans. (1954) S. van den Bergh *Averroes' Tahafut al-Tahafut*, 2 vols, Oxford: Oxford University Press.
Avicenna. (1952) *Madkhal*, edited by M. Khudaryī, F. al-Ahwānī, and G. Anawatī, Cairo: The General Egyptian Book Organization.
Avicenna. (1959) *Avicenna's De anima, Being the Psychological Part of Kitāb al-Shifā'*, edited by F. Rahman, London: Oxford University Press.
Avicenna. (1966) *Burhān*, edited by 'A. Badawī, Cairo: Association of Authorship, Translation and Publication Press.
Avicenna. (2009) *The Physics of The Healing*, edited and translated by J. McGinnis, 2 vols, Provo: Brigham Young University Press.
Black, D. L. (1993) "Estimation (*Wahm*) in Avicenna: The logical and psychological dimensions," *Dialogue* 32: 219–258.
Druart, Th.-A. (1988) "The soul and body problem: Avicenna and Descartes," in *Arabic Philosophy and the West: Continuity and Interaction*, edited by Th.-A. Druart, Washington: Center for Contemporary Arab Studies, Georgetown University.
Hall, R. (2006) "The '*Wahm*' in Ibn Sina's psychology," in *Intellect et imagination dans la Philosophie Médiévale. Actes du XIe Congrès International de Philosophie Médiévale de la Société Internationale pour l'Étude de la Philosophie Médiévale (S.I.E.P.M.), Porto, du 26 au 31 août 2002*, vol. 1, edited by M. Cândida Pacheco and J. F. Meirinhos, Turnhout: Brepols.
Hasnawi, A. (2001) "La définition du mouvement dans la Physique du *Šifā'* d'Avicenne," *Arabic Sciences and Philosophy* 11: 219–255.
Hasse, D. (2000) *Avicenna's De anima in the Latin West*, London: The Warburg Insitute.
Ierodiakonou, K. (2005) "Ancient thought experiments: A first approach," *Ancient Philosophy* 25: 125–140.
Janssens, J. (2004) "Experience (*tajriba*) in classical Arabic philosophy (al-Fārābī–Avicenna)," *Quaestio* 4: 45–62.
Kaukua, J. (2015) *Self-Awareness in Islamic Philosophy: Avicenna and Beyond*, Cambridge: Cambridge University Press.
Knuuttila, S. and Kukkonen, T. (2011) "Thought experiments and indirect proofs in Averroes, Aquinas, and Buridan," in *Thought Experiments in Methodological and Historical Contexts*, edited by K. Ierodiakonou and S. Roux, Leiden: Brill.
Kukkonen, T. (2002) "Alternatives to alternatives: Approaches to Aristotle's arguments *per impossibile*," *Vivarium* 40: 137–173.
Kukkonen, T. (2014) "Ibn Sīnā and the early history of thought experiments," *Journal of the History of Philosophy* 52: 433–459.
Lammer, A. (2016) *The Elements of Avicenna's Physics: Greek Sources and Arabic Innovations*, PhD dissertation, Ludwig-Maximilians-Universität München.
Langermann, T. (2008) "Quies Media: A lively problem on the agenda of post-Avicennian physics," in *Uluslararasi İbn Sînâ Sempozyumu, Bildiriler*, 2 vols, edited by N. Bayhan, Istanbul: Kültür A. Ş. Yayilnari.
Lettinck, P. (1999) "Ibn Sina on atomism: Translation of Ibn Sina's *Kitab Al-Shifa, Al-Tabi'iyyat I: Al-Sama' Al-Tabi'i* Third Treatise, Chapter 3–5," *Al-Shajarah* 4: 1–51.
Marmura, M. E. (1986) "Avicenna's 'flying man' in context," *The Monist* 69: 383–395; repr. in Marmura, M. E. (2005), *Probing in Islamic Philosophy*, Binghamton: Global Academic Publishing.
McGinnis, J. (2003) "Scientific methodologies in Medieval Islam: Induction and experimentation in the philosophy of Ibn Sînâ," *Journal of the History of Philosophy* 41: 307–327.
McGinnis, J. (2006) "A medieval Arabic analysis of motion at an instant: The Avicennan sources to the forma fluens/fluxus formae debate," *British Journal for the History of Science* 39: 189–205.

McGinnis, J. (2007a) "Avoiding the void: Avicenna on the impossibility of circular motion in a void," in *The Proceedings of Classical Arabic Philosophy, Sources and Reception*, edited by P. Adamson, Warburg Institute Colloquia, London: The Warburg Institute.

McGinnis, J. (2007b) "Logic and science: The role of genus and difference in Avicenna's logic, science and natural philosophy," *Documenti e studi sulla tradizione filosofica medievale* 18: 165–187.

McGinnis, J. (2010) "Avicennan infinity: A select history of the infinite through Avicenna," *Documenti e studi sulla tradizione filosofica medievale* 21: 199–222.

McGinnis, J. (2015) "A small discovery: Avicenna's theory of *Minima Naturalia*," *Journal of the History of Philosophy* 53: 1–24.

Morrison, R. (2005) "Quṭb al-Dīn Shīrāzī's hypotheses for celestial motions," *Journal for the History of Arabic Science* 13: 21–140.

Philoponus, I. (1887) *In Aristotelis De caelo Commentaria*, in *Commentaria in Aristotelem*, vol. 7, edited by I. L. Heiberg, Berlin: typis et impensis Georgii Reimeri.

Rashed, R. (1999) "Al-Qūhī vs. Aristotle: On motion," *Arabic Sciences and Philosophy* 9: 7–24.

Simplicius. (1894) *In Aristotelis Physicorum Commentaria*, in *Commentaria in Aristotelem*, vols. 16–17, edited by H. Vitelli, Berlin: typis et impensis Georgii Reimeri.

Smith, A. M. (2015) *From Sight to Light: The Passage from Ancient to Modern Optics*, Chicago: University of Chicago Press.

5
GALILEO'S THOUGHT EXPERIMENTS
Projective participation and the integration of paradoxes

Paolo Palmieri

1 Introduction: the importance of Galileo's thought experiments

Historians and philosophers of science maintain that "fundamental changes in our understanding of the natural world" occurred at the turn of the sixteenth century (Jacob 1999, xiii). Some scholars refer to that series of events as the beginning of the *scientific revolution*. Others have denied that a revolutionary transformation really occurred at the beginning of the seventeenth century and have claimed that it is more fruitful to describe that period in terms of complex exchanges and mutual influences with technological developments, societal practices, and intellectual traditions (cf., for instance, Hadden 1994 and Shapin 1996). Regardless of the historiographic and philosophical perspectives, most would agree that, throughout the seventeenth century, "the gradual rejection of the Aristotelian binary physics of metaphysical *natures* and *places* in favor of the modern physics of universal forces whose behavior can be quantified and expressed in terms of mathematical laws" characterized the emergence, gradual or otherwise, of novel styles of inquiry within the philosophical tradition of Western Europe (Jacob 1999, xiii). Galileo Galilei (1564–1642) was an initiator of processes of transformation which, in the nineteenth century, culminated in the consolidation of the social and intellectual institutions that constitute modern mathematical physics. Over the past four centuries, Galileo has been the subject of passionate debate and acrimonious controversy, for very different reasons, some stemming from the intellectual battles of the Enlightenment philosophers against the Christian church, some from the affirmation of the positivist philosophical movement in the nineteenth century, which elevated science to a form of religion whose first martyr would have been Galileo (recall his notorious abjuration of Copernicanism before the Roman Inquisition in 1633). Yet, paradoxically enough, we still know very little about how Galileo contributed to the mathematization of nature, and what is even more striking is that there is little or no consensus among scholars concerning his achievements.

One methodological element that has attracted considerable attention in the philosophical literature is Galileo's alleged use of thought experiments. James Robert Brown may well be right in claiming, in the wake of Alexander Koyré, that it was by means of thought experiments that Galileo established the principle that all bodies fall at the same speed in the void. Moreover, I agree with Brown that Galileo's celebrated account in *Two New Sciences* (1638) may encapsulate, or trick us into believing that it does, in "the most beautiful thought experiment ever devised."[1] Famously, Koyré came to the thought-provoking conclusion that Galileo's experiments, such as the celebrated inclined plane, are all suspect, and that they may have been imaginary (i.e., instances of a cunning but morally dubious exploitation on Galileo's part of what Koyré calls *expérience imaginaire*), that is, never really performed by Galileo despite the fact that he tells us otherwise (Koyré 1973, 197–245). Hence there is little doubt that understanding Galileo's methodology also means understanding the role that thought experiments played in his work, what they consisted in precisely, and whether they can be neatly distinguished from other forms of inquiry pursued by Galileo and thus opportunely isolated in order to investigate them better.

In my view, the most remarkable advancement that has been made possible by recent research on his methodology suggests that it is virtually impossible to separate Galileo's *thought* experiments from his *real* experiments (assuming for the moment that we agree on what *thought* and *real* roughly mean in this context). In other words, it suggests that the dichotomy real versus thought experiment does not illuminate Galileo's methodology – it does not carve nature at its joints, so to speak – and that we must rethink this presupposition. In this chapter, I will address this intriguing state of affairs, tentatively replacing the questionable dichotomy with the categories of *projective participation* and *integration of paradoxes*. Under the guidance of these two new concepts I will reappraise what I prefer to call Galileo's experiential engagements with his lifeworld, focusing on the patterns that have been interpreted as thought experiments. I will make the suggestion that Galileo's experiential engagements constitute a continuous spectrum of patterns of inquiry, where thought, namely, the projective dynamics of mind (both Galileo's individual psyche and the social mind manifested in cultural traditions such as late Renaissance philosophical currents), and participation, namely, material or bodily activities, are merged together in the attempt to integrate into his lifeworld what for all intents and purposes appeared to him to be paradoxical phenomena (such as, all heavy bodies fall at the same rate in the void). Finally, I will conclude by suggesting that there are important lessons to be learned by aiming the spotlight at Galileo's lifeworld while rethinking the dichotomy of real versus thought experiment.

1.1 Outline of the chapter

In the next section, Section 2, I will discuss recent research, based on the reenactment of Galileo's experiments, that has shown the insurmountable difficulties we encounter when we try to demarcate *thought* from *real* in Galileo's engagements with the lifeworld. In Section 3, I will discuss in more detail Galileo's engagements with the lifeworld that have been interpreted as his "most beautiful thought experiment," analyzing their history, and illustrating the complex dynamics of integration of paradoxes that underlies his coming to terms with falling bodies. In the final section, Section 4, I will reflect on the lessons that we can learn from Galileo's thought experiments, briefly indicating the intersections of historical and philosophical research that might be fruitfully pursued in the future.

2 Projective participation and Galileo's lifeworld

In this section I will begin by inviting readers to enter Galileo's lifeworld by the back door, to come into a universe of alien experiences, to be sure, thus hoping that this exercise in what I will call with Husserl *epochē* will pave the way for helping us suspend our hermeneutic prejudices. Our investigation will proceed by extracting valuable information not only from published texts but also from manuscript sources that often reveal deeper and obscure phenomena. In 1626, Galileo wrote the following report in a letter to a correspondent:

> I have been for three months caught with an admirable affair, that is, the artful multiplication of the lodestone's virtue to hold iron. I have already been able to arrange things so that a 6-ounce lodestone, which by its own virtue holds no more than one ounce of iron, can with art hold 150 ounces, but I hope to improve. I will report to You since You have a speculative mind very much inclined to delight in this sort of accident. As for myself I cannot marvel enough at all of this, when I see such an angry conjunction occurring because of a simply immaterial virtue. I am so much more pleased with it as I know that Gilbert, who speculated deeply about this, and experimented and wrote diligently about it, could not increase the virtue of a lodestone holding one ounce to holding more than three ... The gain, which I have been making day by day gradually, has ensnared me with so much pleasure and marvel that I have almost become a locksmith, and being intrigued by this I have shut away everything else; to the point that, becoming more and more insatiable, like a miser, I cannot be satisfied. At the beginning I thought that it was a huge profit to increase the lodestone's virtue forty times, but now the interest rate of one hundred and fifty times is not enough, and I am at pains to improve as much as I can, while at the same time I am learning what it means to be a miser.
>
> (OGG, XIII, 328)[2]

Throughout his life, for all his deep-seated interests in the phenomena of magnetism, Galileo coped in vain with the elusive power, the immaterial virtue, of armed magnets. He learned how to improve things, as he says in the letter, but never got to grips with the alienating presence of the armed magnet in his lifeworld. Experiential learning about the magnet seems to have been *real* in the sense that here Galileo reports that he has been working hence expending much more physiological energy than required by brain activity, that is, exercising bodily activities, by strenuously manipulating pieces of lodestone with metal sheet (the process of arming magnets). In his lifeworld, consciousness is drawn to the mystery of the *angry* conjunction occurring because of an immaterial virtue; but what does this phenomenon of irresistible attraction towards anger mean? Recurrent bouts of anger in Galileo's professional and private life have been diagnosed by scholars, and in his youth he learned some Greek under the guidance of an unknown humanist master by translating passages from, among other works, Plutarch's tract *On Controlling Anger* (OGG, IX, 276). Anger was a moral issue that the Renaissance revival of Plutarch's writings had contributed to bring to the fore in many guises. When confronted with the mysterious multiplication of the armed magnet's virtue to attract iron,

Galileo unconsciously projected his psychic conflicts on to the phenomenon exhibited by the lodestone. We can understand Galileo's situation better if we suspend our prejudices about current disciplinary divisions and make an effort to see with Galileo's eyes and through the lenses of his epoch's moral dilemmas and his own psychic predispositions. Thus we are urged to conclude that his work with lodestones was not only real in the sense I suggested above, involving bodily exertion, but also imaginary, the projection of the moral quality of anger onto the physics of magnets, as Koyré would have liked. But I prefer to say that it was an instance of projective participation within a lifeworld of material and psychic realities, or validities, in which mind and body are not yet separate. Here I follow Husserl's intuition according to which:

> one can truly say that the idea of nature as a really self-enclosed world of bodies first emerges with Galileo ... Clearly the way is thus prepared for dualism, which appears immediately afterward in Descartes. In general we must realize that the conception of the new idea of 'nature' as an encapsulated, really and theoretically self-enclosed world of bodies soon brings about a complete transformation of the idea of the world in general. The world splits, so to speak, into two worlds: nature and the psychic world.
>
> (Husserl 1970, 60)

We can start breaking down the barrier that divides our philosophical outlook from Galileo's thought experiments by considering a universe where the psychic and the material are not separate.

We can make further progress towards understanding the workings of projective participation within Galileo's non-dualistic lifeworld by turning to his work with pendulums. I will consider the *isochronism* of simple pendulums (i.e., the property of simple pendulums to oscillate at a constant frequency regardless of the amplitude of the oscillations), and the *synchronism* of pendulums of different materials (i.e., the property of simple pendulums whose bobs are of different materials, but whose lengths are the same, to oscillate at the same frequency).

Galileo was steadfast in repeatedly claiming that simple pendulums are isochronous, and that pendulums of different materials are synchronous. For instance, as to the first claim Galileo stated the following:

> The second fact, really marvelous, is that the same pendulum makes its vibrations with the same frequency, or very little, almost negligibly different, regardless of whether they are made along the greatest or the smallest arcs of the same circumference. I say that if we remove a pendulum from the perpendicular, one, two, or three degrees, or if we remove it 70, 80, or even 90 degrees, once released, it will in both cases make its vibrations with the same frequency, both those where it traverses an arc of 4 or 6 degrees, and those where it traverses arcs of 160 degrees, or more. This will be most clearly seen by suspending two equal weights by two strings of the same length, and by removing one from the perpendicular a small distance, and the other a much greater distance. When let go, they will go back and forth under the same times, one along very long arcs, the other along very small ones.
>
> (OGG, VII, 474–476)

As to the second claim, he reported the following account:

> I decided to take two balls, one of lead and the other of cork, the former more than a hundred times heavier than the latter. I attached both to thin strings, equally long, about 4–5 braccia, and fixed above. After removing both from the perpendicular, I let them go at the same instant. While descending along the circumference of the circles described by the equal strings, the balls, after passing beyond the vertical, have come back along the same paths. By reiterating their goings and comings a full hundred times, on their own, they have shown to the senses that the heavy one goes so nearly under the time as the light one, that neither in one hundred, nor in one thousand vibrations, does it anticipate the time by a moment; for, both move with exactly the same pace. Further, the operation of the medium can be discerned, since, by somewhat impeding motion, the medium much more decreases the vibrations of the cork ball than those of the lead ball; yet, it does not make them more or less frequent. On the contrary, if the arcs traversed by the cork ball are no more than 5–6 degrees, and those traversed by the lead ball no more than 50–60 degrees, they will be traversed under the same times.
>
> (OGG, VIII, 128–29)

Reenactment of experiments becomes all important in this context.[3] I have reconstructed Galileo's apparatus and experienced the change in the visual appearance of the pendulums' oscillations as the release angles of the bobs are progressively increased. I call this phenomenon *discrepancy*. As I experimented, the best way to grasp this gradual change in visual appearance (at least the way that worked best for me) is to focus observation on the stopping points of the two bobs, the points where the bobs invert their motions. At those instants, the bobs have zero speed. So at that very moment it is easy to ascertain if their motions do not start again at the same instant, or, conversely, if they do not arrive at the inverting point at the same instant. Before discussing the implications of these surprising findings, I need to stress that the results obtained with my apparatus (i.e., the phenomena of isochronism vs. discrepancy) are very robust, in the sense that they occur over a wide range of the pendulum's parameters; they are not the accidental artifact of a particular choice of parameters. The gradual shift from isochronism to discrepancy challenges the observer's conceptual framework. The discrepancy possesses one very peculiar characteristic. Since the motions of light pendulums slow down rather quickly, because of the loss of energy caused by aerodynamic resistance, what happens is that, after a short period of time from the start, the pendulums enter a region of oscillations where the difference in their periods diminishes, so that the discrepancy, after accumulating for a little while, plateaus and then appears to be rather constant over the remaining interval of observation. This pattern, once again, is consistently true over a wide range of parameters. The discrepancy, in other words, does not "explode," the phenomenon does not degenerate into chaotic behavior. It remains clearly visible at a level which remains rather stable over a long period of observation.[4]

As for synchronism the pendulums in my reenactments again show a gradual shift from synchronism to discrepancy, with the cork ball moving ahead. This is due to the fact that, because it decelerates rapidly, the cork ball enters the region of small oscillations where aerodynamic resistance is smaller, thus starting to move ahead of the lead ball. Do the balls go at the same pace (*con passo egualissimo* ... , says Galileo)? For some time they do. Since Galileo is careful not to say from what angle the balls are supposed to be released, it is quite possible, for small oscillations, to see the balls go *con passo egualissimo* for some time.

Reconstructed pendulums show isochronism, synchronism, and above all discrepancy, manifesting a continuum of patterns of behavior. But in the twenty-first century the observer who reenacts Galileo's experiments observes in a different way, that is, with better discrimination. This reenacting observer relates to his lifeworld through a different modality, which, as I have reported, steers attention towards the strangeness of the discrepancy, its unexpected emergence, a phenomenon for which Galileo's texts do not furnish any indication at all. Initially I spent hours on end in the laboratory trying to learn how to observe in another modality, placing my body in different postures, looking at the scene from different viewpoints, hoping that the disturbing presence of the discrepancy would eventually evade my field of consciousness. I failed. My lifeworld was much more robust than I had anticipated.

Thus, I must conclude that the observer who reenacts Galileo's experiments is part and parcel of a radically different lifeworld, where mathematical physics plays a most prominent role, and where the laws of mechanics, such as the non-isochronism of circular pendulums, are well-established, indeed indelible, unrenounceable notions. There is no such thing, then, as Galileo's *real* as opposed to *thought* experiments with the pendulum. His experiential engagements with pendulums cannot be described by this conceptual dichotomy. I would argue that reenactment of the pendulum affords an experience that is commensurable to Galileo's only in the limit, in the sense that isochronism and synchronism tend to manifest themselves better and better only when the parameters that control the outcome of the experiment tend to certain values. So Galileo's engagements with pendulums are instances of projective participation in a lifeworld of psychic and material events, which are not dissociated in Galileo's consciousness and which therefore challenge our conceptual vocabulary. Galileo does not "see" the discrepancy, for he projects the realities of isochronism and synchronism onto the canvass of his own lifeworld.[5] Psychic constructs are as real as material artifacts.

Consider now the inclined plane. Here is Galileo's celebrated account of the situation:

> In a wooden beam or rafter about twelve braccia long, half a braccio wide, and three fingers thick, a channel was rabbeted in along the narrowest dimension, a little over a finger wide and made very straight; so that this would be clean and smooth, there was glued within it a piece of vellum, as much smoothed and cleaned as possible. In this there was made to descend a very hard bronze ball, which was rounded and polished, the beam having been tilted by elevating one end of it above the horizontal plane from one to two braccia, at will. As I said, the ball was allowed to descend along the said groove, and we noted (in the manner I shall presently tell you) the time that it consumed in running all the way, repeating the same process many times, in order to be quite sure as to the amount of time, in which we never found a difference of even the tenth part of a pulse beat. This operation being precisely established, we made the same ball descend

only one quarter the length of this channel, and the time of its descent being measured, this was found always to be precisely one half-the other. Next making the experiment for other lengths, examining now the time for the whole length [in comparison] with the time for one-half, or with that of two thirds, or of three-quarters, and finally with any other division, by experiments repeated a full hundred times, the spaces were always found to be to one another as the squares of the times. And this [held] for all inclinations of the plane; that is, of the channel in which the ball was made to descend, where we observed also that the times of descent for diverse inclinations maintained among themselves accurately that ratio that we shall find later assigned and demonstrated by our Author. As to the measure of time, we had a large pail filled with water and fastened from above, which had a slender tube affixed to its bottom, thorough which a narrow thread of water ran; this was received in a little beaker during the entire time that the ball descended along the channel or parts of it. The little amounts of water collected in this way were weighed every time on a delicate balance, the differences and the ratios of the weights giving us the differences and ratios of the times, and which such precision that, as I have said, these operations repeated time and again never differed by any notable amount.[6]

I reenacted the experiment with the help of graduate students.[7] An issue has to do with how Galileo measured times of descent. He weighed water collected in a glass from a narrow pipe attached to the bottom of a large bucket (a secchia, in the original). Tom Settle simply measured the volume of water collected in a graduated beaker (1961). We followed Settle in simplifying the time measuring procedure; that is, we did not replicate exactly Galileo's measurements of weights by means of a mechanical balance (but note that he does not say anything about the balance). I will discuss in Section 5 the problems raised by Galileo's weighing procedure. We used a common laboratory electronic balance capable of measuring weights with the precision of 1/10th of gram. Our water clock was a large plastic water tank with a plastic faucet, the opening of which could be easily controlled, similar to those used to dispense drinkable water. We operated the water clock by opening and closing the flow of water from the faucet with our fingers, collecting the water in a glass.

There is a slight ambiguity in the above text. Galileo says that the plane was elevated about 1–2 braccia. So, it is possible that his phrasing (... all inclinations of the plane) refers to all the inclinations of the plane that had been tested within the range of the 1–2 braccia. Another possible reading is that Galileo claims that for all inclinations of the plane, even beyond the limit of 1–2 braccia, he had always found an exact correspondence of the ratios between theory and experiment.

We operated as follows imagining two scenarios. The first scenario is a simplified one and aims at exploring the question of the stability of the pattern of acceleration for balls of different sizes rolling down the whole length of the inclined plane at certain inclinations within the 1–2 braccia range. Let us note that, as the elevation of the plane is increased from about 1 braccio to about 2 braccia (corresponding in our setup to 3.75° and 11.33°, respectively), the times of descent tend to decrease. Heavier bodies consistently travel faster on the plane. As for differences among balls of different sizes at the same elevation of the plane, we can state the following. For the two balls rolling on the groove we can draw the same conclusion, that is, heavier bodies consistently travel faster on the plane. For the three balls rolling inside the groove, however, the situation is less predictable.

The second scenario is more complex. It aims at exploring the question of the stability of the times-squared law for balls of different sizes rolling down the plane, and for a wider range of inclinations than 1–2 braccia. As can be gathered from Galileo's account, this type of experiment was supposed to give evidence of the correctness of the times-squared law of acceleration at different inclinations of the plane. How do the data compare with the expected ratios of the times-squared law? The times-squared law enunciated by Galileo states that the theoretical ratios of the times of descent along fractions of the whole length of the plane are as the square root of the ratios of lengths. For example, the ratio of the time along the whole plane to the time along ¼ of the plane is 2. The ratio of the time along the whole plane to the time along ½ of the plane is the square root of 2. The data suggest that the experiment tends to degenerate markedly approaching lower inclinations. As for higher inclinations, there is a better agreement between the theoretical and measured ratios compared with lower inclinations.

In summary, a phenomenon of discrepancy similar to the pendulum manifests itself also in the inclined plane experiment, where we can observe degenerative tendencies in the patterns of accelerations that for Galileo remained totally "invisible". The reenactment of experiments with historical accuracy has brought to light this intriguing situation in which a phenomenon emerges in the consciousness of the observer in the twenty-first century that had remained virtually inaccessible four centuries ago.

To reiterate, the moral is that Galileo's experiential engagements with inclined planes cannot be described by the conceptual dichotomy of *real* versus *thought* experiment. Once again we are led to the conclusion that our lifeworld has changed so dramatically, which reorients our capacity for observation in such a way that discrepancies, such as lead to instabilities in the patterns of acceleration of balls rolling down on the inclined plane, will nowadays promptly emerge in consciousness. By contrast Galileo's lifeworld prevents the discrepancies from emerging into his consciousness, for he projects the validity of the times-squared law onto the different structures of his lifeworld. His preference for ratios described by the smallest integers is certainly a legacy of the currents of Pythagorean and Hermetic symbolism that runs through the lifeworlds of the Renaissance, and which we know were embraced by Galileo wholeheartedly (as evidenced by his musical theories). I emphasize that I am not suggesting that we have developed a better sensitivity, or a superior capacity for observation, and that poor Galileo must have deluded himself. It is not a question of delusion. We too accept the times-squared law of falling bodies in gravity fields (at least to the extent that we still teach it in physics textbooks) while knowing perfectly well that it cannot be a true representation of reality. The question is that the definition of what constitutes reality cannot escape the lifeworld in which consciousness emerges. We demarcate *real* from *thought* differently than Galileo because we emerge into a different lifeworld, that's all.

We have now reached a point where the examples discussed should have cleared the way for our epochē to begin to work effectively. In the next section, I will plunge into Galileo's lifelong entanglement with falling bodies. I will investigate the integration of paradoxes in his consciousness. Projective participation and integration of paradoxes worked hand in hand in Galileo's lifeworld.

3 "The most beautiful thought experiment": falling bodies as integration of paradoxes

It is important to realize at the outset that Galileo has great fondness for paradoxes. It is not that he likes to boast of solving paradoxes that others have failed to grasp. It is rather that he prefers to find comprehensive arguments that are not aimed at resolving the paradoxes one way or the other, in the sense of making the wonder they provoke disappear, but instead amplify the apparent contradictions into a broader, even more challenging framework of ideas. In Galileo's lifeworld, reason seems to be drawn to paradoxes because they afford him the opportunity to think in terms of the coincidence of opposites (the so-called *coincidentia oppositorum* alluded to by late-medieval and Renaissance philosophers such as Nicholas of Cusa and Giordano Bruno). He feels comfortable on the horns of a dilemma. This tradition of Renaissance philosophy of the opposites also runs through Galileo's lifeworld. Descartes was struck by Galileo showcasing his natural talent for paradoxical reasoning in his last-published book, *Two New Sciences* (1638). He comments that all Galileo says about the infinite (such as his argument that there are as many even numbers as there are integers) is fundamentally flawed since he first announces that the infinite is incomprehensible by us, insofar as we are finite beings, but he then goes on to discuss it as if he comprehended it. Further, says Descartes, Galileo claims that when solid bodies become liquid they turn into an infinity of points, which is a figment of his imagination, all too easy to disprove. Finally, Descartes remarks, Galileo's proof that a line or a surface is equal to a point is a sophism (here Descartes refers to Galileo's discussion of the paradoxes raised by the so-called geometry of indivisibles).[8] Descartes was right in feeling that Galileo's arguments were not aimed at dismantling the paradoxes raised by the infinite and by the geometry of indivisibles. For, Galileo really wanted to integrate them into his mathematical natural philosophy.[9] He did not want to dissolve them. Thus Descartes's scathing comments on Galileo's *Two New Sciences* afford us a rare glimpse into an alien lifeworld that is all the more precious.

Somehow over a period of five decades, Galileo arrived at the general notion that all bodies fall at the same speed in the void. Let us begin by considering the text that Galileo published in 1638, and which has been considered as the most beautiful thought experiment in the history of science. Galileo's spokesman, Salviati, addresses his Aristotelian interlocutor, Simplicio, as follows.

> *Salviati.* ... without other experiences, by a short and conclusive demonstration, we can prove clearly that it is not true that a heavier movable is moved more swiftly than another, less heavy, these being of the same material, and in a word, those of which Aristotle speaks. Tell me, Simplicio, whether you assume that for every heavy falling body there is a speed determined by nature such that this cannot be increased or diminished except by using force or opposing some impediment to it.
>
> *Simplicio.* There can be no doubt that a given movable in a given medium has an established speed determined by nature, which cannot be increased except by conferring on it some new impetus, nor diminished save by some impediment that retards it.

> *Salviati.* Then if we had two movables whose natural speeds were unequal, it is evident that were we to connect the slower to the faster, the latter would be partly retarded by the slower, and this would be partly speeded up by the faster. Do you not agree with me in this opinion?
>
> *Simplicio.* It seems to me that this would undoubtedly follow.
>
> *Salviati.* But if this is so, and if it is also true that a large stone is moved with eight degrees of speed, for example, and a smaller one with four [degrees], then joining both together, their composite will be moved with a speed less than eight degrees. But the two stones joined together make a larger stone than that first one which was moved with eight degrees of speed; therefore this greater stone is moved less swiftly than the lesser one. But this is contrary to your assumption. So you see how, from the supposition that the heavier body is moved more swiftly than the less heavy, I conclude that the heavier moves less swiftly.
>
> (Galilei 1974, 66–67)

Here Galileo explicitly restricts the argument to bodies of the same matter, that is, of the same specific weight. This is confirmed in a subsequent passage, where Galileo has Sagredo, the third interlocutor, say:

> You [Salviati-Galileo] have clearly demonstrated that it is not at all true that unequally heavy bodies, moved in the same medium, have speeds proportional to their weights [*gravità*], but rather have equal [speeds]. You assumed bodies of the same material (or rather, of the same specific gravity), and not (or so I think) of different density, because I do not believe you mean us to conclude that a cork ball moves with the same speed as one of lead.
>
> (Galilei 1974, 71–72)

So it is important to realize that in Galileo's mind this pattern of reasoning does not work for bodies of different material but only for those having the same specific weight. The importance of this restriction cannot be underestimated. The fact is that this text cannot be easily extrapolated from the context of beliefs, material artifacts, and mentalities that are all interwoven in Galileo's lifeworld. Galileo's literary talent represents Simplicio as a very credible character, an inoffensive, docile interlocutor who readily admits that a given movable in a given medium has an established speed determined by nature, that it is evident that, were we to connect the slower to the faster, the latter would be partly retarded by the slower, and so on, and so on. One marvels at the naïveté with which commentators have taken this comedy at face value, not even noticing that the argument is restricted to bodies of the same density. One wonders whether Salviati poking fun at *Simplicio* (does the name resonate with the word *simplicity*?) was really supposed to savagely mock Galileo's Aristotelian adversaries, as we always thought, or was instead an artful ruse to take us on a guided sightseeing tour of Galilean rhetoric. For, when looking carefully at the iceberg of archival documents that have been preserved for four centuries, one finds almost nothing in Simplicio's *simplicity* that had not been Galileo's own honest opinion at some point in his career.[10] Who is Simplicio, then?

In the 1590s, decades before publishing the above text, Galileo jotted down notes which he never published, collectively known as De Motu (OGG, I, 251 ff). These notes are one of the most beautiful documents in the history of science. Here Galileo's lifelong struggle with the integration of paradoxes comes to the fore. He begins by attacking the theory, attributed to Aristotle by himself and by his teachers at Pisa, that all bodies of the same kind fall with speeds proportional to their bulk.[11] Thus, a piece of lead twice as large as another piece of lead will fall twice as fast.

But Galileo is convinced from the very beginning of the paradoxical truth that all bodies of the same material fall downwards at the same speed. He does not start off by offering a counter-argument to the Aristotelian theory, which he thinks is just ridiculous (OGG, I, 263). Galileo is dismayed that anybody could think otherwise than he thinks. His language betrays this emotional modality of thought throughout.[12] The progression of the argumentative strategy points us in the right direction. To repeat, Galileo is already convinced that all bodies of the same material fall downwards at the same speed from the beginning. Recall that De Motu is not for publication. Galileo is jotting down notes by way of self-analysis exploring the situation of fall as opposed to floatation in the context of Archimedean hydrostatics. I surmise that if we insisted on looking for a source from which Galileo draws his stubborn conviction, we would have to concede that it is a projection coming from the unconscious.

Following the emotional outburst of invectives against those who do think otherwise, he has a moment of lucidity when he hits on the brilliant analogy. The reason why mobiles of the same kind, although different in volume, fall at the same speed is the same as why both a chip of wood and a large wooden beam will float (OGG, I, 263). Floatation and fall are states of affairs in which consciousness discerns uniformity of behavior. It is the presence of the surrounding medium, the immersion of bodies in a fluid element, that makes the patterns of falling bodies intelligible. Floatation is arrested fall, or vice versa, fall in a medium is the continuation of floatation from the temporal perspective. Here is how Galileo's thought-processes proceed towards integration, following the sharp contrast between his a priori, unconscious conviction and the flashing discernment in consciousness of an analogy between fall and floatation.

He begins by saying " ... *si mente concipieremus*," that is, if we conceive with mind, or in mind. Allow me to suspend for the time being the question of what words such as "mind" or similar cognates mean in Galileo's time, at the turn of the sixteenth century. I will come back to this delicate point further on. He goes on as follows. Let us consider a wooden beam and a chip of the same wood floating on water. Then, imagine the specific weight of water decreasing, so that at one point water will become specifically lighter than wood. Who could claim, he asks, that the beam will begin to descend before or faster than the chip? The reason why the beam's behavior will be the same as the chip's is that while descending both will have to raise an amount of water equal to their volumes. Thus the volumes of water that are being raised will have the same ratio as that of the chip's and the beam's volumes. In consequence, the ratio of the weight of the beam to the weight of its displaced volume of water is the same as that of the weight of the chip to the weight of its displaced volume of water. With the same easiness, both the chip and the beam will overcome the resistance of the water which has to be displaced (OGG, I, 264). He concludes the train of thought by proposing an embryonic form of the argument that he eventually published five decades later. He assumes that if one of two mobiles moves faster than the other the composite of both will move faster than the slower, yet slower than the faster one. Then he goes on to state that mobiles of the same kind and different volumes will move with the same speed. The strategy is as follows. Let *a* and *b* be the two bodies, and *a* be larger than *b*. If possible, let *a* move faster than *b*. The composite will move faster than *b* yet slower than *a*. But the composite is larger than *a*, therefore a larger body will move slower than a smaller body, which is awkward (OGG, I, 264).

The style of the argument is that of a reductio ad absurdum. Furthermore, whereas in the *Two New Sciences* we find the supposition that bodies are endowed by nature with a speed of their own, easily conceded by Simplicio, in this early form of the argument, Galileo employs the canonic formula to be found in all classical Greek geometry whenever a reductio is introduced; for instance, it is quite common in Archimedes. It runs *if possible, let ...* , etc. It asks the reader to admit what is believed to be impossible by the writer, hence in Galileo's self-analysis, the formulaic introduction rhetorically asks Galileo himself to admit that *a* moves faster than *b*, namely, that it is false that bodies of the same material but different bulk fall at the same speed, which is contrary to his belief. The use of the canonic formula suggests to me that Galileo is already convinced of his claim as being valid in his lifeworld, and that it remains open to question whether he employs the tentative argument as a means of probing the possibility of a deductive proof for the claim and/or boosting his belief in its truth. For all intents and purposes, the reconstruction of the argument in *Two New Sciences*, which is amplified by the intromission of the initial assumption that for every heavy falling body there is a speed determined by nature, appears to have been dictated by the rhetorical exigencies of the dialogue (remember that *Two New Sciences* is written in the form of dialogues among three interlocutors). To see how, let us pursue this question of the dialogic nature of Galileo's thought.

Many years after the *De Motu* writings Galileo received a book written by Antonio Rocco, a libertine philosopher who, in the name of Aristotle, had attacked Galileo's recently published *Dialogue on the Two Chief World Systems* (1632). Galileo undertook to write a response to Rocco that he later abandoned. Fortunately, the copy of Rocco's book in Galileo's possession that was annotated by him has been preserved. There we find numerous comments by Galileo that help us piece together the history of his theories. At one point Rocco has a startling comment. He says that philosophy is the sincere search for the truth of things, not the conjuring of chimeras, let alone the defense of paradoxes repugnant to both reason and sensory experience (OGG, VII, 602). To this comment Galileo replied in the margin, almost shouting, "It is you who, by not understanding, turn true and noble statements into paradoxes and dreams" (OGG, VII, 602). No doubt this anger is suspect. Here Galileo appears to be angrily rejecting the association of truth and overt paradox. Then he gives yet another account of the famous argument:

> I formed an axiom such that nobody could ever object to. I hypothesized that any heavy body whatever which descends has in its motion degrees of speed so limited by nature and fixed, that it would be impossible to alter them, by increasing or decreasing its speed, without using violence in order to speed up, or slow down, its natural course. I then figured in my mind two bodies equal in volume

and weight, such as, for instance, two bricks, which depart from the same height at the same time. These will doubtless descend with the same speed, assigned to them by nature. If this speed has to be increased by another mobile, it is necessary that this mobile move more swiftly. Yet if one imagines the two bricks joining together while descending, which one would be that by adding impetus to the other will double the latter's speed, given that speed cannot be increased by an arriving mobile if it does not move more swiftly?

(OGG, VII, 731)

Galileo tells us that he hypothesized that any heavy body which descends is possessed in its motion of degrees of speed limited by nature and fixed. In this passage written in 1634, four decades after *De Motu*, Galileo is shaping his reasoning about falling bodies in an ideal dialogue with Rocco. It is the dialogue that reinforces in Galileo the need to make the assumption explicit. But one might be more radical in reading this version of the argument from 1634. One might suggest that Rocco's rebuttal is nothing more than a hook for Galileo's imagination to project his own dissatisfaction with the still-unresolved process of integration of the paradox of fall. Galileo clings to the paradox but needs further "therapeutic" assistance in making his own framework of beliefs ever more resilient. Hence there was anger in the reply to Rocco in the margin. He invokes the help of nature in assigning to each and every heavy body a speed that is fixed indelibly, namely, necessarily, in the essence of the body itself. Now, Rocco and Galileo seem to agree on one point, not a particularly original one, despite the controversy. As Rocco pointed out, since God is eternal, nature must also be (OGG, VII, 601). Rocco's sentence falls short of stating explicitly that nature must also be eternal, an obvious heresy for a Christian believing in God's creation from nothing. Yet this is what Rocco, the libertine philosopher and anonymous author of a novel on pedophilia, really thinks. For, he then goes on to equate God with nature quite explicitly, only qualifying his too bold assertion by adding that nature is the immutable instrument of God's own immutability and wisdom. Galileo has this in mind when he enlists the help of nature in making the speed of any heavy body immutably fixed. In other words, Galileo is grounding his argument in God's own immutability in sustaining the order of the universe. The falling-bodies argument in its final form, published by Galileo in *Two New Sciences*, does state this much in between the lines. But from the perspective of the twenty-first century one may easily lose sight of the fact that this background would have been quite obvious to an attentive reader four centuries ago and not in need of amplification. Hence we have come to a point where we can see that Galileo's beautiful thought experiment needs to invoke the immutability of God-Nature for it to be conclusive, at least in the eyes of its inventor.

In circling round this question of falling bodies Galileo realizes that there is a paradoxical center, the truth, around which he can orbit by leveraging an array of thought processes and engagements with material artifacts (such as pendulums, inclined planes, and floating bodies of different shapes and materials, with all of which we know he experimented extensively[13]) but which remains unattainable by human thought. What is being achieved in consciousness by way of integration is not the center, an unconscious image of God and hence of truth, but rather the diffracted vision of the truth, of its paradoxical nature, from different angles. Elsewhere I have recounted the vicissitudes of how Galileo was eventually able to generalize the validity of his claim to all bodies falling in the void (Palmieri 2005a). Since the beautiful "thought experiment" unfortunately never proved to be applicable to bodies of different materials, that story goes beyond the scope of this chapter. But there is another closely related episode of integration of paradoxes in the development of Galileo's theory of fall which helps us illuminate the question of Galileo's projective processes from the broader perspective of his lifeworld. I will consider it in the light of the historical context in which he evolved his theories.

By the time Galileo published his argument in *Two New Sciences* he had long been in possession of a mathematical theory of fall according to which the speed of bodies falling downwards, both vertically and along any inclined plane, is proportional to the elapsed time, while the space traversed is proportional to the square of the elapsed time. It is often referred to as the times-squared law, though Galileo did not call it a law. Thus his mature theory of fall included both the statement that all bodies in the void fall at the same speed and the proportionality of space to the square of time. In order to ground the deductive structure of the theory he postulated that the final speed reached by a heavy body when hitting the horizontal after starting from a given height and falling along any inclination whatever is the same regardless of the inclination. It is another startling paradox among the many discussed by Galileo in his last book. But he had no conclusive argument for the postulate. He then had recourse to the same strategies of paradox integration and projective participation by presenting a situation that involves both material artifacts, the pendulum and the inclined plane, and, as we shall see presently, psychic artifacts. It consists in modeling the fall along the straight incline with the circular arc of a pendulum swinging around a peg positioned along the vertical (OGG, VIII, 206). The experiment can be carried out in practice as Galileo suggests and one can verify his claims. I easily repeated it with students in one of my undergraduate classes. In this instance, there is no discrepancy emerging in our lifeworld, and we can follow Galileo's instructions to projectively participate in the lifeworld setting. The two situations are not identical, though, since the inclined plane has an angular point at the bottom junction with the horizontal, while the pendulum swings along a smooth curvilinear trajectory crossing the vertical at its bottom. For the whole argument to go through, projective participation must combine observation of the material world, i.e., the pendulum returning to almost the same height from which it started, with the act of imagining removing the angular point from the pathway downwards along the straight incline.

Galileo claims that if one imagines removing the hindrance due to the angularity at the bottom of the plane, then the "intellect will remain satisfied that the two impetuses [acquired along the incline and the pendulum arc] will suffice to push the mobile to the same height in both cases."[14] We need not go into the details of the overall argument here. What matters is that Galileo makes use of a conceptual vocabulary from the psychology of the time. It is embedded within his lifeworld. Once again we discover that integrating in consciousness the paradox of the equality of speeds along different inclines, which is Galileo's first strategy for convincing the reader of the validity of his postulate,[15] requires relying on the tacit assumption that the intellect is dependent for its functioning on the powers of God.

In the psychology of Galileo's lifeworld the intellect is regarded as a faculty of the human soul. But what is it exactly, and how does it work? Why does Galileo say that the intellect will remain satisfied after something has been imagined? The idiomatic construction in the original turn of phrase hints at the passivity of the intellect that will remain satisfied once the imagination has removed the hindrance. The emphasis is on the passivity of thought. This does not harmonize well with the notion of thought experiment, which suggests some sort of mental activity. But there is activity also in Galileo's understanding of the intellect, and to find out more about this we need to explore the psychology of Galileo's lifeworld at a much deeper level.

The prevailing view of the human mind in the intellectual milieu of the University of Padua, where Galileo had been a professor for seventeen years, was that of Giacomo Zabarella, a predecessor of Galileo whose theories had risen to prominence not only at Padua but also in Europe, and especially in Germany. His books went through numerous editions which were well received. I will base my succinct account on *De rebus naturalibus* [On natural things], an encyclopedic exposition of natural philosophy which became very popular after Zabarella's death in 1589. The human mind understands by "suffering," i.e., by being the passive recipient of an action that informs it. Thus the human mind is twofold, both active and passive at the same time. But while its passivity is explicable in terms of its own cognitive functions, insofar as it understands by turning itself into the object of understanding, the action that transforms the passive mind into the object of understanding is rather more obscure. The fundamental question concerning the activity of mind was whether this activity was part of the human soul or not. It raised delicate questions that had been debated in Europe since the late Middle Ages. It is a question that leads straight into the realm of Christian theology. It concerns the individuality of the human soul, whether it can be regarded as a principle of individuation, or whether a super-individual soul exists that supervenes on the process of human cognition but is not itself a faculty of the individual human soul. Ultimately it is a question the answer to which defines for Christians the demarcation between orthodoxy and heresy in relation to the immortality of the human soul.

The active part of mind was called *intellectus agens*, acting or active intellect. Zabarella's view is that *intellectus agens* is a so-called separate substance, i.e., a substance that is not material, and which may or may not be one of the intelligences that animates the inferior celestial spheres. The possibility that it is one of the celestial intelligences governing the motions of the heavenly spheres is ruled out by Zabarella on grounds that we need not pursue here. He argues that *intellectus agens* cannot be but the supreme intelligence, namely, God himself. God moves the first heaven, *primum mobile*, and God is the first cause of all things. The passive human intellect is solely an instrument of the divine *intellectus agens*. Things that are intelligible in potentiality must be made intelligible in actuality by *intellectus agens*. But since God is the supreme intelligible and the most intelligible of all things, *intelllectus agens* must be God himself (Zabarella 1590, 933).

When Galileo claims that if one imagines removing the hindrance due to the angularity at the bottom of the rectilinear plane, then the "intellect will remain satisfied," we must pay heed and carefully read his language in the context of a psychology such as Zabarella's. The final act by which the human intellect will remain satisfied is the supervenience of *intellectus agens*, namely, God, that clears the passive mind and makes it into the final object of understanding. Imagination removes the hindrance but understanding is a function of the "information" (in the sense of endowing with form) of passive intellect by God.

Thus the integration of paradoxes in consciousness, such as the paradox of speeds along different inclines – the foundation of the deductive structure of the science of falling bodies in which "the most beautiful thought experiment" ideally culminates – means allowing the supervenience of *intellectus agens*, namely, God, actuating the clearing of the passive mind that turns it into its own finality, the object of understanding; in this instance, the equality of speeds along different inclines having the same height. In Galileo's lifeworld, psychic validities are not separate from material ones, and indeed there is a continuum from the material to the psychic that precedes the subsequent separation of the two, as Husserl had stated.

4 Conclusion: Galileo's heart of darkness and why all this matters

Galileo's self-examination of unconscious convictions is the place of origination of the "most beautiful thought experiment" in the history of science. Its progress through projective participation in the lifeworld leads to the emergence of clarity in consciousness, in the only form that is granted to the human passive intellect, namely, that of a diffracted vision of the reconciliation of opposites from different viewpoints. Husserl spoke of Galileo as "at once a discovering and a concealing genius," who brought to the fore the true mathematical structure of reality, while fatefully covering up the "untruth" of the immediate presence of the lifeworld (Husserl 1970, 52). He also noted that four centuries later the situation has not changed. The radical shift from a classical to a quantum mechanics has not modified the scenario that Galileo envisaged. It is mathematics, Husserl thinks, that illuminates matter, and which is regarded as the ultimately real. Hence the question of the nature of the act that is a discovering and a concealing at the same time remains an urgent one for philosophy today. In this sense, Galileo's thought experiments are more than philosophical relics from a past that does not concern us anymore.

Galileo's self-examination has deep roots in his fascination with Archimedean mathematics. A few marginal postils to the latter's *On the Sphere and the Cylinder*, probably written in the late 1580s, strongly suggest that Galileo scrupulously studied this work. At about the same time, he furnished a solution to the problem of Hiero's crown different from that commonly related in the anecdotes reported in the Archimedean tradition.[16] Though published many years later in *Two New Sciences*, Galileo's theorems on centers of gravity, whose Archimedean inspiration is all too evident, date from the mid-1580s (OGG, I, 187ff). Finally, we have the *De Motu*, the veritable Archimedean manifesto of Galileo's youth that I have already examined. Whence this fascination?

While Euclidean geometry principally deals with diagrams based on circles and straight lines, opening up a vista on the realm of pure forms abstracted from matter, Archimedean mathematics plunges the natural philosopher into the darkness of matter. Though the Renaissance became infatuated with all classical mathematics, the late sixteenth century in particular saw a powerful coming back of Archimedean ideas, especially regarding mechanics, centers of gravity, and floating bodies. Galileo was part of the rescue operation but his interests in the abyss of matter and the paradoxes of fall ran deeper than antiquarianism. The myth of Galileo that has been handed down to us by the high priests of nineteenth-century positivism (and their logical mutants) has it that Galileo was the founder of modern science, chiefly mathematical physics and experimentation, and that his revolutionary achievement consisted in dismantling the constructs of the late medieval cosmos, i.e., eradicating its roots in the doctrines of Aristotle and his late scholastic followers. Yet, by following the lead of the Husserlian "at once a discovering and a concealing genius" and by puzzling together recent advances in Galileo studies, a different picture begins to emerge.

This picture portrays Galileo as a crypto-hermetist whose processes of self-edification bordered on heresy and libertinism though they never overlapped with these elusive early modern practices. Galileo engaged in hermetic work aimed at liberating the self from its thrownness into the darkness of matter. As we now know, such work involved Archimedean mathematics, which united the opposites of the divine forms and the heaviness of material bodies, judicial astrology, as an exploration of the structure of time, reconciliation of conflicting truths through Biblical hermeneutics, an aesthetics of light and darkness, exemplified by the moon washes of the early telescopic observations, and emotional self-control, specifically the subjugation of the vice of anger, clearly evidenced, as we have seen, in Galileo's writings.[17]

In sum, I describe all of this as Galilean hermetism. It was a search for the sublimation of the self into the all-pervading light of the divine, as suggested by his late poetry and by his theory of light, on which his pupils collected many testimonials that have not been properly attended to in Galileo scholarship.[18]

Galileo's thought experiments, when placed in the context of his lifeworld, the heart of darkness of the "discovering and concealing genius," point us in unforeseen directions, for which some of our philosophical categories and disciplinary divisions are not entirely adequate. We must pause and learn a lesson here.

Notes

1 Brown (2004, 24). See the account alluded to by Brown, in Galilei (1974, 66 ff), which will be discussed in this chapter extensively. Cf. also Atkinson & Peijnenburg (2004), Norton (2004, 1996), Palmieri (2003), Budden (1998), Gendler (1998), McAllister (1996), Miščević (1992), Prudovsky (1989), Geymonat & Carugo (1981), and Kuhn (1977).
2 The abbreviation OGG refers to Galilei (1890–1909), the Roman numeral to the volume, and the Arabic numerals to pages. See Reeves (2002) on Galileo's use of the miser simile in regard to magnetism.
3 I take the liberty of referring the reader to my previous work (Palmieri 2008, 2011) for more details and ample discussions of the interpretative problems concerning the reenactment of historical experiments.
4 I have shot numerous videos of these time-consuming experiments, which demonstrate the stability and persistence of the phenomenon of discrepancy. They will be made available upon request to the author.
5 I emphasize this conclusion since it is different than that I reached a few years ago, when I thought that Galileo would hardly have missed the pendulum discrepancy (Palmieri 2008). At that time I failed to realize that Galileo's lifeworld suggests a way out of the conundrum posed by his complete silence about the discrepancy in all the pertinent texts.
6 Galilei (1974, 169–170), translated by Stillman Drake, with minor modifications. Cf. OGG, VIII, 212–13.
7 Eric Hatleback built the wooden structure and conducted trials with myself and Elay Shech. We did not follow Galileo's procedure for lining and polishing the groove since we thought that our machine cut groove was already very smooth. But we coated the groove with a finishing varnish to protect it and improve hardness (the polished vellum used by Galileo would have achieved a similar effect). The total length of our plane was 21 ft. In order to try different elevations of the plane, we decided to build two simple wooden towers, placing one of them at one end of the plane and

8 OGG, XVII, 388. Descartes wrote these negative comments to Marin Mersenne in 1638 after glancing at Galileo's *Two New Sciences*.
9 Occurrences of "paradosso [paradox]" in Galileo are rare but revealing. There is one, for instance, in the *Discourse on Floating Bodies* (OGG, IV, 77), one in the *Assayer* (OGG, VI, 256), a few in the *Dialogue on the Two Chief World Systems* (OGG, VII, 65, 155, 452, for instance), and one in the *Two New Sciences* (OGG, VIII, 68). In Galileo's writings the meaning of this word is very close to that of a marvelous, incredible phenomenon, apparently contradictory. In June 1612, in a letter to Maffeo Barberini (the future pope, Urban VIII), Galileo wrote that some people held in high repute poked fun at the recently discovered sunspots, as if they were a paradox, a gross absurdity, "... mi viene scritto che huomini di molta stima di cotesta città se ne burlano come di paradosso et assurdo gravissimo" (OGG, XI, 305). Cf. Palmieri (2005b), in which Galileo's ingenious strategies for inventing ever-more striking paradoxes are described in the context of Archimedean hydrostatics.
10 Cf., for example, Galileo's early *De motu* writings (ca. 1590s), in which many "false" theories (false in the light of his later ones) are defended by the young Galileo (OGG, I, 251 ff).
11 "De illis mobilibus quae sunt eiusdem speciei dixit Aristoteles, illud velocius moveri quod maius est" (OGG, I, 262–63).
12 OGG, I, 263. "...quis unquam dixerit ... ." The Latin barely conceals Galileo's wrath that anybody could possibly think otherwise.
13 OGG, IV, collates Galileo's writings on floatation. His experiments with floating bodies have an almost 'surrealist' quality. He ingeniously shapes balls mixing beeswax with iron filings so as to only so slightly alter their density with respect to water and thus be able to test limit conditions. He shapes bodies with pointed edges to demonstrate that floatation is neither aided nor hindered by shape and that the only parameter that makes bodies sink or float is their density, in accord with Archimedes's theories. He discovers hydrostatic paradoxes involving pressure that challenge his own and the reader's imagination. See Vergara-Caffarelli (2009), who reconstructed some of Galileo's experiments with floating bodies.
14 OGG, VIII, 207–8. Galileo says, "mi par bene che l'intelletto resti capace."
15 I underline that this is only Galileo's first strategy since he also emphasizes that the validity of the postulate will be confirmed by the correspondence between the truths that will be geometrically demonstrated from the postulate and experiment.
16 Cf. OGG, I, 215ff, 379 (on the problem of Hiero's crown), and ibid., 233ff. (postils to *On the Sphere and the Cylinder*).
17 Cf., for example, Wootton (2010). David Wootton has highlighted unsuspected strands of argument in Galileo's theories and elements in his patterns of behavior that reveal an unorthodox image bordering on religious heresy.
18 Favaro (1907, 1949). Antonio Favaro, the editor of the monumental multi-volume edition of Galileo's works (Galilei 1890–1909), diligently collected and published a number of "strange" opinions and theories that were attributed to Galileo by his closest friends and disciples, but which had so to speak fallen by the wayside of history. Favaro was a staunch positivist opposing the Catholic church in Italy in the aftermath of the political unification of the state in 1861. His faith in the positivist religion prevented him from making sense of the obscure hermetic allusions that he had discovered.

References

Atkinson, D. and Peijnenburg, J. (2004) "Galileo and prior philosophy," *History and Philosophy of Science* 35A: 115–136.
Brown, J. R. (2004) "Why thought experiments transcend empiricism," in *Contemporary Debates in the Philosophy of Science*, edited by C. Hitchcock, Malden: Blackwell.
Budden, T. (1998) "Galileo's ship thought experiment and relativity principles," *Endeavour* 22: 54–56.

Favaro, A. (1907) "Pensieri, sentenze e motti di Galileo Galilei raccolti dai discepoli e pubblicati da Antonio Favaro," *Rivista di fisica, matematica e scienze naturali* 86: 97–109.
Favaro, A. (1949) *Pensieri, Motti e Sentenze Tratti dalla Edizione Nazionale delle Opera*, Florence: Barbèra.
Galilei, G. (1890–1909) *Le Opere di Galileo Galilei*. Edizione Nazionale, edited by A. Favaro, 20 vols, Florence: Barbèra.
Galilei, G. (1974) *Two New Sciences. Including Centres of Gravity and Force of Percussion*, edited and translated by S. Drake, Madison: The University of Wisconsin Press.
Gendler, T. S. (1998) "Galileo and the indispensability of scientific thought experiment," *British Journal for the Philosophy of Science* 49: 397–424.
Geymonat, L. and Carugo, A. (1981) "I cosiddetti esperimenti mentali nei Discorsi Galileiani e i loro legami con la tecnica," in *Per Galileo*, edited by L. Geymonat, Verona: Bertani Editore.
Hadden, R. W. (1994) *On the Shoulders of Merchants: Exchange and the Mathematical Conception of Nature in Early Modern Europe*, Albany: SUNY Press.
Husserl, E. (1970) *The Crisis of European Sciences and Transcendental Phenomenology. An Introduction to Phenomenological Philosophy*, translated by D. Carr, Evanston: Northwestern University Press [original edition *Die Krisis der europäischen Wissenschaften und die transzendentale Phänomenologie: Eine Einleitung in die Phänomenologische Philosophie*, edited by Walter Biemel, The Hague: Martinus Nijhoff, 1954].
Jacob, J. R. (1999) *The Scientific Revolution*, New York: Humanity Books.
Koyré, A. (1973) *Études d'histoire de la pensée scientifique*, Paris: Éditions Gallimard. (First published Paris: Presses Universitaires de France, 1966).
Kuhn, T. S. (1977) "A function for thought experiments," in *The Essential Tension*, Chicago: University of Chicago Press.
McAllister, J. W. (1996) "The evidential significance of thought experiment in science," *Studies in History and Philosophy of Science* 27A: 233–250.
Miščević, N. (1992) "Mental models and thought experiments," *International Studies in the Philosophy of Science* 6: 215–226.
Norton, J. (1996) "Are thought experiments just what you thought," *Canadian Journal of Philosophy* 26: 333–366.
Norton, J. (2004) "Why thought experiments do not transcend empiricism," in *Contemporary Debates in the Philosophy of Science*, edited by C. Hitchcock, Malden: Blackwell.
Palmieri, P. (2003) "Mental models in Galileo's early mathematization of nature," *Studies in History and Philosophy of Science* 34A: 229–264.
Palmieri, P. (2005a) "Galileo's construction of idealized fall in the void," *History of Science* 43: 343–389.
Palmieri, P. (2005b) "The cognitive development of Galileo's theory of buoyancy," *Archive for History of Exact Sciences* 59: 189–222.
Palmieri, P. (2008) *Reenacting Galileo's Experiments: Rediscovering the Techniques of Seventeenth-Century Science*, Lewiston: The Edwin Mellen Press.
Palmieri, P. (2011) *A History of Galileo's Inclined Plane Experiment and Its Philosophical Implications*, Lewiston: The Edwin Mellen Press.
Prudovsky, G. (1989) "The confirmation of the superposition principle: On the role of a constructive thought experiment in Galileo's Discorsi," *Studies in History and Philosophy of Science* 20: 453–468.
Reeves, E. (2002) "Occult sympathies and antipathies: The case of early modern magnetism," in *Wissensideale und Wissenskulturen in der frühen Neuzeit. Ideals and Cultures of Knowledge in Early Modern Europe*, edited by W. Detel and K. Zittel, Berlin: Akademie Verlag.
Settle, T. (1961) "An experiment in the History of Science," *Science* 133: 19–23.
Shapin, S. (1996) *The Scientific Revolution*, Chicago: University of Chicago Press.
Vergara-Caffarelli, R. (2009) *Galileo Galilei and Motion: A Reconstruction of 50 Years of Experiments and Discoveries*, Bologna: Società Italiana di Fisica; Berlin: Springer.
Wootton, D. (2010) *Galileo: Watcher of the Skies*, New Haven: Yale University Press.
Zabarella, G. (1590) *De rebus naturalibus libri XXX*, Cologne: Ioannis Baptistæ Ciotti Senensis ære.

6
THOUGHT EXPERIMENTS IN NEWTON AND LEIBNIZ

Richard T. W. Arthur

There are many notable thought experiments in the writings of the two great natural philosophers Isaac Newton (1642–1727) and Gottfried Leibniz (1646–1716). The one most often cited from Newton's work is his thought experiment with the rotating bucket, by which he undermined Descartes's relational account of motion. Leibniz's most famous work, perhaps, is the thought experiment concerning the mill given in his *Monadology*, which he uses to argue for the non-reducibility of perception to mechanical operations. The former still plays a seminal role in arguments about the ontological status of spacetime; the latter may be considered ancestral to John Searle's Chinese Room thought experiment. Another of Leibniz's work which is still very topical is the thought experiment underlying the so-called Leibniz Shift arguments, where we are asked to imagine whether there would be any discernible change if, without any change in the mutual situations of its constituents, the whole created world were either reflected about a plane so that east is changed to west, or (in response to Samuel Clarke's counterargument) moved along a straight line with a certain velocity. Another of Newton's thought experiment occurs in his *De gravitatione*, in which, imagining God to have endowed certain portions of extension with the properties of mobility and impenetrability (subject to the laws of collision), together with perceptibility, he asks whether we could distinguish these from the bodies apparent to the senses.

One can detect a theme underlying these various thought experiments, and some others besides. This is the attempt to use indistinguishability arguments to throw light on the nature of motion and matter. So rather than proceeding case by case, I will situate these thought experiments in a continuous narrative based on that theme. This will also allow me to introduce along the way one or two lesser-known thought experiments (TEs) that occur in their writings. A case in point is the TE Newton gave in *De gravitatione*, which is very revealing about his views on substance and God's relation to the created world.

1 Newton's "creating matter from space" TE

It is no exaggeration to say that the locus of dispute between Newton and Leibniz, and indeed the very thing that caused them to fall out, was Newton's notion – anathema to

Leibniz – that God could cause things to happen (non-miraculously) in the natural world by dint of his will alone, without any material intermediaries through which his will could be made effective.[1] Newton drew succour for this position by an appeal to the efficacy of the human will (where there is no question of miracles being performed). This is made clear in *De gravitatione*, a manuscript of uncertain date that was not published until 1962, although its importance for understanding Newton's philosophy has been appreciated ever since. There Newton argued as follows:

> Since each man is conscious that he can move his body at will, and believes further that other men enjoy the same power of similarly moving their bodies by thought alone, the free power of moving bodies can by no means be denied to God, whose faculty of thought is infinitely greater and more swift. And for the same reason it must be agreed that God, by the sole action of thinking and willing, can prevent a body from penetrating any space defined by certain limits.
>
> (Newton 2004, 27)

This prompts Newton to construct a thought experiment, the first of the TEs based on indistinguishability arguments that I wish to consider here.

Suppose, Newton writes, that God made some part of space impervious to bodies, so that it might "resist the motions of bodies, and perhaps reflect them, and assume all the properties of a corporeal particle" (2004, 28). Suppose further that this impenetrable part of space could be transferred while retaining its quantity and shape. "I do not see why," he continues, "it would not equally operate upon our minds and in turn be operated upon." In this way, movable spaces of this kind, impervious to bodies and to each other, "would sustain all the vicissitudes of corpuscles and exhibit the same phenomena." He continues:

> And hence these beings will either be bodies or very similar to bodies. If they are bodies, then we can define bodies as *determined quantities of extension which omnipresent God endows with certain conditions*. These conditions are: (1) that they are movable ... definite quantities [of space] which may be transferred from space to space; (2) that two of this kind cannot coincide anywhere, that is, that they may be impenetrable, and hence that oppositions obstruct their mutual motions and they are reflected in accordance with certain laws; (3) that they can excite various perceptions of the senses and the imagination in created minds, and conversely be moved by them, which is not surprising since the description of their origin is founded on this.
>
> (Newton 2004, 28)

So defined, "these beings will be no less real than bodies, nor ... less able to be called substances" (29). Given the indistinguishability of these beings from the bodies we observe, Newton claims, he has "deduced a description of this corporeal nature from our faculty of moving our bodies," so that "God may appear (to our innermost consciousness) to have created the world solely by the act of will, just as we move our bodies by the act of will alone" (30).

Newton stops short of claiming that bodies actually are just movable volumes of extension with these properties; he has too much respect for God's power to do things beyond what he himself can imagine[2]: "I would rather describe a certain kind of being similar in every way to bodies, and whose creation we cannot deny to be within the power of God, so that we can hardly say that it is not body" (2004, 27). He does not infer identity from indiscernibility in principle, as did Descartes with his famous thought experiment with the wax in the second of his *Meditations*. There Descartes asks us to abstract away from all sensible qualities until only extension, together with its properties of shape, size and movability, remains; such a part of extension he then identifies as body, intelligibly conceived.[3] But, argues Newton,

> extension is eternal, infinite, uncreated, uniform throughout, not in the least mobile, nor capable of inducing change of motion in bodies or change of thought in the mind; whereas body is opposite in every respect, at least if God did not choose to create it always and everywhere. For I should not dare to deny God that power.
>
> (Newton 2004, 33)

In fact, Newton explicitly contrasts his thought experiment with Descartes's:

> Let us abstract from body (as [Descartes] demands) gravity, hardness, and all sensible qualities, so that nothing remains except what pertains to its essence. Will extension alone then remain? By no means. For we may also reject that faculty or power by which [the qualities] stimulate the perceptions of thinking things. For since there is so great a distinction between the ideas of thought and of extension that it is not obvious that there is any basis of connection or relation [between them], except that which is caused by divine power, the above capacity of bodies can be rejected while preserving extension, but not while preserving their corporeal nature.
>
> (34)

There are thus two essential properties of bodies lacking in Descartes's movable portions of extension: their capacity to stimulate perceptions in the minds of thinking things, and their receptivity to being moved by such minds, as evidenced in our own ability to move our limbs by force of will.

Although it remained unpublished until the 1960s, this TE did in fact have some indirect historical influence. This was through John Locke's discussion of creation *ex nihilo* in Book IV, Chapter X of his *Essay Concerning Human Understanding*. There he suggested that "if we could emancipate ourselves from vulgar notions," we might conceivably "be able to aim at some dim and seeming conception how *matter* might at first be made, and begin to exist, by the power of that eternal first Being: but to give beginning and being to *spirit* would be found a more inconceivable effect of omnipotent power" (Locke 1894, 321). Somewhat mischievously, though, Locke maintains a discreet silence as to how this might be done, piquing the interest of his contemporaries, including Leibniz and Reid.[4] Locke's translator Pierre Coste was equally baffled until he happened to be discussing this part of the *Essay* with Newton, long after Locke's death: "He told me, smiling, that he himself had suggested to Locke this way of explaining the creation of matter" (Locke 1894, 322). Coste's subsequent description of what Newton told him about how "we might have some rude idea of the creation of matter" corresponds in detail with the account in *De gravitatione*.

Leibniz never saw this thought experiment of Newton's, nor did he know that this is what Locke was alluding to. But by the 1690s he certainly knew that it was Newton's view that God could create things by his will alone, and that his will could act on homogeneous mathematical objects like space even if there was no discriminating factor in the material on which his will was supposed to act. He also became aware that this view was shared by those in Newton's circle, such as Samuel Clarke. For it was one of the main points of dispute in his controversy with Clarke in the last two years of his life. There are several components of this view that Leibniz objects to, all of them pre-dating his apprehension of Newton's own views, concerning what it presupposes about individuation, about free will, about the relation of God to his creation, and about the absoluteness of space.

Let us examine Leibniz's views on individuation first.

2 Leibniz on individuation: the two squares TE

A thought experiment that recurs in Leibniz's unpublished work concerns the Principle of Individuation. This is directed at purely geometrical accounts of body, such as are found in Descartes, and also in his dissident atomist follower, Gerauld de Cordemoy. Like Newton, Leibniz objects that a pure extension without any connection with mind will be inadequate to constitute body. But where Newton contends that God can equip atoms of extension with the necessary properties by his sheer will, the gist of Leibniz's argument is that a geometric atom will lack any principle by which God could individuate it in the first place. Regarded as a purely geometric entity, there will be nothing in it to indicate its place in its own causal history, and therefore nothing to distinguish it from another equivalent entity with a different causal history. He first articulates the thought experiment in a "Meditation on the Principle of Individuation" on 1 April, 1676 (A VI iii 490–91/DSR 51–53), and then reiterates it as a criticism of Cordemoy in his notes of 1685 on the latter's *Treatise*. In the latter it goes as follows:

> Let us suppose two triangular atoms come into contact and compose a perfect square, and that they rest next to each other in this way; and let there be another corporeal substance or atom, a square one equal to the composite of the latter two. I ask, in what respect do these two extended things differ? Certainly no difference can be conceived in them as they are now, unless we suppose something in bodies besides extension; rather they are distinguished solely by memory of their former conditions, and there is nothing of this kind in bodies [geometrically conceived]. How can they become different in themselves afterwards, as in the case where they are struck by some third body in such a way that one breaks into parts and the other does not? This is a difficulty for all atomists, and obliges one to admit that there is something else in matter apart from extension.
>
> (A VI iv 1799/LoC 279)

In the 1676 version of this thought experiment, the two square atoms were imagined as being produced by the merging of two right-angled triangles and two half-square rectangles, respectively. He argues that the effect must involve its cause; but in this case, two different causes or means of production produce the same effect, exactly the same square, bearing no mark of how it was produced. "Neither of these squares can be distinguished from the other in any way, not even by the wisest being" (A VI iii 490–91/DSR 51). Here also Leibniz did not dwell on the idealization of considering atoms in only two dimensions, but was intent on establishing the necessity for a mind in each atom to serve as its principle of individuation.

> And so it is impossible that two squares of this kind should be perfectly similar; for they will consist of matter, but that matter will have a mind, and the mind will retain the effect of its former state. And indeed, unless we admit that it is impossible that there should be two things which are perfectly similar, it will follow that the principle of individuation is outside the thing, in its cause. It will follow that the effect does not involve the cause ... But if we admit that two different things always differ in themselves in some respect as well, it follows that there is present in any matter something which retains the effect of what precedes it, namely a mind.
>
> (A VI iii 490–91/DSR 51)

That Leibniz should single out "mind" as the principle of individuation seems extravagant from a modern point of view. But what he is trying to establish is that there must be some mark within the atom that bears traces of its own history, and that this cannot be found if the atom is conceived as a merely geometrical entity (as it is by Descartes and Cordemoy). Thus it is necessary to concede that in order for two different things to exist, they must "always differ in themselves in some respect as well" – or, conversely, that two existing things that are in principle indiscernible are in fact the same thing. This is the principle that Leibniz will later promote as his Principle of the Identity of Indiscernibles (PIIs). Note that it only applies to existing things, things that have a causal history. It is perfectly possible to conceive two perfectly similar things, such as the two perfectly similar atoms here; but such purely geometric entities, being everywhere similar, do not have sufficient complexity to be regarded as existents. Thus the PII entails both that each existing thing must be internally distinguished from any other existing thing, and that a purely mathematical entity does not have sufficient determining characteristics to qualify as an existing thing.

3 The Leibniz shift TEs

Precisely analogous considerations informed Leibniz's thinking about both space and motion in the same period (1676–77). In what may be regarded as one of the first studies in his *Analysis Situs*, the essay *Principia mechanica*,[5] Leibniz defines a *situs* or situation as "a mode according to which any body can be found, even though we recognize nothing in it specifically by which it can be distinguished from the others" (A VI iii 103/Arthur 2013b, 108). As such, it is a geometrical notion, a body's situation being determined by its angles to and distances from surrounding bodies. Motion, geometrically understood, is simply change of situation. In the essay Leibniz conducts a thought experiment in which he asks the reader to imagine two bodies A and B, moving uniformly toward one another with a relative velocity v. He considers six cases, where first A and then B is considered as being at rest; then each moving toward the other with velocity $½v$, and then moving uniformly in the same direction with a difference in velocities of v; and then viewed from a third body C, first assumed to be at rest, and then moving with uniform velocity in relation to both. In each case the phenomena will appear the same, so that not even an omniscient being will be able to determine which body is in absolute motion: "whatever speed or direction we attribute by assuming an absolute motion for one of the bodies, we will always find that anyone must then understand motion in the others in such a way that everything will appear as before" (109/114). This constitutes Leibniz's most explicit argument for what he will later call the Principle of the Equivalence of Hypotheses.

All this, however, concerns motion insofar as it is *understood geometrically*, that is, as simply change of situation. In the same paper Leibniz adduces an important distinction between *motion understood geometrically* and *motion with respect to cause*. Motion understood as change of situation is entirely relative. But when it is understood with respect to cause, it can be attributed to the thing that involves the cause: "in the case of two bodies, motion is attributed to that one which contains the cause of their mutual situation having changed" (104/109). Identifying the body that involves the cause must be done on the basis of a physical hypothesis, namely one "which involves reference to a cause from which the remaining changes may be derived more easily" (111/115). And this *most intelligible hypothesis*, as Leibniz will later call it, is to be taken as true. On this basis Leibniz argues that the Copernican hypothesis "would certainly seem to be sufficiently corroborated" (105/110), citing numerous empirical phenomena and the fact that "these things can be explained more distinctly by the supposed motion of the earth and its being reduced to a simple cause" (111/115).[6]

This distinction between motion geometrically considered and motion with respect to cause thus perfectly parallels the arguments for the PII in the TE discussed above. In each case no determination can be made by appeal to objects considered geometrically; instead a consideration of cause is required. In early 1677, Leibniz argues that these considerations about the relativity of motion (geometrically conceived) also rule out an absolute or container space with respect to which motions are to be determined:

> If *space* is a certain thing supposed in pure extension, whilst the nature of *matter* is to fill space, and *motion* is change of space, then motion will be something absolute; and so when two bodies are approaching one another, it will be possible to tell which of them is in motion and which at rest; or, if both are moving, with what speed they are moving. And from this will follow those conclusions which I once showed in the *Theory of Motion Abstractly Considered*. But in reality space is not such a thing, and motion is not something absolute, but consists in relation.
>
> ("Space and motion are really relations,"
> A VI iv 1968/ LoC 225)

Here Leibniz abjures the laws of collision he himself had published in the *Theoria Motus Abstracta* (1672) as depending on a preferred space, whereas by 1676 he recognized (perhaps after discussions with Huygens) that the conservation of quantity of motion (and thus the then accepted laws of mechanics) depends only on "relative motion," i.e., velocity difference.[7] Here we can see that his objection to taking space as something absolute predates Newton's public endorsement of absolute space in his *Principia* of 1687 by ten years.

In his famous correspondence with Samuel Clarke in the last two years of his life, Leibniz skilfully develops these arguments into a battery of thought experiments now known as *Leibniz Shift* arguments. In the first of these, given in his Third Paper, Leibniz asks us to consider a scenario where God creates the world in two different ways round with respect to absolute space:

> Space is something absolutely uniform, and without the things placed in it one point of space does not absolutely differ in any respect from another point of space. Now from hence it follows (supposing space to be something in itself, besides the order of bodies among themselves) that 'tis impossible there should be a reason why God, preserving the same situations of bodies among themselves, should have placed them in space after one certain particular manner and not otherwise; why everything was not placed the quite contrary way, for instance, by changing east into west. But if space is nothing else by that order or relation, and is nothing at all without the bodies but the possibility of placing them, then those two states, the one such as now is, and the other supposed to be the quite contrary way, would not at all differ from one another. Their difference therefore is to be found in our chimerical supposition of the reality of space in itself.
>
> (Third Paper, §5; *PPL* 682)

Here Leibniz is putting into play two of his cherished principles. According to his Principle of Sufficient Reason (PSR), "nothing happens why it should be so rather than otherwise." Thus if space is homogeneous, so that the points cannot be individuated save by what is situated in them, it follows that, if we suppose with Newton that such a mathematical space exists as a container of all the bodies prior to God creating them, then God could have no reason to place the bodies (with all their mutual relations preserved) one way in that space rather than another. Since nothing happens without a reason, it could not happen that God would create things in such a space one way round rather than the other. According to his Principle of the Identity of Indiscernibles (PIIs), any two things which are in principle indiscernible are in fact identical. Thus, if God's creating all the things arranged in space one way is indistinguishable in principle from his having created them the opposite way (with east switched with west), then the two arrangements are identical. The alleged difference is an illusion resulting from the supposition that they are created in an independently existing space.

Now, Clarke accepts Leibniz's PSR. But because, like Newton, he regards the will as being able to cause things to happen in the body, he does not accept that the will alone is not a reason.[8] God can will things to happen in the space in which he is omnipresent with infinitely more facility than we can will certain things to happen in our sensorium to which our minds our present. Accordingly, he responds:

> And there is this evident absurdity in supposing space not to be real, but to be merely the order of bodies – that, according to that notion, if the earth and sun and moon had been placed where the remotest fixed stars now are, provided they were placed in the same order and distance they now are with regard to one another, it would not only have been (as this author rightly says,) *la même chose*, the same thing in effect, which is very true; but it would also follow that they would then have been in the same place too as they are now: which is an express contradiction.
>
> (Third Reply, §2; *PPL* 685)

But this reply presupposes that the places of the earth, sun, and moon are places in absolute space that are individuated independently of those bodies, and thus begs the question. Clarke ignores Leibniz's argument that, given the homogeneity of mathematical space, the points can only be individuated by what is situated at them. Perhaps this is easier to see in the second of the thought experiments Leibniz offers, concerning time.

"Supposing any one should ask," Leibniz writes, "why God did not create every thing *one year sooner*; and the same person should infer from thence that God has done something concerning which 'tis not possible there should be a *reason* why he did it *so and not otherwise*" (Third Paper, §6; *PPL* 682–83). To be explicit, suppose Newton is correct that absolute time exists independently of things, and that God created the world at some instant of this time, t_0, on the time axis between $-\infty$ and $+\infty$. Now if we suppose he could have created everything a year sooner, at $t_0 - 1$, with the whole order of things happening in time otherwise remaining the same, then he would have done something for which there could be no reason. For if the instants are all identical, save for their order, there is no way of distinguishing them from one another. So God could not have a sufficient reason for choosing one instant as opposed to the other, since even he cannot distinguish things that have all their properties in common.

To this Clarke objected that "if time was nothing but the order of succession of created things, it would follow that if God had created the world millions of years sooner than he did, yet it would not have been created at all the sooner" (Third Reply, §4; *PPL* 685). This assumes that the times could be identified independently of the things happening at them, just as Clarke had assumed about places. But if time is homogeneous, there is nothing to distinguish t_0 from $t_0 - 1$. If you say we can distinguish t_0 as the instant at which everything is created, the same goes for $t_0 - 1$: "the beginning, whenever it was, is always the same thing" (Fourth Paper, §15; *PPL* 688). Thus, as Leibniz had already concluded:

> the same argument proves that *instants* apart from things are *nothing*, and that they consist only in the successive *order* of things; which order remaining the same, *one* of the two states, for instance that of the imagined anticipation, would not be any different from, and could not be discerned from, the *other* which is now.
>
> (Third Paper, §6; *GP* VII 364/*PPL* 683)

Now Leibniz's concession here that the instants of mathematical time are all identical *save for their order* may seem to open a way of distinguishing them from one another. For in his manuscript *De gravitatione* Newton had explicitly claimed that the parts of duration and place are individuated by their place in the order:

> For ... the parts of duration are individuated by their order, so that (for example) if yesterday could change places with today and become the later of the two, it would lose its individuality and no longer be yesterday, but today; so that if any two could change their positions, they would change their individuality at the same time, and each would be converted numerically into the other. The parts of duration and space are understood to be the same as they really are only because of their mutual order and position; nor do they have any principle of individuation apart from that order and position, which consequently cannot be altered.
>
> (Newton 2004, 25)

But the "parts of duration" are for Newton not to be equated with the temporal locations of any *thing*, actual or possible: for duration is a mode of existence also of God, who exists independently of things. Accordingly he conceives the order as obtaining among the parts of time considered *prior to any states of things* that might individuate them: they are individuated solely by their position in the order. Thus whereas for Leibniz the parts of time, considered in themselves, are completely indiscernible and wholly similar, making time *homogeneous* – each such interval being identical with the ideal temporal continuum – for Newton, on the other hand, they are intrinsically distinguishable by their place in an order which exists absolutely (presumably in the mind of God), making time *inhomogeneous*. It is this very inhomogeneity of time or individuality of its parts prior to their being filled by things or events that makes for the immutability and immovability of absolute space and time, according to Newton:

> Just as the order of the parts of time is unchangeable, so too is the order of the parts of space. Suppose those parts to be moved out of their places and they will be moved (so to speak) out of themselves. For times and spaces are, as it were, the places of themselves and of all things.
>
> (Newton 1999, 410; translation slightly modified)

Leibniz's argument, on the other hand, is precisely that such a shift of everything in time with the mutual positions and intervals remaining intact would produce no discernible difference, because of the homogeneity of time in abstraction from the events happening at the times.[9] This anticipates in an important respect the connection recognized in modern physics between the *homogeneity of time* and the *invariance of the laws of physics under time translations*. That is, it is acknowledged that in a homogeneous time the translation of the dates and times of all events and states, say, backwards one year, can make no real difference to our description of the world. For if time were not homogeneous, then the same laws would not hold at one time as at another, and there would be a way of discerning a privileged time through the application of those laws.

In the case of space, two such "Leibniz Shift" arguments apply: because of the homogeneity of space in all three perpendicular directions, a translation of the whole existing world along any one of the three spatial axes will leave it exactly the same as before; and because of the *isotropy* of space, a *rotation* will also leave it invariant.[10] Also, because motion is at any instant an instantaneous tendency to move in a straight line, a shift of the whole world with a constant velocity in a straight line will again make no discernible difference. (This is the reasoning that Leibniz had applied in 1677 against absolute space: the laws of mechanics depend only on the relative velocities of bodies, and so do not recognize any one space as a preferred rest space.)

Clarke mounts an objection to such a velocity shift as follows:

> If space was nothing but the order of things coexisting, it would follow that if God should remove in a straight line the whole material world entire, with any swiftness whatsoever, yet it would always continue in the same place, and that nothing would receive any shock upon the most sudden stopping of that motion.
>
> (Third Reply, §4; PPL 685)

Of course, this again presupposes that the spaces can be individuated independently of the bodies in them, the very point Leibniz's argument is designed to refute. Newton and Clarke assume that the whole world could have a place in absolute space and a motion in absolute space, and that one could consider the world and its speed and acceleration from the standpoint of that space, considered as immobile. But according to Newton's own Corollaries 5 and 6 to his Laws of Motion,

> Corollary 5: When bodies are enclosed in a given space, their motions in relation to one another are the same whether the space is at rest or whether it is moving uniformly straight forward without circular motion.
>
> Corollary 6: If bodies are moving in any way whatsoever with respect to one another and are urged by equal accelerative forces along parallel lines, they will all continue to move with respect to one another in the same way as they would if they were not acted on by those forces.
>
> (Newton 1999, 423)

So, *contra* Clarke, Corollary 5 says you could not tell if the whole world were moving in a straight line with uniform speed; and Corollary 6 says that a sudden deceleration of all the bodies alike at the same time would not disturb their relative motions either. So, given that you are in that world, you could not discern it either. The vantage point that Clarke assumes for observing the "sudden shock" is non-existent.[11]

As has been observed before, given the equality of (passive) gravitational mass and inertial mass, Newton's Corollary 6 is a version of the Weak Equivalence Principle (WEP). Together they entail that the linear acceleration of a system of bodies will be indistinguishable from that same system of bodies moving inertially. But for Newton, this indistinguishability does not entail identity.[12] The accelerated system of bodies is accelerated with respect to absolute space. His best argument for this was given by him in his celebrated thought experiment with the bucket.

4 The reality of circular motion: Newton's bucket and two balls TEs

"True motion," Newton argued, "is neither generated nor changed except by forces impressed upon the moving body itself, but relative motion can be generated and changed without the impression of forces upon this body" (1999, 412). You can generate a change in a body's motion relative to yourself simply by moving yourself, without applying any force to the other body. But for Newton "absolute motions are determined only by means of unmoving places," the positions that "always remain immovable and constitute the space that I call immovable," namely absolute space (412).

As an example of an effect distinguishing absolute from relative motion, Newton appealed to the "forces of receding from the axis of circular motion" (412). For "in a purely relative circular motion these forces are null, while in true and absolute circular motion they are larger or smaller in proportion to the quantity of motion." In support of this, Newton presented the following TE:

> If a bucket is hanging from a very long cord and is continually turned around until the cord becomes twisted tight, and if the bucket is thereupon filled with water and then, by some sudden force is made to turn around in the opposite direction and, as the cord unwinds, perseveres for a while in this motion; then the surface of the water will at first be level, just as it was before the vessel began to move. But after the vessel, by the force gradually impressed upon the water, has caused the water also to begin revolving perceptibly, the water will gradually recede from the middle and rise up the sides of the vessel, assuming a concave shape (as experience has shown me), and, with an ever faster motion, will rise further and further until, when it completes its revolutions in the same times as the vessel, it is relatively at rest in the vessel.
>
> (Newton 1999, 412–13)

Although Descartes is nowhere mentioned by name, it would not be lost on Newton's contemporaries that his argument constitutes a beautiful refutation of the criterion proposed by Descartes for identifying true motion: "Motion in the strict sense is to be referred solely to bodies which are contiguous with the body in motion" (*Principia Philosophiae* [1644]; Descartes 1985, 234). For, after the bucket has begun to spin, the water in the bucket takes some time to pick up its motion, so that its surface initially remains flat. Here there is maximal relative motion between the two surfaces, but no centrifugal endeavour. But when, after several seconds, the water has picked up the motion of the bucket, its surface takes a concave shape, and it climbs the side of the pail (actually in beautiful spiral arms, like a spiral galaxy). Yet, according to Descartes's criterion, the water is at rest relative to the sides of the bucket, and therefore there is no motion in the strict sense.

So Descartes is wrong: the centrifugal endeavour of the water to rise up the sides of the bucket "does not depend on the change of the position of the water with respect to surrounding bodies," writes Newton, but is rather a unique effect of the "truly circular motion of each revolving body" (Newton 1999, 413). This motion is absolute, not relative to the bucket, and must be represented as such in a presupposed absolute space.

But how could one determine a motion relative to absolute space? Here Leibniz's shift argument appears to be decisive. If we allow that a system of bodies, such as the room in which the bucket experiment is conducted, is a relative space in Newton's sense, then the bucket will also be rotating with the same rotational velocity in any relative space moving inertially with respect to it. So it fails to support Newton's idea that the space in which the rotation is represented is a unique mathematical space.

Leibniz did not address this TE directly. Given his response to the Copernican case, he should have noted that we know the reason for the water's motion, namely the work done in winding up the cord holding the bucket. So the hypothesis that the bucket is rotating and not the whole universe around it is the most intelligible hypothesis, and therefore true. Instead, regarding circular motion, he insisted that "since circulation also arises only from the composition of rectilinear motions, it follows that if the equipollence of hypotheses holds in whatever rectilinear motions are supposed, it will also hold in curvilinear ones" (GM VI 253). This is not the case, and involves a subtle fallacy of composition. Nonetheless, Leibniz was correct in denying that Newton's criterion establishes that the motion must be relative to absolute space.

Newton cedes the difficulty of distinguishing true motions from merely apparent ones, given that "the parts of that immovable space in which the bodies truly move make no impression on the senses" (414). As is well known, the Austrian philosopher Ernst Mach takes him to task for this, arguing that in mechanics we only have access to the relative positions and motions of bodies (Mach 1919, 229). But in an attempt to forestall such criticism, Newton had offered a second thought experiment to show that the centrifugal force due to rotation would be empirically determinable even in an empty space:

> For example, if two balls, at a given distance from each other with a cord connecting them, were revolving about a common centre of gravity, the endeavour of the balls to recede from the axis of motion could be known from the tension of the cord, and thus the quantity of motion could be computed ... In this way, both the quantity and direction of this circular motion could be found in any immense vacuum, where nothing external and sensible existed with which the balls could be compared.
>
> (Newton 1999, 414)

In response, Mach concedes that if the earth is rotating, a centrifugal force will be produced, the plane of Foucault's pendulum will rotate, and so on, and that "all these phenomena disappear if the earth is at rest and the other heavenly bodies are affected with absolute motion round it, such that the same *relative* rotation is produced" (Mach 1919, 231). But, he argues, this is to assume an absolute motion in space, whereas all our knowledge is of relative spaces and motions. "The universe is not *twice* given, with an earth at rest and an earth in motion; but only *once*, with its *relative* motions, alone determinable. It is, accordingly, not permitted us to say how things would be if the earth did not rotate" (232). He suggested that, for all we know, the same phenomena might be produced by the rotation of the whole universe around the earth, and might be the effect of the distribution of distant matter.

The latter idea was developed by Einstein into what he called "Mach's Principle," in his attempt to construct his theory of General Relativity (GR), even though he was later to recognize that it was not supported by the resulting theory. Moreover, it is no more true in GR than in classical or special relativity that rotation is purely relative. Circular motion cannot be transformed away without having to appeal to otherwise unmotivated ad hoc forces to explain the phenomena. In this regard, Newton's argument for the reality of circular motion is vindicated.

5 Physical identity: Locke's day- and night-men and Leibniz's two spheres TE

In his dialogue with the views of Locke on identity, Leibniz reiterated his position that "in addition to the difference of time and place, there must always be an internal *principle of distinction*: although there can be many things of the same kind, it is still the case that none of them is ever exactly alike" (*NE* 230). As we saw above, in his argument for this PII, Leibniz appeals to the causal history of the individual in question as always providing some distinguishing feature consonant with its being up at a particular place and time: "it is by means of things that we must distinguish one time and place from another, rather than *vice versa*; for times and places are in themselves perfectly alike" (*NE* 230). And not finding a basis for such a feature in matter geometrically conceived, he sought it in something analogous to a mind that could possess *memory*.

This provided a basis for some agreement with Locke on the matter of personal identity, since Locke claimed that consciousness is what constitutes personal identity. "Since consciousness always accompanies thinking," Locke argued in his *Essay*, "and 'tis that which makes every one to be, what he calls *self*; and thereby distinguishes himself from all other thinking things, in this alone consists personal identity" (*NE* 235). Up to a point, Leibniz agrees: "I also hold this opinion that consciousness or the sense of *I* proves moral or personal identity" (*NE* 235). But for him, while this is a criterion for distinguishing persons from non-rational animals, it is not a sufficient condition for the identity of any individual substance, since it presupposes the *"real, physical identity"* of the substance in question. For personal identity requires that the soul "should also retain a moral identity which is apparent to us ourselves, so as to constitute the same person, which is therefore sensitive to punishments and rewards" (*NE* 236). Locke, however, rejects the idea of a physical identity constituted by a soul (or soul-like substance) on the grounds that souls, as far as we know anything of them, "are indifferent to any parcel of matter," so that there is no apparent absurdity in the supposition that a soul could pass from one body to another (*NE* 239). To establish that only consciousness is pertinent to personal identity, he proposes the following thought experiment:

> If we could suppose either that two distinct incommunicable consciousnesses might act alternately in the same body, the one constantly by day, the other by night; or that the same consciousness might act by intervals in two distinct bodies; I ask in the first case, whether the *day-* and the *night-man* would not be two as distinct persons as Socrates and Plato; and whether in the second case, there would not be one person in two distinct bodies, as much as one man is the same in two distinct clothings?
> (Bk. II Ch. xxvii, §23; *NE* 245)

Leibniz demurs on two counts. First, whether or not other people were aware of the change, it would have occurred, and God would know of it. More importantly, though, the "divorce" that Locke supposes "between the insensible perceptions which remained in the same substances and the states of awareness which were exchanged would be a miracle" (*NE* 245). So he replies with a TE of his own:

Here is something we could much more fittingly suppose: in another region of the universe or at some other time there may be a sphere in no way sensibly different from this sphere of Earth on which we live, and inhabited by men each of whom differs sensibly in no way from his counterpart among us. Thus at one time there will be a hundred million pairs of similar persons, i.e. pairs of persons with the same appearances and states of consciousness. God could transfer the minds, by themselves or with their bodies, from one sphere to the other without their being aware of it; but whether they are transferred or left where they are, what would your authorities say about their persons or "selves"? ... [S]ince according to your theories consciousness alone distinguishes persons, with no need for us to be concerned about the real identity or diversity of substance, or even about what would appear to other people, what is to prevent us from saying that these two persons who are at the same time in these two similar but inexpressibly distant spheres, are one and the same person? Yet that would be a manifest absurdity.

(Bk. II Ch. xxvii; *NE* 245)

The real identity that Leibniz proposes must underlie that sameness of substance consists in a link between the states of the same substance, a trace in each state of those that had gone before. As he explains in the *New Essays*,

These insensible perceptions also indicate and constitute the same individual, which is characterized by the traces or expressions they preserve of the previous states of this individual, thereby connecting these with its present state; and even when this individual itself has no sense of these traces of previous states, that is to say, when there is no longer any explicit memory of them, they could be known by a superior mind.

(A VI vi 55; *NE* 55)

Thus consciousness is not necessary to physical identity, contra Locke. A rational being will be able (under the right circumstances) to recognize the traces of prior states or perceptions, and it is in this that conscious memory consists. But even unconscious organisms (including comatose humans) must have something analogous to a memory in order to maintain their own identity and thus to constitute selves.

6 Leibniz's mill: the irreducibility of perception

Leibniz did not accept Newton's idea that mind could act on matter, or that in perception matter acted upon the mind. But he did accept that the mind is active, and that only by conceiving it as active could it qualify as an agent. Thus he was led to posit a perfect parallelism: as the mind or soul forms its perceptions and intentions, so the bodies apparently acting on its sensory organs or limbs perform precisely corresponding motions. "The soul does not act upon things, according to my opinion, any otherwise than because the body adapts itself to the desires of the soul, by virtue of the harmony which God has pre-established between them" (Fourth Paper, §31; *PPL* 689). The very idea that perception could be explained in terms of mechanical causation was to Leibniz unintelligible. In the *Monadology* he gave a thought experiment designed to show the absurdity of such a conception:

> Imagine a machine which by its structure produced thought, feeling, and perception. We can imagine it as being enlarged while retaining the same relative proportions to the point where we could go inside it, as we would go into a mill. But if that were so, we would find nothing but pieces pushing against one another, and never anything to account for a perception.
>
> (§17, GP VI 609/PPL 644)

The argument is not that nothing mechanical will be going on physiologically in perception; indeed Leibniz is adamant that to every perception or thought in the mind there must be corresponding motions and resistances in the tissues of the brain. What Leibniz denies is that perception itself is something mechanical. This is not because he is some sort of vitalist; for Leibniz, organism is in fact an exquisite kind of mechanism. But the mechanical organization of any living organism is so complex – infinitely complex, according to him – that it cannot be duplicated by any man-made automaton. In both these respects his argument can be seen as anticipating the arguments given by John Searle through the vehicle of his Chinese Room thought experiment (Searle 1980; Cole 2015). No matter how well the effects of intelligence can be duplicated mechanically, both refuse to accept that such indistinguishability entails identity.

Notes

1 See Leibniz's letter to Hartsoeker, 10 February 1711, published in translation in 1712 in the *Memoirs of Literature*; and Newton's response of May 1712; both given by Andrew Janiak in (Newton 2004, 109–17).
2 As Liam Dempsey writes in a perceptive article on Newton's philosophy of mind, "In deference to God's creative powers, Newton does not wish to say definitively what the actual nature of body is" (Dempsey 2006, 423, n. 10).
3 Here mention should also be made of Thomas Hobbes's thought experiment in *De corpore*, part II, chapter vii, concerning place and time. Hobbes writes that in teaching natural philosophy he can think of no better way to begin "than from privation, that is, from feigning the world to be annihilated" (Hobbes 1905, 43). If we suppose such an annihilation of all things, what remains of space? A "phantasm," is Hobbes's answer; to consider what was in the world, not specifically, but only insofar as it "had a being without the mind" would be to have a "conception of that we call space" (44–45).
4 Leibniz speculated that perhaps he had in mind "the Platonists who took matter for something fleeting and passing," and Reid was led to claim that the system Locke hints at "in every particular ... tallies exactly with the system of Berkeley." See Locke (1894, 321, n. 2). For discussion see Stein (2002, 272–73), and Dempsey (2006).
5 This essay was published in its original Latin in the *Akademie* edition (A VI iii 101–11), and translated with commentary by myself in Arthur (2013b). It was probably written some time between late summer of 1676 and February of 1677.
6 Leibniz continues to uphold this position in his mature dynamics: both the idea that motion conceived geometrically is purely relative, and the idea that the hypothesis that yields the most intelligible explanation should be taken as true. Cf. *Dynamica*, Prop. 19: "Universally, when motion occurs, we find nothing in bodies by which it could be determined except change of situation, which always consists in relation (*in respectu*). Thus motion by its nature is respective. But

7 "The conservation of the quantity of motion must be asserted of the action, i.e. relative motion, by which one body is referred to or acts on another" (*On Motion and Matter* [April 1676], A VI iii 493/*LoC* 79).
8 Cf. Clarke, Third Reply §5 (*PPL* 685), and Fifth Reply: "In which case, the parts of space being exactly alike, 'tis evident there can be no reason, but mere *will*, for not having originally *transposed* their situations" (*GP* VII 422).
9 Tim Maudlin (2012, 41–42) argues that since the "distinct points of absolute space are supposed to be qualitatively identical, the PII implies that there cannot really be more than one of them, but E^3 contains more than one point." But as we have seen, Leibniz conceives the PII to apply to existing things, not to abstractions. Cf. his remark to Clarke: "The supposition of two indiscernibles, such as two pieces of matter perfectly alike, seems indeed to be possible in abstract terms, but is not consistent with the order of things, nor with the divine wisdom, by which nothing is admitted without a reason" (Fifth Paper, §21, *PPL* 699).
10 Another celebrated TE offered by Leibniz that is closely related to these "Leibniz shift" arguments is one that would now be understood as an example of a *gauge symmetry*. "If all the things that we observe in the world were diminished in the same proportion, it is evident that we would not be able to notice the change" (A II i 380; translated from the French quotation given by De Risi in his 2016, p. 51, n. 49). Or, as he expresses it in the *Specimen Geometriae luciferae* of the mid-1690s, "if God made the sphere of the universe [*orbem universum*] greater while conserving the same proportion among all its parts, there would be no principle by which this could be observed" (GM VII 266).
11 The same objection applies to Maudlin's criticisms of these thought experiments of Leibniz, all of which criticisms presuppose that positions and velocities in absolute space are identifiable independently of bodies and their motions. For example, he argues that since God could give the whole world "any absolute velocity in that space without affecting the relative positions and motions of bodies," and in any given direction, he would have no reason for giving it a velocity in any one direction: "there could be no reason to prefer one over another. The *only* absolute velocity that does not require a choice is the zero velocity, absolute rest. So the PSR, far from prohibiting any choice of absolute velocity for the material world, demands exactly one choice" (Maudlin 2012, 48–49). But if there is no basis for distinguishing one velocity from another in absolute space, these different scenarios are indistinguishable even to God, so he could have no reason for choosing any of them.
12 In this respect Einstein can be seen as having followed Leibniz's logic, promoting an indiscernibility in principle to an identity, in order to derive the Strong Equivalence Principle.

References

Arthur, R. T. W. (2013b) "Leibniz's *Mechanical Principles* (c. 1676): Commentary and translation," *The Leibniz Review* 23: 101–116.
Cole, D. (2015) "The Chinese room argument," *The Stanford Encyclopedia of Philosophy*. Available here: http://plato.stanford.edu/archives/win2015/entries/chinese-room/ (accessed 15 November 2016).
Dempsey, L. (2006) "Written in the flesh: Isaac Newton on the mind–body relation," *Studies in the History and Philosophy of Science* 37: 420–441.
De Risi, V. (2016) *Leibniz on the Parallel Postulate and the Foundations of Geometry*, Cham: Birkhäuser-Springer.
Descartes, R. (1985) *The Philosophical Writings of Descartes*, vol. 1, edited and translated by J. Cottingham, R. Stoothof and D. Murdoch, Cambridge: Cambridge University Press.
Gerhardt, C. I. (ed.) (1849–1863) *Leibnizens Mathematische Schriften*, 7 vols, Berlin and Halle: Asher and Schmidt; reprint ed. Hildesheim: Georg Olms, 1971; cited as GM VI 157, etc.
Gerhardt, C. I. (ed.) (1875–1890) *Die Philosophische Schriften von Gottfried Wilhelm Leibniz*, 7 vols, Berlin: Weidmann; reprint ed. Hildesheim: Olms, 1960; cited as GP II 268, etc.

Hobbes, T. (1905) *Metaphysical Writings*, edited by M. W. Calkins, La Salle: Open Court.
Leibniz, G. W. (1923–) *Sämtliche Schriften und Briefe*, Akademie der Wissenschaften der DDR, Darmstadt and Berlin: Akademie-Verlag; cited as A VI III 229, etc.
Leibniz, G. W. (1969) *Philosophical Papers and Letters*, 2nd ed., edited and translated by L. Loemker, Dordrecht: D. Reidel; abbreviated *PPL*.
Leibniz, G. W. (1981) *New Essays on Human Understanding*, translated and edited by P. Remnant and J. Bennett, Cambridge: Cambridge University Press; abbreviated *NE*.
Leibniz, G. W. (1992) *De Summa Rerum: Metaphysical Papers, 1675–1676*, translated by G. H. R. Parkinson, New Haven: Yale University Press; abbreviated *DSR*.
Leibniz, G. W. (2001) *The Labyrinth of the Continuum: Writings on the Continuum Problem, 1672–1686*, edited, selected and translated by R. T. W. Arthur, New Haven: Yale University Press; abbreviated *LoC*.
Locke, J. (1894) *An Essay Concerning Human Understanding*, 2 vols, collated and annotated, with prolegomena, biographical, critical and historical by A. C. Fraser, Oxford: Clarendon Press.
Mach, E. (1919) *The Science of Mechanics*, translated by T. J. McCormack, Chicago: Open Court.
Maudlin, T. (2012) *Philosophy of Physics: Space and Time*, Princeton: Princeton University Press.
Newton, I. (1962) *Unpublished Scientific Papers of Isaac Newton*, edited and translated by A. R. Hall and M. B. Hall, Cambridge: Cambridge University Press.
Newton, I. (1999) *The Principia: Mathematical Principles of Mathematical Philosophy*, edited and translated by I. B. Cohen and A. Whitman, Berkeley: University of California Press.
Newton, I. (2004) *Newton: Philosophical Writings*, edited by A. Janiak, Cambridge: Cambridge University Press.
Searle, J. (1980) "Minds, brains and programs," *Behavioral and Brain Sciences* 3: 417–457.
Stein, H. (2002) "Newton's metaphysics," in *The Cambridge Companion to Newton*, edited by I. B. Cohen and G. E. Smith, Cambridge: Cambridge University Press.

7
THOUGHT EXPERIMENTS, EPISTEMOLOGY AND OUR COGNITIVE (IN)CAPACITIES

Kenneth R. Westphal

1 Introduction

Credible, informative epistemology has been difficult, even before Descartes's *Meditations* elevated it to first philosophy, not least because we must use most if not all of our cognitive capacities to consider and to specify the character, scope and limits of our cognitive capacities. Worse yet, the problem of global perceptual scepticism appears as easy to formulate as it is difficult to solve: simply as a matter of logic, all of our beliefs, thoughts and experiences could appear to us to be just as they are, even if none were veridical (Stroud 1994). Since Gettier, Quine and Davidson, it may well appear that philosophers can only reply to sceptics by telling them to get lost, Rorty (1986) suggested. Gettier's (1963) famous counter-examples to analysing the concept "knowledge" exhaustively into the concepts of "justification," "truth" and "belief" all turn on contextual factors, of which the benighted protagonist of his examples, Smith, is unaware, and of which he could not become aware merely by reflecting upon his own attitudes, beliefs or experiences. Varieties of epistemological externalism flourished in response. Quine (1969, 75) belittled the "make believe" involved in the empiricist attempt to reconstruct the world on the sole bases of logic and one's own (putative) sensory experiences, advising instead to naturalize epistemology by embracing cognitive psychology. Davidson (1987 [2001, 154]) conceded to Rorty's (1986) suggestion.

Does epistemology collapse for lack of resources other than logic, conceptual analysis and descriptions of one's own apparent experiences, thoughts and beliefs? No, but understanding how and why not requires, Kant noted, a "changed method of thinking" (*veränderte Methode der Denkungsart; KdrV* Bxvii, 704). Some of these methodological changes are summarized in §2 in order to identify a philosophical role for thought experiments to help identify logically contingent, though cognitively fundamental capacities and circumstances necessary to human thought, experience and knowledge. As Kant also noted, experiments are only informative in response to posing the right question, indeed: the right kind of question (*KdrV* Bxii–xiv). Accordingly, preparations for these epistemological thought experiments (§2) fill half of this chapter. The second half (§§3–5), examines three such thought experiments, variously developed by Kant, Hegel, C. I. Lewis, Austin, Wittgenstein and F. L. Will.

2 Some critical cautions and a role for thought experiments

To change one's "method of thinking" is not merely to exchange one philosophical method or one set of assumptions for another. It involves changing one's basic ways, means and strategies of *thinking*, one's whole approach to philosophizing, and thereby to change one's ways of using or assessing any philosophical method, or its scope, limits and results. Accordingly, the following remarks can only characterize some relevant changes and, I hope, make them plausible, though not defend them in detail.[1]

2.1 Conceivability, infallibilism and philosophical cogency

Global perceptual scepticism is logically possible. Is this logical possibility, conceivable as it is, epistemologically relevant? Why or how, exactly? Deductive logic concerns avoiding various fallacies by which false conclusions would be drawn from true premises. Although knowledge involves avoiding or minimizing error as far as possible, there is no good reason to think that, in addition to truth (or sufficient accuracy) and belief, the justification condition(s) for knowledge can be specified or satisfied by deductive logic alone – however one may analyse one's concepts, beliefs or apparent experiences. Why suppose that cognitive justification sufficient for knowledge must eliminate any and all logically possible, merely conceivable alternative states of affairs – whether regarding the content of the belief or claim, its origins, or whatever else may be thought to contribute to or to constitute its cognitive justification? If one could exclude or eliminate any and all logically possible alternatives, that would certainly suffice to guarantee the truth of the belief or claim in question, but why think failure to exclude or eliminate all logically possible alternatives is required for knowledge, specifically: for cognitive justification?

Infallibilism about cognitive justification is most familiar from Descartes's attempt to outwit the possibility of a malignant, deceptive genie. Descartes's attempt is vitiated, not by one, but five distinct vicious circularities.[2] The worst concerns the prospect that, not the Divinity, but rather the malignant genie imbued Descartes with exactly the same innate ideas of simple natures as he reports having, including his idea of the Divinity, but so arranges the rest of creation that none of Descartes's ideas (other than that of his own occurrent thinking being) are true – especially his idea that any being with one perfection must have all perfections, because one divine perfection is that, within the Divinity, *all* perfections are simply *one* and unitary.[3] Descartes deliberately wrote meditations rather than disputations, but co-meditating epistemologists who do not receive the divine neo-Augustinian illumination to which Descartes purports to guide our attention, must instead develop a radically different approach to epistemology.

The classic empiricist alternative was to reduce all talk about physical objects and events to talk about elementary sensory episodes and various logical (re)constructions of them. Though often proposed, none came closer to achieving such a reduction or (re)construction than Carnap (1928). The most fundamental problem confronting any such (re)reconstruction is that either the (re)construction takes the temporality of the sequences we experience for granted, and so fails to complete the proposed reduction or (re)construction; or else appeal to unreconstructed temporal ordering is avoided, but then the reduction or (re)construction can only specify symmetrical relations amongst elementary sensory episodes which in principle fail to formulate the asymmetrical temporal relations involved in anyone's experiences, including those historical events investigated and explained by any empirical theory, including their procedures and processes of observation and data collection – all of which are temporally extended processes. Empiricist reductionism fails prior to posing issues about cognitive justification.

Infallibilist standards of cognitive justification would be wonderful, were they within our capacities. "Infallibilism" requires not only that strict logical deduction suffices, but also that it is necessary for cognitive justification. Infallibilism equates cognitive justification with provability. Provability constitutes justification, however, only within strictly formal domains. The one strictly formal domain is a properly reconstructed Aristotelian square of opposition; only within that domain are sentences provable (demonstrable) on the basis of form alone (Wolff 2009). All other domains involve various existence postulates, including semantic postulates. The adequacy and the use of these postulates cannot be assessed by formal methods alone. We can of course formalize various domains or linguistic frameworks (Lewis 1929 [1956], 298; Carnap 1950a), but within such formalized logistic systems, strict deduction can at most be necessary, though never sufficient for the justification of specific claims within their domains. The justification of specific claims always involves the further semantic or existence postulates constitutive of their domain, and requires the assessment of the use of those postulates in connection with the specific claim in question. This is no objection to formalized logistic systems; it is a fact. Problems for epistemology lie in failure to recognize this fact and its implications. One implication of this fact is that infallibilist standards of justification are appropriate *only* to formal domains. Empirical knowledge concerns spatio-temporal objects, events, persons, structures or processes. Accordingly, empirical knowledge is a non-formal domain. Hence infallibilist standards are not "too stringent," as has been frequently claimed: Infallibilist standards of justification are in principle *irrelevant* to empirical knowledge. As Kant noted, deductive logic is a canon for rational judgment, but (outside strictly formal domains) no organon for knowledge (*KdrV* A52–4, 60–1, 795–7/B76–8, 85–6, 823–5).

An important corollary to this interim finding is that the prime methodological problem confronting epistemology is to determine, within the domain of all logical possibilities, which possibilities pertain to human cognition. An important feature of this vast perplexity is highlighted by considering the philosophical fate of Aristotle's model of philosophical knowledge, epistēmē or *scientia*, which he modelled on Euclidean geometry, but which he expressly insisted must be matched to the precision possible within any domain of inquiry. How and why did this flexible model become the strict deductivist infallibilism associated with *scientia* in the Modern period? It was not Descartes's innovation. It was legislated in March 1277 by Étienne Tempier, Bishop of Paris, upon the authority of the Roman Pope, when he condemned as heretical 220 neo-Aristotelian theses in natural philosophy (Piché 1999). It is both explicit in Tempier's condemnation, and implied by many of his comments on those theses, that the Divine Omnipotence can do anything which is not logically self-contradictory, including bringing about any effect without its typical causes. This holds, too, for those "effects" we typically regard as our sensory experiences of our surroundings. Knowledge – *scientia* – requires eliminating all logically possible alternatives to any cognitive claim. All else is either divine revelation or fallible conjecture; natural philosophers can do no more, and no better, than to propose possible explanations of natural phenomena. That edict was later violated by Copernicus and Galileo, though honoured by Descartes (at least officially).[4] Tempier's edict made mere logical conceivability into a mainstay of philosophical analysis, argumentation and (dis-)proof (Boulter 2011), even if its implications for global perceptual scepticism were first explicitly generalized in Descartes's *Meditations*.[5]

Infallibilism about cognitive justification limits epistemology to conceptual analysis, not only because it proscribes appeal to logically contingent empirical premises (other than those pertaining to first-person reports of appearances to oneself), but also because it requires reliable first-person awareness of *all* justificatory factors relevant to any claim at issue: the view now called "access internalism." This includes full, competent reliable access to the factors constitutive of knowledge, so that one can determine whether these factors are, in any specific case, satisfied. This is the strong "K-K" principle: The purported requirement that, to know that x, one must know that one knows that x. These considerations drove "traditional" (pre-Gettier) epistemologists to seek a conceptual analysis of knowledge as consisting in justified true belief, as the conceptually necessary, jointly sufficient conditions for any and all empirical knowledge.

The chief methodological problem confronting epistemology as conceptual analysis is the Paradox of Analysis: How can any conceptual analysis be informative, and yet also be recognized to be complete and adequate? If we can recognize a conceptual analysis to be complete and adequate, we must already understand the concept(s) so analysed, in which case the analysis is uninformative. If instead a conceptual analysis is informative, how can we tell whether it is complete or adequate? This paradox of analysis greatly exercised philosophers from the 1940s into the 1990s, though neglected since. This neglect is reflected, if unwittingly, in how easily philosophers today offer or accept as serious challenges remarks of the form: "But couldn't someone say _____?", or: "But couldn't it be, couldn't it happen that _____?" Such questions presume that any and all logically possible alternatives to any proposed account must be eliminated in order to justify that proposal. Such philosophers have inherited their methodological predilections from Bishop Tempier. Consider again Descartes's statement that one perfection of the Divinity is that within the Divinity all perfections are simply one and unitary (AT 7:137). So saying does not suffice to *conceive* this purported truth; it is as much a contradiction as insisting that within the numerical unit, 1, all numbers are simply one and unitary: Any plurality of perfections is inconsistent with their simple numerical unity. Saying or claiming otherwise does not make it otherwise conceivable. Merely *thinking* that one is speaking or thinking cogently, however sincerely one may so suppose, does not suffice *actually* to think or to speak cogently. Neither our concepts, our meanings, nor the cogency of our own thinking or speaking are transparently self-evident in the ways philosophers still too often and habitually suppose (cf. Burge 2010).

The best solutions to the Paradox of Analysis all, implicitly or explicitly, replace conceptual analysis with conceptual explication (cf. esp. Hare 1960). It is striking and significant that both Kant (*KdrV* A727–31/B755–9) and Carnap (1950b, 1–18) distinguish between conceptual analysis and conceptual explication, in these very terms, and for very much the same reasons and to the same effect. Conceptual explication does not aspire to completeness; conceptual explication is selective and aspires to improve the clarity of the explicated concept(s) and to improve upon their use *in the context(s)* of original use of the concept(s) in question. No conceptual explication is known to be complete; all remain corrigible and partial; their assessment is always in part a function of their improved function within possible contexts of their *actual* use, *not* within merely imagined contexts of their (allegedly) possible use! Because they are context-bound in this way, conceptual explications involve – and invoke – important aspects of semantic externalism, the thesis that the content (intension) of a concept or term may be specified by factors unacknowledged by a competent speaker, S, and which may concern circumstances of which he or she cannot become aware by simple reflection. Simply *calling* a philosophical account of a concept, term, phrase or principle an "analysis" does not suffice for that account to *be* a conceptual analysis. If the content or adequacy of that account depends in part upon its context of actual use, it is an explication. The first methodological maxim is to make such context-dependence into a philosophical virtue. The questions are how to do so, and whether such virtues can aid epistemology.

Gettier's (1963) counter-examples in effect echo Carnap's distinction between conceptual analysis and conceptual explication, insofar as Gettier's counter-examples invite us, his readers, to reconsider how we would use, understand and explicate the concepts "empirical knowledge" and (cognitive) "justification" in the kinds of circumstances of use in which Smith believes he knows something which, in view of contextual factors unknown to him, he cannot know.

2.2 Naturalized epistemology and causal reliability "theories"

Another way of stating the exorbitant demands of infallibilism about cognitive justification is that it requires proving a priori that our cognitive capacities suffice for empirical knowledge in any possible environment, before trusting ourselves to know anything about our actual environment. These a priori, merely analytic aspirations of "traditional" (pre-Gettier) epistemology were discarded by "naturalized" epistemology, which appeals in various ways to various empirical findings in order to understand empirical knowledge. One popular genre of naturalized epistemology takes the form of "causal reliabilism." The popularity of causal "theories" of knowledge, of language or of human mindedness, unfortunately, exceeds their cogency.

Davidson (1980, 80; 2004, 98) noted that we lack knowledge of relevant causal laws and mechanisms in these domains. That is correct, significant, yet insufficient. Dretske's information-theoretic epistemology established three important semantic points:

1 Causal relations are neither necessary to nor sufficient for information relations (Dretske 1981, 30–9).
2 Information relations are necessary for any specifically *semantic* content, and hence also for linguistic meaning or conceptual content (Dretske 1981, 214–30).
3 Information relations are necessary though not sufficient for representations or for relations of representation, whether sensory or conceptual (Dretske 1981, 153–230; 1995[6]).

These points stand, regardless of the (in)adequacy of Dretske's account of the information decoding required for belief or knowledge (Dretske 1981, 57, 144, 219),[7] and regardless of the shortcomings of his attempt to naturalize the mind. Dretske's findings entail that bland appeals to "causality" in matters of human mindedness are, as Pinker (1997, ix) remarked about earlier philosophical views of the mind, "too vapid to be wrong."

If indeed we can know anything (such as how to see, recognize read and understand these printed words), it is in part because our psycho-physio-neurology functions in ways which enable us to know something. The difficulty is to fill in this platitude with sufficient, informative specifics. This, I believe, must be a multidisciplinary task. The proper task can be formulated and pursued only by heeding a major problem with its predecessor at the turn of the twentieth-century CE: "psychologism."

Reviewing that multidisciplinary (also polyglot, robustly international and intercontinental) literature, as I recently did, underscores just how grave and pervasive were problems of psychologism, and why it so exercised not only Frege, but still at midcentury also Carnap (1950b, §11). One chronic error of philosophers is simply to postulate whatever psychological or neurophysiological processes they think are required to fill in between the aspects of human mindedness they describe philosophically; so doing is evident not only, e.g., in Brentano (1874), Lipps (1901, 1912, 1913), or Wundt (1907), but also in Quine (1995).[8] More significantly: to pertain to knowledge or to epistemology, causal regularities or psycho-physiological processes must be, or must satisfy, *proper*, that is: properly *cognitive*, functions. They must be properly responsive to truth, accuracy and in many cases to evidence and analysis. These parameters are inherently normative, even though they are instantiated or effected by our sociopsychological neurophysiology. The recent rise of "virtue epistemology" in effect addresses a gap in epistemology resulting from rejecting anything so psychological as judgment. Yet many beliefs do not just happen to happen; many (if not most or all) beliefs are formed, and they are formed more or less responsibly – if often habitually so. Even Russell's deliberately simple example, "The cat is on the mat," requires not just sensory experience, but noticing the cat, the mat, and their respective locations. Seeing is not believing; believing is not simply seeing. Believing is propositionally structured in ways that sensory perception alone is not (Dretske 1969, ch. 2). In many cases, beliefs result not merely from judgments, but as they should: from considered judgment (Elgin 1999).

2.3 Conceptual content, linguistic meaning and specifically cognitive reference

A more fundamental problem confronting currently popular causal "theories" highlights both the distinctiveness of epistemology and a long-standing methodological shortcoming of much analytic philosophy. Causal theories of human mindedness (language, thought, belief, knowledge, action) describe various intelligent capacities, actions or achievements in causal terms. Whether those causal terms refer, and if so how accurately, to any instantiations within our neurophysiology, are assumed by most so-called "causal" theories; they are neither established nor investigated by causally minded philosophers. Responsible naturalistic epistemologists rightly appeal to results of relevant empirical sciences (e.g. Kornblith 2002; Millikan 2004; Ryder, Kingsbury, and Williford 2012); this is as it should be. Cognitive reference to relevant, specific causal particulars and their kinds can be borrowed in this way – though only from *actual* scientific results.

Too often neglected by causal theorists of human mindedness is a basic distinction between, e.g., uttering a sentence and making a claim. To be a *claim*, even a *candidate* cognitive claim, a sentence must be used to make a statement about some relevant particulars (of whatever kind or scale). The linguistic meaning or the conceptual content (intension) of any sentence or statement in principle does not suffice to determine whether there are any such particulars, or whether there are several, or only one such. However detailed or extensive a description may be (when used to explicate the linguistic meaning or conceptual content of any proposition, sentence, thought or statement), and regardless of whether it includes one or more putative definite referring expressions,[9] intension cannot secure definite singular reference, because there may be no such particular that satisfies the intension, or there may be several such particulars. Predication as a linguistic form does not suffice for predication as a proto-cognitive act of ascribing characteristics *to* any one (or more) particular(s). Conversely, an intension may in part be inaccurate, and yet be used successfully to designate some particular; this is part of Donnellan's (1966) point about successful referential use of inaccurate definite descriptions, such as "The man in the corner holding a Martini," which can pick out one person within a group clustered in the indicated corner, where the others (let us suppose) evidently hold soft drinks, yet the designated individual in fact drinks from his Martini glass only water.

The epistemological significance of the distinction between predication as a grammatical (sentential) form and predication as a proto-cognitive achievement of ascribing a characteristic(s) to some particular individual(s) is augmented by Evans's (1975) account of predication. Evans argued (soundly, I submit) that mastery of predicates within some language requires being able to distinguish particulars or their specific aspects which are properly characterized by the predicate(s) in question, where such discrimination involves identifying by delimiting the relevant region occupied by the relevant particular(s) or their aspect(s). Evans showed that ascription of any characteristic and spatio-temporal localization by delimitation of any particular exhibiting that characteristic are mutually interdependent proto-cognitive achievements.

Donnellan's and Evans's findings hold regardless of considerations about accuracy or precision; sufficient accuracy or precision to discriminate the relevant individual(s) and characteristic(s) from other individuals and characteristics suffices, even if they are approximate. Their points hold regardless of whether a single, particular individual or a plurality of particular individuals may be at issue; they hold regardless of the scale or duration of the relevant individual(s), and they hold regardless of issues about any cognitive or doxastic justification of the relevant attribution. Their findings are decisive for epistemology, for the following reasons.

To make even a candidate claim to know something empirically requires localizing the relevant particular(s) within space and time, and ascribing some characteristic to it (or to them). Predication in the form of ascription of characteristic(s) to some particular individual(s) is necessary for Someone's (S's) claim to *have* any truth value, or any value as an approximation. Such attribution is also necessary to *evaluate* the truth or the accuracy of that attribution. Such attribution is also necessary for S's claim to *have* any cognitive justification, of whatever form(s) and to whatever extent it may be cognitively justified. And – waiving for now issues about error, false belief and radical mis-representation – S's claim having some kind and extent of cognitive justification is required to *assess* its cognitive justification, and whether it suffices for knowledge. (These conditions must be satisfied by any other claims required to determine whether S's attribution errs or fails radically).

Whatever may be the proper account of linguistic meaning or linguistic reference, and likewise whatever may be the proper account of conceptual content (intension), these do not suffice for epistemology, because they do not suffice for specifically *cognitive* reference – even putative, proto-cognitive reference – to localized discriminated individuals. The egocentric predicament posed by global perceptual scepticism voids not only the justificatory resources required for any empirical knowledge, but also the referential resources required to make even *candidate* cognitive claims (within the non-formal domain of putative empirical knowledge). This point holds regardless of theories of linguistic meaning or of conceptual content (intension); it concerns proto-cognitive *reference* to particulars. I stress "proto-cognitive," because such reference is necessary for any empirical claim to know something; it is necessary for any claim even to be a *candidate* cognitive claim; accuracy and sufficient cognitive justification are distinct, further cognitive requirements. Consequently, philosophy of language and philosophy of mind may contribute to epistemology, but they do not suffice for epistemology: accuracy of ascription and specifically *cognitive* justification are not phenomena within the domains of philosophy of language or philosophy of mind (whether singly or combined). Ultimately, this is why philosophers of language such as Quine, Rorty or Davidson could only tell sceptics to get lost (§1).[10] Thinking or supposing that one ascribes various characteristics to something does not suffice for any *actual* ascription. Actual ascription, even putative ascription, requires localizing the relevant particular(s), sufficiently to discriminate them from their neighbours or relatives (i.e., from similar, though relevantly different sorts of individuals).[11]

2.4 *Identifying and exploiting our cognitive dependencies*

The egocentric predicament of global perceptual scepticism purports to rob us of both our justificatory resources *and* our referential resources, required for even candidate empirical claims to know anything. Despite his infallibilist aspirations, one feature of Descartes's strategy in the *Meditations* merits credit: In various regards Descartes seeks to characterize his manifold dependencies, including his cognitive dependencies, and to exploit these for epistemological insight. (Descartes himself did not advocate the disembodied mind invented by his successors; cf. Ferrini 2015).

Here, at last, is a role for thought experiments in epistemology: Can thought experiments be devised to help us identify some of our fundamental cognitive capacities, and our consequent incapacities? Can thought experiments be devised to help us identify how some of our fundamental cognitive capacities are in principle and in practice dependent capacities, in ways which illuminate epistemological issues, without simply dismissing issues about scepticism, or simply replacing epistemology with empirical cognitive science? Can thought experiments contribute philosophically to the multidisciplinary research required to understand human cognition?

Three such thought experiments are considered below (§§3–5). They are thought *experiments*, not merely examples, and they experiment with our human capacities for *thought*. They aim to contribute to our self-knowledge as cognisant beings, by helping us to identify some very basic features of our very finite form of human cognisance, and to appreciate their epistemological implications. In this regard, these examples are not merely conceptual, and concern not merely what is possible, but what is possible *for us* human beings.

Against Strawson's (1966) analytical reconstruction of Kant's "Objectivity Argument," Rorty observed:

> Arguments of the Strawsonian type rest on considerations of which words can be understood independently of which other words. The relevance of these considerations vanishes if we admit the possibility of a being who could experience something as an X but could not use the word "X" nor any equivalent expression.
> (Rorty 1970, 224; cf. 231)

Rorty's observation epitomizes the characteristically "analytical" misunderstanding of Kant's transcendental methods and proofs, a misunderstanding running through the whole discussion of "analytic transcendental" arguments. Conceptual content or linguistic meaning as such cannot suffice for epistemology (per §2.3). Rorty's question, whether "a being who could experience something as an X but could not use the word "X" nor any equivalent expression" is *possible*, itself belongs to the infallibilist tradition inaugurated by Bishop Tempier in 1277 (Boulter 2011), skewered by Carnap (1950b) and Gettier (1963), though superseded by Kant in 1781 (Westphal 2007). Unless *we* are that kind of being whose possibility Rorty supposes, that possibility is irrelevant to *our* human form of finite cognisance.

The prospects for epistemology are not significantly improved by seeking some form of "broad" conceptual necessity; for that, too, we would need adequate criteria for adequate explication of "broad" conceptual necessity, *and* adequate grounds for supposing that any such "broad" conceptual necessity pertains to *us* as the finite cognisant beings we are. Not only metaphysics, but too much epistemology has "merely groped around, and worst of all: amongst mere concepts" (*KdrV* Bxv)![12] Like Kant, some exceptional ordinary language philosophers recognized that epistemological issues cannot be addressed merely in terms of linguistic meaning, conceptual or propositional content (intension) or other forms of conceptual analysis. Specifically epistemological issues are only engaged when we consider how *we* can form and use thoughts to make putative cognitive claims or judgments, whether in specific cases or wholesale.

Consider one point Kant claims to establish in this way. He grants that it is entirely conceivable that there be no space at all, and that we can conceive of space as being entirely empty, but he denies we can *represent* to ourselves the absence or lack of space (*KdrV* A24/B38–9). Kant's point concerns the fundamental role within human cognisance of representing individuals and events spatially, and how spatial representation is required for us to represent anything *as* distinct to ourselves. He makes comparable points about how we experience all appearances temporally, that is, within time (*KdrV* A31/B46). My present point is not to defend these claims, but to highlight Kant's concern with identifying *our* human forms of sensibility, which are (partly) constitutive of our human form of mindedness, namely, that we experience whatever we do spatially and temporally (nothing here turns on whether our experiences are veridical). The logical possibility of other forms of cognisance is altogether beside Kant's elementary epistemological point.

We cannot expect an entire epistemology from a few thought experiments, but we can expect some epistemologically significant results. In view of the manifold constraints on philosophical theory of knowledge reviewed above, that is far from nothing. Here I cannot develop or defend these results in detail; I hope however to make clear how to appreciate and assess these kinds of thought experiments. I shall consider them in systematic rather than chronological order, beginning with singular cognitive reference (§2.3).

3 Hegel on the semantics of singular cognitive reference

Hegel's phenomenological method involves establishing some positive conclusions through strictly internal critique of the views and principles he opposes, considered in connection with their intended domains of use. About Hegel's method Robinson (1977, 2) observed that " ... bad theory makes for bad practice, and the bad practice shows up the logical difficulties of the theory." In *The Phenomenology of Spirit* (1807), and in his subsequent systematic philosophy, Hegel undertakes to revamp and augment Kant's Critical account of rational judgment and justification, whilst dispensing with Kant's Transcendental Idealism (and other such views). These aims, together with Hegel's methodological strictures – especially: to avoid *petitio principii* – require Hegel (inter alia) to argue against aconceptual "knowledge by acquaintance." This he does in the first chapter of the *Phenomenology*, by using thought experiments concerning commonsense cognitive claims, to elicit our recognition of fundamental and pervasive roles of various concepts and our competent use of them within even the apparently "simplest" claims to know anything. The form of consciousness Hegel calls "sense certainty" espouses naïve realism. Hegel's phenomenological presentation of this paradigmatic naïve realist highlights varieties of "mediation" involved in what sense certainty purports is utterly immediate knowledge. Many of the "meditations" revealed by Hegel's examples are conceptual and cognitive, involving the competent use of various concepts.[13]

Anticipating by a century Russell's early view that "this" is a logically proper name, Hegel queries:

> Thus *sense certainty* itself is to be asked: *What is the this?* If we take it in the doubled form of its being, as the *now* and as the *here*, the dialectic which it has within itself will receive just as comprehensible a form as the this itself is. To the question, *What is the now?* we thus answer for example: *The now is night*. A simple experiment suffices to test the truth of this sense certainty. We write this truth down; a truth can lose nothing through writing it down, just as little as by preserving it. If we look *now*, *this noon*, again at this written truth, we must say that it has become stale.
>
> The now, which is night, is *preserved*, that is, it is treated as what it was given out to be, as a *being*; but it proves itself much more to be a non-being. Of course the *now* itself sustains itself, but as a something that is not night; and it sustains itself just as well against day, which it now is, as something that also is not day ... . This self-preserving now is thus not something immediate, but instead something mediated, for it is determined as something remaining and self-preserving *through* the fact that another is not, namely the day and the night. Nevertheless it is still as simple as before, *now*, and in this simplicity it is indifferent to that which occurs in it.
>
> (PhdG 9:64.29–65.11/¶¶95–6)

Hegel's example and discussion may appear either quaint or confused, but he is a master of taking views absolutely literally and identifying what follows from them, *and* what does *not*, and using these findings to identify further assumptions which allow that view to have appeared plausible or tenable. Yes, Hegel does not here distinguish between the "is" of predication, the "is" of being and the "is" of identity – but he is arguing against a view which rejects any and all conceptual distinctions as unnecessary for simple, "immediate" commonsense knowledge of anything. Yes, of course *we* know how to, and we do, sort out and sequence our experiences of various particulars, and our experiential episodes – but not simply by *sensing* whatever transpires around us! Seeing *that* it is now night, or day, or dusk or dawn is a conceptually mediated, propositionally structured cognitive achievement, however commonsensical, automatic or apparently "immediate" it may appear.

Some philosophers have responded (in discussion) to such examples by reporting that they are unaware of using concepts in making any such claims or observations. Perhaps they are unaware of using concepts, but such lack of awareness proves nothing without the further premise of strong Cartesian self-transparency. Descartes deceived himself about how self-transparent were his own clear and distinct ideas (Westphal 2014, §4.1); so too naïve realists. Here we begin to appreciate the point and character of Kant's transcendental inquiries, which Hegel further developed: to try to identify basic capacities we must exercise in order to be sufficiently self-aware as to wonder, e.g., about the scope and character of human cognisance. Like Kant's, Hegel's cognitive psychology accords well with much recent cognitive science (Brook 1994; deVries 1988). As for distinguishing the "is" of identity and the "is" of predication, in "Sense Certainty" Hegel *justifies* this distinction by *reductio ad absurdum* of aconceptual naïve realism, which disregards their distinction.

This point comes to a head when sense certainty retrenches to an alleged specious present awareness of any one particular (*PhdG* 9:67.23–32/¶105). Hegel continues his pursuit:

> The *now* is pointed out, *this now*. *Now*; it has already ceased to be as it is pointed out. The *now* that *is*, is an other than the one pointed out, and we see, that the now is just this: insofar as it is, already no longer to be. The now, as it is pointed out to us, is something that *has been*, and this is its truth; it doesn't have the truth of being. It is therefore of course true that it has been. However what *has been*, is in fact *no being*; *it IS not*, and the concern was with being.
>
> We thus see in this pointing out only a movement taking the following course: 1) I point out the now; it is maintained as the true. But I point it out as passing, or as something sublated. Thus I sublate the first truth and 2) now I maintain as the second truth, that it *has been*, or is sublated. 3) But what has been is not. I sublate the second truth, its having been or its being sublated. Thus I negate the negation of the now, and thus return to what was first maintained: that *now* is. The now and the pointing out of the now are thus so constituted, that neither the now, nor the pointing out of the now, is an immediate simple; instead, each is a movement which contains distinct moments within itself; ... But this first, which is reflected in itself, is not exactly the same as what it first was, namely, something *immediate*. Instead, it is just *something reflected within itself*, or a *simple* which remains what it is in other-being; a now that is absolutely many nows. And this is truthfully the now; the now as a simple day that has many nows within it, hours; such a now, an hour, is just so many minutes, and this now similarly is many nows and so on. – *Pointing*

out is thus itself the movement which pronounces what the now is in truth, namely a result, or a plurality of nows taken together; and pointing is the experience, that now is a *universal*.

(PhdG 9:67.33–68.21/¶107)

If Hegel's points are now obvious to us demonstrative sophisticates, that does not make them insignificant. Hegel points out that any specific *use* of the concept "time" involves specifying in context some relevant *period* of time; in adjoining paragraphs he makes the parallel points about using the concept "space," "region of space" and the personal pronouns (first-, second- or third-person), and how specifying (sufficiently, if approximately) the relevant scope of what is "here" and "now" – and he or she to whom it is so – is required in order to designate any specific individual as *this* particular here and now – or that one there and then, or witnessed by you or by her whenever and wherever it was located and localized by Someone in particular. Our use of none of these concepts or terms is pointillistic, as it were; all of them are determinable concepts; their relevant scope and reference must be – and can only be – fixed in situ. Using these determinable concepts in such determinate ways, specifying their scope in context, is necessary for forming even the most ordinary commonsense knowledge, including any seeing *that* _____ such and so is the case.

In the final two paragraphs Hegel makes the further point, like Evans, that fixing in situ the relevant scope and reference of whatever in particular one claims to know about, requires not just descriptive intension, but *ascriptive* attribution *to* specific, localized individuals (or their aspects) which we (putatively) delimit within space and time. Hegel expressly notes – like Kant, and against Leibniz – that however extensive or detailed a description may be, it may equally well describe several individuals, none at all, or perhaps (by dumb contingent luck) only one: which case obtains is neither specified nor settled by that description (intension, classification), but instead by localizing some putative individual(s) to which one ascribes some characteristics (PhdG 9:70.20–29/¶110).

In this way, Hegel argues by using these and related thought experiments to identify and facilitate our appreciation of logically contingent, though fundamental and pervasive features of *our* cognitive capacities, competences and achievements. Taken together, Hegel's examples constitute a *reductio ad absurdum* of naïve realism, which justifies the Thesis of Singular Cognitive Reference (§2.3). This decisive, incisive thesis is Kant's, though he left his readers to find it in the joint implications of the Transcendental Aesthetic and the Amphiboly of the Concepts of Reflection.[14]

Hegel's initial characterization of a "universal" (concept) matches exactly that introduced by Hume in his account of distinctions of reason (*T* 1.1.7.17–18), which marks the downfall of concept empiricism: Hume's official "copy theory" of sensory impressions and ideas, together with this three official "laws" of psychological association, can at most account for classifications of sensed characteristics, as fine- or coarse-grained as one can perceptually discriminate. However, to account for merely determinable concepts, such as "time," "period of time," "space," "region of space," "I," "physical object" ("body") or "word," Hume can only appeal to our "imagination," but for these capacities of the imagination Hume can offer no *empiricist* account (Westphal 2013).

Finally, the Thesis of Singular Cognitive Reference (§2.3) can be seen to undergird O. K. Bouwsma's (1949) brilliant exposé and critique of Cartesian scepticism. The general corollary to that Thesis is this: Global sceptical "hypotheses" are hypotheses in name only, because they lack any determinate, specifiable reference *to* any particulars alleged to be responsible for blocking the veridicality (or the justification) of any and all sensory experience. They must prescind from any such reference, in order to evade empirical investigation (and self-refutation). By evading reference in these ways, they fail to be even *candidate* cognitive claims; they are mere logical possibilities, with *no* assessable truth-value, accuracy or cognitive justification. In all three regards they lack cognitive standing, and so cannot serve to defeat or to undermine the cognitive justification of any claim with cognitive status, even as putative knowledge (ascriptive attribution to some localized individuals), however approximate or weakly justified it may be. Both Kant and Hegel recognized that fallibilism about cognitive justification is no sceptical capitulation.

4 Kant on the "transcendental affinity" of the sensory manifold

Taunting Leibniz, Hume (*En* 5.21) notes that his view of human concept- and belief-formation through customary habituation affords, as it were, a pre-established harmony between the order of nature and the order of thought. Hume is right about our cognitive dependence upon perceptible natural regularities, though his empiricism precludes its full appreciation. Kant noted that, although all human knowledge begins with experience, it does not for that reason all result from experience (*KdrV* B1). For all the sophistication of Kant's account of the a priori concepts, principles, structures and functions of the human mind, he insisted that our cognitive capacities only become active in response to sensory stimulation from without the mind. Though necessary, sensory stimulation as such is insufficient: it must be such that we can process it, by bringing it under concepts in judgments whereby we classify and identify (at least putatively) various particular objects, events or persons surrounding us. This basic point holds, mutatis mutandis, Kant argues, regarding the contents of sensations, of empirical intuitions, of experiences and of the objects we experience.

Kant's thesis is that unless the contents of one's sensations have a minimum, humanly recognizable degree of regularity and variety they would not admit of perceptual synthesis, and so would provide no basis for even putative cognitive judgments using either a priori or empirical concepts. This "affinity" (associability) of the sensory manifold is transcendental because a priori it is a necessary condition of possible self-conscious human experience. It is formal because it concerns the orderliness of the contents of sensations. However, ultimately it is satisfied neither by the a priori intuitive conditions of experience (spatiality and temporality as forms of our sensory receptivity) nor by the a priori conceptual conditions of cognitive judgment. Its satisfaction is due to the "content" or the "object" of experience (*KdrV*, A112–3, A653–4/B681–2).

Appearances must be associable in order for us to make cognitive judgments at all. This associability, Kant argues, must have an objective, necessary ground in order for experience to be at all possible for us. This ground Kant calls the "affinity" of the sensory manifold; he argues for it using a wildly counterfactual thought experiment:

> Now if this unity of association did not also have an objective ground ... it would be entirely accidental that appearances should fit into a connection in human knowledge. For even though we should have the capacity to associate perceptions,

it would remain entirely undetermined and accidental *whether they themselves were associable*; and in case they were not associable, then a multitude of perceptions, and indeed an entire sensibility would be possible, in which much empirical [sensation] would occur within my mind, but separated, and without belonging to *one* consciousness of myself, which, however, is impossible. For only because I ascribe all perceptions to one consciousness (original apperception) can I say of all perceptions that *I am conscious of* them. There must, therefore, be an objective ground ... upon which rests the possibility, indeed, the necessity, of a law that extends to all appearances – a ground, namely, for regarding all appearances as data of the senses that must be associable in themselves and subject to universal rules of a thoroughgoing connection in their reproduction. *This objective ground of all association of appearances I entitle their affinity* ... According to this principle all appearances, without exception, must so enter the mind or be apprehended, that they conform to the unity of apperception. Without synthetic unity in their connection, which is thus objectively necessary, this would be impossible.

(*KdrV*, A121–3; emphases added)

In this passage Kant points out that an intact and complete human sensibility and understanding, capable of associating perceptions, does not of itself determine whether any appearances or perceptions it has are in fact associable. If they were not, there may be fleeting, random sensations, but there could be no unified, and hence no self-conscious, experience. The necessity of the associability of the sensory manifold is *conditional*; it holds between that manifold and any self-conscious human being. Necessarily, if a human being is self-consciously aware of anything via any sensory manifold (any plurality of sensations), then the content of that manifold is associable. The associability of this content *is* its "affinity." Because such sensory affinity is necessary for possible self-conscious human experience, this affinity is transcendental.

Kant stresses the transcendental status of this issue in the following passage, though here he speaks of a "logical law of genera" instead of the "transcendental affinity" of the sensory manifold:

If among the appearances offering themselves to us there were such a great a variety ... of content [sic], i.e., regarding the manifoldness of existing beings – that even the most acute human understanding, through comparison of one with another, could not detect the least similarity (a case which can at least be thought), then the logical law of genera would not obtain at all, no concept of a genus, nor any other universal concept, *indeed no understanding at all would obtain*, since the understanding has to do with such concepts. The logical principle of genera therefore presupposes a transcendental [principle of genera] if it is to be applied to nature (by which I here understand only objects that are given to us). According to that [latter] principle, sameness of kind is necessarily presupposed in the manifold of a possible experience (even though we cannot determine its degree a priori), because *without it no empirical concepts and hence no experience would be possible*.

(*KdrV*, A653–4/B681–2; emphases added)

Despite Kant's shift in terminology, the minimum condition which satisfies the "logical law of genera" likewise satisfies the "transcendental affinity" of the sensory manifold: Below a certain (a priori indeterminable) degree of regularity and variety amongst the contents of sensations, our understanding cannot make judgments; consequently under that condition we cannot be self-conscious (because we cannot identify ourselves *as* being self-consciously aware *of* anything else). Consequently, this condition is a necessary, transcendental condition for the possibility of self-conscious experience. Above this minimal level of regularity and variety, there is then a reflective issue about the extent to which we can systematize (integrate) our experience of the world. Insofar as we must use concepts to see *that* anything is or is not the case, we can only do so within a world exhibiting humanly identifiable kinds of variety and repeatability amongst the particulars we experience.[15]

Kant's example of what we may call "transcendental chaos" – sensory contents so irregular we could not detect any regularities or varieties amongst them – provides a thought experiment which strongly supports the view now called mental content externalism. Kant expressly grants that transcendental chaos is logically possible; his transcendental point is that such chaos cannot hold of any world (of any environment) of which we human beings can be aware, nor within which we can be aware of ourselves *as* being aware of some appearances occurring before, during or after others. (Kant's link between these forms of awareness cannot be examined here; see Westphal 2016b). If Kant's thought experiment about transcendental chaos is correct, it provides sufficient ground to block the sceptical generalization from occasional possibility of perceptual error or misjudgement to the alleged possibility of universally nonveridical sensory "experience." The point of Kant's thought experiment lies neither in the question whether a world of sensory chaos is logically possible, nor in the question whether an unfortunate human being might possibly be flooded with incomprehensibly chaotic sensations. The reflexive, transcendental character of Kant's thought experiment lies in the question, whether *you*, dear reader, could be self-aware within a world in which your sensibility were flooded only by incomprehensibly chaotic sensations?

Kant's thought experiment may not be decisive, but it is bolstered by his analysis of the kinds of conceptual, judgmental achievements required to integrate sensations into percepts, and percepts into perceptual episodes, and those required to use the first-person pronoun. Those analyses do not rely on thought experiments, but rather upon considerations of what is necessary for us to process and integrate sensory information over time.[16] It is worth noting here, however, that Hegel's thought experiments contra naïve realism (§4) and Kant's thought experiment regarding transcendental chaos nicely complement each other. This holds too of the third thought experiment, from Wittgenstein (§5).

Kant himself did not work out the full implications of his transcendental thought experiment about sensory chaos, for a reason later noticed and exploited by C. I. Lewis (1929). Fully developed, Kant's thought experiment can replace much of the "Transcendental Deduction of the Pure Categories of the Understanding," and it refutes Kant's Transcendental Idealism – supporting instead Lewis's robust pragmatic realism, including his pragmatic conception of the relativized a priori (Westphal 2010a, §2).

5 Wittgenstein on thought and pervasive regularities of nature

The thought experiments considered in this chapter comport with this aim of Wittgenstein's:

> Not empiricism and yet realism in philosophy, that is the hardest thing.
> (Wittgenstein, *RFM* VI, §23; p. 325)

In a note to the *Investigations*, Wittgenstein observes:

> What we have to mention in order to explain [*zur Erklärung*] the significance, I mean the importance, of a concept, are often extremely general facts of nature. Such facts as are hardly ever mentioned because of their great generality.
>
> (*PI* §142 Note)

Wittgenstein sternly advised caution whenever a philosopher starts talking about how things must be.[17] Yet his caution about how things "must" be is consistent with pointing out how things must be, under specified conditions. For example, Wittgenstein showed forcefully that we can use language and can follow rules only within and due to our relatively stable and identifiable social and worldly context (von Savigny 1991; Schroeder 2001; Travis 2006; Wright 1986).

To highlight the character and significance of "extremely general facts of nature" Wittgenstein develops and suggests some very radical, probing thought experiments. One such experiment begins with a chair which disappears, or at least seems to occasionally, though at other times we can touch it (*PI* §80). Occasions such as these are perplexing, but Wittgenstein underscores their significance by radicalizing the suggested instabilities of our surroundings:

> Only in normal cases is the use of a word clearly prescribed to us; we know, have no doubt, what to say in this or that case. The more abnormal the case, the more doubtful it becomes what we now are to say here. And if things behaved quite differently from how they actually behave – if there were for instance no characteristic expression of pain, of fear, of joy; if rule became exception and exception rule; or if both became phenomena of roughly equal frequency – this would make our normal language games lose their point [*Witz*]. – The procedure of putting a lump of cheese on a balance and fixing the price by the turn of the scale would lose its point if it frequently happened that such lumps grew or shrank for no obvious reason.
>
> (*PI* §142)

Wittgenstein draws attention to how our language is governed in ways that suit the nature we know and live in. His considerations highlight a crucial *conditional* necessity, that to have any point or any use at all, the structure of our language must broadly comport with the structure of the world we inhabit (*PI* II §xii).

Wittgenstein invites us to imagine these wildly counterfactual circumstances:

> If a ruler expanded to an extraordinary extent when slightly heated, we would say – in normal circumstances – that that made it *unusable*. But we could think of a situation in which this was just what was wanted. I am imagining that we perceive the expansion with the naked eye; and that we ascribe the same numerical measure of length to bodies in rooms of different temperatures, if they measure the same by the ruler which to the eye is now longer, now shorter.
>
> It can thus be said: What is here called "measuring" and "length" and "equal length," is something different from what we call those things. The use of these words is different from ours; it is *akin* to it; and we too use these words in a variety of ways.
>
> (*RFM* I §5, cf. §140)

Wittgenstein's example is expressly enthymematic. The situation in which the rapidly expanding ruler is "just what was wanted" is one in which there are, not just rooms of various temperatures, but also many other objects which expand readily (and very nearly at the same rate) with changes in temperatures, just like the ruler. Such a regularity would give sense to the imagined, non-standard practice of measuring. This imagined non-standard measuring practice underscores ways in which our standard measuring practices are rooted not only in arithmetic but also in very general regularities of nature: most particulars we ordinarily deal with do not expand dramatically with small changes in temperature. Wittgenstein's examples also underscore the importance of the scientific practice of specifying critical quantities like density by reference to standard temperature and pressure.

Wittgenstein's thought experiments invite us to reflect on cases where "things behave quite differently from how they actually behave, ... if rule became exception and exception rule" (*PI* I §142). This suggests a massive inversion of typical regularities, by which the common rule would become the isolated instance whilst normally bizarre cases would become ubiquitous. Consider a world in which things in our environment did not conserve their quantities, either of volume, or weight or number; imagine that they melded together like drops of liquid or bits of soft dough, but without preserving mass, volume or shape in any noticeable way. If such non-conserving goo congealed or parted relatively slowly, perhaps we might be able to track some portions of it. If instead their behaviour were quite rapid, we could not track them. If this were our environment, we could not identify these items (even if there were "items"), we could not count them, and we could not develop or use arithmetical concepts.

The transcendental character of Wittgenstein's examples is plainest in *On Certainty*.[18] Wittgenstein again stresses the role of identifiable, stable natural regularities for the very point of our language games (*OC* §513, cf. §505); without such regularities truth and falsehood would be impossible (*OC* §514). This is one of Wittgenstein's "fundamental" statements, statements that are neither logical truths nor results of empirical investigation (*OC* §§110, 138, 402, 494, 512); i.e., they defy Hume's fork. Nevertheless, they form the stable basis, rooted in practice (*OC* §§7, 29, 110, 139, 402), without which we simply could not think (*OC* §§403, 506), hence not even about ourselves. Wittgenstein's reflections are genuinely transcendental because they concern the contingent, conditional necessities which must be satisfied if self-conscious human thought or experience is to be at all possible for us.

Inspired by Wittgenstein, Waismann (1945) detailed the "porosity" or "open texture" of all empirical concepts, which precludes any conclusive (empiricist) verification of any empirical claim. Likewise our empirical classifications of individuals, their features and their kinds remain in principle and in practice corrigible. Waismann's points are important scores against infallibilist presumptions about cognitive justification. Similarly inspired, and likewise critical of infallibilist presumptions about cognitive justification, Austin (1946) suggested we consider this radical thought experiment:

> "Being sure it's real" is no more proof against miracles or outrages of nature than anything else is or, *sub specie humanitatis*, can be. If we have made sure it's a goldfinch, and a real goldfinch, and then in the future it does something outrageous (explodes, quotes Mrs. Woolf, or what not), we don't say we were wrong to say it was a goldfinch, we don't know what to say. Words literally fail us.
>
> (Austin 1946, 160; 1979, 86)

Austin is right that infallibility is humanly impossible, certainly within the domain of empirical knowledge. That is important, yet insufficient. Reflecting on these examples and on Wittgenstein's, Frederick Will (1968) observed that not merely words fail us in such bizarre cases: thought itself fails us. We very finite, semi-rational human beings can only think insofar as we inhabit a tolerably comprehensible, negotiable, sufficiently describable, identifiable world.

6 Conclusions

Global perceptual scepticism presumes we have far greater capacities for intelligent thought, speech and "experience" than we do. That can be shown by transcendental use of these sorts of thought experiments, provided philosophers recognize that the tasks of epistemology too – as Kant recognized (*KdrV* A805/B833) – are comprehended within Thales's commandment, inscribed at Delphi: "Know thyself!" Rescinding infallibilism and mere conceptual analysis, and recognizing our manifold if indirect and often implicit dependence upon our environs, both natural and social, are the beginnings of epistemological insight, which can be fostered and informed by transcendental use of epistemological thought experiments, though only if we change fundamentally our philosophical "method of thinking."

Notes

1 For detailed examination, see Westphal (2004, 2016a, 2016b).
2 The five circularities are detailed in Westphal (1987–88). Subsequent defences of Descartes against charges of circularity have neglected the complexities and difficulties confronting his epistemological project in the *Meditations*.
3 Meditations 3, 5; Replies 1/AT 7:49–50, 137, 240, 241; 8.1:12.
4 *Prin.* 3.46, AT 8.1:100–1; *Disc. Meth.*, AT 6:45–6; *Le Monde*, AT 11:36.
5 Widely known to Mediaevalists, the Paris Condemnation of 1277 remains just as widely neglected even by specialists in 17th-century philosophy, including those concerned with philosophical history; most recently, e.g., Lærke, Smith and Schliesser (2013). Papal infallibility was only made official dogma by the First Vatican Council (1870) in its "First dogmatic constitution on the Church of Christ," ch. 4, §9. It became the majority Catholic view during the Reformation, i.e., a century after the Paris Condemnation; see Tierney (1972).
6 This point is developed gradually in Dretske (1995); it concerns the relations between "natural" and "functional" meaning, and how representational systems must function in order to be capable of misrepresentation.
7 For concise discussion, see Westphal (2003), §§26, 27.
8 On Quine, see Murphey (2012) and Westphal (2015). Ignorance if not contempt of our predecessors has reached such extremes that it is worth noting that Lipps's translation of Hume's *Treatise* is excellent, and that much current philosophical "naturalism" is no more cogent than that at the turn of the twentieth-century CE; see Westphal (2016a, 2016b).
9 Such as, e.g., "the," "the one and only," "the very one itself," "those very ones there" or "whoever just entered."
10 Though Quine (1969) appeared to advocate naturalizing epistemology, he never did. His referential "proxy functions" preserved no more than cardinality, but prescinded from any determinate ascription of characteristics to localized particulars. Quine said that physical objects are only a simplifying posit, but his own semantics precludes associating any specific or adequate concept(s) with his physical inscriptions or utterances. Talk is cheap; actually saying something significant is more demanding; see Westphal (2015).

11 I beg the reader's forbearance if I appear to belabour the obvious, but recent literature provides all too much evidence that these elementary points of epistemology and ascription (as distinct to mere description) are widely neglected; e.g., the resurgence of "analytic metaphysics" presupposes it.
12 The pervasive error here illustrated from Rorty (1970) was not due to lack of good information; see Watson (1881), Caird (1889), Bird (1996) and Dryer (1966). The error was made pervasive by philosophers' willingness to heed Russell's (1913; CP 9:39) battle-cry, "back to the eighteenth Century," by which Russell had meant Hume, not Kant. Such default empiricism persists today in much "analytic metaphysics."
13 A critical synopsis of Hegel's method and critique of naïve realism is provided by Westphal (2009); for a full-dress examination and assessment, see Westphal (2000), (2002–03); for the bearing of Hegel's critique on Russell, see Westphal (2010b). Translations are my own. Quotations are brief to curtail the scholarly digressions fuller quotation would require.
14 It was brought to my attention by Melnick (1989); I develop it in Westphal (2004), very much in accord with Bird (2006).
15 I discuss Kant's examples and also Wittgenstein's (in §5) in greater detail in Westphal (2005).
16 See Guyer (1989) and Strawson (1989); on Kant's identification of our basic logical forms of judgment see Wolff (2016, forthcoming).
17 Cf. *PI* §§81, 101, 131; *RFM* II §41, III §§30 ¶2, 31 ¶1, VI §§7, 8, 24, 46, VII §67.
18 My remarks on *On Certainty* are indebted to notes on this topic kindly shared with me by Graham Bird.

References

Austin, J. L. (1946) "Other minds," *Proceedings of the Aristotelian Society* 20(suppl.): 148–187; rpt. in: idem. (1979), 76–110.
Austin, J. L. (1979) *Philosophical Papers*, 3rd ed., edited by J. O. Urmson and G. J. Warnock, Oxford: Clarendon Press.
Bird, G. (1996) *Kant's Theory of Knowledge*, London: Routledge and Kegan Paul.
Bird, G. (2006) *The Revolutionary Kant*, Chicago: Open Court.
Boulter, S. (2011) "The Medieval origins of conceivability arguments," *Metaphilosophy* 42: 617–641.
Bouwsma, O. K. (1949) "Descartes' evil genius," *The Philosophical Review* 58: 141–151.
Brentano, F. (1874) *Psychologie vom empirischen Standpunkt*, 2 vols, Leipzig: Duncker und Humblot.
Brook, A. (1994) *Kant and the Mind*, Cambridge: Cambridge University Press.
Burge, T. (2010) *Origins of Objectivity*, Oxford: Clarendon Press.
Caird, E. (1889) *The Critical Philosophy of Immanuel Kant*, 2 vols, Glasgow: Maclehose.
Carnap, R. (1928) *Der logische Aufbau der Welt*, Berlin: Weltkreis.
Carnap, R. (1950a) "Empiricism, semantics, and ontology," *Revue International de Philosophie* 4: 20–40; 2nd rev. ed. in: Carnap (1956), 205–221.
Carnap, R. (1950b) *Logical Foundations of Probability*, Chicago: University of Chicago Press.
Davidson, D. (1980) *Essays on Actions and Events*, Oxford: Clarendon Press.
Davidson, D. (1987) "Afterthoughts" to "a coherence theory of truth and knowledge," in *Subjective, Intersubjective, Objective*, edited by D. Davidson, 154–157, Oxford: Clarendon Press.
Davidson, D. (2004) *Problems of Rationality*, Oxford: Clarendon Press.
Descartes, R. (1964–1976) *Oevres de Descartes*, rev. ed., edited by C. Adam and P. Tannery, Paris: Vrin; cited as "AT" by vol.:page numbers.
deVries, W. (1988) *Hegel's Theory of Mental Activity*, Ithaca: Cornell University Press.
Donnellan, K. (1966) "Reference and definite descriptions," *The Philosophical Review* 75: 281–304.
Dretske, F. I. (1969) *Seeing and Knowing*, London: Routledge and Kegan Paul.
Dretske, F. I. (1981) *Knowledge and the Flow of Information*, Cambridge: MIT Press.
Dretske, F. I. (1995) *Naturalizing the Mind*, Cambridge: MIT Press.
Dryer, D. (1966) *Kant's Solution for Verification in Metaphysics*, London: George Allen and Unwin.
Elgin, C. Z. (1999) *Considered Judgment*, Princeton: Princeton University Press.
Evans, G. (1975) "Identity and predication," *Journal of Philosophy*, rpt. in: idem. (1985), 25–48.
Evans, G. (1985) *Collected Papers*, Oxford: Clarendon Press.

Ferrini, C. (2015) *L'invenzione di Cartesio. La disembodied mind negli studi contemporanei: eredità o mito?* Trieste: Edizioni dell'Università di Trieste.
Gettier, E. (1963) "Is justified true belief knowledge?" *Analysis* 23: 121–123.
Guyer, P. (1989) "Psychology and the transcendental deduction," in *Kant's Transcendental Deductions*, edited by E. Förster, Stanford: Stanford University Press.
Hare, R. M. (1960) "Philosophical discoveries," *Mind* 69: 145–162.
Hegel, G. W. F. (1807) *Phänomenologie des Geistes*, critical edition by W. Bonsiepen and R. Heede, Bamberg and Würzburg: Goephard; cited as *PhdG* (volume 9 in GW).
Hegel, G. W. F. (1986–2016) *Gesammelte Werke*, 31 vols, Deutsche Forschungsgemeinschaft, with the Hegel-Kommission der Rheinisch-Westfälischen Akademie der Wissenschaften and the Hegel-Archiv der Ruhr-Universität Bochum, Hamburg: Meiner; cited as "*GW*" by vol.:page.line numbers.
Hume, D. (1739–1740) *A Treatise of Human Nature*, critical edition by D. F. Norton and M. J. Norton, Oxford: Oxford University Press: 2000; cited as "*T*" by part.book.paragraph numbers.
Hume, D. (1748) *An Enquiry Concerning Human Understanding*, critical edition by T. Beauchamp, Oxford: Clarendon Press: 2007; cited as "*En*" by paragraph numbers.
Kant, I. (1781) *Critik der reinen Vernunft*, 1st ed., Riga: Hartknoch; cited as "*KdrV*," "A"; rpt. in: idem. (1998) and (2009).
Kant, I. (1787) *Critik der reinen Vernunft*, 2nd rev. ed., Riga: Hartknoch; cited as "B"; rpt. in: idem. (1998) and (2009).
Kant, I. (1998) *Kritik der reinen Vernunft*, edited by J. Timmermann, Hamburg: Meiner, Philosophische Bibliothek 505.
Kant, I. (2009) *Kant im Kontext III – Komplettausgabe*, 2nd ed., edited by K. Worm and S. Boeck; release (XP/Vista) 6/2009. Berlin: InfoSoftWare.
Kornblith, H. (2002) *Knowledge and its Place in Nature*, Oxford: Clarendon Press.
Lærke, M., Smith, J. E. H. and Schliesser, E. (eds) (2013) *Philosophy and its History: Aims and Methods in the Study of Early Modern Philosophy*, Oxford: Oxford University Press.
Lewis, C. I. (1929) *Mind and the World Order*, New York: Charles Scribner's Sons; rpt. with revisions, New York: Dover, 1956.
Lipps, T. (1901) *Das Selbstbewusstsein: Empfindung und Gefühl*, Wiesbaden: Bergmann.
Lipps, T. (1912) *Grundzüge der Logik*, Leipzig: Voss.
Lipps, T. (1913) *Psychologische Untersuchungen*, 2 vols, Leipzig: Engelmann.
Melnick, A. (1989) *Space, Time, and Thought in Kant*, Dordrecht: Kluwer.
Millikan, R. G. (2004) *Varieties of Meaning: The 2002 Jean Nicod Lectures*, Cambridge: MIT Press.
Murphey, M. G. (2012) *The Development of Quine's Philosophy*, Berlin: Springer.
Piché, D. (1999) *La Condamnation parisienne de 1277*, Paris: Vrin.
Pinker, S. (1997) *How the Mind Works*, New York: Norton.
Quine, W. V. O. (1969) "Epistemology naturalized," in *Ontological Relativity and Other Essays*, New York: Columbia University Press.
Quine, W. V. O. (1995) *From Stimulus to Science*, Cambridge: Harvard University Press.
Robinson, J. (1977) *Duty and Hypocrisy in Hegel's Phenomenology of Mind*, Toronto: University of Toronto Press.
Rorty, R. (1970) "Strawson's objectivity argument," *Review of Metaphysics* 24: 207–244.
Rorty, R. (1986) "Pragmatism, Davidson and truth," in *Truth and Interpretation*, edited by E. Lepore, Oxford: Blackwell.
Russell, B. (1911) "Knowledge by acquaintance and knowledge by description," *Proceedings of the Aristotelian Society*, in: idem. (1994), vol. 6: 147–182.
Russell, B. (1913) "*Theory of Knowledge: The 1913 Manuscript*," London: Routledge, in: idem. (1994), vol. 7.
Russell, B. (1994) *The Collected Papers of Bertrand Russell*, edited by J. Passmore, London: Routledge; cited as CP.
Ryder, D., Kingsbury, J. and Williford, K. (eds) (2012) *Millikan and Her Critics*, New York: John Wiley and Sons.
Schroeder, S. (2001) "Private language and private experience," in *Wittgenstein: A Critical Reader*, edited by H.-J. Glock, Oxford: Blackwell.

Strawson, P. F. (1966) *The Bounds of Sense*, London: Methuen.
Strawson, P. F. (1989) "Sensibility, understanding, and the doctrine of synthesis: Comments on Henrich and Guyer," in *Kant's Transcendental Deductions*, edited by E. Förster, Stanford: Stanford University Press.
Stroud, B. (1994) "Scepticism, 'Externalism,' and the Goal of Epistemology," *Proceedings of the Aristotelian Society, Supplement* 68: 291–307.
Tierney, B. (1972) *Origins of Papal Infallibility, 1150–1350*, Leiden: Brill.
Travis, C. (2006) *Thought's Footing. A Theme in Wittgenstein's Investitations*, Oxford: Clarendon Press.
von Savigny, I. (1991) "Self-conscious individual versus social self: The rationale of Wittgenstein's discussion of rule following," *Philosophy and Phenomenological Research* 51: 67–84.
Waismann, F. (1945) "Verifiability," *Proceedings of the Aristotelian Society* 19 (suppl.): 119–150.
Watson, J. (1881) *Kant and his English Critics. A Comparison of Critical and Empirical Philosophy*, London: Macmillan.
Westphal, K. R. (1987–1988) "Sextus Empiricus Contra René Descartes," *Philosophy Research Archives* 13: 91–128.
Westphal, K. R. (2000) "Hegel's internal critique of naïve realism," *Journal of Philosophical Research* 25: 173–229.
Westphal, K. R. (2002–2003) "Analytischer Gehalt and zeitgenössische Bedeutung von Hegels Kritik des unmittelbaren Wissens," *Jahrbuch für Hegel-Forschungen* 8/9: 129–143.
Westphal, K. R. (2003) *Hegel's Epistemology: A Philosophical Introduction to the Phenomenology of Spirit*, Cambridge: Hackett Publishing Co.
Westphal, K. R. (2004) *Kant's Transcendental Proof of Realism*, Cambridge: Cambridge University Press.
Westphal, K. R. (2005) "Kant, Wittgenstein, and transcendental chaos," *Philosophical Investigations* 28: 303–323.
Westphal, K. R. (2007) "Consciousness and its transcendental conditions: Kant's anti-Cartesian revolt," in *Consciousness: From Perception to Reflection in the History of Philosophy*, edited by S. Heinämaa, V. Lähteenmäki, and P. Remes, Dordrecht: Springer.
Westphal, K. R. (2009) "Hegel's phenomenological method and analysis of consciousness," in *The Blackwell Guide to Hegel's Phenomenology of Spirit*, edited by K. R. Westphal, Oxford: Wiley-Blackwell.
Westphal, K. R. (2010a) "Kant's critique of pure reason and analytic philosophy," in *Cambridge Companion to Kant's Critique of Pure Reason*, edited by P. Guyer, Cambridge: Cambridge University Press.
Westphal, K. R. (2010b) "Hegel, Russell and the foundations of philosophy," in *Hegel and the Analytical Tradition*, edited by A. Nuzzo, New York: Continuum.
Westphal, K. R. (2013) "Hume, empiricism and the generality of thought," *Dialogue: Canadian Journal of Philosophy/Revue canadienne de philosophie* 52: 233–270.
Westphal, K. R. (2014) "Autonomy, freedom and embodiment: Hegel's critique of contemporary biologism," *The Hegel Bulletin* 35: 56–83.
Westphal, K. R. (2015) "Conventionalism and the impoverishment of the space of reasons: Carnap, Quine and Sellars," *Journal for the History of Analytic Philosophy* 3: 1–66.
Westphal, K. R. (2016a) "Mind, language and behaviour: Kant's critical cautions *contra* contemporary internalism and causal naturalism," in *Felsefede Yöntem/Method in Philosophy*, edited by S. Babür, special issue of *Yeditepe'de Felsefe/Philosophy at Yeditepe* 10, İstanbul: Yeditepe Üniversitesi Press, 102–149.
Westphal, K. R. (2016b) "Kant's dynamical principles: The analogies of experience," in *Kant's Critique of Pure Reason: A Critical Guide*, edited by J. O'Shea, Cambridge: Cambridge University Press, 184–204.
Will, F. L. (1968) "Thoughts and things," Presidential address to the Western (now Central) Division of the American Philosophical Association; rpt. in: idem. (1997).
Will, F. L. (1997) *Pragmatism and Realism*, edited by K. R. Westphal, Lanham: Rowman and Littlefield.
Wittgenstein, L. (1958) *Philosophical Investigations*, 2nd ed., translated by G. E. M. Anscombe, London: Macmillan; cited as "PI," by part, § numbers.

Wittgenstein, L. (1969) *On Certainty*, edited by G. E. M. Anscombe and G. H. von Wright, translated by D. Paul and G. E. M. Anscombe, Oxford: Basil Blackwell; cited as "OC."

Wittgenstein, L. (1978) *Remarks on the Foundations of Mathematics*, 2nd rev. ed., edited by G. H. von Wright, R. Rhees and G. E. M. Anscombe, translated by G. E. M. Anscombe, Cambridge: MIT Press; cited as "*RFM*."

Wolff, M. (2009) *Abhandlungen über die Prinzipien der Logik*, 2nd rev. ed., Frankfurt am Main: Klostermann.

Wolff, M. (2016) "How precise is Kant's table of judgments?" in *Kant's Critique of Pure Reason: A Critical Guide*, edited by J. O'Shea, Cambridge: Cambridge University Press, 83–105.

Wolff, M. (forthcoming) "Kant's table of judgments: Frege's critique and Kant's counterargument."

Wright, C. (1986) "Does *Philosophical Investigations* I.258–60 suggest a cogent argument against private language?" in *Subject, Thought, and Context*, edited by P. Pettit and J. McDowell, Oxford: Clarendon Press.

Wundt, W. (1907) *System der Philosophie*, 3 vols, 3rd rev. ed., Leipzig: Engelmann.

Part II
THOUGHT EXPERIMENTS AND THEIR FIELDS

8
THOUGHT EXPERIMENTS IN POLITICAL PHILOSOPHY

Nenad Miščević

1 Introduction

At some of the crucial junctures in the history of political philosophy, in the works that have strongly marked its development, we find appeals to the reader to imagine some social arrangement, judge it and then reason from these judgments. In the *Republic*, Plato famously invites us, through his character Socrates, to build a state "in the logos," presumably meaning in thought and speech, observe how it works, and, from there, read off the true nature of justice (369a5–10). J. J. Rousseau, in introducing his *Social Contract*, asks us to "set aside the facts" and turn to "the right and the reason" and think of an arrangement, a contract that will solve the problem of preserving freedom in an organized political society (in his posthumously published methodological introduction, Rousseau 1915, 473).[1] In the twentieth century, John Rawls famously invites us to get in the armchair and imagine that we are behind a veil of ignorance, which hides from us crucially important information about ourselves and about the people we shall be within society, and to consider what kind of political arrangement ("basic structure") and principles we would favour under such circumstances. Like in the *Republic* and in the *Social Contract*, the process of imagining is here supposed to give us the crucial data for building a theory of a just society. These episodes of imagining and judging are pretty clearly examples of what are now called thought experiments. Such experiments, it is clear already from the three famous examples we listed, are normally concerned with properties of imagined political arrangement, and also and more abstractly, of principles guiding and structuring them. Two great works of political philosophy, Plato's *Republic* and Rawls's *A Theory of Justice* are arguably long thought experiments, and elements of thought-experimenting are omnipresent both in utopian (including dystopian) and contractualist thinking. (I shall in the following abridge "political thought experiment" with "PTEs," using "TE" alone for "thought experiment"). The tradition continues, in a most lively and creative manner; see, for instance, Gaus (2011) for an interesting discussion.

Similarly, two and a half decades ago, Dworkin famously proposed a "fantasy answer" (as he puts it) to the challenging problems of distributive justice, inviting the reader to

"Imagine people shipwrecked on an empty island with diverse natural resources. They are each given an *equal number* of clamshells as bidding tokens, and they compete in an auction for individual ownership of the island's resources" (1981). More recently, addressing a similar set of issues, and advocating a more socialist solution, G. A. Cohen in his *Why Not Socialism* (2001/2009) proposed a TE involving a camping trip.[2] Imagining the trip, the reader can come to see the connection between community and equality, and that inequality would destroy community (and, to put it more technically, we come to understand the need for correcting for option luck). If you have leftist leanings, you will like it; if you have rightist ones you will dislike it. In any case, you will better understand the issues. Cohen then uses the camping trip as a model for a socialist society; and he uses the understanding of equality provided by the trip-model to argue for an extremely high level of equality in his socialist society. Of course, if you are skeptical you might ask how plausible such a fine camping trip is, and whether it can be used as a paradigm for much larger arrangements.

Of course, distributive justice is not the only issue for which solutions are these days sought through such imaginative experimenting.[3] Chandran Kukathas in his (2003) presents a "liberal archipelago" consisting of independent political communities. No deep basis is needed for a community, and the proposal is consistent with political community being a product of convention.

As far as political TEs are concerned, a long and intricate debate has been going on concerning one particular case, namely Rawls's veil-of-ignorance, and its place in theories of justice. However, *relatively little has been written on PTEs in general*.[4] Some consolation can be drawn from the fact that insights about moral thinking apply to political thought. However, PTEs present important puzzles of their own, given that they often concern intricate political arrangements to be judged from the philosopher's armchair. There is, therefore, *a growing need to address PTEs directly and specifically*.[5]

We shall explore a series of issues linked to PTEs, each of them only briefly, for obvious reasons of space.[6] First, we ask: what is a PTE, and what are its important characteristics and typical stages? Next, we look at historical and contemporary uses of PTEs, stressing the role of *Republic*-like TEs and their social contract counterparts. We hope that even this brief overview will indicate the indispensability of PTEs for political thought. There are many well-known doubts and objections to the indispensability claim, and they will be dealt with, unfortunately very briefly, in the same section. We shall then propose a typology of the methods of political thought, based on the trichotomy of founding elements – factual, thought-experimental-intuitional and principle-derived – and tentatively suggest that a lot of political thinking can be understood in terms of it. Finally, we shall consider the desiderata for successful PTEs and some of the prospects and advice that may follow from their consideration, briefly addressing the issue of the normative force of thought-experimental results, in connection with the current debates on the status of idealizations and ideal theories in political thinking.

2 Definition and structure

What is a PTE? If it involves appeal to an imagined, counterfactual situation in order to answer a political and moral question, does any act of imagining count? We need a general definition of TEs in order to find the answer. Some authors (Häggqvist 1996 and

Brown 1991 for instance) decline to propose a general definition. Brown offers a hint: "Thought experiments are devices of the imagination used to investigate the nature of things," he writes at the beginning of his Stanford Encyclopedia entry on TEs. Others give proposals that are not helpful for judging if a political-philosophical proposal is a TE. For instance, Ernst Mach gave a pioneering characterization of thought-experimenters and their use: "All of them imagine conditions, and connect with them their expectations and surmise of certain consequences: they gain a thought experiment" (1976, 136).[7] Fortunately, Tamar Szabó Gendler (2004), who concentrates on TEs in science, has proposed a workable definition centered on a particular imagined situation to be reasoned about, the imaginative access to the situation and an epistemic goal motivating the reasoning. Applied to PTEs, her idea would, to my mind, yield the following specification:

(a) Thought-experimental reasoning involves reasoning about a particular set of social and political circumstances, which may be specified in more or less detail.
(b) The thinker's mode of access to the scenario is via imagination rather than via observation.
(c) Contemplation of the scenario takes place with a specific purpose: coming to a judgment about some politically relevant theoretical proposal.

However, more precision is needed. Does any act of imagining count? Is the use of imagination a necessary condition?[8] For the second question, consider Kant's universalizability test in its simplest form (putting aside the recent Kantian literature where it has been developed into a more complex strategy). I want to keep the book I borrowed, and I ask myself what would happen if everyone did the same. Do I have to vividly imagine the reactions of various book owners? Even worse, in cases of cheating a partner or committing murder, vividly imagining everyone doing the same would result in a kind of trash-movie fantasy exercise, the moral relevance of which is highly dubious. Is the use of imagination really a necessary condition for a PTE?

The first question first. I propose to distinguish a wide and a narrow conception, and to keep both at hand. On the wide conception, even small imaginative experiments, like those involved in finding out a categorical imperative concerning some given action (token and type), i.e., imagining everyone performing the action, and considering the consequences, count as TEs. On the narrow conception only systematic, worked-out counterfactual scenarios count as TEs. The ambiguity is not peculiar to TEs, but rather comes from the very wide application of the term "experiment." The *Meriam-Webster Dictionary* offers as its first example a few sentences that depict scientific practice, talking about "simple laboratory *experiments*" and "some *experiments* with magnets." But then it passes to "an *experiment* in living more frugally" and concludes with "the city's *experiment* with a longer school year." These last two are not the province of philosophy of science for sure; and we have no problem distinguishing the full scientific meaning of "experiment" from its less demanding relatives. For us, the most relevant distinction is one between rudimentary experiments or quasi-experiments (available even to children) and full-fledged scientific ones. We might draw the parallel: rudimentary (quasi-)experiments versus full-fledged scientific ones on the scientific side, and rudimentary (quasi-)TEs versus full-fledged philosophical ones on the scientific side. The rough-and-ready tests, like for instance Hare's put-yourself-in-the-other-person's-shoes test, are rudimentary in this sense.

Rousseau's proposed social contract seems to fulfill the demands of the above definition inspired by Tamar Gendler, if we take "imagination" sufficiently widely to encompass "imagining in thought."[9] To start from the end, the purpose has just been specified: it is to solve the cooperation problem. As for (b), we are of course to imagine in thought what the arrangement would be like. Finally (a) is supposed to be satisfied by the claim about the uniqueness of the pact: "The clauses of this contract are so determined by the nature of the act that the slightest modification would render them pointless and ineffectual" (2002, 163). The kernel of the contract is clearly and emphatically unique, it is "a particular set of social and political circumstances" to be arranged for.

Concerning the second question, a possible line of answer would be to allow a kind of concrete, singular *conceiving*, alongside with imagination, as the legitimate mode of access to the scenario. (A long tradition in understanding "intuition," from Descartes, through Hintikka to Bealer counts such conceiving as "intuitional"). In the cheating example, I can just conceive of John, Mary, Peter, Helga and so on cheating their respective partners, without going into imaginative details.

Another issue, which we can here only mention in passing, is the relation between real cases and the ones imagined in PTEs. Let us add presumably real cases as the third category: a philosopher might believe that something is real, and be wrong about it. St. Augustine in his *The City of God* treats the legends from Old Testament as exact history, the great Muslim political thinkers proceed the same way with legends about the four "just caliphs," and Machiavelli treats Livy's stories about Roman kings as hard data.[10] Again, there seems to be a continuum between the three groups: judging the justice or injustice of a real arrangement is in principle very much like judging a merely legendary one (while believing it is real), and can be like passing a judgment of an actual political arrangement about which you learn from CNN. Tim Williamson proposed a similar line in relation to TEs in general, focusing on theoretical ones, in particular the Gettier TE (2007).

Let me briefly mention the typical structure of thought-experimenting in the great works of political theory.[11] Consider the *Republic*. The real construction of the Kallipolis begins with Glaucon's rejection of minimal economy, a "pig state" as he calls it, and his insistence that a good polis needs luxury. Luxury means import, import demands having things to export, this raises the demand for good agriculture, and this the need for a wide territory, which then has to be protected. In short, we need an army. This will bring in its wake a series of arrangements, indeed some very famous ones. Each is tested, in a small TE. It is to be imagined, and then the question of its justness is raised and answered. This ends the small TE, or "micro-TE." Then the interlocutors and the readers are invited to the next arrangement to be imagined. Would it be just? Yes. Then, repeat the procedure. Each such micro-TE is a step within the macro one. In short, Socrates asks: Is arrangement A just? If the answer is "yes" for each question, and if they fit together, the result is the perfectly just polis, the Kallipolis. The *Republic* is the first such macro-TE, Rawls's *A Theory of Justice* the most recent one. How does one arrive at the fit? First, the experimenter needs to aggregate micro-TEs; second, harmonize the results of these micro-TEs and then judge their coherence with other moral intuitions we might have. Let me call the harmonious unification of micro-TEs "the topical narrow reflective equilibrium" and the final narrow result "the general narrow reflective equilibrium." The former, topical one is geared to the unity of narrative structure, plus relevance and coherence between particular micro-TEs and their results.

To summarize, at *stage one*, a question is asked about a particular arrangement. At *stage two*, the question is understood, one hopes correctly, by the interlocutor. At *stage three* comes the tentative conscious production, the building of the "model" of the scenario at the conscious level. The *fourth stage* is more demanding. It concerns the production of the answer, involving the generation of intuition as to whether the arrangement is just or unjust. This probably involves reasoning at the unconscious level. At *the fifth stage*, the thinker comes out with an explicit intuition at the conscious level, usually geared to the particular example and having little generality. If the consideration of a particular scenario is typical, the thinker will have to do some varying and generalizing (deploying both moral and rational competence) at the conscious and reflective level and, perhaps, at the unconscious one too. Sometimes this process is called intuitive induction (Chisholm 1966). This is the *sixth* stage. *Stage seven* finally brings general belief at the reflective level. Three components are prominent in such a procedure: first, the aggregation of micro-TEs; second, the harmonization of the results of these micro-TEs; and finally, the judgment of their coherence with other moral intuitions one might have. In other words, the philosophical unification can be described in terms of narrow reflective equilibrium. This is *stage eight*. One can call the harmonious unification of micro-TEs "topical narrow reflective equilibrium" and the final narrow result "general narrow reflective equilibrium." The former, topical process is geared to the unity of narrative structure, plus the relevance and coherence between particular stages, the micro-TEs. At *stage nine*, general knowledge of a more empirical kind is brought into play for the important and difficult task of comparing the result with all we know about life and politics, from both the personal experiential level and from history, social and natural sciences, reaching a wide reflective equilibrium as the final result (see, for instance, Gaus 2011 for a rich account of the usability and even indispensability of such wider knowledge in political theory).[12]

Attention to the internal structure of TEs is important for judging their viability and value, since criticisms of them often result from the failure to understand the specific requirements and liabilities of each stage. On the methodological side, understanding PTEs in detail could, in the long run, improve reasoning in matters of political theory. It can also help with particular PTEs in applied matters. In contemporary ethical and political debates the participants constantly appeal to results (and intuitions) that derive from counterfactual suppositions and even more complete scenarios typical for TEs. In order to evaluate such proposals, one should have a firm grip on methodological assumptions and their role, from stage to stage, within the biography of a TE.

3 Politics in the armchair: the place of PTEs in political theory

3.1 TEs and their rivals: topical and historical issues

It is time briefly to place political thought-experimenting on the wider map, relating it to its competitors in the methodology of political theory. In contemporary debates, the most popular anti-TE view is the inferentialist one, according to which they can be replaced by inference from empirical and moral premises. But can any given thought experiment be replaced by argument which features only norms and empirical information? The inferentialists (e.g., John Norton) see TEs as "arguments which: (i) posit hypothetical or counterfactual states of affairs, and (ii) invoke particulars irrelevant to the generality of the conclusion" (Norton 1991, 129). Particular items from a TE are anyway irrelevant for its point, so why not make explicit the hidden argument; reconstruct its premises concerning general laws, empirical facts, and (in the case of moral and political TEs) moral norms; and replace the TE with such an argument? This is the most important topical issue in the area; once we point to the (hopefully correct) answer, we can turn to the next task: placing PTEs on the map as against alternatives, and note the historical relations between PTEs and its competitors.

Note that there is an interesting difference between moral-political TEs and the scientific ones. In the later, the inferentialist can rely on empirically tested and mathematically formulated natural laws as the general premises, in the former cases, the situation is drastically different. The first difference is that the very moral principles, which are candidates for general premises, demand testing, and the main testing ground is the armchair and moral intuitions. A consequentialist (e.g., a utilitarian) might claim that the general utilitarian principle is general enough and does not demand testing by intuitions. However, even the most elementary question (e.g., concerning what is to be maximized by human action) leads to disagreements that can be settled only with the help of intuitions. (Take Mill's famous and crucially important claim that it is "better to be Socrates dissatisfied than a fool satisfied"; it is presented as something obvious to the sensible reader; one would say, as an "intuition"). Second, testing is needed in the application of principles. Historical Kantian principles famously lead to unacceptable rigorist conclusions, unless moderated by additional considerations, which again come from the domain of intuitions and TEs. Third, many theoreticians argue that general principles are just too general, and are not to be applied directly. One needs to derive norms and rules, and this again brings in intuitions (see Gaus 2011).

Given these grounds, it seems that one may accept the indispensability of PTEs: a TE is an original and irreplaceable "representational device," which does not reduce to mere illustration of some piece of abstract knowledge or theory. A critic may point out that some of the famous scientific TEs were merely provisional tools of investigation, sooner or later to be replaced by more accurate tools, say, more precise measuring devices (as with Galileo's famous musket ball and cannon ball TE). But what tools do we have for validating the "outcomes" or the "findings" of political (or, for that reason, moral) TEs? (Adding that social sciences might provide a better comparison class than natural sciences, both because they face the same control-of-variables problem and because often there is no clear alternative to thought-experimenting (admittedly, for different reasons, having to do with moral scruples about experimenting on people and social engineering)). These are the difficult questions that confront the whole of ethics and political philosophy, but do not speak particularly against PTEs.

Let me briefly mention another kind of dissatisfaction: how can thinking about arrangements that are hardly possible in real life, and constructed by arbitrarily selecting the features considered to be important, teach us anything about political reality? Both kinds of problem, modal distance and the arbitrariness of selection, are to be encountered elsewhere in philosophy and even science (see Miščević 2013a, 203). Let me add that we do imagine alternatives to the actual world all the time (how would it feel to be famous, or wealthy, or self-confident?), and go on disagreeing about the relevance of particular solutions. A third sort of criticism, focused on the primacy of factual matters and their moral status, is exemplified by Sen (2009).

We can now briefly turn to history.[13] Plato-style thought experiments have a long tradition in political thought, including medieval thinkers like Al-Farabi, renaissance Platonists (Campanella and Morus) and utopian socialists from eighteenth and nineteenth centuries. Another family of PTEs is equally famous, and seems to have a better standing on the contemporary scene: the social contract TEs. Among many differences between the two, one is paramount. Notice that the *Republic*-TE is performed in a dialogue of aristocratic intellectuals who among themselves find out what is best for the concerned population: for instance, any young and healthy women in the Kallipolis have to go through the reproductive program designed by philosophers, and are not free to criticize and opt out. If she demurs, they tell her the noble lie, and make her accept it. In this sense, the fate of the ordinary people is decided by third persons, philosophers; for them the *Republic*-TE is a third person procedure. The main modern competitor to such kinds of experiment is the social contract, where each participant asks herself the crucial question: Would you yourself sign this document? P.J. Proudhon puts the point explicitly and graphically: "The social contract should be freely discussed, individually accepted, signed with their own hands, by all the participants" (1969, 115). In this sense it is a first person political TE; the background probably being the assumption of basic equality and dignity of each participant. The contrast between the expert-oriented, Plato-inspired macro-PTEs and the more egalitarian social contract macro-PTEs is a contrast quite important for political philosophy and its methodology.

Let us take another step in the direction of generality, and note the existence of a strong tradition in political philosophy that is contrary to thought-experimenting, from Aristotle's criticism of the community of children in the *Republic*, through Hume and Burke, all the way to Sen. The modern period brought another central kind of political TEs to the fore: the hypothetical social contract. And the critics reacted. Locke, Rousseau and Kant on the one side contrast with Hume on the opposite one, with Hegel later continuing the tradition of criticism of contractualist thought-experimenting. Arguably, the contrast between defenders and critics of political TEs has been the central contrast in the history of methodology of political philosophy, from Plato and Aristotle to Rawls and Morgenthau.

Here is then one way of systematizing the possible approaches, thought-experimental (-intuitional), factual and principle-derived. We have been looking at PTEs and the intuitions they produce as one source of political theorizing. The second available source, stressed by authors from Aristotle, through Augustine and Machiavelli to Burke, Hegel and the Marxists, are historical facts (or presumed facts). The third traditional source are beliefs concerning political principles. Some great philosophers, from Aristotle through Proclus, and Islamic and Christian scholastics all the way to Hegel, saw our alleged acquaintance with general moral-political principles as independent from singular TEs; others, like Kant and Rawls, saw principles as items either discovered or tested, or both discovered and tested, through intuitions derived from considering particular (types of) cases. Philosophers usually preferred one or two, leaving the third one aside: Machiavelli and Burke prefer facts; Hegel a combination of principles and historical facts; and Rousseau, Kant and Rawls (from *A Theory of Justice*) TEs and principles, with minimal factual background. So, a study of the history of PTEs might help to build a more systematic picture of the history of political philosophy.

3.2 PTEs, utopias and dystopias

Plato's perfectly just polis is the good place to live in, the best in fact. Thomas More helped with the name: the successful macro-TE (or even mega-TE) results in a utopia. This brings us to an interesting characterization of the *Republic*. Indeed, it has arguably given birth to a whole genre of politico-philosophical narrative products: utopias. Malcolm Schofield has argued that the *Republic* is a work of political utopianism thus: "the *Republic* ... is the first great work of political utopianism ever written" (2006, 205). He sees utopian thinking as "the imagining of a blueprint for a desired world which is nevertheless located in present-day concerns, with questions about practicability and legitimacy ... regarded as secondary. Utopianism will always be with us ... Human thought is always dealing with the possible as well as the actual ... [so] there is often no option but to explore alternatives" (ibid). In short, utopia is imagination of alternatives. But, we have seen that the imagination of alternatives as performed in the *Republic* is a PTE. Is there any difference?

Here is my proposal. In presenting an alternative social arrangement one can pursue different goals; for our purpose the main difference is between the epistemic and motivational. In the case of a philosophical TE the explicit goal is epistemic: for instance, find out what justice is. Now, once the blueprint is there the further goal might be motivational: implementing the system as far as possible. (Go to Sicily and try to persuade the local ruler to do it. Or, teach the system to a dissident general, Dion; when he becomes leader, he might implement it. Or, train the elite of your polis in the right way; a member of it could become a ruler one day, and so on). But as long as philosophy is being done, the primary goal is epistemic. Alternatively, one might design a utopia, in the same manner as one designs a macro-arrangement for a TE, but with a primarily practical goal. This is then the proper province of utopian literature. Of course, the same text is sometimes read as more epistemic, or more motivational.[14] A further way to characterize the contrast is to appeal to the order of determination; in theoretical TEs it goes from world to mind, in political TEs to a large extent from mind to world (even if a goal is epistemic: to find objective Good or the Just, etc.). Unfortunately, mistakes in theoretical TEs have different sorts of consequences than mistakes in motivational ones: implementing a utopia brings much more serious problems in its wake. Here is a tentative and very simple division of political TEs and utopias, taking into account the fact that sometimes they are merely implicit (e.g. social contract being presented as a historical fact), and sometimes explicit:

	Epistemic	*Motivational*
Explicit	Plato, Rawls	Plato
Implicit	Hobbes, Locke	most utopias

The columns correspond to the two roles, epistemic and motivational we mentioned above. Let us now return to more general issues.

4 Experimenting and aspiring: the desiderata on PTEs

What makes a TE into a good experiment? Let me briefly present the desiderata for a good PTE, under four very general headings. First, we have to consider the relevance and importance of matters considered, and the width of coverage, including the richness of detail in the scenario imagined. Second, it should be normatively (morally and politically) relevant, teaching the experimenter (author or reader) what kinds of arrangements are just, and what kinds unjust, and possibly more about moral matters crucial for the society one is interested in.

Third, the scenario proposed should be sufficiently realistic. This includes the demand that it should be stable through time; this has been an important consideration since the beginning of political thought. Finally, if the arrangement is morally and politically attractive, it would be fine if something sufficiently like it were at least in principle reachable from our present political position. Each desideratum brings difficult questions. We shall discuss the realism and reachability in a little more detail, since these issues appear in recent discussion in new and interesting forms.

4.1 Controlling the variables

This is the main methodological desideratum. First, the relevance and importance of matters are considered. One important sub-problem is how much, and what kind, of empirical information the political thinker should incorporate into his or her proposed alternative political arrangements. One may ask: have all important variables been taken into account in the construction of the given PTE? Ernst Mach pointed out this desideratum,[15] and Julian Baggini (web) has called the difficulty this point raises the problem of the "control of variables." An alternative way of describing it appeals to the scenario involved as a "counterfactual situation" (or even "world"). How does this situation differ from the actual one, and how distant is it, authors like Tim Williamson would ask (2007)? Are the variables that have been taken into account really relevant? Three examples illustrate the problem with its sub-problems and the desideratum. First, the sub-problem of quantity, or including too few variables. Rousseau's *Social Contract* is notorious for not providing enough information about the contract itself. For instance, the information on what matters is covered by the hypothetical contract; is it just politics, or perhaps also the economy; and what about gender matters and the like? How wide is the group? Options range from the size of his native Geneva to a cosmopolitan contract. And little is clear about practical matters, like getting people ready for the contract, the issue of lying – the legislator inventing myths – and so on.

Second sub-problem: which variables are relevant? Plato is importing from the real world the need for relative luxury, and the need for a strong, standing army of the guardians (central for the whole story). We should postulate, he claims (2.373a) this need as given in order to pass from the "state for pigs" to a more luxurious state. And the whole further development – with guardians and their education by philosophers – will depend on this assumption. Many readers might agree, but certainly not all.

Equally famously, or infamously, Rawls builds some central tenets of his Original Position on the assumption that people are not going to be envious of social inequalities, once they have their basic needs satisfied. But competitiveness seems to be essential to human nature, and many have argued that giving a zero value to this variable threatens the persuasiveness of the whole construction.

The next and related desideratum is the width and detail of the coverage. The most famous TEs in contemporary political philosophy are so much more detailed than scientific ones. Thought experimenting leaves some matters out; but how detailed must the coverage be in order for a PTE to succeed? Importance and coverage seem to allow for trade-offs: if the centrally important variables are correctly represented in TE, the construction can survive without extensive coverage of all details. Rawls is, for instance, in his *A Theory of Justice* very clear about the obedience to laws in ideal theory; but very vague about the character of the Basic Structure, to the point that we do not even know if it has to be statist or not. On the other hand, detailed coverage guarantees that all central variables will be taken into account

4.2 Positive normative status: justice and other moral qualities

The most important claim in the classical PTEs is the following: If the relevant social political matters were arranged in the given way, the arrangement would be just. It is a counterfactual, the antecedent is the description of a micro-scenario (for a micro-TE), or their conjunction – one big proposal (a mega-TE). Justice is usually seen as the main requirement, but other qualities also count: If the relevant social political matters were arranged in the given way, the arrangement

> ... would bring happiness and satisfaction to its members (would be optimitic in the descriptive sense).
> ... would be such that members of the community would be free persons.
> ... would be such that members of the community would be treated with respect.
> ... would be such that members of the community would be equal.

In dystopias, the demand is reversed: the arrangement should be bad enough to serve as a warning. But in philosophy they seem to be almost non-existent; their real home is literature.

Much more needs to be said, but we shall return to the normative issues connecting them with the factual ones below.

4.3 Realism

We pass from normative desiderata to desiderata concerning the reality (or un-reality) of the model, which we may call social and psychological, or metaphysical if you prefer the highest genus. Let me start with an example of a recently proposed PTE that seems quite unrealistic by the ordinary criteria of realism. We already mentioned Kukathas's liberal archipelago (2003), consisting of islands hosting independent political communities, on the whole completely unmanaged. Some communities are extremely tolerant, other intolerant, and a third kind is semi-tolerant. Islands are connected by "the sea of toleration," so they are not literally isolated. On the (imaginary) factual level, the arrangement seems difficult and unstable. We are not told how disagreements are to be settled (for instance, a refinery on one island poisoning hundreds of others). Also, internal intolerance goes ill with external tolerance: domestic violence habituates people to exercising pressure, using threats and force, disregarding others, and it is unclear how this would go with external toleration. The readers probably ask themselves why would one risk such a dissonance in constructing one's ideal society.

Many authors see the realistic character of the imagined situation as the necessary condition for the theoretical relevance of imagining. Joshua Cohen, discussing in his (2010) the ideal of "free community of equals," writes: "But can people live this way? Can human beings really live in a free community of equals, or is that ideal a utopia, well beyond our reach? Here we have ... the problem of realism" (16). He very briefly mentions three kinds of possibility required for the instantiation of desirable communities (2010, 14), (without mentioning PTEs):

> the first is the motivational possibility: people must be such that in principle they can get motivated for such a project ... [second,] a free community of equals must also be socially and politically possible: can an ongoing society meet the conditions described by that ideal? I will call this the problem of institutional possibility.
> (2010, 19)

And there is a third kind: "a third possibility problem": "this problem arises from doubts about 'accessibility': is there any route leading from current circumstances to the society of the general will?" (2010, 14).

He mentions the third possibility only to set it aside. Then he briefly, all too briefly, turns to the impossibilities that make the project "utopian" (in the sense of impossible and unreachable):

> Corresponding to the three problems of possibility, we can distinguish three ways that political thought might be utopian: it might rest on values that simply cannot be jointly realized under any conditions; it might endorse values whose realization is incompatible with human nature; and it might embrace an ideal that cannot be realized by a social trajectory that begins from current conditions.
> (2010, 14)

One can join Cohen in distinguishing the motivational from institutional possibility of a proposed ideal: reasonable people may wonder whether that ideal is humanly possible, whether its motivational demands are compatible with our human nature (2010, 16). And, "A free community of equals must also be socially and politically possible: can an ongoing society meet the conditions described by that ideal?" (2010, 19). How do the proponents of PTEs demonstrate the psychological possibility? Rawls dedicates 200 pages to the issue of stability in his A Theory of Justice (and then to some extent changes his mind in Political Liberalism). He appeals to common knowledge about people, no special insights. So, our access to various kinds of possibilities seems to be holistic in the sense that thinkers appeal to all sorts of knowledge about themselves, people in general, political arrangements and so on. presumably, this knowledge is of an ordinary sort, used in daily interactions. Here is another example.

We might further distinguish two more sets of possibility – possibility in the world considered, and possibility in relation to our world. The first has to do with consistency and coherence, as well as psychological-motivational possibility and institutional possibility there, in the imagined world. We assume that the relevant imagined worlds have the same laws of psychology as our world, so that the arrangement that works for them is psychologically and institutionally possible for us. We shall consider the second one at the end of our list.

An important aspect of possibility and realistic character is related to stability or sustainability of the arrangement considered. If ought implies can, the closest metaphysically possible and morally acceptable world should be also humanly possible and stable. Plato's community of children has an infamous problem in this context, recognized by Aristotle and deployed against the *Republic*. The instability of anarchist arrangements might be the contemporary counterpart. Rawls dedicates to stability a long chapter of his *A Theory of Justice* building upon the assumed virtuous circle between human feelings of justice that prompt just arrangements and the ability of just arrangements to enhance the feeling of justice in their turn. However, in his later writings, the issue of stability is moved out of the domain of thought-experimenting, into considerations of actual liberal tradition and factual overlapping consensus (for an interesting account see Weithman 2011).

4.4 Reachability

Finally, the proposed arrangement, if morally relevant, has to be such that humanity can reach it from its actual situation. Realism is sometimes taken to encompass this desideratum as well.[16] We want it, in other words, to be plausibly reachable from the actual world, and from some given moment of time, preferably from the present (not just reachable with negligible probability) and the price of reaching the model ideal should not be exorbitant (see, for example, Miller 2013). Similarly, in order to be relevant, a dystopian negative model should be a serious and threatening option; not perhaps a clear and present danger, but one that could easily arise from our actual situation.

Let us briefly discuss the last three desiderata together: normative qualities (goodness, justice), possibility and accessibility. Positive big PTEs typically involve understanding of social arrangements, both of the underlying (contra)factual structure and of resulting normative properties (as opposed to mere isolated pieces of knowledge about some microarrangement). The object of understanding is the whole of the model. In positive PTEs it is a relatively (or absolutely) ideal picture. The understanding and appreciation of the model proposed has been the main epistemological locus for theorizing about political ideals, from Plato to Rawls, Dworkin, G.A. Cohen and other present-day philosophers. Thus, on the normative side, PTE is an important means for building ethico-political ideal and/or aspirational theories, as they are called in recent literature (see below). Of course, such normative considerations have interacted in theory building and in the history of debates with the desiderata concerning realism, and there is a natural bridge between them: we want morally valuable arrangements to be somehow humanly achievable, and we hope that at least some stable and achievable arrangements will also have centrally important moral qualities. One can imagine a morally perfect arrangement, which turns out to be politically extremely unstable since it overburdens the members of the community, and one is confronted with a plethora of historically quite stable arrangements, most infamously slavery and serfdom, that are morally extremely bad.

One canonical contrast relevant to our purposes is the one between ideal and non-ideal theory, originally due to Rawls.[17] The contrast has many versions, so let me mention two recent ones. Alan Hamlin and Zofia Stemplowska (2012) distinguish ideal from non-ideal theory through four contrasting pairs. First, full compliance and non-full compliance; as in Rawls, ideal theory assumes full compliance with laws of the just arrangement. The second is idealization, introduction of clear positive contra-factual elements in contrast to mere abstraction, simplification and setting aside of irrelevant features. Further, fact-sensitivity and fact-insensitivity; the ideal theory is less sensitive to facts than the non-ideal one. Finally, we have the contrast between perfect justice (or another value) and local improvement in justice (or another value). Hamlin and Stemplowska talk about "AD-recommendations" "to emphasize that what they recommend is both achievable and desirable. In fact it is precisely the lack of AD-recommendations that is at stake in debates about the uses of ideal theory (2012, 330). Ideal theory thus seems obviously to fall on the side of typical positive PTEs. But what should we do about the lack of recommendations for achieving desirable outcomes?

A beginning of an interesting answer, involving another version of the ideal/non-ideal contrast, has been offered by David Estlund in his "Utopophobia," chapter XIV of his (2008) book.[18] He distinguishes three kinds of political theory: realist, aspirational-hopeless and utopian. The realist one is rather cynical, and its extreme opposite are the utopian theories ("utopia" here being a starkly impossible political model or project). "A normative political theory can be as cynical or as utopian as one wishes, but most theories try to steer between these extremes" (2008, 263). The intermediate theories are called "aspirational":

> Consider a theory that held individuals and institutions to standards that it is within their ability to meet, but which there is good reason to believe they will never meet. So far, the theory has no apparent defect.
>
> (2008, 264)

> It remains aspirational: it sets sound standards that are not met, but could be met, and it tells us to meet them.
>
> (2008, 267)

Finally, he divides aspirational theory into less ambitious ones, that he calls "concessive," and more ambitious ones, described as "pure."

Now, good positive PTE-models seem to be suggesting an aspirational theory; there is a clear connection between thought-experimental considerations, and the ideal/non-ideal theory issues and we can easily bring two traditions together, hoping for a classification that cuts the normative animal at its joints. But, there is more: the main topic of the aspirational discussion is the normative force of different modal statuses: various possibilities and impossibilities, and these options seem to parallel our desiderata for PTEs.

Let us develop matters here just a little bit, in a form acceptable for aspirational theorizing. Our distinction within PTE-models between those that are suitable for some possible world with the same laws of psychology as ours (i.e. psychologically and institutionally possible), and those that are actually reachable from our world at some given time, is not to be found in Estlund, but might be helpful when we come to the contrast between the aspirational and the completely utopian (and to the two degrees within the aspirational status).

Now, we can connect this desiderata with Estlund's partition. First, every PTE-model for an aspirational theory must satisfy desiderata having to do with consistency and stability of the arrangements in the world to which they belong. Second, only those used for concessive aspirational theories must also satisfy the same desiderata in relation to our world; they need to be reachable, at least in principle, from our present situation.

Let me illustrate. Remember the camping trip PTE, proposed by G.A. Cohen. It looks plausible at first sight: if people can be maximally cooperative on a camping trip, why not in other social interactions? The model is psychologically and organizationally possible, its price is not exorbitant, can be low, but, its quality is not guaranteed. (If ten boys and one girl go camping, there will be some competition, and one asks how bad it can get. Well, imagine a more balanced group; still there will be no guarantee that there would not be some other conflict, say, over distribution of boring duties). Finally, camping does not last a whole year, normally, it is over quickly. So, how plausible is it as a long-term model for society as a whole? Consider the close possibilities, first, the psychological one: can one act at one's work place the same way as one would act while camping? Next, the institutional one: is the non-managed, almost anarchist camping arrangement possible on a large scale? Next, the external question: is it implementable in our society (e.g. should the Labor party push for it)? Cohen himself, sounding quite anarchist for a Marxist, thinks it is. If he is right, the model is concessive aspirational, and things are in order. If he is wrong, his PTE-model is just pure aspirational. He would not be happy with this, as shown by dozens of pages dedicated to defending its feasibility. However, we should not despair. We can still argue from the attractiveness of the trip arrangements to the attractiveness of some changes in our society; the model as a whole might be merely purely aspirational but some of its parts can be reworked into a concessive aspirational proposal. So, let me venture an optimistic guess: the almost-unachievable idealized PTE models are epistemically, morally and politically useful since they direct our attention in the right way.

5 Conclusion

Political thought experiments combine normative with factual-causal features. On the one hand, they offer models that are supposed to have important factual properties: durability, psychological and institutional stability, reachability from the present moment in time, and so on. Here, they are close to factual scientific TEs. We have talked about the control of variables and the proximity of the possible world(s) depicted by the TE scenario to our world. On the other, they connect these models with normative matters, most often positive ones (but also sometimes negative, as in dystopian writings). This makes them unique. In most moral TEs the factual background is ordinary, and theoretically minimal, in scientific TEs the moral, normative element plays no role. PTEs combine the two, in a unique and interesting way.

This suggests two sources of indispensability of TEs in political thinking, which make TEs original and irreplaceable "representational devices," which do not reduce to mere illustration of some piece of abstract knowledge or theory. The first is shared by other factually oriented armchair experimentation, in science and in theoretical philosophy: human beings are often much better at detecting counterfactual matters, like the plausibility of a given scenario, when the scenario is particular, and concretely imaginable; no wonder given our evolutionary history, and the role of perception, in contrast to abstract thinking, in our dealings with the world. The other concerns normative matters: in this area facts alone are not enough, so we can depend on intuitions and principles only, and we have no way to test the later empirically, without importing normative assumptions. Therefore, the main test for principles is intuitions, and most of them come from the armchair.

Given the indispensability of thought-experimenting for the political theory, alongside with factual information and appeal to principles, there is no wonder that PTEs play a crucial role in it. From Plato's work and his followers, through early social contract thinking all the way to Rawls and present-day thinkers, the main ideas and proposals were formulated as tasks for TEs. Other great thinkers were less enthusiastic, and there is a parallel line of critics, relying either on factual (or presumed factual) sources, or on principles, or both. One could write the history of political philosophy as the history of interactions of these three lines. Moreover, we noted two possible roles for political TEs: their proper and intrinsic epistemic role in which they serve as heuristic and testing devices (as in Plato, Locke and Rawls), and the motivational role, which makes them into utopias, to be followed, imitated and perhaps implemented in political action. The first is a more philosophical epistemic one, and the second a more activist one. The second often spills over into literature, with literary utopias and dystopias; interestingly, they allow for more ambiguity in conclusions drawn from the material presented, leaving the readers to decide for themselves, and a larger plurality of possible readings counts as a plus, not as a minus to be avoided or vehemently criticized, as is the case with their philosophical counterparts.

Here is the final philosophical motivation: Since TEs are central for other areas of philosophy and for some traditions in fictional writing, once we put the big picture together, we will get a more unified view of the whole, which could help us to integrate the methodology of political philosophy with the methodology of philosophy in general, and finally contribute to a deeper understanding of fictional-literary thought experimenting.

In short, in the contemporary scene, one extensively discusses some particular comprehensive PTEs, above all the Rawlsian veil-of-ignorance, but without putting them into the large methodological framework where they certainly belong, namely the meta-philosophical considerations of PTEs in general. It is time to build a comprehensive theory that will connect PTEs with thought-experimenting in general and help both with methodological and substantive issues.

Acknowledgements

Thanks go to James R. Brown, Tea Logar, Friderik Klampfer, Miomir Matulović, Lukas Mayer, Pranay Sanklecha and Tim Williamson.

Notes

1 In the original French it is in the first person: "Mais je cherche le droit et la raison, et je ne discute pas les faits" (Rousseau 1915, 462).
2 In it, we are invited to imagine a group of people on a camping trip. People camping normally exercise solidarity, treat each other as equals, and help altruistically and without reservation. In exposition, Cohen asks various questions about the imagined situation. For instance, would it be alright if you had in the region your own special high-grade fish pond, and you ate delicious fish

out of it, and did not let anyone else have any? Of course, this would be terrible on the trip. Your group would stop being a "real" small community.

3 A ground-breaking book on TEs in more concrete political research, *Counterfactual Thought Experiments in World Politics* (1996), edited by P. E. Tetlock and A. Belkin has appeared almost two decades ago, and has been followed by a continuous spate of works, to which philosophers of politics should pay due attention.

4 On the positive side, there is a plethora of high-quality work on TEs in general, starting with the pioneering work of James R. Brown (see references).

5 Also, TEs in moral philosophy are a well-discussed topic (see Brun, this volume), and the area of political TEs intersects with the area of moral-philosophical TEs. There is a lot of classical philosophical debate, and the main innovation comes these days from experimental philosophy, which uses psychological methodology to investigate (and often criticize) TEs (see Stich and Tobia, this volume; Ludwig, this volume; and Cohnitz and Häggqvist, this volume).

6 I discuss the majority of these topics in more detail in Miščević (2012, 2013a, 2013b, 2013c).

7 The situation with TEs replicates the one with experiments in general. Some good lexicons of philosophy of science even lack the entry on experiment as such. Thoughtful overviews in good volumes, like Newton-Smith's Blackwell's *Companion to Philosophy of Science* (2000), stress the plurality of "images of experiment" (Gooding 2000, 117); and others, like Theodore Arabatzis's entry on "Experiment," offer a brief sketch of the "epistemology of experiment" (2008, 163), without venturing a definition.

8 To see the relevance of the first question, take Rousseau's famous formulation of the task of political philosophy:

> To find a form of association that may defend and protect with the whole force of the community the person and property of every associate, and by means of which each, joining together with all, may nevertheless obey only himself, and remain as free as before. Such is the fundamental problem of which the social contract provides the solution.
>
> (2002, 163)

The social contract is the pole that enables us to vault from facts to norms. Its clauses,

> properly understood, may be reduced to one – the total alienation of each associate, together with all his rights, to the whole community; for, in the first place, as each gives himself absolutely, the conditions are the same for all; and, this being so, no one has any interest in making them burdensome to others.
>
> (Ibid.)

This is the scenario to be contemplated, the solution proposed by Rousseau. The defence he offers is really laconic: if I give myself to all, then there is no particular person that is my master; therefore, I give myself to nobody (a logical error looms large here, but let us put it aside). Further, he claims that whatever cluster of forces I gave to all, I am getting it back and receive the firm promise of protection, thereby receiving more "force" than I have given to all. So, this is the proposed solution in its barest outline, the one favored by Rousseau. Does it involve imagination at all? Is it a TE?

9 For more historical information about Rousseau's predilection for "empire of imagination" in political matters, the book to read is Miller's *Rousseau: Dreamer of Democracy* (1984, especially chs 2 and 3).

10 Consider a thinker who follows with great interest an important historical development, say the degradation of an idealistic, utopian movement into a repressive, statist and anti-democratic arrangement (early Christianity to Christian monarchies, Red Turbans revolt to the establishment of the Ming dynasty, or leftist movements to Stalinist Soviet Union). He or she then reimagines it in a narrative rich with fantastic elements (Orwell's *Animal farm*, or Le Guin's *The Dispossessed*). Let us agree that the reader is presented with "a particular set of social and political circumstances, which may be specified in more or less detail," that her "mode of access to the scenario is via imagination" and that the author wants the reader to come up with her judgment about both the low moral quality of the circumstances contemplated and about the typical

dynamics that generates the degradation. The main conditions for a PTE are fulfilled. It seems then that there is a continuum between the first, the actual, historical cases; the second, slightly rearranged scenarios that involve abstraction from the actual details; and the third "idealized" scenarios (in the technical sense of introducing unreal, even impossible elements, like the rule of pigs in the *Farm*).

11 I develop the account of the stages in PTEs in a bit more detail in my (2013a).
12 Of course, not every political TE is so detailed and well-structured. Rousseau's *Social Contract* proposes the solution of the main political problem in one sentence, and then does not discuss it the way one might expect from the *Republic* or from Rawls, and the result has been confusion and serious disagreement about even his most basic views. Even the relatively pedantic Kant is less talkative about his social contract than the reader might wish.
13 With apologies for brevity. For more details, see Miščević (2012, 2013a, b).
14 For example, Locke's account of the social contract is epistemic on a traditional reading, but if we follow Ashcraft (1986) and read the *Second Treatise* as a political pamphlet, it will come out as primarily motivational.
15 In his 1976, Chapter XI, sect. 3–5, without using the exact term.
16 On such an understanding, being realistic has two meanings. On the first, a model is realistic if it is psychologically and institutionally possible in some imaginary possible worlds. On the second, a model is externally realistic if it can be implemented in the actual world starting from the present situation.
17 *A Theory of Justice* (1971), ch. 1, sect. 2. See also Simmons (2010).
18 See also his 2011 paper.

References

Arabatzis, T. (2008) "Experiment," in *The Routledge Companion to Philosophy of Science*, edited by S. Psillos and M. Curd, New York: Routledge.
Ashcraft, R. (1986) *Revolutionary Politics and Locke's Two Treatises of Government*, Princeton: Princeton University Press.
Baggini, J. (2007) "On thought experiments." Available here: http://philosophybites.com/2007/12/julian-baggini.html (accessed 15 November 2016).
Brown, J. R. (1991) *Laboratory of the Mind: Thought Experiments in the Natural Sciences*, London: Routledge.
Chisholm, R. (1966) *Theory of Knowledge*, Englewood Cliffs: Prentice Hall.
Cohen, J. (2010) *Rousseau, A Free Community of Equals*, Oxford: Oxford University Press.
Dworkin, R. (1981) "What is equality? Part 1: Equality of welfare," *Philosophy and Public Affairs* 10: 185–246.
Estlund, D. (2008) *Democratic Authority: A Philosophical Framework*, Princeton: Princeton University Press.
Gaus, G. (2011) *The Order of Public Reason, A Theory of Freedom and Morality in a Diverse and Bounded World*, Cambridge: Cambridge University Press.
Gendler, T. S. (2004) "Thought experiments rethought – and reperceived," *Philosophy of Science* 71: 1152–1164.
Gooding, D. C. (2000) "Experiment," in *Blackwell's Companion to Philosophy of Science*, edited by W. H. Newton-Smith, Somerset, UK: Wiley-Blackwell.
Häggqvist, S. (1996) *Thought Experiments in Philosophy*, Stockholm: Almqvist & Wiksell.
Hamlin, A. and Stemplowska, Z. (2012) "Theory, ideal theory and the theory of ideals," *Political Studies Review* 10: 48–62.
Kukathas, C. (2003) *The Liberal Archipelago: A Theory of Diversity and Freedom*, Oxford: Oxford University Press.
Mach, E. (1976) *Knowledge and Error*, Dordrecht: D. Reidel.
Miller, D. (2013) *Justice for Earthlings, Essays in Political Philosophy*, Cambridge: Cambridge University Press.
Miller, J. (1984) *Rousseau: Dreamer of Democracy*. New Haven: Yale University Press.

Miščević, N. (2012) "Plato's *Republic* as a political thought experiment," *Croatian Journal of Philosophy* 35: 153–165.

Miščević, N. (2013a) "Political thought experiments from Plato to Rawls," in *Thought Experiments in Philosophy, Science, and the Arts*, edited by M. Frappier, L. Meynell and J. R. Brown, London: Routledge.

Miščević, N. (2013b) "In search of the reason and the right – Rousseau's social contract as a thought experiment," *Acta Analytica* 28: 509–526.

Miščević, N. (2013c) "A hierarchy of armchairs: Gerald Gaus on political thought experiments," *European Journal of Analytic Philosophy* 9: 52–63.

Norton, J. D. (1991) "Thought experiments in Einstein's work," in *Thought Experiments in Science and Philosophy*, edited by Tamara Horowitz and Gerald Massey, 129–148, Lanham: Rowman & Littlefield.

Proudhon, P. J. (1969) *General Idea of the Revolution in the Nineteenth Century*, New York: Haskell House Publishers.

Rawls, J. (1971) *A Theory of Justice*, Cambridge: Harvard University Press.

Rawls, J. (2005) *Political Liberalism*, New York: Columbia University Press.

Rousseau, J. J. (1915) *The Political Writings of J. J. Rousseau*, edited by C. E. Vaughan, Cambridge: Cambridge University Press.

Rousseau, J. J. (2002) *The Social Contract and the First and Second Discourses*, edited by S. Dunn, New Haven: Yale University Press.

Schofield, M. (2006) *Plato: Political Philosophy*, Oxford: Oxford University Press.

Sen, A. (2009) *The Idea of Justice*, Cambridge: Harvard University Press.

Simmons, J. (2010) "Ideal and nonideal theory," *Philosophy & Public Affairs* 38: 5–36.

Tetlock, P. E. and Belkin, A. (eds) (1996) *Counterfactual Thought Experiments in World Politics*, Princeton: Princeton University Press.

Weithman, P. (2011) *Why Political Liberalism: On John Rawls's Political Turn*, Oxford: Oxford University Press.

Williamson, T. (2007) *Philosophy of Philosophy*, Oxford: Blackwell.

9
THOUGHT EXPERIMENTS IN ECONOMICS

Margaret Schabas

1 Introduction

To an outsider, contemporary economics might seem like one big thought experiment. The perennial joke about three scientists stranded on a desert island, with only a can of food, and the economist naively offering the supposition of a can opener, captures well the proclivity of economists to enter into an imaginary world. Current economic discourse consists mostly of models, which in turn invoke stylized abstractions, idealizations, and ceteris paribus conditions. Moreover, economists privilege the inner working of the human mind. The reason markets purportedly work is because we can extrapolate to other minds and impute a similar instrumental rationality. For these reasons, one might expect enthusiastic appeals to the laboratory of the mind. I will argue here, however, that thought experiments, as distinct from models, are uncommon in economics, past or present. Paul Krugman (2011) has reached a similar verdict, although his definition of a thought experiment is broader than mine.[1]

There are some philosophers, Julian Reiss most prominently, who take a different view on the matter. After noting that mainstream economics is "dominated by mathematical model building," he goes on to say that "I am going to look at a practice that is both older and, arguably, more widely used in economics than mathematical modelling: thought experimentation" (Reiss 2013, 177). Mary Morgan, Uskali Mäki, and Robert Sugden have each, independently, characterized the mental manipulation of models as thought experiments and thus implied their extensive appeal (Morgan 2002; Mäki 2005; Sugden 2005). Most recently, Harro Maas (2014) has argued that both Thomas Robert Malthus and Paul Samuelson made use of thought experiments. I differ with these scholars. We manipulate ideas in our heads all the time, but that is not what counts as a thought experiment. In fact, among contemporary economists, thought experiments are used infrequently and even when the label is applied, as is the case for example in models of climate change, it is not done so properly (see, e.g., Stern 2008; Mankiw 2013).

I argue here for the non-proliferation of thought experiments. I suggest we distinguish the mental manipulation of models, informal conjectures, exhibits, and long-term forecasting, from thought experiments. One missing ingredient, quite simply, is something akin to an experiment. As David Gooding (1992) argued, a thought experiment must resemble an experiment. Otherwise, it is something else, a demonstration, a train of thought, or a set of suppositions. A mathematical proof engages mental manipulation but it is not experimental. And I mean nothing more by the adjective "experimental" than the way it is commonly used in the natural sciences to distinguish those pursuits from the "theoretical." If all mental manipulations of models by economists were to count as thought experiments, then it would be difficult to see what is excluded, especially in the science of economics where modelling is so prevalent. I thus do not share the move by some philosophers of science, such as Nancy Nersessian, who deliberately conflate mental models with thought experiments.[2]

It is important to keep in mind that thought experiments are rare in the natural sciences. If this were not the case, if thought experiments but not laboratory experiments were the dominant mode of inquiry, our sciences would have turned out very differently. As Kuhn (1977) points out, thought experiments tend to congregate at the time of revolutions, precisely because they dredge up deeply held convictions and position them in a new light.[3] In my efforts to delimit the identification of thought experiments in economics, I will conform to its more entrenched usage in the physical sciences, such as the paradigmatic experiments undertaken by Galileo and Einstein. For better or for worse, economists have long sought to emulate the epistemic standards set by physics; taking these as the exemplars is not distortionary.

There are some genuine cases of *Gedankenexperimente* in economics, for example by David Hume and Ludwig von Mises, although neither used the term. But current appeals to thought experiments, as I will argue here, are often misnomers because there is nothing experimental to the line of reasoning. As Roy Sorensen has emphasized, a thought experiment "is an experiment that purports to achieve its aim without the benefit of execution" (Sorensen 1992, 205). The experiment is carried out in the laboratory of the mind, but mimics an experiment that might have been carried out in physical space-time, but at the time is infeasible. For that reason, Newton's famous bucket experiment does not qualify as a thought experiment. Indeed, a careful reading of the *Principia* indicates that Newton is describing an actual experiment, albeit one from which he extracts a theoretical result (the existence of absolute motion).[4]

Conversely, Galileo's thought experiment (1632) to demonstrate the uniform acceleration of falling bodies could not be carried out because there were no good clocks, nor a vacuum pump to remove the air resistance. Had he in fact attempted an experiment (say in Pisa), it would have refuted his law. By the 1660s, however, the first steps toward providing the apparatus necessary to measure g (9.8 meters/second-squared) were taken, by Huygens, who built one of the first mechanical clocks with a minute hand, and by von Guericke, who constructed an air pump to produce a particle vacuum. It remains an open question if all thought experiments are simply experiments-in-waiting, but the main point is not to lose sight of the fact that a thought experiment is still an experiment.

Economics has become more and more an experimental science. Of the 1665 mentions of "experiment" in articles in the *American Economic Review*, founded in 1911, the majority (1100 mentions) have appeared since 2006. Moreover, it can boast some crucial experiments, for example with public goods or rational choice theory. It may well be that as economics increases its experimental reach by devising new tools the need for thought experiments will diminish all the more.

Another important distinction between models and thought experiments draws upon the extent to which we can characterize thought experiments as "expeditions to possible worlds" (Sorensen 1992, 135). A thought experiment, unlike a model, is launched by a jarring, often bizarre counterfactual, but then restores some mental equanimity by introducing familiar objects to assist the mind of the experimenter as she reaches her destination. The initial counterfactual reorients the mind and dredges up some more deeply rooted beliefs that may prove contradictory to others. Were the thought experiment to pile one jarring counterfactual after another, it is unlikely that pre-existing intuitions could be availed upon to do the deliberative work at hand. Precisely because a given thought experiment arrives at a new understanding of the world without appealing to new empirical findings means it functions by realigning existing and familiar beliefs.

A model, by contrast, builds on what Robert Sugden (2005) has aptly called a "credible world." A model aims to establish a structure and internal coherence to a world that one can inhabit, explore, and manipulate further. By living in that world for a period of time, the model-builder and her converts acquire new insights over time, ones that have potential analogues to our actual world. Mary Morgan has brought this out admirably in her recent book (2012). The model-builder is a colonizer, while the thought experimenter is a tourist.

2 Models versus thought experiments

In the nineteenth century, economists defined their science as a set of laws that govern the production and distribution of commodities. In the twentieth century, the list of laws grew considerably and, at its high-water mark circa 1970, economics had over one hundred laws or regularities (theorems, principles, identities, etc.) on the books. But it is now passé to search for laws. In fact, as Stephano Zamagni (1989) has observed, the number of laws has been shrinking quite steadily. Some laws now deceased were long-lived, Say's law or Walras's law, while others were meteoric, the Laffer curve or Phillip's curve. The diminution of laws has been replaced by the construction of models. In the 1930s, the pioneering econometricians, Ragnar Frisch and Jan Tinbergen, transferred the idea of model building from physics to economics (Boumans 2005). Within a decade, models became the most common medium of analysis in economics.[5]

As several leading philosophers have emphasized, every proposition in a model is, strictly speaking, false (see Gibbard and Varian 1978; Hausman 1992a, 1992b). Models necessarily simplify and abstract and assume away extraneous noise. But the whole thrust of the model is to enlighten us about the world we inhabit and for this reason, the model-builder normally points to some empirical verifications for some of the derivations. Models, as Mary Morgan (2012) has argued, create a self-contained world. They enlighten us insofar as the structures they construct correspond to structures we believe hold true in our own world. There is, however, no formal proof to warrant these beliefs. Sugden (2000) has pointed out that the inductive leap between the model and our world is always left implicit, partly because it would undercut the rigor of the model to impose additional bridge conditions (that is, weaken the abstractions and generalizations). What makes for a good model is that each proposition is posited at the precise level of abstraction that the overall structure of the model can withstand and yet still offer new insights.

It is easy to conflate models with thought experiments; both feed on counterfactuals and abstractions, including the appeal to perfect or ideal conditions (although I would submit that thought experiments on average invoke fewer idealizations than models). Both rely heavily on a narrative that weaves a cogent argument. And both are devised with the aim of capturing one or more general truths about our actual world. Moreover, the degree of human intervention to move from a demonstration or observation to the status of an experiment is not always clear and is likely to vary from one science to the next. What counts as an experiment in botany may differ from what counts as an experiment in chemistry, for example. One need only think of the near-contemporaries Gregor Mendel and Dmitri Mendeleev to get a sense of the range.[6] For these reasons, I accept that thought experiments differ from models more by degree than by kind, and fall on a continuum. If thought experiments must be experimental to warrant the label, there will be borderline cases. There are likely some models that are near cousins to thought experiments, and vice versa. One of these, Ricardo's analysis of mechanization, will be discussed below.

If we could obtain a metric for the journey the mind takes to that counterfactual world, then in both cases (models or thought experiments) we might have a better means of settling the distinction. Jon Elster (1978) struggled with this in his quest for the "optimal counterfactual" in doing social science. But the received view, from David Lewis (1973), is that we cannot find that metric. It must be left to judgment, and for that reason as well, it is preferable to construe models and thought experiments as falling on a continuum.

To carry out the return journey, thought experiments rely heavily on a narrative, arguably more than models, especially mathematical models where so much is left implicit. As Sorensen has noted, there are often particular details in the narrative of a given thought experiment that are of no obvious value to the final results. This is not true in models, for the most part, since the aim is to ascend to the highest possible level of abstraction and to create a self-sustaining structure that will prompt further applications. Models are not built with the intention of being used only once, although no doubt that is what happens in most cases. Thought experiments, by contrast, once they are devised to make their point, have no future shelf life; as Ian Hacking (1992) has pointed out, they are analytically stillborn.

To summarize thus far, to count as a thought experiment in economics there ought to be something experimental, something that manipulates and demonstrates. Unlike a model, thought experiments tend to be launched by a jarring counterfactual that transports the mind to a distant alternative world, then offers a narrative peppered with familiar details that facilitate a return journey on the part of the mind. Hume did this well when he supposed that every Briton awoke with an extra five pounds in his pocket, as a way to demonstrate that the interest rate was immune to inflation.

Friedman also carries out a thought experiment, much like Hume's. He supposes that helicopters drop $1,000 bills evenly distributed across the USA such that each person collects (all in an instant) just enough to double their money holdings, from 5.2 to 10.4 weeks of income. Friedman also needs to establish that this is a singular event, insofar as expectations of repetitions would undercut the result. He also rules out that the bizarre event upsets longstanding economic patterns of behaviour, such as the factors that undergird the demand for money holdings. Everything else stays the same, but the doubling of money holdings causes a series of subsequent readjustments to production and prices until the optimal quantity of money is restored.

The helicopter drop is a thought experiment because it meets the two criteria: it is launched with a bizarre counterfactual and it is an experiment. In fact, like the case of Galileo on uniform acceleration of falling bodies, it is an experiment-in-waiting. In 2008, a single nation-wide tax rebate was described as a "helicopter drop." American tax-filers received, by check or direct deposit, a cash injection ranging from $300 to $600. This Economic Stimulus Act did not meet many of the conditions stipulated by Friedman's thought experiment. It was not instantaneous, universal, or equitable; nor was it a singular event. There was an earlier rebate in 2001, for example. Nor did it use helicopters or $1,000 bills. But like many other classic thought experiments in physics, say the measurement of muon decay in particle accelerators to demonstrate Einstein's analysis of time dilation, there is a clear progression toward actual experiments.

One reason thought experiments might not be common in economics is that, as Kuhn recognized, thought experiments tend to come in the wake of a crisis. Economics has had its upheavals; two even fit well the model offered by a Kuhnian revolution, namely the Marginal Revolution of the 1870s and the Keynesian Revolution of the 1930s. But there has been nothing comparable since then; nor did I find thought experiments to coincide with those upheavals. Many key terms were redefined or given a different priority, utility, capital, or the demand for money. None of those terms were novel, however.

Apart from the thought experiments of Hume and Friedman, there are not many more clear-cut cases to be found (see Thoma 2016 for some examples). As Julian Reiss has pointed out, Ludwig von Mises offers a thought experiment with his account of the "evenly rotating economy" (von Mises 2007, 244–50). He constructs this as a contrast to the economy in a "state of rest"; the latter is one in which prices settle dynamically after a series of exchanges. In the rotating economy, both time and market fluctuations are eliminated. It is an "imaginary construction" that cannot ever happen in "reality" (von Mises 2007, 247). Because there is no uncertainty, there is also no choice. As a result, he announces "such a rigid system is not peopled with living men making choices and liable to error; it is a world of soulless unthinking automatons; it is not a human society, it is an ant hill" (von Mises 2007, 248). He then submits that there is no place for money in this imaginary economy, since money is necessarily dynamic. At best, money serves the purpose of a *numeraire*, that is, a unit of account. Von Mises has created a thought experiment of sorts, but not one, it seems, that had much influence on subsequent discourse. Most of the Austrian economists favoured armchair economics, and were thus engaged in long ruminations that might seem at times to resemble thought experiments. Reiss also describes Carl Menger's account of the origins of money as a thought experiment, but in my view it is just a narrative, and lacks the critical ingredient of an experiment. Narratives about the origin of money are found throughout the history of economics and are essentially conjectural history used to motivate current theoretical claims regarding the form and function of money.

The same holds, I believe, for the work of cliometricians. Reiss has characterized Robert Fogel's famous book, *Railroads and American Economic Growth* (1964), as offering an example of a genealogical thought experiment. Fogel considered in great numerical detail the difference in economic growth that would have ensued up to 1890 if America had not adopted the railroad, and reaches the conclusion that it would not have differed by more than five per cent. Hence, it was wrong of historians to deem the advent of the railroad a critical factor in American economic expansion. Cliometrics thrives on counterfactuals, but so do many historians. Indeed, I slipped one in near the start of this chapter, conjecturing an alternative history of the natural sciences dominated by thought experiments rather than actual experiments. Although history hovers in the penumbra of science, it seems yet to become an experimental science. The delay or absence altogether of the railway is also not an outlandish counterfactual. The genesis of human inventions is replete with contingencies, and there is nothing to strain credulity that removes a particular invention from our historical landscape. Cliometrics is better characterized as a project to verify mainstream economics using extensive data-gathering and econometric methods (see Schabas 1995).

3 Ricardo on machinery: an intermediate case

Let me turn now to an example of what strikes me as an intermediate case between the thought experiment and the model. In his third and last edition of the *On the Principles of Political Economy and Taxation* (1821 [1951]), Ricardo famously inserted Chapter 31 entitled "On Machinery." It challenged the widespread belief that Ricardo confessed to have previously held, that new machinery caused only a temporary decrease in employment (frictional unemployment). Because the new machinery would reduce the cost of production for that particular commodity, it would thereby free up capital that would shift to another sector and promptly restore employment to the same prior level. Moreover, everyone would benefit because the good produced by the new machinery was now cheaper.

To overturn this received view, Ricardo devises a case whereby the return on capital (profit-rate) is the same across the entire economy (ten per cent) but the ratio of fixed to variable capital due to mechanization suddenly increases and thus renders a group of workers permanently redundant. He believes that it is entirely possible that the capitalist would be content with the same aggregate return and have no reason to reinvest the hitherto sum of variable capital (wages fund) in a new sector. Ricardo then claims that his analysis is borne out by recent labour disruptions, specifically the Peterloo Massacre of 1819, and that he is "convinced that the substitution of machinery for human labour, is often very injurious to the interests of the class of labourers" (ibid., 388).

To motivate his argument, however, there is one critical step, namely that the "improved machinery is *suddenly* discovered and extensively used" (ibid., 395). Ricardo suggests this may happen in the production of cotton (the power loom that the Luddites attempted to suppress), but he then weakens his stance and suggests that in fact there may never have been such a case. "The truth is, that these discoveries [of new machinery] are gradual, and rather operate in determining the employment of the capital which is saved and accumulated than in diverting capital from its actual employment" (ibid.).

Is this a thought experiment? Well, Ricardo admits that his sudden intervention of a new machine that is extensively used and funded not by credit but by an existing wages fund, strains credulity. Early in his text he acknowledged a proposition established by Adam Smith and others that most capital accumulation was funded by credit and not by accumulated savings. Ricardo must also limit the commodity the machine produces to a wage good, that is, a good universally consumed by workers. In short, Ricardo spins a tall tale out of whole cloth. His account meets the two criteria of an experiment (a sudden intervention) and a jarring counterfactual. But he also wants to extract real-world insights and suggest that recent strife between workers and factory owners are based on sound principles. Machines can permanently displace workers and do not simply produce frictional unemployment. The argument has many flaws and a sign, perhaps, that Ricardo had become too clever for his own good, but it does appear that it fits the example of a thought experiment more than a model.

But there are other aspects of the analysis that resemble a model. The entire argument depends on many stylized assumptions. There are three temporal periods during which everything adjusts instantaneously. The workers who are not employed in building the new machines in period two are able to continue working in the same traditional manner, but it is not clear that this is possible (do the factories close or is the labour input cut in half uniformly?). And if the good produced by the new machine is and was a central commodity in the worker's consumption bundle, what provides for the shortfall during the transition? Everything else about the situation is stylized. There is perfect competition, full employment at a uniform subsistence wage, and a uniform profit rate. Capital moves all of a sudden from variable to fixed, and labour input is perfectly measured by money values. Ricardo's chapter on machinery, I believe, falls somewhere on the continuum between models and thought experiments, but closer to the model. It consists of a string of propositions that invoke idealizations or stylized facts rather than an expedition to an incredible world.

4 Misnomers

Harro Maas has recently classified Malthus's argument that agrarian output will fall drastically behind population growth as a thought experiment. In my view, however, there is nothing experimental about the argument. There is no manipulation. In fact, Malthus wants to emphasize that population growth is driven mostly by the sub-rational passions in the marriage bed and not by anything that is subject to our control (his main recommendation to reduce population is to postpone the age of marriage). Similarly, agrarian output is limited by the unrelenting scarcity of arable land and the principle of diminishing returns. Insofar as Malthus is projecting forward in time, his argument is clearly more inductive than many at the time, certainly compared to the strong deductive structure found in Ricardian economics. But he also makes a number of stylized assumptions at the start (the arithmetic progression of agrarian output for each period and the geometric progression of population growth). He also posits a quarter-century period and thus neatly projects ahead one century. But I do not see his demonstration of the increasing gap between population and food supply as thus qualifying as a thought experiment. There are countless renditions of the Malthusian argument in the form of a model (terse propositions and equations).[7]

Environmental economists now offer "thought experiments" when they propose models that project a century into the future, often in the context of global warming. Nathaniel O. Keohane (2009) offers what he calls "a simple thought experiment" in his efforts to compare the cap and trade policy with carbon taxes projected up to the year 2100. Martin L. Weitzman (1992) also uses thought experiments to motivate intuitions regarding biodiversity as well as address the problems of climate change. The point is that once one bites off any more than about five years, extant models are not easily applicable, if only because most of the capital has been consumed and the production possibility frontier would have shifted. The confidence intervals diverge and the standard models become unstable. Hence, environmental economists use the term thought experiments because they cannot construct formal models. But are they using the term correctly? I think not. There is nothing experimental about their train of thought; the term is used as a placeholder for informal modelling. Again, let us look to the natural sciences. Astronomy, geology and evolutionary biology use significantly greater temporal projections, to the past and the future, and yet do not employ the term thought experiment. The problem lies rather in the short time horizon adopted in mainstream economics.

The Ellsberg paradox is normally described as a thought experiment, both in the original offering and in the substantial journal literature that it spawned. It established the interesting result, now ascribed to us humans, of adversity to ambiguity. Ellsberg describes a series of hypothetical drawings of different coloured balls from different urns and some unexpected outcomes when the parameters are varied. But it seems preferable to deem Ellsberg's original account as simply a description of an experiment that he did not conduct, much like many examples in the theory of probability. Now, given sufficient research funding, Ellsberg's experiments and many variants on that theme have been instantiated in the laboratory (see Helevy 2007). They resemble the set of experiments conducted by Tversky and Kahneman (1981) that establish systematic deviations, under contrived conditions, from the central axioms of rational choice theory.

Robert Sugden (2005, 252) has defined these experiments as "exhibits." At their preliminary stages, he refers to them as thought experiments, particularly in the sense that they focus upon intuitions about such deviations. But insofar as they are carried out more often than not, it seems preferable to view them as accounts of experimental designs, not thought experiments. Furthermore, there is nothing strange or bizarre about these experiments at all. They use everyday objects, balls, bets, cash, or theatre tickets. They are, in short, about credible and not incredible worlds. Nor would I classify them as models, since they do not create an independent or robust structure based on a set of mildly counterfactual propositions. Rather, they demonstrate that prior theoretical assumptions about rationality may need to be revised. They *exhibit* a specific pattern or regularity of human agency.

5 Conclusion

I cannot possibly canvass the entire field of economics, but in my study of the leading journal, the *American Economic Review*, I found that the term "thought experiment" was mentioned 76 times, all in the past 20 years. Since some articles had several mentions, this is trimmed to at best 50 articles out of a total of approximately 2000 articles (for the past 20 years). This comes out as a negligible incidence of 0.025. Thought experiments exist in the mainstream literature, but are not prevalent.

I found one discernable pattern, however. About a dozen economists in the upper echelon of the profession invoke a thought experiment in their invited address to the American Economic Association (the Richard T. Ely annual lecture or the Presidential address). The list is an impressive one: Edmund Phelps (1995), Lawrence H. Summers (2000) and

Robert E. Lucas (2003), to name just a few. These articles are meant for a larger readership, and not subject to the normal peer review process. Each economist would introduce a hypothetical scenario, one that the author had not troubled to instantiate or put to test in a laboratory.

For example, Akerlof (in his 2007 Presidential address) writes: "In a thought experiment, consider a woman living on $50,000 a year who learns that her uncle will die in one year leaving her $2,000,000. Even if she has considerable savings in the bank, it would be unseemly for her to run down her savings in anticipation of the bequest. She is not *entitled* to do so. She should stick to spending from her current income. This gives another example in which norms regarding entitlements to spend are related to current income, in violation of the life-cycle hypothesis" (Akerlof 2007, 17). This is an account of a hypothetical scenario, at best an exhibit like Ellsberg. There is nothing experimental about it, nor is there a jarring counterfactual. Such cases probably happen daily in the U.S.A., where there are more than ten million millionaires. Did Akerlof seek out sociological studies of recently informed heirs? No, he used this so-called thought experiment to take a swipe at the life-cycle theory of consumption behaviour. He sought to show that the Keynesian view that consumption is sensitive to current and not just permanent income still holds a grain of truth.

No doubt there are other examples of thought experiments that have been subject to more rigorous refereeing than the sample I read in the *American Economic Review*. But most are similar to those offered by Akerlof. In another leading journal, Gregory Mankiw (2013) offers a thought experiment about a society with perfect economic equality. He then introduces Steve Jobs, J. K. Rowling, and Steven Spielberg as a way to justify those in the top 1 per cent income bracket. Again, there is no experiment present. We have a strong counterfactual but nothing that introduces variables via human agency.

A more plausible candidate is the one where Larry Summers considers a scenario of a bank such that "everyone would be paid off [in a bank run] as long as no more than one-third of the investors chose to withdraw" (Summers 2000, 7). Although he grants that there are several possible outcomes, he deems the likelihood of a bankruptcy improbable. He then remarks: "I think that this thought experiment captures something real. On the one hand, bank runs or their international analogues do happen. On the other hand, they are not driven by sunspots: their likelihood is driven and determined by the extent of fundamental weaknesses" (ibid).

Is this a thought experiment? Perhaps. Banks are predicated on the supposition that one-third of depositors will never withdraw on a given day. Summers also offers a more formal analysis of the situation to generate the various equilibria and, in that sense, he is devising a model where one of the parameters is highly unusual (a third of depositors withdraw, but credit is forthcoming such that the bank does not collapse). But these scenarios have indeed transpired. One of the reasons the Canadian banks survived so well after the 1929 crash is that they were in close proximity to one another. On a given day of panic, the Bank of Montreal manager would prevail upon the good graces of his neighbouring Toronto Dominion manager to provide the cash necessary for the sudden bank run, thus upholding faith in the banking system. The next day, somewhat like a potlatch ceremony, the TD manager could count on the BofM manager to assist him if he was subject to a run. As Summers concludes, "avoiding situations where the bankrun psychology takes hold ... will depend heavily on strengthening core institutions and other fundamentals" (ibid).

I think he uses the term "thought experiment" to glide quickly over a point that might have been fleshed out with historical support.

Thought experiments that meet the criteria I have proposed here are uncommon in economics. The term is used very infrequently in mainstream economics and, in my view, such references are often misnomers. This may be partly due to the fact that economics has only recently embraced experimentation on a significant scale, or because models are such a dominant method. It seems advisable to keep models distinct from thought experiments while granting that there will be intermediate cases. But, like Hume, I do not wish for anything given here to commit the naturalistic fallacy; if economists have not used thought experiments very often, that does not preclude their using them more frequently in the future. Krugman (2011) thinks this would be a beneficial turn of events. And maybe tourism is a better outcome than colonization.

Acknowledgements

I wish to thank Adam Morton, Alan Love, Julian Reiss, Harro Maas, and John Davis for valuable feedback. This paper has benefited from presentations at the American Social Sciences Association Meetings (INEM), the Pacific American Philosophical Association Meetings, the University of Queensland, the University of Toronto, and the University of Minnesota.

Notes

1 There is very little literature on the subject. A recent editorial by Paul Krugman (2011) is predicated on the view that they are not commonplace. He defines the thought experiment as a model that uses an informal economic argument rather than one with mathematical equations or econometric analyses. Krugman views Hume's monetary thought experiments as the standard, and adds to these a few more examples, a study of a recent babysitting co-op (Sweeney and Sweeney) and the more famous case of the use of cigarettes in POW camps in World War II. They fit his definition but not mine. Another example that Krugman cites, by Karl Smith (a graduate student), uses imaginary gnomes switching people about overnight to challenge standard market assumptions. This example counts; there is a strong counterfactual to launch the experiment, and a follow-up using familiar this-world details, but the example is only on the web; it is not a refereed publication.
2 This not a new claim; Nersessian (1992) also characterizes thought experiments as mental modelling.
3 T. S. Kuhn pointed out that thought experiments undertake conceptual reform and thus sort out a misfit between familiar concepts and the world (Kuhn 1977, 264).
4 According to Newton (1687, 10), the water "will ascend to the sides of the vessel, forming itself into a concave figure (as I have experienced)."
5 There are rare instances of models in economic discourse before the postwar explosion, although no one used that label. Good examples are found in the work of Jean-François Melon (1735), François Quesnay (1757), and Johann von Thünen (1826) (see Morgan 2012). But just as there were instances of decision theory and game theory before the twentieth century (e.g. Blaise Pascal, Daniel Bernoulli, Condorcet, and A.A. Cournot), it is only in the postwar period that models, game theory, and decision theory became widespread.
6 Mendel's breeding of pea plants is commonly referred to as an experiment, but such practices were rare in botany at the time in contrast to chemistry. Most breeders were not conducting scientific experiments. Lorraine Daston (2011) offers an excellent account of the gradual disambiguation of observation from experiment in early modern science.
7 Several are offered in the Norton anthology on Malthus (2004).

References

Akerlof, G. A. (2007) "The missing motivation in macroeconomics," *American Economic Review* 97: 5–36.
Boumans, M. (2005) *How Economists Model the World into Numbers*, London: Routledge.
Daston, L. (2011) "The empire of observation, 1600–1800," in *Histories of Scientific Observation*, edited by L. Daston and E. Lunbeck, Chicago: University of Chicago Press.
Elster, J. (1978) *Logic and Society: Contradictions and Possible Worlds*, New York: John Wiley.
Fogel, R. (1964) *Railroads and American Economic Growth: Essays in Econometric History*, Baltimore: Johns Hopkins Press.
Gibbard, A. and Varian, H. (1978) "Economic models," *Journal of Philosophy* 75: 664–677.
Gooding, D. (1992) "What is experimental about thought experiments?" in *Proceedings of the 1992 Biennial Meeting of the Philosophy of Science Association*, edited by D. Hull, M. Forbes, and K. Okruhlik, vol. 2, pp. 280–290, East Lansing: Philosophy of Science Association.
Hacking, I. (1992) "Do thought experiments have a life of their own?" in *Proceedings of the 1992 Biennial Meeting of the Philosophy of Science Association*, edited by D. Hull, M. Forbes, and K. Okruhlik, vol. 2, pp. 302–308, East Lansing: Philosophy of Science Association.
Hausman, D. (1992a) *The Inexact and Separate Science of Economics*, Cambridge: Cambridge University Press.
Hausman, D. (1992b) *Essays on Philosophy and Economic Methodology*, Cambridge: Cambridge University Press.
Helevy, Y. (2007) "Ellsberg revisited: An experimental study," *Econometrica* 75: 503–536.
Keohane, N. O. (2009) "Cap and trade, rehabilitated: Using tradable permits to control U.S. greenhouse gases," *Review of Environmental Economics and Policy* 3: 42–62.
Krugman, P. (2011, February 2) "Models, plain and fancy," *The New York Times*. Available here: https://krugman.blogs.nytimes.com/2011/02/02/models-plain-and-fancy/?_r=0
Kuhn, T. S. (1977 [1964]) "A function for thought experiments," in *The Essential Tension*, Chicago: University of Chicago Press.
Lewis, D. (1973) *Counterfactuals*, Oxford: Blackwell.
Lucas, R. E. (2003) "Macroeconomic priorities," *American Economic Review* 93: 1–14.
Maas, H. (2014) *Economic Methodology: A Historical Introduction*, London: Routledge.
Mäki, U. (2005) "Models are experiments, experiments are models," *Journal of Economic Methodology* 12: 303–315.
Malthus, T. R. (1798 [2004]) *An Essay on the Principle of Population*, edited by P. Appleman, New York: Norton.
Mankiw, N. G. (2013) "Defending the one percent," *Journal of Economic Perspectives* 27: 21–34.
Morgan, M. S. (2002) "Model experiments and models in experiments," in *Model-Based Reasoning: Science, Technology, Values*, edited by L. Magnani and N. J. Nersessian, Dordrecht: Kluwer.
Morgan, M. S. (2012) *The World in the Model: How Economists Work and Think*, Cambridge: Cambridge University Press.
Nersessian, N. J. (1992) "In the theoretician's laboratory: Thought experimenting as mental modeling," in *Proceedings of the 1992 Biennial Meeting of the Philosophy of Science Association*, edited by Hull, D., M. Forbes, and K. Okruhlik, vol. 2, pp. 291–301, East Lansing: Philosophy of Science Association.
Newton, I. (1934 [1687]) *Principia*, translated by A. Mott, edited by F. Cajori, Berkeley: University of California Press.
Phelps, E.S. (1995) "The structuralist theory of unemployment," *American Economic Review* 85: 226–231.
Reiss, J. (2013) "Genealogical thought experiments in economics," in *Thought Experiments in Philosophy, Science, and the Arts*, edited by M. Frappier, L. Meynell, and J. R. Brown, New York: Routledge.
Ricardo, D. (1821 [1951]) *On the Principles of Political Economy and Taxation*, 3rd ed., edited by Piero Sraffa, Cambridge: Cambridge University Press.
Schabas, M. (1995) "Parmenides and the cliometricians," in *The Reliability of Economic Models: Essays in the Epistemology of Economics*, edited by D. C. Little, Dordrecht: Kluwer.

Sorensen, R. (1992) *Thought Experiments*, Oxford: Oxford University Press.
Stern, N. (2008) "Economics of climate change," *American Economic Review* 98: 1–37.
Sugden, R. (2000) "Credible worlds: The status of theoretical models in economics," *Journal of Economic Methodology* 7: 1–31.
Sugden, R. (2005) "Experiments as exhibits and experiments at tests," *Journal of Economic Methodology* 12: 291–302.
Summers, L. H. (2000) "International financial crises: Causes, preventions, and cures," *American Economic Review* 90: 1–16.
Thoma, J. (2016) "On the hidden thought experiments of economic theory," *Philosophy of the Social Sciences* 46: 1 129–146.
Tversky, A. and Kahneman, D. (1981) "The framing of decisions and the psychology of choice," *Science* 211: 453–458.
Von Mises, L. (1949 [2007]) *Human Action: A Treatise on Economics*, vol. 2, Indianapolis: Liberty Fund.
Weitzman, M. L. (1992) "On diversity," *Quarterly Journal of Economics* 107: 363–405.
Zamagni, S. (1989) "Economic laws," in *The Invisible Hand: The New Palgrave*, edited by J. Eatwell, M. Milgate and Newman, New York: Norton.

10
THEOLOGY AND THOUGHT EXPERIMENTS

Yiftach Fehige

The topic of thought experiments intersects with theology in a number of ways. Six intersection points will be discussed in what follows. (1) Thought experiments have been dismissed as an ill-founded method in ethics on theological grounds. (2) They have been compared to theological reasoning in order to support the view that they are absolutely useless as sources of evidence. (3) In contrast, others have used the fact that thought experiments arise in both theology and science as an argument to the effect that theology is methodologically rational in some of the same ways that science is. (4) Intriguing are the connections between thought experiments and theology that emerge from discussions concerning their literary aspects. (5) The claim that philosophy would be severely impoverished without thought experiments is supported by examples from philosophical theology. (6) Finally, revealed theology – to be distinguished from philosophical theology – has added its own examples of thought experiments. A discussion of these examples can raise new questions, or help to address some of the questions already raised in the philosophical analysis of thought experiments.

1 Divine law versus ethical thought experiments

Peter Geach can be understood as claiming that an important class of ethical thought experiments is to be dismissed. His target are those that pose moral dilemmas such as a person who has to choose between two absolutely binding moral norms (Geach 1969, 128). Geach's dismissal of such thought experiments follows from genuinely theological assumptions.[1] (1) Moral norms are divine commands. They are not conventions, nor do they source their justification primarily from reason. (2) God is perfectly rational, absolutely good, and omnipotent in his care for humanity. Both assumptions are part of so-called classical theism (see Swinburne 2005), which is one of many ways in which philosophers have attempted to schematize the theistic essence of Christianity. The two assumptions lead Geach to reject the possibility of scenarios that involve a person who cannot obey one divine law without disobeying another divine law. Just imagine the infamous thought experiment about the two SS officers knocking at the door of your home. In your home there are Jews hiding and fearing for their lives. Should you lie to the SS officers or is the divine law to love your neighbor overriding the law not to lie. Such scenarios and their use in ethics are ill-founded, argues Geach, because God would simply not allow such genuine moral dilemmas to exist and thereby force a person to choose between different divine commands. If God is perfectly rational and absolutely good then he simply does not command what ought not to be done; if God governs all events by his providence then he can see to it that circumstances in which a man is inculpably faced by a choice between forbidden acts do not occur. Of course, such circumstances (with the clause *and there is no way out* written into their description) are consistently *describable*; but God's providence could ensure that they do not *in fact* arise. In other words, contrary to what unbelievers often say, belief in the existence of God does make a difference to what one can expect to happen in one's moral life.

The upshot of Geach's critique seems to be that some perfectly consistent thought experiments in ethics are methodologically illegitimate. God would simply not allow for the scenarios in an important class of ethical thought experiments to arise. Thus to imagine such scenarios is methodologically pointless from the perspective of a moral philosophy that affirms God's existence. The recognition of God's existence in philosophy makes a difference, and one aspect of it is the pointlessness of an important class of ethical thought experiments.

The emerging skeptical position about thought experiments is weak, because the supporting theological assumptions are extremely problematic. To begin with, no moral norm can source justification from the mere fact that God commands the norm (*God commands it, therefore we have to do it*) nor from facts about the nature of God (*God is absolutely good and what an absolutely good person commands ought to be done*). In either case we end up with a natural fallacy. In the former case we need a moral principle to connect the commands and the fact of God commanding the moral norms, such as: whatever God commands, we ought to do it. This seems obviously wrong, as the example of Moses clearly shows. According to Scripture, Moses challenges God on numerous occasions because he does not think highly of particular divine commands. And he manages even to change God's mind! It is a mistake to construe religion as uncritical submission to God and his commands. In the latter case it is not the fact that God is absolutely good which carries the justificatory force but his or her absolute goodness. And if that is so, reference to God and his existence seems beside the point in deliberations about the moral significance of a divine command. In a nutshell, neither the fact that God is the author of a moral norm, nor facts about God's nature seem sufficient to uphold the rationality of divine moral norms. And, the more reasons we need to find to compensate for that lack of justification arising from the natural fallacies in question, the less justificatory force recourse to God has in justifying the moral norm. Important to note is that we should not confuse our *justification* in following a moral norm and our *motivation to* follow a moral norm. Belief in God may increase the motivation to live a good life. But this has little do to with the justification of moral norms.

In light of these considerations, command theorists such as Geach have the choice of endorsing a kind of positivism in matters ethical. In this case divine laws are treated as exempt from the requirement of justification, period, and this is due to the fact that they are produced by a legitimate process, such as divine revelation. The strategy is to shift the burden of justification away from the moral norms in question to their origin. The central idea is to uphold the obligation not to lie in light of it being revealed by God and the belief that divine revelation is a legitimate process of producing moral norms, comparable to the process in the legislature that results in the passing of a new bill. In fact, I have the impression that most advocates of divine command theories follow this strategy today. They argue for the view that divine revelation is a legitimate source of all sorts of knowledge and justification (see, for example, Swinburne 2007), although particular norms and religious claims that are sourced from divine revelation may seem rationally unsupportable. The most problematic aspect of those attempts is the total absence of a serious engagement with the blatant lack of a theory of divine intervention (see Saunders 2002). This is obviously a great problem because you cannot have divine revelation without divine intervention, at least not from the standpoint of Christian classical theism. God is defined as absolutely transcendent to the course of nature, and the only way to make himself and any of his moral commands accessible to humans is by means of intervention. In other words, Christian classical theism claims an ontologically significant gap between the world and God, and the history of Christianity is, as it were, an impressive series of attempts to bridge that gap. The growing prominence of the principle of causal closure in philosophy of science since the nineteenth century has resulted in the most challenging obstacle to those attempts. This probably explains why even such comprehensive theological systems as the one developed by Richard Swinburne in terms of classical theism entail a theory of divine revelation that remains silent on the topic of divine intervention, and yet results in a defense of most problematic moral norms as divinely sanctioned, such as the immorality of same-sex relations and the inequality of man and woman in heading a family. Swinburne's theory of revelation is also extremely problematic from a genuine Christian theological standpoint (see McLean 2013). Of course, in light of these problems advocates of divine command theories have the option of leaving the framework of Christian classical theism. In this case, however, the second assumption of Geach's case against an important class of ethical thought experiments begins to totter, as the divine attributes of perfect rationality, absolute goodness and providence that are central to the enterprise of classical theism come under close scrutiny. This opens up what many consider today more promising alternatives to classical theism in order to capture the essence of Christianity, such as process theology (see Clayton 2010).

In conclusion, Geach's classical theistic version of Christianity leads to a skeptical position with respect to an important class of ethical thought experiments. It is doubtful, however, that the theological assumptions that support the skepticism are less controversial than the use of thought experiments in ethics.

2 Lack of evidence

Paul Thagard compares the use of thought experiments to professions of religious faith in order to voice his opposition to their use in philosophy (Thagard 2010). In matters of faith we are dealing with beliefs that lack any evidential support. The same is true for beliefs supported by thought experiments. And, without evidence we are not justified in holding those beliefs, and behave irrationally when holding onto beliefs based on faith and thought experiments. In science the potential harm of thought experiments is compensated by alternative methods that can be used to scrutinize outcomes of scientific thought experiments. In the case of religious faith and philosophical thought experiments things are very different, and thus we should refrain from the respective practices. Thagard sees the facts of the history of philosophy on his side. In this respect his main concern is the study of the human mind. All thought experiments in philosophy of mind have been proven ill-founded and simply wrong-headed. They have been of no evidential significance to improve our understanding of the mind. Even more, most often they lead us astray. Only since scientific methods were developed to study the mind have we made progress in understanding the true nature of the mind.

Thagard's position is philosophically extremely problematic and borders at self-contradiction in light of his endorsement and development of computer simulations to study the mind (see Stuart 2014). Even worse, the analogy to religious faith is a categorical mistake insofar as he implies that matters of religious faith are comparable to matters of scientific fact and philosophical investigation. Thagard's assumption is unsubstantiated that religious beliefs, theological statements, and philosophical claims require the same kind of evidence as empirical beliefs and scientific statements. Only empirical matters require empirical methods to be substantiated by the kind of evidence that Thagard declares absolute. But not even all scientific matters are primarily empirical in Thagard's sense, as the discussion about the metaphysical dimension of science illustrates. For example, if it is true that substance dualism and physicalism make empirically hardly any difference in their description of related scientific facts (see Meixner 2004), then, of course, empirical evidence will not help philosophers much in their choice of metaphysics. What helps is to look at the assumptions that defenders of substance dualism and physicalism make and submit them to a philosophical critique that deals with pieces of evidence Thagard's notion of evidence declares illegitimate. That declaration is problematic not only due to a lack of argumentative support, but because of the resulting loss of explanatory power available to historians of science. For example, the shift from Aristotelian physics to Galilean physics and the significance of the famous falling bodies thought experiment is easily misunderstood if we do not take into account that the normative notion of evidential significance shifted at that time (see McAllister 1996). To the Aristotelian back then, Galileo's thought experiment was partly inaccessible in its evidential significance because natural occurrences and not phenomena carried scientific evidence. But Galileo elevates phenomena to the status of scientific evidence, and they play an important role in his advancement of a new way of doing physics. Not natural occurrences but experimentally demonstrated phenomena are the primary unit of evidence in the new physics. Finally, Thagard seeks support for his position from the alleged fact that before the scientific study of the mind no progress was made in understanding its nature. That is presumptuous. It is true that enormous progress was made since the rise of modern science (although less than it is often claimed). But the often-heard claim that today's science of the human mind amounts to a revolution in the way we think about humanity is an exaggeration (see Karafyllis and Ulshöfer 2008). Of interest in the present context is the historical fact that theological thought experiments played an important role in medieval studies of human cognition (see Perler 2008).

In conclusion, Thagard's analogy of religious faith and philosophical thought experiments in support of a skeptical position is a non-starter. It seems more plausible to accept philosophical thought experiments than the assumptions that lead Thagard to reject them.

3 Cousins, not enemies!

The history of science and religion was neither full of conflict (despite radical secularists' claims) nor harmony (despite religious apologetics' claims). John H. Brooke is credited with the complexity thesis that states complexity to be the most accurate characterization of the relationship between science and religion throughout history (see Brooke 1991). For example, "science" and "religion" have a history that requires to be taken into account when assessing the interaction between the corresponding practices, beliefs, institutions, and claims. The view that the two have been in perennial conflict throughout the ages not only is difficult to prove for historiographical reasons, but is simply a fabrication of the nineteenth century. It was a very influential myth. Today, mainly atheists like Richard Dawkins have an interest that it keeps being told to support the view that science and religion are incompatible. Nevertheless the story is unsupportable by historical evidence. Important to note is that claims about a constant harmony are as problematic as those about a perennial conflict. There was conflict and there is conflict between science and religion, although it is often unclear what the actual issues are. Sometimes they are political, sometimes they are ideological, sometimes they are philosophical, and at other times they are theological. Giordano Bruno, for example, was not the first martyr of modern science, as sometimes stated; he had to die at the hand of the inquisition because of his theological views, not his scientific beliefs. Of course, that does not make the incident less tragic. What makes it so easy to misunderstand the case of Bruno is the fact that theology and science were deeply intertwined in his writings, as was common at his time and for much longer after him.

In addition to historiographical and historical problems that plague both militant atheists and religious apologetics, it is philosophically unclear as to how the complexity in question is playing out today. Unlike the early days of modern science, science and religion are separated from one another, and the question is pressing for theologians as to how to relate the two. Many proposals are on the table, some more plausible than others. John Polkinghorne is among the few who take this question very seriously. In some writings he argues for integration, especially when it comes to the relationship between Darwinism and Christian claims about humanity's creation in the image of God. In other writings he advances a more modest view of the relationship between Christianity and science, namely for the possibility of some kind of dialogue between the two. Dialogue requires a high degree of independence of science and religion of one another. In Polkinghorne (2007), for example, he insists on both differences between science and religion and their similarities to support the view that dialogue between stakeholders of each domain is a genuine option. He looks at the way quantum physics and Christian theology are conducted and concludes that both are similar in their use of reason, which he characterizes along the lines of critical realism. Differences between the two are accounted for in terms of quite diverse subject matters. But methodologically there is no reason to consider quantum physics as a rational enterprise and the other not. Of interest in the present context is his comparison of the use of thought experiments in quantum physics and Christian theology. Polkinghorne's central claim is that both disciplines need thought experiments for the sake of conceptual clarity. He supports this claim in the form of a parallel discussion of the thought experiments in the infamous debate between Einstein and Bohr about quantum physics, on the one hand, and a discussion of a biblical thought experiment about the world to come as hoped for in Christianity, on the other. Polkinghorne's observation seems right that Christian theology and quantum physics do share the practice of thought experiments. The conclusion he draws for the relative similarity of the two requires further analysis, however. This is especially true with respect to the difficult question as to whether or not the concepts about the micro-physical world and the supernatural realm are both instances of an analogical use of language or rather a univocal use. If the former are univocal and the later analogical the similarity in the use of thought experiments seems less compelling than Polkinghorne claims.

In conclusion, thought experiments matter in discussions of the relationship between science and religion. It remains questionable at this time what follows in terms of rationality considerations from the fact that both science and religion make use of thought experiments.

4 Analytic theology and thought experiments

Very recently a meta-philosophical dispute arose (see Kraay 2013) that concerns the feasibility of a philosophical enterprise called "Analytic Theology," defined as the "activity of approaching theological topics with the ambitions of an analytic philosopher and in a style that conforms to the prescriptions that are distinctive of an analytical philosophical discourse" (Rea 2009, 7). Critics of this project object that this is not philosophy but Christian theology in disguise (see Schellenberg 2009).

Of interest in the present context is the contribution of Eleonore Stump to the metaphilosophical discussion about the merits and perils of Analytic Theology. While supportive of the philosophical enterprise, she criticizes analytic philosophers' narrowness in approaching theological topics. More specifically, Stump finds that analytic philosophers use thought experiments in thinking about God, instead of literature. More generally, Stump argues that there is a disregard among analytic philosophers of literature as a source of knowledge. This results in a lack of analysis of literary narratives when addressing theological topics. Stump shares a number of the claims that we find advanced in the few existing contributions to the discussion about the literary aspects of thought experiments. One of them is an affirmation of the cognitive significance of literature, "which is explicable less well or not at all by non-narrative philosophical prose" (Stump 2009, 254 n. 6).

While there is agreement with Stump in this respect, her low opinion of thought experiments runs counter to the majority view, however, concerning the literary features of thought experiments. Her derogatory remarks seem to be the result of a narrowness in her own approach to literary narratives. She fails to consider the possibility that literary narratives themselves may be counted as thought experiments, as Elgin (2014) argues. In other words, Stump completely misses the literary aspects of thought experiments and their relevant similarity to those features of literary fiction that she cherishes and motivate other philosophers to think of novels as possible thought experiments. Her views about the philosophical importance of literature require correction in this respect. With that in mind, Stump's critique can be given a positive spin if it is used to support a call for a more extensive use of existing thought experiments in philosophical theology due to their literary aspects – disregarding the important differences between literature and thought experiments.

This is especially true with respect to Stump's central epistemological claim that there is a type of knowledge that is inaccessible in any other way but by means of literary fiction. Stories "transmit a kind of knowledge of persons which is not reducible to knowledge *that*" (Stump 2009, 259). She has a distinction in mind that has been playing an important role in discussions on thought experiments, especially in the debate between James R. Brown and John D. Norton about the right epistemology of thought experiments. Stump insists on a kind of knowledge that complements the type of knowledge that Norton prioritizes at the exclusion of other types of knowledge in his account of thought experiments, namely *propositional* knowledge. Those thought experiments that provide knowledge and justification do so due to their propositional aspects primarily, argues Norton. In addition to the propositional type of knowledge Stump defends a kind of knowledge that is comparable to Brown's Platonic "seeing," although her approach has less metaphysical baggage. Stump is mainly concerned with knowledge provided by first-person experiences and second-person experiences. The former has to do with a person's way of feeling what it is like to undergo certain experiences. The latter concerns knowledge that is acquired in interpersonal interactions. Both first- and second-person experiences may constitute non-propositional knowledge that analytic philosophers cannot ignore when addressing important theological topics. The topic that Stump is most concerned with is the problem of evil, which is not relevant in the present context. The non-propositional knowledge that Stump claims to be inaccessible by any other means but by storytelling is also irreducible to propositional knowledge in its cognitive content. In other worlds, in my reading, Stump advances three claims: (1) storytelling can be cognitively efficacious in philosophical theology; (2) cognitive efficacy can be attributed to the non-propositional aspects of literary narratives; and (3) non-propositional cognition is inaccessible from a third-person perspective and irreducible to propositional knowledge. As stated earlier, there is no reason to exclude thought experiments from the scope of the first and thus from the other two claims. All three claims lead her to conclude that literary fiction is permanently indispensable in philosophical discourse, including philosophical theology, and requires philosophy to include methods of literary criticism. Expository propositional reconstructions of the cognitive backbone of a story cannot replace the story without loss of cognitive content. And to treat literature as merely illustrative of cognitive claims misses the central point of literature, Stump claims.

Another important consequence of Stump's intervention is that insofar as literary fictions are a species of thought experiments conveyed by a narrative (as proposed by Swirski 2007), the inaccessibility and irreducibility that we can claim for them following Stump, provide a nice explanation of the existence of a class of thought experiments that Brown calls "counter thought experiments" (Brown 2007). Counter thought experiments are thought experiments that challenge a thought experiment not by exposing a fallacy in accompanying propositional reasoning but by questioning whether the phenomenon established by another thought experiment would really obtain. Probably the most beautiful example in the history of science is Niels Bohr's counter thought experiment to Einstein's *clock-in-the-box* thought experiment (see Bohr 1949). Extremely simplified the situation was as follows: Einstein presented a thought experiment that meant to establish a phenomenon that amounts to a violation of Heisenberg's uncertainty principle. He imagined an apparatus that allows us to do something that the principle claims to be impossible, namely to measure the exact value of both the time and energy variable of a photon. In Bohr's slightly modified version of the same thought experiment, however, this phenomenon does not obtain. Bohr added details to the imaginary measurement process. What we are seeing in Bohr's thought experiment is not a phenomenon that violates Heisenberg's uncertainty principle but a measuring device that forces us to be precise *either* in determining the value of the energy *or* the time variable of the photon, and thereby it confirmed Heisenberg's uncertainty principle. Most amazingly, Bohr invoked Einstein's own theory of general relativity to show why we could not be precise in both tasks at the same time. And important in the present context is that the whole exchange between Bohr and Einstein progressed by means of thought experiments, which themselves cannot be reconstructed in terms of propositional knowledge without turning the whole exchange irrational (Bishop 1999). To relate this example back to the discussion of Stump's views about literary fiction as being epistemically significant in philosophical theology, in counter thought experiments like this we find an attempt to prevent a possible loss of cognitive content of a story at times when no fully adequate propositional representation is available of the issue addressed by the story. Noteworthy is the fact that an increase in the use of scientific (counter) thought experiments is characteristic of so called "paradigm changes," such as it was happening at the time when Einstein and Bohr wrestled with the implications of the emerging quantum physics.

From Stump's perspective, then, it follows that taking thought experiments seriously will lead to a transformation of the way philosophical theology is conducted. For example, required is the use of methods of literary criticism in philosophical inquiry. It means also a transgression of the well-defined realm of precise, compelling arguments in philosophical conduct, for which defenders of the enterprise of Analytic Theology have a soft spot. Precise, compelling arguments are to be valued but they "are not everything. If we insist on rigour above everything else, we are in danger of getting it above everything else: a fossilized view of the world, unable to account for the richness of reality in which we live our lives" (Stump 2009, 261). Indeed, an overemphasis on conceptual clarity and rigor in propositional reasoning may be the root cause for so many of the distortions of Christianity that we find in the writings of some prominent Christian Analytic Theologians, such as Richard Swinburne (see Hick 2010).

In conclusion, following Stump we have reason to think that the literary aspects of thought experiments are not irrelevant for their philosophical value and raise important questions about the use of methods of literary criticism when incorporating thought experiments and other pieces of literary fiction in philosophical discourse, especially on matters theological.

5 Theology enriches philosophy

Philosophy is among those disciplines that would be unthinkable without thought experiments. Among the many thought experiments that the history of philosophy produced we find a number that are distinctively theological. Sometimes the theological character of a philosophical thought experiment reflects its main subject matter, namely God. Other philosophical thought experiments make genuinely theological assumptions in order to address a non-theological topic. A wonderful example of the latter is John Hick's rejoinder to verificationist claims that theology is vacuous talk because there is no way we could possibly expect theological statements to be verified. When it comes to theological statements we are not only lacking empirical support, but we do not even have an idea about possible methods of verification. Well, argues Hick (1960), since its emergence Christianity has been affirming the coming of a time when all truths of faith will be proven true for all humanity by God. Until that time humanity's epistemic situation is comparable to two travelers on the road to a city of whose existence they have differing views. One of them strongly believes that it exists, the other doubts it. But both continue their travel together on the road to the city in question. As long as the travelers are on the road, contends Hick, we have no reason to reject the hope of the believing traveler as irrational on grounds of unverifiability. In the same way as we have a very good understanding of what it means that the assumed city at the end of the road of our two imaginary travelers verifies either the belief of its existence or the belief of its nonexistence, the Christian creed has meaning. This is Hick's idea of eschatological verification of the Christian creed, which he proposed at the time of the onset of the decline of the verificationism defended by logical positivists.

Among those thought experiments that are theological by their subject matter is the intriguing scenario of a stone too heavy for an omnipotent God to lift. Could an omnipotent God create such a stone? One can read this thought experiment in different ways. Sometimes it is used as an argument against the logical possibility of a God as traditionally conceived, namely as an ultimate being of metaphysical absoluteness. We are good but God is absolutely good. We are free but God is absolutely free. We know things but God knows everything. We can do things but God can do everything. Etc. Accordingly, if there is a stone too heavy for God to lift then God is not omnipotent because there is something she cannot do, namely lift a stone. And, if she could not create such a stone then her alleged omnipotence seems undermined, as well. God seems limited in what she can create. Either way, there is no omnipotent God because such a God is impossible as the thought experiment shows that one cannot even describe such a being coherently. Something that cannot be described by us coherently is impossible, and impossible things do not exist. Used this way, the thought experiment fails, in my view. Divine omnipotence must have limits, and this for a number of reasons. For example, God can do only what is logically possible. Otherwise the claim that God is also absolutely rational is in jeopardy.

The thought experiment seems more useful when put to work in facilitating a discussion about the nature of God's omnipotence (see Swinburne 2005). The stone thought experiment does not bring to light a logical limit but probably limits to divine action that are rooted in the divine nature. Accordingly, it does not require a logical analysis but a theological treatment. God could create such a stone, and if she did she ceased to be omnipotent.

In conclusion, philosophy's dependence on thought experiments extends to philosophical theology.

6 Divine food for mice, and thought

Since thought experiments became the subject of serious discussions in the 1980s, Christian theology, like many other disciplines, has heightened its awareness of the significance of thought experiments for its own endeavors. There are many intriguing examples. Among my personal favorites is one that concerns a central doctrine of Catholic faith, namely the doctrine of transubstantiation.[2] In the Catholic tradition, the priest is believed to change bread and wine into the body and blood of Christ. Due to the priestly act of consecration the host and wine change their substance, which is defined in terms of Aristotelian ontology. Thereby they cease to be bread and wine, and become the body and blood of Christ. They only seem to remain unchanged because what is not substance about them is not affected. Consecration only impacts the substance, not the accidental properties (shape, texture, color, etc.). The reason for this partial change of reality – Thomas Aquinas argued – is that a full change meant that the believer will have to consume real flesh and blood. But that would be unbearable. Nobody wants to eat human flesh and drink human blood, not even Christ's.[3] Thus the properties of bread and wine remain intact, although they become properties of a new substance after consecration.

In the present context, there is no need to delve to deeply into the technical details of the controversial debate surrounding the Catholic doctrine of transubstantiation. Important now is that the priestly act of consecration results in a real, although partial, change in the bread and wine. It is real insofar as the change is not exclusively projected onto bread and wine by the community of believers. Bread and wine assumed a new reality following the consecration, despite their appearance of continuing to be bread and wine. Therefore, the consecrated hosts that are not consumed by the assembled congregation are kept in a tabernacle and venerated. They *are* the body of Christ. Now imagine a church mouse breaking into the tabernacle and eating all of the hosts kept in there. A wonderful thought experiment because it prompts the challenging question if the mouse consumed Christ? The question triggers huge problems for the doctrine of transubstantiation. It seems inevitable that the mouse consumes the body of Christ insofar as anyone can consume the body of Christ. If nobody and thus also not the mouse could consume the body of Christ, we could not speak in any meaningful way of a new reality that obtained in the host by means of a transubstantiation in consequence to the priestly act of consecration. Some theologians think otherwise, and introduce the distinction between the body of Christ and the spiritual benefits resulting from its consumption. The mouse can *eat* the host, but not *consume* the body of Christ because it does not satisfy the preconditions satisfied by those who actually *consume* the body of Christ. Who is worthy of the body of Christ? Who is worthy of enjoying the benefits of the sacrament? It follows that not only the mouse but even some believers cannot consume the body of Christ, even if they were to be given the consecrated host for consumption. They would simply *eat* a consecrated host, but not *consume* the body of Christ. But if there are requirements to be satisfied, the idea of a new reality in the host seems compromised. The change to a substance is not manifest after consecration, but only a change in the disposition to bring about the spiritual effects inherent in the body of Christ. But who puts the spiritual benefits into it when it is consumed by a believer worthy of the body of Christ? It is probably God. But why then to define anything like the doctrine of transubstantiation in the first place? Wouldn't it suffice to say that in the very moment when the consecrated host is consumed by a worthy believer it becomes the body of Christ in all its reality and spiritual richness? Yet, again, the whole idea of spiritual benefits inherent in the body of Christ might be misguided. Aren't sacraments more like windbags that indicate God's omnipresence, instead of bringing God's presence about? Of course, an affirmative answer will undermine the doctrine of transubstantiation defined in terms of a static substance ontology. And, as just demonstrated, a negative answer provokes problems of a different but not less difficult nature. Obviously, the theologian faces quite a challenge, and all this due to an imaginary church mouse breaking into a tabernacle and eating consecrated hosts.

In conclusion, Christian theology is among the many disciplines that make extensive use of thought experiments. It has some intriguing examples of thought experiments to offer.

7 Conclusion

Theology and the topic of thought experiments intersect in many ways. I have reviewed only some of them, and indicated where further discussion is necessary and worthwhile. Further inquiries into the theological dimension of the topic of thought experiments seem timely in light of historical claims that today's conceptions of science and religion along the lines of the propositional are a very recent phenomenon (see Harrison 2015). For example, thought experiments are a wonderful topic to revisit the cognitive power of the imagination in its irreducible non-propositional features. As such they provide the opportunity to look for more promising ways to analyze the relationship between science and religion than those that are widely pursued today.

Notes

1 I am reading Geach here very charitably. His own presentation of his views is more implausible than the reading of them that I am going to discuss. For those who are interested in some of the details of the theological motivation of his skepticism about thought experiments, here only so much: his position is that the question, why obey God's law, is an "insane" question. He is referring to attempts to justify any observance of Christian morals, and dismisses those attempts as misguided. It is not an insane question, however, in my view, at least in the sense of being misguided. It is very reasonable to raise the question why to act in accordance with Christian morals, and this for at least two reasons: (1) the Christian Bible lacks the clarity required of a moral handbook – and since it is the main source of our ideas of God's moral laws, further inquiry is required to determine the precise nature of these laws. Such inquiry is motivated by the simple question, why to observe this or that alleged divine moral law, such as the command not to desire other people's property. (2) But even if we were justified in assuming that Christians know what exactly it is God wants us to do when reading the Christian Scripture, it seems very reasonable to wonder why God would create human beings that have reason, free will, and can chose not to follow God's laws in certain situations for very good reasons. In other words, why does God not leave it to humans to figure out the right moral laws, instead of revealing to them what is right and wrong. This is to raise the question if Christianity is really well understood if characterized as requiring blind submission to divine moral commandments. We are entering here technically challenging terrain, which to address would require more details about both theological anthropology and theology of divine revelation then I have space to offer here.

The theological quintessence of Geach's skepticism about thought experiments is that he thinks that the mere knowledge of God's existence makes a morally significant difference with respect to the cognitive power of situations imaginable but not actual.

2 For some historical context on both the doctrine and the thought experiment, see Wainwright and Westerfield Tucke (2006, 230–7).

3 Thomas deals with the eucharist in the *Summa Theologiae*, third part, questions 73–83 (ST, III, 73–83). The issue of transubstantiation is dealt with in question 75, articles 1–3. The reference to the thought experiment can be found in question 80, article 3, ad 3. The article is about whether only the just person is able to "eat Christ sacramentally."

References

Bishop, M. (1999) "Why thought experiments are not arguments," *Philosophy of Science* 66: 534–541.
Bohr, N. (1949) "Discussions with Einstein on epistemological problems in atomic physics," in *Albert Einstein: Philosopher-Scientist*, edited by P. A. Schilpp, LaSalle: Open Court.
Brooke, J. H. (1991) *Science and Religion: Some Historical Perspectives*, Cambridge: Cambridge University Press.
Brown, J. R. (2007) "Counter thought experiments," *Royal Institute of Philosophy Supplement* 82: 155–177.
Clayton, P. (2010) "Something new under the sun: Forty years of philosophy of religion, with a special look at process philosophy," *International Journal for Philosophy of Religion* 68: 139–152.
Elgin, C. Z. (2014) "Fiction as thought experiment," *Perspectives on Science* 22: 221–241.
Geach, P. (1969) *God and the Soul*, London: Routledge and Kegan Paul.
Harrison, P. (2015) *The Territories of Science and Religion*, Chicago: Chicago University Press.
Hick, J. (1960) "Theology and verification," *Theology Today* 17: 12–31.
Hick, J. (2010) "God and Christianity according to Swinburne," *European Journal for Philosophy of Religion* 2: 25–37.
Karafyllis, N. C. and Ulshöefer, G. (eds) (2008) *Sexualized Brains: Scientific Modeling of Emotional Intelligence from a Cultural Perspective*, Cambridge: MIT Press.
Kraay, K. (2013) "Method and madness in contemporary analytic philosophy of religion," *Toronto Journal of Theology* 29: 245–264.
McAllister, J. W. (1996) "The evidential significance of thought experiments," *Studies in the History and Philosophy of Science* 27: 233–250.
McLean, B. (2013) "Lessons learned from Swinburne: A critique of Richard Swinburne's revelation: From metaphor to analogy," *Toronto Journal of Theology* 29: 369–387.
Meixner, U. (2004) *The Two Sides of Being: A Reassessment of Psycho-Physical Dualism*, Paderborn: Mentis.
Perler, D. (2008) "Thought experiments: The methodological function of angels in Late Medieval epistemology," in *Angels in Medieval Philosophical Inquiry*, edited by I. Iribarren and M. Lenz, Alsdershot: Ashgate.
Polkinghorne, J. (2007) *Quantum Physics and Theology: An Unexpected Kinship*, New Haven: Yale University Press.
Rea, M. C. (2009) "Introduction," in *Analytic Theology: New Essays in the Philosophy of Theology*, edited by O. D. Crisp and M. C. Rea, Oxford: Oxford University Press.
Saunders, N. (2002) *Divine Action and Modern Science*, Cambridge: Cambridge University Press.
Schellenberg, J. L. (2009) "Philosophy of religion: A state of the subject report: the Canadian theological society's inaugural Jay Newman memorial lecture in philosophy of religion," *Toronto Journal of Theology* 25: 95–110.
Stuart, M. T. (2014) "Cognitive science and thought experiments: A refutation of Paul Thagard's skepticism," *Perspectives on Science* 22: 264–287.
Stump, E. (2009) "The problem of evil: Analytic philosophy and narrative," in *Analytic Theology: New Essays in the Philosophy of Theology*, edited by O. D. Crisp and M. C. Rea, Oxford: Oxford University Press.
Swinburne, R. (2005) *Faith and Reason*, 2nd ed., Oxford: Clarendon.
Swinburne, R. (2007) *Revelation: From Metaphor to Analogy*, 2nd ed., Oxford: Oxford University Press.
Swirski, P. (2007) *Of Literature and Knowledge: Explorations in Narrative Thought Experiments, Evolution, and Game Theory*, London and New York: Routledge.
Thagard, P. (2010) *The Brain and the Meaning of Life*, Princeton: Princeton University Press.
Thagard, P. (2014) "Thought experiments considered harmful," *Perspectives on Science* 22: 288–305.
Wainwright, G. and Westerfield Tucke, K. B. (eds) (2006) *The Oxford History of Christian Worship*, Oxford: Oxford University Press.

11
THOUGHT EXPERIMENTS IN ETHICS

Georg Brun

1 Introduction

In normative and applied ethics, thought experiments are frequently used in debates on questions such as: Are we morally obliged to give large amounts to poverty relief? Can the number of lives saved be ethically decisive? Is torture ever morally permissible? At the heart of every thought experiment is a scenario with a question. Here are sketches of some of the best-known ethical thought experiments, which have also become prominent in political discourse:

Trolley: in the so-called *Driver's Two Options* (there are many other versions), a runaway trolley is heading towards five workers on the track who have no escape; is it morally permissible for the driver to steer the trolley onto another track where it will kill one worker? (Foot 2002; Thomson 2008)

Pond: a child has fallen into a pond and is about to drown; ought you hurry to rescue him even if doing so ruins your shoes and thwarts your plans for the day? (Singer 1972)

Violinist: while asleep, your body has been hooked up to the body of a violinist who has an illness that makes it necessary for her to be connected to your metabolism for nine months; is it morally permissible for you to ask to be severed from her even if this will kill her? (Thomson 1972)

Ticking Bomb: a terrorist has hidden a bomb that will kill thousands of people if set off; are we morally permitted to torture her given that we know that only in this way we will learn how to defuse the bomb? (Shue 1978)

Original Position: behind a "veil of ignorance," in a situation in which no one knows his place in society, his status or his natural strengths and weaknesses, which fundamental principles of justice would free and rational persons accept as being in their interest? (Rawls 1999)

In contrast to the first four scenarios, *Original Position* is not a stock example. One explanation for this is that *Original Position* has a specific function in Rawls's theory of justice, whereas the other scenarios are used in more familiar ways as parts of arguments for or against an ethically relevant claim about, for example, abortion, torture or our obligation to help others. However, the first four scenarios are sometimes used differently as well, for example, to illustrate the consequences of some moral principle. This calls for a typology of ethical thought experiments according to their functions, which will be introduced in Section 3. Before this issue can be tackled, we need a more detailed characterization of the structure of thought experiments which explains how scenarios, questions and arguments figure in thought experiments (Section 2). Section 4 then investigates the two most widely discussed functions of thought experiments, namely supporting and refuting ethical claims. Since such epistemic functions cannot be analysed in a metaethically neutral way, I introduce some elements of the method of reflective equilibrium as a more specific background in moral epistemology, which enjoys relatively broad acceptance. In Section 5, I finally discuss a range of challenges and touch upon specifically moral objections to ethical thought experiments.

2 Reconstructing ethical thought experiments

The philosophical literature usually focuses on analysing thought experiments of a certain kind, most often, thought experiments that aim at refuting a general claim. For such thought experiments, specific schemes of reconstruction have been developed, typically tied to some philosophical approach (e.g. Sorensen 1992, ch. 6; Häggqvist 1996, ch. 5, 2009; and see the entries in Part III of this volume). In this chapter, I rely on a simpler reconstruction, which enables us to address the variety of ethical thought experiments and to distinguish two common uses of the term "thought experiment":

(1) A scenario and a question are introduced.
(2) The experimenter goes through (imagines, thinks about, etc.) the scenario and arrives at some result.
(3) A conclusion is drawn with respect to some target (e.g., an ethically relevant claim or distinction).

A "core" thought experiment just comprises (1) and (2). An "extended" thought experiment includes some additional reasoning (3), which can be reconstructed as an argument; the result of (2) is used as a premise from which, typically together with a range of often implicit assumptions, a conclusion is drawn with respect to some target.

In *Trolley*, for example, the scenario describes a situation with a runway trolley, two tracks, a driver, several workers and a switch. The question is whether the driver is morally permitted to throw the switch. The experimenter imagines or thinks about the situation and arrives at, say, the conviction that the driver is permitted to change the switch. This is the result of the core thought experiment. The extended thought experiment then uses this result as a premise in an argument for, say, the target thesis that (body) numbers count morally. An additional assumption involved in this argument may be that the difference in numbers of workers on the tracks is the reason why switching is permissible.

In more complex cases, one extended thought experiment draws on the results of several core thought experiments. Smart (1972, 27–8), for instance, uses two scenarios, one with one and another with two million equally happy people, to illustrate the difference between average (both scenarios yield the same result) and total utilitarianism (the situation with more people fares better).

Conversely, the same core thought experiment can be used in different arguments. This provides a more natural and flexible analysis of reasoning by thought experiment than an analysis which uses "thought experiment" only for extended thought experiments, associating every thought experiment with a specific structure (1)–(3) (see, e.g., Häggqvist 1996, 2009).

The elements (1)–(3) require several explanations. The scenario describes a situation which is declared or assumed to be possible in some sense, for example, (meta)physically, logically or conceptually.[1] If the thought experiment is to be successful, the scenario must be a consistent, meaningful description (see Rescher 2005, ch. 9) and the person running the thought experiment must be able to make appropriate use of the scenario by, for example, conceiving of the described situation or applying a given principle to it. Often, the scenario is qualified as fictional (e.g. Elgin 2014), hypothetical or counterfactual (e.g. Gendler 2000, 17). This is not meant to imply that the described situation must not be real or realizable, but only that it need not be so, and that, if the described situation happens to be realized, this does not affect the thought experiment. Passersby come across drowning children, and *Trolley*-style accidents do in fact happen, but as thought experiments, *Pond* and *Trolley* are independent of those tragedies. This is so because even if situations as described in the scenario are real, the scenario, not these situations, sets the stage for the thought experiment. As all descriptions of non-abstract states of affairs, scenarios are invariably less rich than the actual and possible situations that fit the description (does the violinist like eggplant casserole?). This selectivity serves to establish at least a presumption about which aspects of a situation are relevant for answering the given question, without implying the unrealistic assumption that the scenario explicitly mentions all and only the relevant information. Common ground and implicatures play an important role as well.

The element (2) is deliberately framed in unspecific terms to leave room for a broad range of activities and results. More specific descriptions can be used to characterize specific kinds of thought experiments, for example, thought experiments in which an intuition is prompted by imagining a situation or thought experiments which use modal reasoning. We should, however, resist the temptation to postulate any such specific description as a general characterization. It is, for example, sometimes said that ethical thought experiments are used to elicit intuitions (see Stich and Tobia, this volume). What this boils down to depends on what one means by "intuition." A necessary but not sufficient requirement for a belief (or other propositional attitude) to be an intuition is that it is not held *just* because it has been inferred consciously (see Brun 2014). But as a general characterization of the result in (2), this minimal condition is still too narrow.[2] There are many ethical thought experiments in which the result of (2) is a judgement gained by means of an explicit argument, typically involving additional assumptions not explicitly mentioned in the scenario.

Similar problems result if thought experiments are distinguished from counterfactual or hypothetical reasoning in general by the requirement of having an experimental element in the sense that something is imagined not merely by contemplating propositional content, but visually, tactually or in another perception-related way (Brown and Fehige 2014). If this idea is to be effective at all, the element of experience must be more than the visual, auditory or other associations routinely evoked by any description of a non-abstract situation. Understood in this way, however, an implausibly narrow notion of thought experiment results, which excludes many philosophical (e.g. Putnam's H_2O vs. XYZ on Twin Earth) and ethical thought experiments such as *Ticking Bomb* and *Trolley* if they are described as simply as at the beginning of this section.

The argumentation reconstructed in (3) may take any form of argument ranging from modal and deontic deductive reasoning to arguments from analogies and inference to the best explanation. The target mentioned in (3) allows for many different kinds of conclusions: they can be about a concept, a proposition, a theory, or about a relation between two or more such objects (e.g. a difference between two theories). As Gendler (2000, 25) argues, there is a tendency (but no strict rule) that thought experiments in different disciplines aim at different results in (2). Scientific thought experiments primarily ask what would happen in the situation described in the scenario; thought experiments in metaphysics, epistemology and philosophy of language more often ask how we should describe what would happen; and thought experiments in ethics and aesthetics very commonly ask how what would happen should be evaluated. Accordingly, scientific thought experiments typically target empirical claims; in metaphysics, epistemology and philosophy of language, the target is typically a proposal for a conceptual analysis or, more generally, a characterization of a concept (e.g. Gettier-cases against knowledge as justified true belief); in ethics, the target is usually a claim about a normative concept or some normative principle or theory, for example, that numbers count morally, that abortion is permissible, or that the right to life includes a right to be sustained in living.

The explanations given so far obviously do not amount to a definition of "ethical thought experiment," but together with the examples above they should suffice to give a fairly clear idea of what ethical thought experiments are. On this basis, we can now explore the functions of ethical thought experiments in more detail.

3 Functions of ethical thought experiments

Typologies of extended thought experiments according to their goal are of special importance since the evaluation of a thought experiment must frequently be relative to what it is supposed to achieve. In what follows, I suggest a typology that can accommodate the broad range of functions of thought experiments in ethics (for alternatives, see, e.g., Brown 1991; Walsh 2011; Davis 2012). It is important to keep in mind that core thought experiments are normally put to more than one use, and that their use can change over time, for instance, because they are employed in the context of different background assumptions and with different goals (Elgin 2014). The proposed classification therefore primarily deals with extended thought experiments, and only derivatively with core thought experiments.

To simplify, we can speak of, for example, an "epistemic thought experiment" where we strictly speaking would have to say "extended thought experiment with an epistemic function" or "core thought experiment used in an extended thought experiment with an epistemic function."

3.1 Epistemic thought experiments

The goal of epistemic thought experiments is to provide a reason which speaks in favour of or against a claim with respect to the target.[3] Accordingly, we can draw a basic distinction between constructive and destructive epistemic functions. Constructive thought experiments come in two varieties. Some are meant to show that something is possible. Shue (1978), for example, uses *Ticking Bomb* to show that there are possible exceptional circumstances in which torture is permissible, and according to one analysis, *Violinist* aims at showing "that abortion could be morally permissible even when the fetus has a right to life" (Brown and Fehige 2014). Other constructive thought experiments are intended to provide only some (non-conclusive) support for a claim. *Pond* is regularly interpreted in this way, either as intended to support a general principle that obliges us to help if we can do so without significant moral costs, or as an argument from analogy which supports the claim that we should give significant amounts of money to help poor people. That thought experiments can provide support for an ethical principle at all, is a view that needs metaethical backing. On Singer's own view (2009, 15–17), for example, intuitions are epistemically dubious, including those prompted by *Pond*; and Dancy (e.g. 1985, 1993, 64–6) has argued that analogies from core thought experiments to real cases are inherently problematic. Section 4 discusses epistemic functions in more detail against a specific background in moral epistemology.

Destructive thought experiments provide a counterexample to a target claim. Often, they show that something can be the case and use this in an argument against an incompatible claim. *Violinist*, for example, is standardly reconstructed as providing such a refuting argument against the claim that the right to life of one person under all circumstances outweighs the right of another person to decide what happens with his or her body. Obviously, this type of refuting use of a scenario is most closely related to the possibility-showing constructive use. *Ticking Bomb* shows that torture is permissible in some circumstances just in case it refutes the claim that torture is impermissible under all conditions whatsoever. Another way of using the result of going through the scenario is to turn it against some background assumption. *Violinist*, for example, can also be reconstructed as challenging the tacit assumption that the right to life entails a right to be sustained in living (Brown and Fehige 2014).

It is natural to think that epistemic functions of thought experiments are normally refuting rather than constructive because general claims can be decisively undermined but not conclusively supported by individual cases. And in fact, there is a culture of "counterexample philosophy," which widely employs refuting thought experiments which target a conceptual claim that is part of some account of, for example, moral permissibility, autonomy or consent. The thought experiment then comes to the result that an act described in the scenario does (not) fall under that concept in contrast to what follows from the account in question. Whether that actually amounts to a refutation of this account depends on methodological assumptions, in particular on the conditions an adequate "analysis" or "explication" of a concept is supposed to meet. If the goal is an analysis which preserves all clear-cut cases, counterexamples to such cases invariably refute the proposed analysis. If the goal is an explication that may include some conceptual revision, counterexamples are not automatically decisive.

In the philosophical discussion, epistemic or, more specifically, destructive epistemic functions are generally taken to be the basic or the most important functions of thought experiments. There is, however, not one function all ethical thought experiments essentially have. And even if one considers non-epistemic functions as entirely secondary, it remains important to recognize them because ethical thought experiments usually have an epistemic function non-exclusively, and therefore other, non-epistemic functions can influence the epistemic function or the two functions can get conflated.

3.2 Illustrative and rhetorical thought experiments

Illustrative thought experiments render a concept, a proposition, a theory or some other target clearer and more understandable, but insofar as we focus exclusively on its illustrative function, we do not see a thought experiment as providing reason for or against its target. Singer's original use of *Pond* is clearly intended as an illustration of a principle he independently defends. He writes (1972, 231): "If it is in our power to prevent something very bad from happening, without thereby sacrificing anything morally significant, we ought, morally, to do it. An application of this principle would be as follows." The case of the drowning child makes then vivid what the quoted principle may ask of us in a concrete situation. Another example is the difference between total and average utilitarianism. One may know in abstract terms that it will become manifest only in a comparison of two groups with a different number of people, but going through specific scenarios makes the difference more readily graspable. Furthermore, textbook-examples which are thought experiments are usually illustrative (Cohnitz 2006, 77).

Closely related are rhetorical thought experiments, which are intended to convince people to accept or reject some ethical idea. *Pond* is certainly apt for rhetorical use and actually functions this way in some of Singer's later writings (e.g. 2009). Rhetorical functions very often piggyback on an epistemic function, but certainly not always. Ticking-bomb scenarios, for example, are notorious for having been used in media and political discourse as a means for campaigning in favour of torture and other illegal or contested practices.

Of course, illustrative thought experiments can be misleading, and rhetorical thought experiments can be used in propagandistic or demagogic ways, but this is not necessarily so. We expect successful epistemic thought experiments to have the rhetorical power of convincing us, and there is nothing inherently problematic about that, in contrast to an illustrative or rhetorical function of a thought experiment which is interpreted or sold as epistemic (for a paradigmatic example, see Dennett's 1980 critique of Searle's Chinese room argument as an "intuition pump").

3.3 Heuristic thought experiments

In the simplest case, heuristic thought experiments are just devices for generating ideas. A core thought experiment is run, but its result is then investigated independently. More ambitious heuristic thought experiments systematically explore morally relevant factors and differences.

One possibility is to try to isolate factors which are potentially morally relevant by developing variations of a scenario and seeing whether the resulting moral intuitions or judgements co-vary. Thomson's work on trolley cases is a well-known example. She extensively varies the scenario in order to find whether it makes a difference if, for example, the driver or a bystander can change the switch, or if the choice is described as one between killing five and killing one, or between killing one and letting five die. Actually, this procedure can also run into problems. Many more factors can be tested for moral relevance, including the age of the people on the track, whether they are employees of the train-system, or whether they are members of an ethnic minority. In fact, there is empirical research showing that skin colour has an influence on the judgement of people who are strongly committed to its moral irrelevance (see Uhlmann et al. 2009). This raises the question of whether such an effect undermines the value of the elicited judgements, or whether we should rather conclude that a trolley scenario which alludes to skin colour is badly designed, or that philosophers need to be more careful in running thought experiments (see Stich and Tobia, this volume; Ludwig, this volume).

Another heuristic strategy systematically explores the consequences of various theories for a range of scenarios with the goal of, for example, finding out in which situations two rival theories actually lead to different results. Again, comparisons of various versions of utilitarianism provide examples.

Applications of the two strategies just described can actually be analysed as heuristic or as another type of thought experiment, depending on what we take to be their target. Consider the example of the two versions of utilitarianism. If the target is the claim that there is a difference between total and average utilitarianism, then Smart's thought experiment is most naturally interpreted as illustrating this difference or as having the epistemic function of showing that there is indeed such a difference. If the target is, say, total utilitarianism, then Smart's thought experiment may be interpreted as having the heuristic function of tracking down a situation in which total utilitarianism differs from average utilitarianism, but in itself this neither supports nor undermines total utilitarianism. The last interpretation shows that the heuristic potential of thought experiments can be exploited even by those who are deeply sceptical about epistemic functions of ethical thought experiments (e.g. Dancy 1993, 65).

In the literature there is a tendency to see illustrative and heuristic functions of thought experiments as of merely limited interest, especially in comparison with epistemic functions. However, another view emerges, for example, in Hills's recent discussion of moral understanding. According to her account, to understand that q is why p is morally right or wrong, requires that one has the ability to "draw the conclusion that p' (or that probably p') from the information that q' (where p' and q' are similar to but not identical to p and q)" (Hills 2009, 102). In other words, one needs the ability to run heuristic and illustrative thought experiments. Furthermore, Hills argues that moral understanding is not only instrumental in reliably doing the right thing and justifying yourself to others, but also essential for having a good character and for morally worthy action. On this account, the ability to run thought experiments is of central interest not only to ethical theorists, but to all moral agents.

3.4 *Thought experiment with a theory-internal function*

Borsboom, Mellenbergh and Van Heerden (2002) argue that there are thought experiments which perform some specific function within a theory, different from the functions discussed so far. Their prime example is the scenario of a "counterfactual long run" in frequentist statistics. A prominent example of an ethical thought experiment with a theory-internal function is Rawls's *Original Position*. The scenario models fair conditions for social cooperation as well as restrictions on arguments for principles of justice (Rawls 1999, 16–9; 2001, 17, 83, 85; cf. Gendler 2007 for a different analysis). Also Kant's categorical imperative involves a thought experiment in which we have to test whether we can will the generalization of the maxim guiding some way of acting (see Parfit 2011, 285, 328–9). A closer analysis and evaluation of such thought experiments inevitably requires an in-depth discussion of the respective ethical theories and cannot be undertaken here.

4 Ethical thought experiments and reflective equilibrium

Epistemic functions of thought experiments are philosophically the most prominent and hence deserve a closer analysis. But as pointed out in Section 3.1, such functions depend on metaethical assumptions. I therefore introduce in this section a background in moral epistemology, which is relatively widely accepted, namely reflective equilibrium (Section 4.1). On this basis, the central functions of thought experiments can be characterized more precisely (Section 4.2), and some consequences can be drawn regarding the results of core thought experiments and with respect to what we can expect to accomplish by thought experiments (Section 4.3).

4.1 Reflective equilibrium

The method of (so-called "wide") reflective equilibrium can be characterized most succinctly by two key ideas. Firstly, judgements and principles are justified if judgements, principles and background theories are in equilibrium. Secondly, this state is reached through a process that starts from judgements and background theories, proposes systematic principles and then mutually adjusts judgements and principles (and possibly also background theories).[4]

The contrast between principles and judgements is not to be understood as a matter of their content, but as the contrast between propositions that are part of some given moral theory or system of principles and propositions to which somebody is actually committed. Commitment is to be understood as an epistemically relevant status which implies at least a minimal degree of credibility. Commitments can be expressed explicitly or merely revealed in action and they can have any degree of firmness from feeble to unwavering. In the tradition of Rawls and Daniels, commitments are required to be considered judgements; that is, judgements not made under circumstances prone to error such as inattention, excessive self-interest, etc. Both, commitments and elements of the theory, may be changed in the process of mutual adjustment. Every stage of the process of developing a reflective equilibrium is characterized by a position consisting of the current commitments and the current theory.

4.2 Functions of thought experiments

Within the framework of reflective equilibrium, thought experiments can play several roles. Constructive epistemic thought experiments can generate commitments at any stage in the process of developing a reflective equilibrium. In simple cases, the commitment is just the result of the core thought experiment. The experimenter considers *Trolley*, for example, and resolves that throwing the switch is morally permissible. In more complex cases, a conclusion of an extended thought experiment is supported by the result of a core thought experiment and additional reasoning. In this way, *Trolley* may support the claim that it is morally permissible to kill a person if this is the only way to save several others. While such supportive thought experiments can be independent of the current theory, this need not be the case. Elements of the current theory can enter the reasoning, and candidates for commitments can also be generated just by applying the current theory to the scenario. In *Trolley*, a philosopher with deontologist leanings could argue that the prohibition on killing implies that it is morally impermissible to change the switch, and then conclude that this result should be accepted because it does not conflict with any of her other commitments.

Of course, conflicts will often arise, and then destructive thought experiments become important. In such cases, the result of a core thought experiment is a premise in an argument which shows that there is an incoherence within or between the current commitments and the theory, as in the *Trolley*-examples of the preceding paragraph. On this basis, an extended thought experiment argues for giving up a commitment or some element of the current theory.

If the process of mutual adjustments is to be carried out in a systematic way, heuristic thought experiments play a crucial role as well. They are needed for exploring the results of applying the current theory to systematic variations of scenarios. Again, the many variants of *Trolley* provide an example.

4.3 Consequences

We can now turn to some debated issues in the literature on ethical thought experiments. Let us begin with the results of core thought experiments.

Firstly, the result of a thought experiment is always a commitment that is explicitly expressed in public or in one's mind, not one merely revealed in action – for the thought experiment must not rely on the scenario being real. It has been argued that this is problematic and we should rather rely on how we act in real situations (Davis 2012). As a general strategy to determine what is morally right, this is implausible because, regrettably, we cannot count on our actions being more reliably right than our explicit commitments. The method of reflective equilibrium, however, calls for initially recognizing and also for possibly revising all kinds of commitments, including those resulting from thought experiments and those merely revealed in action.

A second issue concerns the role of intuitions. We have seen in Section 2 that an implausibly narrow conception of thought experiments results if one insists that all core thought experiments elicit intuitions. Many further points about the role of intuitions depend on a theory of intuitions, but some basic results are available independently (for discussion, see Stich and Tobia, this volume; Ludwig, this volume; Copp 2012; Brun 2014). On the relatively uncontroversial assumption that intuitions cannot be based on explicit inference, the method of reflective equilibrium leaves room for intuitions as results of core thought experiments, as long as they are not gained by explicit reasoning; this excludes appealing to the theory we are currently developing when going through the scenario. And the conclusion of an extended thought experiment can be an intuition only if it is not reached by explicit argumentation. Furthermore, reflective equilibrium does not exempt intuitions from critical evaluation. They can be revised just as any other commitment. Sometimes, we will not accept an intuition elicited by a scenario as its proper result because we have good reason to think that the intuition is inadequate. Someone may hold that changing the switch is impermissible even if he or she is not able to get rid of his or her recalcitrant intuition that doing so is permissible in this particular case. In other cases, epistemic background theories may give us reason to discredit intuitions as based upon, say, cultural stereotypes.

Closely related considerations also make clear that requiring commitments to be considered judgements poses no principled obstacles to the use of thought experiments. It just means that the conclusion of the extended thought experiment depends on the (possibly implicit) assumption that the result of the core thought experiment meets certain standards.

Turning to extended thought experiments, we can first note that although destructive thought experiments can play an important role, this does not mean that the result of a core thought experiment always "wins" against incompatible commitments or elements of the current theory. It is rather one of the characteristics of reflective equilibrium that revisions may well take the other direction and lead to overriding the result of a thought experiment (as in the example of the recalcitrant intuition above). A refuting thought experiment can show the need for a revision, but it alone cannot settle what is to be revised.

A second point concerns analogies. It is sometimes assumed that supportive thought experiments paradigmatically take the form of analogies (see Section 5.2). Take *Violinist* as an example: is its main point not that the result of the core thought experiment can be transferred by analogy to cases of abortion? In the context of the method of reflective equilibrium, however, the standard way of transferring a moral judgement from one case to another is not by direct analogy but by explicitly introducing principles that cover both cases.

The most important consequence is more general. If we rely on the method of reflective equilibrium, then the fact that a proposition is the result of a core thought experiment is not sufficient for this proposition to be epistemically justified to the degree required for knowledge (and the same is true a fortiori for conclusions of analogies based on such a result). If reflective equilibrium is necessary for epistemic justification, the primary object of justification is not a single proposition but an entire position consisting of the commitments and the theory in equilibrium. Hence, thought experiments may play important epistemic roles according to the method of reflective equilibrium, but they cannot by themselves justify a commitment or a theory. Defenders of reflective equilibrium should therefore object to the view that a destructive thought experiment alone may suffice to refute a claim and to the idea that being supported by an intuition elicited by a thought experiment or by an analogy based on a core thought experiment may be sufficient for justification.

5 Challenges to ethical thought experiments

Although ethical thought experiments are frequently challenged, wholesale criticism of ethical thought experiments in all their functions is implausible. There are, however, challenges which target a specific function of thought experiments. Well-known examples are

Dancy's attacks on supportive thought experiments, which are briefly discussed below. But most challenges to ethical thought experiments raise a problem that may affect specific thought experiments, and I focus on such challenges in what follows. I first give an overview in Section 5.1 and then discuss three issues which have been prominent in debates about ethical thought experiments (Section 5.2). Finally, I address the question of how thought experiments in ethics can raise specifically moral problems (Section 5.3).

5.1 A general overview of challenges

The structure (1)–(3) from Section 2 can be used as a basis for an overview of challenges which address specific thought experiments in any of the functions distinguished in Sections 3 and 4 (see also Gendler 2000, 22–4). Challenges to core thought experiments frequently point out a problem with the scenario or the question. Sometimes we have difficulties going through the described situation because the scenario is incoherent. In other cases, the situation is difficult to imagine because it is underdescribed; that is, described too schematically and relevant details remain undetermined. Or the scenario in effect undermines the conditions for a meaningful application of the concepts used in the question (this kind of objection is best known from the debate about personal identity, targeting, e.g., Parfit's 1987 teletransportation scenarios; see Rescher 2005, ch. 9). Two points which will be discussed further below are the question of how realistic scenarios should be, and the charge that a scenario or a question is misleading.

Other challenges to core thought experiments point out problems with "going through" the scenario and coming up with a result. Maybe no intuition or judgement results because the situation is underdescribed. In such cases, the problem is not that we cannot imagine a situation as described, but that the scenario does not provide enough information to answer the question in a non-arbitrary way (Wilkes 1988, e.g., claims that this problem arises for personal-identity thought experiments because "person" is not a natural-kind term). In other cases, an intuition or a judgement results, but in a problematic way. Whether thought experiments are unreliable if they rely on intuitions is currently a much debated issue (see Stich and Tobia, this volume; specifically for moral intuitions: Burkard 2012; Copp 2012). Many writers hold that intuitions are not reliable truth-trackers, but frequently the product of prejudice, tradition or stereotypes. One strand of experimental philosophy is devoted to investigating empirically whether such accusations can be substantiated by showing that people's reactions to a scenario co-vary with, for example, cultural factors (see Stich and Tobia, this volume; Ludwig, this volume). If the result of a core thought experiment is arrived at not intuitively but discursively, the reasoning may be criticized as fallacious if it involves an invalid or weak argument, an unwarranted assumption (invited, e.g., by an underdescribed scenario), or a conclusion that is irrelevant in the context at hand.

Challenges to an extended thought experiment attack the reasoning which is supposed to establish the conclusion about the target. One type of criticism is that the reasoning is fallacious in one of the ways just mentioned. Since thought experiments using arguments from analogy are quite common in ethics, such objections often home in on weak analogies (see the discussion below). Other challenges point out that it is not clear enough what the conclusion of the thought experiment is supposed to be or that it misses what is at issue in a given debate. For example, does a refuting thought experiment address utilitarianism in general or only some specific version?

5.2 Common challenges to ethical thought experiments

Let us now turn to three types of challenges which are frequently raised in debates about ethical thought experiments. A first question is whether thought experiments, especially epistemic and heuristic ones, should be realistic. The issue is not whether the scenario gives a vivid and detailed description, nor whether the described situation is improbable or bizarre, but rather whether the described situation is modally remote, involving, for example, biologically or technologically impossible elements such as the fission of humans.

On the one hand, there are reasons for appealing to unrealistic situations. They are relevant to universally valid statements and definitions (Sorensen 1992, 279; Walsh 2011). They can produce results that we have a lot of confidence in (Parfit 1987, 200). And if we want to use heuristic thought experiments to isolate morally relevant factors, we need to compare similar situations which differ just in the factor in question (e.g. would cruel treatment of animals be permissible if animals were insentient?); appeal to unrealistic scenarios is then needed if rival theories agree on realistic situations or if realistic situations differ in additional respects (Sorensen 1992, 91; Kamm 1993, 7).

On the other hand, unrealistic epistemic thought experiments have been challenged on various grounds (see Elster 2011). Firstly, some approaches to ethics seek to develop practical, action guiding, moral principles which are meant to lead to the right results in our world, but not necessarily in unrealistic situations. Unrealistic thought experiments are then irrelevant to the justification of these principles (e.g. Hare 1981, 47–9). However, insofar as an approach to ethics must also deal with "deeper" ethical principles that capture moral truths or definitions of moral terms, unrealistic cases remain relevant.

Secondly, there is the worry that unrealistic scenarios lead to core thought experiments with unreliable results. This challenge needs qualification. Reliability is independent of whether the scenario is realistic overall. Unrealistic problems can have easy answers (If binary fission is iterated three times, how many persons result?), realistic cases can pose hard questions and real situations can include too many factors which distract from important features, trigger biases or interfere with our judgement in other ways. More plausibly, unreliability looms if the unrealistic aspects undermine the resources needed to answer the question at stake (Rescher 2005, ch. 9). Even if the scenario is coherent, we may not be able to determine the morally relevant factors and their exact import, or to work out the necessary background assumptions for the unrealistic situation, especially if the unrealistic aspects concern central elements of our web of belief (Sorensen 1992, 43–4). With respect to unrealistic thought experiments that ask for an intuition, many argue that our capacity for intuitive judgement is unreliable in situations for which it has not been developed by evolution or social practice (e.g. Kitcher 2012). This line of argument sometimes leads to more general scepticism about epistemic thought experiments involving intuitions (see, e.g. Singer 2005; Machery 2011).

As a second type of challenge, many epistemic thought experiments are accused of being misleading (Wood 2011), independently of whether they are realistic. At least three charges can be distinguished. Firstly, the really important moral questions are replaced by dubious problems that do not occur in reality. Instead of, say, "Who is responsible for the trolley disaster?", the experimenter asks "Should you throw the switch?" Secondly, thought experiments use forced-choice questions which artificially limit the range of admissible courses of action ("Change the switch, yes or no?") and thereby rule out giving the right answers (e.g. "Try to save all six."). Thirdly, problematic assumptions are introduced, especially by way of implicature or presupposition. *Trolley*, for example, suggests that it asks an important question, that at least one of the available answers is morally legitimate, that moral decisions are a matter of ranking states of affairs resulting from actions, and that further information about the situation is irrelevant (e.g. "Do the workers have permission to be on the track?").

However, those who advance such objections must deal with the rejoinder that they do not take seriously the thought experiments they reject, either by refusing to deal with them, by filling in details that favour their own views or by insisting on changing the subject. Moreover, unrealistic epistemic thought experiments cannot simply be dismissed as irrelevant if they target a universal moral statement or definition which covers such situations. But it is true that they are often not worked out in sufficient detail and need reconstruction. In *Trolley*, for example, the intuition or judgement that we should change the switch may contribute to refuting the view that numbers are never decisive, though it certainly does not show that consequentialism is right, that numbers always count or that rights and entitlements are unimportant. Suggesting that such conclusions follow is bad rhetoric – just as much as insinuating without further evidence that users of trolley cases draw or implicate such conclusions. Finally, a lot of the scepticism may stem from the worry that scenarios such as *Trolley* or *Ticking Bomb* are used to argue directly for a conclusion about some other situation. Typically such a move involves an analogy, and this leads to a third type of challenge to epistemic thought experiments.

Violinist and *Pond* are routinely interpreted as analogies in which the result of the core thought experiment – "It is permissible to unplug yourself from the violinist." or "You ought to rescue the child." – supports a conclusion about abortion or poverty relief respectively. In Section 4.3, I explained that in the context of method of reflective equilibrium such supportive functions are usually better reconstructed as operating more indirectly. But if extended thought experiments are interpreted as analogies, two sorts of objections need to be considered.

Firstly, Dancy (1985, 1993, 64–6) has mounted an attack on supportive thought experiments, which he assumes to employ an analogy from the result of a core thought experiment to a real case. According to Dancy, such analogies are not reliable because, in contrast to the real case, the information on the situation described in the scenario is inevitably limited. We must therefore either qualify our conclusion about the real case with the condition that it does not relevantly differ from the situation described in the scenario, or admit that any new information about the real case can spoil the analogy. One answer operates on the metaethical level and argues against Dancy's specific form of particularism and holism about reasons, which underwrites his claim that we cannot conclusively evaluate situations which are neither real nor variations of real situations (see Häggqvist 1996, ch. 2.7; Cohnitz 2006, ch. 4.2.2 for discussion). Another answer challenges Dancy's understanding of the analogy involved. He asks for an argument that, given the result of the core thought experiment, conclusively shows a claim about the real case. Arguments from analogy, however, are a form of plausible reasoning resting on a premise which states that the real case is relevantly similar to the situation described in the scenario. Analogies are therefore not deductively valid, and strong analogies can be overthrown by further arguments. Nonetheless, for supporting, in contrast to proving, a conclusion a strong analogy suffices (Rescher 2005, 59).

Objections of the second sort target weak analogies in specific extended thought experiments. Examples abound in the debate about thought experiments which use a ticking-bomb scenario to argue that torture may be morally permissible in real life. Critiques of such arguments very often point out that even if torture should be permissible in *Ticking Bomb*, real-life situations differ from this scenario in ways that effectively undermine the analogy. For example, the scenario (explicitly or implicitly) assumes that we know that only torture will get us the right information in time, but in reality this is uncertain, or that torture is strictly limited to some very specific and rare exceptions, whereas in reality it is always an institutionalized practice with a strong tendency to spread (Luban 2005).

5.3 Moral objections to ethical thought experiments

If an ethical thought experiment in fact suffers from one of the shortcomings discussed so far, this can obviously be morally relevant. Bad ethical thought experiments can lead to bad ethics and consequently to morally wrong action. Accordingly, Parfit's ethical project, for example, has been criticized for employing misleading thought experiments (Wood 2011). And attempts to legitimize post-9/11 torture practice with the help of ticking-bomb scenarios have been criticized as irresponsible because they involve an analogy which is invalidated by discrepancies between the scenario's assumptions and easily knowable empirical facts (Luban 2005).

There is, however, also the worry that some ethical thought experiments raise moral problems in other ways. Specifically, it has been argued that discussing certain scenarios and questions is a symptom of moral corruption or leads to moral corruption of the author or the audience of the thought experiment (see, e.g., Anscombe 2005; Williams 1972, 92). Such worries can hardly be defended as a general critique of (unrealistic) ethical thought experiments. After all, one may also argue that the debate about ticking-bomb scenarios, and especially the analysis of the disanalogies involved, has considerably contributed to a better understanding of how torture might not be justified. What rather seems really problematic is the rhetorical use of thought experiments such as *Ticking Bomb* in political discourse and propaganda (see Luban 2005 for an analysis and examples). Glossing over crucial assumptions and selling gerrymandered questions as well-founded challenges can have morally bad consequences and it is incompatible with an adequate self-understanding of a philosopher.

Acknowledgments

For helpful comments, I thank Christoph Baumberger, Claus Beisbart and Anna Goppel. My research has been supported by the Swiss National Science Foundation (project 150251).

Notes

1 There is also reasoning *per impossibile* with counterfactuals with logically or mathematically false antecedents (see Rescher 2005, ch. 8.8), but as far as I can see, it plays no role in ethics.
2 Cappelen (2012) even argues that there are no philosophical thought experiments that rely on eliciting intuitions as opposed to reasoning; he specifically discusses *Violinist* and *Trolley*.
3 This is a rather narrow sense of "epistemic." In a wider sense, heuristic functions may also be classified as epistemic.
4 These two ideas can be found in all standard accounts of reflective equilibrium, specifically in Rawls (1999) and Daniels (2011). In what follows, I rely on an understanding which also draws on ideas of Elgin (1996); see Brun (2014) for a more extensive outline.

References

Anscombe, G. E. M. (1957 [2005]) "Does Oxford moral philosophy corrupt youth?" in *Human Life, Action and Ethics*, Exeter: Imprint Academic.
Borsboom, D., Mellenbergh, G. J. and Van Heerden, J. (2002) "Functional thought experiments," *Synthese* 130: 379–387.
Brown, J. R. (1991) *The Laboratory of the Mind: Thought Experiments in the Natural Sciences*, London: Routledge.
Brown, J. R. and Fehige, Y. (2014) "Thought experiments," in *Stanford Encyclopedia of Philosophy*. Available here: http://plato.stanford.edu/archives/fall2014/entries/thought-experiment/ (accessed 15 November 2016).
Brun, G. (2014) "Reflective equilibrium without intuitions?" *Ethical Theory and Moral Practice* 17: 237–252.
Burkard, A. (2012) *Intuitionen in der Ethik*, Münster: Mentis.
Cappelen, H. (2012) *Philosophy Without Intuitions*, Oxford: Oxford University Press.
Cohnitz, D. (2006) *Gedankenexperimente in der Philosophie*, Paderborn: Mentis.
Copp, D. (2012) "Experiments, intuitions and methodology in moral and political philosophy," in *Oxford Studies in Metaethics*, vol. 7, edited by R. Shafer-Landau, Oxford: Oxford University Press.
Dancy, J. (1985) "The role of imaginary cases in ethics," *Pacific Philosophical Quarterly* 66: 141–153.
Dancy, J. (1993) *Moral Reasons*, Oxford: Blackwell.
Daniels, N. (2011) "Reflective equilibrium," in *Stanford Encyclopedia of Philosophy*. Available here: http://plato.stanford.edu/archives/spr2011/entries/reflective-equilibrium/ (accessed 15 November 2016).
Davis, M. (2012) "Imaginary cases in ethics. A critique," *International Journal of Applied Philosophy* 26: 1–17.
Dennett, D. C. (1980) "The milk of human intentionality," *The Behavioral and Brain Sciences* 3: 428–430.
Elgin, C. Z. (1996) *Considered Judgment*, Princeton: Princeton University Press.
Elgin, C. Z. (2014) "Fiction as thought experiment," *Perspectives on Science* 22: 221–241.
Elster, J. (2011) "How outlandish can imaginary cases be?" *Journal of Applied Philosophy* 28: 241–258.
Foot, P. (1967 [2002]) "The problem of abortion and the doctrine of the double effect," in *Virtues and Vices and Other Essays in Moral Philosophy*, Oxford: Clarendon Press.
Gendler, T. S. (2000) *Thought Experiment. On the Powers and Limits of Imaginary Cases*, New York: Garland.
Gendler, T. S. (2007) "Philosophical thought experiments, intuitions, and cognitive equilibrium," *Midwest Studies in Philosophy* 31: 68–89.
Häggqvist, S. (1996) *Thought Experiments in Philosophy*, Stockholm: Almqvist and Wiksell.
Häggqvist, S. (2009) "A model for thought experiments," *Canadian Journal of Philosophy* 39: 55–76.
Hare, R. M. (1981) *Moral Thinking: Its Levels, Method, and Point*, Oxford: Clarendon Press.
Hills, A. (2009) "Moral testimony and moral epistemology," *Ethics* 120: 94–127.
Kamm, F. M. (1993) *Morality, Mortality Volume. 1: Death and Whom to Save from It*, New York: Oxford University Press.

Kitcher, P. (2012) "The lure of the peak," *New Republic* 243: 30–35.
Luban, D. (2005) "Liberalism, torture, and the ticking bomb," *Virginia Law Review* 91: 1425–1461. Available here: http://scholarship.law.georgetown.edu/facpub/148
Machery, E. (2011) "Thought experiments and philosophical knowledge," *Metaphilosophy* 42: 191–214.
Parfit, D. (1987) *Reasons and Persons*, Oxford: Clarendon Press.
Parfit, D. (2011) *On What Matters*, vol. 1, Oxford: Oxford University Press.
Rawls, J. (1999) *A Theory of Justice*, rev. ed., Cambridge: Belknap Press.
Rawls, J. (2001) *Justice as Fairness. A Restatement*, Cambridge: Harvard University Press.
Rescher, N. (2005) *What If? Thought Experimentation in Philosophy*, New Brunswick: Transaction Publishers.
Shue, H. (1978) "Torture," *Philosophy and Public Affairs* 7: 124–143.
Singer, P. (1972) "Famine, affluence, and morality," *Philosophy and Public Affairs* 1: 229–243.
Singer, P. (2005) "Ethics and intuitions," *The Journal of Ethics* 9: 331–352.
Singer, P. (2009) *The Life You Can Save. Acting Now to End World Poverty*, London: Picador.
Smart, J. J. C. (1972) "An outline of a system of utilitarian ethics," in *Utilitarianism For and Against*, edited by J. J. C. Smart and B. Williams, Cambridge: Cambridge University Press.
Sorensen, R. A. (1992) *Thought Experiments*, Oxford: Oxford University Press.
Thomson, J. J. (1972) "A defense of abortion," *Philosophy and Public Affairs* 1: 47–66.
Thomson, J. J. (2008) "Turning the trolley," *Philosophy and Public Affairs* 36: 359–374.
Uhlmann, E. L., Pizarro, D. A., Tannenbaum, D. and Ditto, P. H. (2009) "The motivated use of moral principles," *Judgment and Decision Making* 4: 476–491.
Walsh, A. (2011) "A moderate defence of the use of thought experiments in applied ethics," *Ethical Theory and Moral Practice* 14: 467–481.
Wilkes, K. V. (1988) *Real People. Personal Identity Without Thought Experiments*, Oxford: Clarendon Press.
Williams, B. (1972) "A critique of utilitarianism," in *Utilitarianism For and Against*, edited by J. J. C. Smart, and B. Williams, Cambridge: Cambridge University Press.
Wood, A. (2011) "Humanity as an end in itself," in *On What Matters*, vol. 2, edited by D. Parfit, Oxford: Oxford University Press.

12
HAPPIEST THOUGHTS
Great thought experiments of modern physics

Kent A. Peacock

1 Introduction: of chickens and physicists

A physicist can be defined as a person for whom a chicken is a uniform sphere of mass M. The point of this joke (which this author first heard from a physics professor) is that physicists shamelessly omit a lot of detail when they attempt to model and predict the behaviour of complex physical systems; indeed, one of the important skills that physics students must learn is knowing what to *leave out* when setting up a problem. This penchant for simplification does not necessarily mean that physicists are hopelessly out of touch with reality, however; for one can learn a surprising amount about how real things behave by thinking about apparently simplistic models.

A typical textbook example of a physical model might be the block sliding down an inclined plane. The plane is at a definite angle with respect to the force of gravitation; the block (a rectangular chunk of indefinite stuff) has a given mass, and there will be a certain coefficient of friction between the block and the plane. The assignment might be to calculate the coefficient of friction that would be sufficient to prevent the block from sliding down the plane, as a function of the angle of the plane. Now, no block of material in the world is perfectly uniform, no planar piece of material is perfectly flat and smooth, no actual coefficient of friction is known to arbitrary accuracy, and gravity is never exactly uniform in direction and magnitude. And yet, there are many physical systems in the real world which are sufficiently *like* idealized models such as this, to a definable degree of approximation, that their observable behaviour can be predicted using such models. Models are therefore useful not only because they help us to picture how basic physical principles work in a concrete situation, but also as frameworks on which to hang a practical calculation.

Even textbook problems couched in terms of simple models such as the inclined plane amount to thought experiments of a sort. Usually, though, we reserve the honorific *Gedankenexperimente* for idealized scenarios that give us new insights into the meaning or limitations of important physical concepts, usually by testing their implications in extreme or highly simplified settings. Suppose, for example, that I confusedly believe that all objects fall at a rate that is a function of their mass. Galileo has an elegant thought experiment that shows that my notion is a mistake: all objects in a uniform gravitational field must fall with the same acceleration (ignoring air resistance), on pain of outright contradiction.[1]

Galileo's thought experiment, like most typical textbook models, can be translated into experiments that can actually be performed. But sometimes one can learn a lot even from thought experiments that cannot be done, at least in the simple terms in which they are first described. Mach invited us to rotate the entire universe around Newton's bucket of water. No granting agency will fund that feat, and yet Mach's insights contributed (in a complicated way) to the construction of a theory (general relativity) that has testable consequences (Janssen 2014).

In this chapter I describe several thought experiments that are important in modern physics, by which I mean the physical theory and practice that developed explosively from the late 19th century onwards. I am going to mostly skip thought experiments that merely *illustrate* a key feature of physics[2] in favour of those that contributed to the advancement of physics. Some thought experiments (such as Galileo's) provide the basis for rigorous arguments with clear conclusions; others seem to work simply by *drawing attention* to an important question that otherwise might not have been apparent. Many of the most interesting thought experiments have ramifications far beyond what their creators intended. I will pay special attention to one particular thought experiment, defined by Einstein and his collaborators Boris Podolsky and Nathan Rosen (1935). The Einstein-Podolsky-Rosen (EPR) thought experiment dominates investigations of the foundations of quantum mechanics and plays a defining role in quantum information theory; I will suggest that it may even help us understand one of the central problems of cosmology. In the form in which Einstein and his young colleagues first described it, the EPR experiment was another idealization that probably cannot be performed. Despite this, it has evolved into practicable technology. While the thought experiments to be discussed here are key turning points in the history of modern physical theory, in several cases (including the EPR experiment) their full implications remain to be plumbed.

It is an extraordinary fact that most of the decisive thought experiments in 20th-century physics were born from the fertile imagination of one person, Albert Einstein. This forces us to ponder the importance of individual creativity in the advancement of science. Music would be very different, and much diminished, had Beethoven died young. If Einstein had not lived, would others have made equivalent discoveries? It seems likely that many of his advances would have been arrived at by other competent physicists sooner or later—except perhaps for general relativity, for the very conception of the possibility of, and need for, such a theory was due to the foresight and imagination of Einstein alone.

2 Sorting molecules: a thought experiment in thermodynamics

We will start with Maxwell's Demon, a thought experiment that bridges 19th- and 20th-century physics.

James Clerk Maxwell (1831–79) is best known for his eponymous equations for the electromagnetic field. He also made important contributions to statistical mechanics; in particular, he was the first to write the Maxwell-Boltzmann probability distribution which describes the statistics of particles in a Newtonian gas. Although Maxwell did not originate the concept of entropy (which was due to Rudolf Clausius, 1822–88) he was well aware of the Second Law of Thermodynamics, which, in the form relevant to our discussion here, states that no process can create a temperature difference without doing work. Maxwell fancifully imagined a box containing a gas at equilibrium, with its temperature and pressure uniform throughout apart from small, random fluctuations (Norton 2013a). A barrier is inserted in the middle of the box, and there is a door in the barrier. A very small graduate student with unusually good eyesight is given the task of tracking the individual gas molecules and opening or closing the door so as to sort the faster molecules into (say) the left side, and the slower molecules into the right. Apparently, then, a temperature difference can be created between the two sides by means of a negligible expenditure of energy. The problem is to say precisely why such a violation of the Second Law of Thermodynamics would not be possible.

There is a large literature on Maxwell's demon, which we cannot hope to do justice to here. (For entry points, see Maroney 2009; Norton 2013a.) It is well understood that there is a sense in which statistical mechanics would, in principle, allow us to beat the Second Law—albeit, in general, only for extremely brief periods of time. The easiest way to create a temperature difference between the two boxes is simply to leave the door open for a very, very long time. Eventually enough fast molecules will, by pure chance, wander into one side and enough slow molecules, again by pure chance, will wander into another, to create a measurable temperature difference between the gasses in the two boxes, at least until another fluctuation erases the gains made by the first. Now imagine that the hole has a spring-loaded door which could snap shut as soon as a specified difference in temperature ΔT was detected between the two partitions. The thermometer and door mechanism will have some definite energy requirement, but this can be made independent of ΔT. If we want ΔT to be large enough that it implies an energy transfer greater than the energy requirements of the door mechanism, all we have to do is wait long enough and eventually a large enough fluctuation will probably (not certainly) come along—although the larger we want it to be, the longer we (again, probably) have to wait. (Let us call this process "fishing for fluctuations"; like ordinary fishing the result can never be guaranteed.) As soon as the desired temperature difference is detected, the door snaps shut and we would have "trapped a fluctuation" in a way that apparently violates the Second Law. This example underscores the point made by Ludwig Boltzmann (and apparently well understood by Maxwell), which is that the Second Law is a statistical statement. Violations of the Law by pure chance are possible. In trying to exorcise Maxwell's demonic assistant we are dealing with a question of what is overwhelmingly probable, not what is certain in a law-like way. The question is not whether energetically free sorting against entropic gradients (such as temperature or concentration) could be done at all, but whether it can be done reliably, repeatedly, and in a time span shorter than the life of the observable universe.

In 1914 Marian Smoluchowski presented a critique of the Demon in terms of the statistics of fluctuations (see Norton 2013a), which Smoluchowski argued would *almost* always wipe out any gains against equilibrium that any conceivable demon could make. Leo Szilard argued in 1929 (1972) that information-theoretic constraints would prevent the demon from beating the Second Law. The acquisition and manipulation of the information that the Demon would need in order to track the particles would, Szilard argued, inevitably dissipate more waste heat than could be gained by sorting the molecules. John Norton (2013a) champions Smoluchowski's analysis, and argues that the information-theoretic approaches to refuting the Demon popular from Szilard onward are all more or less circular in that they *presume* the validity of the Second Law. More recently, Norton argues (forthcoming) that the question of information is irrelevant and that the Demon can be ruled out on the basis of Liouville's Theorem of statistical mechanics, which shows that the operation of a Maxwell's Demon is strictly impossible in any system that undergoes Hamiltonian evolution (i.e., virtually every conceivable classical system).[3] I will not attempt here to decide upon the correct theoretical analysis of the Demon. Instead, let us invoke the other towering figure of 19th-century science—Darwin—and sketch a view of the Demon from an evolutionary point of view.

In biology it is well known that cell membranes regularly perform a process called *active transport*. This involves the pumping of a wide variety of molecules or ions through tiny pores in a cell membrane against entropic gradients. The intricate molecular machines that perform active transport in the walls of virtually all kinds of cells are the closest things in the biological world to Maxwell's Demon, although they tend to create concentration differences, not temperature differences. The crucial point is that any sort of active transport that has so far been observed and studied by cell biologists requires the expenditure of energy.

As R. N. Robertson puts it,

> Systems which can transport molecules against their concentration gradients or ions against their electrochemical potential gradients are called *active transport* systems ... Such systems use energy provided by the cell to work against the tendency for everything to reach chemical equilibrium ... Formally, active transport is a reversal of the decrease in free energy which occurs when concentration or electrochemical systems tend toward equilibrium.
>
> (1983, 134–5)

Is it conceivable that natural selection could arrive at a form of active transport that does not require the expenditure of some of a cell's budget of metabolic energy?

There is growing evidence that natural selection tends to act so as to minimize the use of available energy. Damian Moran and co-authors (2014) studied a species of eyeless fish which live in underground caves entirely devoid of light. These fish use dramatically less metabolic energy than their surface-dwelling cousins, not only because they have no eyes, but because they do not partake in the energy-intensive circadian rhythm typical of animals exposed to the cycles of night and day. As Moran et al. (2014) put it,

> While it is a strange thought for terrestrial vertebrates to entertain, it may be unnecessary for animals living in caves or the deep sea to rouse their metabolism for the onset of a day that will never arrive.

If there is no particular survival advantage to paying the high metabolic cost of sight and all of the activities that go with it, a species that evolves its eyes away will have a survival advantage over one that does not. And it seems likely that this would apply generally: all things being equal, if there is a way to reduce energy expenditure it will tend to be found—and favoured—by natural selection. Cellular life goes back well over three billion years, and natural selection has had all of that time to sample the possibility space for active transport and to converge on the means that are the most economical and efficient in their use of cellular resources, especially energy. If it were indeed possible to micro-sort molecules against entropic gradients without the expenditure of energy, natural selection almost certainly would have found a way to do it by now.[4] Arguably, then, we can take this as a good sign that Maxwell's busy Demon is *practically* impossible, whether or not the last theoretical loopholes in the arguments against it can ever be closed.

3 Thought experiments in relativity

We turn now to a series of thought experiments that played important roles in the development of the special and general theories of relativity. There is a vast literature on these thought experiments, and we can do little more here than sketch the most interesting ones and point in some directions in which philosophical or scientific questions about them may still linger.

Einstein used a number of elegant models to illustrate how relativity works. For example, he imagined a railway carriage rolling along at constant velocity with respect to a level embankment, and used this scenario to illustrate the relativity of simultaneity (Einstein 1961). However, accounts of these illustrative models are widely available and they do not seem to have played a major role in his discovery of the theory.

3.1 To catch a light beam

In his "Autobiographical Notes," Einstein claims that he "hit upon" a paradox at the age of sixteen:

> If I pursue a beam of light with velocity c ... I should observe such a beam of light as an electromagnetic field at rest though spatially oscillating. There seems to be no such thing, however, neither on the basis of experience nor according to Maxwell's equations. ... One sees in this paradox the germ of the special theory of relativity.
> (Einstein, 1951)

This apparently very simple and intuitive thought experiment is surprisingly difficult to interpret, even though its intended import—that it does not make physical sense to suppose that one could catch up to a light wave—is obvious. There are two puzzles: first, what could the youthful Einstein, circa 1895, have had in mind? Second, exactly what could the Einstein of 1948 have been thinking? I will deal with the second question first.

The odd thing about the 1948 account is that, *prima facie*, Einstein was mistaken when he said that someone who could catch up with a light wave would see "an electromagnetic field at rest though spatially oscillating." Why? Because a field configuration that was "at rest though spatially oscillating" would be a *standing* wave, also known as a *stationary* state. There are indeed stationary solutions of the field equations; it is a question of having the right boundary conditions. (For instance, a standing electromagnetic wave can be set up between two mirrors relatively at rest and facing each other. The nodes are at rest with respect to the mirrors, and so I can be at rest with respect to the nodes if I can catch up to the mirrors). However, Einstein was obviously speaking of free waves in open space, which do not have the sort of boundary conditions that allow for stationary states. Therefore, it seems that he should have said that if an observer could catch up with a light wave he or she would see a *static* or *frozen* electromagnetic wave, with no variation in *any* of its parts with respect to the time coordinate in the co-moving frame of the observer. It would be like a surfer catching up to a wave: the wave surface would appear to be at rest with respect to the surfer (ignoring spray and minor turbulence). (Thanks to John Norton for this analogy). But that is not what Einstein said.

Unlike water waves, light waves are purely transverse (vibrating at right angles to the direction of motion). So perhaps this is what Einstein had in mind (whether in 1895 or 1948): if you were keeping abreast of a light wave, you could still "see" its transverse oscillations. But even this does not quite work. In special relativity, if a reference frame could be moving at the speed of light in vacuum, its proper time would not advance (such a frame would be said to be on a *null trajectory* in spacetime) and so nothing could be oscillating in any direction with respect to the time coordinate in such a frame. In terms of the moving observer's reference frame the light wave would have to be static in the strict sense. However, the one thing that one cannot do according to the rules of special relativity is catching up to an electromagnetic wave *in free space*—although in 1948 this is a logical *consequence* of the invariance postulate, not a ground for it. So again, the interpretational-historical problem is to say whether Einstein in his autobiography was trying to recount what his younger, pre-relativistic self may have (confusedly) imagined, or did he just make a somewhat sloppy (though perhaps understandable) mistake? I am not convinced that there is enough textual evidence to resolve this puzzle—although I lean toward the former interpretation because I find it hard to imagine that the Einstein of 1948 could have made an elementary technical error about relativity.

What *could* Einstein have been thinking in 1895? The precocious youth almost certainly knew something about Maxwell's equations by then, but his formulation of the Principle of Relativity lay ten years ahead. As John Norton explains (2013b), both the exact timing and content of Einstein's youthful insight are open to question; quite likely the Einstein of the late 1940s, as do many of us, had gently revised his recollections decades after the events he describes. In a much earlier account given by Einstein of this thought experiment (Norton 2013b, 130–31) he denied that he had, at age sixteen, a clear notion of the constancy of the velocity of light; rather the function of the thought experiment for the young Einstein simply seems to have been that it raised a striking and suggestive question: precisely what would one see if one could catch up with a light ray? In this respect the light ray experiment is similar to Maxwell's Demon—no clear conclusion, just a question. Thus, we see that unlike Galileo's thought experiment refuting the Aristotelian notion of variable rates of fall, which presents a rigorous *reductio* argument with a definite conclusion, thought experiments can contribute to advances in science simply by vividly directing attention to a problem that no one else seems to have worried about.

It is easy for modern commentators to whiggishly interpret the light ray experiment in the light of what is *now* known about relativity. Norton (2013b) points out that there is good reason to think that if the light ray experiment is to be interpreted as an argument at all, and not merely an unclear question rich with implications, the pre-1905 Einstein was not in fact targeting the ether theory of light, but rather the emission theory of light—the view that the speed of light depends upon the speed of its source. Clearly, if I am moving *away* from a source of light, and if the speed of the light emitted by that source depends upon the speed of the source, then I might not have to move very fast at all to catch up with the light—from *that* source. But, as Einstein realized, this is not the sort of thing we actually observe.

Whatever Einstein may have had in mind at the age of sixteen or seventeen, the upshot is that by 1905 he had arrived at a theory in which Maxwell's equations are taken as laws of nature which are the same for all inertial frames of reference. These equations predict the existence of electromagnetic waves travelling with an invariant velocity, because the speed of light is a *constant* in the equations: "light is always light." Therefore, if Maxwell's equations are laws of nature, the speed of light must be, in effect, a law of nature itself. As such, it must be independent of an observer's state of motion, even when one is moving arbitrarily close to the speed of light. As Einstein demonstrated, this assumption leads to the Lorentz transformations. Then if we wish to make kinematics and dynamics consistent with Maxwell, we have to make them Lorentz covariant as well. If the round Maxwellian peg would not go into the square Newtonian hole, the hole must be made round—and Einstein showed precisely how to do this.

The light beam thought experiment illustrates an important feature of the way physical theories develop: the intuitive or heuristic viewpoint that stimulated a new development in theory is sometimes not preserved by the time that the resulting theory is formalized. The presumption that such formative intuitions must always be preserved in the formalized theory that flows historically from them has been dubbed the "heuristic fallacy" by John Woods (2003). That this presumption is indeed often false is all the more clear when we grasp that thought experiments do not always contribute to the advancement of a science by serving as *arguments* for any particular proposition—at least not in ways that can be unambiguously reconstructed decades after the fact. Einstein himself described his light ray thought experiment as "child-like" and said, "Discovery is not a work of logical thought, even if the final product is bound in logical form" (quoted in Norton 2013b, 130).

3.2 *"The happiest thought of my life"*

By 1907 special relativity was consolidated. After another foray into quantum mechanics, in which he produced the first qualitatively correct quantum theory of specific heats and in effect founded modern solid state physics (Pais 1982, ch. 20), Einstein turned his attention to the problem of unifying gravitation with the principle of relativity. The obvious barrier to writing a relativistic theory of gravitation was that Newton's law of gravitation contains no dependency on time, and is therefore an action-at-a-distance theory (a fact that Newton himself had deplored; see Newton 1692). There was a subtler but no less fundamental problem with Newton's theory: in his picture it is entirely a coincidence that gravitational mass (the "charge" that appears in the force law) and inertial mass (the resistance of an object to an accelerating force) happen to be precisely the same quantity. Einstein reports that in the course of writing a review article on relativity, he was suddenly struck by "the happiest thought of my life" (Pais 1982, ch. 9):

> The gravitational field has only a relative existence in a way similar to the electric field generated by magnetoelectric induction. *Because for an observer falling freely from the roof of a house there exists*—at least in his immediate surroundings—*no gravitational field* ... Indeed, if the observer drops some bodies then these remain relative to him in a state of rest or uniform motion ... The observer therefore has the right to interpret his state as 'at rest.'

Galileo's observation that all bodies in a uniform gravitational field fall with the same acceleration (neglecting air resistance) thus takes on a "deep physical meaning": gravitation is therefore simply a manifestation of inertia, a "fictitious force" such as the centrifugal and Coriolis forces. Most important for Einstein, this fact is a manifestation of the Principle of Relativity:

> if there were to exist just one single object that falls in the gravitational field in a way different from all the others, then with its help the observer could realize that he is [falling] in a gravitational field ... [This is] therefore a powerful argument for the fact that the relativity postulate has to be extended to coordinate systems which, relative to each other, are in non-uniform motion.
>
> (Pais 1982, 178)

On the basis of this thought experiment, Einstein formulated his Equivalence Principle, which expresses the equivalence of gravitation and acceleration: an accelerated frame is equivalent to an inertial frame experiencing a gravitational field.[5] The Equivalence Principle is often illustrated by the elevator thought experiment, which appears in his first exposition of relativity for the general readership, written and published in 1916 (Einstein 1961). If I am floating in the midst of in a windowless elevator car in free-fall, I have no way of telling from any measurements I can perform within the car whether it is falling freely in a uniform gravitational field, or moving inertially in deep space, far from all matter. (Out of a commendable concern for the safety of the experimenter, Einstein advises (66) that he "fasten himself with strings to the floor"). If there is a rocket engine attached to the base of the elevator car, and I am held to the floor of the car by a constant force, I have no way of telling whether the rocket is burning with constant thrust, or whether I am sitting on the surface of a large planet whose gravitational field is such as to generate a uniform acceleration equal to that of the rocket.

The idea that gravitation is an inertial force is simple and beautiful; it had to be right. However, it was incompatible with the long-held presumptions (which Kant thought were *a priori*) that space has to be Euclidean and time has to be absolute. This was apparent to Einstein in at least two ways, which again can be illustrated with elegant thought experiments.

First, go back to the elevator car sitting on the surface of a spherical planet. Small test masses will fall toward the centre of mass of the planet; thus, two test masses released side by side will move toward each other as they fall. Now, the gravitational potential is a function of the distance from the centre of mass of the planet. Therefore, two test masses released one above the other will tend to move apart from each other when they are released and allowed to fall freely. (The one closer to the centre of mass falls with greater acceleration.) The tendency for freely falling matter to be stretched radially and squeezed tangentially is called the *toothpaste tube* effect. It can be described as a manifestation of *tidal forces*, which are due to differences in gravitational potential from point to point. A gravitational field can be detected by the tidal accelerations it produces (which, again, become vanishingly small within a small enough region of spacetime). Here is the catch: if we want to follow the Equivalence Principle and insist that the test particles are moving inertially, and if we accept that inertial motion follows the shortest paths (the "geodesics") in a geometry, then we are forced to the conclusion that in the presence of gravity the geometry of space (more precisely, spacetime) cannot be Euclidean—for in a Euclidean geometry the inertial paths would be parallel.[6]

Second (and here is yet another thought experiment), Einstein considered a circular disk rotating with uniform angular velocity about its centre. Those portions of the disk not at the centre will be Lorentz-contracted in the tangential direction with respect to the centre; the Euclidean relationship between the circumference and diameter of the circle will therefore fail.

In this way the Equivalence Principle combined with well-established conclusions from special relativity led Einstein to the realization that in order to fulfil his ambition to create a fully relativistic theory of gravitation, he would have to radically alter the geometry of spacetime. It might have been less intellectually risky to give up on the notion of gravitation as a manifestation of inertia, but Einstein boldly grasped the second horn of the dilemma and (under Marcel Grossman's tutelage) taught himself the requisite mathematics—Riemannian geometry and tensor analysis. Thus it was that a theory that was sparked by beautifully intuitive and simple thought experiments quickly acquired mathematical complexity so daunting that in 1913 Max von Laue (who had made a key contribution to general relativity by defining the 10-component stress-energy tensor) wrote of the "extraordinary, in fact inconceivable complexity" of the nascent theory as a reason for rejecting it (quoted in Gutfreund and Renn 2015, 115).

The rest is (complicated) history: after a number of false starts, Einstein perfected his field equations of gravitation in late 1915. They received their first experimental confirmation with Eddington's famous eclipse expedition of 1919 that showed Einstein's prediction of the bending of starlight near the limb of the Sun to be correct (to within, at that time, a rather large margin of error). The theory has since then survived every observational test to which it could be subjected. While few experts doubt that general relativity must eventually be replaced with a quantum theory of spacetime, it remains the limit toward which such theories must converge within its very large realm of applicability, just as general relativity itself had to converge to the Newtonian picture where the latter is applicable.

Einstein devoted the larger part of his later research efforts to formulating a unified field theory that would, in principle, provide a geometric picture of all forces in nature (Sauer 2014). In very simple terms, the idea of the unified field theory was to see whether every sort of force could be inertial. This implies further leaps in the complexity of spacetime geometry. It is clear by now that it is impossible to fully account for the structure and behaviour of elementary particles without taking quantum mechanics into account. Einstein's later attempted unified field theories were all classical—local, continuous, and deterministic—and are now generally considered to be magnificent failures (Pais 1982, ch. 17). Perhaps the fact that they were not guided by any clear, intuitive thought experiments had something to do with this.

3.3 Holes in spacetime

We need to also take a quick look at Einstein's "hole" argument, which played a key role in Einstein's tortuous route to the final form of his field equations for gravitation. There is a large literature on this subject, much of it dealing with issues beyond the scope of this paper (see Janssen 2014; Stachel 2014; Norton 2015b). What we need to do here is, again, see the simple, intuitive picture that guided Einstein—or in this case, almost misguided him.

By 1912 Einstein had nearly succeeded in formulating the gravitational field equations that he would publish three years later. However, he was stymied by two difficulties, one technical, the other conceptual. The technical problem was that the field equations he and Marcel Grossman had constructed did not seem to reduce to the Newtonian picture when they should. This glitch disappeared by the time Einstein arrived at the correct equations, but it led him to question whether it would be possible to find field equations that were generally covariant. He formulated his "hole" argument in order to show that the field equations could not be expected to be generally covariant, but instead the argument helped him to clarify the meaning of the concept of covariance.

General covariance was intended by Einstein to be an extension of the special-relativistic Principle of Relativity to all possible states of relative motion. Philosophically, general covariance is an expression of Einstein's realism, which implies among other things that physical realities are not affected merely by how we choose to describe them. In practice, Einstein thought, this would mean that a mere coordinate transformation should make no difference to the observable *predictions* that we should be able to extract from the theory; therefore, the *form* of the equations of the theory should be preserved by any smooth (continuous and differentiable) mathematical transformation. Transforming from one coordinate system to another—for instance, transforming from Cartesian to polar coordinates—should make no difference to what it is that the coordinates are being used to describe. The methods of differential geometry pioneered by Gauss and Riemann were thus ideal for Einstein's purposes, since they enable one to make a distinction between intrinsic properties of a geometric structure (such as curvature) and extrinsic properties which are purely an artefact of the choice of reference frame or coordinate system.

But would it be possible to write a generally covariant theory of gravitation that satisfied the Equivalence Principle, which implies that the mass-energy structure of spacetime determines the inertial paths of matter? Einstein asked what would happen if there were a *hole in spacetime*, a bounded vacuole containing nothing that could serve as a *source* of the gravitational field; i.e., no matter, energy, fields, or particles whatsoever. If determinism holds, the field inside the hole should be fixed in a unique way by the matter outside it. Presumably we can extend our coordinate grid to cover the hole. Now, apply a smooth transformation to the grid-points inside the hole (but not those outside it). This should transform the gravitational field inside the hole, since the field is a function of the metric structure. By general covariance, both the original and the transformed coordinates should be equally acceptable descriptions of the situation inside the hole. And yet, one seems to have two distinct field structures that are somehow a consequence of the *same* mass-energy distribution. Given the stark choice between abandoning determinism or general covariance, Einstein chose the latter.

Einstein seems to have been briefly satisfied with his hobbled field equations of 1913, but it became increasingly apparent that they were not observationally adequate. Spurred by competition from David Hilbert, Einstein returned to general covariance and in late 1915 arrived at the set of field equations that is still by far the best theory of spacetime structure we have. In 1916 Einstein set aside worries about holes in spacetime by arguing that the only things that can actually be observed are coincidences in space and time between "material points":

> All our space-time verifications invariably amount to a determination of space-time coincidences.
> (quoted in Gutfreund and Renn 2015, 115, 51)

These are the only things that we actually observe and so our theory should be built out of them; how we paint coordinates onto those observable point-coincidence events should make no difference to the physics we describe. Carlo Rovelli puts it in more modern terms:

> Reality is not made up of particles and fields on a spacetime: it is made up of particles and fields ... that can only be localized with respect to one another. No more fields on spacetime: just fields on fields.
> (2004, 71)

In short, the best answer to Einstein's "hole" argument is that the notion of an entirely matter-free hole in spacetime has no physical meaning. If a cosmological constant is admitted (as it must be) then even empty space itself has a gossamer "dark energy," but one need not invoke the cosmological constant to see the point. By about 1920 Einstein himself acknowledged (Einstein 1922) that the old ether of the 19th century is reborn in general relativity as a dynamic substance ultimately indistinguishable from the matter that lives within it. As the distinguished relativist Bryce DeWitt explained,

> General relativity not only restores dynamical properties to empty space but also ascribes to it energy, momentum and angular momentum. In principle, gravitational radiation could be used as a propellant. Since gravitational waves are merely ripples on the curvature of spacetime, an anti-etherist would have to describe a spaceship using this propellant as getting something for nothing—achieving acceleration simply by ejecting one hard vacuum into another. This example is not as absurd as it sounds. It is not difficult to estimate that a star undergoing asymmetric (octopole) collapse may achieve a net velocity change of the order of 100 to 200 km s^{-1} by this means.
> (DeWitt 1979, 681)[7]

Will the warp-drive spacecraft of the future climb to the stars on jets of pure ether?

4 The role of thought experiments in Einstein's discoveries

Obviously, Einstein's discoveries were not based purely on thought experiments. By 1905 he was almost certainly aware of the negative result of the real experiment done by

Michelson and Morley (see Pais 1982, ch. 6) though he does not mention it by name in "On the Electrodynamics of Moving Bodies" (1905). Rather, he begins his great paper by objecting to the redundancy and arbitrariness in the way that Maxwell's electrodynamics was "usually understood" at the time (Stachel 2005, 123). In particular, he disliked the fact that the induction of a current in a conductor by a magnetic field was described in different ways depending upon whether the conductor or the magnet were presumed to be at rest, even though the observable effects depend only upon the relative motion of the two. (As several authors have pointed out, this simple consideration in itself constitutes an elegant thought experiment.) Einstein was guided by his acute sense of logical economy as much as his physical intuition. But of course, one should not under-rate Einstein's "muscles of intuition"[8] when he was in the "prime of his age for invention."[9] Einstein trained those muscles during his years in the patent office, where he was constantly required to analyse how alleged inventions were actually supposed to work.[10] As Peter Galison documents (2003), many of these inventions were concerned with the measurement of time or the determination of synchrony.

The role of many of Einstein's thought experiments such as the light beam chase in the formation of his theories seems to have been essentially suggestive, not logical. A comparison can be made with August Kekulé's apocryphal vision of a snake swallowing its tail, which he claimed led him to grasp that benzene has a ring structure.[11] Just as Kekulé envisioned a physical structure, thought experiments such as the light beam chase lead us to picture an argument structure; that is, they do not always constitute an argument, but they suggest one. Consider Einstein's "happiest thought"; in itself, it was simply an observation that a person falling freely in a uniform gravitational field would not feel a force due to gravitation. Much of the impact of this observation for Einstein, from his personal accounts of the event, seems to have been its *affect*; seeing the point of the experiment (that gravitation is remarkably *like* an inertial force) was like grasping the punch-line of a good joke. (Einstein was known for his often-raffish sense of humour.) There is a sense of pleasant surprise, of immediate certainty, like Martin Gardner's *aha!* moment when you *get* the trick that solves a problem (1978). A good thought experiment has the effect of an instantaneous paradigm shift: staring at the duck for a long time, you finally see the rabbit (Kuhn 1970). It is, in itself, not an argument but a perception that suggests an argument. Almost everyone has fallen or jumped off of something at some time; only Einstein noticed the implications. Pasteur famously said that chance favours the prepared mind; so, also, do thought experiments.

5 Thought experiments in quantum mechanics

With the advent of quantum mechanics, physics moved away from the intuitive and the visualizable. Nevertheless, some notable thought experiments played key roles in the growth of quantum theory. There is not space to analyse all of them here in detail. I will make just a few comments about the virtual oscillators that Planck used to justify his black-body radiation law, another elegant model by Einstein which he used in 1909 to demonstrate the wave-particle duality of light, and Heisenberg's microscope and the role it did or did not play in his derivation of the Uncertainty Relations in 1927. I will have a lot more to say about the Einstein-Podolsky-Rosen (EPR) thought experiment and the lead-up to it.

5.1 Planck's resonators

In late 1900 Max Planck finally accepted that he had to adopt Ludwig Boltzmann's discrete counting methods in order to find a derivation for the radiation formula that he had stumbled upon by a combination of interpolation and inspired guesswork a few weeks earlier. But he needed the most general possible model he could devise for the interaction of matter and the radiation field. In 1900, of course, virtually nothing was known of the detailed structure of matter; furthermore, the whole point of the calculation was to arrive at a formula that would be valid for any kind of material whatsoever (for the only defining characteristic of a perfect black body is that it absorbs all the radiation that hits it). So Planck imagined that radiation exchanges energy with "virtual" harmonic oscillators or resonators in the walls of the radiation cavity. Planck's virtual oscillators were "spherical chickens," shorn of all detail except the physically plausible assumption that they could somehow come into resonance with incident radiation. But the model was not enough; in order to get the right formula, Planck had to commit what he called an "act of desperation" (Stone 2013, 59) and assume that radiation exchanged energy with the resonators in discrete chunks of magnitude $E = h\nu$, where ν is the frequency of the incident light and h is a new constant of nature.[12] Thus was quantum mechanics born, though it would take over twenty years more (and much hard work by the "valiant Swabian" and others) before it was widely accepted that the radiation field itself is quantized.

Should Planck's story about his virtual resonators count as a thought experiment, or just as an apt model on which a calculation could be hung? Models can be of specialized systems of narrow interest, while a game-changing thought experiment focusses attention on a key feature of wide generality and suggests what calculations must be done in a large class of cases. Planck used his model to ask, what are the most general features of the way in which radiation must interact with any conceivable kind of matter? It was simply mathematics that forced Planck to introduce energy quantization, because that was the only way he could get the right answer. Quantization for Planck was simply a formal step, for which he could not see any independent physical justification. The defining features of Planck's model were not by themselves sufficient to point to the solution of the problem he set it, but the simplicity and generality of the model clarified the question to the extent that it left Planck only one mathematical option. For this reason I am happy to count Planck's resonator model as one of the most consequential thought experiments of the new physics.

5.2 Of fluctuations and mirrors

Now we turn to another ingenious scenario by Einstein which certainly does count as a thought experiment of the first order (although it requires a good knowledge of statistical mechanics to fully appreciate it). In 1909 Einstein imagined a mirror inside a Planckian cavity, able to travel back and forth freely on a rail perpendicular to its face (Einstein 1909; Pais 1982, 408–9; Stone 2013, 136–40). In the cavity is a quantity of ideal gas and radiation, all in equilibrium at a definite temperature. What we do next is Einsteinian simplicity at its best: ask what is required for the mirror to be in equilibrium with the gas and radiation—for it must be. But this thought experiment is no mere dazzling *aperçu*. Einstein applied his mastery of the statistics of fluctuations, which he had exhibited in his work in 1905 on Brownian motion, and derived a key formula for the radiation fluctuations that the mirror must experience in order to remain in equilibrium. The mirror is subject to pressure fluctuations both from the gas and from the radiation, and the gas and radiation fluctuations must be in equilibrium with each other. The new thing Einstein did was to use Planck's blackbody energy distribution formula to compute the fluctuations due to radiation. Planck gives the energy distribution at the given temperature in terms of frequency, which shows the energy flux to which the mirror is subject. Then the crowning touch: Einstein imagined the mirror to be transparent to all frequencies except a narrow band; using Planck's Law for the energy density in that band, he arrived at an expression for the root-mean square fluctuations in the position of the mirror due to what he called "radiative friction." The key result was that this expression contains two terms. One represents wave-like fluctuations caused by constructive and destructive interference, due to small variations in phase, polarization, and frequency. (In modern terms, the light in the cavity would be said to be incoherent.) The other has the form of fluctuations due to impacts from discrete bundles of energy of magnitude $h\nu$. At low radiation densities, the particle-like fluctuations strongly dominate. Einstein took this result, which is a direct consequence of Planck's well-verified distribution law, as good evidence for his view that "the next state of theoretical physics will bring us a theory of light that can be understood as a kind of fusion of the wave and emission [particle] theories of light" (in Stone 2013, 137).

5.3 Heisenberg's microscope

This is not the place to recount the whole story of how modern quantum mechanics burst on the scene from 1925 to 1927. (For a short version see Peacock 2008; for exhaustive detail, see Mehra and Rechenberg 1982.) By 1927, it was clear that the new quantum theory challenged classical intuitions in a number of related ways. Schrödinger had created wave mechanics in 1926, hoping that it would give a realistic, classical underpinning to quantum statistics. And yet, it soon became apparent that QM only gives us probabilities, which are calculated indirectly from the (complex-valued) wave function by means of the Born Rule, $P(x) = |\psi(x)^2|$. What, then, does $\psi(x)$, which Einstein sarcastically dubbed the *Gerspensterfelder* (ghost field), actually represent? The one thing that Schrödinger's theory did not do was get rid of what he called the "damned quantum jumps" (Stone, 2013, 268); rather, it simply gave a remarkably efficient set of algorithms for using the "ghost field" to calculate the probabilities that those jumps would occur. Why these algorithms work so well remained (and remains) a mystery.

Another profound mystery was the appearance of non-factorability (or non-factorizability, as it is sometimes more awkwardly called). As soon as two or more particles undergo some sort of dynamical interaction, the wave function for the combined multiparticle system has cross-terms which imply much stronger statistical interdependencies between the particles than seemed to be possible. These cross-terms are in general algebraically irreducible (except for the special and limited case of so-called *product states*); once the particles have interacted their observable properties remain closely correlated (or anti-correlated) even when the particles have separated to arbitrary distances. Schrödinger (1935b) coined the term "entanglement" (from the German, *Verschränkung*) to describe this mysterious interdependency of non-factorable systems, and famously stated,

When two systems, of which we know the states by their respective representatives [wave functions], enter into a temporary physical interaction ... and when after a time the systems separate again, then they can no longer be described ... by endowing each of them with a representative of its own. I would call that not *one* but rather *the* characteristic trait of quantum mechanics.

(1935, 555)

A remarkable property of entangled states is that, as Schrödinger suggested, the individual particles in an entangled state cannot be represented as pure states, only as mixtures (classical ensembles of quantum states). They are not "things in themselves"! Einstein hated this feature of quantum mechanics, and he was convinced that it marked a fundamental flaw in the theory.

In 1927 Einstein attempted to construct his own version of wave mechanics (Howard 2007). His aim was to produce a wave mechanics without the pesky cross-terms, and he failed because it cannot be done. The short paper he produced was presented at a meeting but remained unpublished (Einstein 1927). It was his last attempt to make a constructive contribution to quantum mechanics—and definitely not up to his usual standard.[13]

In the same year Werner Heisenberg introduced his indeterminacy relations. Heisenberg was a complex and contradictory character. His ethically dubious participation in the Nazi atomic project during WWII (Rose 1998) sadly tarnishes the brilliance of his contributions to theoretical physics in his dazzling youth, when he laid down the essential principles of modern quantum mechanics at the age of 23.

The central epistemological problem that quantum mechanics will not permit us to ignore is that it is impossible to observe and measure the properties of a particle without physically interacting with it. Einstein based special relativity on operational definitions of quantities such as position and time, constructed so that it would be possible to clearly distinguish between these apparent properties of objects that are partially due to the way they are observed and those that are intrinsic to the objects. Quantum mechanics forces us to ask whether the notion of intrinsic properties has any physical meaning at all.

To investigate this problem, Heisenberg imagined a microscope designed to detect the position and velocity of an electron by scattering gamma rays off it (Heisenberg 1927, 1930). By the wave-particle duality both electrons and gamma rays have both a wave and a particle aspect. It is necessary to use high-energy gamma rays since there is an inverse relationship between wavelength and energy: the lower the wavelength the higher the resolving power of a microscope, so that only high-energy electromagnetic radiation has a short enough wavelength to detect an electron within any reasonable range of error. The key idea of the thought experiment was to apply basic laws of optics to show that the more accurately one could resolve the momentum of the electron, the less accurately one could resolve its position, and *vice versa*. Heisenberg arrived at the now-familiar inequality,

$$\Delta x \Delta p_x \geq h,$$

where the deltas are the uncertainties in position x and momentum p_x, and h is Planck's constant of action. We cannot measure one of the deltas with full precision without rendering the other completely indefinite.

Are the indeterminacy relations merely epistemic, a reflection of our *practical* inability to know the precise values of quantities that are, in fact, pre-existent? The microscope experiment itself suggests that these endemic uncertainties are merely the product of the fact that we cannot avoid using very short wavelength radiation to "see" an electron; because of the inverse relation between wavelength and energy, the more accurately we want to detect the position of the target particle, the more we must change its momentum. This epistemic reading of the thought experiment seems to leave open the possibility that the electron may still have well-defined values of both position and momentum even if we can never hope to simultaneously measure them. The problem, one might think, is only that there is no procedure in which we could reduce our "jiggling" of the observed system to zero.

Heisenberg realized that there are both mathematical and philosophical grounds for rejecting this naïve interpretation of the indeterminacy relations. Mathematically, observable quantities come in *conjugate pairs* defined by commutation relations which show precisely the extent to which the commutative law fails for the linear operators representing those observables. Shortly after Heisenberg's publication of the indeterminacy rules, Schrödinger and others showed that they are simply a mathematical consequence of the commutation relations between position and momentum (Cohen-Tannoudji, Diu and Laloë 1977, 286-7). According to the mathematical formalism that emerged in the years 1926-30, this inability to simultaneously tie down both values of a conjugate pair is not merely due to unavoidable experimental clumsiness due to the finitude of the quantum of action. Rather, in the mathematics of wave mechanics, asking for simultaneous, exact values of position and momentum is a mathematical contradiction in terms, like asking for a square circle. (This is because position and momentum are Fourier transforms of each other). Philosophically, Niels Bohr argued that this was a manifestation of what he called *complementarity*: the types of experiments in which one can measure position are simply incompatible with the types of experiments in which one can measure momentum. We need both wave and particle viewpoints to fully describe physics, and yet at the quantum level these two modalities cannot be applied simultaneously—where "simultaneously" does not necessarily mean "at the same time coordinate" but "in the same procedure." Thus, the microscope thought experiment is not a way of rigorously deriving the indeterminacy rules from the formal principles of quantum theory, but rather a highly suggestive semi-classical approximation.[14]

5.4 Einstein challenges quantum mechanics

Einstein remained stubbornly convinced that the properties of physical systems could not depend upon the types of measurements we choose to perform on them, especially if those properties could be inferred from measurements performed at a distance. He referred to Bohrian complementarity as the "tranquillizing philosophy—or religion?" which, he said, "is so delicately contrived that, for the time being, it provides a gentle pillow for the true believer from which he cannot very easily be aroused" (Fine 1986, 19).

In 1927-30, Einstein brought the full force of his ingenuity to bear on quantum mechanics and the indeterminacy relations in particular, trying to devise thought experiments in which they could be shown to fail. For once his inventiveness failed him; Bohr and others were always able to find loophole in Einstein's arguments that saved Heisenberg. (See Bohr et al., "The Bohr-Einstein Dialogue," in Wheeler and Zurek 1983, 1–50.)

By 1935 Einstein had given up on trying to beat the indeterminacy relations and tried a much subtler approach. In that year he and two younger collaborators, Boris Podolsky and Nathan Rosen, published a short, difficult paper (Einstein et al. 1935) in which they outlined an enigmatic thought experiment aimed at showing that quantum mechanics cannot provide a complete description of the entities for which it purports to account. The Einstein-Podolsky-Rosen (EPR) *gedankenexperiment* has evolved from a hypothetical scenario to become a defining paradigm of modern quantum mechanics.[15]

We have already mentioned two features of quantum mechanics that were the most troubling to Einstein, non-commutativity and the indeterminacy relations that follow from them. Non-commutativity plays an important role in the EPR experiment. However, as Don Howard (2007) says, "[E]ntanglement, not indeterminacy, was the chief source of Einstein's misgivings about quantum mechanics ... Indeterminacy was but a symptom; entanglement was the underlying disease."

The aim of the EPR paper was not to show that QM is incorrect, but rather that it is *incomplete* in the sense that it does not give a description of every "element of physical reality" ("EPR" again) belonging to an entangled state. By this time, Einstein had decided that the indeterminacy relations of Heisenberg point to nothing more than the incompleteness of quantum mechanics itself (incompleteness in the sense that the theory fails to represent properties that particles presumably *do* have). Part of the aim of the EPR paper was to make this notion of completeness precise. A necessary condition for completeness, according to EPR, is that "every element of the physical reality must have a counterpart in the physical theory" (777). And their sufficient condition for reality was this: "If, without in any way disturbing a system, we can predict with certainty (i.e., with probability equal to unity) the value of a quantity, then there exists an element of physical reality corresponding to this physical quantity" (777). The argumentative strategy for the paper would be to use the *sufficiency* condition for reality to show that quantum mechanics fails the *necessary* condition for completeness.

Here is the gist of the argument. Consider a composite system $U + V$ comprised of two particles which interacted dynamically at one point and then separated far from each other in space. Because they interacted they will possess quantities (such as total momentum or difference in position) that must be conserved globally. EPR take pains to show that these quantities commute on the system as a whole. This fact is crucial to the argument, since the mutually consistent global conservation requirements give us a basis for comparing the results of apparently incompatible measurement procedures on the individual particles.

Now, measure (say) position on U at time t. This collapses the entangled state into a product state with V in an eigenstate of position, allowing us to predict its position with certainty. (As Schrödinger put it, this "steers" the V-system into a definite state). But we could have also measured momentum on U at time t, and this would collapse the entangled state into a product with V in an eigenstate of momentum at time t, allowing us to predict its momentum with certainty. We cannot measure both position and momentum on U in the same procedure, but we are entirely at liberty at time t to choose which of the two types of procedures to apply. Thus, measurements we can perform on U enable us to predict presumably non-commuting properties of V with certainty. Therefore, there seems to be only two possibilities: either V was *already* in definite states of both position and momentum (despite Heisenberg), or our choice of measurement strategy on U at time t spookily influenced the state of V—at time t! But EPR say (780), "no reasonable definition of reality could be expected to permit this," precisely because U and V are spatially distant at time t. Therefore, quantum mechanics must be incomplete since *by its own admission* it cannot represent properties that system V *must have already had* at time t.

The EPR argument thus establishes (validly) a disjunction: either QM is incomplete (in the sense they specify) or there is spooky action (or perhaps both!).

EPR illustrated their argument by applying it in detail to an entangled wave function which has some very interesting properties which I would not attempt to analyze here except to note that there seems to be no practical way to prepare particles in this particular state; thus the EPR experiment, as they described it in 1935, is a pure *Gedankenexperiment*. Later on, practicable versions of the experiment would be defined.

Niels Bohr rushed to publish a response (1935). He agreed with EPR that "of course there is in a case like that just considered there is no question of a mechanical disturbance of the system under investigation during the last critical stage of the measuring procedure" (699). However, one cannot hope for a single complete description of the system. Rather, there are complementary descriptions of the system; in one, we can infer the momentum of V from momentum measurements on U, and in the other we can infer the position of V from position measurements on U. But from these facts we cannot infer a pre-existent reality in which V possessed sharp values of both position and momentum, for one cannot infer sharp values of both position and momentum for particle V with a *single* procedure. To ask for anything else would be to ask a foolish question, as Feshbach and Weisskopf put it (1988): "If you ask an inappropriate question, you get a probability distribution as a response." Thus, Bohr's cryptic and complicated response to some extent does clarify what the quantum mechanics of 1935 actually *says* about the EPR scenario, but it is very difficult to avoid the suspicion that a deeper level of analysis is possible—even if it would not be precisely what either EPR or Bohr themselves likely had in mind.[16] Indeed, J. S. Bell would later show that this is the case.

It is often said that EPR argued for a "hidden variable" or "hidden parameter" account of QM (although they did not use those terms themselves). Einstein in later years stated that he thought that there should be an *ensemble* interpretation of quantum mechanics (1969, 668), which he apparently understood as a probability distribution over possible *local* states of the particles. The idea would be that the particles have some sort of complex internal coding (perhaps still far beyond the ken of our present physical theories) which is capable of telling them how to behave in order to obey the observed predictions of quantum mechanics, for all of the possible experimental questions they could be asked.

This notion of hidden variables can be compared to heredity. Why do siblings resemble each other? Not because of anything "spooky," but because of a common *local* cause, namely the shared DNA they got from their parents. Although the role of DNA in heredity was not understood in 1935, EPR in effect implied (although they did not explicitly state) that there has to be some sort of "quantum DNA" encoded in the entangled particles when they interacted at their common source, sufficient to explain how the particles react when they are measured. In 1935 there was no obvious way to test this proposal. And so there matters stayed until after WWII.

The EPR thought experiment is widely misunderstood. Its import was not to demonstrate the existence of entanglement, but rather to use entanglement as evidence that quantum mechanics could not be telling the whole story about the structure of particles. The non-factorability of wave functions for multiparticle systems had been well known as early as 1927 (Howard 2007), although Schrödinger did not introduce the term "entanglement" until 1935. Einstein himself had grasped that light quanta were suspiciously too-well correlated from the time of his pre-1910 pioneering papers on the statistics of electromagnetic radiation. The EPR paper did have the valuable effect of *drawing attention* to the phenomenon of entanglement in a way that its challenge to conventional notions of locality and causality could not be ignored. *Via* the work of Bell (shortly to be described), the EPR thought experiment was one of the key sparks for the modern flowering of quantum information theory. Thus, even though the paper did not accomplish what its authors hoped it would accomplish, it has proven to be one of the most provocative and unexpectedly fruitful of Einstein's great papers.

5.5 *How the EPR debate might have gone*

It seems hard to imagine that anything useful could be added to the reams of analysis of the EPR paper that have already appeared, and yet one essential question has received very little attention. Is it actually the case that there is no dynamical interaction between the two particles "during the last critical stage of the measuring procedure"? Both Bohr and Einstein themselves thought that this question did not even merit discussion, and numerous papers published since their time purporting to demonstrate "signal locality" in entangled states simply follow their lead and assume without argument that entangled systems are dynamically local.[17] The bald assumption that space-like separation guarantees dynamical independence (Einstein's *Trennungsprinzip*, his Separation Principle, as in Einstein 1948) seems so utterly reasonable to most authors that very few have thought seriously to question it. And yet, whether or not the separation principle is correct is one of the first questions that should have been examined, not the last.

Had Einstein and other protagonists in the mid-1930s noticed a short remark by Pauli, published in 1933, the debate over the EPR scenario could have taken a different direction.[18] In a review article on quantum mechanics Pauli includes a discussion of many-particle systems. He notes that when there is no mutual interaction between the particles the system is represented by a wave function which is simply the product of individual wave functions belonging to the individual particles. Pauli seems to suggest that in order for such a wave function to be a solution of the Schrödinger Equation for the system, the algebraic structure of the Hamiltonian (energy operator) must be parallel to the algebraic structure of the state function. For a product state, the total Hamiltonian must be additive (i.e., simply the sum of the Hamiltonians for the individual particles):

> An additive decomposition of the Hamiltonian into independent summands corresponds [*entsprich*] therefore, to a product decomposition of the wave function into independent factors.
>
> (Pauli 1933; quotation from English translation, Pauli 1980)

Pauli does not directly comment on the Hamiltonian structure for non-product (non-factorable) states, but this pregnant remark raises questions that should have been obvious even in 1935. Does Pauli's *entsprich* mean that a state is a product state *if and only if* its Hamiltonian is additive? If so, then many-particle systems represented by *non-factorable* wave functions (such as the special entangled wave-function used as an example by EPR) would have to have *non-additive* Hamiltonians with algebraically irreducible cross-terms. If that is the case, then for any entangled state there must in general be eigenvalues (energy states) of the total system Hamiltonian that are not simply sums of local energy states for the individual particles; let us call this non-local energy the *energy of entanglement*. Such energy eigenstates would be properties of the entangled system as a whole, rather like the way in which the energy of an atomic orbital is a property of the orbital as a whole and cannot be spoken of as localized to the electrons associated with the orbital. It is unclear whether the existence of such non-localized energies can be sensibly described as implying any sort of "action" at a distance, but their existence would be a clear challenge to Einstein's dynamically local realism because they it would mean that the particles in an entangled state are dynamically entailed no matter how far apart they are.

Nothing I have said here is meant to suggest that Pauli himself would have been an advocate of such a flagrant challenge to relativistic orthodoxy. One can surmise from his own dismissive remarks about the EPR paper[19] that he did not think that the EPR argument merited close analysis. Whatever Pauli may have thought, however, there is increasing evidence, both theoretical and experimental, for dynamical non-locality in entangled states. This is not the place to review that evidence in detail; suffice to say that the question of dynamic non-separability in entangled states—and thus the ultimate interpretation of the EPR thought experiment—remains open.[20]

Could it be, then, that both horns of the dilemma offered by EPR must be grasped? Is quantum mechanics both endemically incomplete and dynamically non-local? Could it be the case that, precisely as Pauli indicated in 1933, each implies the other—something that perhaps should have been obvious a very long time ago? To answer questions like these a systematic study of the dynamics of the EPR and other entangled states needs to be carried out, a task that remains to be done. It is notable that entangled (non-additive) Hamiltonians are commonplace in the literature on quantum information; see, e.g., (Dür, Vidal, Linden, and Popescu 2001). No one seems yet to have studied the structure of the Hamiltonian for the special wave function used by Einstein, Podolsky, and Rosen in 1935, although this would be of great foundational interest.

I will conclude the discussion of the EPR thought experiment by making a brief observation that some may find outrageous. Modern cosmology is built upon the Big Bang model, according to which the universe that we observe expanded rapidly (and indeed is still expanding at an increasing pace) from a highly compressed state some 14 billion years ago. (I need not review the very strong evidence for this picture here; see Kirshner 2002). But these are precisely the conditions that lead to quantum entanglement: particles at close quarters interact dynamically and remain statistically entailed thereafter even when they separate in space and time. It would seem that the entire universe is, in effect, a vast EPR apparatus. And if so, what are its dynamics? Is dark energy the entanglement energy of the universe?

5.6 Schrödinger's "hellish device"

Shortly after the EPR paper appeared, Schrödinger published his famous "cat" paradox which was intended to expose the contradictions inherent in quantum mechanics (Schrödinger 1935a, 1983). The key idea of the thought experiment was in part due, again, to Einstein, and was hammered out in an extensive correspondence between the two physicists in 1935 (for detailed analysis, see Fine, 1986). Einstein's first version of the experiment was entirely at the macroscopic level:

> The system is a substance in chemically unstable equilibrium, perhaps a charge of gunpowder that ... can spontaneously combust, and where the average lifespan of the whole setup is a year ... In the beginning, the ψ-function characterizes a reasonably well-defined macroscopic state. But, according to your equation, after the course of a year ... the ψ-function then describes a sort of blend of not-yet and of already-exploded systems ... in reality there is just no intermediary between exploded and non-exploded.
> (Fine 1986, 78)

Schrödinger soon hit upon the idea of coupling a macroscopic system (an unfortunate cat) to a quantum-level system. A bit of radioactive material has a half-life of an hour; if it decays the resulting alpha particle triggers the release of a deadly poison that instantly kills the cat. If this cruel apparatus is described in the language of quantum mechanics, the wave function for the radioactive atoms is entangled with the wave function for the cat, and the cat is presumably in a superposition of states, either alive or dead—until we open the box to see what has happened to it. Schrödinger's version of the experiment is in one respect cleverer than Einstein's, since it shows that macrostates can be infected with quantum uncertainty if they are coupled to microstates in just the right way. Since the idea of the cat being in a superposition of states is presumably absurd, and since the dividing line between the quantum and the macroscopic (classical) level is arbitrary, the idea of quantum systems being in superpositions must also be absurd. Einstein's simpler version of the experiment has the conceptual advantage that it exposes the contradictions that seem to follow from assuming that quantum mechanics (which after all is advertised as a universal theory) is applied to ordinary macrosystems.

A catalogue of responses to the cat paradox is equivalent to a catalogue of proposed solutions to the measurement problem, which is to show how it is that measurements on superposed quantum systems can apparently produce definite, classical results. I cannot do justice to this literature here and I will only make a few general observations.

Einstein and Schrödinger's point can be seen to follow from the EPR sufficient condition for reality. Since opening the box presumably does not disturb the system (here we run into a problem similar to Maxwell's demon), and since we know that when we open the box the cat will definitely be in an alive exclusive-or dead state, it must have been in precisely that state before the box is opened. (That is, if we can think of "alive" as a state, then we can think of "alive XOR dead" as a state.) Thus, one way of challenging Schrödinger's thought experiment is to challenge EPR's reality condition by pointing out that while in quantum mechanics the probability may be unity that a system will be found to be in a certain eigenstate when subject to a certain measurement procedure, that fact does not entitle us to say that the system was in that state before it was measured.

Another obvious problem with the cat experiment is that a real feline, alive or dead, is a complex macrosystem comprised of an enormous number of particles in an incoherent state. In quantum mechanical language it can only be described usefully as a mixture which will behave classically (to an extremely good approximation) even if it is coupled to a quantum-coherent system. To this extent the cat was a poor example, even though it drew attention to the problem in an almost poignant way. However, it is now possible to create "Schrödinger cat states"—macroscopic coherent states (for there is in principle no limit to the size of a quantum-coherent state) that can be in a superposition (Yam 2012).

There are at least two lessons to take from the Einstein-Schrödinger cat. First, it is still not fully understood how quantum processes lead to definite or apparently definite results at the macroscale (this is the measurement problem). Second, the thought experiment emphasizes the key fact that the non-classical features of quantum mechanics cannot be safely sequestered to the micro-level. (Here we have another case of an important thought experiment that does not so much provide a conclusive argument as it memorably draws attention to a problem). As an illustration of this point, another important thing that happened in physics in the 1930s was the discovery of superfluidity and superconductivity, macro-scale phenomena that are entirely manifestations of quantum statistics. If cost were no barrier, it would be possible to create an Olympic swimming pool full of superfluid helium—and recent work in observational cosmology shows that the entire universe is a Planckian cavity (Smoot and Davidson 1993). If physics is quantum all the way down, it is also quantum all the way up.

6 After Einstein

6.1 Neglected potential

In 1951 the young American physicist David Bohm published an illuminating analysis of the EPR thought experiment in his text on quantum theory (1951). Bohm reformulated EPR's experiment in terms of spin observables. His version of the experiment had the great virtue that it could in principle be performed, opening up the possibility of an experimental test of the "quantum DNA" hypothesis.

Bohm then created a whole new version of (non-relativistic) QM, based on the quantum potential, a non-local potential field which is a function of the shape of the envelope of the wave packet (and thus, in effect, of the phase relationships within the wave function) (Bohm 1952a, 1952b; Cushing 1994). Bohm's "interpretation" successfully reproduces the predictions of ordinary quantum mechanics and resolves some challenges (regarding scattering) to a similar theory that had been proposed by de Broglie in 1927 (see discussion in Cushing 1994). His quantum potential contributes to the energy of a composite quantum system as a whole; in general it is distance-independent and it cannot be localized to individual particles. Most physicists were horrified; J. R. Oppenheimer (disgracefully) said, "If we cannot refute Bohm, we must choose to ignore him" (Peat 1997, 133).[21] All horror aside, Bohm had apparently done what John von Neumann had argued could not be done (1955), which was to construct a hidden variable theory that apparently could underpin quantum statistics—although in a way that is explicitly non-local.

6.2 "The most profound discovery of science"

John Stewart Bell, who evidently was unworried about whether his career would be irrevocably damaged if he were known to have read Bohm's papers, noted that Bohm had done what von Neumann had claimed was impossible—namely, constructed a hidden variable underpinning for quantum statistics. As noted, Bohm's approach is explicitly non-local, and Bell set out to determine whether *any* completion of QM had to be non-local.

Bell used Bohm's version of the EPR experiment, and considered correlations between spin measurements taken on the entangled particles (Bell 1964). He took the novel step of considering measurements taken in different directions (which allowed comparison between different spin components), and he showed that if there were local hidden variables—"quantum DNA"—then the correlations must obey certain mathematical inequalities. Bell then showed that according to quantum mechanics, the expectation values for these correlations violate the inequalities for a wide range of relative detector angles—they can be more strongly correlated (or anti-correlated) than quantum DNA would allow for. By the 1980s (Aspect, Dalibard, and Roger 1982), experiments showed that Bell's Theorem (the statement that QM violates "local realism") is almost certainly correct, and recent results are closing the last conceivable loopholes (Miller, 2016). There can be no such thing as quantum DNA! Bell's discovery was called (by H. P. Stapp) the "most profound discovery of science" (1975), and well it might be. It would have been fitting if Bohm and Bell had shared the Nobel Prize sometime in the 1980s—but the academic community did not quite have the courage to make such a radical move.

The experimental devices that have been used to test Bell's Theorem are real-world versions of the hypothetical EPR apparatus. Particles are emitted from a source and sent to remote locations where they interact with measurement devices such as polarizers or Stern-Gerlach devices (which detect spin). A key feature of these modern EPR apparatuses is that they employ *delayed-choice*: the decision about which parameter of the particles to measure (such as spin in various directions) is made (automatically, of course, by a randomizing process) *after* the particles are emitted. The timing is thus such that it would be impossible for information about the detector choice on one side of the apparatus to be transmitted to the detector or particle on the other side at any speed less than or equal to the speed of light. If Einstein's separation principle is correct, then the distant particles should exhibit no stronger correlations than those that could be built into them at the source (by the fact, for instance, that their total spins must add up in certain definite ways). But in fact, the Bell-EPR correlations violate the expectations of separability. Does this mean that there really is "spooky action"? The debate continues.[22]

Bell's Theorem is a special case of a more general result, the Kochen-Specker (KS) Theorem (Kochen and Specker 1967; Redhead 1987; Bub 1997): Quantum statistics cannot in general be underpinned by a Boolean property distribution. The notion of a Boolean structure can be defined precisely in terms of lattice theory (Bub 1997) but it can be grasped intuitively by thinking of every possible measurement on a quantum system as asking the system a question (which can always be formulated so as to yield a yes or no answer). (For instance, "is your spin-x up?") Classical physics presumed that it would always be possible (in principle) to ask such questions in a non-invasive way and that the amount of information to be gathered by asking more and more questions would monotonically increase. But for a quantum system, the list of possible experimental questions must include questions about non-commuting observables. The Bell-Kochen-Specker results state that if we could answer every possible experimental question that could be asked of a quantum system, the set of answers would be logically inconsistent. Bell's Theorem is essentially a special case of the more general Kochen-Specker result, applied to a spatially extended system. As Demopoulos (2004) emphasizes, descriptions of quantum systems are *incompleteable* because the presumption of completeability entails a mathematical contradiction.

This had been anticipated by Schrödinger in 1935:

> ... if I wish to ascribe to the model [of a quantum mechanical oscillator] at each moment a definite (merely not known exactly to me) state, or (which is the same) to *all* determining parts definite (merely not known exactly to me) numerical values, then there is no supposition as to these numerical values *to be imagined* that would not conflict with some portion of quantum theoretical assertions.
> (Schrödinger 1935a; trans. J. D. Trimmer, 1983)

Fitting quantum mechanical predictions to a Boolean substrate is like trying to smooth out a carpet moulded to the surface of a sphere onto a flat floor. There will be a lump! We can move it around and even hide it under furniture, but we cannot make it go away. Thus, it is not entirely accurate to call "no-go" results such as Bell's Theorem "no hidden variable" theorems; more accurately, they are *no Boolean variable* theories. Even more precisely, they are *not enough Boolean variable theorems*, since non-Boolean quantum systems can have Boolean subspaces defined by complete sets of commuting observables.

Bell's Theorem is still not well-understood, even in the professional community. Here is Nobel-winner Frank Wilczek on entanglement:

> Measuring the spin of the first qubit tells you about the result you'll get by measuring the second bit, even though they might be physically separated by a large distance. On the face of it, this "spooky action at a distance" to use Einstein's phrase, seems capable of transmitting information (telling the second spin which way it must point) faster than the speed of light. But that's an illusion, because to get two qubits into a definite [entangled] state we had to start with them close together. Later we can take them far apart, but if the qubits can't travel faster than the speed of light, neither can any message they can carry with them.
> (2008, 117–18)

Wilczek's reasoning is unclear, but he seems to suggest that whatever leads to the correlations manifested in entangled states must have been built into the particles when they were emitted. If so, the correlations of quantum mechanics would be no more mysterious than the fact that many copies of an issue of *Physical Review Letters* contain the same information because they were all printed on one press before they were mailed out to various subscribers. It is distressing that a winner of a Nobel in Physics is seemingly unaware that there is a result called Bell's Theorem whose import is precisely to rule out such "reasonable" explanations.[23]

The entire point of Bell's Theorem is this: the assumption that entangled particles are encoded at their source with instructions sufficient to satisfy the predictions of quantum mechanics is (in general) mathematically inconsistent with the correlations predicted by the theory (and observed in many kinds of experiments). For an elementary but rigorous demonstration of this fact, see (Maudlin 2002, ch. 1).

Bell's momentous result itself is negative: it rules out a certain class of explanations of quantum correlations, but does not by itself say what actually accounts for these correlations (beyond the quantum mechanical algorithms with which one calculates them). The prima facie explanation, if there is one, is that there is indeed some sort of spooky action (faster than light dynamics) going on, precisely as Einstein had feared. An enormous amount of intellectual energy has been expended trying to find some way of explaining or interpreting quantum mechanics so as to avoid this conclusion, which Bell himself and so many others have found so distasteful.[24] It is this author's opinion that the dogged efforts to explain away the appearance of spooky action have become what Imre Lakatos called a "degenerating research programme" (Lakatos 1976) but it is beyond the scope of this paper to defend this claim. It is enough here to say that Bell's momentous result remains poorly understood more than fifty years after its publication.

6.3 Entangled paths

We will conclude our (incomplete) list of important thought experiments in modern physics with a brief look at interferometry, one of the most powerful tools of modern physics. The essential idea of an interferometer is that particle or light waves are emitted from or collected from a common source, directed through different pathways, and brought together and allowed to interfere. The interferometric Michelson-Morley experiment of 1887, no thought experiment, showed that it is impossible to detect the motion of the Earth with respect to the hypothetical luminiferous ether (Taylor and Wheeler 1966, 76–8). Interferometry plays an increasing role in modern quantum information theory. Nielsen and Chuang remark,

> We can now see what an actual quantum computer might look like in the laboratory (if only sufficiently good components were available to construct it), and a striking feature is that it is constructed nearly completely from optical interferometers.
> (2000, 296)

Given that it is still technically impossible to construct most types of quantum computers that have been envisioned, one must say that so far most of the very active field of quantum computing is still in the realm of the thought experiment.

John A. Wheeler, like Mach, was not afraid to think on a cosmological scale. Imagine a quasi-stellar object billions of light years from Earth with a massive galaxy roughly halfway between (Wheeler 1983, 190–5). The galaxy will act as a gravitational lens (an effect predicted by Einstein), and can focus the light from the distant quasar onto detectors in an Earthly observatory. Light emitted from the quasar can take either path on its route to the lab on Earth. Gravitational lensing thus permits interferometry on a cosmological scale. The light is passed through a filter and then through a lens which focusses the light on the input faces of two optical fibres. The experimenters have a choice: they can either interpose a half-silvered mirror at the point at which the two light beams converge, or leave the mirror out. Omitting technical details, the key point is that with the mirror in place the experimenters will see interference between the light waves from the quasar, which is only possible if the waves had travelled through both paths; whereas with the mirror omitted, the experimenters will detect individual photons in one detector or the other and thus be able to tell which path the photons took. It is precisely *as if* the choice of measurement procedure here on Earth determines (determined?) which path the photons took when they were emitted from the quasar billions of years earlier.

Does this literally mean that the past has an indeterminate ontology? Wheeler himself suggests that it does:

> ... we are dealing with an elementary act of creation. It reaches into the present from billions of years in the past. It is wrong to think of that past as "already existing" in all detail. The "past" is theory. The past has no existence except as it is recorded in the present. By deciding what questions our quantum registering equipment shall put in the present we have an undeniable choice in what we have the right to say about the past.
>
> (1983, 194)

As with Bell's Theorem, one could cautiously interpret Wheeler's Cosmological Interferometry experiment in a purely negative way. We have to concede that it is contradictory to say that the particle had a trajectory before we made our detector choice, but we could refuse to say more. In particular, we might stubbornly refuse to say that our experimental choice here on Earth today *creates* something in the past. But even if we take this cautiously agnostic stance, we are committed to the position that the past is ontologically "gappy." On pain of contradiction, there are some claims about the past that we just cannot make; Wheeler's cosmic delayed choice experiment thus may well amount to an instance of the Kochen-Specker Theorem.[25] Arguably it tells against the block universe theory, according to which the universe is a complete four-dimensional, Riemannian plenum, and it may well provide support for the retrocausal interpretation of quantum mechanics, according to which amplitudes from future to past must be included in quantum-mechanical calculations (Cramer 1986). Like many of the thought experiments sketched in this review, there is still much to be learned from Wheeler's grand interferometer.

7 Have thought experiments a future in physics?

Einstein himself had a very unusual ability to visualize—or, more accurately, kinaesthetically to *feel* how things work (Einstein 1945). An ordinary competent physicist may well believe that it is hopeless to attempt to intuitively grasp the workings of nature as fluently as Einstein, any more than an ordinary musician can hope to duplicate the cognitive feats of Mozart. However, one can learn from those with extraordinary skills—one can at least *try* to do what they do. Einstein did one thing that can be done by anyone with sufficient intellectual courage: he deliberately sought out the simple, the obvious, the perception that was right under everyone's nose. One quality that all effective thought experiments have is that the essential insight is both simple and obvious—once you see it.

The willingness to seek out the obvious that is not yet obvious to most people is as much a matter of temperament as raw cognitive ability, because it requires one to be unconventional (as was Einstein)—a risk that sometimes even exceptionally intelligent people are not willing to take.

It is reasonable to ask whether there is still a creative role for thought experiments to play in physics as it grapples with the ever-increasing abstrusity of quantum gravity, particle physics, and string theory. It could be argued that the frontlines of theoretical physics now operate on a level of abstraction that is so far from common experience that the kind of ordinary mechanical and spatiotemporal intuitions at which Einstein excelled may no longer have much relevance. I have great faith in the flexibility and adaptability of the human imagination, and I think it is too soon to draw such a pessimistic conclusion. But even if visualization comes to play a decreasing role in the physics of the future, it will always be good methodology to seek out the obvious—and to question the conventional wisdom that too often prevents us from seeing it.

Acknowledgments

For helpful discussions or advice the author is grateful to Richard T. A. Arthur, Bryson Brown, Saurya Das, John Norton, David Siminovitch, Mike Stuart, and Jesse Supina. The author also thanks the editors of this volume for the opportunity to write this chapter, and James Robert Brown in particular for encouragement at many stages of this author's career. Thanks are also due to the University of Lethbridge and the Social Sciences and Humanities Research Council of Canada for essential financial and material support. Of course, none of these fine persons or institutions are responsible for any errors or misconceptions that may have found their way into this work.

Notes

1 For a nice analysis of Galileo's thought experiment, see Arthur (1999).
2 Such as the double-slit experiment. For a lucid exposition, see Feynman, Leighton, and Sands (1965, ch. 1).
3 Norton also develops the same result for quantum systems.
4 Norton (forthcoming) makes essentially the same argument with respect to ribosomes.
5 There are several readings of the Equivalence Principle; one must in particular distinguish between what Einstein himself seems to have had in mind, which he expressed in more than one way during the years in which he developed General Relativity, and the way it is used in modern formulations of the theory. See Anderson (1967); Misner, Thorne, and Wheeler (1973); and Norton (1986).
6 For an exceptionally clear and user-friendly explanation of how these thought experiments imply the curvature of space-*time*, see Norton (2015a).
7 Note that DeWitt's account of space as capable of possessing momentum is in interesting tension with what Einstein said in 1920: "According to the general theory of relativity space is endowed with physical qualities; in this sense, therefore, there exists an ether ... But this ether may not be thought of as endowed with the quality characteristic of ponderable media, as consisting of parts which may be tracked through time. The idea of motion may not be applied to it" (1922, 23–4).
8 Keynes' famous phrase (Keynes 1978) applies to the young Einstein as much as Newton.
9 This is adapted from the phrase that Newton applied to himself during that fertile period when he created the differential calculus and laid down the elements of his mechanics (Newton 1888).

10 A. Fölsing: "... for young Albert Einstein, examining patents was more than just a livelihood ... His virtuosity with 'mental experiments' was not all that far removed from intellectual penetration of an invention ..." (1997, 103).
11 See Martin (1997, 165–7). Kekulé proclaimed (perhaps with tongue in cheek), "Let us learn to dream, gentlemen, then perhaps we shall find the truth."
12 John Norton (private communication): "The amazing result in thermodynamics is that if systems A and B are in equilibrium, all that matters for A about B is B's temperature ... Whatever properties the matter may have, the equilibrium state of the radiation will be the same." So Planck needed only the sketchiest picture of matter, combined with the assumption of quantization, to get his result.
13 See Peter Holland (2005) for a detailed analysis of Einstein's abortive 1927 wave mechanics.
14 Heisenberg's rules are also often called the uncertainty relations. However, as Richard Arthur (private communication) has pointed out to me, the latter term is potentially misleading since it suggests that the Heisenberg rules merely represent epistemic uncertainty about quantities that do, in fact, have definite values.
15 There is no space in this chapter to consider yet another thought experiment of Einstein's, the box experiment, which makes essentially the same point as the EPR experiment. See Norsen (2005).
16 See Howard (2007) for an insightful analysis of what was at stake between Bohr and EPR.
17 For example, Ghirardi, Rimini, and Weber (1980) and Shimony (1983). For critiques of the orthodox approach to signal locality, see Peacock (1992); Kennedy (1995); and Mittelstaedt (1998).
18 My attention was drawn to this important passage in Pauli's book by an unpublished presentation by Don Howard (2006).
19 "Einstein has once again expressed himself publicly on quantum mechanics ... every time that happens it is a catastrophe" (Aczel 2002, p. 117).
20 Here in brief are two of the many pieces of evidence for non-local dynamics to be considered. Theoretical: although many presentations of "Bohmian mechanics" carefully guard themselves from putting it this way, Bohm's quantum potential, which is implicit in the mathematics of wave mechanics, is a manifestly nonlocal contribution to the total energy of multiparticle systems (Bohm 1952a). Observational: the recent and very important experiment of Lee et al. (2011) prima facie seems to show that two physically distant chips of diamond can be put into the same phonon energy state.
21 Bohm was *persona non grata* not only because of his unorthodox physics but also due to his refusal to testify against his friends who were suspected of left-wing sympathies (Peat 1997). I have heard from a reliable witness that at Princeton in the 1960s it was a career-ender to *mention* Bohm's name.
22 Current orthodoxy states that because of Bell's Theorem, quantum mechanics violates "kinematic" locality but not "dynamic" locality; that is, orthodoxy holds that the dynamics of entangled particles is still local (additive) despite the endemic violation of Bell's Inequalities in a wide variety of entangled systems. In my view this position is hopelessly inconsistent, but this question is beyond the scope of the present paper.
23 J. S. Bell:

> The discomfort that I feel is associated with the fact that the observed perfect quantum correlations seem to demand something like the 'genetic' hypothesis ... For me, it is so reasonable to assume that the photons in those experiments carry with them programs, which have been correlated in advance, telling them how to behave. This is so rational that I think that when Einstein saw that, and the others refused to see it, *he* was the rational man ... So for me, it is a pity that Einstein's idea doesn't work. The reasonable thing just doesn't work.
>
> (Bernstein 1991, 84)

24 In an interview in 1988, Bell stated that according to his theorem, "maybe there must be something happening faster than light, although it pains me even to say that much" (Mann and Crease 1988, 90).
25 This was pointed out to me by Jesse Supina (private communication).

References

Aczel, A. D. (2002) *Entanglement: The Greatest Mystery in Physics*, Vancouver: Raincoast Books.
Anderson, J. L. (1967) *Principles of Relativity Physics*, New York: Academic Press.
Arthur, R. (1999) "On thought experiments as a priori science," *International Studies in the Philosophy of Science* 13: 215–229.
Aspect, A., Dalibard, J. and Roger, G. (1982) "Experimental tests of Bell's inequality using time-varying analyzers," *Physical Review Letters* 49: 1804–1807.
Bell, J. S. (1964) "On the Einstein Podolsky Rosen paradox," *Physics* 1: 195–200.
Bernstein, J. (1991) *Quantum Profiles*, Princeton: Princeton University Press.
Bohm, D. (1951) *Quantum Theory*, Englewood Cliffs: Prentice-Hall.
Bohm, D. (1952a) "A suggested interpretation of the quantum theory in terms of 'hidden' variables, I," *Physical Review* 85: 166–179.
Bohm, D. (1952b) "A suggested interpretation of the quantum theory in terms of 'hidden' variables, II," *Physical Review* 85: 180–193.
Bohr, N. (1935) "Can quantum-mechanical description of physical reality be considered complete?" *Physical Review* 48: 696–702.
Bub, J. (1997) *Interpreting the Quantum World*, Cambridge: Cambridge University Press.
Cohen-Tannoudji, C., Diu, B. and Laloë, F. (1977) *Quantum Mechanics*, vol. 1, New York: John Wiley and Sons.
Cramer, J. G. (1986) "The transactional interpretation of quantum mechanics," *Reviews of Modern Physics* 58: 647–688.
Cushing, J. T. (1994) *Quantum Mechanics: Historical Contingency and the Copenhagen Hegemony*, Chicago: University of Chicago Press.
Demopoulos, W. (2004) "Elementary propositions and essentially incomplete knowledge: A framework for the interpretation of quantum mechanics," *Noûs* 38: 86–109.
DeWitt, B. S. (1979) "Quantum gravity: The new synthesis," in *General Relativity: An Einstein Centenary Survey*, edited by S. W. Hawking and W. Israel, Cambridge: Cambridge University Press.
Dür, W., Vidal, G., Linden, N. and Popescu, S. (2001) "Entanglement capabilities of nonlocal Hamiltonians," *Physical Review Letters* 87: 137901.
Einstein, A. (1905) "Zur Elektrodynamik bewegter Körper," *Annalen der Physik* 17: 891–921.
Einstein, A. (1909) "Entwicklung unserer Anschauungen über das Wesen und die Konstitution der Strahlung," *Physikalische Zeitschrift* 10: 817–825.
Einstein, A. (1922) *Sidelights on Relativity*, translated by G. B. Jeffery and W. Perrett, New York: E. P. Dutton (Dover Reprint).
Einstein, A. (1927) "Bestimmt Schrödinger's Wellenmechanik die Bewegung eines Systems vollständig oder nur im Sinne der Statistik?" Paper presented at the Prussian Academy of Sciences, Berlin.
Einstein, A. (1945) "A testimonial from Professor Einstein," in *The Mathematician's Mind: The Psychology of Invention in the Mathematical Field*, edited by J. Hadamard, Princeton: Princeton University Press.
Einstein, A. (1948) "Quanten-Mechanik und Wirklichkeit," *Dialectica* 2: 320–324.
Einstein, A. (1951) "Autobiographical notes," in *Albert Einstein: Philosopher-Scientist*, edited by P. A. Schilpp, New York: Tudor.
Einstein, A. (1961) *Relativity: The Special and the General Theory*, translated by R. W. Lawson, New York: Crown.
Einstein, A. (1969) "Remarks to the essays appearing in this collective volume," in *Albert Einstein: Philosopher-Scientist*, edited by P. A. Schilpp, La Salle: Open Court.
Einstein, A., Podolsky, B. and Rosen, N. (1935) "Can quantum-mechanical description of physical reality be considered complete?" *Physical Review* 47: 777–780.
Feshbach, H. and Weisskopf, V. F. (1988) "Ask a foolish question ... ," *Physics Today* 9: 11.
Feynman, R. P., Leighton, R. B. and Sands, M. (1965) *The Feynman Lectures on Physics, Volume III: Quantum Mechanics*, Reading: Addison-Wesley.
Fine, A. (1986) *The Shaky Game: Einstein, Realism, and the Quantum Theory*, Chicago: University of Chicago Press.

Fölsing, A. (1997) *Albert Einstein: A Biography*, translated by E. Osers, New York: Viking.
Galison, P. (2003) *Einstein's Clocks, Poincaré's Maps: Empires of Time*, New York and London: W. W. Norton.
Gardner, M. (1978) *Aha! Aha! Insight*, New York: Scientific American.
Ghirardi, G. C., Rimini, A. and Weber, T. (1980) "A general argument against superluminal transmission through the quantum mechanical measurement process," *Lettere Al Nuovo Cimento* 27: 293–298.
Gutfreund, H. and Renn, J. (2015) *The Road to Relativity: The History and Meaning of Einstein's "The Foundation of General Relativity,"* Princeton: Princeton University Press.
Heisenberg, W. (1927) "Über den anschaulichen Inhalt der quantentheoretischen Kinematik und Mechanik," *Zeitschrift für Physik* 43: 172–198.
Heisenberg, W. (1930) *The Physical Principles of the Quantum Theory*, Chicago: University of Chicago Press.
Holland, P. (2005) "What's wrong with Einstein's 1927 hidden-variable interpretation of quantum mechanics?" *Foundations of Physics* 35: 177–196.
Howard, D. (2006) "Early history of quantum entanglement." Available here: www3.nd.edu/~dhoward1/Early%20History%20of%20Entanglement/sld001.html (accessed 15 November 2016).
Howard, D. (2007) "Revisiting the Einstein-Bohr dialogue," *Iyyun: The Jerusalem Philosophical Quarterly* 56: 57–90.
Janssen, M. (2014) "'No success like failure ... ': Einstein's quest for general relativity, 1907-1920," in *The Cambridge Companion to Einstein*, edited by M. Janssen and C. Lehner, New York: Cambridge University Press.
Kennedy, J. B. (1995) "On the empirical foundations of the quantum no-signalling proofs," *Philosophy of Science* 62: 543–560.
Keynes, J. M. (1978) "Newton the man," in *The Collected Writings of John Maynard Keynes*, edited by E. Johnson and D. Moggridge, Great Britain: Royal Economic Society.
Kirshner, R. P. (2002) *The Extravagant Universe: Exploding Stars, Dark Energy and the Accelerating Cosmos*, Princeton: Princeton University Press.
Kochen, S. and Specker, E. P. (1967) "The problem of hidden variables in quantum mechanics," *Journal of Mathematics and Mechanics* 17: 59–87.
Kuhn, T. S. (1970) *The Structure of Scientific Revolutions*, 2nd ed., Chicago: University of Chicago Press.
Lakatos, I. (1976) *Proofs and Refutations: The Logic of Mathematical Discovery*, Cambridge: Cambridge University Press.
Lee, K. C., Sprague, M. R., Sussman, B. J., Nunn, J., Langford, N. K., Jin, X.-M., Champion, T., Michelberger, P., Reim, K. F., England, D. G., Jaksch, D. and Walmsley, I. A. (2011) "Entangling macroscopic diamonds at room temperature," *Science* 334: 1253–1256.
Mann, C. and Crease, R. (1988) "Interview with J. S. Bell," *Omni* 84+.
Maroney, O. (2009) "Information processing and thermodynamic entropy," *Stanford Encyclopedia of Philosophy*. Available here: http://plato.stanford.edu/entries/information-entropy/#MaxDem (accessed 15 November 2016).
Martin, R. M. (1997) *Scientific Thinking*, Peterborough: Broadview Press.
Maudlin, T. (2002) *Quantum Non-Locality and Relativity*, 2nd ed., Oxford: Blackwell.
Mehra, J. and Rechenberg, H. (1982) *The Historical Development of Quantum Theory*, vols. 1–6, New York: Springer-Verlag.
Miller, J. L. (2016) "Three groups close the loopholes in tests of Bell's theorem," *Physics Today* 69. Available here: https://doi.org/10.1063/PT.3.3039 (accessed 15 November 2016).
Misner, C. W., Thorne, K. S. and Wheeler, J. A. (1973) *Gravitation*, San Francisco: W. H. Freeman and Co.
Mittelstaedt, P. (1998) "Can EPR-correlations be used for the transmission of superluminal signals?" *Annalen Der Physik* 7: 710–715.
Moran, D., Softley, R. and Warrant, E. J. (2014) "Eyeless Mexican cavefish save energy by eliminating the circadian rhythm in metabolism," *PLoS One* 9: e107877.
Newton, I. (1692) "Original letter from Isaac Newton to Richard Bentley," *The Newton Project*. Available here: www.newtonproject.sussex.ac.uk/view/texts/normalized/THEM00258 (accessed 15 November 2016).

Newton, S. I. (1888) *A Catalogue of the Portsmouth Collection of Books and Papers Written by or Belonging to Sir Isaac Newton: The Scientific Portion of Which Has Been Presented by the Earl of Portsmouth to the University of Cambridge*, Cambrige: Cambridge University Press.

Nielsen, M. A. and Chuang, I. L. (2000) *Quantum Computation and Quantum Information*, Cambridge: Cambridge University Press.

Norsen, T. (2005) "Einstein's boxes," *American Journal of Physics* 73: 164–176.

Norton, J. D. (1986) "What was Einstein's principle of equivalence?" *Studies in History and Philosophy of Science* 16: 203–246.

Norton, J. D. (2013a) "All shook up: Fluctuations, Maxwell's demon and the thermodynamics of computation," *Entropy* 15: 4432–4483.

Norton, J. D. (2013b) "Chasing the light: Einstein's most famous thought experiment," in *Thought Experiments in Philosophy, Science, and the Arts*, edited by M. Frappier, L. Meynell, and J. R. Brown, New York and London: Routledge.

Norton, J. D. (2015a) "General relativity," Available here: www.pitt.edu/~jdnorton/teaching/HPS_0410/chapters/general_relativity/index.html (accessed 15 November 2016).

Norton, J. D. (2015b) "The hole argument," *The Stanford Encyclopedia of Philosophy* (Fall 2015). Available here: http://plato.stanford.edu/archives/fall2015/entries/spacetime-holearg/ (accessed 15 November 2016).

Norton, J. D. (forthcoming) "Maxwell's demon does not compute," in *Physical Perspectives on Computation, Computational Perspectives on Physics*, edited by M. E. Cuffaro and S. C. Fletcher, Cambridge: Cambridge University Press.

Pais, A. (1982) *"Subtle is the Lord ... ": The Science and the Life of Albert Einstein*, Oxford: Oxford University Press.

Pauli, W. (1933) *Die allgemeinen Principien der Wellenmechanik*, edited by H. Geiger and K. Scheel, 2nd ed., vol. 24, Berlin: Julius Springer.

Pauli, W. (1980) *General Principles of Quantum Mechanics*, translated by P. Achuthan and K. Venkatesan, Berlin: Springer-Verlag.

Peacock, K. A. (1992) "Comment on 'tests of signal locality and Einstein-Bell locality for multiparticle systems,'" *Physical Review Letters* 69: 2733.

Peacock, K. A. (2008) *The Quantum Revolution: A Historical Perspective*, Westport: Greenwood Press.

Peat, D. (1997) *Infinite Potential: The Life and Times of David Bohm*, Reading: Addison-Wesley.

Redhead, M. (1987) *Incompleteness, Nonlocality, and Realism: A Prolegomenon to the Philosophy of Quantum Mechanics*, Oxford: Oxford University Press.

Robertson, R. N. (1983) *The Lively Membranes*, Cambridge: Cambridge University Press.

Rose, P. L. (1998) *Heisenberg and the Nazi Atomic Bomb Project: A Study in German Culture*, Berkeley: University of California Press.

Rovelli, C. (2004) *Quantum Gravity*, Cambridge: Cambridge University Press.

Sauer, T. (2014) "Einstein's unified field theory program," in *The Cambridge Companion to Einstein*, edited by M. Janssen and C. Lehner, New York: Cambridge University Press.

Schrödinger, E. (1935a) "Die gegenwärtige Situation in der Quantenmechanik," *Naturwissenschaften* 23: 807–812, 828–849.

Schrödinger, E. (1935b) "Discussion of probability relations between separated systems," *Proceedings of the Cambridge Philosophical Society* 31: 555–563.

Schrödinger, E. (1983) "The present situation in quantum mechanics," in *Quantum Theory and Measurement*, edited by J. A. Wheeler and W. H. Zurek, translated by J. D. Trimmer, Princeton: Princeton University Press.

Shimony, A. (1983) "Controllable and uncontrollable nonlocality," in *Foundations of Quantum Mechanics in the Light of New Technology*, edited by S. Kamefuchi, Tokyo: Physical Society of Japan.

Smoot, G. and Davidson, K. (1993) *Wrinkles in Time: Witness to the Birth of the Universe*, New York: William Morrow and Co.

Stachel, J. (ed.) (2005) *Einstein's Miraculous Year: Five Papers that Changed the Face of Physics*, Princeton: Princeton University Press.

Stachel, J. (2014) "The hole argument and some physical and philosophical implications," *Living Reviews in Relativity* 17: 1. Available here: https://doi.org/10.12942/lrr-2014-1 (accessed 15 November 2016).

Stapp, H. P. (1975) "Bell's theorem and world process," *Il Nuovo Cimento B* 29: 270–276.
Stone, A. D. (2013) *Einstein and the Quantum: The Quest of the Valiant Swabian*, Princeton: Princeton University Press.
Szilard, L. (1972) "On the decrease of entropy in a thermodynamic system by the intervention of intelligent beings," in *The Collected Works of Leo Szilard: Scientific Papers*, Cambridge: MIT Press.
Taylor, E. F. and Wheeler, J. A. (1966) *Spacetime Physics*, San Francisco: W. H. Freeman and Co.
Von Neumann, J. (1955) *Mathematical Foundations of Quantum Mechanics*, Princeton: Princeton University Press.
Wheeler, J. A. (1983) "Law without law," in *Quantum Theory and Measurement*, edited by J. A. Wheeler and W. H. Zurek, Princeton: Princeton University Press.
Wheeler, J. A. and Zurek, W. H. (eds) (1983) *Quantum Theory and Measurement*, Princeton: Princeton University Press.
Wilczek, F. (2008) *The Lightness of Being: Mass, Ether, and the Unification of Forces*, New York: Basic Books.
Woods, J. (2003) *Paradox and Paraconsistency: Conflict Resolution in the Abstract Sciences*, Cambridge: Cambridge University Press.
Yam, P. (2012) "Bringing Schrödinger's cat to life," *Scientific American*, Available here: www.scientificamerican.com/article/bringing-schrodingers-quantum-cat-to-life/ (accessed 15 November 2016).

13
THOUGHT EXPERIMENTS IN BIOLOGY

*Guillaume Schlaepfer
and Marcel Weber*

1 Introduction

Unlike in physics, the category of thought experiment is not very common in biology. At least there are no classic examples that are as important and as well-known as the most famous thought experiments in physics, such as Galileo's, Maxwell's or Einstein's. The reasons for this are far from obvious; maybe it has to do with the fact that modern biology for the most part sees itself as a thoroughly empirical discipline that engages either in real natural history or in experimenting on real organisms rather than fictive ones. While theoretical biology does exist and is recognized as part of biology, its role within biology appears to be more marginal than the role of theoretical physics within physics. It could be that this marginality of theory also affects thought experiments as sources of theoretical knowledge.

Of course, none of this provides a sufficient reason for thinking that thought experiments are really unimportant in biology. It is quite possible that the common perception of this matter is wrong and that there are important theoretical considerations in biology, past or present, that deserve the title of thought experiment just as much as the standard examples from physics. Some such considerations may even be widely known and considered to be important, but were not recognized as thought experiments. In fact, as we shall see, there are reasons for thinking that what is arguably the single most important biological work ever, Charles Darwin's *On the Origin of Species*, contains a number of thought experiments. There are also more recent examples both in evolutionary and non-evolutionary biology, as we will show.

Part of the problem in identifying positive examples in the history of biology is the lack of agreement as to what exactly a thought experiment is. Even worse, there may not be more than a family resemblance that unifies this epistemic category. We take it that classical thought experiments show the following characteristics: (1) They serve directly or indirectly in the *non-empirical epistemic evaluation* of theoretical propositions, explanations or hypotheses. (2) Thought experiments somehow appeal to the *imagination* (so a purely mechanical deduction or calculation from theoretical principles would not count as a thought experiment). (3) They involve *hypothetical scenarios*, which may or may not be fictive. In other words, thought experiments suppose that certain states of affairs hold (irrespectively of whether they obtain in the actual world or not) and then try to intuit what would happen in a world where these suppositions are true.

We want to examine in the following sections if there are episodes in the history of biology that satisfy these criteria. As we will show, there are a few episodes that might satisfy all three of these criteria, and many more if the imagination criterion (2) is dropped or understood in a lose sense. In any case, this criterion is somewhat vague in the first place, unless a specific account of the imagination is presupposed. There will also be issues as to what exactly "non-empirical" means. In general, for the sake of discussion we propose to understand the term "thought experiment" here in a broad rather than a narrow sense. We would rather be guilty of having too wide a conception of thought experiment than of missing a whole range of really interesting examples.

2 Darwin

There are several places in the work of Darwin where he resorts to hypothetical scenarios in the course of presenting his theories. The best known cases are those from Darwin's *On the Origin of Species* (1859) discussed by Lennox (1991), but similar imaginary cases can be found in *The Descent of Man* (1871) as well as in his essay of 1844 and it is likely that there are even more. The reason is that Darwin, due to the speculative character of his endeavor, very often presents hypothetical explanations and each of them could potentially qualify as a thought experiment. In any case, we will have to restrict ourselves here to the presentation of the canonical cases discovered by Lennox and discuss their epistemic role in the context of the *Origin* as well as their specific features.

Lennox argues that Darwin's hypothetical cases play a crucial role in his argumentation in the *Origin*. According to him, their role is to show the explanatory potential of Darwin's theory rather than to serve as evidence for the theory's truth. Thus, they aim at showing that the theory of natural selection *can* explain such things as species transformation, appearance of new species, and the extraordinary adaptation of organisms to their environment, but not that it actually *does* explain these phenomena. The following "imaginary illustrations," as Darwin calls them, probably prompted the well-known criticism by Fleeming Jenkin (Hull 1973), in which Jenkin also uses hypothetical scenarios against Darwin's idea of natural selection.[1] Jenkin thus provided what Brown (1991) calls *counter thought experiments*, which led Darwin to refine his original thought experiments.

The following case is one of the two "imaginary illustrations" presented by Darwin at the end of the fourth chapter of the *Origin*. It is the paradigm of Lennox's "Darwinian thought experiments":[2]

> Let us take the case of a wolf, which preys on various animals, securing some by craft, some by strength, and some by fleetness; and let us suppose that the fleetest prey, a deer for instance, had from any change in the country increased in numbers, or that other prey had decreased in numbers, during that season of the year when the wolf is hardest pressed for food. I can under such circumstances see no reason to

doubt that the swiftest and slimmest wolves would have the best chance of surviving, and so be preserved or selected ...

Now, if any slight innate change of habit or of structure benefited an individual wolf, it would have the best chance of surviving and of leaving offspring. Some of its young would probably inherit the same habits or structure, and by the repetition of this process, a new variety might be formed which would either supplant or coexist with the parent-form of wolf.

(Darwin 1859, 90–1)

Lennox considers this passage to contain a thought experiment, for it displays an imaginary situation and provides support to Darwin's theory. Furthermore, he points out three aspects of Darwin's illustrations, which, he claims, constitute jointly sufficient criteria for characterizing a thought experiment: First, the thought experiment should evoke concrete objects or processes in order to "give ... the feeling of experimentation," which cannot be obtained by staying at the level of abstract theories. Second, the described situation should be plausible. This is normally ensured by referring to familiar objects and processes that "could happen, in a fairly robust sense of 'could.'" Finally, it should relate to the theoretical claim to which it lends support by instantiating some of its essential features (see Lennox 1991, 229–30).

Concerning the epistemic role of these thought experiments, Lennox's thesis that Darwin did not intend them as providing direct evidence for natural selection is supported in several ways. Darwin's use of the expression "imaginary illustrations" as well as the subjunctive mood already give quite strong indications. Furthermore, Darwin makes explicit that the aim of the chapter is not to provide a proof for the theory of natural selection: "whether natural selection has really thus acted in nature ... must be judged of by the general tenour and balance of evidence given in the following chapters" (Darwin 1859, 127). In addition, the claim according to which these thought experiments aim at showing the explanatory power of the theory also fits the general plan of the *Origin*. They are located in Chapter Four, which, according to a synoptic view of "Darwin's argument" proposed by Waters (2003), has the role of showing that natural selection is an "adequate" explanation in the Herschelian sense of establishing a *vera causa*, which precisely amounts to showing that the theory could explain speciation and adaptation.[3]

The view that the role of thought experiments is to evaluate a theory's explanatory potential is shared also by Kuhn (1977). But according to Kuhn, thought experiments can advance science only by showing a theory's failure. According to Lennox, there is no such asymmetry. Thought experiments, like in the case presented above, can also provide positive support regarding a theory's explanatory potential. This probably constitutes the most specific feature of Lennox's concept of "Darwinian thought experiments."

Restricting the role of thought experiments to an assessment of the potential or possible truth of an explanation grants them a legitimate role in science even if that role is "independent of empirical support of a theory's truth" (Lennox 1991, 237). To illustrate this, Lennox takes the case of the philosophical debate over adaptationism (Gould and Lewontin 1979; Kitcher 1982, 60; 1985, 226, cited by Lennox 1991, 240). This debate is rooted in a criticism of the tendency to explain everything in nature with help of natural selection, which amounts to considering any feature of an organism as an adaptation. On Lennox's view, adaptationism helps to explore natural selection theory's explanatory potential no matter whether the theory is true or false. In the same way, thought experiments do not speak for the truth or falsity of a theory, but they can serve to fathom the theory and bring support to its explanatory potential.

Lennox's account of Darwinian thought experiments raises many interesting issues. A first issue concerns the identification and the limits of the epistemic category of thought experiments, another one the psychological aspects related to the evaluation of the explanatory power of a theory by means of Darwinian thought experiments. We shall discuss these two issues in turn.

Concerning the first issue, it should be noted that, although Darwin calls them "imaginary illustrations," the thought experiments of chapter four in the *Origin* are supported by observational data. For instance, in the wolf pack case, Darwin appeals to evidence regarding the heritability of fleetness observed in greyhounds or of the tendency to prey on specific animals observed in domestic cats. He also mentions two varieties of wolves observed in the Catskill Mountains in New York that may instantiate the process proposed in the thought experiment. Lennox interprets this appeal to experimental data as a way to improve the plausibility of the thought experiments, but it also restricts the extent in which these illustrations can be considered as imaginary. The imaginary part of the illustration here seems to be the explanatory process rather than the particular case at stake, which is real. The same can be said of other Darwinian thought experiments in the *Origin*.

Should any hypothetical scenario pertaining to a theoretical claim about a particular matter of fact be considered a thought experiment? If not, then what restriction could prevent such an explosion of the category? Kuhn (1977), on his part, provides a restriction by limiting thought experiments to situations of conceptual conflict arising during scientific crisis. But why should this be so? By extending Kuhn's definition to imagined cases directly supporting a theory, thought experimenting appears to be a much broader category than is usually supposed. The only distinction between a thought experiment and the a priori evaluation of any theoretical claim seems to be, in Lennox's view, the appeal to concrete objects or processes.

This brings us to the second issue, the psychological aspects of thought experimenting and the requirement of concreteness. To what extent and how does the appeal to concrete objects or processes help in evaluating the explanatory potential of a theory? It should be noted that one of the main differences between the mind and the laboratory is that the objects manipulated within the mind are abstract to begin with, therefore it is not obvious why thought experiments should be restricted to imagining *concrete* cases. A possible argument might be that supporting a theory must necessarily involve a reference to one of its particular instances, as suggested by Lennox's third sufficiency condition. But even if such a principle is granted for *empirical* support, it is not clear that it transfers to *thought* experiments, which often seem to appeal to a *type* of instance, not any concrete case (cf. Maxwell's demon-type scenarios, which seem to be generic rather than particular; see Peacock, this volume).

3 Population genetics and natural selection theory

Darwin's theory of natural selection was thoroughly transformed in the early twentieth century due to the work of mathematical population geneticists, most notably R. A. Fisher,

J. B. S. Haldane and S. Wright (Provine 1971). These scientists provided a series of mathematical models describing the evolution of gene frequencies in populations of sexually reproducing organisms under the influence of evolutionary forces such as natural selection or random drift. This work culminated in a synthesis of Darwinian thought with more recent discoveries in genetics, in particular Mendel's laws as well as the chromosomal mechanisms of inheritance. Before these mathematical models existed, the theory of natural selection was still controversial and thought to be incompatible with modern genetics. The reason was that genetics was seen as being concerned only with discrete mutations, which seemed to suggest a saltationist theory of evolution, i.e., evolution through discontinuous leaps or "hopeful monsters" rather than Darwin's idea of a gradual adaptive process (Mayr 1982). But especially the work of Fisher proved that Mendelian inheritance can give rise to continuous variation that provides the material for natural selection to act on, and that selection is theoretically effective in changing the frequencies of genes in a population. In addition, Fisher provided theoretical models that could explain the abundance of species that reproduce sexually as well as other frequently encountered traits.

The introduction to Fisher's extremely influential book *The Genetical Theory of Natural Selection* (Fisher 1930) appears to announce a thought experiment:

> No practical biologist interested in sexual reproduction would be led to work out the detailed consequences experienced by organisms having three or more sexes; yet what else should he do if he wishes to understand why sexes are in fact, always two?
>
> (Fisher 1930, ix)

In this passage, Fisher seems to suggest that, in order to understand why actual organisms normally come in two sexes, it is necessary to examine hypothetical organisms with three or more sexes. Only if the evolutionary consequences of having one, two, three or more sexes are understood, can we hope to understand why two sexes are so common. While this looks like the sketch of a thought experiment, the curious reader will look for it in vain in the rest of the book. Fisher does not come back to the issue; he only offers a model describing the advantages of sexual reproduction in general over asexual reproduction. Furthermore, as Weisberg (2013) has pointed out, the problem as stated in Fisher's book is underspecified. For example, he does not say if all the 3 or n sexes are supposed to be necessary for producing offspring or if different mating types (i.e., subtypes of a species that can only produce offspring with members from a different type) would also count. Depending on how the 3- or n-sex biology is understood, it is not fictive at all but has well-known precedents in nature (see Weisberg 2013, 131–4). However, Fisher's intention was clearly to describe a non-existent entity with his three or more sexes.

Perhaps Fisher's example should not be taken too literally; in fact, its purpose according to Fisher is only to illustrate the advantages of approaching evolutionary problems from a mathematical point of view, which Fisher claims, is characterized by a specific kind of imagination.[4] But Fisher's thought experiment also illustrates a general strategy that characterizes his approach and that is very often used in evolutionary biology: When considering a trait, biologists first define a character space that contains all the possible values that the trait can take. For example, take the ratio of male and female offspring that the female of a given species produces on average. In many species, this ratio is close to 1:1, but in theory it could take any value, so long as it is a rational number. Let us call this space of values the character space. This space defines a set of *logical* possibilities; thus the idea is not that each value of the space could actually be realized. As Darwin already noted, there could be "laws of growth" that prevent some character values of being realized. Thus, there will be a subspace of character values that is logically as well as biologically possible. Evolution will only be capable of producing organisms within the subspace of biologically possible character values.

This approach can be seen at work in a field known as "life history theory" (Stearns 1992). Life histories (or life cycles) involve traits such as the age of onset of reproduction, the number of offspring produced, as well as the average life span or longevity. Variation in these traits is enormous; some organisms go through a long larval phase before they mature, just to reproduce once and then die quickly. Other species enjoy a steady output of offspring almost throughout their lifetime, some over hundreds of seasons. Life history theory tries to explain why each species has the life history traits it does. But in order to do so, it needs to consider the space of all logically possible trait combinations. Typically, life history theorists will try to show that an organism's life cycle is somehow adapted or optimized. But of course, evolution cannot produce any combination of life history traits. There are constraints or trade-offs that limit the range of possible values that the different life history characters can take. For example, it is widely thought by life history theorists that reproduction has a cost: Producing more offspring reduces longevity, both because it is inherently dangerous and because the metabolic resources used for reproduction are diverted from the maintenance of the body. Thus, it is not possible to maximize both the number of offspring and longevity at the same time.

The role of such constraints or trade-offs is sometimes explained with the help of a fictive creature known as a "Darwinian demon." This is an organism "which can optimize all aspects of fitness simultaneously" (Law 1979, 399). By an "aspect of fitness," Law means a character such as the number of offspring or the life span. Obviously, a genotype that produces more offspring and lives longer than his conspecifics would quickly dominate the population, such that this genotype will be the only one present. His fitness would be vastly superior. So why do not naturally occurring organisms become fitter and fitter, eventually turning into Darwinian demons? This is one of the central questions of life history theory. There are many answers that have been given to this question, but they usually involve some kind of trade-off or constraint that prevents a species from maximizing all aspects of fitness at the same time.

Thus, even if Fisher's example of a three- or *n*-sex biology is questionable, the principle that he was trying to illustrate is an important one: When giving an evolutionary explanation, biologists cannot be content to consider just actual organisms. They must also examine a range of logically possible organisms that are defined by a character space. The explanation will then show why the traits of actual organisms take certain values within this character space. The explanation will typically be based on the assumption that all other trait combinations have been eliminated by natural selection or prevented by some "laws of growth" or other constraints. But showing that some trait combination is actually the fittest that is available given the constraints, trade-offs, etc., requires that the fitness values for different possible organisms be estimated. Of course, the same strategy is necessary in order to show that some trait has *not* been optimized by natural selection, so there is no presumption of adaptationism here (cf. Gould and Lewontin 1979).

Fisher's example aside, can we find in the explanatory practice that we have just outlined any use of thought experiment? What about the idea of a Darwinian demon, this "mythical entity ... that grows quickly, breeds fast, outcompetes all and never ages" (Bonsall 2006, 120)? Is this demon comparable to Maxwell's demon? In fact, there are interesting parallels in terms of the role that these two demons play. Maxwell imagined two chambers filled with gas of different temperatures (see Peacock, this volume). In between the two chambers there would be a door that is controlled by the demon. The demon would open the door whenever a faster-than-average molecule were about to pass from the cooler to the warmer gas, and also when a slower-than-average molecule was about to pass from the warmer to the cooler side. Thus, heat would spontaneously flow from the cooler to the warmer body, in violation of the Second Law of thermodynamics. Maxwell's demon describes a scenario that is supposed to be *physically impossible* and challenges theoretical physics to give an explanation of what physical principles prevent Maxwell's imaginative scenario from being realized. (The standard answer is that Maxwell's demon would need to acquire information about the velocity and trajectory of gas molecules, which would generate enough entropy to offset the entropy reduction generated by the demon's gate controlling of molecules). It could be suggested that the role of the Darwinian demon is similar: It describes a biologically impossible scenario such that biologists are challenged to explain why it is impossible. While Maxwell's demon scenario seems more imaginative, both are fictions and thus involve the imagination.

But it should also be noted that the Darwinian demon is hardly indispensable for evolutionary biologists to do their work (unlike, perhaps, some thought experiments in physics). This is evident because there was important theoretical work done in life history theory before the demon was introduced in 1979 (by Richard Law). Fisher's own work is a case in point. The evolutionary biologist Michael B. Bonsall refers to the Darwinian demon as an "iconic representation" that serves to "focus the thoughts and ideas presented" (120). This would suggest a mainly pedagogical role for the Darwinian demon, perhaps much like Fisher's case of three sexes.

Are there any reasons for thinking that thought experimenting plays a more prominent role in population genetics, i.e., a role that goes beyond mere illustration? In fact, there could be such reasons. Sober (2011) has argued that some mathematical models of evolutionary biology provide *a priori* causal knowledge. This seems like quite a radical claim at first, as causal knowledge is widely thought to be empirical in nature (due to the extremely influential arguments by David Hume). However, Sober's claim is not that population genetic models such as Fisher's sex ratio model mentioned above can provide any knowledge about *actual* causes. Rather, what these models can do is to tell the biologist that under certain conditions, conditions that may be real or hypothetical, some state of a population of organisms *would promote* some other state. For example, an unbalanced state of a population with respect to sex ratio *would promote* an increase, on an evolutionary time scale, in females that have a tendency for producing more offspring of the minority sex.

Sober's argument is philosophically sophisticated and we lack the space here to give it a proper treatment. Clearly, Sober's "would promote"-locution is in need of explication; it is not clear if it can be interpreted causally while at the same time maintaining its *a priori* status (see Lange and Rosenberg 2011).

4 Molecular biology

For the most part, discussion about thought experiments in biology has focused on evolutionary biology. However, there are also candidates to be found in other fields of biology. We shall discuss two examples from mid-twentieth-century molecular biology. The first example concerns protein synthesis and the genetic code, the other is about protein folding and the so-called "Levinthal paradox."

In 1958, the co-discoverer of the double-helix structure of DNA Francis Crick published a remarkable paper simply titled "On Protein Synthesis" (Crick 1958). In this paper, he attempted to draw together all that was known at that time about the synthesis of proteins by living cells and then formulate the outlines of a mechanism. The paper became famous for containing a hypothesis that Crick dubbed the "Central Dogma of Molecular Biology" (it was really a hypothesis at this stage; Crick later reported that he misapplied the term "dogma"). According to the Central Dogma, genetic information flows from DNA to RNA to protein, but not in the other direction. What Crick meant by this is that the sequence of DNA nucleotide bases determines the sequence of RNA bases, which in turn determines the sequence of amino acids in proteins. The converse is not true according to Crick; RNA does not determine DNA sequence (which turned out to be incorrect) and protein sequence does not determine RNA sequence (which is still considered to be correct today).

For Crick, this hypothesis was a solution to one of the great puzzles of biology: namely, the question of how a living cell can make thousands of different specific protein molecules. While much was known in 1958 about how a cell can make other biomolecules (carbohydrates, lipids), the case of the proteins was trickier. The reason was the following: Other biomolecules are typically made by specific enzymes. But obviously, this cannot be how the cell can make different proteins because enzymes are proteins themselves. So to make a specific protein such as hemoglobin, the cell would need a specific enzyme. But to make this enzyme, it would need another enzyme and so on. This mechanism would thus generate an infinite regress. Crick concluded that some kind of code was necessary to specify the amino acid composition of all the different proteins made by a cell. According to this idea, the amino acid sequence of each protein was determined by the DNA base sequence of a gene. The code, which came to be known as the "genetic code" later, determines which amino acid sequence is specified by any arbitrary DNA sequence, just like the Morse code determines what letter of the alphabet is specified by a combination of short and long signals.

Crick thus not only predicted the existence of a genetic code, he also provided some constraints as to what this code might look like. (We are simplifying the history here. Crick was not the first to engage in such considerations, but his speculations turned out to be remarkably accurate. For historical details see Judson 1979.) Since there are exactly 20 different naturally occurring amino acids that compose all the proteins in any living organism, it was clear that more than one nucleotide base was necessary to encode these amino acids. For there are only four nucleotide bases, usually abbreviated as A, T, G and C. Let us imagine that each amino acid was specified by two bases in the genetic code. Because there are $4^2 = 16$ combinations of nucleotides, this would not be enough for 20 amino acids. Therefore, the code had to be at least a triplet code. But there are already $4^3 = 64$ triplet combinations of four bases, therefore the code had to be redundant.

This means that at least some amino acids must correspond to several base triplets, or else there would have to be meaningless codons.

Remarkably, all this is exactly what was found in the 1960s through much painstaking experimental work using protein-synthesizing cell extracts that were programmed with artificial polynucleotides. The genetic code was "cracked" and the exact mapping of base triplets to amino acids was unraveled. But Crick (with some help from other scientists) had figured out some of this on the basis of theoretical considerations alone.

We suggest that some parts of Crick's reasoning show some of the characteristic marks of a thought experiment: In particular, Crick examined several hypothetical or counterfactual scenarios, including a scenario where each protein is made by a specific enzyme as well as a scenario with a duplet code. He then showed that these scenarios were not possible, thus lending support to other scenarios such as the triplet code. Thus, as in the other cases discussed so far, thought experimenting was used in order to explore logical spaces of possibility and to identify some regions in these spaces as not only logically but biologically possible. Having thus noticed an important similarity to classic thought experiments, we should also point out that some aspects of this example fit the category less well. In particular, can we say that Crick used his imagination when reasoning about the genetic code? The difficulty with this is that his considerations appear to be quite abstract and based more on a principle of causality and simple math than on imagining a fictive scenario (such as in the case of Maxwell's demon). But the same may be true of some of the classical thought experiments, e.g., Galileo's (see Palmieri, this volume). Thus, it is difficult to say if this is a case of imagining or not.

Another issue is the exact epistemic role of Crick's considerations. Did it consist in the non-empirical evaluation of theoretical hypotheses? In a sense, one could say that Crick was examining the truth of certain hypotheses about the mechanism of protein synthesis. On the other hand, it is also clear that he did not consider these considerations as definitive proof of any theoretical hypothesis. The mechanism of protein synthesis was clearly to be established experimentally, which it eventually was. So perhaps one could say that what we have here is a different epistemic use of thought experiment, perhaps a use that is properly located in the context of discovery rather the context of justification (cf. Weber 2005, ch. 3). In other words, the thought experiment was used here in order to *generate* rather than *evaluate* theoretical hypotheses.

Another example from the history of molecular biology is the so-called "Levinthal paradox." In 1969, Cyrus Levinthal surprised the scientific community with a simple argument that called into question the received view of how protein chains fold into their three-dimensional structure (Levinthal 1969). According to the received view, a newly synthesized protein chain will randomly twist and move about until it has found the three-dimensional structure that corresponds to its lowest energy state. This state is given by the intramolecular interactions (hydrophobic interactions and hydrogen bonds) that are possible between the different parts of the molecule. Now, Levinthal made a very simple calculation. He first observed that a protein consisting of 150 amino acid residues has about 450 degrees of freedom, of which 150 are due to possible variation in bond angles of the side chains while 300 are due to rotations of peptide bonds (the chemical bonds that keep a chain of amino acids together to form a protein). Assuming that each peptide bond can assume 10 different states per rotational degree of freedom (a conservative assumption), there will already be 10^{300} different protein configurations. But this would mean that it takes far too long for a protein to find its state of lowest energy by a random process. For many proteins fold into their correct conformation within just a few seconds. Levinthal calculated that even when a protein tries different conformations extremely rapidly, there would not be time to try out more than about 10^8. Therefore, the assumption that proteins fold into their state of lowest energy must be wrong. It is much more likely that it finds some local (as opposed to global) energy minimum in a series of steps or "nucleation points" that are due to local interactions in neighboring amino acids.

It is remarkable that a simple consideration such as Levinthal's can topple a widely held theoretical assumption based on an established physical theory (thermodynamics). The case is similar to Crick's: Levinthal also imagined a fictive scenario that defines a space of logical possibilities. Then, he showed that only a small region of this logical space is actually accessible for real proteins to occupy. This, we suggest, is the hallmark of a thought experiment in biology.

5 Artificial life and computational modeling in biology

Several authors have suggested that artificial life and other computational approaches are a form of thought experimenting (Dennett 1994; Swan 2009), therefore it is appropriate to briefly discuss these approaches here.

Traditionally, simulation is used to calculate possible fates of dynamical systems for which there is no analytic solution describing their trajectory. This is often the case in systems described by coupled differential equations, but also in so-called agent-based models, where a number of agents behave according to simple rules, but collectively produce complex emerging patterns. By revealing these patterns, simulation allows scientists to evaluate whether a particular model possibly explains a phenomenon (Winsberg 2014).

Agent-based models are much used in artificial life (A-life). An example is the virtual world of Tierra created by the evolutionary biologist Thomas S. Ray (1993), in which the supposed conditions for biological evolution are reproduced *in silico* to explore the consequences of current theoretical assumptions. More specific studies aim at simulating population behaviors such as the grouping of bird flocks, mammal herds or fish schools, by implementing individual behavioral rules and testing their effect at the population level. These studies suggest possible explanations and proved to be particularly useful in showing what minimal abilities are required from individual agents in order to achieve the complex patterns observed at population level (see Reynolds 1987, cited in Swan 2009).

A philosophical analysis of A-life simulations as a kind of thought experimenting has been proposed by Swan (2009), who takes up Daniel Dennett's idea of considering A-life as a way of constructing "thought experiments of indefinite complexity" (Dennett 1994). The starting point of her account is that both in simulations as well as in classical thought experiments the systems under study can be manipulated at will. Specifically, it is possible to examine how a system obeying certain rules will behave. This feature provides a mean to "reason from effects back to probable causes" (Swan 2009, 696), which is also the hallmark of abduction as described by Charles Sanders Peirce (1958).[5]

Although these computer simulations seem to perfectly fit the role suggested above – providing hypothetical scenarios to explore the logical field defined by a theoretical framework – they do not satisfy the requirement that thought experiments must involve the imagination.[6] Thus, it seems that in the current literature on thought experiments, the term is used at least in two different senses. In one, wider sense, the label "thought experiment" is given to any kind of theoretical model (including computational models) that involve hypothetical or counterfactual scenarios. In the other, narrower sense, thought experiments also involve the mental powers of imagination.

6 A constructive role for thought experiments?

A common feature of all the cases presented here is the exploration of a field of possibilities followed by an evaluation of statements about what is *biologically* possible. The relevant possibilities can include logical possibilities, as in Fisher's sex-ratio model discussed in Section 3. Alternatively, the salient possibilities may be constrained by the principles of a theoretical framework, like in the case of Crick's discussion of the genetic code (Section 4), in Levinthal's paradox (Section 4), life history traits (Section 3), or evolutionary simulations of the A-life application Tierra (Section 5). The outcome of the thought experiment is the evaluation of a statement expressing a logical or theoretical possibility pertaining to the explored space. This evaluation seems to depend on the accordance of the tested statement with further biological constraints pertaining to the particular region of the space of possibilities that is visited. In general, it seems that antecedent theoretical or practical knowledge plays a major role, so biological thought experiments for the most part do not just rely on untutored intuitions.

In some cases, thought experiments reveal constraints that have not yet been taken into account in the theoretical framework. Examples for this include the time constraints in Levinthal's paradox, the impossibility of an infinity of specific biosynthetic enzymes in Crick's reasoning about the mechanism of protein synthesis or the inexistence of a Darwinian demon. When the general theoretical framework cannot cope with the particular constraints involved in the hypothetical case, thought experimenting seems to serve the purpose of pinpointing explanatory insufficiency or eventually the existence of a problematic assumption in the theoretical framework. In other cases, the thought experiment seems to support the idea that the proposed theoretical framework sufficiently explains typical hypothetical cases, like in Darwin's thought experiments or some A-life simulations.

Some of the experiments discussed above seem to occur in a context of discovery in a wider sense, where novel hypotheses are produced and evaluated prior to experimental verification. Since thought experiments carry some evidential power in the assessment of possible explanatory hypotheses, but seem nevertheless unable to provide sufficient confirmation, their role might be construed along the line of Curd's (1980) "assessment" of research hypotheses, which occurs in the context of discovery rather than the context of justification because it cannot provide sufficient justification, but has some justificatory value since it allows us to make informed choices among possible hypotheses. When the thought experiment does not provide a selection of testable hypotheses, it may reveal a lack of explanatory constraints and the need for further theoretical hypotheses, like in the case of some A-life simulations, Levinthal's paradox or Darwin's demon.

This picture of thought experimenting as exploring and evaluating a field of theoretical possibilities suggests two kinds of theorizing activities that relate to the imagination criterion. The first activity is the choice of theoretical assumptions that should constitute the most relevant constraints pertaining to the particular situation. The second activity consists in inferring the consequences following from these constraints. These consequences seem mainly to be obtained either by deduction or by computational simulation, but other means have been proposed, like the appeal to mental models suggested by Nersessian (1992) or Miščević (1992).[7] Since in simulations the step of inferring the consequences of a set of assumptions is delegated to a computer, their status as thought experiment may be denied (Chandrasekharan, Nersessian and Subramanian 2012; cf. also Lenhard, this volume), but the choice of the assumptions still depends on the theoretician's imagination and this may suffice to view, with Dennett and Swan, computational simulations as extended thought experiments, just like the use of paper and pencil suitably enhances geometrical thought experiments. Our examples seem to provide a continuum of cases where some rely more on the evaluation of theoretical assumptions, like in the Darwinian thought experiments, whereas others highlight more the inferential aspects, be it deductive or computational, like in the case of Levinthal's paradox or A-life simulations. But it seems that both assumption evaluation and inferential work are present as aspects in all the cases.

The examples presented in this chapter suggest that thought experimenting may be widely used in scientific modeling as a means of evaluating the relevance of a theoretical model as well as its consistency with more general models pertaining to similar cases. In this picture, thought experiments are less important than sometimes assumed for the justification of particular statements, but they appear to be much wider spread in the scientific practice. They may play an important role for the integration of theoretically scattered scientific fields and provide guidance for scientific research.

The results provided here should be relativized in any case to the selection of cases we made in the first place. Our broad criteria allowed us to choose what we consider the most significant cases of thought experimenting in biology, but philosophers assuming a more specific view of thought experimenting may end up with a different picture.

Notes

1 Although Jenkin falsely concludes from his imaginary cases that natural selection cannot explain speciation, his criticism highlights the importance of the frequency of variation and the problem of inheritance type, which led Darwin to slightly modify his thought experiments in the later versions of the *Origin* (Lennox 1991; Morris 1994; Bulmer 1999).
2 This thought experiment is directly followed by another one, which we will not reproduce here for the sake of brevity. It pertains to the explanation of mutual adaptations of bees and flowers. Other thought experiments can be found in Chapters Six, on the evolution of complex organs and Seven, on the evolution of instincts.
3 See also Love (2010).
4 Fisher suggests that "the intelligence, properly speaking, is little influenced by the effects of training. What is profoundly susceptible of training is the imagination, and mathematicians and biologists seem to differ enormously in the manner in which their imaginations are employed" (Fisher 1930, viii). Furthermore, "it seems impossible that full justice should be done to the subject in this way, until there is built up a tradition of mathematical work devoted to biological problems, comparable to the researches upon which a mathematical physicist can draw in the resolution of special difficulties" (Fisher 1930, p. x).

5 Abduction as characterized by Peirce is the process by which one constructs hypotheses to explain a particular fact. Today, it is sometimes referred to as "inference to the best explanation" (Lipton 2004).
6 This is the reason why Chandrasekharan, Nersessian and Subramanian (2012) do not consider computer simulations as thought experiments but rather as an alternative approach. See Lenhard (this volume) for more distinctions between simulations and thought experiments.
7 It is not clear in the case of the view involving Platonic insights defended by Brown (1991), whether these insights occur at the level of the choice of assumptions, inference of their consequences or both.

References

Bonsall, M. B. (2006) "Longevity and ageing: Appraising the evolutionary consequences of growing old," *Philosophical Transactions of the Royal Society of London B* 361: 119–135.
Brown, J. R. (1991) *The Laboratory of the Mind: Thought Experiments in the Natural Sciences*, London: Routledge.
Bulmer, M. (1999) "Did Jenkin's swamping argument invalidate Darwin's theory of natural selection?" *The British Journal for the History of Science* 37: 281–297.
Chandrasekharan, S., Nersessian, N. J. and Subramanian, V. (2012) "Computational modeling: Is this the end of thought experiments in science?" in *Routledge Studies in the Philosophy of Science, Thought Experiments in Science, Philosophy, and the Arts*, edited by M. Frappier, L. Meynell, and J. R. Brown, London: Routledge.
Crick, F. H. C. (1958) "On protein synthesis," *Symposia of the Society for Experimental Biology* 12: 138–163.
Curd, M. V. (1980) "The logic of discovery: An analysis of three approaches," in *Scientific Discovery, Logic, and Rationality*, edited by T. Nickles, Boston: Springer.
Darwin, C. (1859) *On the Origin of Species by Means of Natural Selection, or the Preservation of Favoured Races in the Struggle for Life*, London: John Murray.
Darwin, C. (1871) *The Descent of Man, and Selection in Relation to Sex*, New York: D. Appleton and Company.
Dennett, D. (1994) "Artificial life as philosophy," *Artificial Life* 1: 291–292.
Fisher, R. A. (1930) *The Genetical Theory of Natural Selection*, Oxford: Clarendon.
Gould, S. J. and Lewontin, R. C. (1979) "The spandrels of San Marco and the panglossian paradigm: A critique of the adaptationist programme," *Proceedings of the Royal Society of London. Series B, Biological Sciences* 205: 581–598.
Hull, D. L. (1973) *Darwin and His Critics: The Reception of Darwin's Theory of Evolution by the Scientific Community*, vol. 1, Chicago: University of Chicago Press.
Judson, H. F. (1979) *The Eighth Day of Creation: Makers of the Revolution in Biology*, New York: Simon and Schuster.
Kitcher, P. (1982) *Abusing Science: The Case Against Creationism*, Cambridge: MIT Press.
Kitcher, P. (1985) *Vaulting Ambition: Sociobiology and the Quest for Human Nature*, Cambridge: MIT Press.
Kuhn, T. S. (1977) "A function for thought experiments," *The Essential Tension*, Chicago: University of Chicago Press.
Lange, M. and Rosenberg, A. (2011) "Can there be a priori causal models of natural selection?" *Australasian Journal of Philosophy* 89: 591–599.
Law, R. (1979) "Optimal life histories under age-specific predation," *The American Naturalist* 114: 399–417.
Lennox, J. G. (1991) "Darwinian thought experiments: A function for just-so stories," in *Thought Experiments in Science and Philosophy*, edited by T. Horowitz and G. Massey, Savage: Rowman and Littlefield.
Levinthal, C. (1969) "How to fold graciously," in *Mossbauer Spectroscopy in Biological Systems: Proceedings of a Meeting Held at Allerton House, Monticello, Illinois*, edited by J. T. P. DeBrunner and E. Munck, Champaign-Urbana: University of Illinois Press.
Lipton, P. (2004) *Inference to the Best Explanation*, 2nd ed., London: Routledge.

Love, A. C. (2010) "Darwin's 'imaginary illustrations': Creatively teaching evolutionary concepts and the nature of science," *The American Biology Teacher* 72: 82–89.

Mayr, E. (1982) *The Growth of Biological Thought*, Cambridge: Harvard University Press.

Miščević, N. (1992) "Mental models and thought experiments," *International Studies in the Philosophy of Science* 6: 215–226.

Morris, S. W. (1994) "Fleeming Jenkin and *The Origin of Species*: A reassessment," *The British Journal for the History of Science* 27: 313.

Nersessian, N. J. (1992) "In the theoretician's laboratory: Thought experimenting as mental modeling," in *Proceedings of the 1992 Biennial Meeting of the Philosophy of Science Association*, edited by D. Hull, M. Forbes, and K. Okruhlik, vol. 2, pp. 291–301, East Lansing: Philosophy of Science Association.

Peirce, C. S. (1958) *Collected Papers of Charles Sanders Peirce: Reviews, Correspondence, and Bibliography*, edited by A. W. Burks, Cambridge: Harvard University Press.

Provine, W. B. (1971) *The Origins of Theoretical Population Genetics*, Chicago: University of Chicago Press.

Ray, T. S. (1993) "An evolutionary approach to synthetic biology: Zen and the art of creating life," *Artificial Life* 1: 179–209.

Reynolds, C. W. (1987) "Flocks, herds and schools: A distributed behavioral model," *ACM SIGGRAPH Computer Graphics* 21: 25–34.

Sober, E. (2011) "A priori causal models of natural selection," *Australasian Journal of Philosophy* 89: 571–589.

Stearns, S. C. (1992) *The Evolution of Life Histories*, Oxford: Oxford University Press.

Swan, L. S. (2009) "Synthesizing insight: Artificial life as thought experimentation in biology," *Biology & Philosophy* 24: 687–701.

Waters, C. K. (2003) "The arguments in the *Origin of Species*," in *The Cambridge Companion to Darwin*, edited by J. Hodges and G. Radick, Cambridge: Cambridge University Press.

Weber, M. (2005) *Philosophy of Experimental Biology*, Cambridge: Cambridge University Press

Weisberg, M. (2013) *Simulation and Similarity: Using Models to Understand the World*, Oxford: Oxford University Press.

Winsberg, E. (2014) "Computer simulations in science," in *The Stanford Encyclopedia of Philosophy*, edited by E. N. Zalta. Available here: http://plato.stanford.edu/entries/simulations-science/ (accessed 15 November 2016).

14
THOUGHT EXPERIMENTS IN MATHEMATICS

Irina Starikova and Marcus Giaquinto

It is not news that we often make discoveries or find reasons for a mathematical proposition by thinking alone. But does any of this thinking count as conducting a thought experiment? The answer to that question is "yes," but without refinement the question is uninteresting. Suppose you want to know whether the equation $[8x + 12y = 6]$ has a solution in the integers. You might mentally substitute some integer values for the variables and calculate. In that case you would be mentally trying something out, experimenting with particular integer values, in order to test the hypothesis that the equation has no solution in the integers. Not getting a solution the first time, you might repeat the thought experiment with different integer inputs.

The fact that there are such mundane thought experiments is no surprise and does not answer the question we are really interested in.[1] The numerical thought experiment just given involves nothing more than applying mathematically prescribed rules (such as rules of substitution and calculation) to selected inputs. It would be more interesting if there were mathematical thought experiments in which the experimental thinking goes beyond application of mathematically prescribed rules, by using sensory imagination as a way of eliciting the benefits of past perceptual experience.[2] In what follows, we will try to show that there are such thought experiments and to assess their epistemic worth.

Our method will be to present some candidate thought experiments with what we hope is enough background explanation and in sufficient detail for you, the reader, to perform the relevant mental operations yourself; without this participation the chapter will be neither convincing nor engaging. We have tried to avoid run of the mill examples by staying out of universally familiar mathematical areas; but to keep the material accessible, the examples are mathematically quite simple, with something a bit more advanced reserved for the end. The chapter has three main parts, corresponding to the mathematical areas from which the examples are drawn: knot theory, graph theory and geometric group theory. In the last two parts later exposition depends on earlier; so the material is best read in the order presented.

1 Candidates from knot theory

1.1 Preliminaries

For the examples to be intelligible, some background about knots in mathematics is needed. Here it is with a minimum of technical detail.

A *knot* is a tame closed non-self-intersecting curve in Euclidean 3-space.

The word "tame" here stands for a property intended to rule out certain pathological cases, such as curves with infinitely nested knotting. Knots are just the tame curves in Euclidean 3-space which are homeomorphic to a circle.[3] In Figure 14.1, on the left is a diagram of a knot and on the right a pathological case.

A knot has a specific geometric shape, size and axis-relative position, but if it is made of suitable material, such as flexible yarn that is stretchable and shrinkable, it can be transformed into other knots without cutting or gluing. Since our interest in a knot is the nature of its knottedness regardless of shape, size or axis-relative position, the real focus of interest is not just the knot but all its possible transformations. A way to think of this is to imagine a knot transforming continuously, so that every possible transform is realized at some time. Then the thing of central interest would be the object that persists over time in varying forms, with knots strictly so called being the things captured in each particular freeze frame. Mathematically, we represent the relevant entity as an equivalence class of knots.

> Two knots are *equivalent* iff one can be smoothly deformed into the other by stretching, shrinking, twisting, flipping, repositioning or in any other way that does not involve cutting, gluing, passing one strand through another or eliminating a knotted part by shrinking it down to a point.[4]

In practice equivalent knots are treated as the same, with a knot strictly so called regarded as just one of the forms a knot can take. This practice will be followed here. More precisely, the word 'knot' without the qualification 'strict' will be used to refer to an equivalence class of strict knots. Figure 14.2 presents diagrams of the same knot.

Diagrams like these are not merely illustrations; they also have an operational role in knot theory. But not any picture of a knot will do for this purpose. We need to specify:

> A *knot diagram* is a regular projection of a strict knot onto a plane (as viewed from above) which, where there is a crossing, tells us which strand passes over the other.

Regularity here is a combination of conditions. In particular, regularity entails that not more than two points of the strict knot project to the same point on the plane, and that

 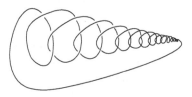

Figure 14.1

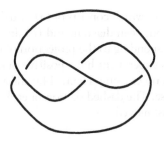

Figure 14.2

two points of the strict knot project to the same point on the plane only where there is a crossing.

A knot diagram with one or more crossings tells us at each crossing which strand passes over the other, but it does not tell us how far above the other it goes. So distinct strict knots can have the same knot diagram. But this does no harm, because strict knots with the same knot diagram are equivalent. This is all the background we need in order to proceed to examples.

1.2 A thought experiment with knots

An important and obvious fact is that a knot has many knot diagrams. As we represent knots by knot diagrams, a major task of knot theory is to find ways of telling whether two knot diagrams are diagrams of the same knot. In particular we will want to know if a given knot diagram is a diagram of *the unknot*, which is the only knot representable by a knot diagram without crossings. To warm up, here are some exercises. Using your visual imagination on the two knot diagrams in Figure 14.3, see if you can tell whether either is a diagram of the unknot.

In fact it is not possible to deform the knot represented on the left so that the result is a diagram without crossings, but you will probably have no difficulty with the one on the right. Figure 14.4 indicates a simple way.

Before considering what you can reasonably conclude from the results of your efforts, try to visualize deforming the knot represented by this more complicated knot diagram, Figure 14.5, to get a diagram without crossings.

It can be done, but it is difficult without actually producing physical diagrams representing the knot at one or more intermediate stages of the complete deformation. To conduct this thought experiment one performs one or more trials, a trial being a finite sequence of

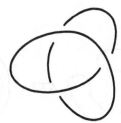

Figure 14.3

steps, each of which consists of (a) visualizing a deformation in 3-space of a knot as represented by one seen diagram and (b) drawing (or otherwise producing) another knot diagram corresponding to the projection of the knot at the end of the visualized deformation so far. The experiment has a positive outcome when one of the trials ends with a diagram which has no crossing. Figure 14.6 illustrates the intermediate stages of a successful trial for this case. The dashed section of each diagram indicates the part about to be moved or the part just moved.

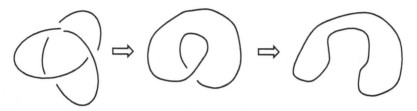

Figure 14.4

Figure 14.5

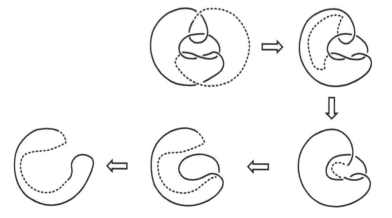

Figure 14.6

1.3 Assessment and objections

One charge laid against so-called thought experiments in physics is that they are not experiments at all, but "merely picturesque arguments" for a claim that is already believed (Norton 1996). Is that true of the process of visual imagining and diagram making just described? Picturesque it may be. But one may embark on the process in order to find out whether the knot represented by the initial diagram in Figure 14.6 (matching Figure 14.5) is an unknot, lacking any conviction either way; one may even doubt that it is the unknot. So one may really be experimenting, in the sense of performing a series of actions in order to test the hypothesis that the original diagram is a diagram of the unknot.

Granting that it is a genuine experiment, another worry concerns its epistemic value. Can we really make discoveries this way, relying heavily on visual imagination? Are we not simply replacing proper experiments by "fantasies of the imagination" (Norton 1996)? There is an important distinction between veridical imagining and fantastical imagining.[5] Veridical imagining is aimed at finding out the true answer to some question, and is constrained by the accumulated effects of past perceptual experience. Of course this does not make veridical imagining infallible; the adjective "veridical" is intended to describe an aim, not a result, of imagining. Fantastical imagining is not constrained in that way, as it is not aimed at answering a question, but serves psychological ends such as wish-fulfilment, horror thrill, sensory fascination and so on. Veridical imagining is common and useful. Wanting a desk for a particular room, you visit a furniture showroom; there you see an attractive desk, somewhat bigger than you had in mind. Would it fit reasonably well into the room with its other furniture? In this situation it is reasonable to visualize the room to reach a judgement. This is veridical imagining. Other examples readily come to mind: Can I prepare a tolerable evening meal from the ingredients I now have at my disposal? Can five normal adults sit comfortably in my car? We do in fact rely on sensory imagination to answer such questions, and we get correct answers frequently enough for this practice to persist.

This still leaves open the question of epistemic value in *this* case. Here are two questions we need to answer:

(1) Can our visual imagination be sufficiently reliable here?
(2) How do we reliably reach a conclusion about a mathematical question from information about physical situations?

The question of reliability is a serious one when trying to imagine deformations starting from a complicated knot diagram. But in our case the complexity is quite small and there is no real worry. Let us call a maximal part of a knot diagram between undercrossings an *arc*. Then the first step in Figure 14.6 involves flipping the rightmost arc over the central part of the diagram and shrinking it until it falls just within the leftmost arc. This clearly preserves knot identity (up to equivalence, of course). The remaining steps are clearly identity preserving atomic moves known as Reidemeister moves.[6] When one makes a non-atomic move in getting from one diagram to another, as in the first step of Figure 14.6, one can check its permissibility by seeing if one can break it down into a sequence of Reidemeister moves. Returning to the rightmost diagram of Figure 14.3, it is easy to see that (with two Reidemeister moves) it can be turned into a diagram without crossings, as shown in Figure 14.4. So the answer to the first question is: yes, a person's visual imagination can be (and often is) sufficiently reliable for this task. Your own experience in following the examples should provide you with supporting evidence.

In these cases we are visualizing a physical possibility, at least partly based on experience with string, yarn, cotton thread or suchlike. How do we get from an empirical discovery of a physical possibility to a mathematical possibility? The highly informal way in which the subject has been presented here hides the conceptual distance between the physical thought and the corresponding mathematical proposition. In these cases the conclusion is that a strict knot which projects the starting diagram is ambient isotopic to a strict knot which projects a diagram without crossings. But what does "ambient isotopic" mean? To get a sense of the full mathematical content of such a claim, note first that a strict knot is mathematically identified with a homeomorphism γ from the unit circle S^1 into R^3 (not the image of S^1 under the homeomorphism), with an additional condition on the homeomorphism to rule out wild knots.[7] Ambient isotopy is defined as follows:

> Strict knots γ_0 and γ_1 are *ambient isotopic* iff there is a continuous map $F: R^3 \times [0,1] \to R^3$ such that for each r in [0,1], $F(x, r)$ is a homeomorphism of R^3, $F(x, 0)$ is the identity map on R^3, and $F(x, 1) \cdot \gamma_0 = \gamma_1$.

This definition makes clear that visualizing *alone* does not enable us to discover a full mathematical fact expressed in saying, of two strict knots, that they are ambient isotopic. This is because one cannot tell by visualizing alone that there is a continuous map fulfilling the stated conditions. But we have been assuming that visualizing can make it reasonable to believe the mathematical claim and lead to discovery. How is this possible?

The answer is that these visual thought experiments take place in the context of background knowledge about the links between the mathematical definitions and idealized physical objects and transformations that can be visualized. These links belong to what is referred to as the foundational aspect of knot theory, and often expositions of the foundations reveal that the mathematical definitions are tailored to represent the intended kind of visualizable objects and transformations. Sometimes promising definitions are put forward only for the sake of showing their inadequacy for representing the intended visualizable material, before proper definitions are given.[8] Moreover, mathematically inequivalent definitions of tame knots are given in different texts, but it is known that each adequately represents what is intended, much as real numbers can be defined as Dedekind cuts of rational numbers or as Cauchy equivalence classes of Cauchy convergent sequences of rational numbers.

For foundational purposes there needs to be some way of fixing the subject matter in mathematical terms, so that the correctness of basic assumptions and methods can be proven. But once that job has been done, we may proceed without adverting to our foundational definitions. This is the situation with regard to basic knot theory. The foundational definitions are needed for proving Reidemeister's Theorem: two strict knots are equivalent if and only if there is a finite sequence of Reidemeister moves taking a diagram of one to a diagram of the other. Once that has been established we can go a long way with visual thought experiments.

THOUGHT EXPERIMENTS IN MATHEMATICS

1.4 Another example: the trefoil and the unknot

Let us return to the leftmost diagram of Figure 14.3, reproduced in Figure 14.7.

Figure 14.7

This is a trefoil knot. If you have been visualizing properly your attempts to visualize a deformation of this trefoil so that it projects a diagram without crossings will have been unsuccessful. After a few trials you may have become convinced that this trefoil is not the unknot. The diagram is cognitively quite simple. So, unless your visual imagination is poor, a few negative trials provides evidence that the trefoil is not the unknot.

For more conclusive evidence, we can use a knot invariant known as colourability.[9]

> A knot diagram is *colourable* if and only if each of its arcs can be coloured one of three different colours so that (a) at least two colours are used and (b) at each crossing the three arcs are all coloured the same or all coloured differently.

Colourability is knot-invariant in the sense that if one diagram of a knot is colourable every diagram of that knot is colourable.[10] This fact can be proved using Reidemeister's theorem. Since any diagram of a knot can be reached from any other diagram of that knot by a finite sequence of Reidemeister moves, to prove the invariance of colourability it suffices to show that if a Reidemeister move is performed on a colourable knot diagram the resulting diagram is again colourable.

A standard diagram of the unknot, a diagram without crossings, is clearly not colourable because it has only one arc (the whole thing) and two colours cannot be used. So in order to show that the trefoil is distinct from the unknot, it suffices to show that the trefoil diagram is colourable. So here is a thought experiment to test the hypothesis that the trefoil represented in Figure 14.7 is colourable: while looking at the diagram, visualize each of the arcs as coloured red, green or blue using at least two colours; alternatively, when looking at the diagram, mentally label each arc with one of the words "red," "green" or "blue" using at least two of them.[11] Then check that at each crossing all three arcs have the same colour or all three have different colours.

Because the trefoil diagram of Figure 14.7 is visually so simple, this thought experiment can be carried out reliably, thereby giving the thinker very strong reason to believe that the trefoil is colourable, as in fact it is, hence not equivalent to the unknot. With more complicated diagrams, it is difficult to hold the relevant information in visual imagination, and one is forced to colour or label arcs on the page or screen and then check that the conditions are met.

2 Examples with graphs

2.1 Cycle graphs

We often represent mathematical objects by a configuration of dots connected by line segments, such as a tree or a cycle. This gives rise to the algebraic notion of a graph G which consists of a set V_G, the "vertices" of G, and a set E_G of pairs of members of V_G, the "edges" of G.[12] We will be concerned with cycle graphs:

G is a *cycle graph* iff $V_G = \{v_1, v_2, \ldots, v_k\}$ for $k \geq 3$ and every edge in E_G occurs just once in the sequence $\{v_1, v_2\}, \{v_2, v_3\}, \ldots, \{v_n, v_{n+1}\}, \ldots, \{v_k, v_1\}$.

A cycle graph has an obvious representation as a regular polygon; there are just as many edges as vertices. The spatial representation of graphs makes us notice not only kinds of graphs, but also various graph-theoretic properties and relations.

A *path* between vertices u and v is a non-empty sequence of edges $\{y_1, y_2\}$, $\{y_2, y_3\}, \ldots, \{y_{n-2}, y_{n-1}\}, \{y_{n-1}, y_n\}$, with the y_j distinct, and $u = y_1$ and $v = y_n$.

A graph is *connected* iff between any two of its vertices there is a path. The *length* of a path is the number of edges in the path. For connected graphs we define:

The *distance* between two vertices u and v, d(u, v) = the length of a shortest path between u and v.

The *diameter* of a graph is the maximum distance between vertices, i.e. max $\{d(x, y) : x, y \in V_G\}$.

Suppose we want to express the diameter of a cycle graph with n vertices in terms of n. A thought experiment can help us here. Imagine the vertices of the graph to be small but heavy pearls of equal size and weight, adjacent pearls connected by a fixed unit length of strong flexible thread, like a necklace. Then imagine holding the necklace by any one pearl, letting the rest of it go. What will happen? The rest will fall as far as the thread will let it; so the maximum distance between the top pearl (the held pearl) and any other will be the number of units of thread (representing edges) between the top pearl and a lowest pearl. What if we hold the necklace by any other pearl, say k units of thread further on? As the necklace is a cycle, by visualizing what happens each time we rotate the necklace by a unit, we can tell that the configuration made by the hanging necklace remains unchanged, and so the distance between the new top pearl and the new lowest pearl (or pearls) will be the same. So the number of units of thread between the top pearl and a lowest pearl is the maximum distance between pearls. This represents the diameter of the graph.

But what is this number, for a given number n of unit threads in the whole necklace? The thought experiment continues. We now visualize the dangling necklace with fine-grained attention to discover its form. At the top is a single pearl with its two neighbouring pearls hanging next to each other at a distance of one unit below the top; if there are

THOUGHT EXPERIMENTS IN MATHEMATICS

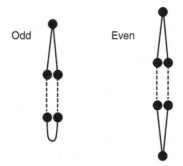

Figure 14.8

at least two more pearls, the next pair of pearls will hang at a distance of two units from the top; if there are at least two more, the next pair will hang at a distance of three from the top, and so on. That will be the same whether the number of pearls is even or odd. Now visualize the lowest few pearls of the dangling necklace. How will they be arranged? If the number is odd, below the top pearl the remaining pearls will hang in pairs, the lowest pair having a unit of thread connecting them, illustrated on the left in Figure 14.8. If the number is even, at one unit below the top pearl will be one pair of pearls, at one unit below them another pair of pearls, and so on until we run out of pairs and just one pearl remains (as the total number of pearls is even). By visualizing attentively the bottom of the image necklace in this situation, one can discern that this lowest single pearl will be connected by unit threads to each of the lowest pair of pearls just above it, as on the right in Figure 14.8.

To make use of these results, we reason as follows. Let the total number of unit threads (edges) be n. If n is even, we notice that there are two equal length paths from top to bottom; so we merely need to divide by 2. If n is odd, noticing that the thread between the bottom pair of pearls does not belong to any path between top and bottom pearls, we subtract that one thread from the total; then we can notice that there are two equal length paths from the top to either bottom pearl; so we only need to divide the remaining $n-1$ edges by 2. Either way we get $\lfloor n/2 \rfloor$, the greatest integer $\leq n/2$. So here is a discovery one can make with the help of a thought experiment: the diameter of a cycle graph with exactly n vertices is $\lfloor n/2 \rfloor$.

To assess this candidate thought experiment, the two questions we need to answer are: (1) Is what we have called a thought experiment in this case really an experiment, as opposed to a picturesque argument for a claim already believed? (2) Given that it is an experiment with certain outcomes, is it a reliable way of getting those outcomes?

The relevant mental actions here are (a) visualizing the cycle graph as a physical object, the necklace of pearls, and then visually imagining the result of holding the necklace by one pearl while letting go of the rest of it; (b) visualizing what happens to the configuration as we change top pearls, going from one pearl to an adjacent pearl; and (c) visualizing the spatial forms of the result of letting the necklace dangle, for odd and even numbers of pearls, with special attention to the top and the bottom. It seems right to say that parts and (a) and (b) are unrevealing: we already know that the necklace will dangle, pulled down by gravity as far as the connecting thread will allow, and that changing the pearl by which the necklace is held will leave the configuration unchanged. Part (c), however, may be revealing. Finer grained imagery results from taking into account the parity information. The forms of the lower end of the necklace in the two cases are revealed to us by the visualizing. So (a) followed by (b) and then (c) constitutes a series of mental actions, not to test a hypothesis, but to find the forms the necklace would take. That is a thought experiment. The results of the experiment are the forms we find; we use them as input to further thinking leading to our mathematical conclusion.

Is our visual imagination reliable here? If you agree that we would get the same results if we performed the experiment physically with actual necklaces matching the description in the thought experiment, you should accept that this use of visual imagination is reliable.[13] This is not surprising: our visual experience of physical situations relevantly similar to the described situation is sufficiently extensive to produce reliable dispositions for veridical imagining. Mathematically the result is quite trivial. For something a bit more interesting mathematically we focus on Cayley graphs.

2.2 Cayley graphs

Cayley graphs are representations of groups with a finite set of generators. Recall that a *group* is a set G together with a binary function $x \bullet y$ satisfying exactly these conditions:

Closure: For all x, y in G, $x \bullet y$ is in G.
Associativity: For all x, y, z in G, $(x \bullet y) \bullet z = x \bullet (y \bullet z)$.
Identity: For some z in G, for every x in G, $x \bullet z = x = z \bullet x$
Inverse: For any z in G satisfying the identity condition, for every x in G there is a y in G such that $x \bullet y = z = y \bullet x$.

It is easy to prove from the identity condition that there is just one identity, often denoted e. It is easy to prove from the inverse condition that each member x of G has just one inverse, denoted x^{-1}. As $\bullet$ is associative, we can omit brackets and the function symbol and use juxtaposition instead. This improves legibility.[14]

Let S be a finite subset of G. S is a set of *generators for* G iff every member of G is the product of a finite sequence of members of S or their inverses. More formally, putting S^{-1} for the set of inverses of members of S, this is:

For every x in G, there are y_i $(1 \leq i \leq n)$ in $S \cup S^{-1}$ such that $x = y_1 y_2 \ldots y_n$.

In this case, $((G, \bullet), S)$, usually written simply (G, S), is a *generated group*. Here are some examples of finitely generated groups:

- Let n be an integer greater than 2. The domain of the group is the set C_n of rotations of a regular n-sided polygon about its centre by $k2\pi/n$ radians for integers k. The function $\bullet$ is composition. Let anticlockwise rotation by $2\pi/n$ be the sole generator.
- The set of integers Z under addition, with generator 1.
- The set S_3 of permutations of a triple $\{a, b, c\}$ under composition, with generators $\{r, f\}$, where r (for 'rotation') takes $\langle a, b, c \rangle$ to $\langle c, a, b \rangle$, and f (for 'flip') takes $\langle a, b, c \rangle$ to $\langle c, b, a \rangle$.[15]

266

Some groups are not finitely generated. An example is the set Q of rationals under addition.[16] Many finitely generated groups have different sets of generators. For example, C_5 is generated by $\{2\pi/5\}$; it is also generated by $\{4\pi/5\}$. The group (Z, +) is generated by $\{1\}$; it is also generated by $\{2, 3\}$.[17]

Cayley graphs represent finitely generated groups in the following way: each group member is represented by a unique vertex, and each vertex represents exactly one group member; for any group member g and generator s there is a directed edge from the vertex representing g to the vertex representing sg.[18]

Let us look at some examples. A graph for C_6 is suggested by the general geometrical description of C_n given above. Put c for the generator, anticlockwise rotation by $2\pi/6$ radians; for $k > 0$, put c^k for this operation repeated k times, that is, anticlockwise rotation by $k2\pi/6$ radians, and c^{-k} for clockwise rotation by $k2\pi/6$ radians. Put e for the identity, that is, anticlockwise rotation by 2π. We can represent this generated group as in Figure 14.9.

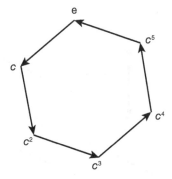

Figure 14.9

As the generated group (Z, +, { 1 }) is infinite, we can only show part of its graph, as in Figure 14.10; but it is obvious how it continues. The identity e is 0, the sole generator is 1, and any integer n results from adding 1 or −1 $|n|$ times.

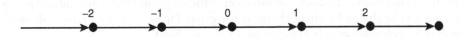

Figure 14.10

Groups with two or more generators have more complicated structures than their single generator counterparts. This can be seen by comparing diagrams of their Cayley graphs. Here are a couple of examples. Figure 14.11 is a diagram of the Cayley graph of (Z, +, { 2, 3 }). We use different shades for composition with the different generators, black for an edge from n to n + 2 and grey for an edge from n to n + 3.

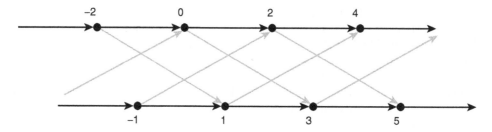

Figure 14.11

Figure 14.12 depicts the graph of S_3 with generators r and f. We use grey for an edge from x to rx and black for an edge from x to fx. Also, for each generator s which is its own inverse, there will be two edges between adjacent vertices, one from x to sx, the other from sx to x, as $x = ssx$. In this case it is visually easier to read the image if we merge the two edges using arrowheads both ways. We do this for edges between x and fx, as f (= flip) is its own inverse.

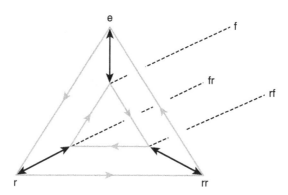

Figure 14.12

Although in practice we often ignore the difference between the visual image and the graph, they are not the same, as there can be visually divergent images of the same graph. The lines could be arcs of a circle, for instance; or the shape, size and positioning of polygonal faces can be changed without changing the graph. Figure 14.13 for example shows the graph of S_3 with generators {r, f} as a prism (without labels).

The Cayley graph of a finitely generated group represented by these diverse images is a graph-theoretic object, not a drawing. We can be precise about this. Let G be a group generated by a finite set S. The *Cayley graph* of (G, S) is the graph (V, E) with V = G and E = the set of ordered[19] pairs ⟨x, sx⟩ for x in G and s in S.

Why bother with the visible diagrams of Cayley graphs? Because they can help us grasp the nature of the Cayley graphs they represent; they can help us reason about them; they can suggest to us hypotheses about them; they can help us to discover or explain facts about them.[20]

Figure 14.13

Here is a simple example. Recall that a single line segment with arrowheads both ways represents two edges with opposite directions between the same pair of vertices. Then inspection of the visual representations of graphs so far will show that all the vertices of a graph have the same number of edges coming into them and the same number leaving them. Is this true for all Cayley graphs? A little reflection shows that it is. Let v be any vertex of the Cayley graph of (G, S). Then for each s in S, $\langle v, sv \rangle$ is an edge leaving v; moreover, every edge leaving v is $\langle v, sv \rangle$ for some s in S. So the total number of edges leaving v is $|S|$. Again, for each s in S, $\langle s^{-1}v, v \rangle$ is an edge into v (as $v = ss^{-1}v$) and all edges into v are of this form. So the total number of edges into v is $|S|$. So all vertices of the graph have the same number of edges coming in and the same number leaving: in the terminology of graph theory, every Cayley graph is regular. In this case, visual inspection of some visual graphs (the standard visual representations of Cayley graphs) led to a general conjecture about Cayley graphs (the mathematical entities), a conjecture that is confirmed by reasoning.

2.3 Thought experiments with Cayley graphs: vertex transitivity

In the case just considered, attentive visual *inspection* of the visual graphs suggested a conjecture. Now we claim that operations in visual *imagination* can do the same kind of work. Looking at the visual graph for C_6 with anticlockwise rotation through $2\pi/6$ as generator, it is clear that we can move any vertex to any other by a transformation of the whole configuration that maps vertices one-to-one onto vertices, in such a way that edge relations are preserved. Putting g for the mapping, this means that $\langle v, w \rangle$ is an edge if and only if $\langle g(v), g(w) \rangle$ is an edge. The transformation is simply a rotation of the whole about the centre by as much as is required to take v to w, and this is made obvious to us by visual imagination.

A one-to-one mapping of the vertices of a graph onto those vertices (i.e. a permutation of the vertices) which preserves edge relations is said to be an *automorphism* of the graph. So the property of the Cayley graph of (C_6, {r}) which visual imagination revealed to us is this: for any of its vertices v and w there is an automorphism which maps v to w. A graph with this property is said to be *vertex transitive*.

For the finite cyclic groups (C_n, {r}) and the infinite-cyclic group (Z, {1}), finding an automorphism is very easy. Take any v and w in the group. If $v = w$, the identity function does the job. Otherwise, there will be some non-zero integer k such that $w = r^k v$. This is k rotations through $2\pi/n$ (or k unit translations) with direction depending on whether k is negative or not. But this same operation applied to all members of the group will preserve edge relations of the Cayley graph, as can be recognized from visualizing the operation on the graph as a whole.

What about finitely generated groups with more than one generator? Let us look at the Cayley graph for S_3 with generators r and f as depicted in Figure 14.13, the prism. A grey directed edge represents one application of r, i.e., a step from a vertex v to a vertex rv; a black edge is the merging of two edges with opposite directions, each representing one application of f. Let v and w be any distinct vertices. The thought experiments involve visualizing spatial operations on the whole prism until one finds one (or a sequence of them) which maps v to w and takes edges to edges without exception. There are three possibilities to consider. In each case we describe a visualizable operation (sequence) which clearly does the job.

(1) v and w belong to the same triangle, that is, $w = rv$ or $w = r^2 v$. Visualize a rotation of the whole prism about the axis through the centre of both triangles (the "horizontal" axis) by one- or two-thirds of a revolution in the direction of the grey edge from v. For example, let v and w be as in Figure 14.14. Anticlockwise rotation of the whole prism by two-thirds of a revolution maps v to w leaving edge relations undisturbed.[21]

(2) v and w lie at opposite ends of the same black edge. Then reflection in a plane parallel to the triangles cutting the prism in half maps each vertex with its counterpart at the

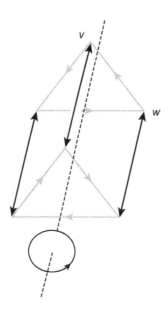

Figure 14.14

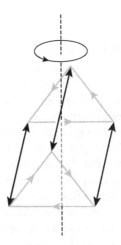

Figure 14.15

other end of a black edge and preserves edge relations. This is the mapping that takes each x to fx. An alternative is to rotate anticlockwise about the horizontal axis until the black edge between v and w is at the top, and then rotate about the vertical axis through the centre by half a revolution as in Figure 14.15. If v and w start at the bottom left edge, this is the mapping that takes each x to fr^2x.

(3) v and w do *not* lie at opposite ends of the same black edge and do *not* belong to the grey same triangle. It is easiest to consider two cases. (i) Let v and w be diagonally opposite vertices on the bottom face of the prism. Then a half revolution about the vertical axis as in Figure 14.15 takes v to w and leaves edge relations undisturbed. (ii) Let just one of v and w be a vertex at the top of a triangle. Then half a revolution about the vertical axis followed by one- or two-thirds of an anticlockwise revolution, will take v to w and preserve edge relations.

We can visualize these whole-prism operations using a picture of the prism with vertices appropriately labelled v and w, and in so doing we readily discern that vertices are mapped one-to-one onto vertices and that edges are taken to edges. This is not surprising. Each whole-prism revolution we have mentioned is a bijection of vertices onto vertices which preserves edge relations; so the composite operation of performing one of these revolutions after another is a bijection which preserves edge relations: a composition of automorphisms is an automorphism.

We can conclude that for any v and w in the Cayley graph of S_3 there is an automorphism taking v to w: the Cayley graph is vertex transitive. What if we replace the triangular faces of the prism with matching regular polygons of more than three sides? The same three cases for pairs of distinct vertices need to be considered (with reference to triangles replaced by reference to n-gons), and using a power of schematic imagination it is not difficult to discern that the same kinds of transformation will provide the needed automorphisms. The only difference is that in this case, the whole-prism rotations about the central horizontal axis which are available to us are k/n of a revolution for each integer k such that $1 \leq k \leq n$, instead of 1/3 or 2/3 of a revolution. As this works regardless of the number of polygon sides, we have a way of telling that the Cayley graphs of an infinite class of groups with two generators (the dihedral groups D_n) are vertex transitive.

Against the background knowledge that all groups with a single generator (the cyclic groups) have vertex transitive graphs, this finding raises the questions: Is the Cayley graph of every group with two generators vertex transitive? Is every Cayley graph vertex transitive? There are many kinds of groups with two generators that we have not considered; so it would be wrong to regard the thought experiments described here as providing significant evidence for the hypothesis that all two-generated groups have vertex transitive graphs. A *fortiori* our thought experiments do not provide much evidence for the hypothesis that all Cayley graphs are vertex transitive. But the outcomes of our thought experiments make these hypotheses worthy of investigation, by trying to find a proof or a counterexample. In fact there is a fairly straightforward proof that every Cayley graph is vertex transitive.

What we have shown is that in some cases one can use one's visual imagination to find the required automorphisms, without already knowing that there are any, hence in a truly experimental way. This active use of visual imagery, first studied by cognitive scientists in the 1970s (see Shepard and Cooper 1982), is a useful part of the toolkit of mathematicians and students of mathematics, though the results are usually recorded symbolically, without trace of the mental experimentation which led to them. The utility of visual imagination depends on confining our efforts to images and image transformations which are simple enough for us to manipulate reliably in imagination. But the variety of images and image transformations that we can handle reliably suffices to make visual imagination a potent instrument of mental experimentation in mathematics.

3 A case from geometric group theory

The example we will now present is the first step of a revolutionary advance in geometric group theory due to Russian mathematician Mikhail Gromov. To keep the exposition short and digestible, we omit some of the technical details.

If S and T are distinct finite subsets of a group G and both generate G, the Cayley graphs (G, S) and (G, T) will not in general be isomorphic. For example, the Cayley graphs of (Z, {1}) and (Z, {2, 3}), illustrated by Figures 14.10 and 14.11, are not isomorphic. How, if at all, can we use Cayley graphs of a group to discover properties of the group itself, that is, properties which are invariant with respect to generating sets?

The seminal thought is that we may be able to find group properties which do not depend on the generating set by ignoring the fine-grained local features of the different Cayely graphs of a given group and attending only to the coarse, global features shared by all the group's Cayley graphs. But how, given a particular Cayley graph of a group, can we tell what its coarse global features are?

A Cayley graph of an infinite (finitely generated) group is an infinite graph; so only finite portions of it can be visually represented. But we can imagine viewing ever-larger portions of the graph in the hope that large-scale features of the group may emerge. We can give this idea mathematical articulation by regarding a Cayley graph as a metric space, as follows.

For every pair g, h of members of a generated group (G, S) there is at least one path in its Cayley graph from g to h. The length of a path is just the length of the sequence of consecutively adjacent edges which constitutes the path, and the distance between g and h, denoted $d_S(g, h)$, is the length of a shortest path starting at g and ending at h. This distance function is the *shortest path metric*.[22] Viewing ever-larger portions of the Cayley graph amounts to successively viewing diagrams representing the parts of the Cayley graph containing vertices at most n units away from the identity e, for increasing n.[23] We call this kind of visual transformation "zooming out."

Now let G be any infinite group with different finite sets of generators S, T and maybe others. From a visual representation of the Cayley graph of (G, S) or (G, T) – it does not matter which – we can try zooming out in visual imagination *so far* that the fine details of the Cayley graph are lost and features of the large-scale geometry (or "coarse" geometry) of the object now come into view. The hope is that the large-scale geometry is the same for whichever Cayley graph we start with, that is, regardless of generating set. If this works, then we might find that algebraic properties of the group G itself, properties which are invariant with respect to generating set, can be discovered by attending to the coarse geometry of the object we reach by zooming out. Here is how Gromov put it:

> This space [the space of the Cayley graph of $\Gamma = (G, S)$ with the shortest path metric] may appear boring and uneventful to a geometer's eye since it is discrete and the traditional local (e.g. topological and infinitesimal) machinery does not run in Γ. To regain the geometric perspective one has to change his/her position and move the observation point far away from Γ. Then the metric in Γ seen from a distance d becomes the original distance divided by d and for $d \to \infty$ the points in Γ coalesce into a connected continuous solid unity which occupies the visual horizon without any gaps or holes and fills the geometer's heart with joy.
>
> (Gromov 1993)

To get Gromov's point one must bear in mind that a Cayley graph is not a geometric object: its "edges" are just pairs of vertices and so contain no points between endpoints. A Cayley graph with shortest path metric is a metric space, but the metric (the distance function) is discrete, as the distance between any two vertices is a non-negative integer. By "moving the observation point far away from" the Cayley graph metric space (i.e., by zooming out from it), the discrete object is transformed in appearance into a space with a dense and continuous metric, having (non-negative) real values.

What happens if we imagine zooming out from a visual presentation of a Cayley graph? If, actually looking at one, we zoomed out perceptually far enough the whole thing would disappear from view. To avoid this, an idealization is involved in our mental exercise: we suppose that while distances between vertices shrink as we zoom out, the vertices themselves do not fade at all. The experimental question is: what would happen to one's view of a standard diagram of a Cayley graph as one moved the observation point away by distances without upper bound, if vertices remained in view like points of starlight? What kind of space would emerge as a result? The answer depends on the Cayley graph one starts with, and is obtained by a combination of visual imagination and physical reasoning.

What happens then to standard diagrams of Cayley graphs of (Z, {1}) and (Z, {2, 3}), shown partially in Figures 14.10 and 14.11? Both become indistinguishable from the traditional representation of the real numbers as a single uninterrupted line without ends. In this case at least, differences due to different generating sets have been wiped out, as desired. What happens to the integer points of the plane (ZxZ, {⟨1, 0⟩, ⟨0, 1⟩})? The vertices in each horizontal string coalesce, and at the same time the vertices in each vertical string coalesce; that is, spaces between the points shrink and disappear, resulting in a continuous plane. What happens to the appearance of a *finite* Cayley graph as we imagine zooming out? Eventually its vertices coalesce to a single tiny dot. Does this nullify the whole exercise? Not at all: we are looking for *asymptotic* properties, properties that emerge at the limit of zooming out or properties that emerge at a late stage and persist, and so our focus is naturally on infinite groups (with finite generating sets.)

There is no reason to think that what we have described as an idealized mental operation of zooming out in visual imagination is really a disguised argument for something we already believe. For the question would then arise how we came to believe it, if not by the kind of thinking we describe. It is true that there is more to the mental operation than a simple transformation in visual imagination, for we add conditions. We ask how the appearance of the diagram of the Cayley graph of (Z, {2, 3}), for instance, would be transformed by zooming out under the condition that vertices remained visible, though not necessarily distinguishable. This indicates that the cognitive processes involved are complicated and probably also not fully open to introspection. But it is clear that visual imagination of a spatial change is involved and that the thinking as a whole does not reduce to the application of mathematically prescribed rules. Reliability is going to be limited by the fact that the kind of spaces we can easily visualize are Euclidean or embeddable in a Euclidean space. But the examples given fall within these limits.

The direct outcomes of these experiments do not count as mathematical results and, as just mentioned, the outcomes are limited. This is not a problem, because the real rewards of the zooming-out thought experiments are not their direct outcomes, but their effects in suggesting three mathematical possibilities. First, zooming-out suggests that there is a way of filtering out differences due to the different generating sets of the same group. Secondly, zooming out suggests that there is a way of thinking of an infinite generated group in terms of a metric space with a continuous metric (so that a group may have properties determined by geometric properties of the continuous metric space). Thirdly, zooming out suggests that we will sometimes get the same continuous metric space from distinct groups (not just the same group with different generating sets), perhaps giving us an equivalence relation on groups.

To benefit mathematically from these effects, we need to find a mathematically precise account of a suitable relation that holds between the Cayley graph of a finitely generated group (G, S) with the shortest path metric – call it $\Gamma(G, S)$ – and the continuous metric space we arrive at by zooming out from $\Gamma(G, S)$. The relation is suitable only if for any infinite group G generated by finite subsets S and T, $\Gamma(G, S)$ and $\Gamma(G, T)$ stand in this relation to the same continuous metric space.

The mathematization of the intuitive relation meeting these requirements is so neat that we present it now. An isometric mapping between metric spaces is one that preserves distances; a quasi-isometric mapping is one that preserves distances to within fixed linear bounds:

A map f from (S, d) to (S', d') is a *quasi-isometric mapping* iff there are real constants $K \geq 0$ and $L > 0$ such that for all x, y in S

$$d(x, y)/L - K \leq d'(f(x), f(y)) \leq L \cdot d(x, y) + K.$$

Quasi-isometric mappings are not in general surjective on the intended target space, and we will fail to capture the intuitive relation if we impose surjectivity as an extra condition.[24] But we would like to find an equivalence relation on metric spaces which is a suitable loosening of isometry. So some extra condition is needed. The condition is that the mapping be surjective to within a fixed bound. Precisely put, the mapping f from (S, d) to (S', d') is *quasi-surjective* on S' iff there is a real constant $M \geq 0$ such that every point of S' is no further than M away from some point in the image of S under f. Putting these together, we define:

A map f from (S, d) to (S', d') is *a quasi-isometry* iff f is a quasi-surjective quasi-isometric mapping from (S, d) to (S', d').

(S, d) is *quasi-isometric to* (S', d') iff there is a quasi-isometry from (S, d) to (S', d').

This is an equivalence relation, which works as intended. First, a discrete space can be quasi-isometric to a dense continuous space. The inclusion (identity) mapping from $\Gamma(Z, \{1\})$ to R, with constants $L = 1$ and $K = 0$, is a quasi-isometric mapping; and it is quasi-surjective as every real number is at most $1/2$ a unit distance away from an integer. So $\Gamma(Z, \{1\})$ is quasi-isometric to R with standard distance metric.[25]

Moreover, $\Gamma(Z, \{2, 3\})$ also is quasi-isometric to R with standard distance metric; so $\Gamma(Z, \{1\})$ and $\Gamma(Z, \{2, 3\})$ are quasi-isometric spaces. This fact generalizes: for any infinite group G with finite generating sets S and T, $\Gamma(G, S)$ and $\Gamma(G, T)$ are quasi-isometric spaces, as intended. This means that properties of G which are quasi-isometric invariants will be independent of the choice of generating set, and therefore informative about the group itself.

Furthermore, for some *different* groups G and H with generating sets S and S' respectively $\Gamma(G, S)$ and $\Gamma(H, S')$ are quasi-isometric; in this case the groups G and H are said to be quasi-isometric. So finitely generated infinite groups fall into equivalence classes modulo quasi-isometry.

Finally, an immensely rewarding outcome: there are some kinds K of *geometric* space such that groups with Cayley graph spaces which are quasi-isometric to a space of kind K (though not necessarily the *same* space) share significant algebraic properties. This turns out to be the case for groups which are quasi-isometric to hyperbolic geodesic spaces, but that is a story for another occasion (see Starikova 2012).

4 Summary and defence

We have presented examples from knot theory, graph theory and geometric group theory of a kind of thinking which involves active use of visual imagination and goes beyond the application of mathematically prescribed rules, as a way of answering questions or overcoming obstacles. Is a trefoil knot equivalent to the unknot? What is the diameter of a cyclic graph in terms of the number of its edges? Is the Cayley graph of $(S_3, \{f, r\})$ vertex transitive? What spatial representations enable us to discover properties of a finitely generated group which are invariant with respect to generating sets?

Our impression is that the role (or roles) of this kind of experimental thinking in the advance of mathematical knowledge is under-appreciated, though we have not justified that opinion here. Our aim has been merely to substantiate the view that there are thought experiments in mathematics which involve visualization of physical situations or transformations, often with an idealized aspect.

These visual thought experiments neither are, nor serve in place of, mathematical *proofs* of the conclusions reached, even when those conclusions are true and the thought experiments are reliable ways of reaching them. But we hope that the cases we have presented support our view that the thought experiments can give the thinker good reason to believe them.

This raises a general philosophical worry. If visual thought experiments of the kinds we have described can provide reasons for mathematical beliefs, they would provide empirical reasons. But mathematics, as opposed to the application of mathematics to non-mathematical subject matter, is an *a priori* science. How then can there be empirical evidence for a mathematical fact?

The main problem here lies with the dictum that mathematics is an *a priori* science. It is ambiguous. If it means that any knowable mathematical truth can be known without empirical justification, it is consistent with the claim that we can have empirical reasons for believing a mathematical proposition. But it may mean something much stronger, ruling out the possibility that we can have empirical reasons for believing a mathematical proposition. If the dictum has this stronger meaning, so much the worse for the dictum. Here is a simple example. How many vertices does a cube have? Your background knowledge includes the facts that cubes do not vary in shape and that material cubes will not differ from geometrically perfect cubes in number of vertices. To find out the answer one can inspect a material cube and count its vertices. (Or you can visualize a cube to find four at the top surface and four at the bottom). The visual experience in this case provides evidence for your conclusion that a cube has eight vertices. "But is this really a *mathematical* fact?" Why not? It is a very simple fact, but we can extend the problem: Do all platonic solids have the same Euler characteristic? Surely the answer to *that* is a mathematical fact. And it can be verified in the same way. Physical models of each of the five platonic solids can be visually inspected to find out whether $V - E + F$ is the same for all of them. The visual inspection provides empirical evidence for a positive answer. There are plenty of other examples, and a good case can be made that our initial knowledge of some single-digit addition facts is acquired empirically, from experiences of counting.

Empirical evidence has a much larger role in the epistemology of actual mathematical belief acquisition than is often thought. Even so, one may resist the idea that visual imagination is a way of providing us with empirical evidence. But visual imagination is not just a way of indulging in fantasy. It is also a way of harnessing the amalgamated memories of past experiences of visual perception to come to conclusions about physical situations. In this role it provides empirical evidence. Of course there is always the question, for any particular use of visual imagination to answer a question, whether it is reliable. There is no general test for reliability, but in the context of mathematics we have a way of resolving doubts: we look for a proof.

For these reasons we see no general bar to accepting that full blooded thought experiments are instruments, alongside proofs, for the advancement of mathematical knowledge.

Acknowledgements

Irina Starikova would like to thank the Brazilian Coordination for the Improvement of Higher Education Personnel (CAPES) and the Russian Foundation of Basic Research (RFBR).

Notes

1 For this reason we find that the category of thought experiments as characterized in Van Bendegem (2003) to be too broad.
2 For a different focus, see Glas (2009). Glas says that "imagery, mental or experiential, is not essential" to the aspect of thinking that he counts as thought experiment (even when accompanied by imagery). For this reason, the kinds of thinking that we discuss in this paper do not fall under what Glas counts as thought experiment.
3 We are setting aside higher dimensional knot theory.
4 There are mathematically precise definitions of knot-equivalence. It is clearly not enough to say that equivalent knots are homeomorphic, as all knots are homeomorphic to the circle hence to each other. They are equivalent iff there is an ambient isotopy taking one to the other. More about that shortly.
5 Articulated by Paul Boghossian in a New York Institute of Philosophy workshop on the a priori in June 2013.
6 Every introductory text on knot theory and some more advanced texts define the Reidemeister moves, and they can be readily found on the web. For an introduction see Adams (2001).
7 Even here there is some oversimplification. First, the homeomorphism is usually required to preserve orientation (which has not been defined here), to avoid identifying chiral knots with their mirror images. Also, for the advantages of operating in a compact space the co-domain of the homeomorphism is usually taken to be S^3 instead of R^3.
8 See for example Greene (2013).
9 Colourability is sometimes called "tricolourability."
10 There is a combinatorial version of colourability. If instead of colouring the arcs one labels them 0, 1 or 2, the colourability conditions together have a numerical equivalent: (a) at least two of the numerical labels are used and (b) at each crossing if x is the value of the overcrossing arc and y and z are the values of the other two arcs, $2x - y - z = 0$ (mod 3). This mod 3 labelling readily generalizes to other invariants known as "mod p labelling," where p is an odd prime.
11 This can be done either by visually imagining a written colour word placed next to an arc or, just as easily, by aurally imagining uttering a colouring word as a label of an arc one is visually attending to.
12 Strictly speaking, E_G is a multiset, so that an element $\{u, v\}$ can occur more than once, the number of occurrences being the number of edges with endpoints u and v. Those edges with endpoints u and v are said to be *parallel* to one another. Also, there can be one or more edges $\{u, u,\}$, known as *loops*. Cycle graphs are *simple* graphs, in the sense that they have no loops and no two edges are parallel.
13 We clearly could perform this experiment physically as well as in thought; the same goes for the thought experiments on knots illustrated in Figures 14.4 and 14.5. This refutes Buzzoni's claim that a mathematical thought experiment "leaves no room for a separate real performance of the experiment" (Buzzoni 2011).
14 So for example, we write $ab^{-1}aab$ for $(a \cdot (b^{-1} \cdot a)) \cdot (a \cdot b)$.
15 S_3 is also the group of symmetries of an equilateral triangle. If we take a, b, and c to be vertices of an equilateral triangle, r (rotation) and f (flip) are obvious operations (symmetries) of the triangle.

16 Take any finite set of rationals with denominators $d_1, d_2, \ldots, d_n$. Any sum of those rationals could be expressed as a rational n/m with denominator $m = d_1 \times d_2 \times \ldots \times d_n$. But not all rationals could be so expressed: consider p/q where p and q are primes and q > m.
17 To see that $\{4\pi/5\}$ generates C_5, note that a sequence of three anticlockwise rotations by $4\pi/5$ = anticlockwise rotation by $2\pi/5$; two anticlockwise rotations by $4\pi/5$ = *clockwise* rotation by $2\pi/5$. To see that {2, 3} generates Z note that +3+(−2) = +1 and +2+(−3) = −1.
18 As the group operation is so often function composition, we maintain the convention that s applied to g (i.e. s after g) is sg, so that an edge goes from g to sg.
19 The pairs are ordered because all edges of a Cayley graph have a direction. Notice that edges can run in both directions between a given pair of vertices: both ⟨e, f⟩ and ⟨f, e⟩ are edges in the Cayley graph represented by Figure 14.12.
20 For more on the roles of diagrams of Cayley graphs see the following articles by Starikova (2010, 2012).
21 We should be careful here when specifying the mapping mathematically, because the whole-prism rotation does not coincide with rotation r of the group: for *x* in the near triangle the mapping takes *x* to r*x*, but for *x* in the far triangle it takes *x* to r^{-1}*x*.
22 This *shortest path metric* d_S is the same as the *word metric* for (G, S). Suppose each element of S is assigned a unique name of the form "s_k". Let a symbol of the form "s_k^{-1}" name the inverse of what is named by "s_k". A *word in* S is a finite sequence of elements of the form "s_k" or "s_k^{-1}", so that a word denotes a product of members of G. The word metric for (G, S) is defined: $d_S(g, h)$ = least length of a word w in S such that w denotes hg^{-1}. Note that left multiplying g by hg^{-1} takes g to h.
23 In customary terms, we bring into view (representations of) the *n*-balls for (G, S) for increasing *n*, where the *n*-ball = {g∈ G: $d_S(e, g) \leq n$}.
24 This is because the intuitive relation holds between Γ((Z, {1}) and R with the normal distance metric, but |R| > |Z|; so there is no surjection from Z to R.
25 For a quasi-isometry from R to Z, the mapping which takes each real number r to the nearest integer or, if r is half-way between integers, to the greatest integer less than r, is a quasi-isometric mapping (with L = 1 and K = 1) and is surjective, hence trivially quasi-surjective.

References

Adams, C. (2001) *The Knot Book*, Providence: American Mathematical Society.
Buzzoni, M. (2011) "On mathematical thought experiments," *Epistemologia* XXXIV: 61–88.
Glas, E. (2009) "On the role of thought experiments in mathematical discovery," in *Models of Discovery and Creativity*, edited by J. Meheus and T. Nickles, Boston: Springer.
Greene, J. (2013). "Combinatorial methods in knot theory." Available here: www2.bc.edu/joshua-e-greene/MT885S13/Lecture%201.pdf (accessed 15 November 2016).
Gromov, M. (1993) "Asymptotic invariants of infinite groups," in *Geometric Group Theory*, vol. 2, edited by G. A. Niblo and M. A. Roller, London Mathematical Society Lecture Notes 182, Cambridge: Cambridge University Press.
Norton, J. (1996) "Are thought experiments just what you thought?" *Canadian Journal of Philosophy* 26: 333–366.
Shepard, R. and Cooper, L. (eds) (1982) *Mental Images and Their Transformations*, Cambridge: MIT Press.
Starikova, I. (2010) "Why do mathematicians need different ways to present mathematical objects? The case of Cayley graphs," *Topoi* 29: 41–51.
Starikova, I. (2012) "From practice to new concepts: Geometric properties of groups," *Philosophia Scientiae* 16: 129–151.
Van Bendegem, J. P. (2003) "Thought experiments in mathematics: Anything but proof," *Philosophica* 72: 9–33.

Part III
CONTEMPORARY PHILOSOPHICAL APPROACHES TO THOUGHT EXPERIMENTS

15
THE ARGUMENT VIEW
Are thought experiments mere picturesque arguments?

Elke Brendel

Thought experiments have played an important role in scientific progress throughout the history of science, and are employed to serve various purposes. Some thought experiments function primarily as illustrative examples designed to improve our understanding of a theory. Scientifically and epistemically more important, however, are thought experiments that attempt to test theories, hypotheses, claims, definitions or conceptual analyses. Many thought experiments aim to disprove or undermine existing theories by revealing contradictions, paradoxical implications, counterintuitive or unintended results of these theories. Some thought experiments have not only dismissed theories, but also paved the way for better ones. So it seems that by mere reflection on imaginary scenarios we can learn something interesting and new. Of course, thought experiments can fail. They can miss the point they intend to make and otherwise go astray. Some thought experiments are less reliable or less convincing than others. So thought experiments seem to be the kind of entities that warrant critical examination. We can rationally assess thought experiments with respect to their correctness, plausibility and reliability, and we can specify general criteria for the legitimate use of thought experiments (see, for example, Brendel 2004).

In light of the above considerations about the epistemic status and function of thought experiments, the following questions arise: How can we learn something new from a thought experiment if thought experiments are entirely executed in the "laboratory of the mind"? What kinds of entities are thought experiments, given the fact that they can be fallible or defective? How can we rationally assess the success and failure of thought experiments? These and other questions have been discussed extensively in the literature about thought experiments. John D. Norton famously contends that the answers to those questions lie in the typical *argumentative structure* of thought experiments. Norton claims that thought experiments are nothing more than arguments, albeit disguised in a pictorial or narrative form (see, for example, Norton 1996, 2004a, 2004b). The knowledge delivered by thought experiments can be seen as the result of transforming the (explicit and tacit) premises of an argument by some kind of logical reasoning. So according to Norton's "argument view," the knowledge we gain by a thought experiment does not transcend the informational resources already implicit in the premises of an argument. Since we do not overlook all the consequences of what we already know, and since some thought experiments transform and rearrange our given knowledge in a new, unusual and creative way, the results that thought experiments produce can be highly informative – although no new input from outside is involved. For Norton, reflecting on a thought experiment is nothing over and above the engagement in a process of argumentation. Norton's argument view also provides an easy explanation for the fallibility of thought experiments, as well as for our ability to critically assess a thought experiment's correctness and persuasiveness: thought experiments are to be evaluated in the same way as standard arguments. Thought experiments can fail when they are based on implausible, unjustified or incoherent premises, or when the conclusion is not adequately supported by a legitimate logical inference – or when they suffer from other argumentative shortcomings, such as *petitio principii* etc. On the other hand, successful thought experiments will be those that rest on sound arguments.

James Robert Brown is one of the most prominent and persistent critics of Norton's argument view. Brown contends that not all thought experiments can be seen as mere picturesque arguments. According to Brown, there are some thought experiments, the so-called "Platonic thought experiments" (see, for example, Brown 1991, 77), that provide a priori knowledge by a non-experiential perception of abstract entities. For Brown, a Platonic thought experiment allows us "to see with the mind's eye" (Brown 2004b, 32), i.e., to grasp abstract entities in an intuitive and non-inferential way. Brown stresses the point that this kind of a priori knowledge acquisition via a Platonic thought experiment is qualitatively different from the inferential means of knowledge acquisition via argumentation.

How should we conceive of such Platonic thought experiments that are, according to Brown, "telescopes into the abstract realm" (Brown 2004a, 1131)? Brown characterizes Platonic thought experiments as certain kinds of thought experiments that are simultaneously destructive and constructive. They "destroy an old or existing theory and simultaneously generate a new one" (Brown 1991, 77). For Brown, a Platonic thought experiment allows us to "perceive" the new theory without relying on any new evidence and without deriving the new theory completely from already (and maybe tacitly) known old data. Brown's favourite Platonic thought experiment – the "most beautiful thought experiment ever devised" (Brown 2004b, 24) – is Galileo's experiment on falling bodies. The main target of this thought experiment is the Aristotelian view according to which bodies of different weights move in the same medium in proportion to their weights with different speeds (see Galileo 1954/1638, 61). But this assumption leads to a contradiction. Consider a case where a heavy body A is attached to a lighter body B. The compound object A + B is heavier than the body A alone – and thus, according to Aristotle, must fall faster than the body A alone. But, on the other hand, object B when combined with object A will slow down object A such that the compound object A + B will fall more slowly than the single object A. So, we have reached the contradictory result that object A + B falls both faster and slower than A alone. This is not only "the end of Aristotle's theory," as Brown claims, but we can now go further and intuit the correct law of free-falling bodies: all bodies must move at the same speed (Brown 2004a, 1127).

According to Brown, Galileo's thought experiment "provides us with a priori knowledge of nature ... there are no new empirical data used when we move from Aristotle's to Galileo's theory of free fall. It is not a logical truth either" (Brown 2004a, 1129). Thus, Galileo's thought experiment enables us to perceive (in a non-sensory way) the abstract realm of a law of nature. According to Brown, the knowledge we gain from Galileo's thought experiment cannot be seen as a conclusion derivable via logical inferences from given empirical premises. Brown therefore holds that Galileo's thought experiment does not amount to a mere argument: so he claims that Norton's argument view must be false.

The question of whether thought experiments are mere arguments has been the subject of intense debate over the last two decades. Without giving up their basic ideas, Norton and Brown have altered and modified their views in reaction to criticism. The dialectical moves Norton and Brown have made in order to shore up their positions indicate that the argument view is a kind of moving target. Norton's argument view does not consist in a single claim, but decomposes into different parts. In order to arrive at a differentiated evaluation of the Norton–Brown debate, let us distinguish the following five sub-claims of the argument view. As far as I can tell, these five sub-claims have been the main targets in the debate about the argument view:

(1) *Identity Thesis*: Thought experiments are (type)-identical with arguments.
(2) *Reconstruction Thesis*: Thought experiments "can always be reconstructed as arguments based on explicit or tacit assumptions that yield the same outcome" (Norton 2004a, 1142).

The *Reconstruction Thesis* encompasses the following two theses (2a) and (2b):

(2a) *Reliability Thesis*: "If thought experiments can be used reliably epistemically, then they must be arguments (construed very broadly) that justify their outcomes or are constructible as such arguments" (Norton 2004b, 52). A thought experiment is a "reliable mode of inquiry" only if the argument into which it can be reconstructed justifies its conclusion.
(2b) *Elimination Thesis*: "Any conclusion reached by a (successful) scientific thought experiment will also be demonstrable by a non-thought-experimental argument" (Gendler 2000, 34).

(3) *Epistemic Thesis*: Thought experiments and the arguments associated with them have the same epistemic reach and epistemic significance. Thought experiments are not epistemically superior to their corresponding non-thought-experimental arguments – and *vice versa*. In particular, we cannot learn things from a thought experiment over and above the things we can learn from its associated argument: "... all there is to learn about a thought experiment's epistemic power can be recovered from considering it as an argument" (Norton 2004b, 55). Furthermore, a thought experiment epistemically justifies its outcome to the same degree as its associated argument justifies its conclusion.
(4) *Empirical Psychological Thesis*: "The actual conduct of a thought experiment consists of the execution of an argument ..." (Norton 2004b, 50).
(5) *Empiricist Thesis*: The result of a thought experiment can only come from experience: "The result of a thought experiment must be the reformulation of ... experience by a process that preserves truth or its probability ..." (Norton 2004a, 1142).

Some philosophers have attacked the argument view by criticizing the *Identity Thesis*, claiming that the entities thought experiments deal with are *ontologically* different from the entities arguments are composed of. Arguments seem to consist of *propositions* and logical manipulations of them. Intuitively, as Sören Häggqvist claims, the objects of thought experiments are not propositions, but some kind of psychological process "inside the thought experimenter's skull." He contends that thought experiments unlike arguments "are not composed of truth-valued entities. Nor are they valid or invalid in any formal sense (although they may be more or less felicitous or successful)" (Häggqvist 2009, 61). But intuitions about the ontological status of the things we refer to with the terms "argument" and "thought experiment" are quite shaky. Is it really so odd to call a thought experiment "valid" or "invalid" – and do not we often speak of an argument as more or less "felicitous" or "successful"? Häggqvist admits that his claim "begs the question against Norton" (Häggqvist 2009, 61 n. 21). Our intuitions about the ontological status of arguments and thought experiments seem to be already influenced by our previous attitude towards the argument view. So, Häggqvist's critique of the *Identity Thesis* needs to be supported on independent grounds.

Another argument against the *Identity Thesis* was put forward by Roy Sorensen. For Sorensen, "thought experiments should be studied as if they were experiments" (Sorensen 1992, 214). According to Sorensen, we should therefore embrace the following parity thesis: "thought experiments are arguments if and only if experiments are arguments" (Sorensen 1992, 214). Of course, real experiments do not consist of arguments. They consist of physical objects, measuring instruments, magnets, cloud chambers, particle colliders, etc. Thus, we can conclude from the parity thesis that thought experiments do not consist of arguments. But why should we accept the parity thesis in the first place? To be sure, thought experiments share with real experiments many important features. Thought experiments are not just any kind of hypothetical reasoning about imaginary scenarios. Like real experiments, thought experiments investigate what happens if we change some factors in a specific and controlled way within a given situation. Like real experiments, thought experiments are based on background assumptions and background theories. A proponent of the argument view is happy to admit all of this. But there are also differences between thought experiments and real experiments. Since thought experiments are conducted in the "laboratory of the mind" and involve sometimes highly counterfactual and unreal scenarios or use idealized assumptions, their success (or failure) depends in a crucial way on whether the reasoning processes they invoke are plausible. So, there are good reasons to treat thought experiments and real experiments unequally with respect to the question whether they can be plausibly classified as arguments. The parity thesis is thus a non-starter in arguing against the *Identity Thesis*.

Michael Bishop has offered another much-discussed argument against the *Identity Thesis* (Bishop 1999). Bishop claims that identifying thoughts experiments with arguments "cannot make sense of the historical trajectory of certain thought experiments. In particular, it cannot account for episodes in which different thinkers disagree about a thought experiment" (Bishop 1999, 535). Of course, the fact that there are thought experiments that come in different narrative and picturesque clothing does not necessarily speak against the *Identity Thesis*. There are, for example, a great variety of different versions of Edmund Gettier's famous thought experiment against the traditional analysis of knowledge as justified true belief (see Gettier 1963). The longer the discussion about Gettier's thought experiment has lasted, the more Gettier-style examples have been invented. But they all seem to be tokens of one general type of thought experiment which can be associated with instances of one argument type, i.e., with instances that obey the same logical structure (see, for example, Williamson 2007, ch. 6, for a logical analysis of a Gettier-style thought experiment; see also Cohnitz and Häggqvist, this volume). The *Identity Thesis* would only be undermined if, for example, two tokens of *one* thought experiment type corresponded to two tokens of *different* argument types. According to Bishop, there are many episodes in the history of science where we encounter such a situation. As an example, Bishop discusses Einstein's famous clock-in-the-box thought experiment presented at the Solvay Conference on magnetism 1930 in order to falsify Heisenberg's Uncertainty Principle. In this thought experiment, Einstein imagined a box containing a source of radiation that emits photons. The box has a shutter that opens at an exact moment. The opening of the shutter is controlled by a clock. We can thus measure the exact time when the photon is released. The difference in the weight of the box before and after the photon was released gives us the mass of the photon. By using Einstein's equation $E = mc^2$, we can now measure the photon's exact energy. So, contrary to the Uncertainty Principle, it seems that we can exactly and simultaneously measure a photon's energy at an arbitrarily precise moment in time. Niels Bohr, however, showed that due to the effects of relativistic spacetime, the accuracy of the measurement devices in the clock-in-the-box thought scenario is limited to a certain degree and the minimal uncertainty which is left when measuring the photon's energy and its time of passage is in fact predicted by Heisenberg's principle. So it seems that Einstein and Bohr use the same thought experiment, but since they draw completely different conclusions, their arguments are different: "Since we have two different arguments but just one thought experiment, the thought experiment cannot be the arguments" (Bishop 1999, 540).

Norton has objected to Bishop's argument against the *Identity Thesis* by claiming that Einstein and Bohr use similar but *different* thought experiments that correspond to different arguments: where Einstein uses the scenario in the framework of classical spacetime, Bohr uses relativistic spacetime. So, Einstein and Bohr come to different conclusions "because of the differences in the premises pertaining to spacetime setting" (Norton 2004b, 64).

How shall we decide the debate between Bishop and Norton? Surely, Bishop is right with respect to the observation that we are willing to subsume various instances of thought experiments under one thought experiment type, even though their underlying argumentative structures are different. But Norton could, of course, reply that this does not show that thought experiment types are not *actually* identical to argument types. If the arguments are different, then the corresponding thought experiments must differ at some point. Norton could claim that for pragmatic reasons of simplicity we sometimes use one name for actually different but sufficiently similar thought experiment types. So in a way, Bishop and Norton seem to beg the question against each other.

Let us now turn to the *Reconstruction Thesis*, which has the *Reliability* and *Elimination Thesis* as its parts. The *Reconstruction Thesis* allows for different readings and thus needs some specification. Norton's explications of this thesis suggest a quite strong empirical reading. Norton does not seem to hold the less stringent view that thought experiments can *in principle* be reconstructed as arguments. In particular, he does not seem to retreat to the view that all thought experiments are reconstructible as arguments, at least by ideal reasoners who are in possession of all the relevant facts (see Stuart 2015, ch. 2.3; 2016, 453).

Norton has taken great pains to reconstruct Galileo's thought experiment of falling bodies, which Brown conceives as a Platonic thought experiment (see Norton 1996, 341–3). His reconstruction reveals the fact that we can only reach the conclusion of the constructive part of the thought experiment (that all bodies fall at the same speed) if we add the assumption that the speed of falling bodies depends only on their weights. But this assumption is false for arbitrary media, as Salviati remarked in the *Discorsi* (see Galileo 1954/1638, 65). However, that all bodies fall at the same speed in a *vacuum* was nothing more than a bold conjecture in Galileo's day (see also McAllister 2004 or Schrenk 2004 for similar non-Platonist reconstructions of Galileo's thought experiment). That is why Norton concludes that "this final step now looks more like a clumsy fudge or a stumble than a leap into the Platonic world of laws" (Norton 1996, 345).

Besides Galileo's thought experiment, Norton has managed to reconstruct many other thought experiments as arguments, in particular, typical thought experiments in physics. Since Norton has not come across upon any non-reconstructible thought experiment, he is convinced that there are no examples of thought experiments that resist (actual) argumentative reconstruction: "The ease of their reconstruction suggests that a counterexample will not be found. The reconstructions are generally rather straightforward and often differ little from the original narrative of the thought experiment" (Norton 2004b, 50).

In order to examine the *Reconstruction Thesis* in the light of the Norton-Brown debate, it is essential to understand Norton's conception of *argument* or *argumentation*. Broadly and formally speaking, an argument consists in a set of premises and a conclusion, where the premises and the conclusion are inferentially related by some kind of logical reasoning. Norton adopts this general notion of an argument. However, he is quite liberal on the question of what counts as a valid logical inference that leads to a justified conclusion within an argument. The *Reliability Thesis* connects the reliability of a thought experiment to the justifiedness of the conclusion of the argument into which the thought experiment is reconstructed. Principally, the more logical inferences Norton allows as argumentatively valid, the more possibilities are available to reconstruct thought experiments as reliable tools of scientific inquiry. Whereas Norton initially identified thought experiments with classical deductive and inductive forms of arguments, he later expanded the scope of logic to inference to the best explanation (Norton 1996, 349), the rules of Bayesian confirmation theory (Norton 2004b, 53), and indeed to reasoning based on *informal logic*. According to Norton, thought experiments are just governed by a "very general notion of a logic" (Norton 2004b, 54). In reaction to a mathematical example that Brown discusses as a potential candidate for a Platonic thought experiment (see, for example, Brown 2004b, 38ff.), Norton even allows a thought experiment to be reconstructed by a kind of *argument from analogy*. In order to present an alleged example of a mathematical Platonic thought experiment, Brown draws on Christopher Freiling's "refutation" of the continuum hypothesis. Since the continuum hypotheses is independent of the standard ZFC set theory (Zermelo-Fraenkel set-theory with the axiom of choice), Freiling's "disproof" of the continuum hypothesis cannot completely be carried out within ZFC set theory. His "disproof" rests, in particular, on some kind of visual or figurative evidence, namely dart throws at the real line, from which mathematical conclusions are drawn. Of course, visual "proofs" from analogy have only limited epistemic significance, in particular in mathematics (though see Starikova and Giaquinto, this volume). They can also be misleading, as, for example, Zeno's paradoxes have taught us. I do not want to elaborate on the question of whether Freiling's "refutation" of the continuum hypothesis can be regarded as successful. As Brown has often pointed out, Platonic perception can be fallible. However, Norton challenges Brown's view by claiming that insofar as Freiling's thought experiment works at all (which Norton denies), there is no reason to regard it as a *Platonic* thought experiment: "I just find it [the recognition of the outcome of Freiling's thought experiment] to be the result of prosaic argumentation of an informal kind – just the sort of thing I say arises commonly in thought experiments. The recognition depends on seeing that there is a zero probability of picking a number at random from a measure zero set. We infer that result from reasoning by analogy with dart throws. On a real dartboard, there is only a small probability of hitting the thin wires. The probability drops to zero for infinitely thin wires, the analog of a measure zero set" (Norton 2004b, 58). Norton claims that he has "always urged that thought experiments may be informal arguments." Furthermore, he contends that although Freiling's "refutation" of the continuum hypothesis is beyond the means of classical ZFC set theory, it "certainly could be derived if suitable premises were allowed" (Norton 2004b, 58). Given such a flexible conception of argument in which even all kinds of informal arguments (including arguments from analogy) are allowed, the worry arises that Norton's *Reconstruction Thesis* is immune to falsification and thus amounts to a thesis that is simply vacuously true. It seems impossible to come up with a thought experiment that cannot be reconstructed by an argument in Norton's sense (see also Stuart 2015, ch. 2.8; 2016). Just add enough "suitable premises" and allow deductive, inductive and informal derivations, and thought experiments of all kinds can be reconstructed as arguments.

In another line of critique, it has been argued that thought experiments cannot generally be eliminated in favour of arguments since an important aspect of a thought experiment could get lost when we replace the thought experiment by an argument. Some critics of the *Elimination Thesis* contend that thought experiments are indispensable, since a non-thought-experimental argument cannot by itself account for the question of how we have to adjust our belief system in order to resolve an actually occurring contradiction. Tamar Szabó Gendler, for example, has argued against the *Elimination Thesis* by claiming that arguments simply reveal contradictions but do not tell us how to revise our given belief system such that we obtain a satisfying and non-trivial way out of the contradiction (Gendler 1998). In reply to this line of criticism, Norton assures us that many thought experiments do have the power "to reconfigure conceptual schemas." For example, the argument of Russell's paradox reveals that the "naïve" comprehension axiom has to be revised in order to avoid a contradictory set theory. Norton also contends that, compared to arguments, thought experiments do no better in revealing the culprit when a contradiction arises. The narrative presentation of a thought experiment can be misleading, and can prevent us from taking the right steps in overcoming a contradiction (see Norton 2004a, 1148).

In order to address Gendler's argument against the *Elimination Thesis*, one could again try to extend the notion of logic and allow logical systems that are able to model the phenomenon of revising and adapting belief systems in light of upcoming contradictions. These logical systems also need to incorporate a kind of priority ordering of premises that indicates the degree to which the premises are entrenched in the given belief system. As Rafal Urbaniak has shown, systems of *prioritized adaptive logics* can satisfy these requirements (see Urbaniak 2012). But it has to be recognized that a prioritized adaptive logic deviates from "normal" classical logical reasoning to a large extent. As Urbaniak's formally complex proof of Galileo's thought experiment shows, a system of prioritized adaptive logic provides an adequate formal framework to reconstruct the phenomenon of rejecting beliefs and coming to a non-trivial positive theory in reaction to a contradiction. But it seems highly implausible that we actually execute arguments of this elaborate logical form when we conduct thought experiments. Extending the scope of logic can be an effective means to surmount the observed insufficiencies of the *Reconstruction Thesis*. But if we allow, for example, systems of dynamic adaptive logic to argumentatively reconstruct thought experiments, the plausibility of the *Empirical Psychological Thesis* of the argument view decreases.

Although his challenge to the *Reconstruction Thesis* was unsuccessful, Brown did not admit defeat in the debate. Instead, he claimed that the *Reconstruction Thesis* in itself does not provide sufficient reason to support Norton's view that thought experiments are mere arguments disguised in a pictorial or narrative form: "Even if every thought experiment could be reconstructed in Norton's argument form, this would not guarantee that this is what thought experiments essentially are ... mere reconstruction is not enough. He [Norton] must also make the case that a thought experiment gives some sort of clue to the (hidden) argument ..." (Brown 2004a, 1133). In particular, Brown holds that the *Elimination Thesis* can be met for a thought experiment without this thought experiment actually being an argument. The mere fact that the outcome of a thought experiment is fully derivable within a non-thought-experimental argument does not necessarily mean that the non-thought-experimental argument adequately accounts for the essence of the thought experiment and the actual reasoning processes that leads to its result. So Brown objects that, in order to defend the argument view, Norton needs to do more than just reconstruct thought experiments by more-or-less elaborate systems of logical argumentation. In particular, the non-thought-experimental argument has to reveal the *epistemic significance* of the reconstructed thought experiment and accurately model the reasoning processes that govern the thought experiment: i.e., Brown accuses Norton of not having provided sufficient proof that a thought experiment also conforms to the *Epistemic* and *Empirical Psychological Thesis* of the argument view.

Philosophers have pointed to apparent epistemic dissimilarities between some thought experiments and their associated non-thought-experimental arguments. They contend that the reasoning processes that govern thought experiments are different to the logical reasoning processes that are operative in an argument. Furthermore, they claim that thought experiments and arguments can differ in the way we use them to acquire and justify knowledge. Proponents of the "mental model" view of thought experiments, such as Tamar Szabó Gendler, Nenad Miščević and Nancy Nersessian (see, for example, Gendler 2004; Miščević 1992; Nersessian 1992, 2007), argue that in contrast to the propositional form of argumentative reasoning, thought experimenting involves some kind of "simulative model-based reasoning" (Nersessian 1993, 296). Nersessian, for example, refers to research into narrative comprehension by Johnson-Laird and others (see Nersessian, this volume). This research has shown that we construct and manipulate mental models of the situation depicted in a story in such a way that "the reader calls upon a combination of pre-existing conceptual and real-world knowledge and employs the tacit and recursive inference mechanisms of her cognitive apparatus to integrate this with the information contained in the narrative" (Nersessian 1992, 294). This process of mental modelling enables the reader to understand the story, to grasp the relevant parts of the narrative and to draw conclusions from the depicted text. Since, according to Nersessian, thought experiments are special kinds of narratives, the construction and executing of thought experiments are subject to similar processes of mental modelling: "... the function of the narrative form of presentation of a thought experiment ... is to guide the reader in constructing a structural analog of the situation described by it and to make inferences through simulating the events and processes depicted in it" (Nersessian 1992, 297).

In the same vein, Gendler draws on data from empirical psychology in order to show that the sort of reasoning that is operative in belief-formation processes based on contemplating imaginary scenarios is cognitively and epistemically different to the sort of reasoning that is going on when we infer a conclusion from premises in an argument. She disagrees with Norton's view that the "picturesque clothing" of thought experiments can only give them "special rhetoric powers" (Norton 2004a, 1139) and does not contribute to their *epistemic* significance. In contrast, Gendler claims that there are some cases where "the imagery" is "epistemically crucial" (Gendler 2004, 1161). For Gendler, imaginary scenarios evoke "quasi-sensory intuitions" that could lead us to form new beliefs via a "quasi-observational" imagistic kind of reasoning (see, for example, Gendler 2004). In particular, Gendler points to empirical research by Roger Shepard and others which has shown that judgements about topological similarity are based on some kind of quasi-perceptual mental manipulation of images. Gendler argues that even if one could construe the process of drawing a conclusion from this mental imaging as a kind of deductive or inductive reasoning, the "quasi-observation" on which the conclusion was based cannot be conceived as a kind of inferential argumentative reasoning (Gendler 2004, 1159f.). She also refers to research by Antonio Damasio that seems to indicate that so-called "somatic markers" (certain physically encoded emotional responses to imaginary or real situations) can have an influence on our inclination to study the scenario and "place ourselves in it." Therefore, Gendler argues that "imaginative rehearsal can bring us to new beliefs that may be unavailable to us if we reason in a disinterested purely hypothetical way" (Gendler 2004, 1160).

It has to be noted that although the proponents of the "mental model" view reject the *Empirical Psychological Thesis* as well as the *Empiricist Thesis* of the argument view, they do not ally themselves with Brown's Platonic account of thought experiments. Nersessian, for example, admits that thought experimenting is a "truly creative part of scientific practice," but claims that the reasoning processes governed by a thought experiment are rooted in "non-exceptional" abilities, such as "our abilities to anticipate, visualize, and re-experience from memory" (Nersessian 1992, 292). For Gendler, the "quasi-observational" belief-forming processes that are operative in the contemplation of an imaginary scenario of a thought experiment are quite mundane empirical reasoning mechanisms that "might bring us to new beliefs about contingent features of the natural world" (Gendler 2004, 1154). But they are by no means a priori vehicles into the realm of abstract entities. In particular, they do not enable us to intuit necessary laws of nature.

Most philosophers who attack the *Epistemic Thesis* of the argument view attempt to show that, due to their specific pictorial and narrative form, thought experiments are *epistemically superior* to their corresponding non-thought-experimental arguments. As we have seen, Gendler, for example, argues that by contemplating imaginary scenarios certain intuitions are evoked that allow us to gain insights into (contingent features of) the world that might be inaccessible by "mere" argumentation. Additionally, Brown has tried to show that there are examples where we are more confident in believing the result of a thought experiment than in believing the conclusion of the corresponding non-thought-experimental argument (Brown 1992). But we have to bear in mind that, precisely because they depict imaginary scenarios in a fictional and narrative form, thought experiments can be a less reliable source of knowledge acquisition than arguments. The fictional and narrative character of thought experiments can sometimes conceal argumentative shortcomings. Fancy imaginary scenarios can appeal to our intuition in a way that leads us astray. Some thought experiments can be mere "intuition pumps," as Daniel Dennett has called them, i.e., thought experiments that "are not supposed to clothe strict arguments that prove conclusions from premises. Rather, their point is to entrain a family of imaginative reflections in the reader that ultimately yields not a formal conclusion but a dictate of 'intuition'" (Dennett 1984, 12). Some thought experiments can be very persuasive, although they do not stand up to scrutiny by argumentative reconstruction. A precise argumentative reconstruction of a thought experiment abstracts from distracting details of the imaginary scenario and can therefore better reveal possible flaws, inconsistencies or lack of clarity in the design of the thought experiment. Whereas a thought experiment can appear to be reliable and seem to justify its outcome, the associated non-thought-experimental argument can show that the thought experiment rests on erroneous reasoning. So, thought experiments can also be *epistemically inferior* to their associated non-thought-experimental arguments. To be sure, in mathematics a mere thought experiment that is not supported by a strict logical argument does not have the epistemic power to verify or falsify a mathematical claim.

In light of the above-mentioned evidence from empirical psychology which the "mental modelists" draw upon in order to show that there are differences in the reasoning processes between thought experiments and arguments, the *Empirical Psychological Thesis* does not stand up to scrutiny. Recall that the *Empirical Psychological Thesis* states that we actually execute an argument when we conduct a thought experiment. So, the thesis ascribes a kind of psychological actuality to the inferential processes that govern the argument into which a thought experiment is reconstructed. But this kind of psychological actuality is not supported by empirical research. Furthermore, we have seen that the *Epistemic Thesis* conflicts with some observed differences between thought experiments and arguments with respect to their epistemic importance and epistemic reach.

Let us finally briefly analyse the *Empiricist Thesis*. For Norton, one basis for his *Reconstruction Thesis* is empiricism. We learn from thought experiments, according to Norton, by "drawing on our experience of the world" (Norton 2004a, 1142). Thought experiments do not transcend experience since they can be reconstructed as arguments in which conclusions are logically inferred from only empirically justified premises. But Norton's *Empiricist Thesis* seems to be quite strong, since to falsify this thesis it would be enough to find at least one premise in an argument which is not justified on purely empirical grounds. Axioms and rules of logic cannot function as premises in an argument, otherwise Norton has to give up the a priori character of logic. Since Norton allows systems of deductive logic, inductive and informal logic (and, as shown above, maybe even systems of non-classical logic), there have to be reasons that justify the choice of the specific logic being used as the tool to reconstruct an argument. So, one tacit premise in an argument seems to be the assumption that a certain logic is the correct logic to reconstruct the thought experiment. It is unclear, however, whether and how this premise can be justified in a completely empirical way. Furthermore, as Boris Grozdanoff has pointed out, sometimes the available evidence does not justify the premises and conclusions of an argument. In connection with Einstein's Train thought experiment, Grozdanoff argues that the principle of the constancy of the speed of light, which figures as one premise in the argumentative reconstruction of the thought experiment, was not experimentally justified at the time the thought experiment was framed. Grozdanoff further concludes that "no experience that could have possibly confirmed PRS [the principle of relative simultaneity], the conclusion of the TTE [train thought experiment], was available at all. Since it has to be a relativistic experience that involves speeds at substantial fractions of the speed of light and experientially, and even laboratory-experientially, this was not the case" (Grozdanoff 2007, 79). Of course, Norton could reply that in Einstein's day the train thought experiment was not successful, since its associated argument was not adequately supported by evidence. But that suggests that many thought experiments which we find intuitively successful have to be rejected. Additionally, the *Empiricist Thesis* restricts the argument view to thought experiments in the *empirical sciences*. As we have seen, the debate between Norton and Brown also includes examples of thought experiments in *mathematics* where empiricism is a highly contestable position. Furthermore, although Norton and Brown have not explicitly extended their views to *philosophical* thought experiments, it would be desirable if their views could so generalize. So, the *Empiricist Thesis* unnecessarily restricts the argument view's scope of application.

Let us take stock. I have argued that Norton's argument view can be divided into at least five sub-claims which do not seem to be equally well supported. Arguing against the *Identity Thesis* begs the question against Norton. The *Reconstruction Thesis*, with the *Reliability Thesis* and the *Elimination Thesis* as its parts, can be defended against Brown's Platonic account of thought experiments. But it has to be noted that with its very broad construal of the notion of logic, the *Reconstruction Thesis* runs the risk of amounting to an almost trivially true thesis. We have seen that neither the *Epistemic Thesis* nor the *Empirical Psychological Thesis* stands up to scrutiny. The *Empiricist Thesis* is much too strong. It also confines the scope of the argument view in an unnecessary way and excludes all those thought experiments (in particular, from mathematics and philosophy) whose premises are not empirically justified.

It has finally to be noted that denying the *Epistemic*, *Empirical Psychological* and the *Empiricist* theses does not commit us to a Platonic view of thought experiments. Brown's Platonism and his commitment to a faculty of non-inferential and non-experiential perception evoked by a certain kind of thought experiment have their own philosophical problems. Furthermore, even if we have to reject those theses, it still remains true that we can and should reconstruct thought experiments into arguments. A precise argumentative reconstruction of a thought experiment can reveal merits and shortcomings of a thought experiment. Thought experiments can only function as a driving force in the development of scientific inquiry if they are carefully reconstructed as arguments.

References

Bishop, M. A. (1999) "Why thought experiments are not arguments," *Philosophy of Science* 66: 534–541.
Brendel, E. (2004) "Intuition pumps and the proper use of thought experiments," *Dialectica* 58: 89–108.
Brown, J. R. (1991) *The Laboratory of the Mind. Thought Experiments in the Natural Science*, London: Routledge.
Brown, J. R. (1992) "Why empiricism won't work," *Proceedings of the Biennial Meeting of the Philosophy of Science Association* 2: 271–279.
Brown, J. R. (2004a) "Peeking into Plato's heaven," *Philosophy of Science* 71: 1126–1138.
Brown, J. R. (2004b) "Why thought experiments transcend empiricism," in *Contemporary Debates in Philosophy of Science*, edited by C. Hitchcock, Malden: Blackwell.
Dennett, D. C. (1984) *Elbow Room*, Oxford: Oxford University Press.
Galilei, G. (1954 [1638]) *Dialogues Concerning Two New Sciences*, translated by H. Crew and A. de Salvio, New York: Dover.
Gendler, T. S. (1998) "Galileo and the indispensability of scientific thought experiments," *British Journal for the Philosophy of Science* 49: 397–424.
Gendler, T. S. (2000) *Thought Experiment: On the Powers and Limits of Imaginary Cases*, New York: Routledge.
Gendler, T. S. (2004) "Thought experiments rethought–and reperceived," *Philosophy of Science* 71: 1152–1163.
Gettier, E. L. (1963) "Is justified true belief knowledge?" *Analysis* 23: 121–123.
Grozdanoff, B. (2007) "Reconstruction, justification and incompatibility in Norton's account of thought experiments," *Croatian Journal of Philosophy* 19: 69–79.
Häggqvist, S. (2009) "A model for thought experiments," *Canadian Journal of Philosophy* 39: 55–76.
McAllister, J. W. (2004) "Thought experiments and the belief in phenomena," *Philosophy of Science* 71: 1164–1175.
Miščević, N. (1992) "Mental models and thought experiments," *International Studies in the Philosophy of Science* 6: 215–226.
Nersessian, N. J. (1992) "In the theoretician's laboratory: Thought experimenting as mental modeling," *Proceedings of the Philosophy of Science Association* 2: 291–301.
Nersessian, N. J. (2007) "Thought experiments as mental modelling: Empiricism without logic," *Croatian Journal of Philosophy* 7: 125–161.
Norton, J. D. (1996) "Are thought experiments just what you thought?" *Canadian Journal of Philosophy* 26: 333–366.
Norton, J. D. (2004a) "On thought experiments: Is there more to the argument?" *Philosophy of Science* 71: 1139–1151.
Norton, J. D. (2004b) "Why thought experiments do not transcend empiricism," in *Contemporary Debates in Philosophy of Science*, edited by C. Hitchcock, Malden: Blackwell.
Schrenk, M. (2004) "Galileo versus Aristotle on free falling bodies," *Logical Analysis and History of Philosophy* 7: 81–89.
Sorensen, R. A. (1992) *Thought Experiments*, Oxford: Oxford University Press.
Stuart, M. T. (2015) *Thought Experiments in Science*, PhD thesis, University of Toronto, Canada.
Stuart, M. T. (2016) "Norton and the logic of thought experiments," *Axiomathes* 26: 451–466.
Urbaniak, R. (2012) "'Platonic' thought experiments: How on Earth?" *Synthese* 187: 731–752.
Williamson, T. (2007) *The Philosophy of Philosophy*, Malden: Blackwell.

16
PLATONISM AND THE A PRIORI IN THOUGHT EXPERIMENTS

Thomas Grundmann

This chapter presents and evaluates the Platonic account of thought experiments that is currently most prominently advocated by James Robert Brown. The introductory section will locate Brown's position within a general taxonomy of thought experiments. The second section will give an outline of Brown's own view and elucidate the main concepts involved in it. In the third section, Brown's two main arguments for epistemological Platonism will be critically discussed. The fourth section is devoted to Brown's Platonic account of the laws of nature. Major problems and possible advancements will be explored. The fifth section discusses general objections to the Platonic epistemology. Finally, the sixth section will consider the viability of Platonism if it is restricted to *philosophical* thought experiments.

1 Introduction

A thought experiment is an experiment of a very special kind. Just by considering a particular hypothetical case in our mind we come to believe that a certain target category applies (or does not apply) to the case, or that something specific would happen if the case became reality. Apart from purely heuristic uses, thought experiments are widely regarded as potential sources of knowledge. This is a view that is shared by many philosophers and scientists. However, there is much disagreement about how thought experiments manage to generate knowledge and when they do. On the one hand, there is the empiricist view that thought experiments are sources of *empirical* knowledge. Ernst Mach famously claimed that our knowledge about what would happen if certain conditions obtained is based on our empirically informed instinct (Mach 1933, 27–8). More recently, Timothy Williamson put forward the similar view that our knowledge of counterfactuals is based on imagination that is strongly shaped by experience (Williamson 2007; 2016). Moreover, John Norton has claimed that thought experiments are nothing but disguised arguments with empirical premises (Norton 1996). On the other hand, there is the rationalist view.

Its adherents believe that thought experiments can generate *a priori* knowledge. But again, there is much disagreement about the sources of this a priori knowledge. We can distinguish between *conceptualist, transcendental* and *Platonic* views here. According to conceptualism, thought experiments generate knowledge of analytic truths based on the thinker's conceptual competence (Ludwig 2007). According to transcendentalism, thought experiments reveal the cognitive boundaries of worlds as creatures like us can experience them (Strawson 1966, 15). According to Platonism, thought experiments facilitate an intellectual perception (often called "rational intuition") of an abstract reality that exists outside of space and time (Brown 1991; BonJour 1998).[1] There is the further question of whether thought experiments (of a particular type) have the same epistemological status in all disciplines. Someone who answers this question in the negative might, e.g., believe that when we use philosophical thought experiments to investigate the nature of some philosophical category, this will provide us with a priori knowledge. At the same time, she might also believe that when we use physical thought experiments in order to find out how material things would behave under certain counterfactual conditions, we can at most acquire empirical knowledge. I will call someone who gives a separate treatment to the epistemology of thought experiments within different disciplines a *separationist*.[2] The proponent of the opposing view will be called *unificationist*.[3]

Within this framework, James Robert Brown holds a remarkably radical position.[4] Brown claims that there are thought experiments of a special type ("Platonic thought experiments") that provide us with an intellectual perception of abstract reality. So, he is a *Platonist*. But at the same time he is also committed to *unificationism*. Brown believes that Platonic thought experiments are at work in philosophy, mathematics, and physics (Brown and Fehige 2014). Accordingly, we are able to grasp some of the laws of nature by an act of rational intuition that is independent of sensory experience.[5]

2 Brown's a priori Platonism

Within his general classification of thought experiments (Brown 1991, 33), Brown distinguishes between destructive and constructive thought experiments. A *destructive thought experiment* is directed against an existing theory by either showing that the theory is internally inconsistent or by demonstrating that the theory is in tension with well-supported other beliefs (ibid., 36). Among the constructive thought experiments I will just focus on the *direct* ones: They justify a new theory. The special case of *Platonic thought experiments* belongs simultaneously to the category of destructive and direct thought experiments. It is this latter kind of thought experiment that, according to Brown, generates a priori knowledge of abstract entities (ibid., 77).[6]

Brown's classification can be illustrated by some paradigm cases. The famous Gettier case in epistemology is a paradigm of a destructive thought experiment. According to the standard definition of knowledge, knowledge is justified true belief. The Gettier case defeats this definition by presenting a possible case of justified true belief that is not a case of knowledge. Here is one such case (taken from Malmgren 2011, 272): *Smith believes that Jones owns a Ford, on the basis of seeing Jones drive a Ford to work and remembering that Jones always drove a Ford in the past. From this and the fact that Jones works in Smith's office, Smith infers that someone in his office owns a Ford. In fact, someone in Smith's office does own a*

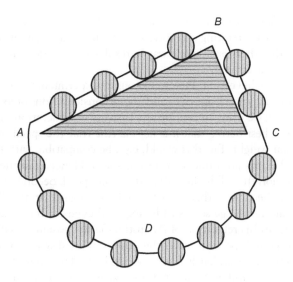

Figure 16.1

Ford – but it is not Jones, it is Brown. Jones sold his car and now drives a rented car. Confronted with this hypothetical case, people tend to judge that Smith justifiedly and truly believes but does not know that someone in his office owns a Ford. This intuitive judgment defeats the standard definition of knowledge without suggesting a correct definition of knowledge in its place. So, it is an instance of a destructive thought experiment that has no constructive power.

Brown's paradigm case of a direct thought experiment is Stevin's case of the inclined plane (cf. Figure 16.1). *Suppose that a chain of weights is draped over a prism-like pair of inclined planes. The chain begins at A and ends at C. Would the chain rest or would it move either towards A or towards B?* Stevin claims that the chain would remain in a static equilibrium. For imagine we would close the loop by adding further weights to the chain. The resulting closed chain would clearly remain at rest. But since closing the chain by adding further weights in this way does not add unbalanced forces, we realize that the chain reaching from A to C would not move, either.

Stevin's case of the inclined planes is, according to Brown's classification, a direct thought experiment since it establishes a new theory, namely that weights over inclined planes remain in equilibrium, where there was no theory before.

Brown's paradigm case of a Platonic thought experiment is Galileo's thought experiment about falling bodies (Brown 1991, 1–2, 43). It was meant both to refute Aristotle's view that the speed of falling bodies is proportional to their weight and at the same time to establish Galileo's new theory that all bodies fall at the same speed. In his *Discorsi* Galileo introduces his thought experiment in roughly the following way: *Suppose that we attach a heavy cannon ball to a light musket ball by using a rope and then release them together. When we apply the Aristotelian theory to this case we can derive a contradiction. On the one hand, the combined system will move with a slower speed than the isolated cannon ball since the slower moving musket ball slows down the cannon ball. On the other hand, the combined system is heavier than the isolated cannon ball, so it should fall faster than it. Hence, on the Aristotelian view, we can conclude that the combined system will move slower and faster than the cannon ball.* However, Galileo does not rest with refuting Aristotle's view. He thinks that, at this point, we can rationally perceive that there is only one way to resolve the paradox, namely by suggesting that all bodies fall at the same speed.

Why does Brown believe that Platonic thought experiments like Galileo's involve some kind of substantial knowledge over and above considerations of logical consistency? First, if the only thing we bring to bear on the case are considerations about logical consistency, we could at best derive that *it is not the case* that the speed of falling bodies is proportional to their weight. But this would, e.g., be compatible with the view that the color of falling bodies has an influence on their speed. Hence, a further step is required to reach the conclusion that all bodies fall at the same speed. Second, it seems intuitively implausible that Galileo's new theory of free fall is a logical truth (Brown 1991, 78). Anyway, substantial knowledge seems to be required even for the *reductio* of Aristotle's theory. Here is why: in his refutation of Aristotle, Galileo assumes that if we attach two bodies of different natural speed to each other, the combined system will move at a speed that is slower than the independently faster moving body. This might be a plausible claim. But it certainly does not follow from Aristotle's view that the speed of falling bodies is proportional to their weight. Why should not the Aristotelian claim that the combined system of the two balls falls faster than any of its two component bodies? Moreover, that bodies with a different natural speed influence each other's speed is only plausible as long as they are connected with a flexible rope. But then it is unclear whether we are permitted to treat the combined system as a body of its own when we apply the Aristotelian theory to the case. Put it in a nutshell: the reductio of Aristotle's theory depends on substantial background knowledge. It remains to be seen whether this knowledge is empirical or a priori.

What is characteristic of a priori knowledge? According to the currently prevailing view that has its roots in Kant, a priori knowledge is only negatively defined, i.e., what is known *a priori* is known independently of sense experience (cf., e.g., Kant 1965, B2; Chisholm 1966, 73; Casullo 2003, 147). This negative definition rules out sense experience from the epistemically relevant entitling or warranting factors. It does not, however, exclude sense experience from the causal or enabling conditions of knowledge. The distinction between entitling and enabling conditions (Burge 1993) helps to explain how we can, e.g., know a priori that red is a color. In order to acquire the empirical concepts RED and COLOR we clearly have to rely on sense experience. But this merely enables our concept acquisition. What warrants our belief that red is a color is only our competence with the concepts that are involved in this belief. There is also a broad consensus among current epistemologists that being known independently of sense experience does require neither infallibility nor indefeasibility by empirical evidence. In paradoxes, for example, typically all the assumptions seem to be a priori justified although not all of them can be true; or, to give an example of empirical defeasibility, the conclusion of someone's non-experiential mental calculation may be defeated by the observation of a conflicting expert judgment (Bealer 1998; BonJour 1998; Casullo 2003). Moreover, the negative definition of a priori knowledge allows for different positive sources of a priori knowledge, such as conceptual knowledge, innate or transcendental knowledge, or knowledge from Platonist rational intuition (Grundmann 2015). Brown subscribes to all the above-mentioned features of a priori knowledge: to the negative definition (1991, 77), to the moderate fallibilist account of the a priori (1991, 92), and to a pluralistic rationalism that allows for different sources of a priori knowledge (1991, 86–7).

What does it mean that the knowledge-entitling factors are independent of sense experience? The evidentialist suggests that this condition is satisfied if the relevant knowledge is not based on *empirical evidence* (Audi 2003, 101; Jenkins 2008, 436). Brown seems to be committed to this view (1991, 77). But real-life cases of intuitively empirical knowledge suggest that the evidentialist condition is not sufficient. Suppose you are on a hiking trip in the mountains and you want to cross a small river by jumping to the other side. In order to find out whether you would succeed in doing so you may use your imaginative skills to develop the consequences of your supposed jumping in the perceived situation. If your imaginative skills are reliable, imagination will provide you with empirical knowledge of what would happen if you jumped. You may also use these skills "offline," without actually perceiving anything at all. In this case you start by imagining a certain hypothetical situation and then continue with imagining what would happen in that situation. Again, this procedure will result in empirical knowledge if your imagination works properly. When your imagination operates "offline" as in this case, the judgment about what would happen is not based on any evidence that is accessible from the agent's perspective. Nevertheless, the knowledge acquired in this way seems to be *empirical* rather than a priori since it is based on an empirically shaped faculty of imagination. This suggests that knowledge that is not based on empirical evidence need not be a priori. It is empirical if it is based on an empirically acquired skill (cf. Williamson 2013[7] and forthcoming).[8]

Let us now turn to Platonism, which is primarily an ontological view and only derivatively the epistemological view that there is a special, Platonic kind of perceptual access to entities in the Platonic realm. Within ontology we can distinguish between nominalism, Aristotelianism, and Platonism (cf. Armstrong 1989). According to nominalism there are only concrete, particular things in space and time. Aristotelianism claims that in addition to concrete particulars there are also universals, each of which is identical through all its particular instances. Although Aristotelianism accepts two different kinds of entities (i.e., particulars and universals) it ties the existence of universals to their instantiation in concrete particulars. In contrast, Platonism makes room for the existence of universals and other entities outside of space and time. This abstract domain of things contains mathematical entities, like numbers or sets, uninstantiated properties, and all kinds of necessary facts. Brown holds the unorthodox view that the laws of nature also belong to this domain of abstract Platonic entities.

Brown's Platonist account of the laws of nature contrasts radically with the standard Humean view. The latter assumes that laws of nature are nothing but generalized conditionals of the form $\forall x\ (Fx \rightarrow Gx)$. If laws of nature are reducible to generalizations, it should be obvious that our knowledge of them must be empirical since it is based on inductive generalizations from the observed co-instantiation in particular cases. The Humean view gives rise to a number of standard problems. Simple versions lack, e.g., the resources to distinguish between genuine laws and accidental generalizations like "All the things in my pocket are coins." Moreover, it cannot explain why the observed regularity holds. But it also cannot account for the fact that laws support counterfactual conditionals. In the 1970s, Dretske, Tooley, and Armstrong independently put forward an alternative view of the laws of nature (DTA, for short). According to DTA, laws are relations between first-order universals. These relations are necessitating second-order universals. The core idea is expressed by the following formula, where the "N" stands for the necessitation relation, and F and G stand for first-order universals: N(F,G). It is, however, crucial for this view that the necessitating relation is itself only contingently instantiated. So, its modal force is not absolute but restricted to a subset of all possible worlds. For this reason there are possible worlds in which the laws of nature differ from the actual world. Whereas the more naturalistically oriented philosophers Armstrong and Dretske reject Platonism, Tooley explicitly endorses the Platonic idea that laws exist even if they do not have any actual instances (Tooley 1977, 671, 686). Brown adopts Tooley's version of DTA. The DTA account seems to solve the main problems of the Humean account straightforwardly (Psillos 2002, ch. 6). First, the distinction between laws and merely accidental generalizations corresponds to the distinction between N(F, G) and the mere generalization $\forall x\ (Fx \rightarrow Gx)$. Second, on DTA laws seem to explain why a particular regularity in the concrete world obtains. This is because N(F, G) implies $\forall x\ (Fx \rightarrow Gx)$. Finally, since N(F, G) is a modal truth it can support counterfactuals.

3 Brown's arguments for his epistemological Platonism about physical thought experiments

Brown offers two arguments in support of his epistemological Platonism, i.e., his view that when we perform the relevant physical thought experiments, we gain a priori knowledge of certain laws of nature by rationally perceiving abstract reality. His *first argument* is a deficiency argument, according to which the knowledge we gain from the thought experiment cannot be explained empirically.[9] As Brown puts it:

> My reasons for claiming [Galileo's] thought experiment provides a priori knowledge are rather simple and straightforward. For one thing ... there are no new empirical data being used when we move from Aristotle's to Galileo's theory of free fall. It's not a logical truth, either.
>
> (Brown 2004, 1129)

This argument can be reconstructed as follows (cf. Clatterbuck 2013, 311[10]):

(1) We gain knowledge from Galileo's thought experiment.
(2) We are provided with no new empirical input in the process of the thought experiment.
(3) If knowledge is acquired independently of new empirical input, then it is a priori.
(4) Thus, the knowledge acquired through Galileo's thought experiment is a priori. (1, 2, 3)
(5) The conclusion of Galileo's thought experiment is not logically true.
(6) Thus, the knowledge acquired through Galileo's thought experiment is non-logical. (5)
(7) The thought experiment gives us non-logical a priori knowledge of physical facts. (4, 6)

Let us address three possible objections to this argument. First of all, premise (3) is doubtful. New *empirical* knowledge might be gained even if there is no new empirical *input*. This might simply be due to the fact that new conclusions are derived from old empirical data. This is exactly what Norton (1996) claims in his reconstruction of physical thought experiments. In Galileo's thought experiment of the falling bodies, one might use the empirical background premise that the speed that results from attaching two bodies that move at a different speed to each other will be intermediate. In Stevin's thought experiment, the relevant empirical background premise might be that there is no perpetual motion.

In reply to this objection, the Platonist has to admit that (3) does not survive scrutiny and has to be substantially revised. She must explicitly rule out that the knowledge newly gained from the thought experiment depends, at least in part, on old empirical background knowledge of the indicated kind. But this can be done. It is hard to believe that whoever gains the knowledge that all bodies fall at the same speed relies on knowledge about how in general the speed of combined bodies will aggregate. The same applies to Stevin's thought experiment. To gain knowledge that the chain will remain at rest one need not rely on the general knowledge that perpetual motion does not exist.

Let us consider a second objection to premise (3). Knowledge can be gained independently of empirical input, or evidence, if it is based on belief-forming skills or capacities that have been informed and shaped by sense experience. In Section 2 it has already been argued that not being based on empirical evidence (or input) is not sufficient for a priori knowledge. It will suffice if the underlying processes are informed by sense experience. As mentioned above, Williamson has made the case that imagination is a cognitive process of this kind (Williamson 2016). It is shaped by (generally reliable) experience, but generates counterfactual judgments that are not simply inferred from empirical premises. In imagination, we often consider a hypothetical case and then develop substantial consequences about what would happen under these conditions. But developing the consequences in imagination is not the same as deriving a conclusion from premises. So this seems to be a theoretical option that conflicts with premise (3). Moreover, Williamson's model of imagination might offer a good explanation of what really goes on in the thought experiments at hand. When we consider Galileo's case of the falling balls we recognize *through imagination* that if the balls were to move at a different speed, then the slower moving ball would slow down the faster moving one. And when we consider Stevin's case, we recognize *through imagination* that the closed chain would remain at rest. But if it is true that the reliability of imagination in these cases depends on reliable sense experience, the resulting knowledge is empirical rather than a priori.

There is also this third objection: if the argument were successful, it would at most establish that one gains non-logical a priori knowledge from thought experiments. This rules out logical sources of knowledge. But it is not sufficient to demonstrate that Platonic perception is the relevant source at work. The argument's conclusion is compatible with other non-logical sources as well, e.g., an innate cognitive module for "folk physics" (Gendler 2000).

Brown's second argument for Epistemological Platonism about physical thought experiments is an argument from parity. It starts with the premise that Platonism in mathematics is uncontroversial. According to it, mathematical entities like numbers or sets are abstract entities that are accessible through rational intuition. If one adds the premise that laws of nature are abstract entities as well, as it is claimed by DTA, then it seems to follow that we can use the same Platonist method as in mathematics to get access to the laws of nature. In Brown's words:

> According to mathematical Platonism we can perceive the abstract entities in mathematics ... So, it's possible to perceive abstract entities ... But laws are abstract entities, so they could be perceivable, too.
>
> (Brown 2004, 1131)

A charitable interpretation would reconstruct Brown's argument as an inductive rather than a – obviously fallacious[11] – deductive inference, such that the truth of its premises makes the truth of its conclusion highly likely. Brown's following remark suggests this reading:

> Suppose Gödel is right: we can 'see' some mathematical objects (which are abstract entities). And suppose the Armstrong-Dretske-Tooley account of laws of nature is also right; laws are relations among universals (which are abstract entities). Wouldn't it be a surprise and indeed something of a mystery if we couldn't 'see' laws of nature, as well?
>
> (Brown 1991, 86)

We can thus reconstruct Brown's argument as follows:

(1) There are abstract entities that can be rationally perceived by us.
(2) Laws are abstract entities.
(3) Therefore, it is highly likely that we can rationally perceive laws.

But even on the inductive interpretation the inference remains dubious. Inductive generalizations rely on relevant similarities between its basis and the domain of generalization. This similarity seems to be absent in the present case. Although mathematical entities and, at least according to DTA, laws of nature are both abstract entities, there are crucial differences between them: (a) Whereas mathematical facts are necessary in the absolute sense, laws of nature hold only contingently. (b) Whereas laws of nature tell us what will happen if some antecedent condition becomes reality, mathematical equations describe an unchanging reality. If we take these differences into account, we cannot infer that laws of nature are accessible in the same way as mathematical truths.

4 Objections to Brown's Platonism about laws of nature

As the considerations above suggest, Brown's arguments for a Platonic understanding of physical thought experiments are inconclusive. Moreover, his account of laws of nature is problematic in itself and in tension with his Platonist epistemology, as the following three objections suggest.

(1) On DTA, laws are *contingent* relations among universals. So, whether a particular statement of a law is true depends on whether the claimed relation holds in the relevant modal neighborhood of the *actual* world. Knowing this, however, requires knowing what the actual world is like. But this knowledge cannot be gained on the basis of perceiving abstract reality alone. In addition, we need to rely on our *empirical* knowledge of the actual world. Hence, grasping the laws of nature cannot be a purely a priori matter.

Notice that this objection is significantly different from a general objection to a priori knowledge of contingent truths.[12] In the face of Kripke's seminal insight (Kripke 1980, 54–6), the existence of a priori knowledge of contingent truths seems no longer deniable in general. By using sentences like "The meter stick is one meter long" (when it is introduced as the standard), "I am here," or "Heat is the dominant source of heat sensations" we express propositions that are only contingently true. The standard meter could have been longer or shorter than it actually is; I could have been somewhere else; heat does not cause heat sensations in worlds without living creatures. Nevertheless, in all worlds in which I actually use one of the above sentences (with the same linguistic meaning as in our actual world) it turns out to be true. So, although the expressed propositions are false in at least some counterfactual worlds, the corresponding sentences are true in any world in which they are uttered. There is a semantic explanation of this striking fact. In the above examples, the attributed property is part of those properties that fix the reference of the sentence's subject term in the utterance world (whichever it is). For this reason a competent speaker can know independently of any empirical knowledge about the utterance world that the expressed propositions are true *in this world*. But at the same time they are not true in every counterfactually possible world. For at least two reasons, such a Kripkean explanation is not available to the Platonist about contingent laws of nature. First, the Platonist explicitly commits himself to the view that the source of her knowledge is intellectual perception rather than semantic competence. Second, it is simply false that claims about the actual laws of nature are true in every possible world in which the speaker asserts them. We can easily imagine a world in which we assert that the laws of quantum physics obtain although they are false. According to DTA this imagined world should correspond to a real possibility. Unless we have at least some empirical knowledge about the world we live in, we cannot know any law of nature that holds in this world. So, even if one has to admit that a priori knowledge of contingent truths is possible in principle, one can still make the case that a priori knowledge of laws of nature is impossible as long as those laws do not hold across all possible worlds.[13]

(2) DTA is also deeply problematic in itself. The following two objections are especially prominent in the literature. First, according to DTA the same property can play different causal roles in different worlds since lawful relations among properties hold only contingently. In consequence, the essence of a property cannot be captured by its causal role. So, the critics argue, it must be constituted by some primitive quiddity of the property that is not essentially related to the property's behavior. Many metaphysicians find this inexplicability of the nature of properties deeply mysterious (Mumford 2006, ch. 6). Second, one of the apparent advantages of DTA over the Humean account of laws is that it seems to explain observable regularities. The explanation is given by an inference from the law to the regularity: $N(F, G) \rightarrow \forall x\ (Fx \rightarrow Gx)$. van Fraassen most prominently objected that it is far from obvious why this inference should be valid. If we understand laws as irreducible relations among universals in the abstract realm, why should this imply that those properties are always co-instantiated in the concrete actual world (van Fraassen 1989)? Although there have been many attempts to give an answer to this problem, there is no consensus that the proponents of DTA have come up with a viable solution.

The proponent of Platonism might think that the main source of the current problems is the DTA account of laws rather than Platonism itself.[14] Indeed, what causes the trouble is the fact that, according to DTA, laws of nature remain – to a certain extent – contingent.

And it is this specific contingency that is, as we have learnt above, incompatible with a priori knowledge and the causal individuation of properties. In contrast, Platonism is only committed to the claim that laws are made true by abstract reality. This is clearly compatible with the view that laws of nature are necessary in the unrestricted, absolute sense which rules out any kind of contingency. Currently, some philosophers, the so-called *necessitarians*, claim that laws are absolutely necessary relations among properties (Ellis 2001; Bird 2005).[15] Admittedly, necessitarianism comes typically in a package with Empiricism and Naturalism, and not with Platonism. Ellis, e.g., believes that the necessary modal relations among properties together with the laws of nature are firmly rooted in the actual world we live in. So, he does not locate the necessary laws of nature in any abstract reality that is accessible only through rational perception. However, a Platonist version of necessitarianism does not seem to be an incoherent view, although I do not know of anyone who actually endorses it. If the Platonist adopts this approach he or she can avoid the preceding objections. But he or she will face a new one. Humeans usually argue for the contingency of laws by relying on the observation that conflicting laws are conceivable. If we can conceive of laws that conflict with our actual ones and if, furthermore, conceivability is a way of gaining knowledge of metaphysical possibilities, laws cannot be necessary in the absolute sense (Sidelle 2002). For example, we can conceive of light traveling twice as fast as it actually does, although this is incompatible with the theory of relativity. Now of course, a Platonic rationalist might simply dispute that conceivability is a reliable guide to possibility. For, according to him or her, rational insight into modal facts primarily relies on rational perception rather than conceivability considerations. In any case, the Platonic rationalist has to pay a considerable epistemological price for giving up conceivability as a reliable indicator of possibility altogether.

(3) Finally, Brown does not address the question why, if the laws of nature are accessible to rational intuition, we have so little a priori knowledge of the fundamental laws of nature. Even if he were right about Platonic thought experiments in physics, they seem to be the rare exceptions.[16] The bulk of the work of physicists is based on real-life experiments. This is strongly disanalogous to mathematics where, if mathematical Platonism is correct, all the axioms are known by rational perception.

The above arguments suggest two things: First, the prospects of Brown's Platonist explanation of physical thought experiments are limited. Second, there might be a better explanation that relies on empirically informed imagination.

5 General objections to Platonist epistemology

Even if one accepts the above criticism, one might still feel attracted to the view that Platonism is the correct view of *philosophical* thought experiments. Admittedly, it is hard to understand how we should have a priori access to *contingent* relations between properties. Philosophy, however, is primarily interested in the essence of properties like, e.g., knowledge, truth, free will, or justice. Essential relations among properties hold in all possible worlds. In this respect, philosophical properties seem to be better candidates for rational perception than the laws of nature. Before turning to Platonism about philosophical thought experiments, we must deal with the question whether there are any fatal objections to Platonist epistemology in general.[17] Here I will consider three objections:

(1) A notorious objection to Platonist epistemology is based on the worry that rational perception of an abstract reality is a completely mysterious process whose function is not even rudimentarily understood. Nobody has a good theory about how it is possible that we can have cognitive access to a domain of things that are outside of space and time. Plato himself suggested that the immortal soul has prenatal cognitive access to this domain that can later be remembered by the embodied soul. But apart from being deeply implausible for other reasons, this narrative does not provide a real explanation because it does not tell us how prenatal contact itself was possible in the first place. Plato's account only postpones the original problem.

Brown's reply to this objection is twofold (1991, 65–6). First, he claims that contrary to appearances, more mundane cognitive processes such as perception are not fully understood, either. Physics, cognitive science and neurobiology tell us a detailed story about how light waves are reflected by the perceptual object, how they stimulate the retina, how this stimulation is transformed into neural activity, and how this activity finally is transmitted within the brain. However, the last step from neural activity to conscious experience or perceptual beliefs still remains a mystery unless the problem of mind-brain interaction has been solved. Although this is true, the mystery of rational insight into abstract reality is, in contrast to what Brown suggests, not fully analogous to the mystery of perception. Within Platonist epistemology there is the mystery of the mind-brain interaction, but there is a second mystery about the interaction of abstract reality with the physical world of the body and the brain (compare Häggqvist 2007, 57). More important is Brown's second reply, according to which gaining knowledge in a certain way does not require that one has a sufficient understanding of one's respective way of knowing. Even in ancient times when people had queer and radically mistaken views about perception they were able to gain perceptual knowledge. Today, we are still lacking a good explanation of how introspection works. Nevertheless, introspective knowledge of, e.g., my current headache is among the paradigm cases of knowledge.

(2) The second objection to Platonist epistemology is related to the causal conception of knowledge. Accordingly, S knows that p if and only if S has the true belief that p and this belief is caused by its truthmaker (Goldman 1992). Paradigm cases of knowledge, such as perception, memory or introspection, seem to satisfy the causal requirement. But for a number of reasons it seems impossible that the domain of abstract reality has any causal influence on the concrete natural world to which our beliefs about abstract reality belong. First, both domains are fundamentally different from each other in such a way that we cannot imagine how this kind of causal interaction might work. Second, the causal closure of the natural world seems to rule out any external influence (Benacerraf 1973). Third, causal relations involve some kind of counterfactual dependency. Usually, this is expressed by the following counterfactual conditional: if the cause had not occurred, the effect would not have occurred either. Now, consider the metaphysically modal facts that constitute abstract reality. Their modal status seems to be necessary itself. So, what is metaphysically necessary is necessarily necessary and what is metaphysically possible is necessarily possible. Since these modal facts could not have been different from what they actually are, the antecedent of

the relevant counterfactual conditionals can never be true. Thus, all causal counterfactual conditionals are vacuously true when applied to the relation between abstract reality and concrete mental states or events. But vacuously true counterfactual conditionals cannot express any causal relations. So, abstract reality cannot have any causal influence on the natural world. This suggests the following argument:

(1) Knowledge requires that a known fact is causally responsible for one's belief about it.
(2) Abstract reality cannot have any causal influence on one's beliefs.
(3) Thus, abstract reality cannot be known.

As recent debates in current epistemology have shown, the prospects of the causal theory of knowledge are dim. That a causal relation to the believed fact is not necessary for knowledge is suggested by many counterexamples, such as scientific predictions that constitute knowledge about future facts. So, the argument from the causal conception of knowledge fails.

(3) In the vicinity of the argument from the causal conception of knowledge, there is a third objection to Platonist epistemology (cf., e.g., Field 1989, 26; BonJour 1998, 157; Casullo 2003, 144–5; Grundmann 2007). It starts with the assumption that knowledge requires an objectively reliable truth-connection between our beliefs and their truthmakers. This assumption is suggested by the conceptual analysis of knowledge. It is further assumed that the required truth-connection cannot be a bare fact but must be grounded either in a reductive relation between truthmakers and the relevant known beliefs or in a causal relation between them. Why should that be so? Imagine that beliefs about a particular domain of mind-independent facts are not typically caused by these facts. Then it seems easily possible that these facts could have been different (or that these facts change) without our beliefs being sensitive to this difference (or change). And this undermines the reliable truth-connection between facts and beliefs. If we now add the further assumption that abstract reality is neither reducible to the concrete natural world nor causally connected to it, we can conclude that knowledge of abstract reality is impossible.

Although this objection looks compelling at first glance, it relies on an assumption that is only plausible for knowledge of contingent facts, yet not for knowledge of modally robust facts, such as knowledge of abstract reality. As long as we just consider contingent truthmakers, it seems undeniable that without a reductive or causal relation between truthmakers and the relevant beliefs a reliable connection between them is impossible. Unless there is such a relation it can in fact happen that one relatum changes without the other. The reliable coordination of both must be metaphysically grounded, it seems. But now consider our beliefs about abstract reality. If these beliefs happen to be actually true, and if they are generated in a way that is modally robust, then it simply cannot happen that they are false in nearby worlds. Why so? Because abstract reality is itself constituted in a modally robust way. Abstract facts do not vary from world to world. Since there is this deep modal difference between the concrete and the abstract world, a metaphysical grounding of reliable truth-connection is only needed for our beliefs about contingent facts, yet not for our beliefs about abstract reality – or so one might argue (for a more detailed version of this reply, cf. Pust 2004; Grundmann 2007).

The above discussion of general objections to Epistemological Platonism suggests that none of them is actually fatal. Epistemological Platonism, therefore, is an option that cannot be dismissed so easily. Let us thus explore whether Platonism provides a fruitful account of the analysis of philosophical thought experiments.

6 The Platonic view of philosophical thought experiments

Philosophers try to give an account of the nature or essence of core philosophical categories. They want to answer Socratic questions such as, e.g., what knowledge, truth, meaning, freedom of the will, or justice really are. So, their primary goal is knowledge of essences rather than the counterfactual behavior of things. In order to test received views about a category's essence philosophers typically ask themselves whether a considered hypothetical case would be an instance of the target category. This is the philosophers' paradigmatic use of thought experiments. Philosophical thought experiments such as the above-mentioned Gettier case have two striking features. First, they seem to provide a priori knowledge. Just by considering the given case description we know that Smith has a justified true belief but does not know that someone in his office owns a Ford. In order to gain this knowledge we need not rely on any past experiences of the actual world. Further empirical knowledge over and above the case description is simply irrelevant to our ability for determining that Smith has a justified true belief but does not know (Ichikawa and Jarvis 2009; Malmgren 2011; Grundmann and Horvath 2014). Second, philosophical thought experiments are not committed to the actual existence of instances of the target category. It might turn out that, on the resulting account of knowledge (or free will), there simply is no knowledge (or free will) in the actual world. These observations are very friendly to Platonism with respect to philosophical thought experiments. It may thus seem quite natural to hold that philosophical thought experiments provide us with an intellectual perception of abstract reality.

Conceptualism, however, gives a much more parsimonious explanation of philosophical thought experiments. Concepts do not only have conditions for their correct application, they are also plausibly associated with application dispositions of those who possess them. With respect to a particular class of concepts, the so-called semantically transparent concepts,[18] application conditions and application dispositions match each other across possible worlds, at least under ideal circumstances. If this story is basically correct for key philosophical concepts, we can use our application dispositions to determine the extension of a concept across possible worlds and thereby, inductively, gain an understanding of the essence of the concept's referent. There is some evidence that favors this conceptualist account of philosophical thought experiments over the Platonist one. Paradigm cases of philosophical thought experiments are destructive rather than constructive. Confronted with a Gettier case we realize that justified true belief is not sufficient for knowledge. But we do not directly discover what knowledge might be instead, or in addition to that. On the Platonic account we would expect a direct grasp of the true relation between our target properties. In contrast, conceptualism predicts only particular correct judgments about the extension of a given concept in a possible case. Knowing fragments of its extension does not directly suggest the true definition of the target concept. It only provides an inductive basis for testing prevailing definitions. The best explanation of this fact is that this knowledge is generated by conceptual competence rather than by Platonic insight.

7 Conclusion

The above considerations suggest the following conclusions concerning the epistemology of thought experiments. First, there are good reasons against treating physical and philosophical thought experiments alike, i.e., to endorse a separationist strategy. Physical thought experiments about the counterfactual behavior of spatiotemporal bodies ultimately involve empirical knowledge, e.g., based on one's imagination. Second, Brown's Platonic account turned out deeply problematic when it is used to explain how rational insight into the laws of nature is possible. Third, philosophical thought experiments seem to generate a priori knowledge of philosophical properties. But in this case, conceptualism seems overall superior to Platonism, even though there are no knockdown objections to the latter.

Acknowledgments

I am grateful for extremely helpful comments from and discussion with Dominik Balg, Joachim Horvath, Jens Kipper, Dirk Koppelberg, Michael Stuart, and Jan Wieben.

Notes

1 However, proponents of rational intuition need not be Platonists (cf., e.g., Bealer 1998).
2 Bealer (1998, 207–8) is a staunch separationist. He even wants to restrict the use of the term "thought experiments" to physical cases and distinguishes rational intuitions about whether a concept applies to a hypothetical case from physical intuitions (about what would happen) that are elicited by physical thought experiments.
3 Häggqvist (2007, 58) commits himself to such a unificationist treatment of thought experiments.
4 Cf. Koyré (1968, 75, 88) for a closely related view.
5 Notice that Brown is not a radical unificationist. He is not committed to the view that all thought experiments are Platonic.
6 Rowbottom (2014) points out that it is not fully clear why Brown thinks that the distinction between direct and Platonic thought experiments is a deep and substantial one. Whether a direct thought experiment is also of the Platonic kind depends exclusively on contingent historical facts, i.e., whether there already exists a theory that is in conflict with the one established by the direct thought experiment.
7 In contrast to what I argue here, Williamson (2013) concludes that there is no epistemologically significant a priori/a posteriori distinction.
8 In order to explain empirical knowledge from imagination the reliabilist can offer the following account: *knowledge-entitling factors are independent of sense experience if the reliability of the judgment does not depend on reliable sense experience.* For a reliabilist account of the a priori/a posteriori distinction, cf. Grundmann (2015).
9 Deficiency arguments show that by embracing a priori knowledge, the shortcomings of empiricist theories can be avoided. See Casullo (2003, 100–1).
10 My reconstruction closely follows Clatterbuck (2013), except with respect to premise (5).
11 On a deductive interpretation, Brown's argument would run as follows:

(1) Some abstract entities (i.e., mathematical facts) can be rationally perceived by us.
(2) Laws are abstract entities.
(3) Therefore, laws can be rationally perceived by us.

The general form of this argument is:

(1') Some Bs are C.
(2') All A are B.
(3') Therefore, all A are C.

The following instance of this general form is a counterexample to its validity:

(1") Some light waves can be perceived by us. (T)
(2") Ultraviolet light consists of light waves. (T)
(3") Therefore, ultraviolet light can be perceived by us. (F)

12 Thanks to Michael Stuart for drawing my attention to this possible misunderstanding.
13 Critical comments by Jens Kipper helped me to improve on this point.
14 Thanks to Michael Stuart for pressing me on this point. In Stuart (2012) he already expresses some doubts about DTA as the correct account of laws.
15 Of course, necessitarians face the obvious objection that laws are never exceptionless since interfering factors are always possible. In reply, necessitarians might claim that truly necessary laws are *ceteris-paribus* laws. Or, maybe more plausibly, they could simply restrict their claim to fundamental laws. For reasons of space, I cannot go into any of the details of this debate here.
16 Cf. Häggqvist (2007, 51—3) for a similar observation.
17 Here I do not address objections to philosophical appeals to intuitions that are independent of the specific commitments of the Platonist account, e.g., the objection from the variance of intuitions with irrelevant factors, or the objection from the absence of calibration, as they have recently been raised by experimental philosophers and methodological naturalists. Cf. for these objections Weinberg, Nichols, and Stich (2001) and Weinberg (2007). For critical replies cf., e.g., Grundmann (2010) and Horvath (2010).
18 These concepts are such that whoever possesses them knows (at least in the sense of practical knowledge) their application conditions across possible worlds. Semantically transparent concepts contrast with, e.g., natural kind concepts, indexical concepts, proper names, or partially understood concepts whose application conditions are (partly) fixed by external factors that need not be known by the subjects who possess them.

References

Armstrong, D. (1989) *Universals: An Opinionated Introduction*, Boulder: Westview Press.
Audi, R. (2003) *Epistemology. A Contemporary Introduction to the Theory of Knowledge*, London: Routledge.
Bealer, G. (1998) "Intuition and the autonomy of philosophy," in *Rethinking Intuition: The Psychology of Intuition and Its Role in Philosophical Inquiry*, edited by M. DePaul and W. Ramsey, Lanham: Rowman & Littlefield.
Benacerraf, P. (1973) "Mathematical truth," *The Journal of Philosophy* 70: 661–679.
Bird, A. (2005) "The dispositionalist conception of laws," *Foundations of Science* 10: 354–370.
BonJour, L. (1998) *In Defense of Pure Reason*, Cambridge: Cambridge University Press.
Brown, J. R. (1991) *The Laboratory of the Mind: Thought Experiments in the Natural Sciences*, London: Routledge.
Brown, J. R. (2004) "Peeking into Plato's heaven," *Philosophy of Science* 71: 1126–1138.
Brown, J. R. and Fehige, Y. (2014) "Thought experiments," *Stanford Encyclopedia of Philosophy*. Available here: http://plato.stanford.edu/archives/fall2014/entries/thought-experiment/ (accessed 15 November 2016).
Burge, T. (1993) "Content preservation," *The Philosophical Review* 102: 457–488.
Casullo, A. (2003) *A Priori Justification*, Oxford: Oxford University Press.
Chisholm, R. (1966) *Theory of Knowledge*, Englewood Cliffs: Prentice Hall.
Clatterbuck, H. (2013) "The epistemology of thought experiments: A non-eliminativist, non-Platonic account," *European Journal of Philosophy of Science* 3: 309–329.
Ellis, B. (2001) *Scientific Essentialism*, Cambridge: Cambridge University Press.
Field, H. (1989) *Realism, Mathematics and Modality*, Oxford: Oxford University Press.
Gendler, T. S. (2000) *Thought Experiment: On the Power and Limits of Imaginary Cases*, London: Routledge.
Goldman, A. (1992) "A causal theory of knowing," in *Liaisons. Philosophy Meets the Cognitive and Social Sciences*, edited by A. Goldman, Cambridge: MIT Press.
Grundmann, T. (2007) "The nature of rational intuitions and a fresh look at the explanationist objection," *Grazer Philosophische Studien* 74: 69–87.
Grundmann, T. (2010) "Some hope for intuitions: A reply to Weinberg," in *Experimental Philosophy and Its Critics*, edited by J. Horvath and T. Grundmann, London: Routledge.
Grundmann, T. (2015) "How reliabilism saves the a priori/a posteriori distinction," *Synthese* 19: 2747–2768.
Grundmann, T. and Horvath, J. (2014) "Thought experiments and the problem of deviant realizations," *Philosophical Studies* 170: 525–533.

Häggqvist, S. (2007) "The a priori thesis: A critical assessment," *Croatian Journal of Philosophy* 19: 47–61.
Horvath, J. (2010) "How (not) to react to experimental philosophy," in *Experimental Philosophy and Its Critics*, edited by J. Horvath and T. Grundmann, London: Routledge.
Ichikawa, J. and Jarvis, B. (2009) "Thought-experiment intuitions and truth in fiction," *Philosophical Studies* 142: 221–246.
Jenkins, C. (2008) "A priori knowledge: Debates and developments," *Philosophy Compass* 3: 436–450.
Kant, I. (1965) *Critique of Pure Reason*, New York: St. Martin's Press.
Koyré, A. (1968) *Metaphysics and Measurement*, London: Chapman & Hall.
Kripke, S. (1980) *Naming and Necessity*, Cambridge: Harvard University Press.
Ludwig, K. (2007) "The epistemology of thought-experiments: First person versus third person approaches," *Midwest Studies in Philosophy* 31: 128–159.
Mach, E. (1933) *Die Mechanik in ihrer Entwicklung*, Leipzig: Brockhaus.
Malmgren, A.-S. (2011) "Rationalism and the content of intuitive judgements," *Mind* 120: 263–327.
Mumford, S. (2006) *Laws in Nature*, London: Routledge.
Norton, J. (1996) "Are thought experiments just what you thought?" *Canadian Journal of Philosophy* 26: 333–366.
Psillos, S. (2002) *Causation and Explanation*, London: Routledge.
Pust, J. (2004) "On explaining knowledge of necessity," *Dialectica* 58: 71–87.
Rowbottom, D. P. (2014) "Intuitions in science: Thought experiments as intuition pumps," in *Intuitions*, edited by A. Booth and D. Rowbottom, Oxford: Oxford University Press.
Sidelle, A. (2002) "On the metaphysical contingency of laws of nature," in *Conceivability and Possibility*, edited by T. S. Gendler and J. Hawthorne, Oxford: Clarendon Press.
Strawson, P. F. (1966) *The Bounds of Sense*, London: Methuen.
Stuart, M. T. (2012) "Review of James R. Brown, *The Laboratory of the Mind*," *Spontaneous Generations: A Journal for the History and Philosophy of Science* 6: 237–241.
Tooley, M. (1977) "The nature of laws," *Canadian Journal of Philosophy* 2: 667–698.
van Fraassen, B. (1989) *Laws and Symmetry*, Oxford: Oxford University Press.
Weinberg, J. (2007) "How to challenge intuitions empirically without risking skepticism," *Midwest Studies in Philosophy* 31: 318–343.
Weinberg, J., Nichols, S. and Stich, S. (2001) "Normativity and epistemic intuitions," *Philosophical Topics* 29: 429–460.
Williamson, T. (2007) *The Philosophy of Philosophy*, Malden: Blackwell.
Williamson, T. (2013) "How deep is the distinction between a priori and a posteriori knowledge?" in *The A Priori in Philosophy*, edited by A. Casullo and J. Thurow, Oxford: Oxford University Press.
Williamson, T. (2016) "Knowing by imagining," in *Knowledge Through Imagination*, edited by A. Kind and P. Kung, Oxford: Oxford University Press.

17
COGNITIVE SCIENCE, MENTAL MODELING, AND THOUGHT EXPERIMENTS

Nancy J. Nersessian

1 Introduction

Wherever one stands on the issues of how a thought experiment is executed and how it provides novel insights into the real world, clearly thought experiments utilize the human capacity for imaginative thinking. A simple exemplar of that capacity is one that Herbert Simon liked to provide audiences in his talks on mental imagery. He would ask the question: "How many windows are in your house?" His expectation, overwhelmingly confirmed, was that you would envision each room and simulate walking through your house until you arrived at an answer. At the end, you had gained information about your house that you are unlikely to have been aware of previously. This exemplar shares the imaginative dimension of thought experiments, though the capacity equally enables humans to entertain riding on a flying pig. Importantly, unlike the flights of fancy humans are capable of, thought experiments in science are developed to provide novel insight into real-world phenomena or to confirm or disconfirm hypotheses. Considerable metacognitive control is exercised over their development, likely requiring numerous iterations even though they are mostly recorded in finished form. Several hypotheses have been advanced as to how an experiment only in thought can provide novel data applicable to the real world or "promote basic conceptual reform" (Kuhn 1977, 291). Surprisingly, thought experiments per se, and the various empirical hypotheses offered about them, have not been investigated in the experimental literature in cognitive science. I say "per se" because, as will be advanced here, there is literature in experimental psychology that can be recruited to examine the cognitive basis of thought experimenting, which, on a hypothesis that Nenad and I introduced independently (Nersessian 1991, 1992; Miščević 1992), also provides insight into how they are executed, promote conceptual reform, and provide novel real-world insights in the absence of new data. Our joint hypothesis was that thought experimenting is a form of mental modeling. I have since extended that hypothesis to incorporate a wider range of empirical investigations (Nersessian 2002, 2008). In *Creating Scientific Concepts* (Nersessian 2008), I argued that thought experimenting is a form of *simulative model-based reasoning*, where inferences are made through constructing and manipulating models, whether conceptual, physical, or computational (see also Chandrasekharan, Nersessian, and Subramanian 2013; Chandrasekharan and Nersessian 2015). Providing the cognitive basis of this form of reasoning requires a synthesis of research including on various kinds of mental models (logical reasoning, discourse models, situation models), mental imagery, mental spatial simulation, mental animation, and embodied mental representation (perceptual-motor, perception-based).

The general hypothesis is that thought experimenting is a species of reasoning rooted in the ability to imagine, anticipate, visualize, and re-experience from memory.[1] When a thought experiment is successful it can provide novel empirical data in the sense that although they are contained in current representations, the means to access them were not available until someone figured out how to conduct the thought experiment. Why an outcome is warranted is a function of the circumstance that the representations and transformative manipulations used in reasoning derive from experiences in the world and current understandings of these and of the problem-solving context of the specific practice in which the objective is to gain a specific kind of understanding. In the case of science, the thought experiment is constructed to produce an outcome that is a candidate for having scientific import. This distinguishes it from fictive imaginings, but just as with real-world experiments, something can go wrong with well-executed thought experimental reasoning. Further a thought experimental outcome, just as a real-world experimental outcome, needs to be interpreted and usually investigated further. It often pinpoints the locus of a problem but often does not in itself provide a solution to the problem without additional work.

Each of the experimental literatures considered here is vast, so I briefly survey the cognitive science findings and theories most relevant to the hypothesis that thought experimenting is a species of simulative model-based reasoning and then consider some implications of the hypothesis. My focus is on thought experiments in science, though the hypothesis should extend to other forms as well.

2 A mental models framework

Since the early 1980s a "mental models framework" has developed within cognitive science and has guided a significant portion of experimentation and interpretation of experimental results. This explanatory framework postulates models as organized units of mental representation of knowledge used in various cognitive tasks including reasoning, problem-solving, and discourse comprehension. What is a "mental model?" How is it represented? What are the mental mechanisms that create and execute mental models? How does mental modeling engage external representations and processes? These foundational issues are not often addressed explicitly in the literature and where they are, there is no clear consensus. Thus, I have chosen the word "framework" to characterize a wide range of research on mental models that is particularly relevant to the hypothesis of thought experimenting as simulative model-based reasoning. Additionally, I contend that addressing the processing and mechanisms issues will require incorporating the broader research to be surveyed here systematically into that framework.

The notion of a "mental model" was introduced by the psychologist and physiologist Kenneth Craik (Craik 1943). Craik hypothesized that in many instances people reason by carrying out thought experiments on internal models of physical situations, where a model is a structural, behavioural, or functional analog to a real-world phenomenon. It is an analog in that it preserves constraints inherent in what is represented. He based this hypothesis on the predictive power of thought and the ability of humans to mentally explore real-world and imaginary situations. A new edition of Craik's book with a postscript replying to critics in 1967 fell on fertile ground since the "cognitive revolution" was underway, and it has since had considerable impact on contemporary cognitive science. Simply googling the words "mental model" will bring up a vast number of references.

In the early 1980s several, largely independent, strands of research emerged introducing the theoretical notions of mental model and mental modeling into the cognitive science literature. One strand introduced the notion to explain the effects of semantic information in logical reasoning (Johnson-Laird 1980, 1983). Another strand introduced the notion to explain the empirical findings that people seem to reason from a representation of the structure of a situation rather than from a description of a situation when performing reasoning related to discourse comprehension ("discourse" and "situation" models) (see, e.g., Johnson-Laird 1983; Perrig and Kintsch 1985). These two strands focused on the nature of the representations constructed and manipulated in working memory during reasoning and problem-solving tasks. A third strand introduced the notion in relation to long-term memory representations of knowledge drawn upon in understanding and reasoning, especially about physical systems. This literature introduced the notion to explain a wide range of experimental results indicating that people use organized knowledge structures relating to physical systems when attempting to understand manual control systems and devices in the area of human – machine interactions (see Rouse and Morris 1986 for an overview) and in employing qualitative domain knowledge of physical systems to solve problems (Gentner and Stevens 1983). Early work relating to physical systems that began with psychological studies migrated into AI where computational theories of "naive" or "qualitative" physics were developed to explore issues of knowledge organization, use, access and control, such as in understanding the behaviour of liquids (Hayes 1979) or the motion of a ball in space and time (Forbus 1983). Pioneering research in these last two strands, primarily concerned with mental models as long-term memory representations used in problem-solving, appeared in the edited collection, *Mental Models* (Gentner and Stevens, 1983), in the same year as Johnson-Laird's (1983) monograph of the same name that brought together the working memory strands.

Philip Johnson-Laird's 1983 book is the locus classicus of working memory accounts of mental modeling. Although Johnson-Laird rooted his account in the earlier proposal of Craik, his focus on mental modeling in the domains of deductive, inductive, and modal logics and his desire to distinguish mental models from what is customarily understood as mental imagery led to not developing what I see as a central insight of Craik: reasoning about physical systems via mental simulation. Accounting for simulative reasoning about physical systems, and thought experimenting in science in particular, requires more kinds of model manipulation than logical reasoning requires. Tacit and explicit domain knowledge of entities, behaviours, and processes, especially causal knowledge, is needed in constructing models of physical systems and creating new states via mental simulation. Craik's notion of a mental model is useful here.

Craik's notion emphasized *parallelism* with the real world both in form and in operation in internal modeling: "By 'relation – structure' I do not mean some obscure non-physical entity which attends the model, but the fact that it is a physical working model which works in the same way as the process it parallels, in the aspects under consideration at any moment" (Craik 1943, 51). I interpret him to mean by this that the internal model complies with the constraints of the real-world phenomena it represents, not that it is run like a movie in the mind. Craik based his hypothesis on the need for organisms to be able to predict the environment, thus he saw mental simulation as central to reasoning. He maintained that just as humans create physical models, for example, physical scale models of boats and bridges, to experiment with alternatives, so too the nervous system of humans and other organisms has developed a way to create internal "'small scale model[s]' of external reality" (61) for simulating potential outcomes of actions in a physical environment. I interpret his use of quotation marks around "small scale models" to indicate that he meant it figuratively, and not that the brain quite literally creates, for example, a vivid image of small-scale boat whose motion it simulates. They are what we would call perceptual-motor representations. Mental simulation of these occurs, he claimed, by the "excitation and volley of impulses which parallel the stimuli which occasioned them ..." (60). Thus the internal processes of reasoning result in conclusions similar to those that "might have been reached by causing the actual physical processes to occur" (51). In making the hypothesis Craik drew on existing research in neurophysiology and speculated that the ability "to parallel or model external events" (51) is fundamental to the brain.

Modern advocates of mental modeling, too, speculate that the capacity is fundamental to the brain and that it evolved as a means for simulating possible ways of maneuvering within the physical environment. It would be highly adaptive for an animal to possess the ability to anticipate the environment and potential outcomes of actions, so many animals should have the capacity for mental simulation. The linguistic capabilities of modern humans make it likely that mental models can be created from both perception and description, which is borne out by the research on narrative and discourse comprehension that will be discussed below. Further, it ought to be possible for skill in mental modeling to develop in the course of learning, as studies of expert/novice reasoning show (Chi, Feltovich, and Glaser 1981). This research indicates that the nature and richness of models one can construct and one's ability to reason develops in learning domain-specific content and techniques. Thus, facility with mental modeling is a combination of an individual's biology and learning and develops in interaction with an external, natural, social, and cultural reality, which gives credence to the idea that scientists could refine and extend this capability in service of creative reasoning about nature.

Research within the mental models framework has now become so extensive and varied that an inventory will not be attempted. Given the focus on thought experimenting I consider here only the psychological accounts that hypothesize reasoning as involving the construction and manipulation of a model in working memory during the reasoning process and not the accounts of the nature of representation in long-term memory. My objective here is to outline an account of mental modeling that is consistent with the literature on mundane cases and adequate as a cognitive basis for thought experimenting. As noted, to do so requires going beyond the literature specifically on mental modeling and integrating findings from the literatures on mental imagery, mental animation, and perception-based representation relevant to the cognitive practice of mental modeling. One caveat needs to be made at the outset. Vivid, picture-like or movie-like imagery is not required in mental modeling processes. Mental modeling can make use of perceptual and motor representations and processes without the reasoner experiencing an image. Conflating a mental model with visual imagery has let opponents of the latter to dismiss or underplay the potential of the former in cognitive processes.

2.1 Discourse and situation models

There are many ways in which a mental model of a physical situation could be constructed, but narratives are the means through which many thought experimental situations are conveyed. In earlier work (Nersessian 1991, 1992) I took the narrative form of presentation to be cognitively important, and, as is borne out in the cognitive science literature, a narrative is a particularly good way to produce a working memory mental model. Reading, comprehending, and reasoning about stories would seem to epitomize thinking with language. Yet, there is a significant body of cognitive research that supports the hypothesis that the inferences participants make from these activities are derived through constructing and manipulating a mental model of the situation depicted by the narrative, rather than by applying rules of inference to a system of propositions representing the content of the text (Johnson-Laird 1982, 1983; Dijk and Kintsch 1983; McNamara and Sternberg 1983; Perrig and Kintsch 1985; Zwann and Radvansky 1998; Zwann 1999). A major strategy of this approach is to differentiate the structure of the text from the structure of the situation depicted in the text, and investigate which of the structures the cognitive representations follow. Johnson-Laird in psycholinguistics and others in psychology, formal semantics, and linguistics have proposed that mental representations in inferences related to narratives take the form of working memory "discourse models" or "situation models." On this proposal, the linguistic expressions assist the reader/listener in constructing a mental model through which they understand and reason about the situation depicted by the narrative. That is, in reasoning, the referent of the text would be an internal model of the situation depicted by the text rather than an internal description. The central idea is that "discourse models make explicit the structure not of sentences but of situations as we perceive or imagine them" (Johnson-Laird 1989, 471). The principal tenets of the theory, as outlined by Johnson-Laird, are as follows. As a form of mental model, a discourse model would have a representation of the spatial, temporal, and causal relationships among the events and entities of the situation described by the narrative. In constructing and updating a model, the reader would call upon a combination of tacit and explicit conceptual and real-world knowledge and employ the tacit and recursive inferencing mechanisms of his or her cognitive apparatus to integrate the information with that contained in the narrative.

A large number of experiments have been conducted to investigate the hypothesis. When queried about how they had made inferences in response to an experimenter's questioning, although no instructions were given to imagine or picture the situations, most participants reported that it was by means of "seeing" or "being in the situation" depicted. That is, the reader sees himself or herself as an "observer" of a simulated situation. Whether the view of the situation is "spatial" (a global perspective) or "perspectival" (from a specific point of view) is still a point of debate, though recent investigations tend to support the perspectival account where the reference frame of the space is that of the body (Mainwaring, Tversky, and Schiano 1996; Glenberg 1997b; Bryant and Tversky 1999).

Significantly, the interpretation given to these experimental outcomes is that a situation represented by a mental model could allow the reasoner to make inferences without having to carry out the extensive operations needed to process the same amount of background information to make inferences from an argument in propositional form. The situational constraints of the narrative are built into the model, making many consequences implicit that would require considerable inferential work in propositional form. For example, consider a case where a subject is asked to move an object depicted in a model. Moving an object changes, immediately, its spatial relations to all the other objects. The reasoner should be able to grasp this simply by means of the changes in the model and not need to make additional inferences, and thus the reasoning should be discernibly faster, which is borne out by the studies listed above. Finally, reasoning by means of a model of a situation should restrict the scope of the conclusions drawn. For example, moving an object in a specified manner both limits and makes immediately evident the relevant consequences of that move for other objects in the situation detailed by the narrative, which the literature supports. Additionally this literature demonstrates that it is much more difficult to make inferences – and sometimes they are not made at all – when participants are required to reason with the situation represented in propositional form.

2.2 Mental spatial simulation

An extensive literature provides evidence that humans can perform various simulative transformations in imagination that mimic physical spatial transformations. The literature on mental imagery establishes that people can mentally simulate combinations, such as with the classic example where participants are asked to imagine a letter B rotated 90 degrees to the left, place an upside triangle below it and remove the connecting line and the processes produce an image of a heart. People can perform imaginative rotations that exhibit latencies consistent with actually turning a mental figure around, such as when queried as to whether two objects presented from different rotations are of the same object (Kosslyn 1980, 1994; Shepard and Cooper 1982; Finke and Shepard 1986; Finke 1989; Finke, Pinker, and Farah 1989; Tye 1991). Further, there is a correlation between the time it takes for participants to respond and the number of degrees of rotation required. Mental rotational transformations can be performed with both plane figures and three-dimensional models. Recent studies have shown that infants are able to predict the orientation of a rotating physical object when it disappears from view (Hespos and Rochat 1997) and that learning through physical manipulation of blocks improves the performance of children on mental rotation tasks (Newcombe and Huttenlocher 2000). As Kosslyn (1994, 345) summarizes, psychological research provides evidence of rotating, translating, bending, scaling folding, zooming, and flipping of images. The combinations and transformations in mental imagery are hypothesized to take place according to internalized constraints assimilated during perception. Kosslyn also notes that these mental transformations are often accompanied by twisting and moving one's hands to represent rotation, which indicates motor as well as visual processing (see also Jeannerod 1993, 1994; Parsons 1994).

Other research indicates that people combine various kinds of knowledge of physical situations with imaginary transformations, including real-time dynamical information (Freyd 1987). When given a problem about objects that are separated by a wall, for instance, the spatial transformations exhibit latencies consistent with the participants having simulated moving around the wall rather than through it, indicating at least tacit use of physical knowledge that objects cannot move through a wall (Morrow, Bower, and Greenspan, 1989). This kind of knowledge is evidenced also in other chronometric studies in which participants are shown a picture of a person with an arm in front of the body and then one with the arm in back and report imagining rotating the arm around the body rather than through it, which is consistent with the latencies (Shiffrar and Freyd 1990). Although physical knowledge other than spatial appears to be playing a role in such imaginings, it has not been explored systematically in this literature. The kinds of transformations considered thus far are spatial: structural/geometrical/topological transformations. However, recent experiments in the perception-action (ideomotor) literature discussed below link together imagery, perception, and action (Brass, Bekkering, and Prinz 2002; Brass and Heyes 2005).

In general, the mental imagery literature on spatial simulation provides significant evidence for the hypothesis that the human cognitive system is capable of transformative processing in which spatial transformations are made on non-propositional representations. There is also significant evidence from neuropsychology that the perceptual system plays a significant role in imaginative thinking initiated by Martha Farah (Farah 1988) and Stephen Kosslyn (Kosslyn 1994), which adds support to this hypothesis. Again, this makes sense from an evolutionary perspective. The visual cortex is one of the oldest and most highly developed regions of the brain. As put by Roger Shepard, perceptual mechanisms "have, through evolutionary eons, deeply internalized an intuitive wisdom about the way things transform in the world. Because this wisdom is embodied in a perceptual system that antedates, by far, the emergence of language and mathematics, imagination is more akin to visualizing than to talking or to calculating to oneself" (Shepard 1988, 180). Although the original ability to envision, predict, and infer by imagining developed as a way of simulating possible courses of action in the world, as humans developed, this ability has been "bent to the service of creative thought" (ibid.). On this account, the mundane ability to imagine and visualize underlies some of the most sophisticated forms of human reasoning as evidenced in creative reasoning in science. To stress once again, though, the format of mental imagery should not be conflated with that of external pictorial representations. No account of visual imagery argues that the representations need be vivid or picture-like. As various researchers have shown, such as with Gestalt figures (Chambers and Reisberg 1985), internal representations appear sketchier and less flexible in attempts at reinterpretation. Furthermore, congenitally blind individuals can carry out classic imagery tasks, though the source of such transformational knowledge would be haptic perception and the imagery, likely kinesthetic in nature (Marmor and Zaback 1976; Kerr 1983; Arditi, Holtzman, and Kosslyn 1988). The point is that the mental representations are such that perceptual and motor mechanisms can be used in their construction and manipulation.

2.3 Mental animation/simulation

There are growing psychology and neuroscience literatures that investigate the hypothesis that the human cognitive system possesses the ability for mental animation. Investigations of physical reasoning have moved beyond spatial and temporal transformations to examining the role of causal and behavioral knowledge in mental simulation. Much of this research involves inferring motion from static (diagrammatic) representations. Prominent research in this vein includes Mary Hegarty's (Hegarty and Just 1989; Hegarty 1992; Hegarty and Ferguson 1993) investigations of reasoning about the behavior of pulley systems and Daniel Schwartz's (Schwartz 1995; Schwartz and Black 1996a, 1996b) studies focusing on gear rotations. These studies, respectively, provide evidence that people are able to perform simulative causal transformations of static figures provided of the initial set-up of the pulleys and of the gears. Several findings are important here. Protocols of participants indicate that they do not mentally animate the pulley systems all at once as would happen in the real-world experience, but animate in segments the causal sequence, working out in a piecemeal fashion the consequences of previous motion for the next segment. The response times for the participants in the gear problems indicate these, too, are animated in sequence, and when given only one set of gears, their response time was proportional to the rate of the angle of rotation. Participants in these kinds of studies often use gestures, sometimes performed over the given diagram, that simulate and track the motion (see, e.g., Clement 1994, 2003; Hegarty and Steinhoff 1994; Golden-Meadow, Nusbaum, Kelly, and Wagner 2001).

Participants perform better when given more realistic external representations of gears than highly schematic ones, such as those of circles with no cogs. In these cases they seem to use physical knowledge, such as friction, directly to animate the model, whereas in the schematic case they revert to more analytic strategies such as comparing the size of the angles that gears of different sizes would move through. Schwartz's research also indicates that mental animation can make use of other non-visual information such as of viscosity and gravity. When participants are well trained in rules for inferring motion, however, they often revert to these to solve the problem more quickly (Schwartz and Black 1996). Mental animation, on the other hand, can result in correct inferences in cases where the participant cannot produce a correct description of the animation (Hegarty 1992). Further, people can judge whether an animation is correct even in cases where the self-produced inference about motion is incorrect (Hegarty 1992).

The interference paradigm provides another strand of experimental research on mental simulation. For instance, when participants execute an action A (e.g., tapping fingers on a flat surface) while watching a non-congruent action on a screen (e.g., an object moving in a direction perpendicular to the tapping) the speed of action A slows down compared to the condition when the subject is watching a congruent action (Brass, Bekkering, and Prinz 2002).This effect also occurs when only the terminal posture of the non-congruent action is presented on screen. While doing mental rotation, if participants move their hands or feet in a direction non-compatible to the mental rotation, their performance suffers. Wexler, Kosslyn, and Berthoz (1998) show that unseen motor rotation in the Cooper-Shepard mental rotation task leads to faster reaction times and fewer errors when the motor rotation is compatible with the mental rotation than when they are incompatible. Even planning another action can interfere with mental rotation (Wohlschlager 2001). A range of neuroimaging experiments showing that action areas are activated when participants passively watch actions on screen (Brass and Heyes 2005 provides a good review) support the behavioral data.

Neuroimaging experiments add to evidence supporting mental simulation. These show that similar brain areas are activated during action and motor imagery of the same action. Gallese, Ferrari, Kohler, and Fogassi (2002) report that when we observe goal-related behaviors executed by others (with effectors as different as the mouth, the hand, or the foot) the same cortical sectors are activated as when we perform the same actions. Whenever we look at someone performing an action, in addition to the activation of various visual areas, there is a concurrent activation of the motor circuits that are recruited when we ourselves perform that action. We do not overtly reproduce the observed action, but our motor system acts as if we were executing the same action we are observing. This effect exists in monkeys as well, and such motor-area activation results even with abstract stimuli, such as when a monkey hears the sound of a peanut cracking. This effect has been replicated across a series of studies (particularly the work on mirror neurons and canonical neurons, Hurley and Chater 2005, vols 1 and 2, provides a good review).

2.4 Embodied mental representation/perceptual mental models

Thought experimenting as a form of mental modeling would need to allow for the possibility of simulative thinking about physical entities, situations, and processes. Considerable experimental knowledge would be needed for this kind of mental simulation, not just what can be derived from perception as it is usually understood as separate from conceptual understanding. The behaviors of the parts of the model, for example, need to be connected to knowledge of how these function, much of which is tacit. For example, people can usually infer how water will spill out of a cup without being able to make explicit or describe the requisite knowledge. Although we have only been considering mental modeling as a working memory process, of course information from long term memory plays a role in this process, as does information from short-term memory. Thus, mental modeling needs to maintain a connection to long-term memory representations, and so an account is needed of how stored, tacit information connects to the working memory representation. How this connection is made is still an open question for cognitive and neurosciences. However, a developing line of research that focuses on the implications of the interaction of human perceptual and motor systems with the environment for representation and processing offers some promising insights.

Traditionally, cognitive processes have been conceived as separate from those of perception and action. Researchers on *embodied* mental representations contend that a wide range of empirical evidence shows perceptual content is retained in all kinds of mental representations, and that perceptual and motor processes play a significant role in many kinds of cognitive processes, including memory, conceptual processing, and language comprehension (Johnson 1987; Lakoff 1987; Greeno 1989; Kosslyn 1994; Yeh and Barsalou 1996; Glenberg 1997b; Barsalou 1999, 2003; Barsalou, Solomon, and Wu 1999; Craig, Nersessian, and Catrambone 2002; Barsalou, Simmons, Barbey, and Wilson 2003; Solomon and Barsalou 2004; Catrambone, Craig, and Nersessian 2006). One area of embodiment research concerns the representation of spatial information in mental models. This research leads to the conclusion that spatial representation is not 3-D Euclidian (the "view from nowhere") relative to the orientation of one's body and to gravity. Sometime ago Irwin Rock hypothesized, there is a "deeply ingrained tendency to 'project' egocentric up-down, left-right coordinates onto the [imagined] scene" (Rock 1973, 17). This hypothesis is borne out by later research (Perrig and Kintsch 1985; Franklin and Tversky 1990; Bryant, Tversky, and Franklin 1992; Glenberg 1997a; Bryant and Tversky 1999).

In particular, Barbara Tverksy and colleagues have found that mental spatial alignment depends on how the participant is oriented in the external environment and corresponds with bodily symmetry (up-down, front-back, and gravity). When asked to imagine objects surrounding an external central object, mental model alignment depends on whether the object has the same orientation as the observer. Arthur Glenberg argues that this bodily orientation is tied to preparation for *situated action* that occurs in real-world situations (Glenberg 1997a).

A second line of research focuses on concept representation. From an embodied cognition perspective, as expressed by George Lakoff and Mark Johnson, a "concept is a neural structure that is actually part of, or makes use of, the sensorimotor system of our brains" (Lakoff and Johnson 1998, 20). Lawrence Barsalou has reinterpreted an extensive, existing experimental literature in behavioral and neuroscience research as supporting the contention that mental representations retain perceptual features and that many cognitive functions involve re-enactment or simulation of perceptual states (summarized in Barsalou 2003). These include perceptual processing, memory, language, categorization, and inference. Barsalou distinguishes between "modal" and "amodal" representations. Amodal representations have an arbitrary relation to their referent in the world, such as the relation between a string of symbols "c-a-t" and a cat. Modal representations retain perceptual features of their referent in the world. On Barsalou's account cognitive processing employs "perceptual symbols," which are neural correlates of sensorimotor experiences (Barsalou 1999). These representations "result from an extraction process that selects some subset of a perceptual state and stores it as a symbol" (Barsalou and Prinz 1997, 275). Perceptual symbols would form a common representational system that underlies both sensorimotor and conceptual processing and make use of perceptual and motor mechanisms. Such representations would possess simulation capabilities; that is, perceptual and motor processes associated with the original experiences would be re-enacted when perceptual symbols are employed in thinking. On this account, concepts are separable neural states underlying perception and constituting the units of long-term memory representation, which in turn can be organized into knowledge units such as schemas, mental models, or frames. In addition to reinterpreting existing experiments, the behavioral experiments he and colleagues have devised to test the implications of this account make a compelling case (Barsalou, Simmons, Barbey, and Wilson 2003, Barsalou, Solomon, and Wu 1999).

Barsalou (1999) stresses that one should not conflate perceptual representations with recording systems in which images are captured but not interpreted (Haugeland 1991). Unlike recordings, perceptual symbols are schematic and allow for infinite possibilities of recombination during a perceptual simulation. One needs neither to be consciously aware of mental imagery, which requires extra cognitive effort to produce or of the simulation process, nor to be "running" anything resembling a kind of motion picture in the head. Perceptual symbols are not holistic, as are images, and their componential, schematic, and dynamic nature allows for abstraction and infinite combination and recombination. Perceptual representations can make use of the information represented without an accompanying perceptual experience, while at the same time allow for the possibility that in some instances there could be such an imagistic experience. On this account, to have a concept is to possess a skill for constructing an infinite number of simulations tailored to one's immediate goals and needs for action. In situated action, "a concept is a skill that delivers specialized packages of inferences to guide an agent's interactions with specific category members in particular situations. Across different situations, different packages tailor inferences to different goals and situational constraints" (Barsalou 2003, 27). These tacit affordances and constraints of situational information would be at play even in the solely imaginative cases, where only conceptual understanding is used. Just how a simulation is performed in reasoning via mental modeling (what I have called "simulative model-based reasoning") is an open research question requiring more knowledge about the cognitive and neural mechanisms underlying such processes.[2]

3 Thought experimenting as simulative model-based reasoning

The claim that thought experimenting is a form of simulative model-based reasoning can now be explicated in terms of the mental modeling framework, components of which were outlined in Section 2. The general claim is that in certain problem-solving tasks people reason by constructing a mental model of the situations, events, and processes that in dynamic cases can be manipulated through simulation. The framework interprets numerous experimental findings as demonstrating that mental modeling is a fundamental form of human reasoning. It is hypothesized to have evolved as an efficient means of navigating and anticipating the environment and solving problems significant for surviving in the world. Humans have extended its use to more esoteric situations, such as scientific problem-solving. Connecting the literatures surveyed in Section 2 provides a framework in which a thought-experimental mental model is an organized representation that embodies and complies with represented constraints of the phenomena being reasoned about. Constraints used in constructing and manipulating mental models are conditioned by experience and by current understanding. These include tacit and explicit knowledge of spatio-temporal relations, the represented situations, entities, processes, and other pertinent information such as causal structure. In the processes of constructing, manipulating, and revising the mental model, information deriving from various representational formats, including linguistic, formulaic, visual, auditory, kinesthetic, can be used. Operations on thought experimental models require transformations be consistent with the constraints of the domain, which can be tacit or explicit for the experimenter. What transformations are legitimate derive from the constraints. Causal coherence, spatial structure, and mathematical consistency are examples of kinds of constraints. The models represent demonstratively (as opposed to descriptively). How good a model it is for the purposes at hand requires evaluating how well the situation conforms to *the kind* of phenomena it is supposed to represent and the usefulness of the inferences that flow from simulating it. Finally, as embodied representations, thought experimenting would be a form of situated action, where "action" can be fully imaginative or carried out in interaction with external representations (e.g., sketches and diagrams) which can facilitate the reasoning processes (see Nersessian 2008, ch. 5 for an extensive discussion).

Scientific thought experiments are a more complex form of reasoning than anything investigated in the current cognitive literature. However, the primary data for examining these thought experiments are narratives, and they are likely to function cognitively much like other narratives. My intuition is that the carefully crafted thought-experimental narrative focuses on the construction of a model of a *kind* of situation and manipulating that model through simulation affords epistemic access to certain features of current representations in a way that manipulating propositional representations using logical rules cannot. I do not claim that the original experimenter need be aware of the cognitive import of the narrative form of communication. Rather, thought experiments likely have been presented in narrative form because the experimenter is attempting to convey the experiment in a way he or she has found particularly salient for their own understanding (and likely through many iterations), albeit the narratives might be crafted with a bit more window dressing.

Experimental data on comprehending and reasoning with narratives support the interpretation that people construct mental models of the situations depicted by the narratives and make inferences through manipulating these, rather than by performing logical operations on proposition-like representations. That is, the referent of the text of the narrative is an internal model of the situation rather than an internal description. Even though scientific thought experiments are more complex than the cases of reasoning investigated in this literature, it is reasonable to assume that these narratives would serve much the same functions. My hypothesis is that the carefully crafted thought-experimental narrative leads to the construction of a mental model of a kind of situation and that simulating the consequences of the situation as it unfolds in time affords epistemic access to specific aspects of a way of representing the world. I construe "narrative" sufficiently broadly to encompass the range from straightforward descriptions such as Galileo's sparse description of imagining two stones of different weights, joined together and falling, in his exploration of the possible differences in the rates of falling bodies to more elaborate "stories" such as his description of an artist drawing on a ship on a voyage from Venice to Alexandretta in exploring whether one can perceive common motion.

As we have seen, many instances of mental modeling in general aim at deriving real-world consequences. For instance, when reasoning about how to get a large piece of furniture through a doorway, one intends that one's thought simulations of various rotations of the shape will result in a successful real-world manipulation. However, humans are capable of endless fictive imaginings that have no such empirical consequences, and scientific thought experiments need to be distinguished from these. That many thought experiments do indeed "work" so well that one feels compelled to accept the outcome contributes to the sense that thought experimenting is an "epistemically potent" form of reasoning. The compelling and generalizable outcomes of thought experiments contribute to why John Norton has advocated that thought experiments are arguments executed by deductive or inductive reasoning (Norton 1991, 2004). Norton's conception of thought experiments as arguments, however, makes them too epistemically potent. One only needs the argument interpretation of thought experimenting if one wants to maintain that thought experiments produce candidate truths about nature. On this view they can provide new knowledge about the world because logic provides reliable reasoning schemas such that based on true (or highly probable) premises they lead to true (or highly probable) conclusions. As Norton says: "If thought experiments are to produce knowledge, then we must require that the transformations they effect preserve whatever truth is in our existing knowledge; or that there is at least a strong likelihood of its preservation" (Norton 2004, 7). Further, he claims that the epistemic potency of thought experiments comes from its revealing "what is common to the many formulations," which for him is "the argument" (op cit., 22). However, the outcomes of simulative model-based reasoning can have the generality he is seeing, i.e., they are interpreted as "generic," that is, as referring to *this kind of* phenomena, not just to the specific situation, and are epistemically potent without having to resort to the notion of truth. I briefly address these claims in turn.

First, it is important to recognize that thought experimenting takes place within a context and a set of practices. Unlike the mental modeling in the context of getting the furniture through the doorway, scientific thought experimental models are not intended to represent just the situations depicted. The model and thus inferences made from it are understood to represent *kinds* of objects, events, and processes in situations of *this kind*. Galileo's thought experiment on falling bodies is interpreted as pertaining to what is common to all kinds of falling bodies. The generality of thought experimenting lies in the capacity of the mind to grasp that – and in what ways – an inference from a specific situation applies to situations of that kind. Real-world experimental reasoning in science functions in a similar way. The practices of science, in general, aim at isolating and extracting what is common to phenomena of the kind under investigation. For instance, an inference made from a specific spring or from a model of a spring can be interpreted as applying to the class of simple harmonic oscillators such that features specific to the spring, such as coils, are abstracted from the interpretation of the representation as irrelevant to the context.

Second, science employs a wide range of reliable methods for which there is no expectation that they will produce truth. Scientists do not contend that idealizations, for instance, are *true* of the real world – not even that they are candidate truths. Their function is different, in particular, it is to enable mathematization. Catherine Elgin (Elgin 1996, 2004) has argued that for a scientific practice to produce epistemically significant outcomes it need not be required to produce truths, but only meet its cognitive goals. Science makes extensive use of practices, such as limiting case demonstrations, idealizations, curve smoothing, and computational modeling, such that insisting on equating truth and epistemic acceptability leads clearly to falsehoods. Yet science accepts the outcomes of such practices as advancing scientific goals, such as deriving a mathematical representation or predicting real-world experimental outcomes on the basis of a computational simulation. Building on the notion of "exemplification" introduced by Nelson Goodman in *Languages of Art* (Goodman 1968), Elgin advocates that the epistemic value of these kinds of strategies used in science lies in their *exemplifying* features relevant to the goals of an investigation. An exemplification "at once refers to and instantiates a feature" (Elgin 1996, 171). What I have been calling "same kind" can be understood as exemplification. Construing thought experiments and their outcomes as exemplifying situations of a certain kind, a thought experimental model facilitates epistemic access to features of representations by abstracting away distracting, irrelevant features, thereby focusing attention on those features salient to the problem-solving context. There often are "irrelevant particulars" (Norton 1991) in the thought experimental narrative, but the narrative is either crafted in such a way that one understands these as irrelevant or it uses the irrelevant particular, such as the inebriated state of the physicist in the chest, to focus attention on the quite relevant feature, such as that he or she cannot know or be aware of certain features of the situation. Understanding what claims can be made about the behavior of all falling objects on the basis of a simulation of specific rocks derives not from inductive generalization but from understanding how the specific situation exemplifies certain features of all such situations. As Elgin points out, scientists devise exemplifications physically as well, such as when they refine a lump of ore to have it consist only of iron. The physical abstraction, then, affords epistemic access to the properties of iron in the context of real-world experimentation. The cognitive capacity for generic abstraction enables understanding the specific situation (represented mentally or physically) as referring to situations of this kind – as belonging to this class of phenomena. The situation exemplifies the kinds of features and relations that are relevant to the problem-solving context. Through it we are able to grasp insights and gain understanding and are warranted in pursuing where the experimental outcomes might lead. Just as with real-world experiments, thought experimental outcomes are in need of interpretation, can require further experimental investigation, and can fail.

4 Conclusion

The practice of thought experimenting enables scientists to follow through the implications of a way of representing nature by simulating an exemplary or representative situation that is feasible within that representation. This chapter argues that the cognitive basis of thought experimenting lies in the mundane cognitive capacity for mental modeling. Reasoning by means of a thought experiment involves constructing and simulating a mental model of a representative situation. It is not a mystery why scientific thought experiments are a reliable source of empirical insight. Thought experimenting uses and manipulates representations that derive from real-world experiences and our conceptualizations of them. Models are constructed and inferences made using cognitive mechanisms that have proven reliability in making empirical predictions. What kind of thought experiments one is capable of conducting and how well one can conduct a thought experiment are functions of learning and expertise. Thought experimenting takes place within a problem-solving context and needs to conform to the constraints of that context and of the practices in which it is being conducted. Within science, experimental situations are devised and understood to exemplify selected features or situations such that inferences made from the experiment are interpreted as generic, as pertaining to the kind and not just the instance. How acceptable an outcome is depends on the understandings that frame it. As with real-world experiments, the outcome does not stand on its own – interpretation and often further investigation are needed.

Notes

1 This general form would seem to also encompass Tamar Gendler's (1998) hypothesis that the epistemic efficacy of thought experiments lies in their employing imagistic representations that are manipulated by drawing on real-world tacit knowledge. Paul Harris (2000) has conducted experimental research that provides significant evidence that young children draw on such knowledge in their imaginings.
2 The discovery of mirror neuron systems is a significant development in that it provides neurophysiological evidence that humans and other primates mentally simulate behaviors and emotions corresponding to others they are observing. These systems are hypothesized to play a central role in understanding and interpreting actions and in empathy (for a review, see Rizzolatti and Craighero 2004).

References

Arditi, A., Holtzman, J. D. and Kosslyn, S. M. (1988) "Mental imagery and sensory experience in congenital blindness," *Neuropsychologia* 26: 1–12.
Barsalou, L. W. (1999) "Perceptual symbol systems," *Behavioral and Brain Sciences* 22: 577–609.
Barsalou, L. W. (2003) "Situated simulation in the human conceptual system," *Language and Cognitive Processes* 18: 513–562.
Barsalou, L. W. and Prinz, J. J. (1997) "Mundane creativity in perceptual symbol systems," in *Creative Thought: A Investigation of Conceptual Structures and Processes*, edited by T. Ward, S. M. Smith, and J. Vaid, Washington: American Psychological Association.
Barsalou, L. W., Simmons, W. K., Barbey, A. K. and Wilson, C. D. (2003) "Grounding conceptual knowledge in modality-specific systems," *Trends in Cognitive Science* 7: 84–91.
Barsalou, L. W., Solomon, K. O. and Wu, L. L. (1999) "Perceptual simulation in conceptual tasks," in *Cultural, Typological, and Psychological Perspectives in Cognitive Linguistics. The Proceedings of the 4th Annual Conference of the International Cognitive Linguistics Association*, vol. 3, edited by M. K. Hiraga, C. Sinha, and S. Wilcox, Amsterdam: John Benjamins.
Brass, M., Bekkering, H. and Prinz, W. (2002) "Movement observation affects movement execution in a simple response task," *Acta Psychologica* 106: 3–22.
Brass, M. and Heyes, C. (2005) "Imitation: Is cognitive neuroscience solving the correspondence problem?" *Trends in Cognitive Science* 9: 489–495.
Bryant, D. J. and Tversky, B. (1999) "Mental representations of perspective and spatial relations from diagrams and models," *Journal of Experimental Psychology: Learning, Memory, and Cognition* 25: 137–156.
Bryant, D. J., Tversky, B. and Franklin, N. (1992) "Internal and external spatial frameworks for representing described scenes," *Journal of Memory and Language* 31: 74–98.
Catrambone, R., Craig, D. L. and Nersessian, N. J. (2006) "The role of perceptually represented structure in analogical problem solving," *Memory and Cognition* 4: 1126–1132.
Chambers, D. and Reisberg, D. (1985) "Can mental images be ambiguous?" *Journal of Experimental Psychology: Human Perception and Performance* 11: 317–328.
Chandrasekharan, S. and Nersessian, N. J. (2015) "Building cognition: The construction of computational representations for scientific discovery," *Cognitive Science* 39: 1727–1763.
Chandrasekharan, S., Nersessian, N. J. and Subramanian, V. (2013) "Computational modeling: Is this the end of thought experiments in science?" in *Thought Experiments in Philosophy, Science and the Arts*, edited by M. Frappier, L. Meynell, and J. Brown, London: Routledge.
Chi, M. T. H., Feltovich, J. and Glaser, R. (1981) "Categorization and representation of physics problems by experts and novices," *Cognitive Science* 5: 121–152.
Clement, J. (1994) "Use of physical intuition and imagistic simulation in expert problem solving," in *Implicit and Explicit Knowledge*, edited by D. Tirosh, Norwood: Ablex Publishing Corporation.
Clement, J. (2003) "Imagistic simulation in scientific model construction," in *Proceedings of the Cognitive Science Society*, vol. 25, pp. 258–263, edited by D. Alterman and D. Kirsch, Hillsdale: Lawrence Erlbaum Associates.
Craig, D. L., Nersessian, N. J. and Catrambone, R. (2002) "Perceptual simulation in analogical problem solving," in *Model-Based Reasoning: Science, Technology, Values*, edited by L. Magnani and N. J. Nersessian, New York: Kluwer Academic/Plenum Publishers.
Craik, K. (1943) *The Nature of Explanation*, Cambridge: Cambridge University Press.
Dijk, T. A. V. and Kintsch, W. (1983) *Strategies of Discourse Comprehension*, New York: Academic Press.
Elgin, C. Z. (1996) *Considered Judgment*, Princeton: Princeton University Press.
Elgin, C. Z. (2004) "True enough," *Philosophical Issues* 14: 113–131.
Farah, M. J. (1988) "Is visual imagery really visual? Overlooked evidence from neuropsychology," *Psychological Review* 95: 307–317.
Finke, R. A. (1989) *Principles of Mental Imagery*, Cambridge: MIT Press.
Finke, R. A. and Shepard, R. N. (1986) "Visual functions of mental imagery," in *Handbook of Perception and Human Performance*, edited by K. R. Boff, L. Kaufman, and J. P. Thomas, New York: Wiles.

Finke, R. A., Pinker, S. and Farah, M. (1989) "Reinterpreting visual patterns in mental imagery," *Cognitive Science* 13: 51–78.

Forbus, K. (1983) "Reasoning about space and motion," in *Mental Models*, edited by D. Gentner and A. Stevens, Hillsdale: Lawrence Erlbaum Associates.

Franklin, N. and Tversky, B. (1990) "Searching imagined environments," *Journal of Experimental Psychology* 119: 63–76.

Freyd, J. J. (1987) "Dynamic mental representation," *Psychological Review* 94: 427–438.

Gallese, V., Ferrari, F., Kohler, E. and Fogassi, L. (2002) "The eyes, the hand, and the mind: Behavioral and neurophysiological aspects of social cognition," in *The Cognitive Animal*, edited by M. Bekoff, C. Allen, and M. Burghardt, Cambridge: MIT Press.

Gendler, T. (1998) "Galileo and the indispensability of thought experiments," *British Journal of the Philosophy of Science* 49: 397–424.

Gentner, D. and Stevens, A. L. (1983) *Mental Models*, Hillsdale: Lawrence Erlbaum.

Glenberg, A. M. (1997a) "Mental models, space, and embodied cognition," in *Creative Thought: An Investigation of Conceptual Structures and Processes*, edited by T. Ward, S. M. Smith, and J. Vaid, Washington: American Psychological Association.

Glenberg, A. M. (1997b) "What memory is for," *Behavioral and Brain Sciences* 20: 1–55.

Golden-Meadow, S., Nusbaum, H., Kelly, S. D. and Wagner, S. (2001) "Explaining math: Gesturing lightens the load," *Psychological Science* 12: 332–340.

Goodman, N. (1968) *Languages of Art*, Indianapolis: Hackett.

Greeno, J. G. (1989) "Situations, mental models, and generative knowledge," in *Complex Information Processing*, edited by D. Klahr and K. Kotovsky, Hillsdale: Lawrence Erlbaum.

Harris, P. L. (2000) *The Work of the Imagination*, Oxford: Blackwell.

Haugeland, J. (1991) "Representational genera," in *Philosophy and Connectionist Theory*, edited by W. Ramsey, S. Stitch, and D. E. Rumelhart, Hillsdale: Lawrence Erlbaum Associates.

Hayes, J. (1979) "The naive physics manifesto," in *Expert Systems in the Micro-Electronic Age*, edited by D. Mitchie, Edinburgh: Edinburgh University Press.

Hegarty, M. (1992) "Mental animation: Inferring motion from static diagrams of mechanical systems," *Journal of Experimental Psychology: Learning, Memory, and Cognition* 18: 1084–1102.

Hegarty, M. and Ferguson, J. M. (1993) "*Strategy Change with Practice in a Mental Animation Task*," Paper presented at the Annual Meeting of the Psychonomic Society, Washington.

Hegarty, M. and Just, M. A. (1989) "Understanding machines from text and diagrams," in *Knowledge Acquisition from Text and Picture*, edited by H. Mandl and J. Levin, Amsterdam: Elsevier Science Publishers.

Hegarty, M. and Steinhoff, K. (1994) "*Use of Diagrams as External Memory in a Mechanical Reasoning Task*," Paper presented at the Annual Meeting of the American Educational Research Association, New Orleans.

Hespos, S. J. and Rochat, P. (1997) "Dynamic representation in infancy," *Cognition* 64: 153–189.

Hurley, S. and Chater, N. (eds) (2005) *Imitation, Human Development, and Culture*, Cambridge: MIT Press.

Illies, C. F. R. (2007) "Orientierung durch universalisierung: Der kategorische imperativals test für die moralität von maximen," *Kant-Studien* 98: 306–328.

Jeannerod, M. (1993) "A theory of representation-driven actions," in *The Perceived Self*, edited by U. Neisser, Cambridge: Cambridge University Press.

Jeannerod, M. (1994) "The representing brain: Neural correlated of motor intention and imagery," *Brain and Behavioral Sciences* 17: 187–202.

Johnson, M. (1987) *The Body in the Mind: The Bodily Basis of Meaning, Imagination, and Reason*, Chicago: University of Chicago Press.

Johnson-Laird, P. N. (1980) "Mental models in cognitive science," *Cognitive Science* 4: 71–115.

Johnson-Laird, P. N. (1982) "The mental representation of the meaning of words," *Cognition* 25: 189–211.

Johnson-Laird, P. N. (1983) *Mental Models*, Cambridge: MIT Press.

Johnson-Laird, P. N. (1989) "Mental models," in *Foundations of Cognitive Science*, edited by M. Posner, Cambridge: MIT Press.

Kerr, N. H. (1983) "The role of vision in 'visual imagery,'" *Journal of Experimental Psychology: General* 112: 265–277.
Kosslyn, S. M. (1980) *Image and Mind*, Cambridge: Harvard University Press.
Kosslyn, S. M. (1994) *Image and Brain*, Cambridge: MIT Press.
Kuhn, T. S. (1977) "A function for thought experiments," in *The Essential Tension*, Chicago: University of Chicago Press.
Lakoff, G. (1987) *Women, Fire, and Dangerous Things: What Categories Reveal about the Mind*, Chicago: University of Chicago Press.
Lakoff, G. and Johnson, M. (1998) *Philosophy in the Flesh*, New York: Basic Books.
Mainwaring, S. D., Tversky, B. and Schiano, D. J. (1996) "Effects of task and object configuration on perspective choice in spatial descriptions," in *AAAI Symposium*, edited by P. Olivier, Stanford: AAAI Press.
Marmor, G. S. and Zaback, L. A. (1976) "Mental rotation by the blind: Does mental rotation depend on visual imagery?" *Journal of Experimental Psychology: Human Perception and Performance* 2: 515–521.
McNamara, T. and Sternberg, R. J. (1983) "Mental models of word meaning," *Journal of Verbal Learning and Verbal Behavior* 22: 449–474.
Miščević, N. (1992) "Mental models and thought experiments," *International Studies in the Philosophy of Science* 6: 215–226.
Morrow, D. G., Bower, G. H. and Greenspan, S. L. (1989) "Updating situation models during narrative comprehension," *Journal of Memory and Language* 28: 292–312.
Nersessian, N. J. (1991) "Why do thought experiments work?" in *Proceedings of the Cognitive Science Society*, vol. 13, Hillsdale: Lawrence Erlbaum.
Nersessian, N. J. (1992) "In the theoretician's laboratory: Thought experimenting as mental modeling," in *Philosophy of Science Association 1992*, vol. 2, edited by D. Hull, M. Forbes, and K. Okruhlik, East Lansing: Philosophy of Science Association.
Nersessian, N. J. (2002) "The cognitive basis of model-based reasoning in science," in *The Cognitive Basis of Science*, edited by P. Carruthers, S. Stich, and M. Siegal, Cambridge: Cambridge University Press.
Nersessian, N. J. (2008) *Creating Scientific Concepts*, Cambridge: MIT Press.
Newcombe, N. S. and Huttenlocher, J. (2000) *Making Space: The Development of Spatial Representation and Reasoning*, Cambridge: MIT Press.
Norton, J. (1991) "Thought experiments in Einstein's work," in *Thought Experiments in Science and Philosophy*, edited by T. Horowitz and G. Massey, Savage: Rowman and Littlefield.
Norton, J. (2004) "Why thought experiments do not transcend empiricism," in *Contemporary Debates in the Philosophy of Science*, edited by C. Hitchcock, Oxford: Blackwell.
Parsons, L. (1994) "Temporal and kinematic properties of motor behavior reflected in mentally simulated action," *Journal of Experimental Psychology: Human Perception and Performance* 20: 709–730.
Perrig, W. and Kintsch, W. (1985) "Propositional and situational representations of text," *Journal of Memory and Language* 24: 503–518.
Rizzolatti, G. and Craighero, L. (2004) "The mirror neuron system," *Annual Review of Neuroscience* 27: 169–192.
Rock, I. (1973) *Orientation and Form*, New York: Academic Press.
Rouse, W. B. and Morris, N. M. (1986) "On looking into the black box: Prospects and limits in the search for mental models," *Psychological Bulletin* 100: 349–363.
Schwartz, D. L. (1995) "Reasoning about the referent of a picture versus reasoning about a picture as the referent," *Memory and Cognition* 23: 709–722.
Schwartz, D. L. and Black, J. B. (1996a) "Analog imagery in mental model reasoning: Depictive models," *Cognitive Psychology* 30: 154–219.
Schwartz, D. L. and Black, J. B. (1996b) "Shuttling between depictive models and abstract rules: Induction and fall back," *Cognitive Science* 20: 457–497.
Shepard, R. N. and Cooper, L. A. (1982) *Mental Images and their Transformations*, Cambridge: MIT Press.

Shepard, R. N. (1988) "Imagination of the scientist," in *Imagination and the Scientist*, edited by K. Egan and D. Nadaner, New York: Teachers College Press.

Shiffrar, M. and Freyd, J. J. (1990) "Apparant motion of the human body," *Psychological Science* 1: 257–264.

Solomon, K. O. and Barsalou, L. W. (2004) "Perceptual simulation in property verification," *Memory and Cognition* 32: 244–259.

Tye, M. (1991) *The Imagery Debate*, Cambridge: MIT Press.

Wexler, M., Kosslyn, S. M. and Berthoz, A. (1998) "Motor processes in mental rotation," *Cognition* 68: 77–94.

Wohlschlager, A. (2001) "Mental object rotation and the planning of hand movements," *Perception and Psychophysics* 63: 709–718.

Yeh, W. and Barsalou, L. W. (1996) "The role of situations in concept learning," in *Proceedings of the Cognitive Science Society 18*, edited by G. W. Cottrell, Hillsdale: Lawrence Erlbaum Associates.

Zwann, R. A. (1999) "Situation models: the mental leap into imagined worlds," *Current Directons in Psychological Science* 8: 15–18.

Zwann, R. A. and Radvansky, G. A. (1998) "Situation models in language comprehension and memory," *Psychological Bulletin* 123: 162–185.

18
KANTIAN ACCOUNTS OF THOUGHT EXPERIMENTS

Marco Buzzoni

1 Introduction

Kant did not distinguish between thought experiment (TE) and real-world experiment (RE), nor did he use the German term *Gedankenexperiment*. But he is of great importance in the history and theory of TEs. Many aspects of Kant's critical philosophy are connected with the concept of TE, including the definition of scientific experiment, the distinction between knowing and thinking, and the fact that "experiments" of pure and practical reason embody the specific method of philosophy (Section 2).

However, the main reason Kant plays such an important role in the history of the concept of TE is because the expression was first used not by Mach, as was believed until a few decades ago, but the Danish scientist Hans-Christian Ørsted, who introduced it (not only in Danish: *Tankeexperiment*, but also in German: *Gedankenexperiment*; Ørsted 1811 [1920]) in order to clarify the relation between mathematics and physical knowledge in Kant. Section 3 will be devoted to Ørsted's account, the first explicitly Kantian theory of TEs.

As we shall see, Ørsted wavers between two positions: sometimes he claims that TEs are merely the hypothetical aspect of REs while other times he assigns to them the capacity of determining a priori some fundamental laws of natural science. The latter position recalls the "material" aspect of the Kantian a priori, a notion which was abandoned by the philosophy of science at the end of the nineteenth century.

This is probably the main reason Ørsted's point of view had no real influence on the historical development of the concept of TE and why some recent Kantian or neo-Kantian accounts of TE depart from Ørsted's concept of the a priori. I, on the other hand, have defended an interpretation of the a priori as purely functional by retaining the necessary and universal character of Kant's a priori while rejecting the material a priori, since content can be given only by experience. On this view, TE and RE are complementary in a sense similar to the complementarity of form and matter in Kant: TEs without REs are empty; REs without TEs are blind (Section 4). On the other hand, Yiftach Fehige has defended a relativized and contingent notion of the a priori which has been recently advocated by many authors, notably by Michael Friedman. Unlike myself, Fehige rejects the universality and necessity of Kant's a priori but retains the idea that the a priori, as a constitutive element of experience, is endowed with material content that may be made explicit by thought experimentation (Section 5).

2 Kant's concept of scientific experiment and the "experiments of pure reason"

In the present section, we shall briefly discuss a few of the many aspects of Kant's critical philosophy that are intimately connected with today's theories of TE, such as the definition of scientific experiment, the distinction between knowing and thinking, and the fact that Kant held that the "experiments" of pure and practical reason embody the special method of (transcendental) philosophy.

According to Kant, scientific experiments are "questions" put to nature (KrV B xiii–xiv, AA 10, lines 17 and 27). These questions are guided, as it were, by hypothetical thinking; as Kant puts it, the experimenter is not viewed "in the character of a pupil who listens to everything that the teacher chooses to say, but of an appointed judge who compels the witnesses to answer questions which he has himself formulated" (KrV B XIII, AA III 10).

This definition is important for two reasons. First, because it assumes an internal conceptual space, a kind of space of reason where immediate intuition is questioned from a conceptual standpoint. Secondly, because it implicitly assumes that, in some sense, answers may be hypothesized before the verdict of experience. Later on, in the Preface to the *Metaphysical Foundations of Natural Science*, Kant radicalizes the autonomy of this conceptual space to the point that all genuine natural science is deemed to include a "pure part" (*reiner Theil*), which is the object of a "pure rational knowledge" of "the a priori principles of all the other explanations of nature" (cf. AA, IV, Vorrede, 469, lines 2–22). As we shall see, the relative autonomy of this space of reason paved the way for Ørsted's theory of TEs.

Many of Kant's conceptions bear a close relation to today's notion of TE. Among the most important of Kant's conceptions in this respect are the distinction between "knowing" (*Denken*) and "thinking" (*Erkennen*) and the notion of "experiments of pure reason" (*Experimente der reinen Vernunft*).

With respect to Kant's well-known unity and distinction between knowing and thinking, I refer to Kant's key objection to the ontological argument, namely the confusion between "to exist" and "to be conceived of as existing," the confusion between actual existence and existence only in thought ("gedachte[r] Existenz") (*Der einzig mögliche Beweisgrund zu einer Demonstration des Daseins Gottes*, AA II 156, line 14). Parallel with and related to this distinction is that between "to exist only in thought" (*existiren nur in Gedanken*) and "to have only in thought" (*nur in Gedanken haben*). These expressions are used by Kant in the many passages in which he speaks of reason's ability to think something as merely possible or to abstract material from formal (a priori) components (for example, in order to obtain the idea of a pure, non-empirical and absolute space; cf. MAN, AA, IV, 481–2 and 506–7).

Finally, the concept of "experiments of pure reason" introduced by Kant in the Preface to the second edition of the *Critique*, has important connections both terminologically and conceptually with today's debate on TEs. This concept addresses a problem which, with very few exceptions, has received little attention in the literature on Kant in general (cf. Kalin 1972; Westphal 2003, 2004; Shi-Hyong 2008; Fulkerson-Smith 2013) and on TEs in particular (see Kühne 2005; Buzzoni 2011; Fehige 2012; Fehige and Stuart 2014).

Experiments of pure reason are intended to clarify the method of transcendental philosophy: this is why they are central to a Kantian appraisal of philosophical TEs, a task yet to be accomplished. In philosophy, unlike the natural sciences, one cannot test claims by experimenting with the relevant objects (cf. KrV B XX–XXI Anm., AA III 14 Anm.). Accordingly, for transcendental arguments not to be arbitrary there must be a criterion which enables one to distinguish true arguments from false ones. This criterion, given by the "method" of the experiments of pure reason, consists in considering objects "from two different points of view," namely "as objects of the senses and of the understanding for experience [*für die Erfahrung*]" on the one hand and "as objects which are thought merely" on the other. If, when considering things from this dual standpoint, we find that "there is agreement with the principle of pure reason," while if we adopt a single point of view there arises an "unavoidable self-conflict" of reason, then "the experiment decides in favour of the correctness of this distinction." (KrV B XVIII–XIX Anm., AA III 13 Anm.)

In other words, an experiment of pure reason consists in showing that a certain distinction (say, the distinction between things as appearances and things in themselves) is true because it is both a necessary and a sufficient condition for avoiding a contradiction of pure reason with itself:

> The *analysis of the metaphysician* separated [*schied*] pure *a priori* knowledge into two very heterogeneous elements, namely, the knowledge of things as appearances, and the knowledge of things in themselves; his *dialectic* combines these two again, in *harmony* with the necessary idea of the *unconditioned* demanded by reason, and finds that this harmony can never be obtained except through the above distinction, which therefore is the true one [*welche also die wahre ist*].
>
> (KrV B XX–XXI Anm., AA III 14 Anm.)

From this point of view, Kalin's thesis that Kant's transcendental arguments "can be characterized ... as Gedankenexperimente" (Kalin 1972, 322) can be applied to the entire *Critique of Pure Reason*. The whole book can be seen as an experiment of pure reason, a philosophical TE whose truth is guaranteed by the fact that human understanding loses itself in antinomies when it ventures beyond the limits of possible experience and attempts to deal with things in themselves (Buzzoni 2011, 105).

Experiments of this kind are not unique to theoretical reason: they may also be used to avoid self-contradiction in the practical use of reason. To begin with, they are instantiated in the first formulation of the categorical imperative: one should act only according to that maxim whereby one can, at the same time and without contradiction, will that it should become a universal law (cf., e.g., MAN, AA IV, 421, 07–08; for the first formulation of the categorical imperative as a TE, see Illies 2007, 313). Secondly, Kant talks explicitly about an "experiment" of practical reason in a passage of the *Critique of Practical Reason*. Exactly as he does in the *Critique of Pure Reason*, Kant remarks that philosophy has an additional problem with respect to natural science or mathematics, since a philosopher cannot use intuition as a foundation but, "almost like a chemist" (*beinahe wie der Chemist*), he or she can at any time conduct "an experiment with every man's practical reason" identifying the relevant moral (pure) principle of determination. The chemist adds alkali to a solution of lime in hydrochloric acid, in order get the lime to precipitate. Similarly, we may add, even if "only in thought" (*nur in Gedanken*), the moral law (as a determining principle) to the empirically affected will, in order to avoid a contradiction of reason with itself (cf. *Kritik der praktischen Vernunft*, AA, V, 92–3, lines 33–7 and 1–10). Finally, Kant uses the expression "experiment of pure reason" also in the essay "On Eternal Peace." By abstracting all empirical matters (such as the various relationships between citizens or between states) from the idea of public law, Kant extends the first formulation of the categorical imperative to the definition of public law. How may we judge whether the "form" of the law is realized in any particular case? By means of "an experiment of pure reason," which is "a criterion which is easy to use in experience and is presented a priori in reason." We have to judge whether the "form" of the law can or cannot be combined with the principles of a moral agent. If not, we can "immediately recognize the falsity (illegality) of a legal claim (*praetensio juris*)" (*Zum ewigen Frieden. Ein philosophischer Entwurf*, AA, VIII 381, 04–18).

To the extent that experiments of pure reason are methodologically similar to scientific experiments, one may agree with Shi-Hyong (2008) and Fulkerson-Smith (2013) that "experiments of pure reason" show Bacon's influence on Kant. However, one should not stress similarities at the expense of fundamental differences between the two kinds of experimentation. It is true that Kant associates reason's capacity to abstract the material from the formal (a priori) components of a phenomenon with the chemist's activity of experimenting. However, it is the use of experiments of pure reason that distinguishes transcendental philosophy from the empirical sciences and mathematics. For this reason we cannot accept Westphal's claim that transcendental arguments have the status of psychological, "epistemic reflections," which attempt to find out "whether Kant's inventory of cognitive capacities holds true *of us*" (Westphal 2003, 141) "by using wildly counter-factual TEs" (Westphal 2004, introduction; see also 18–34). Kant's idea should be developed such that it reconciles a difference between scientific and philosophical TEs with a methodological naturalism that admits no difference in kind between the methods of science and philosophy (see Buzzoni 2016).

3 Novalis', Lichtenberg's, and Ørsted's concept of TE

Among the authors cited as precursors of neo-Kantian accounts of TEs there are Novalis (1772–1801) and Georg Christoph Lichtenberg (1742–1799) (cf. Schöne 1982; Daiber 2001, 24; Schildknecht 1990, 123–69; Kühne 2005, 220–21; Fehige 2012; Fehige and Stuart 2014, 181–98).

Though we find in Novalis the notions both of an "experimental physics of the mind" and of "complete experiments" as a synthesis of physical experiments and poems of productive imagination (cf. Fehige 2012, 156), his importance in the history of the Kantian approaches to TEs should not be overestimated. First, a generic Kantian influence is insufficient to qualify one as a "Neo-Kantian" (cf. Anderson 2005, 289). Secondly, this influence in Novalis is overlaid with many others (Fichte, Schelling, Spinoza, Plotinus, Plato, Schiller, Goethe, Böhme, Baader, etc.). Thirdly, scientific experiments for Novalis are no more reliable than philosophical or fictional ones – a thesis that blurs, in full accord with

German *Naturphilosophie* and Romanticism, Kant's distinction between physics, mathematics and philosophy.

More important than Novalis was Lichtenberg, who spoke of "experimenting with thoughts" ("mit Gedanken ... experimentieren") and of "*experimenting* with ideas" ("mit Ideen *experimentieren*") (Lichtenberg 1968 [1994], K308). Lichtenberg is also well aware that TEs share with REs the character of questions put to nature (Lichtenberg 1971 [1994], K 308 and 310). Moreover, he maintains that the careful use of the subjunctive mode may be used experimentally to break apart conceptual connections that limit scientific creativity (cf. Fehige and Stuart 2014, 187). Finally, Lichtenberg notes that TEs require hypothetical idealizations (cf. Lichtenberg 1971 [1994], K 311) which consist in carrying to the limit the value of a variable (Lichtenberg 1971 [1994], J 1644) – an idea later to be taken up by Mach.

The first theory of TEs that can be defined as Kantian or neo-Kantian in a more rigorous sense was developed by Hans Christian Ørsted. Ørsted adopts Kant's idea of scientific experiment: "To make experiments is to ask questions of nature, but no one can do this usefully unless he knows what to ask about" (Ørsted 1811 [1920], §14. English translation, 294). However, Ørsted criticizes Kant for not considering chemistry as a proper natural science because it was not amenable to mathematization: TE is for Ørsted a particular a priori method for studying dynamic chemical processes (cf. Witt-Hansen 1976, 53–4; Kühne 2005, 92–165; Cohnitz 2008; Buzzoni 2011, 97–99; Fehige 2012, §4; Wilson 1998 [2014], XXII–XXIII; Christensen 2013, 267).

According to Ørsted, TEs are widely used in mathematics, where they consist in the construction of concepts in the intuition: "When we allow a point to move in our imagination in order to produce a line, or a line to rotate around one of its *extremities* to describe a circle with the other, what is this but a TE? Differential and integral calculus consist of nothing but such thought experiments and considerations of them" (Ørsted 1811 [1920], English translation, 296). But TEs are not only demonstrations in the sense of Kant's *Critique of Pure Reason*, which have no "point of contact with today's use of the expression in philosophy of science" (Cohnitz 2008, 407–8). As I said earlier, TEs constitute an a priori method that can be extended to any field of the natural sciences, including chemistry (cf. Ørsted 1822, 482–3; cf. also Fehige 2012, 151–52, who provides a detailed criticism of Cohnitz's point of view).

Kühne 2005 argued that Ørsted wavers between two positions: on the one hand he claims that TEs are only a necessary precondition of empirical science, which is always ultimately founded on REs (cf. Ørsted 1811, §19; Christensen 2013, 271); on the other hand he ascribes to TEs the capacity of determining some fundamental laws of natural science with a degree of certainty in principle identical with that of mathematics (cf. Ørsted 1851, 7–8, and Ørsted 1850/1851, vol. 2 (1851), §§14 and 15; Kühne 2005, respectively 138 and 149–50; Wilson 1998 [2014]).

This wavering depends upon the fact that the status of Kant's a priori is ambiguous and open to opposing interpretations. As is well-known, according to Kant, (1) all "a priori knowledge" is independent of experience (KrV B 3, AA 28, B 117, 269, AA 99–100, 187); (2) the a priori is the condition upon which all experience depends (KrV B 269, AA 188); and (3) the distinctive traits of the a priori are "unconditional necessity" (*unbedingte Notwendigkeit*) and "true," (*wahre*) "strict," (*strenge*) or "absolute universality" (*absolute Allgemeinheit*) (cf. KrV B 3–5, AA 28–30, B 64, AA 68). However, Kant oscillates between two distinct and ultimately contradictory interpretations of the a priori thus defined, one functional and one material. On the one hand, Kant says that the a priori determines only the formal conditions of experience and is devoid of material content; on the other hand, he ascribes content to the (synthetic) a priori since he believes that his transcendental philosophy provides a genuine metaphysical foundation for Newton's natural philosophy, and that part of Newton's *Principia* (its "pure part") provides us with universal and necessary knowledge in need of no further substantial modification (cf. Friedman 1992, 4).

Ørsted's account of TEs, under the influence of German romantic *Naturphilosophie*, develops Kant's a priori in the second (material) rather than the first (functional) sense. In this respect, it is important to note that Ørsted's method of TE is reminiscent of Kant's so-called "transition project" (published posthumously), concerning a possible transition from the special metaphysics of nature contained in the *Metaphysical Foundations* to physics itself (Christensen 2013, 267; on Kant's "transition project," cf. also Hall 2009).

As I stated above, Ørsted's point of view had no real influence on the historical development of the concept of TE. A glance at the history of the philosophy of science in the light of the previous considerations is sufficient to explain this fact. According to Moritz Schlick, the question "Is there a material a priori?" must be answered in the negative: "The empiricism which I hold believes itself to know with certainty that, as a matter of principle, all statements are either synthetic *a posteriori* or tautological; according to it, synthetic *a priori* statements seem to be a logical impossibility" (Schlick 1932 [1969], 25). This rejection of the material a priori was ultimately accepted not only by the Logical Empiricists but also by principal exponents of the philosophy of science, since the birth of the discipline at the end of the nineteenth century. The material a priori was rejected either in the empiricist spirit of Mach, Neo-positivism, Bridgman, and Popper, or in the conventionalist spirit of Poincaré and Duhem, later taken up by the relativist philosophy of science of the 1960s and the "sociological turn," which construed the a priori as a changeable function of historically shifting pragmatic interests. Kant's a priori was therefore regarded as an error, perhaps as an inevitable one before Riemann, Einstein, and the founders of quantum physics, but nevertheless as an error (cf., for example, Mach 1883 [1933], 458–9; Poincaré 1902 [1968], 74–5; Reichenbach 1920, 1–5, and 1938, 12 and 346; Einstein 1924, 1688–9; Bridgman 1927, 3–9; Popper 1963, ch. 7).

It was therefore no accident that broadly Kantian approaches to TEs grew out of concepts of the a priori that were essentially different from Ørsted's. I myself view the a priori as universal but purely formal or functional, that is, devoid of any content. Yiftach Fehige views the a priori as material, but contingent and relativized. In both cases we find the same rejection of an essentially idealistic notion of the a priori in the sense that was fully developed by Hegel. We shall devote the rest of this chapter to examining these two neo-Kantian approaches to TEs.

4 TEs from a neo-Kantian point of view: the transcendental-operational account

After Ørsted, my own transcendental-operational account was the first "Kantian treatment" of TEs (Brown 2011, 202). As Lichtenberg and Ørsted did, I began with Kant's definition of "experiment," according to which a RE is a "question" put to nature; however,

I interpreted the notion of experiment from the viewpoint of an a priori that is devoid of any particular content. It is true that Kant ascribes some content to the (synthetic) a priori, but only a functional reading of the a priori agrees with the spirit of Kant's philosophy and can be used for developing a consistent account of TEs. In fact, there is in Kant a fundamental tendency to consider the synthetic a priori in a purely formal (or rather, *functional*) sense which he contrasts with the *material* conditions, which are given through sensation. For example, Kant emphasized that categories not applied to sense content are "merely functions of the understanding for concepts" and "cannot ... be employed in any manner whatsoever," whether empirical or transcendental (cf. respectively KrV B 187, AA 139, B 305, AA III 208). It is in connection with this sense of the a priori that Kant claims that the manifold is given through the "I think" as the supreme condition of the possibility of experience: the "I think" cannot have a content of its own and must be conceived as a mere form or function (KrV B §16, AA 110).

On the basis of this concept of the a priori, I developed an account that mediates between Brown and Norton by considering TEs from two distinct but connected points of view: transcendental and operational (Buzzoni 2004, 2007, 2008, 2011). On the one hand, the account is transcendental in a very usual sense of the word (cf. Hatfield 1990, 79): TEs are the condition of the possibility of REs because, without the a priori capacity of the mind to reason counterfactually, we could not devise any hypothesis and would be unable to plan the corresponding RE that should test it. This capacity underpins the distinction in principle – a properly transcendental distinction – between TEs and REs. This distinction "cannot be suppressed, since it is the same distinction between the hypothetical-reflexive domain of the mind (which can always contradict itself) and reality (which can always occur and develop in only one way)" (Buzzoni 2013a, 99–100).

But while there is a distinction in principle between TE and RE on the transcendental level of the a priori capacity of the mind to reason counterfactually, the exclusively functional character of the a priori entails that, on the operational-methodological level, TEs – considering their empirical content and actual performance within a discipline – are and function essentially like REs (cf. Buzzoni 2013a, 98).

At the operational-methodological level, an empirical TE "anticipates ... a hypothetical experimental situation so that, on the basis of previous knowledge, we are confident that certain interventions on the experimental apparatus will modify some of its aspects (or 'variables') with such a degree of probability that the actual execution of the experiment becomes superfluous." (Buzzoni 2013a, 97, italics dropped; cf. also 2008, 93) Now, how ought we to interpret this "previous knowledge" in the light of a functional, non-hypostatized a priori? If pure reason cannot provide any content, the entire content of empirical TEs must come in principle from empirical-operational interventions on reality, that is, from actual experimentation. In this sense, a TE would be devoid of empirical meaning (that is, it would not be a TE proper to empirical science) if it did not possess, even while it is still in our minds, an (at least implicit) reference to experience.

The operational-methodological similarity and the transcendental distinction of TEs and REs are best illustrated by Kant's example of a hundred dollars (cf. KrV B 627, AA III 401).

On the one hand, from the perspective of the analysis of the intensions of the respective concepts, our conception of a hundred dollars remains the same irrespective of whether I own them or not. In the same sense, every (empirical) TE corresponds to a RE that satisfies the same conceptual characteristics, and vice versa. All REs may also be thought of as realizations of TEs; conversely, all empirical TEs must be conceivable as preparing and anticipating REs: They must, that is, anticipate a connection between objects which, when thought of as realized, makes the TE coincide completely with the corresponding RE (cf. Buzzoni 2008, 110). For this reason, TEs have the same operational-methodological traits as REs: both are constituted by a theory and a particular, well-specified experimental apparatus (Buzzoni 2013a, 97–8); both ask questions about nature and its laws; both apply Mach's method of variation, whereby some variables are systematically modified to establish which relation of dependence, if any, holds between them; both do that in a theory-laden and idealized way, so that the meaning of both must always be interpreted; both exemplify an "inductive-experimental use of reason" (Buzzoni 2008, 69 and 109; more recently the same claim is made by Clatterbuck 2013); in both cases visualization, perspicuity, intuitive appeal, and clarity are important because empirical TEs apply hypotheses to specific particular cases (those relevant for testing their truth or falsity).

On the other hand, from the transcendental perspective, thought dollars, like TEs, exist only in the sphere of the possible, while real dollars, like REs, occupy a specific place among the interactions between our bodies and the surrounding reality (cf. Buzzoni 2008, 113).

An important consequence of this unity and distinction of REs and TEs is that neither would be what it is outside their mutual relationship. On the one hand, despite their conditioned empirical power, TEs are very important in science for the following reasons: (1) at the most fundamental (transcendental) level, without TEs there would not be REs (we would not know how to put our questions to nature); (2) at the operational-methodological level, TEs, to the extent that they are based on well-established scientific facts and laws of nature, even if they are not realized or we decide not to realize them, can "inductively extend our knowledge" (Buzzoni 2008, 96) and support, at least provisionally, fresh scientific claims. On the other hand, without already realized TEs there would be no reliable empirical laws on which new TEs can base their anticipated answers to new questions. To sum up, they are complementary in a typical Kantian sense: "(empirical) TEs without REs are empty; REs without TEs are blind" (Buzzoni 2013a, 100).

A number of objections have been raised against my account. Brown and Fehige 2014 have objected that, "given the many scientific TEs that cannot be realized in the real-world, Buzzoni might be conflating TEs with imagined experiments to be carried out in the real-world." (cf. also Fehige 2013, 62–3). Now, is an imagined (real) experiment a TE? Yes and no. Surely not, if it is considered apart from any intentional planning. On the other hand, an imagined (real) experiment is a TE if mental "images" are thought of as mental *projects* with experimental value, that is, if they are seen in connection with the ability to reason about the outcomes of a series of possible actions. Remembering or imagining a hundred dollars is not an empirical TE. But this imagining becomes a TE if we place it in a planning context: for example, if we see it from the standpoint of a forger who anticipates in thought how to illegally produce the money (maybe without putting his project into practice because of technical difficulties or because it is too risky).

Another important objection is that for many TEs the requirements of empirical realizability and technical-operational testability appear to be either in principle unsatisfiable or superfluous (Fehige 2013). I have replied to this objection by insisting on the difference between *de facto* and *in principle* realizability. Obviously, there are good empirical

TEs that, *de facto*, neither are nor will ever be REs: limitations of our intelligence or resources may indefinitely postpone the realization of a TE, perhaps certain technical barriers will remain forever unsurmountable, and so on. More than this: many TEs are as important as they are exactly because we are either technically incapable of realizing them or unwilling to carry out the corresponding REs, even though we have good reasons to regard them as in principle realizable. The crucial point is that no empirical TE can ever be absolutely unrealizable without losing its empirical character. We believe that empirical TEs are scientifically useful and reliable because we presuppose that, if they were realized, the sequence of events *that they describe according to causal connections which we assume to be operative in the real world*, would occur in the way they anticipate, and would lead to the consequences that they predict. This holds in principle, no matter how remote the realizability of certain TEs may be. If this assumption is abandoned, TEs cease to be scientific in any important sense. A narrative TE can be incompatible with reality without this having any immediate implications for its truth. On the contrary, if we suppose that Einstein's lift scenario is physically impossible not just in practice, but in principle, it would then no longer be directly relevant to science. Without the assumption of the possibility of a practical realization, we abandon science and are left with only the play of imagination (cf. Buzzoni 2013b, 280–1).

A third and final objection is that I do not give a criterion for distinguishing good from bad TEs independently of physical experiments (Fehige 2013, 63). My reply is that, while it is true that in cases of doubt we must turn to real experiments, which remain the ultimate criterion for all empirical TEs, the general criterion of realizability is, on its own, insufficient to distinguish good from bad empirical TEs. In order to do that, the general criterion of realizability must be translated into concrete and detailed criteria and methods, which are as numerous as the different problems of human life itself. Since the number of these problems is indeterminate, no complete list of criteria or methods can be given *a priori* or (what comes to the same thing) they cannot be reduced to a single criterion or method. For example, we may examine whether a TE only uses widely accepted empirical generalizations, unquestionable assumptions, or everyday abilities so that the carrying out of the corresponding RE could only lead to a foregone conclusion. Otherwise we may detect ambiguities in the meaning of the question that the TE puts to nature. It may also be possible to investigate critically whether a TE rests upon or is consistent with inductively well-supported laws (provided these laws are relevant to the case at hand). Or we may resort to indirect means of assessing a TE, i.e., to methods which are only indirectly related to its realizability in principle, for example, by asking questions such as, "Does the TE answer an important question or does it sidetrack thought into collateral issues?" "Is it fruitful, for example in the sense of opening up new prospects for research?"

It is only through a process of interpretation and reinterpretation of the past history of knowledge (in this case, of the past evaluations of TEs) that we know anything about such methods and criteria (this process is an aspect of the hermeneutic aspect of TEs: cf. Buzzoni 2008, ch. 3 §3). Only by reconstructing past evaluations of TEs can one discover criteria that form a body of fairly stable methods for the attainment of good evaluations. These methods are, in the last analysis, authorized by past experience and successful REs, but they are not a fixed and unchangeable catalogue: the evaluator applies them to new cases and transforms them so that the discussion about the set of good methods never ends (cf. Buzzoni 2013b).

Developing some points of my view, Mike Stuart has tried to interpret the a priori in the light of Kant's notion of transcendental "schemata" which connect the senses with the understanding. Stuart claims that for Kant, the schemata are not concepts themselves, nor rules for application of concepts (Schaper 1964, 272). They are the action or performance of connecting concepts to experience or other concepts. Applying and connecting concepts to real-world activity requires exercising the faculty of judgment, which cannot be taught via rules, but has to be practiced and improved, usually by the use of examples (cf. Allison 1983 [2004], 207). Adopting my notion of the a priori, which relies on the capacity of the mind to consider things counterfactually, Stuart contends that TEs can fix the meaning of difficult theoretical structures (principles, equations, concepts, models, etc.) through the use of imaginary examples. This increases understanding for Stuart, not knowledge. He emphasizes that while understanding is an important step on the path to new knowledge, it is not new knowledge itself. Therefore on the one hand, Stuart sees imagination as the *necessary* a priori condition of (meaningful) "understanding" alone, not of (true) "knowledge": the bare use of the imagination in science cannot be justified by cognitive science or by philosophy. It is only justified in a transcendental sense because it is always necessarily presupposed by both. That is why it is a *sine qua non* of scientific understanding" (Stuart 2017). And on the other hand, this idea is developed from the perspective of cognitive science. In accordance with the top-down processing accepted by many cognitive scientists today, TEs can connect theoretical structures to experience or other theoretical structures that are already meaningful. Stuart agrees with me that at bottom, scientific knowledge and understanding result from operationalization. However, in difficult cases, as in the development of quantum mechanics, the connection between partially operationalized structures must be made via the imagination.

5 TEs from a neo-Kantian point of view: the relativized a priori account

As we have seen, under the influence of German romantic *Naturphilosophie* Ørsted's account of TEs developed Kant's a priori in a sense that may be called material and that was rejected by later schools of philosophy of science. I moved in the opposite direction by retaining the universality and necessity of Kant's a priori, while subtracting from it any particular content, which instead comes only from experience. On the contrary, Yiftach Fehige provided a third way of defending a neo-Kantian approach to TEs: under the influence of Michael Friedman, Fehige retained the material character of the a priori, while abandoning its necessity and universality (Fehige 2013).

Reichenbach distinguished two meanings of Kant's notion of a priori knowledge: "Kant's concept of a priori has two different meanings. First, it means 'apodictically true' (*apodiktisch gültig*), 'true for all times' and secondly, 'constituting the concept of object'" (Reichenbach 1920 [1965], 46. English translation slightly modified). Many authors followed Reichenbach by rejecting the first meaning while retaining the second. The result is "a relativized and dynamical conception" of the Kantian a priori: a priori principles are not universal and necessary (and therefore fixed for all times), but they are preconditions for knowledge, in the sense that they are constitutive of the objects of knowledge according to a given theory, with respect to which they are thus relative. A priori principles may provide an answer to Kuhn's challenge because they guarantee the unity of science "across revolutionary paradigm-shifts" (Friedman 2002, 185; cf. also Friedman 2010, 716; on the "relativized a priori" see, for example, Philström and Sitonen 2006; Richardson 2010, 282; Tanona 2010, 423–4; De Boer 2010).

The idea in itself is not new. Not only Poincaré and Reichenbach (cf., for example, Friedman 2002, 173–5), but also philosophers as different as Lorenz (1941/42, 1959, 1973 [1977]), Wittgenstein, Popper, Kuhn, Miller (1941), Pap (1944 and 1946), Milmed (1961), Scheffler (1967), Körner (1969 [1979]), and perhaps also Lewis and Dewey (cf. Stump 2011, 247) shared a view of this kind. What is new is the application of the relativized a priori to the understanding of TEs. This notion assumes a content for the a priori that can be made explicit through TEs, without suffering under Ørsted's delusion that TEs are capable of establishing some kind of necessity with respect to empirical statements concerning nature. In fact, this concept of the a priori has much less to do with Husserl's material a priori (cf., for example, Husserl 1950, I, §§9 and 16), which was criticized by Schlick, than with the conception – to mention only one of many possible examples – of Arthur Pap (cf. 1944 and 1946), who distinguished between a "material," a "functional," and a "formal" (or analytic) a priori. In this way, the material aspect of Kant's a priori, which for me was a limit that needed to be overcome, becomes for Fehige a point of departure for developing an alternative neo-Kantian account of TEs. More precisely, according to Fehige the kind of synthetic a priori knowledge that Kant ascribed to the "pure part" of natural science is the strongest reason to return to Kant in order to find a middle ground between Platonism and empiricism: a Kantian theory of TEs dispenses with Platonic entities and intellectual intuition of any kind, while taking seriously "the idea that TEs can reveal information about the world that goes beyond pure empirical input" (Fehige and Stuart 2014, 206; cf., in the same vein, see Fehige 2012, 147).

For Fehige, this neo-Kantian account is an extension and refinement of Kuhn's views about TEs. It must be admitted that the challenge to the analytic-synthetic dichotomy inherent in Kuhn's idea that TEs teach us both about our concepts and about the world, clearly moves in the direction of some sort of synthetic a priori and posits an intrinsic connection between real and TEs. Moreover, Kuhn did not try to overcome the separation between analytic and synthetic judgements at the transcendental level, but rather at the historical-empirical level of the relativity of Wittgenstein's language games (Buzzoni 2005).

Fehige is therefore right to see the relationship between his own views and those of Gendler (2000) and McAllister (1996, 2004), who have also taken up Kuhn's point of view. Gendler's theory is a development of Kuhn's conception in the sense that TEs lead to new knowledge of the world by reconfiguring and revising pre-existing epistemological meta-frameworks. Similarly, James McAllister argued that the Galileo's TE against Aristotle's theory of motion, which involves dropping cannon balls of different weights, could not have been of intrinsic evidential significance without important changes in the epistemological meta-framework. In any case, it would be impossible in principle to deduce a contradiction from a theory, thus falsifying it, if there were no shared epistemological meta-framework in the sense of a relativized a priori (cf. Fehige 2013, 69–71).

From the point of view of a relativized and contingent a priori, Fehige develops a straightforward and plausible answer to the main epistemological challenge raised by TEs, namely how can TEs, which do not rely on new material drawn from experience (as REs do), lead to unexpected conclusions sometimes capable of casting doubt on well-confirmed empirical theories. The relevant new information that comes through "reconceptualization" is not empirical, but "philosophical and relates to the Kantian a priori à la Friedman ... It is a reconfiguration of internal conceptual space which depends on changes in the epistemological meta-framework that explains the progress on an empirical matter ... without new empirical information about the world" (Fehige 2013, 69).

Moving from this idea of the a priori, Fehige also provides a plausible answer to the problem of finding criteria for assessing the quality of a TE. Einstein's clock-in-the-box TE suffers from an important shortcoming in comparison with Galileo's falling bodies TE. While Einstein's TE "does not establish sufficiently a link between the Kantian a priori à la Friedman and the empirical matter under consideration," Galileo's TE "is successful in that it moves even the Aristotelian to accept the changes in the Kantian a priori enabling new conceptual possibilities which help the Aristotelian to perceive a familiar anomaly in a new light" (Fehige 2013, 71).

The neo-Kantian account of TEs based on the contingent a priori raises two questions. The first one relates to a theoretical rather than to a historical context, and concerns the tenability of Friedman's answer to Kuhn's challenge of incommensurability and relativism across revolutions. The second question is to what extent the account of TEs based on the contingent a priori can be said to be truly Kantian. As to the first issue, it has been observed that Friedman's neo-Kantian account ascribes to changeable principles a role that they cannot have (cf. Howard 2010) and that it is incapable of solving the main problem which it was intended to solve, that is the problem of incommensurability between paradigms in Kuhn's sense (Buzzoni 2013b, 289–91). Unfortunately I lack the space to address this controversial issue here (but see, for example, Boghossian and Peacocke 2000).

As far as the second question is concerned, we certainly have to preserve the spirit of Kant's philosophy more than its letter. But the question arises whether we can obey the spirit of Kant's philosophy without obeying considerable parts of its letter as well. First, to say that Friedman's a priori is Kantian because it is material in character and has the function of making experience possible seems to allow too many positions to be called "Kantian" (Buzzoni 2013b, 286–91). Secondly, although Kant's a priori is not entirely free from material elements (and in this sense it has something in common with Friedman's a priori), the utility of turning it into something that has all the properties found in the empiricist concept of experience – relativity, variability, particularity – is very doubtful. Some authors have argued that, if Kant's a priori is understood as phylogenetically or psychologically a posteriori, the independence from experience, which is the main characteristic of Kant's a priori, is lost (Kuhle and Kuhle 2003, 214; cf. also Haller 1987, 19–20).

Whatever answer one may give to these questions, which must here remain open, the current state of discussion shows that the relativized a priori account is likely to remain an important reference point in the debate about TEs: all the more important, to the extent that the conception of the contingent a priori is a very widespread one today.

6 Conclusion

We have outlined in this contribution a critical history of the concept of TE from a broadly Kantian viewpoint. The thread of our discussion has been Kant's position on the nature of the a priori and how each neo-Kantian theory of TEs can be understood in terms of its own position on this issue. Section 1 examined some aspects of Kant's philosophy that are related to today's debate on TEs. Section 3 was devoted to Ørsted's first important Kantian theory of TE, which had no effective influence on the historical development of the concept because his commitment to romantic *Naturphilosophie* led him to see TE as a special method for an a priori physics.

Given the rejection of a material a priori by the most important schools of philosophy of science, it was no accident that a broadly Kantian approach to TEs was recently taken up by moving to quite different interpretations of the a priori, namely as universal and necessary, but devoid of content (myself and Mike Stuart), and as a set of principles which are taken as constitutive of experience, but only in a contingent and relativized way (Yiftach Fehige).

References

Allison, H. (1983 [2004]) *Kant's Transcendental Idealism*, New Haven: Yale University Press.
Anderson, R. L. (2005) "Neo-Kantianism and the roots of anti-psychologism," *British Journal for the History of Philosophy* 13: 287–323.
Boghossian, P. and Peacocke, C. (2000) *New Essays on the A Priori*, Oxford: Oxford University Press.
Bridgman, W. (1927) *The Logic of Modern Physics*, New York: MacMillan.
Brown, J. R. (1991 [2011]) *Laboratory of the Mind: Thought Experiments in the Natural Sciences*, London: Routledge (quotations are from the 2nd ed., 2011).
Brown, J. R. and Fehige, Y. (2014) "Thought experiments," *Stanford Online Encyclopedia of Philosophy*. Available here: http://plato.stanford.edu/entries/thought-experiment/ (accessed 15 November 2016).
Buzzoni, M. (2004) *Esperimento ed esperimento mentale*, Milan: Angeli.
Buzzoni, M. (2005) "Kuhn und Wittgenstein: Paradigmen, Sprachspiele und Wissenschaftsgeschichte," in *Zeit und Geschichte/Time and History*, edited by F. Stadler and M. Stöltzner, Kirchberg: Ludwig Wittgenstein Gesellschaft.
Buzzoni, M. (2007) "Zum Verhältnis zwischen experiment und Gedankenexperiment in den Naturwissenschaften," *Journal for General Philosophy of Science* 38: 219–237.
Buzzoni, M. (2008) *Thought Experiment in the Natural Sciences: An Operational and Reflexive-Transcendental Conception*, Würzburg: Königshausen and Neumann.
Buzzoni, M. (2011) "Kant und das Gedankenexperiment," *Deutsche Zeitschrift für Philosophie* 59: 93–107.
Buzzoni, M. (2013a) "Thought experiments from a Kantian point of view," in *Thought Experiments in Philosophy, Science, and the Arts*, edited by M. Frappier, L. Meynell, and J. R. Brown, London: Routledge.
Buzzoni, M. (2013b) "On thought experiments and the Kantian a priori in the natural sciences: A reply to Yiftach J. H. Fehige," *Epistemologia* 36: 277–293.
Buzzoni, M. (2016) " Thought experiments in philosophy: A neo-Kantian and Experimentalist point of view," *Topoi*, DOI 10.1007/s11245-016-9436-6
Christensen, D. Ch. (2013) *Hans Christian Ørsted: Reading Nature's Mind*, Oxford: Oxford University Press.
Clatterbuck, H. (2013) "The epistemology of thought experiments: A non-eliminativist, non-platonic account," *European Journal for Philosophy of Science* 3: 309–329.
Cohnitz, D. (2008) "Ørsteds 'Gedankenexperiment': eine Kantianische Fundierung der Infinitesimalrechnung?" *Kant-Studien* 99: 407–433.
Daiber, J. (2001) *Experimentalphysik des Geistes. Novalis und das romantische Experiment*, Göttingen: Vandenhoeck und Ruprecht.
De Boer, K. (2010) "Kant, Reichenbach, and the fate of a priori principles," *European Journal of Philosophy* 19: 507–531.

Einstein, A. (1924) "Review of Elsbach, Alfred. Kant und Einstein. Untersuchungen über das Verhältnis der modernen Erkenntnistheorie zur Relativitätstheorie (Berlin-Leipzig: de Gruyter)," *Deutsche Literaturzeitung* 45: 1688–1689.

Fehige, Y. (2012) "'Experiments of pure reason': Kantianism and thought experiments in science," *Epistemologia* 35: 141–160.

Fehige, Y. (2013) "The relativized a priori and the laboratory of the mind: Towards a neo-Kantian account of thought experiments in science," *Epistemologia* 36: 55–73.

Fehige, Y. and Stuart, M.T. (2014) "On the origins of the philosophy of thought experiments: The forerun," *Perspectives on Science* 22: 179–220.

Friedman, M. (1992) *Kant and the Exact Sciences*, Cambridge: Harvard University Press.

Friedman, M. (2002) "Kant, Kuhn, and the rationality of science," *Philosophy of Science* 69: 171–190.

Friedman, M. (2010) "Synthetic history reconsidered," in *Discourse on a New Method: Reinvigorating the Marriage of History and Philosophy of Science*, edited by M. Domski and M. Dickson, Chicago: Open Court.

Fulkerson-Smith, B. (2013) "Kant's illuminating experiment: On the placement, purpose and essential procedure of the experiment of pure reason in the critique of pure reason," *Society and Politics* 7: 62–83.

Gendler, T. S. (2000) *Thought Experiment: On the Power and Limits of Imaginary Cases*, London: Garland.

Hall, B. (2009) "'Effecting a transition': How to fill the gap in Kant's system of critical philosophy," *Kant-Studien* 100: 187–211.

Haller, R. (1987) "Kommentar zu dem Vortrag von Konrad Lorenz über Evolution und Apriori," in *Die evolutionäre Erkenntnistheorie. Bedingungen-Lösungen-Kontroversen*, edited by R. Riedl and F. Wuketits, Berlin: Parey.

Hatfield, G. (1990) *The Natural and the Normative: Theories of Spatial Perception from Kant to Helmholtz*, Cambridge: MIT Press.

Howard, D. (2010) "'Let me briefly indicate why I do not find this standpoint natural': Einstein, General Relativity, and the contingent a priori," in *Discourse on a New Method: Reinvigorating the Marriage of History and Philosophy of Science*, edited by M. Domski and M. Dickson, Chicago: Open Court.

Husserl, E. (1950) *Ideen zu einer reinen Phänomenologie und phänomenologischen Philosophie*, Den Haag: Martinus Nijhoff.

Kalin, M. G. (1972) "Kant's transcendental arguments as Gedankenexperimente," *Kant-Studien* 63: 289–328.

Körner, S. (1969 [1979]) *Fundamental Questions of Philosophy: One Philosopher's Answers*, Brighton, UK: The Harvester Press; fourth edition 1979: Atlantic Highlands, NJ: Humanities Press.

Kuhle, M. and Kuhle, S. (2003) "Kants Lehre vom Apriori in ihrem Verhältnis zu Darwins Evolutionstheorie," *Kant-Studien* 94: 220–239.

Kühne, U. (2005) *Die Methode des Gedankenexperiments*, Frankfurt: Suhrkamp.

Lichtenberg, G. Ch. (1968 [1994]) *Schriften und Briefe. Erster Band: Sudelbücher I*, edited by W. Promies, Wien: Carl Hanser. Aphorisms are quoted by the letter assigned to a book, namely A–L, and the number of the aphorism within that book. Quotations are from the 1994 edition.

Kühne, U. (2005) *Die Methode des Gedankenexperiments*, Frankfurt: Suhrkamp.

Lichtenberg, G. Ch. (1971 [1994]) *Schriften und Briefe. Zweiter Band: Sudelbücher I. Materialhefte, Tagebücher*, edited by W. Promies, Wien: Carl Hanser. Aphorisms are quoted by the letter assigned to a book, namely A–L, and the number of the aphorism within that book. Quotations are from the fifth 1994 edition.

Lorenz, K. (1941–1942) "Kants Lehre vom Apriorischen im Lichte gegenwärtiger Biologie," *Blätter für deutsche Philosophie* 15: 94–125.

Lorenz, K. (1959) "Gestaltwahrenehmung als Quelle Wissenshaftlicher Erkenntnis," *Zeitschrift far experimentelle and angewandte Psychologie* 6: 118–165.

Lorenz, K. (1973 [1977]) *Die Rückseite des Spiegels*, München: Piper. English translation: *Behind the Mirror*, London: Methuen.

Mach, E. (1883 [1933]) *Die Mechanik in ihrer Entwickelung. Historisch-kritisch dargestellt*, Leipzig: Brockhaus (quotations are from the 9th ed., 1933).

McAllister, J. W. (1996) "The evidential significance of thought experiments in science," *Studies in History and Philosophy of Science* 27: 233–250.

McAllister, J. W. (2004) "Thought experiments and the belief in phenomena," *Proceedings of the Biennial Meeting of the Philosophy of Science Association* 71: 1164–1175.

Miller, D. L. (1941) "The a priori in contemporary thought," *Philosophy of Science* 8: 20–25.

Milmed, B. K. (1961) *Kant and Current Philosophical Issues: Some Modern Developments of His Theory of Knowledge*, New York: New York University Press.

Ørsted, H. C. (1811 [1920]) "Første Indledning til den almindelige Naturlære," in *Naturvidenskabelige Skrifter*, vols I–III, edited by K. Meier, Copenhagen: Høst and Søn, 1920, 151–190. English translation: "First introduction to general physics: A prospectus of lectures in this science," in *Selected Scientific Works of Hans Christian Ørsted*, 282–309, translated and edited by K. Jelved, A. D. Jackson, and O. Knudsen, Princeton: Princeton University Press.

Ørsted, H. C. (1822) "Über Geist und Studium der allgemeinen Naturlehre," *Gehlens Journal für Chemie und Physik* 36: 458–488.

Ørsted, H. C. (1850–1851) *Der Geist in der Natur*, 2 vols, Munich: Cotta. Translated by L. Horner and J. B. Horner, London: Bohn, 1952.

Ørsted, H. C. (1851) *Der mechanische Theil der Naturlehre*, Braunschweig: Vieweg und Sohn.

Pap, A. (1944) "The different kinds of a priori," *Philosophical Review* 13: 465–484.

Pap, A. (1946) *The A Priori in Physical Theory*, New York: King's Crown.

Philström, S. and Sitonen, A. (2006) "The transcendental method and (post) empiricist philosophy of science," *Journal for General Philosophy of Science* 36: 81–106.

Poincaré, H. (1902 [1968]) *La Science et l'Hypothèse*, Paris: Flammarion (quotations are from the 1968 edition).

Popper, K. R. (1963 [1972]) *Conjectures and Refutations: The Growth of Scientific Knowledge*, 4th ed., London: Routledge and Kegan Paul.

Reichenbach, H. (1920 [1965]). *Relativitätstheorie und Erkenntnis a priori*, Berlin: Springer. English translation by M. Reichenbach, *The Theory of Relativity and A Priori Knowledge*, Berkeley: University of California Press.

Reichenbach, H. (1938) *Experience and Prediction*, Chicago: University of Chicago Press.

Richardson, A. (2010) "Ernst Cassirer and Michael Friedman: Kantian or Hegelian dynamics of reason?" in *Discourse on a New Method: Reinvigorating the Marriage of History and Philosophy of Science*, edited by M. Domski and M. Dickson, Chicago: Open Court.

Schaper, E. (1964) "Kant's schematism reconsidered," *The Review of Metaphysics* 18: 267–292.

Scheffler, I. (1967) *Science and Subjectivity*, Indianapolis: Bobbs-Merrill.

Schildknecht, C. (1990) *Philosophische Masken: Literarische Formen der Philosophie bei Platon, Descartes, Wolff und Lichtenberg*, Stuttgart: Metzler.

Schlick, M. (1932 [1969]) "Gibt es ein materiales Apriori?" in *Wissenschaftlicher Jahresbericht der Philosophischen Gesellschaft an der Universität zu Wien – Ortsgruppe Wien der Kant-Gesellschaft für das Vereinsjahr 1931/1932*, Wien: Verlag der Philosophischen Gesellschaft. Quotations are from M. Schlick, Gesammelte Aufsätze 1926–1936, Hildesheim: Olms 1969, 19–30.

Schöne, A. (1982) *Aufklärung aus dem Geist der Experimentalphysik: Lichtenbergsche Konjunktive*, Munich: C. H. Beck.

Shi-Hyong, K. (2008) *Bacon und Kant: Ein Erkenntnistheoretischer Vergleich Zwischen dem 'Novum Organum' und der 'Kritik der reinen Vernunft'*, Frankfurt: de Gruyter.

Stuart, M. T. (2017) "Imagination: A sine qua non of science," *Croatian Journal of Philosophy*.

Stump, D. J. (2011) "Arthur Pap's functional theory of the a priori," *HOPOS: The Journal of the International Society for the History of Philosophy of Science* 1: 273–289.

Tanona, S. (2010) "Theory, coordination, and empirical meaning in modern physics," in *Discourse on a New Method: Reinvigorating the Marriage of History and Philosophy of Science*, edited by M. Domski and M. Dickson, Chicago: Open Court.

Westphal, K. R. (2003) "Epistemic reflections and cognitive reference in Kant's transcendental response to skepticism," *Kant-Studien* 94: 135–171.

Westphal, K. R. (2004) *Kant's Transcendental Proof of Realism*, Cambridge: Cambridge University Press.

Wilson, A. D. (1998 [2014]) "*Introduction*" to the English Translation of Ørsted 1811 [1920], XV–XL.

Witt-Hansen, J. (1976) "H. C. Ørsted, Immanuel Kant, and the thought experiment," *Danish Yearbook of Philosophy* 13: 48–65.

19
PHENOMENOLOGY AND THOUGHT EXPERIMENTS
Thought experiments as anticipation pumps

Harald A. Wiltsche

The aim of this chapter is to present an outline of a phenomenological theory of thought experiments (henceforth *TEs*). In doing so, I am dealing with a topic that is currently starting to receive increased attention from philosophers with phenomenological leanings. However, since no serious attempt has been made to tackle the issue in a systematic fashion, I will not merely review existing phenomenological work on TEs (such as Mohanty 1991; Kujundzic 1995; Froese and Gallagher 2010; Fehige and Wiltsche 2013; Wiltsche 2013; Hopp 2014). For the most part, my chapter is programmatic: its aim is to suggest some basic directions in which a phenomenological theory of TEs should be developed.

The chapter is structured as follows. I will begin by saying a word or two on what phenomenology is and on why I believe that it can contribute to the ongoing debate on TEs. I shall then introduce five phenomenological concepts that will prove crucial for an understanding of TE-reasoning: *fulfillment, frustration, horizon, anticipation* and *background knowledge*. My strategy is to first give a brief sketch of how knowledge acquisition works in the perceptual realm. It is against this backdrop that I will then outline how knowledge is generated in the realm of TE-reasoning. It is one of my main theses that TEs should be understood as *anticipation pumps*.

Before I begin, however, two qualifying remarks are in order. The first concerns my use of the term "phenomenology": Just as there is more than *one* analytic method, there is no general agreement within the phenomenological community on what *the* phenomenological method precisely is. It is thus important to bear in mind that the following portrayal of phenomenology reflects my own background in (a liberal reading of) Edmund Husserl's philosophy. Secondly, much of what I will have to say about TEs concerns TE-reasoning in science and not TE-reasoning in philosophy. To a certain extent, this limitation again reflects my own background in the philosophy of science. However, since I believe that scientific and philosophical TEs differ only in degree and not in kind, I am confident that the proposed framework can also be applied to non-scientific TEs.

1 Getting phenomenology off the ground

When phenomenology entered the philosophical stage in the early twentieth century, Neo-Kantianism was still in full swing. Otto Liebmann had coined the unifying motto "Back to Kant!" under which the Neo-Kantians sought to overcome the dispute between materialism and idealism that had dominated much of the philosophical discourse in Germany and Austria up until the mid-nineteenth century. It was against this motto that the first generation of phenomenologists directed their own slogan "Back to the *things themselves!*" Yet, it was not particularly Kant of whom Husserl and his followers were critical. The first wave of phenomenologists disapproved of any kind of philosophy that looks at its problems through the glasses of pre-established theories, systems or schemes. Instead of forcing problems into a particular (and potentially artificial) theoretical mould, phenomenologists were (and still are) driven by a deep respect for the *phenomena*, i.e., the things exactly as they are given in experience. On a phenomenological view, many philosophical problems could be solved – or even better: made to evaporate – if we resisted the temptation to interfere with ready-made theoretical schemes and put more effort in a faithful description of the phenomena.

Paradigmatic for this approach is Husserl's sixth Logical Investigation (Husserl 2001b, 177–348): The aim of this book-length treatise is to tackle one of the most fundamental issues in philosophy, namely to understand the concepts "truth," "knowledge" and "knowledge acquisition," as well as the relations between them. On Husserl's view, the trouble with many existing approaches to this issue is that they are infected with pre-established theoretical schemes already at the level of the formulation of the problem. For instance, a common way to start is to ask how a self-enclosed subject is able to reach the external world in order to attain justified true beliefs about reality by relying on acts of visual, auditory or olfactory perception. However, built into this question are a number of far-reaching assumptions such as common-sense realism or the view that a gap between the interiority of the mental and the exteriority of the world in fact exists. Husserl accepts that these and similar other assumptions may be useful or, in some cases, even indispensable in certain practical contexts. Yet, since the job of philosophy is not to simply adopt existing assumptions, but rather to scrutinize them, philosophical analysis must proceed from a standpoint that is not already contaminated with pre-established theoretical schemes. It is for this reason that Husserl actively "brackets"[1] all kinds of metaphysical, scientific and commonsensical assumptions and starts with a careful and unbiased *description* of the types of conscious experiences in which different types of objects become present from a first-person point of view. To be sure, nothing prevents the phenomenologist from eventually taking sides in traditional metaphysical disputes about, say, dualism, realism or physicalism. But whatever he or she will end up saying on such matters must result from a description of the phenomena and not from the mere stipulation of basic maxims or principles.

As I have pointed out, phenomenologists are driven by a deep respect for the phenomena, i.e., for the things as they appear in conscious experience. This general tenet – which, in my view, captures much of what makes a phenomenological account truly phenomenological[2] – also yields important consequences for how phenomenologists should approach the issue of scientific TEs. Let me begin by briefly summarizing how the discussion is usually framed: It is beyond dispute that TEs are part of scientific practice in core disciplines such as physics or biology. Most commentators also agree that at least some scientific TEs are successful in generating knowledge about the empirical world. But how is this possible? Since, by definition, they are experiments *in thought*, TEs do not seem to establish direct cognitive contact with the world. This makes the success of TEs indeed puzzling: How can we learn something about the world by merely thinking about it? It has become common to refer to this question as the *paradox of TEs* (cf. Horowitz and Massey 1991, 1).

Much of the contemporary discussion about scientific TEs is devoted to the task of solving this paradox. Hence, the existence of apparently successful TEs is usually treated as the explanandum to which suitable theoretical explanations are directed. On one such theory, the success of (some) TEs is explained by means of a Platonist construal of the laws of nature and by the ancillary epistemological thesis that TEs allow us to directly grasp these laws with our mind's eye (e.g., Brown 2004, 2011). Another theory explains the success of TEs by declaring them to be arguments in disguise. On this view, scientific TEs lead us to knowledge because they are, in reality, chains of inductive and/or deductive inferences (e.g., Norton 1996, 2004). On a third popular account, the success of TEs is explained by means of a psychological theory according to which the manipulation of mental models allows us to trigger knowledge formations that are not cognitively available otherwise (e.g., Miščević 1992; Nersessian 1992).

A good deal of ink has been spilled over these proposals and I will add to this discussion below. For the moment, however, I want to emphasize that much of the plausibility of each of these theories depends on quite substantial metaphysical, epistemological and ontological assumptions whose scope goes well beyond their actual subject matter. Take, for instance, Platonism: The plausibility of a Platonist explanation of TEs largely depends on our willingness to accept a rationalist epistemology, an ontology that includes universals and the view that the laws of nature are contingent necessitation relations between universal properties. If one accepts these assumptions, then Platonism is a perfectly good explanation for the existence of TEs in science history as well as of their apparent success. If, on the other hand, one thinks that we should be parsimonious in ontological and metaphysical matters and that sense perception is the only source of knowledge about the world, then one will likely opt for one of the empiricist alternatives to Platonism. Hence, although it would be too strong of a claim that the available theories on TEs are evaluated *only* on the basis of their commitments to certain metaphysical and epistemological stances, it is at least safe to say that these commitments play a decisive role in how the discussion normally evolves. And, supposedly, it is also due to these commitments that certain strands of the contemporary debate on TEs appear to be a mere sideline of the age-old battle between rationalism and empiricism.

Now, my point is not to deny that the TE-debate may have implications for the quarrel between rationalists and empiricists. Since it is at least initially plausible to regard TEs as prima facie cases of knowledge acquisition *minus* sense perception, the onus seems to be on philosophers with empiricist leanings to come up with a deflationary account on TE-reasoning. Rather, my point is that, if we wish to address TEs phenomenologically, the issue should be approached in a way that is not already contaminated with pre-established assumptions concerning metaphysical, ontological or epistemological matters. To construct one's theory on the basis of *either* rationalist *or* empiricist intuitions not only clashes with the phenomenological demand to proceed from an unbiased description of the phenomena; it also harbours the danger of begging the question against the respective opponent, of distorting the subject matter before the actual analysis can even begin and of ending up in a stalemate between irreconcilable epistemological and metaphysical systems.

Hence, what sets phenomenology apart from other theoretical alternatives is, first of all, its point of departure: Instead of treating TEs as explananda that call for theoretical explanations whose credibility depends on more general metaphysical, ontological and epistemological intuitions, phenomenology actively brackets such intuitions and proceeds from an unbiased description of the *phenomenon* of TE-reasoning instead. In other words: The main objective, at least at the initial stage, is not to construct a theory that seeks to bring TEs in line with certain pre-established standpoints. The main objective of a phenomenological account is rather to give a faithful description of the *actual performance* of TEs from a first-person perspective and to go on from there.

2 Filling up the phenomenological toolbox

As I have pointed out, phenomenology differs from other theories in its basic approach: A phenomenological account of TEs brackets all kinds of metaphysical, epistemological and scientific assumptions and proceeds from a faithful description of the *phenomenon* of TE-reasoning. However, what does this mean exactly? Where do we have to start if we wish to describe the performance of TE-reasoning from a first-person perceptive? How do we identify certain mental episodes as TEs? And how could we possibly tell if these mental episodes embody instances of successful knowledge acquisition?

In the face of these questions, my strategy in the remaining parts of this chapter will be as follows: Since I am interested in the question of whether TEs fall under the rubric of successful knowledge acquisition, I will have to say a few words on a phenomenological theory of knowledge first. It is mainly through the discussion of examples that I will introduce five concepts that are crucial for a phenomenological understanding of knowledge acquisition in the perceptual realm. These concepts will form the background against which I will then take a closer look at the imagination,[3] the medium in which TEs are performed. My aim is to highlight the similarities as well as the differences between perception and imagination in order to elucidate how knowledge is generated through the use of TEs.

2.1 Fulfillment and frustration

What is knowledge? When are we dealing with cases of successful knowledge acquisition? In line with the general tenets of the phenomenological research program, these questions, too, are to be answered by way of a description of those types of conscious experience in which the relevant distinctions become evident. Take the following two cases as a starting point: (1) I am judging that my bike is in the office while I am still in the cafeteria; and (2) I am judging that my bike is in the office while I am standing right in front of it. Phenomenologically construed, these two cases have a lot in common. To begin with, both experiences are experiences *of the same type*, namely experiences of judging (in contrast to experiences of doubting, imagining, fearing etc.). In addition, both experiences also have the same intentional object, namely my bike in the office. But, clearly, there is a striking difference as well: While the judgement about my bike's whereabouts may just be a wild guess as long as I am still in the cafeteria, the direct acquaintance with my bike (i.e., my standing right in front of it) warrants the judgement about my bike's location beyond all reasonable doubt.

The acknowledgement of this difference allows us to make a first step towards the notion of *fulfillment*, one of the main pillars of phenomenological epistemology: If – like in the first case – I am directed towards an object in its absence, then my intention towards the object is *empty*. If, on the other hand, I am directed towards an object in its actual presence – if the object is given in its "'bodily' selfhood" (*leibhaftige Selbstheit*) (Husserl 1983, 9–10; translation modified) – then my intention towards the object is *fulfilled* by the presence of that very object. Fulfillment, i.e., the congruence between the object as it is emptily intended and the object as it is intuitively given, is the ideal limit towards which our judging strives, "the measure of its success or failure" (Crowell 2006, 14). If this kind of congruence not only takes place, but is also registered by a cognizing subject, then we are dealing with what Walter Hopp aptly calls "knowledge at its best" (Hopp 2011, chapter 7).[4]

Let me summarize: *Fulfillment* takes place if there is a relation of congruence between an object as it is emptily intended and the object as it is intuitively given. Conversely, *frustration* occurs when the intuitive experience of an object is non-congruent with the empty intention towards that same object. In an ideal case of fulfillment, I realize that the object is exactly like I thought it would be. In cases of frustration, the intended object turns out to be different than initially thought. On a phenomenological view, all epistemic concepts such as evidence, justification or falsification ultimately lead back to the basic concepts of fulfillment and frustration.

2.2 Horizon and anticipation

The concepts of fulfillment and frustration are crucial for the phenomenological understanding of knowledge and knowledge acquisition. Fulfillment, i.e., the congruence between an object-as-intended and the object-as-given, is the ideal limit to which all of our knowledge claims aspire. On closer inspection, however, this turns out to be only part of the story, especially – but not only – with respect to the acquisition of empirical knowledge. Consider again the example of the veridical perception of my bike. At first glance, the direct perceptual givenness of my bike seems to clearly fulfil the judgment that my bike is in the office. But a more accurate description reveals that what is really experientially given in this situation is not simply *my bike*, but only *one single profile of my bike*, its current front side. To be sure, I could alter my position and make the current backside the new front side, and vice versa. But this does not change the fact that my bike is always given *in perspectives* and that, more generally, things always and necessarily have more parts, functions and properties than can be actualized in a single intentional act. My bike – as it is intended – is *transcendent*, not only in the sense that it can be seen from indefinitely many more perspectives than I can take up at a given point in time. It is also transcendent in the sense that it has, for instance, a momentarily hidden internal structure, a history, certain practical functions and many other properties that are not in the centre of attention right now.

So, a closer look at how things appear to us reveals that our intentions towards these things always "transcend" or "go beyond" the actual experiences that give rise to them.

As the example of my bike shows, there is a describable discrepancy between what is meant through a particular intentional act (my bike over there) and what is experientially given (my bike's facing side with its momentarily visible features). Phenomenologically construed, this discrepancy does not represent a problem that must be somehow remedied, e.g., by proposing a theory that explains how a number of seemingly disconnected profiles add up to a homogeneous thing to which we then attribute these profiles. The fact that our intentions towards things always transcend the sphere of intuitive givenness is rather to be treated as a phenomenologically discoverable feature of experience itself: Intending is, as Husserl puts it, always and necessarily an *"intending-beyond-itself"* (Husserl 1960, 46). In being intentionally directed towards material things, we "know" that there is more to them than is revealed in one single glance. This "knowing" is not a matter of inferential belief or judgement over and above the experiences in which things are perspectivally given; it is rather an essential part of any such experience.

The important lesson to draw from these considerations is that "each individual percept is a mixture of fulfilled and unfulfilled intentions" (Husserl 2001b, 221). Or, to put it in an alternative terminology: Intentional experiences are always embedded in implicit *horizons* of intentions that are momentarily unfulfilled, but that could be fulfilled in the course of further acts. Even though I can now only see my bike's facing side with its momentarily visible features, my bike appears to me as something that could be explored more fully. I "know" that I could alter my vantage point and explore its momentarily hidden back side. I "know" that I could look more closely and explore its surface in more detail. I "know" that I could cut the frame in half and explore its internal structure. It is these and indefinitely many other potentialities that add up to the implicit horizon against the background of which singular intentions towards things always stand out.

Phenomenological descriptions reveal that intentional acts towards things always point to implicit horizons of empty intentions. Hence, on a phenomenological view, experience is never exhausted by what is actual; experience is always already saturated with implicit references to future experiences that are possible insofar as they could be actualized in the course of further acts. However, in order to get a more complete understanding of the phenomenological notion of horizon, two more aspects have to be stressed: The first thing to note is that an act's horizon is, as I have already indicated, *implicit* to the act itself. This is to say that the horizon is no theoretical construct that is *retrospectively* ascribed to the initial act. An act's horizon is rather *co-given* with the initial act even though we usually are not aware of this. That my bike has a backside is not something that can only be asserted after I have changed my vantage point. It is also not something that is the product of some sort of inferential process. Rather, it is something that belongs to the very meaning of being intentionally directed towards material things.

The second important aspect is this: On the basis of what I have said so far, one could define horizons as sets of empty intentions against the background of which particular fulfilled intentions always and necessarily stand out. But this definition is somewhat misleading: Although it is correct to say that a horizon consists of empty intentions and thus can be described as a "halo of emptiness," it is crucial to stress that "this emptiness is not a nothingness," but rather that "the sense of this halo ... is a *prefiguring* that *prescribes a rule* for the transition to new actualizing appearances" (Husserl 2001c, 42; my emphasis). What Husserl is saying here can be elucidated with the help of my earlier example: If I perceive my bike, my intention towards the bike's facing side is conjoined with a horizon of empty intentions and thus with the anticipation that there is *more* to the bike than is revealed in one single act. However, this *more* is far from being indeterminate: In perceiving my bike, I implicitly anticipate concrete courses of experiences that are compatible with what was originally intended. The perception of the greyish blue of my bike's facing side, for instance, comes with the implicit anticipation that the momentarily hidden backside will exhibit the same colour as well. To be sure, it is possible that this anticipation is frustrated by future experiences. But if I were to find out that my bike's backside is not greyish blue, but coated with diamonds and rubies, then I would probably start to wonder whether I am really dealing with *my* bike at all.

So, typically, horizons are not indeterminate in the sense that a given act points to the entirety of acts that are logically compatible with the initial act. Horizons are rather *structured*: they prescribe implicit rules of anticipation that restrict how things could appear if the corresponding experiences were still to qualify as experiences of the same thing.

2.3 Background knowledge

The point of the previous considerations is that our experience of things is "thoroughly interwoven with anticipations" (Husserl 2001c, 47). Things are always and necessarily given in horizons and these horizons prescribe rules through which we anticipate the course of future experiences. Under normal circumstances, these rules remain implicit and largely unnoticed. It is mainly in cases of frustrated anticipations that their existence even becomes manifest.[5]

Given the view outlined so far, an obvious question arises: Where do the aforementioned anticipations come from? How are they generated? And what is their status? As David Woodruff Smith and Ronald McIntyre have pointed out (Smith and McIntyre 1982, ch. 5; Smith 2004, ch. 5), both horizons and the rules of anticipation that are given through them are dependent on highly heterogeneous stocks of background knowledge that, in their totality, make up our fundamental background image of the world. In large part, this background knowledge is empirical and thus highly contingent in nature. Just think of the earlier example of my anticipation that my bike's backside will exhibit the same colour as its facing side: Clearly, my anticipation in this case depends on the fact that I have had countless previous encounters with my bike. Hence, a more determinate horizon with more determinate anticipations is co-given with *my* experiences of *my* bike than would be co-given with *your* experiences of *my* bike.

Other parts of our background knowledge are not empirical, but theoretical in nature: Psychologists conducted experiments in which students were asked to observe the falling of two objects (a metal sphere and a plastic sphere of the same diameter) and to record their observations (Gunstone and White 1981). Students who initially held that heavier objects fall faster were much more likely to report observations that supported their theory. Experiments such as these suggest that our anticipations of further courses of experience are sometimes strongly influenced by theoretical components of our background knowledge.

Finally, as phenomenologists typically stress, there is a third type of background knowledge that belongs to neither of the two aforementioned categories: Take, for instance, the anticipation that my bike will exhibit, not a particular colour on its backside, *but rather some kind of rear side at all*. Since we fail to even imagine a material thing that does not exhibit a backside *of some sort*, phenomenologists claim that the corresponding anticipation is not governed by a contingent piece of background knowledge; it is rather governed by a "*necessary la[w]* which determine[s] what must necessarily belong to an object in order that it can be an object of this kind" (Husserl 1973, 352). That material things, unlike, say, geometrical objects, are necessarily given in perspectives is determined by "a universal essence which ... *prescribes an intellectually seen generical rule* for every particular object becoming intended to in multiplicities of concrete mental processes" (Husserl 1983, 341).

3 Perception and imagination: the return of the paradox

My approach in the previous sections was to use examples from the perceptual sphere in order to introduce five phenomenological key concepts. Yet, on closer inspection, the applicability of these concepts is not restricted to the perceptual realm. Consider, for example, "horizon" and "anticipation": As I have pointed out, material things are necessarily given in horizons through which we anticipate further courses of experience. Horizontal givenness, however, is by no means exclusive to perception: "Imaginings ... present their objects within exactly the same horizons" (Husserl 1973, 169). Imagine, for instance, Bart Simpson writing "No one cares what my definition of 'is' is" on Mrs. Krabappel's blackboard. If you do so, then the object of your attention is a yellow cartoon character that is scribbling on a blackboard. Yet, co-given with this initial experience is a set of empty intentions through which you anticipate further features of the imagined scenario. Although they are not in the centre of your attention right from the start, you automatically anticipate further features such as the spikiness of Bart's hair, the wall behind the blackboard or the colour of Bart's pants. If the focus of attention shifts and objects from the margin move to the centre, certain other objects fade into the background, without, however, disappearing completely. Like in the previous examples from the perceptual sphere, you "know" that there is more to the imagined objects than can be grasped in one single act.

Horizontal givenness is not the only commonality between perception and imagination. Remember the crucial distinction between empty and fulfilled intentions: If I am merely thinking of my bike, then my intention towards my bike is empty. If, on the other hand, I perceive my bike, my intention towards the intended thing is intuitively fulfilled by the thing's presence. But is perception the only means by which the empty intention towards my bike can be fulfilled? Not at all. If I imagine my bike, then this, too, fulfills the mere thought of my bike – what was empty before (the bike as the object of my thought) is now fulfilled by the quasi-experience of my imagined bike. Hence, perception and imagination reveal a close parallelism not only with respect to the structural characteristic of horizontal givenness: Since "the objective intention directed toward the imagined object has its filling in the experienced phantasms, just as the objective intention in perception has its filling in sensations" (Husserl 2005, 93; translation modified), the parallelism between perception and imagination involves the crucial concept of fulfillment too.

There are, as we have seen, important essential features that are common to perception and imagination. But, of course, there are crucial differences as well. The most obvious concerns the fact that, unlike imagination, perception is an "*originally presentive* mode [of consciousness]" (Husserl 1983, 327). What this means can again be illustrated with recourse to the earlier example: If I perceive my bike standing in my office, then this act is *self-giving* with regard to actual things (my bike) and states of affairs (that my bike is standing in my office). Thus, it is not only the case that the perceptual givenness of my bike intuitively fulfills the thought that my bike is in my office. Even more importantly, the perceptual act "gives its object itself in the flesh" (Husserl 2001c, 140) and thus exhibits a particular quality that is discussed in the contemporary analytic literature under labels such as "presentational feel" (Foster 2000, 112), "scene-immediacy" (Sturgeon 2000, 24) or "presentational phenomenology" (Chudnoff 2013, ch. 1.2). On a phenomenological view, this quality is a main reason why we take perceptual acts to confer justification on empirical beliefs. I see my bike leaning against the bookshelf and it instantly seems to me that what I see is a truthmaker for the proposition "My bike is in the office." The fact that the visual experience of my bike instantiates the quality of having a "presentational feel" explains why this is so.

But now compare this with the case of imagination: If I imagine my bike standing in the office, then this, as I have pointed out, also counts as a case of fulfillment: What was empty before is now fulfilled by the quasi-sensory experience of my imagined bike. However, clearly, the quasi-experience of an imagined bike is no justifier for the belief that my bike is in my office. Phenomenologically construed, this is because imaginative quasi-experiences do not instantiate the property of having a "presentational feel" with respect to actual things and states of affairs. While "[p]erception makes a present reality appear to us as present and as a reality ... [imagination], on the other hand, lacks the consciousness of reality in relation to what is [imagined]" (Husserl 2005, 4). It is for this reason that the imagination does not count as a direct source of justification of empirical beliefs.

Perception is an act that gives its object as actual. An act of imagination gives its object as non-actual. This, in a nutshell, is the reason why the imagination does not count as a direct source of empirical justification. But there is a second, even more fundamental difference that concerns the conditions under which anticipations and expectations[6] are frustrated in each respective realm. Here is an example that illustrates the point: Suppose that I perceive the greyish blue of my bike's facing side. And suppose furthermore that – for whatever reasons – the horizon in which this perception is embedded comes with the anticipation that my bike's backside is coated in pure gold. What will happen? Since a bike that is both mine *and* ridiculously expensive is not part of the inventory of the actual world, this anticipation will be frustrated by further perceptual experiences. And, obviously, there is nothing I can do about this: By and large, our perceptual experiences are not under our voluntary control; their occurrence as well as their content is systematically fixed by our external environment.

But things are entirely different in the imagination. Suppose that I imagine my bike. And suppose furthermore that the horizon in which my imagined bike is given comes with the anticipation that its backside is coated in pure gold. Obviously, nothing prevents me from imagining my bike in a way so that the anticipation of a gold-coated backside would be intuitively fulfilled. Generally speaking, we know that we can do all sorts of crazy things in the sphere of imagination: I could imagine my bike as almost transparent or tall like a mountain. I could imagine that it is accelerated to 90% of the speed of light. Or I could imagine that my bike transmutes into a honeybee and flies away. It is in my freedom to project these and indefinitely many other scenarios with the help of my imaginative capacities. Hence, while the persistency of anticipations and expectations is strictly regulated by the external world in the perceptual sphere, the imagination seems to be distinguished by "its *optional character* [and] therefore, speaking ideally, [by] its unconditioned arbitrariness" (Husserl 2005, 642). "It remains," as Husserl puts it elsewhere, "within the province of our freedom to allow the indeterminateness of ... horizons to be quasi-fulfilled in an arbitrary way by imagining" (Husserl 1973, 171).

Given this rough-and-ready comparison, one could come to the following conclusion: Imagination is like perception in many ways. But beneath the surface of similarities, two crucial differences remain: First, perception gives its objects as actual. The objects of imagination, on the other hand, exhibit the "characteristic of inactuality" (Husserl 2005, 320). Secondly, perceptual anticipations and expectations are fixed by the external world. Imaginative anticipations and expectations, on the other hand, seem to be essentially unrestricted.

If we take this result as conclusive, then this also has serious consequences for the phenomenological understanding of TEs. In particular, the paradox of TEs seems to return within the framework of phenomenology in its original force: Scientific TEs are supposed to justify beliefs about the empirical world. But since TEs rely on our imaginative capacities, and since the imagination is no direct source of empirical justification, we are in need of a plausible story about how TEs could possibly achieve this aim. But whatever story we tell, we will have to confront the following worry: The principal reason for regarding physical experiments as epistemically significant is that our expectations towards them can be and quite regularly are frustrated by perceptual experiences whose occurrence and content is not controlled by us. To put it bluntly: When we perform physical experiments, reality sometimes "kicks back" at us. And when it does, we learn something utterly important, namely that the world is different from what we had expected. But what could possibly "kick back" at us in TEs? Since TEs exploit our imaginative capacities, and since, apparently, these capacities are characterized by the unconditional freedom to imagine whatever we like, the conditions of fulfillment and frustration in TEs appear to be completely under our control. If that is the case, however, then it is hard to see how TEs could possibly qualify as a serious method of knowledge acquisition. Viewed in this light, TEs are similar to children's games. Of course, they are fun to play. But since their rules can change erratically at any time during the process, they are also somehow pointless from an adult's perspective.

4 Three types of constraints

Here is the upshot of the previous section: In order to solve the paradox of TEs, we need to tell a story about why the imagination can be regarded as a source of stable evidence. But there is an obstacle to any such story: One of the principal reasons for regarding perception as epistemically valuable is that what is perceived is not entirely up to us. The occurrence as well as the content of our perceptual experiences is systematically fixed by our external surroundings. Imaginings, on the other hand, seem to lack external constraints: Apparently, we are free to imagine whatever we like, whenever we like.[7] Hence, the conditions of fulfillment and frustration appear to be entirely under our control in the sphere of the imagination. But if this is true, then it is unclear how the imagination could possibly generate stable evidence.

On the basis of what has just been said, a sceptical attitude towards the epistemic value of imagination (and, consequently, of TEs) is fuelled by the view of imagination as being essentially unrestricted. But is this view correct? In what follows I will try to convince you that it is not. My aim in this section is to go through a couple of examples in order to make clear *that*, *how* and *to what extent* the course as well as the content of our imaginings are subject to three different types of external constraints. Getting clear on the nature of these types will finally bring us closer to a phenomenological understanding of how knowledge is generated through TEs.

Suppose, that I ask you to imagine Bart Simpson writing "I will not use abbrev." on Mrs. Krabappel's blackboard. If you do so, then the object of your attention is a yellow cartoon character that is scribbling on a blackboard. Yet, co-given with this initial experience is the anticipation of further features of the imagined scenario: Although these features are not in the centre of attention right from the start, you automatically anticipate further aspects such as the spikiness of Bart's hair, the purple wall behind the blackboard, Bart's depraved behaviour or his red pants. But wait! While the sequence of imaginings evolves in more and more detail, you suddenly realize that something is not right. Even though you cannot quite figure out what it is, the whole scenario does not feel like it should. It is only through careful reflection that you finally notice what bothered you: Bart's pants are blue, not red!

What happened in the situation just described? To begin with, by following my instruction to imagine Bart Simpson, you immersed yourself in the quasi-world of *The Simpsons* and thus accepted certain limitations to your imagining. The concept "Bart Simpson" contains what has become known to you and your epistemic community about the kind of object in question. Hence, by applying the concept "Bart Simpson" in order to determine what you were about to imagine, you activated certain parts of your background knowledge that, in turn, motivated a horizon through which further quasi-experiences were anticipated. It is of course true that the imagination, unlike perception, gives you the freedom to produce quasi-experiences that are at odds with what is contained in the initial concept: You could either consciously decide to imagine quasi-experiences that are not compatible with the concept "Bart Simpson." Or you could just inadvertently fail to stay within the boundaries of what the concept prescribes. But, in any case, if you imagine a white cartoon character that has a yellow bill and wears a sailor shirt with a red bow tie, then you obviously failed to immerse yourself into the quasi-world of *The Simpsons*.

There are further lessons to draw from this example: First, it underscores the fact that normally, when we employ our imaginative capacities, we are not imagining series of disconnected figments. Rather, most imaginative processes consist of sequences of related imaginings that, in their temporal succession, form a coherent whole. And, given the example above, it is easy to see where the coherence is coming from: it is ensured by the background knowledge that enters the imagination through the concepts with which we determine what we intend to imagine and from which our imaginative processes take their basic direction. This is not only true when we are asked to imagine Bart Simpson. It is also true when we are using our imaginative capacities to decide whether the sofa at Ikea will fit through the hallway at home. In both of these cases, the concepts through which we determine what we intend to imagine refer to chunks of background knowledge that, in turn, put constraints on how our imagining can evolve. To be sure, we could always break the coherence by imagining quasi-experiences that stand in no relation to what has been imagined before. But, given our practical ends at Ikea, imagining a sofa that suddenly transforms into a swarm of butterflies just isn't the rational thing to do.

What the example of Bart Simpson also shows is that, secondly, frustration is by no means impossible in the sphere of the imagination. Other than in the perceptual realm, however, anticipations and expectations are not frustrated by quasi-experiences alone. Imaginative anticipations are frustrated by way of a comparison between quasi-experiences and the background knowledge that enters the imagination through the concepts with which we determine the course of our imagining. This is exactly what happened in the example above: Initially, the content as well as the course of our imaginative endeavours were determined by the concept "Bart Simpson." And it was through reflection on the background knowledge to which the concept refers that certain quasi-experiences could be singled out as being at odds with what the concept prescribes. Hence, there turns out to be a close relationship between the conditions of frustration on the one hand and the concepts that determine the course of our imagining on the other. Given this relationship, we can formulate an important conclusion: If we want to learn about the conditions of fulfillment and frustration in a given imaginative process, we have to look closely at the concepts through which the horizontal anticipations are determined.[8]

What I have tried to do so far in this section is take some first steps towards undermining the view according to which the imagination is epistemically inept due to the lack of external constraints to the conditions of fulfillment and frustration. Following my analysis, the imagination indeed gives us the freedom to produce random quasi-experiences that are not related to earlier imaginings. However, it is also possible to use our imaginative capacities differently: We can choose to immerse ourselves in a quasi-world by staying within the boundaries that are prescribed by the concepts through which we determine what we actually wish to imagine. And if we do so, the conditions of fulfillment and frustration are externally fixed; they are fixed by the background knowledge that enters the imagination through the concepts that give our imaginings their basic direction.

Assume for the moment that the foregoing analysis is correct. Even if it is, however, one could still wonder whether it really captures what is truly characteristic of scientific TEs. One could argue as follows: It may be true that the conditions of fulfillment and frustration are relatively well defined as long as we use the imagination in a fairly conservative fashion by sticking to concepts such as "Bart Simpson" or "bike." Concepts like these prescribe clear rules of anticipation because they refer to rather uncontroversial chunks of empirical background knowledge that have been acquired through common experiential sources. In the case of "Bart Simpson," for instance, we know what to imagine because we have spent many hours watching the respective TV show. But isn't it characteristic of TEs to employ our imaginative capacities in a much more exceptional manner? Of course, at first glance, scientific TEs also seem to utilize fairly conventional concepts such as "bucket," "car," "train," "cat" or "tower." But the point of most scientific TEs is to imagine these objects under conditions to which the more common parts of our background knowledge do not apply. Our common background knowledge may prescribe clear rules of anticipation if, for instance, we imagine a car that is rushing towards a garage with 100 km/h. But what determines the conditions of fulfillment and frustration if we are imagining a car rushing toward a garage *with 90% of the speed of light?*

Even a cursory look at the practice of TE-reasoning in science reveals that TEs indeed employ our imaginative capacities in a quite exceptional way. In order for most scientific TEs to be performed, we have to immerse ourselves in quasi-worlds that differ from our actual world in more or less drastic ways. As the following examples show, "immersion" consists in the active bracketing and/or modification of certain parts of our background knowledge: Immersion into the quasi-world of Galileo's ship consists in bracketing the background knowledge according to which ships at sea are always subjected to rocking motions. Immersion into the quasi-world of Stevin's chain consists in bracketing the background knowledge according to which objects moving down inclined planes are always subjected to kinetic friction and air drag. Immersion into the quasi-world of Newton's bucket consists in bracketing the background knowledge according to which the material universe consists of more objects than just a water bucket and a rope.

As we shall see in the next section, the ability to be selective with regard to the background knowledge that determines the content as well as the course of our imaginings is indeed crucial for TEs in science. In the present context, however, this ability is still a reason for concern. Our problem was this: In standard cases of imaginative activity, the conditions of fulfillment and frustration are determined by the relevant parts of our background knowledge that have been acquired in the course of previous encounters with the world. But what determines the conditions of fulfillment and frustration in cases where the imagination takes us well beyond our ordinary experiential grasp?

The obvious answer is that much of what we anticipate and expect in scientific TEs is determined by the *theories* that work in the background of these TEs. The aforementioned car/garage-TE from Special Relativity is a case in point: If we are asked to imagine a car that is rushing towards a garage with 90% of the speed of light, then, obviously, our anticipations and expectations are not guided by previous perceptual encounters with this kind of scenario. What determines the course of our imaginings is rather a theory according to which the measured length of an object decreases noticeably at velocities close to c.[9] The point is even more obvious considering examples such as Heisenberg's gamma-ray microscope or EPR: In cases like these, not only the course, but even the content of our imaginings is almost entirely determined by theoretical components of our background knowledge. To put it bluntly: We just would not know what to imagine if we did not know a thing about quantum mechanics.

Many constraints that impinge on our imaginative activities are due to empirical components of our background knowledge. Others are due to theoretical parts of our background knowledge. This, in a nutshell, is the upshot of this section. However, phenomenologically construed, there is yet a third type of constraints that are neither empirical nor theoretical in nature. Here is an example that might help to make my point: Suppose that I ask you to imagine a brick that is thrown against a windowpane. And suppose furthermore that I ask you to bracket everything you know about the behaviour of bricks and windowpanes. Hence, what I ask you to imagine is a quasi-world in which bricks and windowpanes look like actual bricks and windowpanes, but in which their behaviour is absolutely unpredictable. Now the question is this: Are your anticipations and expectations concerning the behaviour of the brick and the windowpane indeterminate? Are the conditions of fulfillment and frustration entirely up to you?

At first sight, this question might seem odd. If you are serious about bracketing your background knowledge about bricks and windowpanes, then, apparently, there is nothing left that could possibly determine your anticipations and expectations in the scenario described above. You could imagine a quasi-world in which windowpanes are shattered upon impact. But you could also imagine a quasi-world in which it is the bricks that crumble to dust whenever they hit a windowpane. Or you could imagine a quasi-world in which windowpanes transmute into sprays of flowers whenever they are hit by bricks. In short: After bracketing your background knowledge, no anticipation is too outlandish to be in principle unfulfillable by matching quasi-experiences. Or so, at least, it seems.

In fact I think this view is descriptively wrong. There are restrictions to what we can or cannot imagine, even after we have bracketed our entire background knowledge about the objects in question. Consider, for instance, the anticipation of a windowpane that is completely shattered and completely unshattered, both at the same time. As you can easily verify by trying to actually imagine this scenario, it is impossible to intuitively fulfill this anticipation. Or consider the anticipation of a brick that is red and blue all over. Here too, we fail to imagine a fulfilling quasi-experience. Or consider the anticipation of a brick that is seen from all sides at once or whose redness can be smelled. Again, it is impossible to imagine a quasi-world in which these anticipations would be fulfilled by matching quasi-experiences. In all of these cases the problem is not that a particular quasi-experience contradicts a rule of anticipation that suggests itself in the light of previous encounters with the actual world or in the light of a theory. Rather, the problem is that certain quasi-experiences are impossible to imagine, no matter how hard we try. In all of the aforementioned cases we have to realize that the "freedom [of voluntarily producing quasi-experiences] is limited insofar as essential laws of possible *quasi*-fulfillment are inherent here within the boundaries of the unity of an identical possible objectivity understood as intentional and still indeterminate" (Husserl 2005, 671). Hence, the content and course of our imaginings is not only determined by empirical and theoretical components of our background knowledge. Phenomenologically construed, our imaginings are also constrained by "*necessary laws* which determine what must necessarily belong to an object in order that it can be an object of this kind" (Husserl 1973, 352).

In a recent paper, Walter Hopp has drawn particular attention to the role this kind of essential knowledge plays in TE-reasoning. One of Hopp's main theses is "that thought experiments, at their best, are in fact founded on acts of fulfillment in which we intuit universals and the relations among them, and that the actual instantiation of those universals and relations is immaterial" (Hopp 2014, 81). In advancing this claim, Hopp emphasizes the similarities between Brown's Platonism and a phenomenological theory of TEs. According to Hopp's analysis, both accounts agree in their acknowledgement of a knowledge-yielding faculty that is independent of the five senses and that is operative in at least some TEs.[10]

What I have tried to do in this section is to undermine the view of the imagination as essentially unrestricted. If my analysis is correct, then our imaginative capacities are subject to three types of constraints: First, there are constraints that are due to the empirical parts of our background knowledge. Secondly, there are constraints that result from the theories that we have incorporated into our background knowledge. Thirdly and finally, there are constraints that are due to "essential laws which govern acts as *intentional* experiences, in all their modes of sense-giving objectivation, and their fulfilling constitution of 'true being'" (Husserl 2001b, 319).

5 Putting the pieces together

With the above findings in place, we can finally turn to the heart of this chapter. Drawing on the results from the previous sections, I will now take a first stab at a phenomenological description of TE-reasoning in science. On my view, TE-reasoning is a process that occurs in three stages: the preparatory stage, the performance stage and the conclusion stage. I will comment on each of these stages in turn.

5.1 The preparatory stage

Before we can even begin to perform a TE, we need to know a couple of things. First of all, and most obviously, we must know to what end the TE is performed. This is to say that we need a sufficiently clear grasp of the target thesis that the TE is meant to refute, to corroborate or to clarify. Secondly, and no less importantly, we need information about the kind of scenario we are supposed to imagine. This information is encapsulated in the TE-narrative in which the details of the TE-setup are specified. Of course, TE-narratives differ significantly with respect to detail, complexity and style. Some of them are text-only. Others also make use of visualizations. Some of them are colourful and filigreed. Others are strictly technical and reduced to the bare essentials. In any case, however, TE-narratives pursue a twofold task: On the one hand, TE-narratives tell us something about the objects of which the TE-scenario is composed. On the other hand, TE-narratives specify the characteristics of the quasi-worlds in which a TE-scenario is to be imagined. Consider, for instance, the following excerpt from a TE-narrative from a standard physics textbook:

> A man has an $l = 5$ m long garage and buys and $l_0 = 7$ m long car (proper length of the car). He reasons that, if he drives sufficiently fast, the car will fit in the garage due to length contraction (ignore the fact that he is going to ruin his new car by smashing it against the garage wall).
>
> (Faraoni 2013, 25)

In order to understand this TE-narrative, we must have different types of background knowledge at our disposal: While concepts such as "car" or "garage" refer to conventional chunks of empirical background knowledge, concepts such as "proper length" or "length contraction" refer to information about the kind of physics that forms the theoretical framework of the TE. It is only if these pieces of information are part of our general background knowledge that we are able to set up the TE accordingly. If, for instance, knowledge about Lorentz contraction is lacking, then we inevitably fail to set up the TE according to the intentions of its presenter.

But TE-narratives not only give us information about the kinds of objects and processes that we need to imagine in order to carry out the experiment. TE-narratives also contain information about the quasi-world in which the TE ought to be performed. While this information is only implicit in many cases, the above-quoted TE-narrative hints at the specifics of the required quasi-world by remarking that no actual car would remain intact under the imagined conditions. Of course, we know that no actual brake system could decelerate the car from velocities close to c. And we know that the car would melt in less than a blink of an eye. But these and similar other components of our background knowledge must be bracketed if we want to immerse ourselves into the quasi-world that suits the TE we are about to perform. Like many other TEs in physics, the car/garage-TE just would not work in a quasi-world that resembles our actual world too closely. The TE only works in an idealized quasi-world in which many factors that determine the behaviour of the actual world are neglected.

5.2 The performance stage

The purpose of a TE-narrative is to prime its audience for the performance of the ensuing TE. The main tools for doing so are the concepts of which the narrative is composed. These concepts refer to the kind of background knowledge that is necessary in order for the TE to be set up. It is only if the right kind of background knowledge is already in place that we are in a position to imagine the TE-setup as well as the quasi-world in which the TE ought to be embedded. Hence, I fully agree with David Gooding's observation that "a TE becomes possible [only] when a world is sufficiently well-represented that experimental procedures and their likely consequences can be described within it" (Gooding 1992, 281). Whether or not a TE manages to lead us to its desired outcome largely depends on our familiarity with the quasi-world in which the TE ought to be embedded according to its presenter.[11]

Assume that we have successfully completed the preparatory stage in our current example, the car/garage-TE. This is to say that we have a sufficiently clear grasp of the target thesis, we possess the right kind of background knowledge and we understand the specifics of the quasi-world in which the TE-scenario ought to be imagined. We are now in a position to imagine the required TE-setup. If we do so, then the primary object of our intentional directedness is a scenario that consists of an imagined car that is about to rush towards an imagined garage at a speed close to c. However, on the basis of our earlier reflections on the horizontal structure of intentionality, it is clear that the imagined car and the imagined garage is by no means all that is given to us in this situation. Co-given with the quasi-experience of the primary object is an array of empty intentions that point towards possible future states of the imagined TE-scenario. In imagining the TE-setup, as it is laid out in the TE-narrative, we automatically co-intend a horizon that prescribes anticipatory rules concerning the course of further quasi-experiences. These rules of anticipation are motivated by the background knowledge that is necessary for imagining the TE-setup in the first place. And it is through these anticipatory rules that our background knowledge restricts how the imagined scenario could evolve if the corresponding quasi-experiences were still to qualify as experiences of the initial scenario.

The point I am trying to make is this: If we imagine a particular TE-setup, we are not merely imagining a particular arrangement of imagined objects that are embedded in a particular quasi-world. Since the objects of our intentional directedness are necessarily given in horizons, we also co-intend rules of anticipation that restrict how the TE-setup could evolve if the ensuing phases were still to qualify as phases of the initial setup. This way of putting things also makes clear what it actually means to carry out a TE: To perform a TE is to immerse oneself into a particular quasi-world, to imagine a TE-setup within this quasi-world and then to let the TE-setup evolve according to the anticipatory rules that are co-given with each and every quasi-experience of the unfolding TE. Or, to put it in slightly different terms: To perform a TE is to "live through" the anticipatory horizons against the background of which fulfilled intentions towards particular phases of the imaginative process always stand out.[12] With each new phase a new horizon comes to fruition, "a new system of determinable indeterminacy, a new system of progressive tendencies with corresponding possibilities of entering into determinately ordered systems of possible [quasi-] appearances, of possible ways that the aspects can run their course, together with horizons that are inseparably affiliated with these aspects" (Husserl 2001c, 43). In this whole process of "living through" the anticipatory horizons in which each phase of the imaginative process is given, processes of explicit inferential reasoning are mostly absent. This explains one of the most intriguing features of scientific TEs, namely the ease with which they are performed and the apparent effortlessness with which we reach the desired outcome.

According to the view developed so far, the way the initial TE-setup pans out is predelineated by the rules of anticipation that come with every new quasi-experience of the unfolding TE. This, however, raises an obvious question: At any point during the performance of a TE, there are far more empty intuitions towards future quasi-experiences than are relevant for the actual outcome of the TE. If we imagine a car rushing towards a garage, for instance, we implicitly anticipate the car to have a backside. Or we anticipate the garage to have a specific colour. But, obviously, anticipations such as these are entirely irrelevant for what the TE is supposed to show. Hence, the question arises as to how relevant anticipations are distinguished from irrelevant ones.

I opened this section with the remark that the aim of TE-narratives is to prime their audience for the ensuing TE. In the light of the question that has just been raised, this remark must be further clarified: On the one hand, TE-narratives tell us what we are supposed to imagine. They do so by employing particular concepts that activate particular components of our background knowledge. Anticipatory rules that are motivated by these components then restrict how the ensuing TE can unfold. But on the other hand, and equally important, TE-narratives also give us information about what we are *not* supposed to imagine (cf. Davies 2007, 35). In part this is done through the target-thesis that automatically narrows our focus to certain aspects and leaves out others. But it is also done through the determination of the quasi-world in which the TE must be embedded. By bracketing certain parts of our background knowledge in order to immerse ourselves in a particular quasi-world, we prevent certain rules of anticipation from even becoming operative. Our normal anticipations concerning objects sliding down inclined planes, for instance, are determined by the background knowledge according to which such objects are always subject to kinetic friction and air drag. However, as reliable as this background knowledge may be under standard circumstances, the resulting rules of anticipation are entirely impractical for the performance of TEs like Stevin's chain. Hence, in order to let the imagination in such TEs be guided by the right kinds of anticipatory rules, parts of our common background knowledge must be bracketed already at the outset. Thus construed, bracketing is an essential tool for channelling our anticipations in desired ways.

The previous remarks on the role of bracketing also allow me to finally explicate my thesis according to which TEs should be understood as *anticipation pumps*.[13] On the view proposed here, TE-narratives are well designed if they accomplish two objectives: First, they must trigger the right kind of background knowledge in order to motivate the right kinds of anticipatory rules. And secondly, they must ensure that these rules of anticipation are not interfered by anticipations that are inessential or even an impediment for reaching the desired outcome of the imaginative process. Hence, to put it in a slogan: A TE is well-designed if the TE-narrative is successful in "pumping" the right rules of anticipations. The "right" rules are those that lead us from the initial TE-setup to the desired end point with a minimum of unnecessary distractions.

5.3 The conclusion stage

To perform a TE means to successfully "live through" the anticipatory horizons against the background of which fulfilled intentions towards particular phases of the imaginative process always stand out. The performance stage of a TE is completed when we reach that state of the TE-scenario which the presenter deems relevant for the projected target-thesis. Like in the case of physical experiments, we can now ask whether the outcome of the TE supports the conclusion that its presenter draws. For instance: Do the changing states of a water-bucket-system in an otherwise empty universe really force us to accept the existence of absolute space? Does a light ray that enters an elevator horizontally really force us to accept that the effects of gravity and inertial acceleration are indistinguishable?

But scrutinizing the relation between the outcome of the imaginative process and the projected target thesis is not all that happens at the conclusion stage. In many cases it is also natural to reflect on whether the course of the imaginative process itself was inevitable, independently from its purported impact on the target thesis. Here is an example that might illustrate the point: Consider a modern version of Galileo's tower-TE in which we imagine a cannon ball that is tied to a musket ball. We are then asked to throw the combined system from a tower and to see what happens. If the speed of fall of bodies is really proportional to their weights, as the Aristotelian theory suggests, then the combined system will fall faster *and* slower. This outcome is usually taken to show that the Aristotelian law of falling bodies is false and must be replaced with Galileo's.

Now, critical reflection on this TE can occur on two different levels:[14] On the one hand, it is natural to wonder whether both conclusions – the rejection of the Aristotelian law and the proclamation of the Galilean law – are equally supported by the outcome of the imaginative process. Yet, on the other hand, it is also possible to ask whether the outcome itself is inevitable. Is it really the case that the anticipations in this TE unavoidably lead us to two conflicting scenarios in which the combined system falls *both* faster *and* slower? Or do our anticipations vary depending on how tightly the musket ball and the cannon ball are connected? Do our anticipations vary depending on whether the two objects are connected with a rope or with a rubber band? Can a cannon ball that is connected to a musket ball really be treated as *one* object, as the TE seems to presuppose? (For versions of these and similar other objections, cf. Koyré 1968, 51; Gendler 1998, 404–6.) Such questions obviously do not concern the relation between the outcome of the TE-process and the projected target thesis. Rather, such questions concern the TE-process itself.

How can questions concerning the inevitability of the TE-process be resolved? Given what has been said so far, an answer to this question goes along the following lines: Since the evolution of a TE-setup is determined by the rules of anticipation that govern the TE, scrutinizing the outcome of the TE-process can only proceed by way of explicating the background knowledge that initially motivated the relevant rules of anticipation. During the performance stage, i.e., during the process of "living through" the horizons in which the phases of the TE are given, this background knowledge is tacit. However, if we wish to critically reflect on the strength with which the outcome of the TE-process imposes itself on us, the relevant parts of our background knowledge must be made explicit.[15] The strength with which the outcome of a particular TE-process imposes itself on us will depend, among other factors, on the type of background knowledge that motivates the relevant rules of anticipation: If, for instance, a particular set of anticipations is motivated by a theory that operates in the background of a TE, then the degree to which we accept the outcome of the TE depends on the degree of belief in the underlying theory. If, on the other hand, a particular set of anticipations turns out to be determined by an essential law, then the outcome of the imaginative process will be regarded as necessary.

Let me conclude this section by briefly commenting on one last issue: On the view proposed here, to perform a TE is to "live through" the rules of anticipation that are co-given at each stage of the imaginative process. These rules are motivated by the background knowledge that is triggered during the preparatory stage, i.e., through the concepts of which the TE-narrative is composed. Hence, the course as well as the outcome of a TE is ultimately determined by chunks of pre-established background knowledge. But this raises an obvious question: How can we learn something *new* from TEs if their outcome is determined by background knowledge that must already have been acquired before the TE can even be set up? Is not it a consequence of the view defended here that the performance of a TE is the mere recalling of what was already known?

Since scientific TEs are a very diverse lot, it is, I think, impossible to give a principled answer to how TEs manage to go beyond the knowledge one already has to possess in order to perform the TE. It is thus mainly for the sake of brevity that I will reduce myself to one single aspect that seems to be of particular importance in this context: As I have pointed out, TEs require us to immerse ourselves into quasi-worlds that differ from the actual world in more or less drastic ways. One of the reasons why immersion is epistemically significant is that it gives us the opportunity to test our background knowledge under conditions that could not be replicated otherwise. Of course, there is also a danger in projecting quasi-worlds that are far removed from the actual world: The more outlandish the quasi-world, the higher the risk that our anticipations eventually become ungrounded. But one of the things a well-designed TE accomplishes by way of projecting idealized quasi-worlds is to provoke collisions between parts of our background knowledge that would not even come close under normal circumstances.[16] It is in this way that TEs allow us to detect and get rid of inconsistencies in our existing background knowledge, to explicate and scrutinize background assumptions that were previously left unquestioned and, in some particularly impressive cases, even to reconfigure the conceptual apparatus with which we approach the world (Kuhn 1977; Gendler 1998).

6 Concluding remarks

The goal of this chapter was to set out some basic directions in which a phenomenological framework for the analysis of scientific TEs should be developed. On my view, phenomenology differs from the existing approaches, among other things, in its starting point: The main objective, at least initially, is not to construct a theory that seeks to bring TEs in line with certain pre-established epistemological, ontological and metaphysical views. The main objective of a phenomenological account is rather to give a faithful description of the *actual performance* of TEs from a first-person perspective and to go on from there. One of the aims in the preceding sections was to indicate how such a description might actually go. But, of course, much work remains to be done in order to position phenomenology as a serious contender in the ongoing debate on TEs.

Acknowledgements

In developing my views over the last couple of years, I profited from the conversations I had with Jim Brown, Keizo Matsubara, Danny Goldstick, Sonja Rinofner-Kreidl, Walter Hopp, Mike Stuart, Yiftach Fehige, Geordie McComb, Hanne Jacobs, Sebastian Luft, Jeff Hilderley, George Heffernan, Michael Wallner and James McGuirk. I would also like to say "thanks" to the Austrian Science Fund for the generous support of my ongoing research on TEs (project number: J 3114).

Notes

1 The notion of "bracketing" comes from Husserl's mathematical background, specifically from the concept of absolute value (the notation "$|x|$" was introduced by Husserl's teacher Karl Weierstrass). The absolute value $|x|$ of a real number x is the non-negative value of x without regard to its sign. So, for instance, 3 and −3 have the same absolute value: 3. Hence, to bracket a natural number means to be indifferent with regard to a number's property of being positive or negative and to focus on its magnitude instead. Accordingly, to bracket assumptions means neither to endorse nor to deny them. It merely means to focus on what is given independently from all assumptions.

2 It should be emphasized that it is mainly for the sake of brevity that I am working with a rather restricted conception of phenomenology here. For the purposes of this chapter, I am conceiving of the phenomenological method roughly along the lines of Charles Siewert's "plain phenomenology." On this view, one is doing phenomenology if (1) one explains mental distinctions; (2) one shows how such explanations have significant theoretical consequences; (3) one's explanations rely on a source of warrant special to some *first-person* applications of the distinctions explained; and (4) one does not assume that such first-person warrant as one relies on is derived from third-person evidence (cf. Siewert 2007, 202). However, I would also like to stress that this understanding of phenomenology does not do full justice to all the subtleties of Husserl's account. Readers interested in a more comprehensive treatment may refer either to Crowell (2006) for a highly instructive introductory essay or to Smith (2007) for a more detailed, book-length study.

3 "Imagination" is an umbrella term that is notoriously hard to define (cf., e.g., Kind 2013). In what follows, I will take it to denote a type of mental event in which we are intentionally directed towards imagined objects or scenarios and not, for instance, towards propositions. Hence, I am distinguishing between acts of imagining (in which imagined objects or scenarios are given in a quasi-sensory manner) and acts of conceiving (in which the objects of our intentional directedness are propositions). It should be noted, however, that my terminology departs from Husserl's who uses the notion "phantasy" in order to denote what I call "imagination."

4 It must be noted that the concept of fulfillment is not restricted to the realm of perceptual experiences. Although it is true that veridical perceptions are model cases of fulfillment (cf., e.g., Husserl 1983, 5–6, 82–83, 154, 327), fulfillment is a functional concept that goes along with a functional object concept. This is to say that fulfillment takes place whenever an empty intention towards an object is in congruence with a fulfilling intention towards the same object. However, as Husserl makes clear, "an object ... may as readily be what is real as what is ideal, a thing or an event or a species of a mathematical relation, a case of being or a what ought to be" (Husserl 2001a, 145).

5 Here is an example that illustrates the issue: Imagine you are asked to bring a shopping bag into the kitchen. You go to the car, you see the bag in the trunk, you get ready to lift it and – Oops! – your arms go up way too easy and you almost topple over. What happened? Well, the bag is significantly

lighter than you anticipated because it is filled with paper towels. What is remarkable about this case is, first of all, the funny feeling that you had when you lifted the bag. Since you have lifted many light items before, this feeling is certainly not a consequence of the fact that you lifted something light. What makes the experience stand out is rather how it compared to your (frustrated) anticipations. What is more, cases like these also highlight the fact that many of our anticipations correspond to pieces of non-propositional, practical and sensorimotor knowledge about how things are done and how we use our bodies to do them (cf., e.g., Husserl 1997; Noë 2004).

6 A word on terminology: Anticipations are non-independent parts of perceptual experiences. If, for instance, I enter the kitchen and flip the light switch, the experience of the flipping of the switch comes with the tacit anticipation that the light will go on. This anticipation is neither an act in its own right nor is it consciously experienced in the normal course of events. However, anticipations can become the basis for separate acts of *expectation*. If, for instance, I have just repaired the light switch and check it for the very first time, the flipping of the switch may come with the expectation that the light will go on. In this case, the expectation is an act in its own right and has the status of an explicit prognosis of future events.

7 Sartre seems to follow this line of reasoning when he comes to the conclusion "that it is impossible to find in the [mental] image anything more than what one puts into it; in other words, the [mental] image teaches nothing" (Sartre 2004, 103). But similar views can also be found outside of phenomenology: Consider, for instance, Ludwig Wittgenstein's remark that "it is just because imaging is subject to the will that it does not instruct us about the external world" (Wittgenstein 1980, §80). Or take Alan White's more recent assessment that "one can't be surprised by the features of what one imagines, since one put them there" (White 1990, 92).

8 This, of course, is not only true of the imagination. Suppose that you see an object that looks like a barn. If you apply the concept "barn" to the seen object, then you will anticipate the object to have a backside that resembles its facing side. Accordingly, the experience of a backside that does not resemble the facing side (for instance, a backside that is characteristic of fake barns) will frustrate your initial intention. If, on the other hand, you apply the concept "fake barn" to the seen object, a backside that does not resemble the facing side is exactly what you anticipate. Hence, a close relation between concepts and the conditions of fulfillment and frustration is not only to be found in the sphere of the imagination, but also in the perceptual realm (cf. also Hopp 2011, ch. 2.1).

9 On closer inspection, the car/garage-TE is particularly interesting because it is not at all clear which part of Special Relativity should actually determine what we are supposed to imagine in this TE: On the one hand, Special Relativity tells us that objects moving with velocities close to c are Lorentz-contracted. On the other hand, we know since the 1930s that Lorentz-contracted objects would not appear contracted, but rotated (Lampa 1924; Penrose 1959; Terrell 1959). This raises the question as to whether it is relevant for the success of TEs to imagine objects realistically (cf. Brown 2013).

10 It must be noted, however, that Hopp is well aware of the differences between a phenomenological theory of TEs and Brown's (cf. Hopp 2014, 89–90). While phenomenologists will typically not be at odds with the rationalist part of Brown's story – particularly with his claim that sense experience is not the sole source of knowledge about the world – they will most certainly take issue with his construal of the laws of nature and with his Platonist two-world ontology. Hence, building on Davies' useful distinction between extreme and moderate deflationism on the one hand and (two kinds of) moderate and extreme inflationism on the other (Davies 2007, 37–42), phenomenology positions itself somewhere between (the second kind of) moderate and extreme inflationism.

11 This point also has implications for the historiography of TEs. As historically inclined philosophers such as James McAllister (1996) or Paolo Palmieri (2005) have emphasized, it is common in the philosophical literature to make use of the history of TE-reasoning in a rather idiosyncratic, sometimes even "cartoonish" (Palmieri 2005, 223) manner. Not only that case studies are presented without paying sufficient attention to their context; many philosophers also approach the history of TE-reasoning in an overtly "presentist" or "Whiggish" way. In the case of Galileo's famous tower-TE, for instance, it has been objected that it is only if *we today* "look at this thought experiment from an historically distant perspective and with the knowledge of modern physics concerning falling bodies in a vacuum [that] the inference from the contradiction to the 'right' conclusion ... *seems* to be immediate and untutored by any empirical or logical reasoning"

(Brendel 2004, 95; cf., for a similar complaint, Norton 1996, 344–5). What seems right to me about this objection is the almost trivial truth that we cannot presuppose our contemporary background knowledge if we wish to determine the epistemic weight that a TE carried in its original historical context. However, I also believe that the framework of phenomenology is particularly well suited to draw a meaningful distinction between the epistemic weight a TE carries for us, relative to our modern background image of the world, and the epistemic weight a TE originally carried for a given historical community. Cf., for a couple of first steps towards employing the phenomenological tool of the "epoché" in dealing with science history, Arabatzis (2012) and Palmieri (this volume).

12 This echoes Gooding's remark that "to explain the force of an experiment it helps to understand it as a process to be worked through, rather than as a logical structure" (Gooding 1992, 283).

13 Of course, in using this terminology, I take a cue from Daniel Dennett who famously dubbed TEs "intuition pumps." However, my agreement with Dennett's view is rather superficial. While I agree that the hallmark of a well-functioning TE is that it is "cunningly designed to focus the reader's attention on 'the important' features, and to deflect the reader from bogging down in hard-to-follow details" (Dennett 1984, 12), I do not share the dismissive attitude that is characteristic of Dennett's early remarks on TEs.

14 The two levels I am referring to here resemble Brown's distinction between experiment in the broad sense and experiment in the narrow sense: "In the narrow sense, an experiment includes the set up and the observation ... In the broad sense, the experiment includes background assumptions and initial theorizing, the set-up, observation, additional theorizing, calculating, and drawing the final conclusion" (Brown 2007, 157–8). What I call the level of the TE-process is roughly similar to Brown's experiment in the narrow sense.

15 It should be noted, however, that the explication of tacit background knowledge usually comes at the price of diminishing the cognitive efficacy and elegance of a given TE. This point has been emphasized by David Gooding (1992, 286).

16 An example might help make this point more vivid. As noted earlier (cf. fn. 6), our background image of the world is in part composed of pieces of non-propositional, practical and sensorimotor knowledge about how things are done and how we use our bodies to do them. At first blush, one might think that, since TEs are performed in the laboratory of the mind, implicit sensorimotor and kinaesthetic knowledge is irrelevant for the practice of TE-reasoning. However, as Gooding (1992) and Yiftach Fehige and I (2013) have argued, this is far from being the case. While Gooding employs a broadly naturalistic framework to make this point, Fehige and I have approached the issue from a phenomenological perspective. The aim of our chapter was to (a) show that implicit body knowledge is operative in many instances of TE-reasoning and (b) illustrate this claim by means of an analysis of Newton's bucket-TE.

References

Arabatzis, T. (2012) "Hidden entities and experimental practice: Renewing the dialogue between history and philosophy of science," in *Integrating History and Philosophy of Science. Problems and Prospects*, edited by S. Mauskopf and T. Schmalz, Dordrecht: Springer.

Brendel, E. (2004) "Intuition pumps and the proper use of thought experiments," *Dialectica* 58: 89–108.

Brown, J. R. (2004) "Why thought experiments transcend empiricism," in *Contemporary Debates in Philosophy of Science*, edited by C. Hitchcock, Malden: Blackwell.

Brown, J. R. (2007) "Counter thought experiments," *Royal Institute of Philosophy Supplement* 61: 155–177.

Brown, J. R. (2011 [1991]) *The Laboratory of the Mind. Thought Experiments in the Natural Sciences*, London: Routledge.

Brown, J. R. (2013) "What do we see in a thought experiment?," in *Thought Experiments in Science, Philosophy, and the Arts*, edited by M. Frappier, L. Meynell, and J. R. Brown, London: Routledge.

Chudnoff, E. (2013) *Intuition*, Oxford: Oxford University Press.

Crowell, S. G. (2006) "Husserlian phenomenology," in *A Companion to Phenomenology and Existentialism*, edited by H. Dreyfus and M. Wrathall, Malden: Blackwell.

Davies, D. (2007) "Thought experiments and fictional narratives," *Croatian Journal of Philosophy* 19: 29–45.
Dennett, D. C. (1984) *Elbow Room. The Varieties of Free Will Worth Wanting*, Oxford: Clarendon Press.
Faraoni, V. (2013) *Special Relativity*, Springer: Dordrecht.
Fehige, Y. and Wiltsche, H. (2013) "The body, thought experiments, and phenomenology," in *Thought Experiments in Science, Philosophy, and the Arts*, edited by M. Frappier, L. Meynell, and J. R. Brown, London: Routledge.
Foster, J. (2000) *The Nature of Perception*, Oxford: Oxford University Press.
Froese, T. and Gallagher, S. (2010) "Phenomenology and artificial life: Toward a technological supplementation of phenomenological methodology," *Husserl Studies* 26: 83–106.
Gendler, T. S. (1998) "Galileo and the indispensability of scientific thought experiment," *British Journal for the Philosophy of Science* 49: 397–424.
Gooding, D. C. (1992) "What is experimental about thought experiments?" *Proceedings of the Biennial Meeting of the Philosophy of Science Association*, vol. 2, Chicago: University of Chicago Press.
Gunstone, R. and White, R. (1981) "Understanding gravity," *Science Education* 65: 291–299.
Hopp, W. (2011) *Perception and Knowledge. A Phenomenological Account*, Cambridge: Cambridge University Press.
Hopp, W. (2014) "Experiments in thought," *Perspectives on Science* 22: 76–97.
Horowitz, T. and Massey, G. J. (eds) (1991) *Thought Experiments in Science and Philosophy*, Lanham: Rowman and Littlefield.
Husserl, E. (1960) *Cartesian Meditations. An Introduction to Phenomenology*, translated by Dorion Cairns, The Hague: Martinus Nijhoff.
Husserl, E. (1973) *Experience and Judgement. Investigations in a Genealogy of Logic*, translated by J. S. Churchill and K. Ameriks, Evanston: Northwestern University Press.
Husserl, E. (1983) *Ideas Pertaining to a Pure Phenomenology and to a Phenomenological Philosophy. First Book: General Introduction to a Pure Phenomenology*, translated by Fred Kersten, The Hague: Martinus Nijhoff.
Husserl, E. (1997) *Thing and Space: Lectures of 1907*, translated by Richard Rojcewicz, Dordrecht: Kluwer.
Husserl, E. (2001a) *Logical Investigations*, vol. 1, translated by J. N. Findlay, London and New York: Routledge.
Husserl, E. (2001b) *Logical Investigations*, vol. 2, translated by J. N. Findlay, London: Routledge.
Husserl, E. (2001c) *Analyses Concerning Active and Passive Synthesis. Lectures on Transcendental Logic*, translated by Anthony Steinbock, Dordrecht: Kluwer.
Husserl, E. (2005) *Phantasy, Image Consciousness and Memory (1898–1925)*, translated by John B. Brough, Dordrecht: Springer.
Kind, A. (2013) "The heterogeneity of imagination," *Erkenntnis* 78: 141–159.
Koyré, A. (1968) "Galileo's treatise 'De Motu Gravium': The use and abuse of imaginary experiment," in *Metaphysics and Measurement: Essays in the Scientific Revolution*, Cambridge: Harvard University Press.
Kuhn, T. S. (1977) "A function for thought experiments," in *The Essential Tension. Selected Studies in Scientific Tradition and Change*, Chicago: University of Chicago Press.
Kujundzic, N. (1995) "Thought experiments: Architecture and economy of thought," *Journal of the British Society of Phenomenology* 26: 86–93.
Lampa, A. (1924) "Wie erscheint nach der Relativitätstheorie ein bewegter Stab einem ruhenden Beobachter?" *Zeitschrift für Physik* 27: 138–148.
McAllister, J. W. (1996) "The evidential significance of thought experiment in science," *Studies in History and Philosophy of Science* 27: 233–250.
Miščević, N. (1992) "Mental models and thought experiments," *International Studies in the Philosophy of Science* 6: 215–226.
Mohanty, J. N. (1991) "The method of imaginative variation in phenomenology," in *Thought Experiments in Science and Philosophy*, edited by T. Horowitz and G. Massey, Savage: Rowman and Littlefield.

Nersessian, N. J. (1992) "In the theoretician's laboratory," *PSA: Proceedings of the Biennial Meeting of the Philosophy of Science Association* vol. 2, pp. 291–301, East Lansing: Philosophy of Science Association.

Noë, A. (2004) *Action in Perception*, Cambridge: MIT Press.

Norton, J. (1996) "Are thought experiments just what you thought?," *Canadian Journal of Philosophy* 26: 333–366.

Norton, J. (2004) "Why thought experiments do not transcend empiricism," in *Contemporary Debates in Philosophy of Science*, edited by C. Hitchcock, Malden: Blackwell.

Palmieri, P. (2005) "'Spuntar lo scoglio più duro': Did Galileo ever think the most beautiful thought experiment in the history of science?" *Studies in History and Philosophy of Science* 36: 223–240.

Penrose, R. (1959) "The apparent shape of a relativistically moving sphere," *Mathematical Proceedings of the Cambridge Philosophical Society* 55: 137–139.

Sartre, J.-P. (2004) *The Imaginary: A Phenomenological Psychology of the Imagination*, London: Routledge.

Siewert, C. (2007) "In favor of (plain) phenomenology," *Phenomenology and the Cognitive Sciences* 6: 201–220.

Smith, D. W. (2004) *Mind World. Essays in Phenomenology and Ontology*, Cambridge: Cambridge University Press.

Smith, D. W. (2007) *Husserl*, London: Routledge.

Smith, D. W. and McIntyre, R. (1982) *Husserl and Intentionality. A Study of Mind, Meaning, and Language*, London: Reidel.

Sturgeon, S. (2000) *Matters of Mind: Consciousness, Reason and Nature*, London: Routledge.

Terrell, J. (1959) "Invisibility of the Lorentz contraction," *Physical Review* 116: 1041–1045.

White, A. R. (1990) *The Language of Imagination*, Oxford: Blackwell.

Wiltsche, H. A. (2013) "How essential are essential laws? A thought experiment on physical things and their givenness in adumbrations," in *Wahrnehmen, Fühlen, Handeln. Phänomenologie im Wettstreit der Methoden*, edited by I. Günzler and K. Mertens, Münster: Mentis.

Wittgenstein, L. (1980) *Remarks on the Philosophy of Psychology*, Oxford: Blackwell.

Part IV
ISSUES, CHALLENGES AND INTERACTIONS

20
INTUITION AND ITS CRITICS

Stephen Stich and Kevin Tobia

1 Introduction

The term "intuition" has a long history in philosophy, and it has had many different meanings (Osbeck and Held 2014). As Jaakko Hintikka (1999) noted, the term was rarely used in twentieth-century analytic philosophy until Noam Chomsky and his followers popularized its use in linguistics. In Chomskian linguistics, an intuition is a spontaneous judgment about the grammatical properties or relations of sentences. The linguist proposes one or more sentences and asks a question about them: Is this sentence grammatical? Are these two sentences related as active and passive? The person whose intuitions are being probed finds that an answer almost immediately comes to mind, though typically she has never heard the sentences before and is aware of no conscious reasoning about them. The linguistic intuition is the judgment the speaker makes.

For Chomsky and his followers, intuitions are used as evidence about the grammar of the speaker's "I-language" – the language whose rules are actually represented in the speaker's mind (Chomsky 1986). Though the rules of the I-language are not consciously accessible, Chomskian linguists assume that, when things go well, the rules are used by the language processing system to infer the answer to the grammatical question that the linguist has posed.[1] But, of course, things do not always go well. Failure to pay attention, limits on short-term memory, and a host of other factors can cause a speaker to make "performance errors" leading to intuitions that do not accurately reflect what the speaker's mentally represented grammar actually says about the sentences.

A similar practice has played an important role in philosophy since antiquity. The philosopher describes a hypothetical situation and asks whether the people, objects, or events described have some philosophically interesting property or relation. When things go well, the person to whom the question is posed finds that an answer almost immediately comes to mind, though she has never considered the hypothetical situation before and is aware of no conscious reasoning about it. Philosophers quickly noted the similarity between this practice and the one used by Chomsky and his followers, and the term "intuition" became widely used for the spontaneous judgments that people make about philosophical thought experiments. That is how we will use the term here.[2]

2 Two ways intuitions are used as evidence in philosophy

During the decades prior to the emergence of Chomskian linguistics, Logical Positivists and "ordinary language" philosophers argued that philosophers' main job is conceptual analysis. On one influential account, concepts are mentally represented packets of information that characterize a category or an individual, though the details of these mentally represented packets are typically not consciously accessible (Goldman 2007, 2010). The strategy of assembling intuitions about thought experiments – sometimes called "the method of cases" – was widely used by philosophers as a way of gathering evidence about philosophically interesting concepts, and some philosophers have justified the use of this strategy along lines that are quite similar to the Chomskian justification of the use of linguistic intuitions as evidence about a mentally represented grammar. Here is how Alvin Goldman makes the point:

> It's part of the nature of concepts ... that possessing a concept tends to give rise to beliefs and intuitions that accord with the contents of the concept. If the content of someone's concept F implies that F does (doesn't) apply to example x, then that person is disposed to intuit that F applies (doesn't apply) to x when the issue is raised in his mind.
>
> (Goldman 2007, 15)

On views like the one Goldman is endorsing, intuitions are appropriately used as evidence about the extension or the content of a person's concepts. Thus, for example, suppose that Dannisha reads a thought experiment about a runaway trolley that is about to kill five innocent people. By throwing a switch a bystander could redirect the trolley to another track where it would kill only one innocent person. After hearing the story, Dannisha is asked whether it is morally permissible for the bystander to throw the switch and redirect the trolley, and she has the intuition that it *is* morally permissible. For Goldman, and for those who hold similar views, this would count as evidence that the action described is included in the extension of Dannisha's concept of moral permissibility.

There is another family of views according to which philosophical intuitions are often appropriately used in projects that are importantly different from conceptual analysis. On views of this sort, intuitions are frequently used as evidence for or against theories about philosophically important phenomena, like knowledge, justice, causation, and moral permissibility, not some person or group of people's *concepts* of these things. In "Philosophical Theory and Intuitional Evidence," Goldman and Pust distinguish two different kinds of "targets" of philosophical analyses or theories:

> Broadly speaking, views about philosophical analysis may be divided into those that take the targets of such analysis to be in-the-head psychological entities versus outside-the-head non-psychological entities. We shall call the first type of position *mentalism* and the second *extra-mentalism*.
>
> (1998, 183)[3]

Concepts – mentally represented packets of information – are among the leading targets of mentalist analyses, and as we have seen, there is a plausible story to be told about why intuitions can be used as evidence in conceptual analysis. Implicit or tacit theories are another, closely related, target of mentalist philosophical analyses (Jackson, Mason, and Stich 2008). Philosophers who take implicit theories to be the targets of their analyses also claim that these theories play a role in generating (or as Jackson puts it, "driving") our intuitive classifications. So it is clear why intuitions are taken to be good evidence about tacit theories.

In contrast to mentalist targets, the exact nature of the targets of extra-mentalist analyses is less than clear. Goldman and Pust discuss three possibilities: (i) universals or Platonic Forms (like the Platonic Form of knowledge or of justice); (ii) modal truths (like the putative fact that it is possible for a belief to be justified and true, but not an instance of knowledge); and (iii) natural kinds. Moral facts or moral truths are another important target of extra-mentalist analysis that Goldman and Pust do not mention (see, e.g., Audi 2013).

What all of these have in common is that the correctness or incorrectness of an extra-mentalist theory does not depend on what is in the head of a person whose intuitions are used as evidence. When an extra-mentalist theory takes knowledge or moral permissibility as its target, the goal is to specify what knowledge really is, or what really is morally permissible. And when philosophers engaged in extra-mentalist projects use intuitions as evidence, they assume that the content of the intuition is likely to be *true*. If we have the intuition that the protagonist in a Gettier thought experiment does not know the proposition that is the focus of the experiment, then it probably is the case that he does not know that proposition. So an extra-mentalist analysis of knowledge that entails that the protagonist does know the proposition is challenged, while an analysis that entails the protagonist does not know is supported. Similarly, if we have the intuition that it is morally permissible for the protagonist in the trolley case to throw the switch that will divert the trolley, then it probably *is* morally permissible.

Goldman and Pust (1998) are skeptical about this strategy of using intuition as evidence for extra-mental philosophical analyses, because we have no good account of how the content of intuitions could be reliably linked to the facts about Platonic Forms, or natural kinds, or modal and moral truths that the extra-mentalist theory seeks to capture. We agree; it is indeed puzzling how the contents of intuitions could provide reliable evidence about these extra-mental facts. But for most of human history, perception posed a comparable mystery, and the appeal to intuition in mathematics still does. Thus we do not think that the fact that we have no account of how intuitions about philosophical thought experiments could be reliably linked to the extra-mental facts that are the targets of philosophers' analyses provides a compelling reason to be skeptical about the use of intuitions as evidence in these projects.

3 The experimental philosophy critique of using intuitions as evidence for extra-mentalist theories

Over the last dozen years, the emerging field of experimental philosophy has provided what we believe to be a much better reason to be skeptical about the use of intuitions as evidence for extra-mentalist theories. Recall that when philosophers use intuitions as evidence for extra-mentalist theories, they assume that intuitions are likely to be reliable indicators of the *truth* about the extra-mentalist phenomenon they are studying. But recent findings in experimental philosophy have cast doubt on the reliability of some philosophical intuitions by demonstrating, in a growing list of cases, that intuitions vary between demographic groups, and that they are influenced by other factors that are obviously irrelevant to the truth of the content of the intuition. Though space does not permit a detailed discussion of these studies, we will offer a brief overview of what we take to be some of the more important findings.

3.1 Studies showing that philosophical intuitions vary across demographic groups

In one of the first experimental philosophy studies, Weinberg et al. (2001) reported that the epistemic intuitions of American students whose cultural background is East Asian are significantly different from those of students whose cultural background is European, though this finding has since been challenged by a number of authors (for a detailed discussion, see Machery et al. 2015; see also Starmans and Friedman 2013; Nagel, San Juan, and Mar 2013a; Kim and Yuan 2015; Seyedsayamdost 2015a). More recently, Starmans and Friedman (2012) have shown that, in a range of cases, the epistemic intuitions of non-philosophers differ from the epistemic intuitions usually reported by philosophers (but see Nagel, San Juan, and Mar 2013b). And in a particularly striking study, Starmans and Friedman (2014) find that among academics, intuitions about knowledge are influenced by one's academic discipline. In a series of studies, Machery and colleagues have shown that the sort of semantic intuitions that philosophers have used as evidence for theories of reference differ across cultural groups (Machery, Mallon, Nichols, and Stich 2004; Machery, Olivola, and De Blanc 2009; but see Lam 2010, and Sytsma and Livengood 2011 for non-replications with modified materials). In ethics, Ahlenius and Tännsjö (2012) have found cross-cultural differences in intuitions on trolley cases, and in a very well designed study, Abarbanell and Hauser (2010) found cultural differences in intuitions relevant to the act versus omission distinction. More recently, Fessler et al. (2015) report substantial variation in contextual contingency in moral judgment across seven societies. Buckwalter and Stich (2014) survey a number of findings suggesting that some philosophical intuitions vary with the gender of the participant (for further data, including non-replications of some earlier findings, see Adleberg, Thompson, and Nahmias 2015 and Seyedsayamdost 2015b). Colaço, Buckwalter and Stich (2014) found that epistemic intuitions vary with the age of the participants. Feltz and Cokely (2009) and Schulz, Cokely, and Feltz (2011) report that intuitions about free will and responsibility depend on one's personality, specifically on whether one is an introvert or an extrovert. Tobia (2016) finds that intuitions about the strength of arguments in the philosophy of religion vary with respect to the intuiter's commitment to theism or atheism. To sum up, philosophical intuitions have been found to vary with culture, academic discipline, gender, age, and personality. Of course, the degree, scope, and replicability of these findings remain open to further empirical study.

3.2 Studies showing that philosophical intuitions vary with language

Vaesen, Peterson, and Van Bezooijen (2013) found that a cluster of epistemic intuitions elicited from philosophers differed depending on their native language. Native English speaking philosophers had different intuitions from those whose native language was Dutch, German, or Swedish, though all the participants were fluent in English and all the thought experiments used to elicit the intuitions were presented in English. Costa et al. (2014) found that the moral intuitions of participants who read experimental vignettes in their native language were different from the moral intuitions of participants who read the vignettes in one of their non-native languages. They found this striking effect across five groups of native/non-native speakers: English/Spanish, Spanish/English, Korean/English, English/French, and English/Hebrew.

3.3 Studies showing that philosophical intuitions vary with the order in which the thought experiments are presented

In an early study, psychologists Petrinovich and O'Neill (1996) found that participants' moral intuitions varied with the order in which the vignettes were presented. Similar findings have been reported by Liao, Wiegmann, Alexander, and Vong (2012), Wiegmann, Okan, and Nagel (2012), and Schwitzgebel and Cushman (2011). The Schwitzgebel and Cushman study is particularly striking, since they set out to explore whether order effects in moral intuitions were smaller or non-existent in professional philosophers. Surprisingly, they found that this is not the case, even though the thought experiments used were well known to most professional philosophers. They also report that in some cases philosophers' intuitions show substantial order effects when the intuitions of non-philosophers do not! Order effects have also been reported for epistemic intuitions (Swain, Alexander, and Weinberg 2008; Machery et al. forthcoming) and for intuitions about intentional action (Cushman and Mele 2008; Feltz and Cokely 2011).

3.4 Studies showing that philosophical intuitions are subject to framing effects

As we use the term, a framing effect is an effect produced by a minor feature of the wording or presentation of a thought experiment that is irrelevant to the substantive issue being explored. Since the pioneering work of Tversky and Kahneman (1981), there has been an explosion of interest in the phenomenon in psychology, economics, political science, and elsewhere (Sunstein 2005; Kahneman 2011, ch. 34). Framing has been reported in moral philosophy thought experiments by Petrinovich and O'Neill (1996) and by Nadelhoffer and Feltz (2008) who found that some moral intuitions are subject to an "actor-observer effect" – participants' intuitions about moral permissibility were affected by whether the moral scenario is presented in the second person or the third person. Tobia, Buckwalter, and Stich (2013a) found that actor-observer framing can also affect the moral intuitions of philosophers. Nahmias, Coates and Kvaran (2007) and Nichols and Knobe (2007) report striking framing effects in intuitions about free will and responsibility. In a very different vein, both Weinberg and colleagues (Weinberg, Alexander, Gonnerman, and Reuter 2012; Gonnerman, Reuter, and Weinberg 2011) and Tobia and Stich (unpublished) have found that participants' intuitions about epistemological thought experiments are affected by the font in which the thought experiment is presented. In the Tobia and Stich study, the effect was found both in ordinary folk and in professional philosophers.

3.5 Studies showing that philosophical intuitions are affected by the physical and social environment in which the intuition is elicited

There is now a growing body of research reporting that intuitions evoked by moral thought experiments are affected by factors like dirty pizza boxes and a whiff of fart spray (Schnall, Haidt, Clore, and Jordan, 2008a), the use of soap (Schnall, Benton, and Harvey 2008b) or an antiseptic handwipe (Zhong, Strejcek, and Sivanathan 2010), or even the proximity of a hand sanitizer dispenser (Helzer and Pizarro 2011). Tobia, Chapman, and Stich (2013b) found that the moral intuitions of both students and professional philosophers are affected by spraying the questionnaire with a disinfectant spray. Valdesolo and DeSteno (2006) reported that viewing a humorous video clip can have a substantial impact on participant's moral intuitions. And more recently, Strohminger, Lewis, and Meyer (2011) have shown that hearing different kinds of audio clips (stand-up comedy or inspirational stories from a volume called *Chicken Soup for the Soul*) has divergent effects on moral intuitions.

3.6 The implications of these experiments for the use of intuitions as evidence for extra-mentalist theories

The problem that these findings pose for philosophers who use intuitions as evidence for extra-mentalist theories is obvious. In each case it appears that participants' intuitions are varying as a function of some variable that is not relevant to the extra-mental phenomenon being investigated. Thus some of these intuitions must be unreliable. The point was made nicely by Walter Sinnott-Armstrong in a paper that reviewed the literature on order effects in moral intuitions.

> The truth about what is morally right or wrong in the cases did not vary with [the order in which they were presented]. Hence moral [intuitions] fail to track the truth and are unreliable insofar as they are subject to such order effects.
> (Sinnott-Armstrong 2008, 67)

Similarly, the truth about the nature of knowledge, moral permissibility, reference, intentionality, and free will does not depend on the personality or cultural background of the person asked about these things, or on whether she is a native speaker of English, has just seen a funny video clip, or is standing near a dispenser for hand sanitizer. So to the extent that intuitions vary with these irrelevant factors, they are not a reliable source of evidence.

Though we have not yet mentioned it, there is another feature of most of the studies we have cited that poses a further problem for the use of intuitions as evidence for extra-mentalist theories. We have been focusing on findings indicating that intuitions vary across groups of different sorts or across experimental conditions. However, in all of these studies there is considerable variation *within* groups and *within* conditions. Participants with the same cultural background disagree about whether the protagonist in a Gettier case has knowledge; participants who see funny video clips disagree about whether it is morally permissible to push a large man off a footbridge to prevent a runaway trolley from killing five other people; participants who are presented with the second-person version of a moral thought experiment disagree about what is morally required. Some of this disagreement may simply be experimental noise, resulting from participants not understanding the thought experiment, not paying attention, interpreting important words in different ways, or making mistaken assumptions about what the experimenter really wants them to do (cf. Sosa 2007a, 2009). But to the extent that these within-group and within-condition disagreements reflect genuine differences in intuition, they pose an obvious problem for philosophers who would use these intuitions as evidence about extra-mental phenomena, since some of these intuitions must be mistaken.

4 The implications of experimental philosophy findings for the use of intuitions as evidence for mentalist theories

With one important exception, what we have said about extra-mentalist projects applies, mutatis mutandis, to mentalist projects as well. In mentalist projects, intuitions are used as evidence about the concept or tacit theory that putatively plays a central role in generating the intuition. The assumption underlying the use of intuitions as evidence in these projects is that a person's intuitions are a reliable source of evidence about whether her concept applies to cases set out in thought experiments, or about what her tacit theory entails about the cases. But when the presence of dirty pizza boxes or hand sanitizers influences people's intuitions, this assumption cannot be correct, since whether one of a person's moral concepts applies to the behavior recounted in a thought experiment, or what the relevant tacit theory entails about that behavior, does not vary with presence of pizza boxes or hand sanitizers. Nor does the application of a concept to cases depend on the order in which the cases are encountered or on the font in which the thought experiment is printed.

The situation is importantly different for demographic differences, since evidence of demographic differences in intuition suggests that people in different demographic groups have different tacit theories or different concepts. So, for example, Starmans and Friedman's finding that people in different academic disciplines have different intuitions about whether the protagonists in epistemic thought experiments know a specified proposition may indicate that people in different disciplines have different concepts of knowledge. And the discovery, by Abarbanell and Hauser (2010), that the moral intuitions of rural Tseltal-speaking Mayans are not sensitive to the distinction between actions and omissions suggests that the tacit moral theory of these Mayans is importantly different from the tacit moral theory of American and European internet users who reported quite different intuitions in response to similar moral thought experiments. While these are fascinating findings, they pose no problem for the use of intuitions as evidence for mentalist theories, though they make it clear that philosophers pursuing mentalist projects should specify *whose* concepts or tacit theories they are analyzing. Of course, philosophers who engage in conceptual analysis often want to use their analyses in a variety of other projects. And if there are different concepts of knowledge or reference or moral permissibility in different demographic groups, then a philosopher who wants to use one of these concepts must specify *which* demographic variant she is invoking, and why that one is a better choice than the variants used in other demographic groups. Underscoring the need to address questions like this is, we believe, one of the most valuable contributions of experimental philosophy.[4]

5 Responses to the experimental philosophy challenge

The findings surveyed in Section 3 pose a challenge to the use of intuitions as evidence in both mentalist and extra-mentalist projects. In this section we will consider two sorts of responses to that challenge. The first focuses on the alleged expertise of professional philosophers. The second proposes more restrictive accounts of philosophical intuition.

5.1 Three versions of the "expertise defense"

One common response to the experimental philosophy critique of using intuitions as evidence is the claim that the experimental findings, however interesting they may be, tell us nothing about actual philosophical practice, because the experiments use the wrong participants. Experimental philosophers typically collect data about the intuitions of students in classrooms, or internet users, or people in public places. In a few studies, data have been collected from indigenous people in remote corners of the world. But when professional philosophers use intuitions to test their theories, they do not use *those* intuitions. Rather, they use their own intuitions and the intuitions of other professional philosophers. And, the critics continue, this is entirely appropriate, because professional philosophers are *experts* at dealing with philosophical thought experiments. When we rely on intuition in other fields, ranging from medicine to physics to chess, it is rational to attend to the intuition of experts and ignore the intuition of untrained amateurs. The same is true in philosophy. So studies of the philosophical intuitions of people untrained in philosophy pose no threat at all to standard philosophical methodology.[5]

It is important to note that there are several different ways in which this "expertise defense" can be elaborated. One of them, suggested in the following quote from Horvath, maintains that the intuitions of professional philosophers are significantly less likely to be influenced by irrelevant factors like order of presentation, framing, or ambient odors.

> Why should professional philosophers grant ... that their own intuitions about hypothetical cases vary equally with irrelevant factors as those of the folk? Surely, no chess grandmaster, mathematician or physicist would grant anything remotely like that to an experimental psychologist.
>
> (Horvath 2010. Cf. Nado 2014)

Two other versions of the expertise defense maintain that the philosophical intuitions of professional philosophers are more likely to be *accurate* than the intuitions of untrained folk. For philosophers pursuing extra-mentalist projects, the claim is that the content of philosophers' intuitions are more likely to be *true*, while for philosophers engaged in mentalist projects the claim is that philosophers' intuitions are more likely to correctly reflect what their concept or tacit theory actually entails about the case at hand.

The first version of the expertise defense, which predicts that philosophers' intuitions are less likely to be influenced by irrelevant factors, has been the focus of a number of recent experimental studies. In our survey of the literature, in Section 3, we mentioned most of these studies; none of them confirm the prediction made by this version of the expertise defense. Indeed, to the best of our knowledge, there are *no* studies confirming that prediction. Rather, what this growing literature suggests is that philosophers are no less susceptible to language effects, order effects, framing effects, and environmental effects than non-philosophers. Of course, it is possible that the studies done so far are outliers, and that future studies will support those who urge this version of the expertise defense. But at this point, we think it is fair to say that their prediction does not look promising.

Michael Devitt has been by far the most indefatigable defender of the second version of the expertise defense – the version that focuses on extra-mentalist projects and maintains that the contents of philosophers' intuitions are more likely to be true (Devitt 2011a, 2011b, 2015). In a series of papers, he has set out a theoretical framework that, he argues, makes it plausible that philosophers' intuitions will be more accurate than those of ordinary folk – at least in the philosophy of language.[6] But Devitt acknowledges that this theoretical framework must ultimately be tested empirically. And, to his credit, he has designed and conducted a series of experiments intended to do just that. Unfortunately, by his own admission, the experiments were a complete failure (Devitt 2015). Perhaps Devitt or others will ultimately design better experiments. But for now the version of the expertise defense that claims that in the philosophy of language, the contents of philosophers' intuitions are more likely to be true has no empirical support. Things are no better in other areas of philosophy. Indeed, we find it hard to imagine how one might empirically test the claim that the contents of philosophers' moral or metaphysical or epistemological intuitions are more likely to be true than those of ordinary folk. So we are not surprised that no one has tried.

The situation is much the same for the third version of the expertise defense, which claims that philosophers are better than non-philosophers at intuiting what their concepts actually entail about a case. Conceivably clever psychologists or philosophers could design experiments to test this claim. But we suspect that the conceptual and empirical challenges would be daunting. So here, too, we are not surprised that no one has tried. A decade ago, Machery and colleagues (2004) said that the claim that philosophers' intuitions are superior to those of non-philosophers "smacks of narcissism in the extreme." It still does.

5.2 Restrictive accounts of philosophical intuition

We have been working with a very inclusive account of philosophical intuitions modeled on the Chomskian account of linguistic intuitions. Philosophical intuitions, we have been assuming, are immediate responses to questions about whether the people or objects or events in philosophical thought experiments have some interesting philosophical property or relation; they are accompanied by little or no conscious reasoning. In adopting this account, our goal has been to do justice to what Williamson memorably describes as the "promiscuous role the term ['intuition'] plays in the practice of philosophy" (Williamson 2007, 218). However, many philosophers have urged much more restrictive accounts of philosophical intuitions. One motive for constructing more restrictive accounts is to defend the use of intuitions as evidence in philosophy by explaining why intuitions (narrowly defined) are likely to be trustworthy. Another, closely linked, motive is to fend off the challenge posed by experimental philosophy. If the experiments are not eliciting the sort of judgments that comport with the restrictive characterization of intuitions that the author has proposed, then they pose no threat to the evidential use of the narrower class of intuitions. One author who clearly shares both motives is Kirk Ludwig. According to him,

> It is only if a judgment is *solely* an expression of one's competence in the contained concepts and their mode of combination that it counts as an apprehension of a conceptual or a priori truth. Insofar as we think of intuitions as insights into conceptual truths, they are to be conceived as judgments or beliefs which are the product of our competence in the deployment of the concepts involved.
> (Ludwig 2010, 433; emphasis in the original)

For Ludwig, a judgment or belief that is influenced by factors other than conceptual competence will not count as an intuition. Among those factors, surely, are many that were investigated in the experimental studies surveyed in Section 3. A judgment that is influenced by order of presentation, or font size or fart spray is not *solely* the expression of conceptual competence. Thus when intuitions are characterized in this way, the studies pose no challenge to the use of intuitions as evidence in philosophy. But we are inclined to think that in making this move, Ludwig is hoist on his own petard. For the effects discussed in Section 3 are almost always *covert*; people have no conscious awareness that their beliefs or judgments are being affected. So on Ludwig's restricted account, the only way to determine whether one's beliefs or judgments are intuitions is to do well designed and carefully controlled experiments. Rather than showing that the experimental studies are irrelevant to philosophical practice, Ludwig's restricted account of intuition leads directly to the conclusion that the sorts of studies that experimental philosophers have undertaken are required before we can begin to use intuitions as evidence, since without such studies we have no way of knowing which of our beliefs or judgments *are* intuitions.[7,8]

While some authors who propose restricted accounts of intuition want to fend off the experimental philosophy challenge by characterizing a set of judgments or beliefs – or "seemings," as Sosa (2007b) prefers to describe them – that are immune from the sort of irrelevant influences that the experimentalists have documented, Cappelen (2012) takes a more radical approach. He offers an account of intuition that is so restrictive that he can find no evidence that philosophers ever actually use intuitions. And, of course, if philosophers do not use intuitions, then the experimentalists' challenge is irrelevant to philosophical practice. The feature that does most of the work for Cappelen is the one he calls "Rock." As Weinberg (2014) notes,

> [Cappelen] claims that [Rock] is a special kind of epistemic status – "special" recurring frequently in the book, whenever he discusses it – one that is immediate, "glowing", "privileged", and highly controversial. It is a kind of justification so fundamental, unshakeable, indubitable, that an author's saying pretty much anything at all in defense of p, even expressing any hesitancy about whether to endorse p, or about what p's significance might be, is a clear sign that p lacks Rock... .
>
> That Rock is so freaky and fragile, and so completely absent in all of the case studies [that Cappelen presents] ... should have been a sign not to attribute Rock to intuition theorists in the first place. Cappelen adduces almost no textual evidence to support his claim that "most intuition theorists" take intuitions to have this feature.

Since neither philosophers who defend the use of intuitions as evidence nor those who challenge this use show any inclination to accept Cappelen's radically restrictive account of what they have in mind, we think his claim that philosophers do not actually use intuitions as evidence can safely be ignored.[9]

6 The take-home message

In Section 3, we reviewed a number of studies indicating that a substantial list of philosophical intuitions vary across demographic groups and that they are influenced by a number of *prima facie* irrelevant factors, ranging from language and order of presentation to smells, fonts, and funny video clips. We went on to argue that these findings cast doubt on the use of these intuitions as evidence for extra-mentalist theories. In Section 4, we argued that many of the findings also challenge the use of these intuitions as evidence for mentalist projects. Some writers, most notably Jonathan Weinberg and Joshua Alexander, have urged that these findings justify a thoroughgoing skepticism about the use of intuitions as evidence in philosophy (Alexander and Weinberg 2007; Weinberg 2007; Weinberg and Alexander 2014). But we think this conclusion is much too strong.

A growing body of evidence suggests that intuitions in different areas of philosophy are subserved by different psychological and neurological mechanisms (Nado 2011). And in at least one area of philosophy, viz., ethics, there is evidence that intuitions about different questions (e.g., blame, responsibility, and punishment) derive from different mental mechanisms (Cushman 2008; Cushman and Young 2009). This work strongly suggests that philosophical intuition is not a natural kind. Thus, the discovery that intuitions about an issue in one branch (or sub-branch) of philosophy are influenced by some irrelevant factors gives us no reason to think that intuitions about issues in some other branch or sub-branch of philosophy will also be influenced by that factor, or by any other irrelevant factor.

The skepticism about the use of intuitions as evidence that we voiced in Sections 3 and 4 should be directed primarily at intuitions that have been shown to be susceptible to irrelevant influences, and at other intuitions that are the product of psychological mechanisms that are likely to be vulnerable in similar ways. And which are these? The answer is that at this point we do not know, and we are not going to find out without a great deal more sophisticated work in psychology and neuroscience. On our view, this sort of research should be viewed as quite central to experimental philosophy. So the take-home message from this chapter is *not* that intuitions should not be used as evidence in philosophy. Rather, it is that experimental philosophy, broadly construed, has a crucial role to play in assessing and improving philosophical methodology.

Notes

1 For a recent challenge to this Chomskian assumption, see Devitt (2006). For replies, see Antony (2008) and Longworth (2009).
2 "Intuition" was used by twentieth-century philosophers before Chomsky – particularly by ethicists. Until Chomsky, however, "intuition" was used much less frequently in philosophy of mind, philosophy of language, metaphysics, and epistemology. See Pust (2000, ch. 1) for examples of the use of intuitions as evidence in philosophy. Alexander (2012, ch. 1) and Pust (2000, ch. 2) provide

useful overviews of competing accounts of the nature of philosophical intuitions, and Andow (2015) offers some impressive quantitative evidence that there was indeed a dramatic increase in the use of the term "intuition" in philosophy starting about 1970.

3   In more recent work, Goldman (2010) abandons the "mentalist" and "extra-mentalist" terminology. We continue to use it because it provides suggestive labels for two broad conceptions of philosophical analysis.

4   For more on this theme, see Mallon, Machery, Nichols, and Stich (2009) and Machery, Mallon, Nichols, and Stich (2013).

5   For views in this vicinity, see Williamson (2005, 2011), Ludwig (2007), Horvath (2010), Grundmann (2010), and Devitt (2011b).

6   Devitt (2011a, 427) extends the claim to a range of metaphysical intuitions, and in talks he has extended the claim to intuitions in epistemology and ethics as well (personal communication, 28 August 2014).

7   In his chapter in this volume, Ludwig again insists that "not every response to a question on a survey about a scenario expresses an intuition. The survey data then is not straightforwardly data about intuitions. To use surveys for traditional philosophical purposes, we need to filter responses that are not intuitions ..." (Ludwig, this volume, 388). Though he is less explicit here than in Ludwig (2010) about what sort of "filtering" is required, he would presumably insist that spontaneous judgments influenced by order of presentation, or dirty pizza boxes, or proximity of a hand sanitizer dispenser do not count as intuitions, as he prefers to use the term. And since that influence is rarely obvious, it seems that the philosopher, as Ludwig portrays him, must *begin* by doing experimental philosophy. How else can Ludwig's philosopher reliably "filter responses that are not intuitions"?

Ludwig is also rather cavalier in his claims about what other philosophers would count as intuitions. Many "experimental philosophers," he tells us, "have simply misunderstood the sort of intuition (or judgment) sought in philosophical thought experiments. They are not 'spontaneous judgments ... for which the person making the judgment may be able to offer no plausible justification' ..." (Ludwig, this volume, 388; the embedded quote is from Nichols, Stich and Weinberg 2003, 19). However, as Yuri Cath notes, both Nelson Goodman and David Lewis seem to endorse this account of intuitions, or perhaps something even more permissive (Cath forthcoming). Perhaps Ludwig would not count Goodman and Lewis as philosophers.

8   A similar situation confronts the "conceptualist" view of thought experiments that Grundmann espouses in his contribution to this volume. On Grundmann's view,

> conceptualism ... gives a much more parsimonious explanation of philosophical thought experiments. Concepts do not only have conditions for their correct application, they are also plausibly associated with application dispositions of those who possess them. With respect to a particular class of concepts, the so-called semantically transparent concepts, application conditions and application dispositions match each other across possible worlds, at least under ideal circumstances. If this story is basically correct for key philosophical concepts, we can use our application dispositions to determine the extension of a concept across possible worlds and thereby, inductively, gain an understanding of the essence of the concept's referent
>
> (Grundmann, this volume, 305)

Grundmann is careful to note that "application dispositions" (which are a close kin of what we have been calling "intuitions") can only be used in this way *under ideal circumstances*. And while Grundmann does not pause to tell us what ideal circumstances *are*, it seems reasonable to suppose that application dispositions that are influenced by irrelevant factors like order of presentation or proximity to a hand sanitizer dispenser are not being studied under ideal circumstances. Since the influence of irrelevant factors is often covert, the methods of experimental philosophy will have to play an important role in Grundmann's conceptualist program.

9   In their chapter in this volume, Cohnitz and Häggqvist, citing Langkau, note a very different reason to be skeptical of Cappelen's claim that philosophers do not use intuitions as evidence. Cappelen takes the fact that a philosopher argues for a claim to be strong evidence that the philosopher is not

treating the claim as having "Rock" status. But as Langkau observes, there are a number of reasons why an author might offer an argument for a claim, even though she did take it to have "Rock" status. It might, for example, "be required in order to get a paper published" (Langkau forthcoming, cited in Cohnitz and Häggqvist, this volume, 419).

References

Abarbanell, L. and Hauser, M. (2010) "Mayan morality: An exploration of permissible harms," *Cognition* 115: 207–224.
Adleberg, T., Thompson, M. and Nahmias, E. (2015) "Do men and women have different philosophical intuitions? Further data," *Philosophical Psychology* 28: 615–641.
Ahlenius, H. and Tännsjö, T. (2012) "Chinese and Westerners respond differently to the trolley dilemmas," *Journal of Cognition and Culture* 12: 195–201.
Alexander, J. (2012) *Experimental Philosophy: An Introduction*, Cambridge: Polity Press.
Alexander, J. and Weinberg, J. (2007) "Analytic epistemology and experimental philosophy," *Philosophy Compass* 2: 56–80.
Andow, J. (2015) "How 'intuition' exploded," *Metaphilosophy* 46: 189–212.
Antony, L. (2008) "Meta-linguistics: Methodology and ontology in Devitt's *Ignorance of Language*," *Australasian Journal of Philosophy* 86: 643–656.
Audi, R. (2013) *Moral Perception*, Princeton: Princeton University Press.
Buckwalter, W. and Stich, S. (2014) "Gender and philosophical intuition," in *Experimental Philosophy*, vol. 2, edited by J. Knobe and S. Nichols, Oxford: Oxford University Press.
Cappelen, H. (2012) *Philosophy without Intuitions*, Oxford: Oxford University Press.
Cath, Y. (forthcoming) "Reflective equilibrium," in *The Oxford Handbook of Philosophical Methodology*, edited by H. Cappelen and T. Gendler, Oxford: Oxford University Press.
Chomsky, N. (1986) *Knowledge of Language: Its Nature, Origin, and Use*, New York: Praeger.
Colaço, D., Buckwalter, W. and Stich, S. (2014) "Epistemic intuitions in fake-barn thought experiments," *Episteme* 11: 199–212.
Costa, A., Foucart, A., Hayakawa, S., Aparici, M., Apesteguia, J., Heafner, J. and Keysar, B. (2014) "Your morals depend on language," *PLoS ONE* 9: e94842.
Cushman, F. (2008) "Crime and punishment: Distinguishing the roles of causal and intentional analyses in moral judgment," *Cognition* 108: 353–380.
Cushman, F. and Mele, A. (2008) "Intentional action: Two and half folk concepts," in *Experimental Philosophy*, edited by J. Knobe and S. Nichols, Oxford: Oxford University Press.
Cushman, F. and Young, L. (2009) "The psychology of dilemmas and the philosophy of morality," *Ethical Theory and Moral Practice* 12: 9–24.
Devitt, M. (2006) *Ignorance of Language*, Oxford: Clarendon Press.
Devitt, M. (2011a) "Experimental semantics," *Philosophy and Phenomenological Research* 82: 418–435.
Devitt, M. (2011b) "Whither experimental semantics?" *Theoria* 72: 5–36.
Devitt, M. (2014) "Abstract of 'Philosophy with Intuitions: A Response to Herman Cappelen,'" a lecture given at St. Andrews, Spring 2014 (unpublished manuscript).
Devitt, M. (2015) "Testing theories of reference," in *Advances in Experimental Philosophy of Language*, edited by J. Haukioja, London: Bloomsbury Press.
Feltz, A. and Cokely, E. T. (2009) "Do judgments about freedom and responsibility depend on who you are? Personality differences in intuitions about compatabilism and incompatabilism," *Consciousness and Cognition* 18: 342–350.
Feltz, A. and Cokely, E. T. (2011) "Individual differences in theory-of-mind judgments: Order effects and side effects," *Philosophical Psychology* 24: 343–355.
Fessler, D. M., Barrett, H. C., Kanovsky, M., Stich, S., Holbrook, C., Henrich, J., Bolyanatz, A. H., Gervais, M. M., Gurven, M., Kushnick, G., Pisor, A. C., von Rueden, C. and Laurence, S. (2015) "Moral parochialism and contextual contingency across seven societies," *Proceedings of the Royal Society B* 282: 20150907; doi: 10.1098/rspb.2015.0907.
Goldman, A. (2007) "Philosophical intuitions: Their target, their source, and their epistemic status," *Grazer Philosophische Studien* 74: 1–126.

Goldman, A. (2010) "Philosophical naturalism and intuitional methodology," *Proceedings of the American Philosophical Association* 84: 115–150.

Goldman, A. and Pust, J. (1998) "Philosophical theory and intuitional evidence," in *Rethinking Intuitions: The Psychology of Intuition and its Role in Philosophical Inquiry*, edited by M. DePaul and W. Ramsey, Savage: Rowman and Littlefield.

Gonnerman, C., Reuter, S. and Weinberg, J. (2011) "More oversensitive intuitions: Print fonts and could choose otherwise," Paper presented at the 108th meeting of the American Philosophical Association, Central Division, Minneapolis.

Grundmann, T. (2010) "Some hope for intuitions: A reply to Weinberg," *Philosophical Psychology* 23: 481–509.

Helzer, E. and Pizarro, D. (2011) "Dirty Liberals! Reminders of physical cleanliness influence moral and political attitudes," *Psychological Science* 22: 517–522.

Hintikka, J. (1999) "The emperor's new intuitions," *Journal of Philosophy* 96: 127–147.

Horvath, J. (2010) "How (not) to react to experimental philosophy," *Philosophical Psychology* 23: 447–480.

Jackson, F., Mason, K. and Stich, S. (2008) "Folk psychology and tacit theories: A correspondence between Frank Jackson, and Steve Stich and Kelby Mason," in *Conceptual Analysis and Philosophical Naturalism*, edited by D. Braddon-Mitchell and R. Nola, Cambridge: MIT Press.

Kahneman, D. (2011) *Thinking, Fast and Slow*, New York: Farrar, Straus and Giroux.

Kim, M. J. and Yuan, Y. (2015) "No cross-cultural differences in Gettier car case intuition: A replication study of Weinberg et al. 2001," *Episteme* 12: 355–361.

Lam, B. (2010) "Are Cantonese speakers really descriptivists? Revisiting cross-cultural semantics," *Cognition* 115: 320–332.

Langkau, J. (forthcoming) "Experimental philosophy: Against undermining the challenge."

Liao, M., Wiegmann, A., Alexander, J. and Vong, G. (2012) "Putting the trolley in order: Experimental philosophy and the loop case," *Philosophical Psychology* 25: 661–671.

Longworth, G. (2009) "Ignorance of linguistics," *Croatian Journal of Philosophy* 9: 21–34.

Ludwig, K. (2007) "The epistemology of thought experiments: First person versus third person approaches," *Midwest Studies in Philosophy* 31: 128–159.

Ludwig, K. (2010) "Intuitions and relativity," *Philosophical Psychology* 23: 427–45.

Machery, E., Mallon, R., Nichols, S. and Stich, S. (2004) "Semantics, cross-cultural style," *Cognition* 92: B1–B12.

Machery, E., Mallon, R., Nichols, S. and Stich, S. (2013) "If folk intuitions vary, then what?" *Philosophy and Phenomenological Research* 86: 618–635.

Machery, E., Olivola, C. Y. and De Blanc, M. (2009) "Linguistic and metalinguistic intuitions in the philosophy of language," *Analysis* 69: 689–694.

Machery, E., Stich, S., Rose, D., Chatterjee, A., Karasawa, K., Struchiner, N., Sirker, S., Usui, N. and Hashimoto, T. (2015) "Gettier across cultures," *Nous*, DOI: 10.1111/nous.12110.

Machery, E., Stich, S., Rose, D., Chatterjee, A., Karasawa, K., Struchiner, N., Sirker, S., Usui, N. and Hashimoto, T. (forthcoming) "Gettier Was framed!", to appear in *Epistemology for the Rest of the World*, edited by M. Mizumoto, E. McCready, J. Stanley and S. Stich, Oxford: Oxford University Press.

Mallon, R., Machery, E., Nichols, S. and Stich, S. (2009) "Against arguments from reference," *Philosophy and Phenomenological Research* 79: 332–356.

Nadelhoffer, T. and Feltz, A. (2008) "The actor-observer bias and moral intuitions: Adding fuel to Sinnott-Armstrong's fire," *Neuroethics* 1: 133–144.

Nado, J. (2011) *Intuition and Inquiry*, Ph.D. thesis, Department of Philosophy, Rutgers University.

Nado, J. (2014) "Philosophical expertise," *Philosophy Compass* 9: 631–641.

Nagel, J., San Juan, V. and Mar, R. (2013a) "Lay denial of knowledge for justified true beliefs," *Cognition* 129: 652–661.

Nagel, J., San Juan, V. and Mar, R. (2013b) "Authentic Gettier cases: A reply to Starmans and Friedman," *Cognition*, 129: 666–669.

Nahmias, E., Coates, D. and Kvaran, T. (2007) "Free will, moral responsibility and mechanism: Experiments on folk intuitions," *Midwest Studies in Philosophy* 31: 214–241.

Nichols, S. and Knobe, J. (2007) "Moral responsibility and determinism: The cognitive science of folk intuitions," *Nous* 41: 663–685.

Nichols, S., Stich, S. and Weinberg, J. (2003) "Meta-skepticism: Meditations on ethno-epistemology," in *The Skeptics*, edited by S. Luper, Aldershot: Ashgate Publishing.

Osbeck, L. and Held, B. (2014) Rational Intuition: Philosophical Roots. Scientific Investigations, Cambridge University Press.

Petrinovich, L. and O'Neill, P. (1996) "Influence of wording and framing effects on moral intuitions," *Ethology and Sociobiology* 17: 145–171.

Pust, J. (2000) *Intuitions as Evidence*, New York: Garland Publishing.

Schnall, S., Haidt, J., Clore, G. and Jordan, A. (2008a) "Disgust as embodied moral judgment," *Pers Soc Psychol Bull* 34: 1069–1109.

Schnall, S., Benton, J. and Harvey, S. (2008b) "With a clean conscience: Cleanliness reduces the severity of moral judgments," *Psychological Science* 19: 1219–1222.

Schulz, E., Cokely, E. and Feltz, A. (2011) "Persistent bias in expert judgments about free will and moral responsibility: A test of the expertise defense," *Consciousness and Cognition* 20: 1722–1731.

Schwitzgebel, E. and Cushman, F. (2011) "Expertise in moral reasoning? Order effects on moral judgment in professional philosophers and non-philosophers," *Mind and Language* 27: 135–153.

Seyedsayamdost, H. (2015a) "On normativity and epistemic intuitions: Failure of replication," *Episteme* 12: 95–116.

Seyedsayamdost, H. (2015b) "On gender and philosophical intuition: Failure of replication and other negative results," *Philosophical Psychology* 28: 642–673.

Sinnott-Armstrong, W. (2008) "Framing moral intuitions," in *Moral Psychology*, vol. 2, *The Cognitive Science of Morality: Intuition and Diversity*, edited by W. Sinnott-Armstrong, Cambridge: MIT Press.

Sosa, E. (2007a) "Experimental philosophy and philosophical intuition," *Philosophical Studies* 132: 99–107.

Sosa, E. (2007b) "Intuitions: Their nature and epistemic efficacy," *Grazer Philosophische Studien* 74: 51–67.

Sosa, E. (2009) "A defense of the use of intuitions in philosophy," in *Stich and His Critics*, edited by D. Murphy and M. Bishop, Malden: Wiley-Blackwell.

Starmans, C. and Friedman, O. (2012) "The folk conception of knowledge," *Cognition* 124: 272–283.

Starmans, C. and Friedman, O. (2013) "Taking 'know' for an answer: a reply to Nagel, San Juan and Mar," *Cognition* 129: 662–665.

Starmans, C. and Friedman, O. (2014) "No, no, KNOW! Academic disciplines disagree about the nature of knowledge," Paper presented at the Common-Sense Beliefs and Lay Theories Preconference at the Fifteenth Annual Society for Personality and Social Psychology, Austin, Texas.

Strohminger, N., Lewis, R. and Meyer, D. (2011) "Divergent effects of different positive emotions on moral judgment," *Cognition* 119: 295–300.

Sunstein, C. (2005) "Moral heuristics," *Behavioral and Brain Sciences* 28: 531–573.

Swain, S., Alexander, J. and Weinberg, J. (2008) "The instability of philosophical intuitions: Running hot and cold on Truetemp," *Philosophy and Phenomenological Research* 76: 138–155.

Sytsma, J. and Livengood, J. (2011) "A new perspective concerning experiments on semantic intuitions," *Australasian Journal of Philosophy* 89: 315–332.

Tobia, K. P. (2016) "Does religious belief infect philosophical analysis?" *Religion, Brain and Behavior* 6: 56–66.

Tobia, K. and Stich, S. (Unpublished manuscript) "A big and bold argument about expert intuition."

Tobia, K., Buckwalter, W. and Stich, S. (2013a) "Moral intuitions: Are philosophers experts?" *Philosophical Psychology* 26: 629–638.

Tobia, K., Chapman, G. and Stich, S. (2013b) "Cleanliness is next to morality, even for philosophers," *Journal of Consciousness Studies* 20: 195–204.

Tversky, A. and Kahneman, D. (1981) "The framing of decisions and the psychology of choice," *Science* 211: 453–458.

Vaesen, K., Peterson, M. and Van Bezooijen, B. (2013) "The reliability of armchair intuitions," *Metaphilosophy* 44: 559–578.

Valdesolo, P. and DeSteno, D. (2006) "Manipulations of emotional context shape moral judgment," *Psychological Science* 17: 476–477.

Weinberg, J. (2007) "How to challenge intuitions empirically without risking skepticism," *Midwest Studies in Philosophy* 30: 318–343.
Weinberg, J. (2014) "Cappelen between a rock and a hard place," *Philosophical Studies* 171: 545–553.
Weinberg, J. and Alexander, J. (2014) "The challenge of sticking with intuitions through thick and thin," in *Intuitions*, edited by A. Booth and D. Rowbottom, Oxford: Oxford University Press.
Weinberg, J., Alexander, J., Gonnerman, C. and Reuter, S. (2012) "Restrictionism and reflection: Challenge deflected, or simply redirected?" *The Monist* 95: 200–222.
Weinberg, J. M., Nichols, S. and Stich, S. (2001). "Normativity and epistemic intuitions," *Philosophical Topics* 29: 429–460.
Wiegmann, A., Okan, Y. and Nagel, J. (2012) "Order effects in moral judgment," *Philosophical Psychology* 25: 813–836.
Williamson, T. (2005) "Armchair philosophy, metaphysical modality and counterfactual thinking," *Proceedings of the Aristotelian Society* 105: 1–23.
Williamson, T. (2011) "Philosophical expertise and the burden of proof," *Metaphilosophy* 42: 215–229.
Williamson, T. (2007) *The Philosophy of Philosophy*, Oxford: Blackwell Publishing.
Zhong, C.-B., Strejcek, B. and Sivanathan, N. (2010) "A clean self can render harsh moral judgment," *Journal of Experimental Social Psychology* 46: 859–862.

21
THOUGHT EXPERIMENTS AND EXPERIMENTAL PHILOSOPHY

Kirk Ludwig

1 Introduction

Much of the recent movement organized under the heading "experimental philosophy" has been concerned with the empirical study of responses to thought experiments drawn from the literature on philosophical analysis.[1] I consider what bearing these studies have on the traditional projects in which thought experiments have been used in philosophy. This will help to answer the question what the relation is between experimental philosophy and philosophy, whether it is an "exciting new style of [philosophical] research," "a new interdisciplinary field that uses methods normally associated with psychology to investigate questions normally associated with philosophy" (Knobe et al. 2012), or whether its relation to philosophy consists, as some have suggested, in no more than the word "philosophy" appearing in its title, or whether the truth lies somewhere in between these two views.

Section 2 distinguishes different strands in experimental philosophy. Section 3 reviews some ways in which experimental philosophy has been criticized. Section 4 considers what would have to be true for experimental philosophy to have one or another sort of relevance to philosophy, whether the assumptions required are true, how we could know it, and the ideal limits of the usefulness experimental philosophy to philosophy. Section 5 is a brief conclusion.

2 Varieties of experimental philosophy

Broadly construed, experimental philosophy is philosophy informed by empirical work.[2] Experimental philosophy in this sense stretches back to antiquity. Here we will be concerned with a narrower conception of experimental philosophy characterized by the adoption of the survey as a central methodological tool, with a yes-or-no question, or a graduated range of answers from "strongly disagree" to "strongly agree" or the like, typically about a scenario in a philosophical thought experiment. Given this, experimental philosophy, in the sense we are interested in it, might more aptly be called "survey philosophy."

The most important division among experimental philosophers is between those who conceive of its project negatively and those who conceive of it positively. The negative (x-phi⁻) and the positive projects (x-phi⁺) both share the assumption that a central philosophical activity involves eliciting (what are often called) intuitions about actual and hypothetical cases, the latter involving conducting what we call thought experiments, with the aim of conceptual articulation or analysis. The traditional attempts to provide a satisfactory analysis of the concept of knowledge surrounding the literature on the Gettier cases (Gettier 1963) is a paradigm of the sort of activity they have in mind. In this case, the judgment (or intuition) that a subject with a justified true belief that p that is based on a justified false belief does not *thereby* know that p is taken to show that justified true belief is not sufficient for knowledge.

The negative project seeks to show that the results of surveys of undergraduates or others without much philosophical sophistication cast doubt on the probative value of intuitions and the use of thought experiments by philosophers. The negative project argues that the standard use of thought experiments makes certain empirical assumptions which can easily be tested by the survey method, and that (surprisingly) the assumptions (never tested) turn out to be false (Weinberg, Nichols, and Stich 2001; Nichols, Stich, and Weinberg 2003; Machery, Mallon, Nichols, and Stich 2004; Alexander and Weinberg 2007; Swain, Alexander, and Weinberg 2008; Liao, Wiegmann, Alexander, and Vong 2012). Among these alleged assumptions are that philosophers' intuitions are shared by everyone; that they are not biased, based on irrelevant factors, or theory-driven; and that they are not relative to cultural or socio-economic background, and the like.

There are two main ways of taking the positive project. The first is the Continuity Account, and the second the Psychological Account.[3]

1 The Continuity Accounts. X-phi is an enterprise with the same goals that philosophers have when they use thought experiments (the investigation of the application conditions of words or concepts, or of entailment relations between propositions, or implications of sentences), except that we crowdsource the answers (Malle and Knobe 2001; Knobe 2003a, 2003b, 2004 and 2006; Nahmias, Morris, Nadelhoffer, and Turner 2006; Pettit and Knobe 2009; Genone and Lombrozo 2012; Buckwalter and Schaffer 2013). There are two further subcategories.

   a Replacement Accounts: We add that survey philosophy should replace traditional "armchair" methods (Alexander and Weinberg 2007).

   b Supplement Accounts: We urge only that survey philosophy can provide a useful supplement to traditional methods (Papineau 2011; Talbot 2013).

2 Psychological Accounts. X-phi is not the pursuit of traditional philosophical goals (or at least analysis) by appeal to surveys of the philosophically unsophisticated but instead a psychological inquiry,[4] as opposed to a philosophical inquiry, into

   a concepts that philosophers have been interested in (Knobe and Burra 2006; Sarkissian et al. 2010; Nichols 2011), or

   b psychological mechanisms generating responses, whatever they might reveal, that people have (in various groupings) about philosophical thought experiments (Young et al. 2006; Knobe 2007, sec. 2; Nichols and Knobe 2007; Sarkissian et al. 2011).[5]

I will consider each of these programs within x-phi, but focus most attention on the Continuity Account as the most promising case of the *positive* relevance of x-phi to the traditional projects of philosophy.

3 Criticisms of experimental philosophy

Experimental philosophy has been criticized on a number of different grounds (not all these will be completely independent of, or consistent with, one another).

1 Negative x-phi has been directed against positive x-phi, on the assumption that it is pursuing what philosophers have traditionally been trying to do (Alexander, Mallon, and Weinberg 2010). If intuitions are not probative, then they are not probative period, whether you are gathering them in the armchair or in Central Park.
2 Critics have argued that x-phi has been taken in by an illusion widespread among philosophers themselves, namely, that contemporary analytic philosophers rely on intuitions as a source of evidence for philosophical theories. Herman Cappelen in his (2012) book *Philosophy without Intuitions* argues that this is simply an illusion, and experimental philosophers have been taken in by it. While philosophy goes the way it always has, experimental philosophers are engaged both in their critical and in their constructive projects in pursuing a will o' wisp. X-phi⁻ is tilting at windmills while x-phi⁺ is simulating in surveys, a practice that philosophers have never actually been engaged in. (See also Cappelen 2014; and see Cohnitz and Häggqvist in this volume for discussion, §4.)
3 An allied criticism of x-phi⁺ is that concepts philosophers are interested in are not amenable to conceptual analysis because they are of natural kinds and, hence, their real essence is to be discovered by empirical investigation of the world, not in empirical investigation of speakers' dispositions to classify things under the concept. (Cf. Hilary Kornblith's view (2002) that knowledge is a natural kind and therefore not amenable to investigation by conceptual analysis).
4 Another criticism of the continuity version of x-phi⁺ is that there are no (at least interesting) conceptual truths, since there are no (at least interesting) analytic truths, and, hence, the x-phi⁺ conceived of as pursuing conceptual analysis is aiming for a non-existent or uninteresting target (Quine 1953; Putnam 1965), and, in any case, in fact philosophy has all along been aiming at general synthetic a posteriori truths (Papineau 2013).
5 Yet another criticism that focuses on the relation of x-phi to philosophy is that it assumes in both its negative and its positive versions an overly simplified and narrow role for thought experiments in philosophical theorizing, focusing on an overly simplified conception of the "case method," whereas in fact thought experiments are used for illustration, to draw analogies, to raise puzzles (as in Thomson's (1976) contrasting the switch and fat man trolley cases), to draw attention to the range of cases that a theory must deal with, to draw out the consequences of theories, to illustrate arguments and bring out the limitations of our use of language (e.g., thought experiments involving sorites series), and to draw out how we think about certain matters, assumptions we make or principles we reply on, without the suggestion that we are drawing attention to conceptual truths (Sosa 2007a, 101–2). (See also Cohnitz and Häggqvist, this volume, in this connection.)

6 Even in the so-called case method, x-phi operates with a caricature of philosophical method. Philosophers aim to arrive at a reflective judgment about a case and then to review it in the light of other judgments (their own and others) and more general theoretical considerations. They do not simply record their spontaneous judgments and take the third-person stance toward them as neutral observations to be explained. They do not present themselves with scenarios out of the blue and like a medium at a séance wait for the spirit to move them to say something. It is an intellectual exercise like figuring out how to construct a proof of something in logic, or figuring out a mathematical problem, turning something on all sides to get the right view of it, reviewing a range of cases, testing for things that might be misleading by "turning the knobs" as Douglas Hofstader puts it, and looking out for familiar pitfalls. We often enough (though not always) have a sense of not being clear, and we withhold judgment until it becomes clearer (it is not a forced choice). Where it seems relevant, many of us think it is important to be familiar with contiguous domains of scientific investigation, which, while not immune from conceptual confusion, often present us with important puzzle cases and problems and insights. And we do not do this like hermits in the woods: we try out ideas and thought experiments on others, give and publish papers, take criticism, make revisions, try out new ideas generated in this process, and so on (see Bealer 1998; Ludwig 2007; Jackson 2011, §5).

7 Experimental philosophy has been criticized more narrowly on methodological grounds (these are all intertwined – see Ludwig 2007, 2010; Deutsch 2009; Sommers 2010; Williamson 2011 and Kauppinen 2014, 5–6 for general discussion; see Cullen 2010 for empirical refutations of assumptions behind some celebrated survey results).

   a Poor Design. In some surveys which have gotten wide attention, the scenarios or questions have been unclear, misleading, or ambiguous, and insufficiently informed by the relevant knowledge of the issues, so that the interpretation of the results depends upon further untested assumptions about how respondents understood the scenarios and questions.

   b Misunderstanding Intuitions. Experimental philosophers (many) have simply misunderstood the sort of intuition (or judgment) sought in philosophical thought experiments. They are not "spontaneous judgments ... for which the person making the judgment may be able to offer no plausible justification" (Nichols, Stich, and Weinberg 2003, 19), nor are they expressions of *what we would say* or *how things seems to us*. They are rather, for example, judgments that draw solely on the concepts contained in the question in relation to the description of the scenario (there are a variety of views about the form and basis of the judgment, but they *all* reject the spontaneous judgment account). (See Goldman 2007, 2010; Sosa 2007a, 2007b, 2009; Ludwig 2010; Booth and Rowbottom 2014) for further discussion.)

   c Confusion about what data surveys supply. Surveys do not ipso facto elicit intuitions (6b encourages the conflation). Not every response to a question on a survey about a scenario expresses an intuition. The survey data then is not straightforwardly data about intuitions. To use surveys for traditional philosophical purposes, we need to filter responses that are not intuitions, or show the noise level is not so high it makes the data unusable.

   d Controlling for Factors Relevant to Eliciting Relevant Responses. Surveys typically do not control for a variety of factors that are relevant to getting useful results, such as

    i proper understanding of the point of the survey, namely, that it is to elicit responses that on the basis of the content of the scenario itself and the content of the concepts involved in the question about it;
    ii the motivation of respondents in responding;
    iii their level of effort;
    iv the general intellectual capacities of respondents, including their capacity to make and keep track of relevant distinctions;
    v responses to pragmatic implicatures;
    vi extraneous factors in experimental design that introduce confounds like implicit biases and emotional responses that skew judgments.

e Impracticality. Doing philosophy by the survey method is unwieldy, even if it can be done. Philosophers can run through a large number of scenarios relevant to assessing various aspects of an account in a short time. Doing the same thing using the survey method would take a lot more time, with nothing more to show for it in the end. Doing philosophy by surveys, while it would generate more journal articles, would slow progress to a glacial pace.

f Failure to take into account the relevance of competence. Taking the responses of unsophisticated people to thought experiments to be on a par with those of philosophers rests on the false assumption that professional philosophers are no better than their undergraduates in sorting out subtle conceptual issues. Taking the responses of unsophisticated undergraduates and laypeople as being on a par with the responses of philosophers (even controlling for other factors) is to fail to recognize that people differ in how good they are at it and that one can develop a competence in conceptual analysis (inter alia, making distinctions, getting clear on the issues, understanding the point, framing questions and scenarios in the right way, being sensitive to things that might mislead, being ready with alternative cases to check for confusions, etc.) in the same way that one can develop a competence in mathematics or color matching and so on, and that training in philosophy develops such a competence.[6]

g Over quick generalization from studies. Some of the most celebrated and provocative early studies of the x-phi movement (Weinberg, Nichols, and Stich 2001; Nichols, Stich, and Weinberg 2003; Machery, Mallon, Nichols, and Stich 2004; Swain, Alexander, and Weinberg 2008), as well as more recent studies (Buckwalter and Stich 2014) alleging a divergence between "intuitions" of women and men, have failed replication tests: on epistemic intuitions see Nagel (2012), Nagel, San Juan, and Mar (2013), Adleberg, Thompson, and Nahmias (2014), Kim and Yuan (2015), and Seyedsayamdost (2015a); on theories of reference for names see Lam (2010); and on gender differences see Wright (2010), Adleberg, Thompson, and Nahmias (2014), and Seyedsayamdost (2015b). See Seyedsayamdost (2014) for a more wide-ranging critique. In this, x-phi shares in the larger replication crisis of psychology (see the articles in *Social Psychology* 45(3), and Collaboration 2015).[7]

8 Failure to yield the right kind of knowledge of results (Ludwig 2013). In philosophy, like mathematics, we are interested in understanding whether something is so from the first-person standpoint. It is one thing to be told that the Pythagorean theorem is true. It is another to see that (and why) it is true. If you survey high school math teachers, you will find that most think that the Pythagorean theorem is true. You may

be justified in accepting that if they all say that it is true, then it is. But you do not thereby see that (and why) it is true. And if you are interested in mathematics, it is not enough to know that it is true, you want to see that it is true. You want to know on the basis of the exercise of your own reasoning abilities that it is true. And that is the same kind of knowledge that we seek in philosophy. The results of surveys cannot supply it.

I will come back to the last of these below in assessing the question of the relevance of x-phi surveys involving thought experiments and their use in philosophy.

4 What are the ways experimental philosophy might be relevant to philosophy?

What, put abstractly, are the ways in which x-phi *might* be relevant to philosophy?

1 It might give us reason to think that there is something deeply problematic about the use of thought experiments in philosophy (for some purposes at least).
2 It might give us reason to think that some response to a thought experiment is the correct one.
3 It might give us insight into ways in which people can fall into error when responding to thought experiments.

We take these up in turn.

4.1 Can experimental philosophy show that there is something deeply problematic about the use of thought experiments in philosophy?

The negative project in x-phi aims to show that intuitions are not probative. This can take either a moderate or aggressive form. The moderate form merely says that in some cases the results of x-phi show that we should be more cautious about the consensus philosophers have reached about some thought experiments (e.g., whether in Gettier cases subjects lack knowledge), and should be less sanguine perhaps generally than they (allegedly) have been. The aggressive form says that the results of surveys show that reactions to thought experiments never yield any knowledge.

It is difficult to take the aggressive form seriously. Thought experiments rely on our ability to tell when one proposition entails another. We describe scenarios as if about particular individuals, but in fact their content is general. In a Gettier case, we are asked whether if there is someone with a justified true belief that p in a circumstance in which he infers it from a justified false belief, he knows that p or does not know that p. We are supposed to answer on the basis of whether instances of the antecedent entail corresponding instances of the consequent.[8] A general skepticism about our ability to respond correctly to questions about thought experiments calls into question our ability to tell when one proposition entails another or does not. If we cannot tell that with a reasonable degree of reliability in appropriate conditions and with adequate training, then all inquiry collapses. There is nothing special about the abilities that we call upon in philosophy. We call upon them in everyday life and in all areas of inquiry.[9]

The moderate form cannot be dismissed out of hand, but even there it is difficult to establish a conclusion of the form: in such and such an area or on such and such a question, we are simply not in a position to come to know whether a test proposition is true given the description of the scenario. We might be provided, however, with evidence for the presence of confounding factors, which can alert us to the need to guard against them.[10] We return to this below.

The mere fact (*if* it is a fact) of diversity of response to thought experiments, within or across cultural, ethnic, or socio-economic groups (Weinberg, Nichols, and Stich 2001; Nichols, Stich, and Weinberg 2003; Machery, Mallon, Nichols, and Stich 2004), does not show that the application conditions of concepts like the concept of knowledge are relative to different cultures or social milieus.[11] As many people have observed, if the participants are deploying the same concepts (and otherwise they just understand the words differently – and this may explain some diversity of responses (Sosa 2007a, 104)), all that could be shown by these results is that that not everyone is getting it right, and that there can be factors that correlate with different cultural, ethnic, or socio-economic backgrounds that can contribute to errors (Ludwig 2007, 2010; Sosa 2011, 466; Sosa 2007a, 107). It does not show that if there is a consensus among philosophers about what the right answers are, they are wrong, or that they do not know that they are right. Similarly, that you might get variations in responses to simple mathematics questions across different cultural, ethnic, and socio-economic groups does not entail that the consensus among mathematicians about the right answers is wrong or that they do not know that they are right.

4.2 The positive program of contributing to conceptual analysis

What has to be true for x-phi (in the survey mode) to have a positive contribution to make to philosophy?

Responses to surveys are never uniform. Consider a yes-no survey on whether a concept applies in a scenario (for example, whether someone with a Gettierized belief has knowledge or not). There are three possible outcomes: a majority say "yes," a majority say "no," or the respondents are split evenly between "yes" and "no." The positive program (on the Continuity Account) aims to use the results to say something about the application conditions of the concept of knowledge. If answers are split evenly, we can draw no conclusions. If a majority favors one answer, it is natural to suggest the majority is right (parallel considerations to those brought up below would apply if we held that the minority is right).

What has to be true for this to be so? An assumption that would justify it is that the respondents have a positive bias toward a correct response. Given this, and that their responses are independent, we can show that the larger the group surveyed, the higher the probability that the majority is right. In fact, as long as none is invariably right, we can show that after a certain number of voters (as we can call them) the majority always outperforms anyone in the group. More precisely, according to the Condorcet Jury Theorem, where agents' choices are independent of one another, they all have the same bias p ($1 < p < 0$), the decision rule is simple majority, and there are two alternatives one of which is correct, where P_N is the probability for N agents of the majority being right, and prior odds as to which of the two alternatives is correct are even (Grofman, Owen, and Feld 1983, 264):

If $1 > p > 0.5$, then P_N is monotonically increasing in N and $\lim_{n \to \infty} P_N \to 1$; if $0 < p < 0.5$, then P_N is monotonically decreasing in N and $\lim_{n \to \infty} P_N \to 0$; while if $p = 0.5$ then $P_N = 0.5$ for all N.

Even more impressively, the rate of convergence can be quite rapid. If $p = .8$ then $P_{13} > .99$. Figure 21.1 shows the rise in the probability that the majority is right with the probability each individual is right for a group with 95 members.[12] Figure 21.2 shows the increasing probability that the majority is right, given that the probability that each individual is right of .6, with increasing numbers of members. Both of these show only data points for odd numbered groups – ties for even numbered groups reduce the reliability of the majority though it still tends to 1 in the long run.

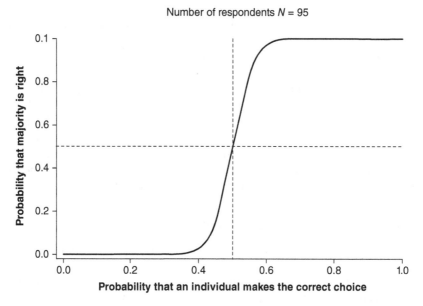

Figure 21.1

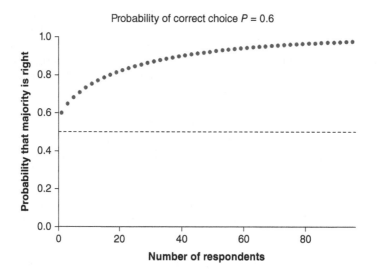

Figure 21.2

Even more striking are related theorems that relax some of these rather idealized assumptions, and, in particular, the assumption of uniform competence. Thus, with p_a representing the average competence of members of the group, if the distribution of p_i is symmetric, then (op. cit. 268)

> If $1 > p_a > 0.5$, then P_N is monotonically increasing in N and $\lim_{n \to \infty} P_N \to 1$;
> if $0 < p_a < 0.5$, then P_N is monotonically decreasing in N and $\lim_{n \to \infty} P_N \to 0$; while
> if $p_a = 0.5$ then $P_N = 0.5$ for all N.

Furthermore (op. cit., 269),

> For heterogeneous groups, if $p_i > 0.5$ for all i, then the greater the size of the majority in favor of an alternative, the more likely is that alternative to be the correct choice.

Finally, there is a Generalized Condorcet Jury Theorem:

> If $p_a > 0.5$ then $\lim_{N \to \infty} P_N \to 1$; if $p_a < 0.5$ then $\lim_{N \to \infty} P_N \to 0$; while if $p_a = 0.5$,
> $1 - e^{1/2} < \lim_{N \to \infty} P_N < e^{1/2}$, i.e., $0.39 < P_N < 0.61$.

What this means is that, so far as the positive program goes, all we need to know is that the participants have a positive bias toward truth and are independent, and to have enough participants, in order to get results that are probative. Ladha (1992) has extended this to show that even when there are correlations among judgments, in a wide range of conditions for large groups the majority outperforms any individual. Abstracting a bit from details, let us call the assumption that enough members of groups surveyed on thought experiments have a sufficiently positive bias and make judgments sufficiently independently of one another for the majority results to have a significant probability of being right the Positive Bias Assumption.[13]

It is an empirical question whether for any given group, e.g., of philosophically unsophisticated undergraduates, or random people enjoying a Saturday in Central Park, the Positive Bias Assumption is correct, in the sampling context. In connection with this, I want to raise three questions.

1 Is it presupposed by the standard view of the method of thought experiments?
2 Do we have reason to believe it?
3 What would it take to establish the needed assumption?

I raise the first question because if it is a presupposition of the method of thought experiments in philosophy that for any random group of individuals (or for most random groups of individuals) most will have a positive bias toward the truth (let this stand in for the constellation of conditions required), then survey philosophers do not need to argue against their traditionalist opponents that the assumption is correct. Their opponents will be committed to it already, and so they would have to regard the results as probative, and as the numbers surveyed get larger and larger, other things being equal, the results would have to be given more and more weight.

However, while the traditional philosopher is committed to it being possible to make advances in analysis by careful consideration of thought experiments, she is certainly not committed to thinking that most of those in groups being surveyed in the conditions of survey philosophy have a positive bias toward providing a correct response. Competence-based accounts are committed to concept possession putting us in a position to articulate the application conditions of concepts. But they do not entail that it is easy, or that individuals might not for various reasons, in various circumstances, particularly for subtle questions, in an unfamiliar practice, be more likely than not to answer a question about a scenario incorrectly.

This makes the next two questions salient. Do we have reason to think that the Positive Bias Assumption is correct? There is no question that it is *always* correct. For example, the gambler's fallacy is quite common (similarly the hot hand fallacy, the assumption that one's probability of guessing correctly an outcome goes up after having guessed correctly a number of times in a row). Someone subject to the gambler's fallacy will think it more likely that the flip of a fair coin will yield a tails if it comes after a series of flips that turned up heads. The prevalence of the gambler's fallacy has been demonstrated both in laboratory and in real-world settings (see Figure 21.3 and Croson and Sundali 2005).

The standard explanation is that the gambler's fallacy is the result of a representativeness bias. People expect short sequences to reflect the underlying probabilities, and so think a string of heads should be balanced by a tail.

Similarly, data from surveys also show that we cannot in general assume that the majority in a group is correct. This is shown by the fact that there can be variations in the majority judgments between groups which differ with respect to culture and socio-economic background, at least on some occasions (Nichols, Stich, and Weinberg 2003;

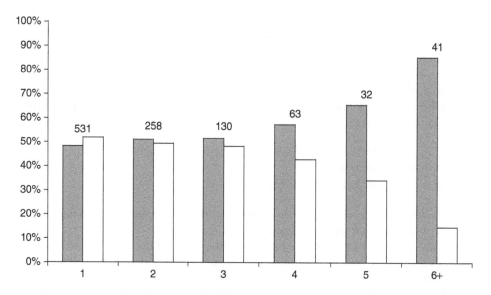

Figure 21.3 Proportion of gambler's fallacy outside bets after a streak of at least length N from data gathered at a large casino in Reno, Nevada, from 18 hours of security videotape of the roulette table (Croson and Sundali 2005, 203).

Machery, Mallon, Nichols, and Stich 2004), as well as relative amount of training in philosophy and so on. Since different runs with different groups yield different results, we cannot say that whatever the majority says is correct. Moreover, the fact that ordering effects make a difference to the distribution of responses in some cases shows that judgments can be affected by factors that are not truth-related (Liao, Wiegmann, Alexander, and Vong 2012).

We can seek larger groups, but it seems unlikely, as the case of the gambler's fallacy shows, that simply increasing the size itself guarantees that most members of the group will have a positive bias toward truth in the relevant conditions. There are other sorts of errors we would expect to be systematic as well, such as responding to standardized conversational implicatures, rather than to what is literally expressed in a scenario.

Thus, in some cases, we know that the majority result is not correct and this cannot be corrected simply by increasing the size of the group. Can we assume nonetheless that in most cases the majority result will be correct? Well, in most cases of what? We might say: in most cases in which the judgment is very simple, and there are no distorting or distracting features of the case or the conditions, and subjects understand what they are doing and are motivated to try to respond in the right way in response just to what the scenario says. Maybe so. But, first, how are we to test for whether or not there are distorting or distracting features of the case? We might find something that obviously is irrelevant to truth correlated with responses – like the choice of names of characters in a scenario or ordering effects or cultural background or personality type – but if there is nothing obvious, can we assume there are no distracting features of the case? Second, are not many of the cases we are interested in not simple cases? Third, in the end, don't we want to know in *particular cases* whether or not the majority result is likely to be true?

This brings us to the last of the three questions I want to take up: what would it take to establish the Positive Bias Assumption? We have a method that purports to help us discern the truth about the domain of conceptual truths. The method is indirect in the sense that it appeals to data about the judgments of agents relative to the assumption that they have a positive bias toward the correct judgment. We third-person observers of the majority response in a group of subjects to questions about the scenario in a thought experiment want to know whether this is a correct expression of their conceptual competence. If our only access to the domain is through their judgments, however, we have no independent method of checking whether they are getting it right or not. It looks as if, in order to support the Positive Bias Assumption, we need to sample the domain independently of the response of the majority. Can we do this?

Yes, why not? Isn't that how we determine that the gambler's fallacy is a fallacy? It is a fallacy, we can see, because each flip of a fair coin is independent of the others, and, hence, for each flip, the probability that a heads or a tails comes up remains constant. On the assumption that the coin is fair, the probability that it comes up heads or tails is .5 each time it is flipped. That *follows* from the assumptions. We have independent access to the domain in question. We can see ourselves what the correct thing to say is. And seeing that, we can see that what most people may say or think about the probability of tails after a sequence of heads is a mistake, and explain to them why it's a mistake, and why they made it.

So it is in the case of surveys of the philosophically unsophisticated. If we want to know whether the majority opinion is correct or probative, and so whether something like the Positive Bias Assumption is correct, we can check to see whether most of our subjects get it right. If they do, then that is evidence that the Positive Bias Assumption is correct. Then, having provided evidence for the Positive Bias Assumption, we can use the survey data to advance one or another particular thesis about a concept's application conditions on that basis.

But wait a minute! *If* to confirm the Positive Bias Assumption, in a particular case, we have to *independently* decide the truth of the matter about what we were interested in testing, then ... we don't need it. Once we are in a position to use the Survey Data to contribute to a philosophical problem, we have settled the matter. Furthermore, it could give us no more justification than we already had, since any confidence we have in the majority being right, or even in the probability that the majority is right, rests on our confidence that the Positive Bias Assumption is right, and that rests on our confidence that we have independently made the right judgment. To try to raise our confidence by this means would appear to be a kind of illegitimate bootstrapping of our epistemic position.

Perhaps it was evident from the start that the solution offered was a poison pill. While it seems the most straightforward way for one to try to establish that for a given population the Positive Bias Assumption is correct, it would undermine the point of survey philosophy (on the continuity approach). It is obvious also, though, that one cannot simply assume that it is true. It needs defense, and it needs defense on a case-by-case basis. Is there an indirect method of arguing in particular cases that we should give some credence to the Positive Bias Assumption, especially when the results might seem to have the most potential for overturning philosophical orthodoxy, that is, when most philosophers do not agree with the majority in survey results? We could try to test for general competency and then try out thought experiments with subjects who have been confirmed to be good at making the right judgment. Perhaps that is what we do informally in philosophy already. But this seems unlikely to be much help in cases in which there is controversy.

4.3 Does x-phi deliver what we want?

Suppose that we can solve the confirmation problem for x-phi, so that we can provide reasons to think that in particular cases the Positive Bias Assumption is true without independently establishing the right result, so that it could actually contribute to advancing a thesis about the application conditions of a concept. Would this deliver what we wanted?

Why not? After all didn't we want to know what the application conditions for a certain concept were? Suppose that the concept were the concept of justice, for example, and suppose that we had someone construct a theory of justice using the results of surveys in an especially clever and sophisticated way. There we would have it, finally, we would know what justice is!

Suppose that a young Greek philosopher in antiquity is interested in the question what justice is, and she has learned of the Oracle at Delphi. She decides then to travel to Delphi to ask the Oracle. Suppose that the Oracle does not speak in riddles, and that it tells her that justice in the state is when individuals receive benefits according to their merits. Suppose that she justifiably believes that the Oracle has a high positive bias toward the truth. She writes down what the Oracle has told her, and she is justified in believing that it is true. Should she be satisfied?

Now suppose an undergraduate student is interested in the nature of justice. She decides to survey faculty who teach courses related to justice in political science, philosophy, cognitive science, sociology, and so on. A majority of those she surveys agree that justice is that state of society represented by arrangements which people would choose were they to have been constrained to choose it behind a veil of ignorance, not knowing their natural abilities or position in society or their sex or race, culture, or individual tastes, but knowing that in any society there would be a distribution of abilities, differences in sex, race, culture, individual tastes, and so on. Suppose that she justifiably believes that the faculty she has surveyed have a positive bias toward the truth. She accepts what they say and is justified in believing it to be true on the basis of their authority. Should she be satisfied?

She should not be satisfied. Why not? The problem is not that what she believes is not true. Let us grant, in one or the other case, it is true, and in fact, we can grant, let us say, that our undergraduate student knows what justice is on the basis of authority. She knows what justice is in the sense that she can give a correct statement of it and she is justified (in a non-deviant way) in her belief. But what she does not have is any understanding of why *that* is what justice is. Or if she does, it does not come from the mere fact that she has ascertained that most of the people in positions of authority that she has asked about it agree on a characterization, and that the majority is likely to be right.

The situation would be the same for the undergraduate who learns that the Pythagorean theory is true (or the Condorcet jury theorem) from reading it in a textbook but not from being given a proof of it. She would know the Pythagorean theorem, but she would not know why it was true. She would not have any understanding why the area of the square on the hypotenuse of a right triangle is the sum of the areas of the squares constructed on its sides. The textbook for her is an oracle, a known reliable source, but not a reliable source that conveys an understanding of the ground for the truth. (Imagine that you told a freshman who is not too sophisticated mathematically but also not completely ignorant that $1 = .99999999....$ She might accept it on authority but find it puzzling. Everything changes when you point out that $1 = 3 \times \frac{1}{3} = 3 \times .333333... = .9999999....$ [14])

What is missing from the x-phi conception of philosophical method is only the most important thing about philosophy. What we want in philosophy is not to know things on the basis of their being the pronouncements of someone who is competent to say, but to know them out of our own competence, to see why they are true. Even if we could trust surveys, they would never give us the kind of knowledge we seek in philosophy. You might as well ask an oracle.

4.4 Can experimental philosophy help philosophy?

Suppose you grant that x-phi is not a replacement or supplement for philosophy, even in the relatively narrow domain of philosophical activity that it concerns itself with. Is that the end of the line for x-phi? Is all the elaborate surveying of the unsophisticated to be relegated to some niche branch of psychology, for whoever might be interested in it? Or is there still some role for it to play as a kind of aid to core philosophical activities?

Experimental philosophy conceived of as a psychological enterprise can still be of some help. Psychology is not irrelevant to philosophical methodology. Our cognitive abilities are impressive, but we are not perfectly rational, we do not always get things right, and there are sometimes interesting explanations of this that only come to light with empirical investigation. The systematic study of the conditions under which we are liable to make mistakes helps us to guard against them. It can help us in teaching students as well, in choosing examples, and giving appropriate context.

That there are order effects in the judgments that people make about cases is an important insight for example (Schwitzgebel and Cushman 2012).[15] That people respond differently depending on the variance of factors that we are convinced are irrelevant to the correctness of a judgment provides a caution about our own judgments. This can help us to think about good thought experiment design, especially in the context of testing ideas with others. This does not show that we can never figure out what the right thing to say is, but it does show that figuring it out can be a complicated matter, and that we need to think systematically about the subject matter and to take into account all of the possible factors that may incline us to error, and to try to correct for them so far as possible. All of this is familiar, of course, but details help.

How much does the identification of misleading factors in particular cases show about how far we can or cannot trust our judgments? In this volume, Stich and Tobia suggest that what it shows is that we cannot get started using thought experiments in inquiry without first undertaking the experimental study of intuitions. This is an overreaction. They make this claim in responding to the point (made in an earlier paper of mine: Ludwig 2007) that responses to surveys are not *ipso facto* philosophical intuitions.

> For Ludwig, a judgment or belief that is influenced by factors other than conceptual competence will not count as an intuition ... A judgment that is influenced by order of presentation, or font size or fart spray is not *solely* the expression of conceptual competence. Thus when intuitions are characterized in this way, the studies pose no challenge to the use of intuitions as evidence in philosophy. But we are inclined to think that in making this move, Ludwig is hoist on his own petard. For the effects discussed in §21.3 are almost always *covert*; people have no conscious awareness that their beliefs or judgments are being affected. So [i] on Ludwig's restricted account, the only way to determine whether one's beliefs or judgments are intuitions is to do well designed and carefully controlled experiments. Rather than [ii] showing that the experimental studies are irrelevant to philosophical practice, [iii] Ludwig's restricted account of intuition leads directly to the conclusion that the sorts of studies that experimental philosophers have undertaken are required before we can begin to use intuitions as evidence, since without such studies we have no way of knowing which of our beliefs or judgments *are* intuitions.
>
> (378; lower case roman numerals added)

There are a number of points to be made in response.
  (i) The first is a point of interpretation. In the article that Stich and Tobia cite, I argued that extravagant claims made on the basis of surveys pose no threat to traditional philosophical methods, but I did not argue that surveys were irrelevant to philosophical practice, as here implied [ii]. Instead, I suggested, as I have above, that they can help us think about good thought experiment design and to identify pitfalls. In fact, except for the absence of the triumphalist tone, and my rejection of the (false and ungrounded) assumption that survey philosophy is essential to

success in philosophy, my conclusion is not that different in its details from Stich and Tobia. Why all the fuss?

(ii) The second is about the claim (in [i] and [iii]) that (a) the fact that in some cases there are factors that distort responses to thought experiments shows that (b) "we [generally] have no way of knowing which of our beliefs or judgments are intuitions" without first undertaking surveys about scenarios in thought experiments. In fact, the inference from (a) to (b) is a *non sequitur*. It does not follow from the fact that there are sometimes distorting influences at work in thought experiments that there always are. And it does not follow that because there are sometimes distorting influences at work in responses to thought experiments that we can never know that our responses are intuitions – just as it does not follow from the fact that we sometimes make mistakes in calculations that we never know that we have made a correct calculation! In response to the charge that there is no way we can ever tell whether we are in the good condition or the bad condition, and that if we cannot, then we can never trust our intuitions, there are several things to say. The first is that it has not been demonstrated that we can never tell when we are in the good condition, and that it does not follow from the fact that if we are in the bad condition we cannot tell (which has also not been demonstrated), that if we are in the good condition we cannot tell (cf. Bernard Williams's discussion of the cases of dreaming and anoxia (Williams 1978, appendix 3)). The second is that, waiving the last point, on the assumption that mistakes are not the norm, we can apply the method of reflective equilibrium to sort out what to say. The third is that there is empirical work that supports the common sense thesis that we are often implicitly aware of cases in which intuition instability (e.g., due to order effects) is a threat and that there are reliable methods for tracking it (introspective confidence and belief strength) (Wright 2010).

(iii) The third is that the general claim Stich and Tobia make is self-defeating. Intuitions, on the view in question, are conceptually grounded judgments about entailments. Therefore, as a completely general thesis about judgments about entailments, it is clearly self-defeating to claim that we must first engage in surveys before we can ever tell whether our judgments about entailments are correct, since in evaluating what the surveys show us we must make judgments about entailments. For example, the judgment that order effects show that there is something problematic about responses to a thought experiment rests on the claim that order of presentation is irrelevant to the correct judgment. That order is completely irrelevant to the correct judgment and that judgments are influenced by order entails that the judgments are being distorted by truth-irrelevant features of the experimental set-up. I trust that readers feel confident that they know, in this case, that the one proposition entails the other. It a point of mild irony that the use of survey results to argue against the use of thought experiments in philosophy relies on an epistemology which could only be supported by the sources which it aims to undermine.

(iv) The fourth is that it does not follow from the fact that, in some cases, there are factors that distort responses to scenarios, that to discover and correct this we need to do surveys. In actual philosophical practice, as noted earlier, Section 3, #6, we aim to survey a range of cases, vary the cases studied, test them on others, compare results with previously established results, bring to bear general theoretical considerations, and when we notice a problem, try to get a clearer view of what is going on, in much the same way that we sort through a problem in geometry or mathematics. The journal literature in philosophy, among other things, carries out this task over time, just as the journal literature in the sciences carries out the task of self-correction and revision that is an ongoing part of the advancement of science.

(v) The fifth is that to arrive at the right view, survey methods alone will not suffice, for in cases in which we suspect that there are distorting factors, the question of whether the positive bias assumption is correct for a group surveyed becomes urgent. Intuitions are ultimately methodologically basic in this domain.

Finally, perhaps another way that x-phi is relevant to philosophy is that it can (potentially) throw up challenges to philosophical theories (though one might wonder whether it will raise challenges that would not be raised anyway). For example, those who want to maintain the Simple View in the philosophy of action, that if someone intentionally Fs, then she intended to F, must confront the fact that there are circumstances in which many people say that someone intentionally F-ed but did not intend to F. Philosophers of course noticed this first, and indeed this was the impetus for the surveys (Harman 1976). Proponents of the Simple View need to offer an explanation for why people get it wrong. These explanations are of course empirical claims about distorting factors. It is not clear the extent to which these can actually be resolved using the survey method (or whether it is the best method; see Levin 2009), but it seems plausible enough that some testing of these theories could be conducted by the survey method, and that this can have some value.

5 Conclusionj

What is the relation of x-phi to philosophy? A pessimist might say:

> The connection is that people who do x-phi are largely housed in philosophy departments, just as people who do religious studies are sometimes housed in philosophy departments. There is a social and an administrative connection. In addition, there is the appearance of the word "philosophy" in "experimental philosophy," and the fact that scenarios from philosophical thought experiments are featured in its surveys. They also sometimes publish in philosophy journals. In short: "experimental philosophy is a cuckoo-bird in the nest of philosophy."
>
> (Sorensen 2014)

Not so fast! X-phi is not promising as a positive program for contributing to the articulation of application conditions of concepts or conceptual connections. First, we have to have independent access to the domain to validate the assumptions that would enable us to use the data, which renders it otiose for our primary purpose, and, second, the kind of knowledge we want in philosophy is not supplied by asking an oracle. But even philosophers dismissive of x-phi⁻ and skeptical of the continuity account should be interested in the results of surveys, for they provide a map of the reactions of the unsophisticated (and in some cases of the sophisticated) and evidence bearing on influences on responses and mechanisms involved that are not related to truth. We can learn something from this, and it can help to make us more sophisticated about the construction and use of thought experiments. In addition, some testing of empirical claims about errors that are made in response to thought experiments can be pursued fruitfully in this way. What then is the relation of x-phi to philosophy? X-phi is philosophy from the sociological point of view. From the standpoint of the tradition in philosophy, in far as it is to be of aid to philosophy, it is more properly thought of as a non-philosophical activity or an adjunct to philosophical activity that has relevance to philosophy in the way in which the investigation of the foibles and frailties of human reasoning has relevance to the practice of human reasoning. We should use all the tools we can assemble to advance our understanding.

Notes

1 Contemporary experimental philosophy is roughly 15 years old, with the first papers that practitioners look back to for inspiration appearing in 2001 (e.g., Weinberg, Nichols, and Stich 2001). An important precursor was *Rethinking Intuition: The Psychology of Intuition and Its Role in Philosophical Inquiry* (DePaul and Ramsey 1998). At the time of this writing, the experimental philosophy bibliography in Philpapers has 824 entries, across philosophy of action, language, mind, ethics, epistemology, metaphysics, the nature of experimental philosophy, cross-cultural research, and miscellaneous other topics. Not all of these papers, however, fit the paradigm of survey philosophy examined here. There are some earlier antecedents to the use of the survey method in philosophy in the work of Arne Naess (1953). Two useful collections are Knobe and Nichols (2008, 2014).

2 An example is the use of experimental work from social psychology to argue that virtue ethics makes false empirical assumptions about character traits (Doris 1998, 2002; Harman 1999, 2000). This is still a matter of controversy (Kamtekar 2004; Snow 2010). Rose and Danks (2013) make a plea not to use the label just for the narrower conception.

3 And there can be mixtures as well, and sometimes it is a little difficult to tell, and the lack of clarity is often aided by a failure to distinguish between different senses of the world "concept" or confusion about what sense of "concept" is at issue in philosophical analysis.

4 There has been some dispute over the use of the term "philosophy." For example, Knobe has urged that the question how people think when they respond to surveys (asked as an empirical question about their psychology and not in the mode of conceptual analysis) *is* a philosophical question. To adopt this terminology, though, would obscure the issue whether these psychological studies bear on the projects for which thought experiments have been deployed in philosophy in the tradition in the last century.

5 Some experimental philosophers gloss this as answering the question "what concepts ordinary people operate with?" In these cases, it seems likely that they have in mind by "concept" something like "psychological-causal structure that guides behavior and speech." It would be a mistake to think this is the same project that the tradition in philosophy was interested in when asking for an analysis of, for example, the concept of justice.

6 It is hard to deny that competence is relevant, but x-phi[-] researchers have aimed to turn this into a challenge to philosophy by arguing we have no reason to think philosophers are more competent in setting up and responding to thought experiments than the completely untutored – alone apparently among all the academic disciplines, philosophical training induces no epistemic benefits. Or at least: we need a positive reason to think so before we can trust philosophers' judgments. All the more reason to do x-phi! Now: let us try the same form of argument on the mathematicians. (In connection with this, see Ludwig 2007; Weinberg 2007; Weinberg, Gonnerman, Buckner and Alexander 2010; Grundmann 2010; Sosa 2011; Williamson 2011; Hales 2012; Hitchcock 2012; Rini 2013; De Cruz 2014; Pritchard 2014; Sorensen 2014; Buckwalter 2014.)

7 Proponents of negative x-phi often repeat the conclusions of the early studies without concern for criticisms that point out methodological flaws in the studies, without concern for evidence that they are not replicable, and without concern for whether the conclusions are even coherent; see for example Stich and Tobia in this volume, Section 3.1, who state flatly: "To sum up, philosophical intuitions have been found to vary with culture, academic discipline, gender, age and personality." But responses to surveys are not ipso facto philosophical intuitions, and philosophical intuitions, taken as the target response to a thought experiment in the method of cases, cannot vary with culture or anything else (given that the target is the expression of a competence to judge entailments), and in fact the data about even responses does not appear to be replicable in many cases. I do not advocate throwing out all the studies, which as I will say below, have their place in our thinking about philosophy, but I do advocate more methodological caution and greater epistemic humility than is often displayed by proponents of x-phi who see their surveys as relevant to philosophy.
8 On this way of understanding the question, we are not asking whether a necessitated conditional is true, or whether a counterfactual judgment is true. If the proposition that p entails the proposition that q, then necessarily, if p, then q, but not vice versa. Similarly for the counterfactual judgment that if p were the case q would be the case. Entailment, as understood here, is an internal relation between propositions. But if it is possible that p and not q, then p does not entail q, and so that suffices to answer the question negatively.
9 See Ludwig (2007) and Jackson (2011, §2). See Talbot (2014) for discussion of the sizable empirical burden of showing that standard procedures in philosophy are not adequate.
10 With respect to the worry that the presence of distracting factors or order effects in some cases shows a general problem because we cannot tell when something like this is going on, see Wright (2010).
11 As noted above, the studies suggesting systematic variation in responses to thought experiments across cultures and socio-economic groups have not fared well in replication tests.
12 These graphs were generated in Mathematica using source code due to Tetsuya Saito.
13 See Talbot (2014) for an argument, based on these kinds of considerations, for the probative value of current philosophical practice with thought experiments, and the point at the end of Section 3, #6.
14 Suppose that survey philosophy became firmly established as the dominant philosophical methodology. Philosophers cease to place any emphasis on their own reactions to thought experiments. They just survey their undergraduate students. And they tell their undergraduate students what the right answers are to traditional philosophical problems in accordance with what the majority say. Administrators find out about this, and decide they can cut out the middleman, and they find that student evaluations of philosophy courses go up because most students find that what they are taught in philosophy courses accords pretty well with what they already thought.
15 Though as Cullen (2010) shows, it is not always plausible that what generates order effects in survey responses has relevance to philosophical practice.

References

Adleberg, T., Thompson, M. and Nahmias, E. (2014) "Do men and women have different philosophical intuitions? Further data," *Philosophical Psychology* 28: 615–641.
Alexander, J. and Weinberg, J. (2007) "Analytic epistemology and experimental philosophy," *Philosophy Compass* 2: 56–80.
Alexander, J., Mallon, R. and Weinberg, J. M. (2010) "Accentuate the negative," *Review of Philosophy and Psychology* 1: 297–314.
Bealer, G. (1998) "Intuition and the autonomy of philosophy," in *Rethinking Intuition: The Psychology of Intuition and Its Role in Philosophical Inquiry*, edited by M. DePaul and W. Ramsey, New York: Rowman & Littlefield.
Booth, A. and Rowbottom, D. P. (eds) (2014) *Intuitions*, Oxford: Oxford University Press.
Buckwalter, W. (2014) "Intuition fail: Philosophical activity and the limits of expertise," *Philosophy and Phenomenological Research* 89: 378–410.
Buckwalter, W. and Schaffer, J. (2013) "Knowledge, stakes, and mistakes," *Noûs* 49: 201–234.

Buckwalter, W. and Stich, S. (2014) "Gender and philosophical intuition," in *Experimental Philosophy*, vol. 2, edited by J. Knobe and S. Nichols, Oxford: Oxford University Press.
Cappelen, H. (2012) *Philosophy Without Intuitions*, Oxford: Oxford University Press.
Cappelen, H. (2014) "X-Phi without intuitions?" in *Intuitions*, edited by A. R. Booth and D. P. Rowbottom, Oxford: Oxford University Press.
Collaboration, Open Science. (2015) "Estimating the reproducibility of psychological science," *Science* 349: 6251.
Croson, R. and Sundali, J. (2005) "The gambler's fallacy and the hot hand: Empirical data from casinos," *The Journal of Risk and Uncertainty* 30: 195–209.
Cullen, S. (2010) "Survey-driven romanticism," *Review of Philosophy and Psychology* 1: 275–296.
De Cruz, H. (2014) "Where philosophical intuitions come from," *Australasian Journal of Philosophy* 93: 233–249.
DePaul, M. and Ramsey, W. (eds) (1998) *Rethinking Intuition: The Psychology of Intuition and Its Role in Philosophical Inquiry*, New York: Rowman & Littlefield.
Deutsch, M. (2009) "Experimental philosophy and the theory of reference," *Mind and Language* 24: 445–466.
Doris, J. (1998) "Persons, situations, and virtue ethics," *Noûs* 32: 504–530.
Doris, J. (2002) *Lack of Character: Personality and Moral Behavior*, Cambridge: Cambridge University Press.
Genone, J. and Lombrozo, T. (2012) "Concept possession, experimental semantics, and hybrid theories of reference," *Philosophical Psychology* 25:1–26.
Gettier, E. (1963) "Is justified true belief knowledge?" *Analysis* 23: 121–123.
Goldman, A. (2007) "Philosophical intuitions," *Grazer Philosophische Studien* 74: 1–26.
Goldman, A. (2010) "Philosophical naturalism and intuitional methodology," *Proceedings of the American Philosophical Association* 84: 115–150.
Grofman, B., Owen, G. and Feld, S. L. (1983) "Thirteen theorems in search of the truth," *Theory & Decision* 15: 261–278.
Grundmann, T. (2010) "Some hope for intuitions: A reply to Weinberg," *Philosophical Psychology* 23: 481–509.
Hales, S. D. (2012) "The faculty of intuition," *Analytic Philosophy* 53: 180–207.
Harman, G. (1976) "Practical reasoning," *Review of Metaphysics* 79: 431–463.
Harman, G. (1999) "Moral philosophy meets social psychology: Virtue ethics and the fundamental attribution error," *Proceedings of the Aristotelian Society New Series* 119: 316–331.
Harman, G. (2000) "The nonexistence of character traits," *Proceedings of the Aristotelian Society* 100: 223–226.
Hitchcock, C. (2012) "Thought experiments, real experiments, and the expertise objection," *European Journal for Philosophy of Science* 2: 205–218.
Jackson, F. (2011) "On Gettier holdouts," *Mind and Language* 26: 468–481.
Kamtekar, R. (2004) "Situationism and virtue ethics on the content of character," *Ethics* 114: 458–491.
Kauppinen, A. (2014) "The rise and fall of experimental philosophy," in *Experimental Philosophy*, edited by J. Knobe and S. Nichols, Oxford: Oxford University Press.
Kim, M. J. and Yuan, Y. (2015) "No cross-cultural differences in Gettier car case intuition: A replication study of Weinberg et al. 2001," *Episteme* 12: 355–361.
Knobe, J. (2003a) "Intentional action and side effects in ordinary language," *Analysis* 63: 190–194.
Knobe, J. (2003b) "Intentional action in folk psychology: An experimental investigation," *Philosophical Psychology* 16: 309–324.
Knobe, J. (2004) "Intention, intentional action and moral considerations," *Analysis* 64: 181–187.
Knobe, J. (2006) "The concept of intentional action: A case study in the uses of folk psychology," *Philosophical Studies* 130: 203–231.
Knobe, J. (2007) "Experimental philosophy," *Philosophy Compass* 2: 81–92.
Knobe, J., Buckwalter, W., Robbins, P., Sarkissian, H., Sommers, T. and Nichols, S. (2012) "Experimental philosophy," *Annual Review of Psychology* 63: 72–73.
Knobe, J. and Burra, A. (2006) "Experimental philosophy and folk concepts: Methodological considerations," *Journal of Cognition and Culture* 6: 331–342.
Knobe, J. and Nichols, S. (2008) *Experimental Philosophy*, Oxford: Oxford University Press.
Knobe, J. and Nichols, S. (2014) *Experimental Philosophy*, vol. 2, Oxford: Oxford University Press.

Kornblith, H. (2002) *Knowledge and Its Place in Nature*, Oxford: Clarendon Press.
Ladha, K. K. (1992) "The Condorcet jury theorem, free speech, and correlated votes," *American Journal of Political Science* 36: 617–634.
Lam, B. (2010) "Are Cantonese speakers really descriptivists? Revisiting cross-cultural semantics," *Cognition* 115: 320–332.
Levin, J. (2009) "Experimental philosophy," *Analysis* 69: 761–769.
Liao, M., Wiegmann, A., Alexander, J. and Vong, G. (2012) "Putting the trolley in order: Experimental philosophy and the loop case," *Philosophical Psychology* 25: 661–671.
Ludwig, K. (2007) "The epistemology of thought experiments: First person versus third person approaches," *Midwest Studies in Philosophy* 31: 128–159.
Ludwig, K. (2010) "Intuitions and relativity," *Philosophical Psychology* 23: 427–445.
Ludwig, K. (2013) "Methods in analytic philosophy," in *Philosophical Methodology: The Armchair or the Laboratory*, edited by M. Haug, New York: Routledge.
Machery, E., Mallon, R., Nichols, S. and Stich, S. (2004) "Semantics, cross-cultural style," *Cognition* 92: B1–B12.
Malle, B. F. and Knobe, J. (2001) "The distinction between desire and intention: A folk-conceptual analysis," in *Intentions and Intentionality: Foundations of Social Cognition*, edited by B. F. Malle, L. J. Moses, and D. A. Baldwin, Cambridge: MIT Press.
Naess, A. (1953) *Interpretation and Preciseness: A Contribution to the Theory of Communication*, Oslo: I Kommisjon Hos J. Dybwad.
Nagel, J. (2012) "Intuitions and experiments: A defense of the case method in epistemology," *Philosophy and Phenomenological Research* 85: 495–527.
Nagel, J., San Juan, V. and Mar, R. (2013) "Lay denial of knowledge for justified true beliefs," *Cognition* 129: 652–661.
Nahmias, E., Morris, S. G., Nadelhoffer, T. and Turner, J. (2006) "Is incompatibilism intuitive?" *Philosophy and Phenomenological Research* 73: 28–53.
Nichols, S. (2011) "Experimental philosophy and the problem of free will," *Science* 331: 1401–1403.
Nichols, S. and Knobe, J. (2007) "Moral responsibility and determinism: The cognitive science of folk intuitions," *Nous* 41: 663–685.
Nichols, S., Stich, S. and Weinberg, J. (2003) "Meta-skepticism: Meditations on ethno-epistemology," in *The Skeptics*, edited by S. Luper, Aldershot, UK: Ashgate Publishing.
Papineau, D. (2011) "What is x-phi good for?" *The Philosophers' Magazine* 52: 83–88.
Papineau, D. (2013) "The poverty of conceptual analysis," in *The Armchair or the Laboratory*, edited by M. Haug, New York: Routledge.
Pettit, D. and Knobe, J. (2009) "The pervasive impact of moral judgment," *Mind and Language* 24: 586–604.
Pritchard, D. (2014) "Sceptical intuitions," in *Intuitions*, edited by A. R. Booth and D. P. Rowbottom, Oxford: Oxford University Press.
Putnam, H. (1965) "It ain't necessarily so," *Journal of Philosophy* LIX: 658–671.
Quine, W. V. O. (1953) "Two dogmas of empiricism," in *From a Logical Point of View*, Cambridge: Harvard University Press.
Rini, R. A. (2013) "Analogies, moral intuitions, and the expertise defence," *Review of Philosophy and Psychology* 5: 169–181.
Rose, D. and Danks, D. (2013) "In defense of a broad conception of experimental philosophy," *Metaphilosophy* 44: 512–532.
Sarkissian, H., Chatterjee, A., De Brigard, F., Knobe, J., Nichols, S. and Sirker, S. (2010) "Is belief in free will a cultural universal?" *Mind and Language* 25: 346–358.
Sarkissian, H., Park, J., Tien, D., Wright, J. and Knobe, J. (2011) "Folk moral relativism," *Mind and Language* 26: 482–505.
Schwitzgebel, E. and Cushman, F. (2012) "Expertise in moral reasoning? Order effects on moral judgment in professional philosophers and non-philosophers," *Mind and Language* 27: 135–153.
Seyedsayamdost, H. (2014) *Reproducibility of Empirical Findings: Experiments in Philosophy and Beyond*, Ph.D. thesis, London School of Economics, London.

Seyedsayamdost, H. (2015a) "On normativity and epistemic intuitions: Failure of replication," *Episteme* 12: 95–116.
Seyedsayamdost, H. (2015b) "On gender and philosophical intuition: Failure of replication and other negative results," *Philosophical Psychology* 28: 642–673.
Snow, N. (2010) *Virtue as Social Intelligence: An Empirically Grounded Theory*, New York: Routledge.
Sommers, T. (2010) "Experimental philosophy and free will," *Philosophy Compass* 5: 199–212.
Sorensen, R. (2014) "Novice thought experiments," in *Intuitions*, edited by R. Booth and D. P. Rowbottom, Oxford: Oxford University Press.
Sosa, E. (2007a) "Experimental philosophy and philosophical intuition," *Philosophical Studies* 132: 99–107.
Sosa, E. (2007b) "Intuitions: Their nature and epistemic efficacy," *Grazer Philosophische Studien* 74: 51–67.
Sosa, E. (2009) "A defense of the use of intuitions in philosophy," in *Stich and His Critics*, edited by D. Murphy and M. Bishop, Malden: Wiley-Blackwell.
Sosa, E. (2011) "Can there be a discipline of philosophy? And can it be founded on intuitions?" *Mind and Language* 26: 453–467.
Swain, S., Alexander, J. and Weinberg, J. (2008) "The instability of philosophical intuitions: Running hot and cold on true-temp," *Philosophy and Phenomenological Research* 76: 138–155.
Talbot, B. (2013) "Reforming intuition pumps: when are the old ways the best?" *Philosophical Studies* 165: 315–334.
Talbot, B. (2014) "Why so negative? Evidence aggregation and armchair philosophy, *Synthese* 191: 3865–3896.
Thomson, J. J. (1976) "Killing, letting die, and the trolley problem," *The Monist* 59: 204–217.
Weinberg, J. (2007) "How to challenge intuitions empirically without risking skepticism," *Midwest Studies in Philosophy* 30: 318–343.
Weinberg, J., Gonnerman, C., Buckner, C. and Alexander, J. (2010) "Are philosophers expert intuiters?" *Philosophical Psychology* 23: 331–355.
Weinberg, J., Nichols, S. and Stich, S. (2001) "Normativity and epistemic intuitions," *Philosophical Topics* 29: 429–460.
Williams, B. (1978) *Descartes: The Project of Pure Enquiry*, London: Pelican.
Williamson, T. (2011) "Philosophical expertise and the burden of proof," *Metaphilosophy* 42: 215–229.
Wright, J. (2010) "On intuitional stability: The clear, the strong, and the paradigmatic," *Cognition* 115: 491–503.
Young, L., Cushman, F., Adolphs, F., Tranel, D. and Hauser, M. (2006) "Does emotion mediate the effect of an action's moral status on its intentional status? Neuropsychological evidence," *Journal of Cognition and Culture* 6: 291–304.

22
THOUGHT EXPERIMENTS IN CURRENT METAPHILOSOPHICAL DEBATES

Daniel Cohnitz and Sören Häggqvist

1 Introduction

Although thought experiments were first discovered as a *sui generis* methodological tool by philosophers of science (most prominently by Ernst Mach), the tool can also be found – even more frequently – in contemporary philosophy. Thought experiments in philosophy and science have a lot in common (cf. the discussion in Sorensen 1992; Häggqvist 1996; Cohnitz 2006). However, in this chapter we will concentrate on thought experiments in philosophy only. Their use has been the centre of attention of metaphilosophical discussion in the past decade, and this chapter will provide an overview of the results this discussion has achieved and point out which issues are still open.

In metaphilosophy, thought experimentation is also often referred to as "the method of cases"; and there sometimes seems to be an assumption in metaphilosophy that there is a common methodological role that thought experiments play throughout philosophy. In the next section, we will first argue that this assumption is mistaken, by pointing out two other methodological roles that thought experiments play in philosophy (there are, arguably, more; cf. Cohnitz in preparation). However, there is one role which seems to be the most interesting from a metaphilosophical point of view, namely the use of thought experiments as counterexamples or "alethic refuters." In Section 3 we will discuss several attempts at reconstructing the logical structure of such refutations by thought experiments. As we will learn from these reconstructions, thought experimentation typically involves several *modal* judgements. This leads us to the epistemology of thought experimentation: why are we entitled to these modal judgements? A prominent answer is that we know the truth of the modal claims intuitively. This line has come under attack in the last decade by "experimental philosophers," who empirically challenge the reliability of intuitive judgements about the kind of subject matter that philosophical thought experiments deal with. In Section 4 we will look at this discussion. Another prominent epistemology of modality tries to explain the modal knowledge involved in thought experimentation via the notion of conceivability. This will be the topic of Section 5. In Section 6 we will conclude with a few general remarks about the prospects of metaphilosophy and modal epistemology.

2 Roles of thought experiments

Talking of "the method of cases" or the "method of thought experimentation" suggests that there is only one (or at least one dominant) way in which philosophers put the considerations of hypothetical cases to use in philosophy. However, just as there are different functions for thought experiments in the sciences, there are different functions for thought experiments in philosophy. Let us characterize a thought experiment (in philosophy) as the consideration of a hypothetical case in the domain of things at issue. This characterization is intentionally vague. There are many things that can count as "considerations" (including, for example, being modelled in a computer simulation), and also many that count as being in a domain of things "at issue."

Nevertheless, this liberal characterization excludes some hypothetical scenarios in philosophy from the class of thought experiments proper. For example, it excludes mere analogies, i.e., cases which are merely in some respect analogical to what is at issue (as, for instance, Plato's cave-scenario, which is supposedly analogical to our actual epistemic situation, which it is intended to illustrate).

It allows us, though, to speak of "illustrative thought experiments." These are thought experiments that are meant to illustrate the intended content of a theory or of a definition by providing a hypothetical example which exemplifies the content of that theory (perhaps in contrast with a rival theory) particularly well. Consider – as an example from physics – what would happen to the earth if the sun were suddenly to explode. According to the Newtonian theory, the earth would immediately depart from its usual elliptical orbit, while Einstein's theory predicts that the earth would stay in its usual orbit for another 8 minutes, the time it takes for light to travel from the sun to earth. Here, the hypothetical case (the sun suddenly exploding) is used to illustrate the difference between Newton's and Einstein's theories. Thought experiments with this function are very common in philosophical texts.

The liberal characterization also allows to count "puzzle cases" as thought experiments. Puzzle cases are hypothetical scenarios which are intended to provoke a philosophical investigation. A prominent example is the trolley case-pair as it is often presented in ethics textbooks (and was presented as a pair in Judith Jarvis Thomson's 1985). One case of that pair is the so-called "standard trolley problem." In the standard trolley problem you are standing by a railroad track when you notice that an uncontrolled trolley is rolling down the track, heading for a group of five railroad workers. You know that they will all be killed if the trolley continues on its path. The only thing you can do to prevent these five deaths is to throw a switch that will divert the trolley onto a side track, where it will kill only one person. When considering what you should do in such case, it seems that you should throw the switch and save the lives of five for the life of one.

The other case of the pair, the "footbridge case" is very similar. Again, the trolley is about to kill five people. This time, however, you are not standing near the track, but on a footbridge above the track. Also, this time you cannot divert the trolley by throwing a switch. You can only stop the trolley by putting something in its way that is heavy enough. You consider throwing yourself in front of the trolley, but you know that you are not heavy enough to stop it. Standing next to you, however, is a very large stranger. The only way you can stop the trolley killing the five people is by pushing this large stranger off the footbridge, in front of the trolley. If you push the stranger off, he will be killed, but you will save the other five. Again, considering what you should do, this time it seems wrong to push the stranger off the bridge even though, as before, you would save the lives of five for the life of one.

In Thomson's presentation of the two cases, her intention was to provoke a theoretical analysis of why it is that we react differently to the two cases although they seem on a par with respect to their morally relevant aspects (it seems that in both cases you need to decide whether you should kill one in order to save the lives of five by active intervention). Puzzle cases are cases in which it is either not clear what we should say about the case, or where our pre-theoretic judgement about the case seems incoherent (as in the trolley case), and they are typically intended to provoke or motivate a theoretical analysis.

A third way to use thought experiments is to use them as counterexamples against already existing theories. This is the use that most metaphilosophers seem to have in mind when speaking of thought experiments. Here is an example, borrowed from Jackson (1982). Physicalism in the philosophy of mind is the view that all facts (including all facts about the mind) are physical facts. Now imagine Mary, a woman who was born and raised in a black and white room and has never seen any colour in all her life. However, in her black and white prison she was trained to become an expert in colour perception. She now knows every physical fact that there is to know about the process of colour vision and colour experience. When for the first time confronted with a red tomato, Mary forms the thought "So that's what it is like to see red." It seems that Mary at that point learns something new; she learns what it is like to see red. This is knowledge of a fact about colour experience. But by stipulation, Mary already knew every physical fact there is concerning colour vision. Thus, the physical facts do not exhaust all the facts and physicalism is false.

The use of thought experiments as counterexamples, (or – following Sorensen 1992 – "alethic refuters") gives rise to interesting epistemological and methodological questions that we will discuss in detail below. These questions include the general puzzle of thought experimentation: how a merely hypothetical case can teach us anything interesting about the world and can even count as a counterexample to some (often well-established) theory. Moreover, how do we know what is possible and what is not, and what would be the case in such a possible scenario?

The other uses, however, do not seem to give rise to the same questions. Whether a puzzle case is actual or merely hypothetical does not seem to matter for its heuristic value. Likewise, that an illustrative thought experiment presents a merely hypothetical case does not in any way diminish its pedagogical value. Also, there is no question of how we know what is the case in a hypothetical scenario. In an illustrative thought experiment, we know what is the case because we stipulated it, and in the puzzle case, there is no claim to knowledge anyway (it is the point of the puzzle that we do not know what to say about the hypothetical case).

Another observation about these different functions is of importance: Thought experiments can have histories and "lives of their own" (pace Hacking 1992). A hypothetical scenario C was perhaps once introduced with the intention of providing a puzzle case, but in the process of deliberating about it, it became clear what one should say about the case. Perhaps this judgement, let us call it (or, rather, its propositional content) J, became so convincing, that the case could then serve as a counterexample to a theory T1 which predicted a different evaluation for that case, while a rival theory T2 would predict precisely C → J. At some point, textbooks explaining the content of T2 might cite C and its paradigmatic evaluation when explaining the content of T2. Also, a thought experiment might start as an illustration of a theoretical alternative and later become used in an argument for that alternative. Because one and the same hypothetical case might play such different functional roles, it can be difficult to determine in which function a thought experiment is intended (a thought experiment in one and the same text might even serve several such functions, either simultaneously for the same reader, or different ones for different readers).

The existence of these different functional roles is a source of confusion in contemporary metaphilosophical discussion. For example, some experimental philosophers (which we will discuss below) are critical about the use of intuitive judgements when thought experiments are used counterexamples. Herman Cappelen (2012) in his work argues that this scepticism is unwarranted, because intuitions play no decisive role in thought experiments. However, Cappelen focusses in his argumentation mainly on thought experiments that are used as puzzle cases (cf. Cohnitz 2012; Chalmers 2014), while the experimental philosophers were criticizing thought experiments that play a role in theory choice, viz. alethic refuters.[1] (We will return to the matter below in Section 4.)

3 Content and form of alethic refuters

In the previous section we stressed the diversity of roles that thought experiments may play within various theoretical disciplines. This section concerns the particular role we called "alethic refuters" (after Sorensen 1992): hypothetical cases intended to falsify a statement or theory by constituting a counterexample to it, in analogy with how ordinary experiments may falsify theories by providing negative instances. Viewed in this way, the use of thought experiments as alethic refuters falls under the broad rubric of hypothesis testing.

Just as philosophers of science have turned to logic in order to understand how testing of theories and hypotheses works, theorists of thought experiments have tried to use logic to study the fine mechanics of alethic refutation. In particular, an aim is to understand how certain thought experiments may be analyzed as arguments issuing in the conclusion that the theory under testing is false. Before briefly looking at some of these attempts, a few preliminary points need to be clarified.

The first concerns the tendency to focus on cases purporting to falsify theories (as hinted by Sorensen's term). This is not due chiefly to any Popperian complaints about the notion of confirmation in general. Rather, there are many more influential instances of thought experiments used to oppose theories than there are of attempted confirmations. This is widely recognized (cf. Sorensen 1992; Williamson 2007; Malmgren 2011). Moreover, the fact that thought experiments involve hypothetical scenarios freely invented by their creators means that whatever problems surround the notion of confirmation in ordinary, non-hypothetical testing are exacerbated. Surely the claim that I can invent a possible case which fits a certain general theory does not carry much weight towards showing that the theory is true. Such cases may abound, but they may often more naturally be taken as illustrations (for various purposes; see Section 2) of theories rather than tests of them, or as puzzle cases for which a theory that makes sense of them is sought (cf. Section 2).

Second, the fact that thought experiments are hypothetical means that any formal reconstruction has to be done in modal logic. Of course, this does not imply that any particular thought experimental scenario cannot also be actual (cf. Malmgren 2011, 279), or that the point it is used to make cannot also be made by an actual case (cf. Williamson 2005, 15; 2007, 192; Malmgren 2011, 273).

Third, it is important not to conflate the issues discussed in this debate (and this section) with the debate over whether thought experiments are identical to arguments, or may be replaced by them without epistemic loss. That question was prompted by John Norton's claim that thought experiments are just arguments adorned with particular details that are strictly irrelevant to their conclusions (Norton 1991). Norton offered this claim in response to Brown's suggestion that thought experiments constitute a peculiar vehicle for a priori knowledge (Brown 1986, 1991a, 1991b); prolonged debate ensued, mostly between Brown and Norton (Norton 1996, 2004a, 2004b; Brown 2004a, 2004b).

The current debate with which we are here concerned takes no stand on this question, however. Just as one may look at the argument form of a piece of reasoning for the conclusion that a theory is false when the premises concern an experiment – and loosely talk of this is as the logical form of falsification – one may be interested in the structure of the corresponding reasoning in connection with thought experiments.

The parallel with ordinary experiments serves to amplify the difference between these debates, and to introduce a final preliminary point. When thought experiments are used to test theories, it seems natural to hold with Sorensen that they "are arguments if and only if experiments [in general] are arguments" (Sorensen 1992, 214). It also seems natural to hold that experiments in general are not arguments: the former, but not the latter, are entities with a spatio-temporal location; the latter, but not the former, have properties like validity and soundness and contain parts with truth-values. Regardless of whether experiments *are* arguments, however, they are, as we just noted, clearly connected with arguments, and one of the benefits of achieving "a fine-grained understanding of the arguments that underlie thought experiments," as Williamson (2007, 180) puts it, is that we may get a clearer picture of the epistemic challenges posed by the premises – that is, what the experiment itself, understood as a process or event, is supposed to supply.[2]

Now just as an ordinary experiment in the field or a laboratory involves particulars – a particular set-up, particular unfoldings, and particular observations and reports of these – a thought experiment typically involves a particular hypothetical scenario. This suggests that the premise reporting the "outcome" of the thought experiment should also be particular (as in the case of ordinary experiments).

3.1 Motivations

Why should we try to formalize alethic refuters? One motivation has already been mentioned above: if we are able to connect an interesting and sizeable class of such thought experiments with arguments sharing a common form, or a few forms, we may be in a better position to see what epistemic challenges they present, and the prospects of meeting them. Of course, just as individual arguments are distinct when the statements composing them are, different thought experiments will be connected with distinct arguments. But insofar as these arguments share logical form, they already have an interesting (if abstract) property in common. This standing motivation for seeking logical structure and form extends to the theory of thought experiments partly for the same reason as in other domains.

An interest in the epistemology of alethic refuters may take different forms. It may also be informed by various methodological and meta-philosophical preconceptions. The debate between Norton and Brown mentioned above was largely driven by Brown's suggestion that the importance of thought experiments in science shows science to have a partly a priori character. The current debate concerning the form of alethic refuters in philosophy is sometimes informed by the goal of demonstrating the methodological integrity of philosophers' use of such thought experiments without thereby construing this use as peculiarly a priori (Williamson 2007). Sometimes, however, a stated aim is precisely to make room for a distinctively aprioristic view of alethic refuters and, with them, philosophy (Ichikawa and Jarvis 2009, 2012; Malmgren 2011). A subsidiary aim for some writers has been to provide an analysis reflecting psychologically real or possible routes to the argument's premises.

3.2 Three recent proposals

Early proposals concerning the form of alethic refuters employed propositional modal logic (Sorensen 1992; Häggqvist 1996). They also sought to apply proposed formal schemata to several influential alethic refuters in philosophy. By contrast, recent proposals tend to employ quantified modal logic. They have concentrated almost exclusively on one sort of closely related alethic refuters, viz., Gettier cases used as counterexamples to the JTB theory of knowledge. But the authors of these proposals also express the claim or hope that the proposal generalizes. Williamson says, for instance: "The discussion can be generalized to many imaginary counterexamples that have been deployed against philosophical analyses and theories in ways more or less similar to Gettier's" (2007, 180). As he immediately concedes, much work remains in order to show his proposal to be generally applicable. Similarly, Malmgren says that "the aim is to capture an argument form that is common to at least a core set of negative experiments" (2011, 272). But neither proceeds to actually attempt application to other cases.

To fix what we are talking about, let us consider a specific instance of a Gettier-like vignette (from Malmgren 2011, 272):

> (S) Suppose that Smith believes that Jones owns a Ford, on the basis of seeing Jones drive a Ford to work and remembering that Jones always drove a Ford in the past. From this, Smith infers that someone in his office owns a Ford. Suppose furthermore that someone in Smith's office does own a Ford – but it is not Jones, it is Brown. (Jones's Ford was stolen and Jones now drives a rented Ford).

Now, does Smith know that someone in his office owns a Ford? The expected judgement is that while having a justified and true belief in this proposition, Smith does not know this.

Williamson suggests that the argument connected with a case like this has the form

(W)   (i)$_w$ $\Diamond \exists x \exists p\ GC(x,p)$
        (ii)$_w$ $\exists x \exists p GC(x,p)\ \Box\!\!\rightarrow \forall x \forall p(GC(x,p) \supset (JTB(x,p)\ \&\ \neg K(x,p)))$
       ∴ $\neg \Box \forall x \forall p(K(x,p) \leftrightarrow JTB(x,p))$,

where the variables "x" and "p" respectively range over subjects and propositions, "GC(x,p)" says that x stands to p in the relation specified by (S), "JTB(x,p)" that x has justified true belief in p, and "K(x,p)" that x knows that p. (We will use this lexicon throughout this subsection.)

On this rendering, as on the others shortly considered, the conclusion is that the JTB theory of knowledge, here understood as a metaphysical claim rather than conceptual analysis, is false. A thinker coming to this conclusion on the basis of Gettier's alethic refuter does so because she accepts, after contemplating the case as presented in (S), the premises of (W). The first premise asserts the metaphysical possibility of someone being related to some proposition in the same way as (S) specifies. The second premise expresses the claim that if someone were thus related to a proposition, she would have justified true belief in it without knowledge.[3] The latter judgement is of particular interest, since it is intended to capture what is usually called the intuition, or intuitive judgement, concerning Gettier cases. On Williamson's proposal this is a counterfactual conditional. But it also highlights the claim that the scenario described in the vignette is possible. For most Gettier cases, this claim is trivial. But without it, the argument would not be valid.

It is important to note that the hypothetical scenario of the vignette – the "GC" predicate of (W) – is itself neutral with respect to epistemic properties: a person's and a proposition's satisfying "GC(x,p)" is itself compatible both with her knowing and with her not knowing that proposition: the scenario itself holds no prejudice with respect to the outcome. This is analogous to the distinction between set-up and observation (or data) in an ordinary experiment: one may know the former without being in any way committed about the latter.

Williamson's proposal has been criticized on various grounds, all (notably) concerned with its internal viability as an analysis of Gettier cases, rather than with any difficulties of generalization. Specifically, Ichikawa (2009) and Malmgren (2011) both complain that the major premise

(ii)$_w$ $\exists x \exists p GC(x,p) \;\square\!\!\rightarrow\; \forall x \forall p (GC(x,p) \supset (JTB(x,p) \;\&\; \neg K(x,p)))$

may be false for reasons apparently unrelated to what it is aiming to capture. Consider that someone may satisfy the antecedent in the nearest world where it is true (perhaps even the actual world) but also, as it happens, have "good reasons to believe that he is prone to hallucinate people driving Fords to work and prone to misremember what cars people drove in the past" (Malmgren 2011, 279). Since such a person will not have justified true belief, the judgement will be false if construed as (ii)$_w$. Someone might also satisfy the antecedent but have grounds for believing the proposition, additional to and independent from those mentioned in (S). (ii)$_w$ may then be false because such a person does have knowledge. But – the objection continues – such instances are *deviant* in relation to what the intuitive judgement about Gettier cases should be. Hence (ii)$_w$ does not capture the intuitive judgement made about such cases.

Moreover, since the consequent of (ii)$_w$ is a universal statement, (ii)$_w$ may be false simply because among the persons in the closest antecedent-world standing in the relation to a proposition specified by (S), only some, but not all, happen to have justified true belief in this proposition without knowing it. This case arises because (ii)$_w$ does not exactly match the anaphoric binding suggested in Williamson's own version of the judgement in English:

"If a thinker were Gettier-related to a proposition, he/she would have justified true belief in it without knowledge" (Williamson 2007, 195).

Williamson's chief reply is that we should accept that our judgements about alethic refuters may be mistaken.[4] In cases like those broached by Ichikawa and Malmgren, we should admit that our judgement was wrong (should we discover this), and amend it accordingly by strengthening the stipulations in the vignette so as to rule out the unwanted instantiations of the "GC" predicate (Williamson 2009). His response is thus, in effect, to chalk such unwanted instantiations up to general fallibility, rather than admitting them as deviant: "We cannot realistically expect that the method of thought experiments in philosophy will turn out to be much more reliable than the methods of the natural sciences" (2009, 469).

Just what the "GC" predicate expresses depends on what the stated scenario of a given Gettier cases stipulates, of course. Hence, Ichikawa notes, the risk of $(ii)_w$ being false due to unintended, accidental realizations seems inverse to the specificity of the scenario. This is why strengthening the scenario is a way of doing away with such realizations. It may seem odd, however, that a thought experiment should be better – in the sense of running less risk of such deviant instantiations – simply for mentioning more specific facts even if these seem entirely irrelevant to its point. Take (S) again. Clearly, stipulating not only the make of the car (a Ford) but also its production year diminishes the risk of deviant instantiations of the antecedent. Ichikawa complains that such specificity should not be viewed as improvement (Ichikawa 2009, 440).

Ichikawa's concern with deviance is largely epistemological: "Williamson's account renders it much too difficult to know the Gettier intuition" (Ichikawa 2009, 440). Malmgren emphasizes what she sees as a semantic mismatch between what $(ii)_w$ expresses and what is actually judged concerning (S), and that this is shown by the fact that $(ii)_w$ does not rule out deviant realizations (2011, 279). She also notes that her complaint appears parallel to the considerations that lead Williamson himself to reject, inter alia

$$\Box \forall x \forall p (GC(x,p) \supset (JTB(x,p) \& \neg K(x,p)))$$

as capturing the judgement (Malmgren 2011, 275–80; Williamson 2007, 184–5).[5]

These criticisms are connected with a concern that a formal account of alethic refuters should allow them to be epistemically successful. On this view, a proposal should render knowledge of the "outcome" premise practicable; Ichikawa and Jarvis's (2009) and Malmgren's (2011) proposals are motivated by a claim that it should be knowable a priori. Ichikawa and Jarvis (2009) and Malmgren (2011) worry that Williamson's account makes the central premise too hard to know, since knowing the counterfactual requires knowing that there are no counterinstances to it. They also offer alternative proposals which eschew construing the judgement as a counterfactual.

Ichikawa and Jarvis (2009) argue that we may reasonably take contemplators of a thought experiment to "fill out" the scenario with propositions beyond those explicit in a vignette. Thus a more complete scenario is contemplated; they suggest that the judgement concerning such a scenario of a Gettier case may be construed as a strict conditional:

$$(ii)_{IJ} \quad \Box(g \supset \exists x \exists p (JTB(x,p) \& \neg K(x,p))),$$

where "g" denotes the enriched scenario, identified in thought by a demonstrative "things are like *that*." Together with the possibility premise

$$(i)_{IJ} \quad \Diamond g$$

this entails the sought conclusion (as understood by Williamson, i.e.: $\neg \Box \forall x \forall p (K(x,p) \leftrightarrow JTB(x,p))$. In contrast to Williamson's $(ii)_W$, Ichikawa and Jarvis's $(ii)_{IJ}$ renders the outcome judgement as a necessity judgement, so as to safe-guard it against the vicissitudes of contingency (2009, 223).

Williamson rejoins that the enrichment supposedly blocking deviant instantiations cannot consist in explicit consideration of various alternative ways of filling out the fiction, hence must consist in dispositions to enrich the scenario beyond the stated text; that such dispositions are likely to vary between different contemplators of a case, thereby threatening public debate about it; and that competing dispositions to enrich may coexist within a subject, thereby threatening the plausibility of the first premise $(i)_{IJ}$. Moreover, he claims, even a richer scenario constructed along the lines envisaged by Ichikawa and Jarvis (2009) and Ichikawa (2009) may be subject to deviant realizations; thus, even if construed as $(ii)_{IJ}$, the judgement risks unintended falsity (Williamson 2009, 466–8). If Williamson is right about the intrasubjective coexistence of competing dispositions to enrich the scenario, this presumably also threatens a contemplator's demonstrative thought ("things are like *that*") with failure to refer to a determinate proposition g.

Malmgren argues that construing alethic refuters as fiction lets in deviant realizations because what is a legitimate enrichment for a fiction need not be one for a scenario in the vignette of a thought experiment, and vice versa: "What is true/false/indeterminate in a problem case does not line up (across the board) with what is true/false/indeterminate in a fiction" (Malmgren 2011, 304).

Her own proposal is that the Gettier judgement is a possibility judgement (Malmgren 2011, 281):

$$(i_M) \quad \Diamond \exists x \exists p \, (GCx,p \, \& \, JTBx,p \, \& \, \neg Kx,p).$$

As in the other proposals, the modality here is metaphysical. (i_M) yields the same conclusion as the other accounts without additional premises. It also, Malmgren argues, meets the demand of being knowable a priori (though it will presumably not be necessary unless S5 is assumed).

3.3 A few comments

Williamson's account has been criticized on the grounds that it makes judgements about alethic refuters contingent. The felt force of such objections will vary depending on one's general views about what philosophy is. To someone for whom the subject matter of many branches of philosophy is not well characterized as conceptual analysis, but rather to be regarded as continuous with the attempts of science to learn about various domains, these objections may be less pressing; whereas they will carry force with adherents of what Ichikawa and Jarvis call "the traditional view of thought experiments and intuitions" (2009, 223). Clearly one's attitude will also depend on whether one takes the distinction between a priori and a posteriori knowledge (or justification) to be valid and important, or not. Williamson has repeatedly expressed the view that this distinction "is a superficial one, of little theoretical interest" (2013; see also Williamson 2007). Although in a spirit very different from the gradualism between philosophy and science endorsed by Quine, he has also repeatedly stressed that the target of alethic refuters such as Gettier's is not an analysis of the concept of knowledge, but a theory about the phenomenon of knowledge.

Parties to these debates tend to be non-sceptics about alethic refuters (at least within philosophy). They also operate within what might loosely be called a non-Platonist epistemology. Hence, they recognize that the premises of their accounts should be non-mysteriously knowable to contemplators of cases in at least some instances (and the focus on Gettier cases is probably motivated partly by the recognition that such cases appear to be successful alethic refuters). Williamson (2007) appeals to a general human capacity for evaluating counterfactuals, which, while fallible and not distinctly a priori, is reliable enough to allow such knowledge. Ichikawa and Jarvis claim that "whatever explains our capacity for everyday knowledge should also be able to explain knowledge of thought-experiment intuitions" (2009, 235–6), arguing that this should make a priori knowledge of the premises of alethic refuters – construed as metaphysical possibility and necessity claims – non-mysterious. While both Williamson and Ichikawa and Jarvis do elaborate on these suggestions, it is fair to say there these issues are unresolved at present.

4 Intuitions and metaphysical modality

Whatever the exact genesis of our knowledge of the premises of an alethic refuter may be, many philosophers hold that the major premise of a thought experiment is in any case judged *intuitively*. Philosophers disagree about what exactly they mean by "intuitive," but it seems that they at least hold that it means that the major premise is not arrived at via any conscious inference from other knowledge.

4.1 The experimental challenge

In the last decade, a number of so-called "experimental philosophers" (or "*xphiles*") have criticized the use of thought experiments in philosophy on the basis of the idea that the crucial premise of thought experiment arguments is established by intuitive judgement. In a series of empirical experiments they try to show that non-inferential judgements about philosophical thought-experiment scenarios vary with philosophically irrelevant factors and hence should not be trusted. For example, the experiments show that a particular version of a Gettier case (as described above) will elicit (on average) different spontaneous evaluations depending on whether the person making the judgement is (a non-philosopher) from a Western or from an East-Asian cultural background (Weinberg, Nichols and Stich 2001; Machery et al. 2004). Similar studies show that judgements may vary with socio-economic status, gender, the order of the cases presented, or whether or not the judgement was made in a clean or a messy environment.

Xphiles draw different conclusions from their results. The most modest conclusion is that philosophers should not simply assume that their intuitive judgements are widely shared, but should empirically check whether they really are (Weinberg, Nichols, and

Stich 2001). More radical *xphiles* demand a moratorium on the use of intuitions in philosophy until we know under which conditions our intuitions are not subject to such variation (Weinberg 2007), and the most radical suggest that we should give up on whole branches of theoretical inquiry, since we do not at present possess reliable methods for finding out the truth in these areas of inquiry (Mallon et al. 2009).

Experiments typically involve a description of a thought experiment scenario, followed by a forced choice question. Such a vignette, as used by Weinberg, Nichols, and Stich in their (2001), reads as follows:

> Bob has a friend, Jill, who has driven a Buick for many years. Bob therefore thinks that Jill drives an American car. He is not aware, however, that her Buick has recently been stolen, and he is also not aware that Jill has replaced it with a Pontiac, which is a different kind of American car. Does Bob really know that Jill drives an American car, or does he only believe it?
>
> REALLY KNOWS   ONLY BELIEVES

When Weinberg, Nichols, and Stich tested the probe on undergraduates at Rutgers university, it turned out that the majority of students with an East-Asian cultural background as well as the majority of students with a cultural background from the Indian subcontinent would judge that Bob *knows* that Jill drives an American car, while the majority of students with a Western cultural background judged that Bob *only believes* it.

If one does not want to conclude from such results that knowledge is culturally relative, one seems forced to conclude that intuitive judgements about hypothetical cases are not providing us with reliable evidence. There are several ways, however, to endorse the second of these disjuncts, without giving up on the method of thought experimentation.

4.2 The expertise defense

One way is to agree that intuitive judgements are not reliable, if the judgements are made by non-experts. As we said above, early x-phi studies tested the judgements of undergraduate students with little or no training in philosophy. The so-called "Expertise Defense" against the challenge coming from x-phi holds that the intuitive judgments of undergraduate students might well be unreliable, however the intuitive judgments that play a role in theory choice in philosophy are the judgments of philosophical *experts*. That *their* intuitions vary has, however, not been shown (and they presumably do not, because otherwise thought experiments could play no role in theory choice).

There are (at least) three ways in which this defense can be fleshed out, only one of which seems somewhat promising. One way to argue for the superior expertise of philosophers and its relevance for the evaluation of hypothetical cases is to point out that intuitive judgments, just as all judgments, are theory-laden. If so, then we should trust those judgments more that are more likely to be influenced by correct theories rather than incorrect theories. Since professional philosophers are likely to be informed by correct theories, and undergraduates are not, we should trust the judgment of philosophers, and discard the judgments by undergraduates as unreliable (for a defense along these lines, see Devitt 2006, 2011).

The problem with that strategy is that this particular view on the epistemology of intuitive judgements undermines the kind of evidential role they are supposed to play. If intuitive judgements are a mere expression of one's theoretical commitments, then intuitive judgements about hypothetical cases can never provide us with new evidence against our currently held theories, since we already need to be committed to a better theory in order to generate recalcitrant judgments that are informed by good theory.

An alternative way of fleshing out the Expertise Defense is to point out that philosophers are experts about the subject matter at issue because of having paid a lot of attention to cases of, say, knowledge and mere belief. On this view, philosophers are more reliable in making correct judgments about hypothetical cases because they are familiar with a bigger data set from which to generalize (Devitt 2011, 2012).

The problem with this version of the Expertise Defense is that it makes a certain *empirical* claim. It claims that people who are professionally more exposed to cases of certain kinds should also become more reliable in their judgment. Unfortunately, this claim does not seem to hold up. In a study that tested this empirical assumption for an Expertise Defense of semantic intuitions, Machery (2012) found that experts of different fields of semantics had significantly different judgments about hypothetical cases in philosophical semantics than their philosophical colleagues, although they are professionally just as much confronted with the same linguistic phenomena as their colleagues. Thus, the homogeneity in philosophical judgments about hypothetical cases is not explained by the expertise of philosophers that stems from exposure and attention to relevant cases.

A third way of fleshing out the Expertise Defense would highlight that philosophical evaluations of hypothetical cases are more likely to be reliable because (i) they are more familiar with the specific use of thought experiments in their area of inquiry and (ii) they know better which kind of intuitive reaction is of relevance and which terminology properly reports that reaction. (i) is based on the observation that the description of a hypothetical scenario in a philosophical text does not settle every detail of the case. We already discussed above that a hypothetical scenario can be enriched to "deviant instances" which would not any longer support the same intuitive evaluations. This is a feature that thought experiment descriptions share with other fictional texts.[6] In the latter case it is a matter of familiarity with the relevant *genre* to know how the open details of a story may or may not be filled out by the reader in order to draw conclusions from the text that are merely implicitly contained in it. Likewise, it is a matter of familiarity – not just with the genre "thought experiment" – but with the genre *thought experiment in this particular theoretical context* that enables the philosopher to fill out the details of the hypothetical case in the way relevant for the function the thought experiment is supposed to play in a particular theoretical inquiry (Cohnitz 2006; Ichikawa and Jarvis 2009). (ii) is based on the observation that philosophers typically know better what is at stake, and how to use the relevant terminology. To see what we mean, consider the use linguists make of grammaticality judgements. Instead of asking lay persons whether a certain string seems "grammatical" to them, they sometimes ask about whether the string seems "acceptable," in order to prevent whatever views on grammar the subject might have to taint the judgment. However, there is a danger that this "fix" does more harm than good because a string of words can seem acceptable or unacceptable in many ways, while the linguist is only interested in its *grammatical* acceptability. A linguist, unlike a lay person, would know that, and is hence less likely to misunderstand the intended sense of "acceptability" if she were given the same task. Moreover, since the linguist knows what is at issue, she would also be able to answer questions framed in terms of "grammaticality" directly in the intended way. Likewise, philosophers might be better placed than lay persons to evaluate thought experiments, since they might know better how to apply the relevant theoretical terminology in reports of their intuitive judgments (Cohnitz and Haukioja 2015).

Of course, also this last version of fleshing out the Expertise Defense is based on certain empirical assumptions.[7] They might seem plausible, but there is still work to do to show that is really what explains the difference in intuitive judgment between the test subjects that participated in the x-phi studies and the professional philosophers.

4.3 *The irrelevance of intuitions for the method of cases*

Herman Cappelen (2012) and Max Deutsch (2015) argue for another response to the Experimental Challenge. According to them, the challenge is simply misplaced, because intuitive judgments do in fact not play any evidential role in contemporary analytic philosophy. The main premises of thought-experiment arguments are not presented and are not established as based on intuitions, but based on argument and reasoning. Hence, the empirical result that intuitions vary a lot with irrelevant factors is an interesting result in itself but of no relevance for philosophical methodology.

Both Cappelen and Deutsch support their claim by showing that philosophers typically back up their evaluation of a hypothetical case by arguments. Now, surely, in order to establish that a certain claim holds in generality for philosophy, this kind of empirical analysis is the way to go. However, there are some issues that have not been sufficiently addressed in Cappelen's or Deutsch's studies.

The first issue has to do with the selection of cases. As we explained above, thought experiments may serve different functions in philosophy. At least Cappelen's selection of cases has been criticized for being somewhat idiosyncratic and for focussing on puzzle cases, rather than on alethic refuters, which is where the metaphilosophical action is (Cohnitz 2012; Chalmers 2014).

The second issue is that it might be difficult to determine whether something is an argument for a conclusion (where the premises of the argument carry the evidential weight for the conclusion), or whether something is a retrospective explanation of an intuitive judgment (where the evidential weight is carried by the judgment). Perhaps the apparent argument is just cited for heuristic purposes or as a mere rhetorical maneuver, as Julia Langkau explains:

> There could be other, not purely epistemic reasons why an author may give arguments. First, the arguments could serve a purely heuristic purpose, i.e., they could help us to get to the truth without actually playing a justificatory role. Usually, one would think that intuitions are used for heuristic reasons, and that the arguments in support of their contents bear the epistemic burden. However, a view according to which our intuitions have Rock [default justificatory] status and our arguments merely serve to rationalize them is not completely implausible. Second, an author might give arguments merely for conversational or rhetorical reasons. While it is

obvious to the author that the intuition has Rock status, it is not to their audience. In order to convince the audience, it might be easier to give arguments for the truth of the content of the intuition than for the claim that the intuition has Rock status. Third, arguments might be required in order to get a paper published. Surely there are certain presentational requirements on philosophical texts which favour certain methods over others. Maybe it is not sufficient in academic philosophy to simply give the thought experiment without support from arguments. In all three cases just mentioned, intuitions could still provide the relevant justification.

(Langkau forthcoming)

In a rational reconstruction of an argumentation, it might well be possible to argue that the apparent argument for the relevant claim is not intended as an argument. For example, if the premises of the proposed argument are question begging in the dialectical situation at issue, it might be more reasonable to suppose that this was in fact a retrospective explanation of the intuitive judgment. However, neither Cappelen[8] nor Deutsch seem to pay sufficient attention to this problem.[9]

Finally, there are several philosophical projects in which the targeted subject matter is explicitly conceived as grounded in psychological competences which manifest themselves in certain intuitive reactions (for example, concept applications, interpretations or productions of utterances, and attributions of mental states). Given the aim of these projects, it makes total sense to "psychologize" their evidence, because psychological processes are what these projects are after. Cappelen and Deutsch seem to assume that they are a clear minority or that they are methodologically confused, but – as these projects often make their intentions explicit – we know they do exist in considerable number, and it is not clear (and not addressed sufficiently by Deutsch or Cappelen) why one should regard all such projects as confused or flawed or unphilosophical. However, for philosophical projects in which the targeted subject matter is not supposed to be grounded in psychological competences, but rather concerned with metaphysical truth, it seems that intuitions should not and probably also do not play a substantial evidential role in philosophy. But that still leaves the matter open how we know that the premises of a thought experiment argument are true.

5 Conceivability and metaphysical modality

As mentioned in Sections 2 and 3, reconstructing thought experiments as (valid) modal arguments pinpoints the question of how we are to know the premises of such arguments. The previous section dealt with the prospects of appealing to intuition. In this section, we will briefly canvass appeals to conceivability. In line with the main proposals mentioned in Section 3, it will be understood here that the modality at issue is so-called metaphysical modality (i.e., modality *de re*).

Metaphysical modality is usually contrasted with so-called conceptual modality. As its name suggests, however, conceivability appears to concern in the first instance what is conceptually possible. Since it is widely thought that what is conceptually possible need not be metaphysically possible, and that what is metaphysically necessary need not be conceptually so, the conceivability theorist needs to somehow account for the difference.

Currently popular versions of appeals to conceivability do this by appealing to collateral, a posteriori, information about the actual world.

Adherents of two-dimensional semantics – to wit, Jackson (1998) and Chalmers (1996) – prefer to gloss such information rather as information about which world is actual. On their view, the applicability of a term at a world w may be judged either in accordance with the assumption that w is the actual world, or in accordance with whatever *is* the actual world. A terms thus has both what they call a primary extension (and intension) and a secondary extension (and intension).[10] For some terms, these diverge. Since it is the secondary intension that determines the metaphysically modal profile of a term, this is what a thinker needs to know in order to know what is metaphysically possible, impossible, or necessary. However, although the secondary intension may be knowable a priori *conditional* on what world is the actual one, the antecedent – that is, what is the actual world – can only be known a posteriori. Thus, Jackson, says, "our best reasons for concluding that certain claims which aren't conceptually necessary are metaphysically necessary derive from claims that are about what is or is not conceptually necessary conjoined with a posteriori claims based on experimental results in some broad sense" (Jackson 2009, 106). To illustrate, the claim that water is H_2O is metaphysically necessary is supposed to flow from conceptual knowledge that *if* water is H_2O, it is so necessarily, together with empirical knowledge that water is actually H_2O.[11]

Another recent exploitation of this idea is what Ichikawa and Jarvis (2012) call their moderate modal rationalism (or MMR). On their suggestion, a claim is metaphysically possible just in case it is conceptually possible and no falsity about the actual world is conceptually necessitated by it. Thus (with the subscript "M" indicating metaphysical and "C" conceptual modality, and "@" an actuality operator):

MMR: $\Diamond_M p \leftrightarrow (\Diamond_C p \ \& \ \neg\exists q(\neg @q \ \& \Box_C(p \supset @q)))$.

(Ichikawa and Jarvis 2012, 147)

Since what is conceptually possible and conceptually necessitated may plausibly be within epistemological reach of conceivability, MMR holds out hope for a route to knowledge of metaphysical modality based on conceivability together with broadly speaking empirical knowledge, just as two-dimensionalism.[12]

Space considerations prevent extensive discussion of these proposals here. We will just make two brief remarks. A dialectical oddity about two-dimensionalism, in this context, is that the schema or grid specifying secondary intensions conditional on which world is (taken as) actual appears itself to depend on consideration of various thought experiments and their outcomes. Concerning Ichikawa and Jarvis's MMR, one may note that the second clause of its right-hand side requires only absence of conceptual necessitation of potential defeaters. It seems fair to ask whether this is enough.

Although very different in outlook, Williamson's own modal epistemology might (perhaps with some strain and probably against his wishes) be regarded as a species of conceivability approach. This epistemology makes central appeal to counterfactuals and our capacity to evaluate them. Williamson suggests that they are evaluated by supposing the antecedent and adding further judgements by using imagination, logic, and constraining background knowledge. A counterfactual is to be accepted just in case such development eventually leads one to add its consequent; it is rejected when the consequent robustly fails to emerge after suitably diligent and varied development (Williamson 2007, 152–3). Insofar as "supposing" is kin with "conceiving," this approach is perhaps at least a relative of conceivability accounts. Like others, it allots a role to factual knowledge about the world; ineliminably so since counterfactuals (often enough) express worldly connections and dependencies (and so are "metaphysical"). As Williamson says, evaluation of them "can in principle exploit all our background knowledge" (2007, 143).

Williamson is happy to let knowledge of metaphysical modality be fallible, and not distinctively a priori. As we saw in Section 3, other theorists, including Ichikawa and Jarvis, insist that this makes thought experimental knowledge too hard to come by, and complain that "Williamson's account leaves intuitions [i.e., judgements about thought experiments] as mere judgments about contingent matters of fact" (Ichikawa and Jarvis 2009, 226). However, it should be noted that none of the conceivability-based accounts of knowledge of metaphysical modality broached in this section eliminates dependence on contingent matters of fact entirely.

6 Theory of thought experiments and the prospects of metaphilosophy

As this survey shows, the discussion of thought experiments is very lively in current metaphilosophy. However, it seems to us that there are at least two issues that the current debate is not sufficiently taking into account.

One issue we already alluded to above. Philosophy is a very diverse field with different areas of inquiry, each of which containing a wide variety of views of how the subject matter of the area should be thought of, and how we can have knowledge of that subject matter. This by itself is not in the way of there being one particular methodological tool that could still serve all of philosophy. For example, pretty much regardless of how you conceive of the subject matter you think you are dealing with and the epistemic access you believe you have, to argue for your view in a logically sound way seems almost always to be a good methodological advice. But as our survey has probably shown, the method of thought experimentation is not quite the neutral arbiter that logic is.[13] Reconstructing the method of cases involves substantial assumptions about the subject matter that philosophy is dealing with, the nature of the relevant evidence, and an epistemology concerning that evidence. This will make it unlikely that there is one reconstruction of the method of cases that fits all its instances in philosophy. We noted already that there are different functions for thought experiments in philosophy. We suspect that the functional characterisation "alethic refuter" might be still be too broad, and that there are different ways in which a thought experiment can serve as an alethic refuter which would require different stories about how the crucial major premise of an alethic refuter gets established. Perhaps metaphilosophy could make better progress in narrowing its scope, and confining its claims only to certain subareas of philosophy, which plausibly have a common epistemology.

In another sense, metaphilosophy should perhaps broaden its scope. Currently thought experiments in philosophy are discussed in isolation from thought experiments in the sciences, despite the fact that several authors have pointed out strong similarities between the use of hypothetical cases in both (Sorensen 1992; Häggqvist 1996; Cohnitz 2006). And, indeed, one might learn from the analysis of thought experiments in the sciences for the case of philosophy. As Chalmers (2014) points out, the special epistemic status of philosophical intuitions should perhaps best be thought of as their *dialectical* justificatory status. As he puts it, "what is distinctive about appeals to intuition is that intuitive claims are taken to have a dialectical justification that is broadly noninferential" (537). This is not necessarily far from the view of Cappelen (2012), who holds that what matters about the crucial premises in thought experiment arguments is not so much their intuitiveness, but their being in the common ground.

This observation matches a view that has been defended for thought experiments in the sciences (Gendler 2000; Kühne 2005; Cohnitz 2006). These authors argue that thought experiments are best analysed when considered in the dialectical context in which they were presented. They also emphasize that considering a thought experiment in its dialectical context provides us with the constraints a hypothetical scenario has to satisfy in order for it to constitute a relevant counterexample. Moreover, this perspective on thought experiments enables us to understand the very point of thought experimentation: why scientists use an imaginary *concrete* or particular case in their argumentation. The idea is that a thought experiment manages to present a case for which a certain judgment is in the common ground between all parties to the debate, even though no generalization of that judgment is available (at the time) that would likewise be in the common ground. For example, as Tamar Gendler (2000) argued, in his famous falling bodies thought experiment Galileo Galilei would have needed a claim like "Entification is not physically determined" in order to argue with general premises against the Aristotelian. However, there would have been various ways for the Aristotelian to avoid accepting such a claim. On the other hand, for the concrete case of a cannon ball chained to a musket ball there is no room to claim that how tightly they are connected (and thus, whether you should consider them as one physical body or two) will matter for how they fall. That this was true for this concrete case was in the common ground – although the general principle was not.

Something similar can be said for some philosophical thought experiments. Consider Frank Jackson's thought experiment with Mary the colour scientist again. For the concrete case it is in the common ground (for most participants to the debate) that Mary learns something new, when seeing the red tomato for the first time. On the other hand, it is safe to assume that no general premise establishing learnability of something new despite full knowledge of physical details would have been dialectically accessible to Jackson (cf. Cohnitz 2006). Again this would explain why Jackson chooses to argue with a thought experiment in the first place. We believe that it is here that metaphilosophy could gain important insights from philosophy of science, further clarifying the dialectical function of thought experimentation.

Acknowledgements

Sören Häggqvist acknowledges support from the Swedish Research Council (grant 421-2012-1004).

Notes

[1] On an alternative interpretation, the debate between Cappelen and the experimental philosophers is not confused about which thought experiments should matter for settling the dispute about whether intuitions play a role in philosophy, but Cappelen just (falsely) believes that all thought experiments function as puzzles.

2 It is not clear why Williamson here talks of arguments *underlying* thought experiments; it would seem more natural to say that certain arguments are based on certain experiments. But quibbles about directional metaphors need not detain us here.
3 It does not quite say this, a point we will return to shortly. Williamson discusses the merits of (ii)$_w$ at some length (2007, 195–9).
4 He also hints at domain restriction, but notes its limits as remedy (2007, 200). Cf. Ichikawa (2009, 437 and 440–2).
5 Deviance considerations also appear to lead Williamson to reject $\forall x \forall p(GC(x,p) \Box\!\!\rightarrow (JTB(x,p) \& K\neg(x,p)))$ as unviable (see Williamson 2007, 196–7).
6 For example, in a Sherlock Holmes story it will be safe to assume that the standard laws of nature and biology hold (at least to the extent they were known to the author of the story); on the other hand, when reading a fantasy novel this is not safe to assume.
7 And, at least for linguistics, the empirical assumptions seems not to hold, as is argued in Culbertson and Gross (2009).
8 Cappelen (2012) briefly discusses the issue in his work, and dismisses it by shifting the burden of proof to the other side.
9 As Ole Koksvik (2013) argues in his work, a judgment that is intuitively true can be arrived at through conscious reasoning. But its intuitiveness might still be what determines its evidential status, and an author might describe a reasoning-route towards the judgment to help others see the truth of the judgment.
10 Jackson (1998, 48) uses the labels "A-extension" and "C-extension" respectively.
11 This is perforce sketchy. For a fuller exposition of two-dimensionalism's modal epistemology, as well as elaborations of it, see especially Chalmers (1996, 2002).
12 Ichikawa and Jarvis (2012, 135) explicitly reject two-dimensionalism. Although its commitments are weaker, however, their proposal retains the element under discussion here. The strategy of invoking conceivability, broadly speaking, informed by or conjoined with a posteriori knowledge of the world is of course exemplified by many more accounts, including ones as diverse as Armstrong (1989) and Yablo (1993).
13 And even logic is not a completely neutral arbiter either (cf. Williamson 2014).

References

Armstrong, D. (1989) *A Combinatorial Theory of Possibility*, Cambridge: Cambridge University Press.
Brown, J. R. (1986) "Thought experiments since the scientific revolution," *International Studies in the Philosophy of Science* 1: 1–15.
Brown, J. R. (1991a) *The Laboratory of the Mind: Thought Experiments in the Natural Sciences*, London: Routledge.
Brown, J. R. (1991b) "Thought experiments: A platonic account," in *Thought Experiments in Science and Philosophy*, edited by T. Horowitz and G. Massey, New York: Rowman and Littlefield.
Brown, J. R. (2004a) "Why thought experiments transcend empiricism," in *Contemporary Debates in Philosophy of Science*, edited by C. Hitchcock, Malden: Blackwell.
Brown, J. R. (2004b) "Peeking into Plato's heaven," *Philosophy of Science* 71: 1126–1138.
Cappelen, H. (2012) *Philosophy without intuitions*, Oxford: Oxford University Press.
Chalmers, D. (1996) *The Conscious Mind*, Oxford: Oxford University Press.
Chalmers, D. (2002) "Does conceivability entail possibility?" in *Conceivability and Possibility*, edited by T. S. Gendler and J. Hawthorne, Oxford: Oxford University Press.
Chalmers, D. (2014) "Intuitions in philosophy: A minimal defense," *Philosophical Studies* 171: 535–544.
Cohnitz, D. (2006) *Gedankenexperimente in der Philosophie*, Paderborn: Mentis.
Cohnitz, D. (2012) "Review of Herman Cappelen: *Philosophy without Intuition* (OUP 2012)," *Disputatio* 33: 546–553.
Cohnitz, D. and Haukioja, J. (2015) "Intuitions in philosophical semantics," *Erkenntnis* 80: 617–641.
Culbertson, J. and Gross, S. (2009) "Are linguists better subjects?" *British Journal for Philosophy of Science* 60: 721–736.
Deutsch, M. (2015) *The Myth of the Intuitive*, Cambridge: The MIT Press.

Devitt, M. (2006) "Intuitions in linguistics," *British Journal for the Philosophy of Science* 57: 481–513.
Devitt, M. (2011) "Experimental semantics," *Philosophy and Phenomenological Research* 82: 418–435.
Devitt, M. (2012) "Whither experimental semantics?" *Theoria* 27: 5–36.
Gendler, T. (2000) *Thought Experiments: On the Power and Limits of Imaginary Cases*, London: Routledge.
Hacking, I. (1992) "Do thought experiments have a life of their own? Comments on James Brown, Nancy Nersessian and David Gooding," *PSA: Proceedings of the Biennial Meeting of the Philosophy of Science Association* 1992: 302–308.
Häggqvist, S. (1996) *Thought Experiments in Philosophy*, Stockholm: Almqvist and Wiksell International.
Ichikawa, J. (2009) "Knowing the intuition and knowing the counterfactual," *Philosophical Studies* 145: 435–443.
Ichikawa, J. and Jarvis, B. (2009) "Thought-experiment intuitions and truth in fiction," *Philosophical Studies* 142: 221–246.
Ichikawa, J. and Jarvis, B. (2012) "Rational imagination and modal knowledge," *Noûs* 46: 127–158.
Jackson, F. (1982) "Epiphenomenal qualia," *Philosophical Quarterly* 32: 127–136.
Jackson, F. (1998) *From Metaphysics to Ethics*, Oxford: Oxford University Press.
Jackson, F. (2009) "Thought experiments and possibilities," *Analysis Reviews* 69: 100–109.
Koksvik, O. (2013) "Intuition and conscious reasoning," *Philosophical Quarterly* 63: 709–715.
Kühne, U. (2005) *Die Methode des Gedankenexperiments*, Frankfurt: Suhrkamp.
Langkau, J. (forthcoming) "Metaphilosophy and the role of intuitions."
Machery, E. (2012) "Expertise and intuitions about reference," *Theoria* 73: 37–54.
Machery, E., Mallon, R., Nichols, S. and Stich, S. (2004) "Semantics, cross-cultural style," *Cognition* 92: B1–B12.
Mallon, R., Machery, E., Nichols, S. and Stich, S. (2009) "Against arguments from reference," *Philosophy and Phenomenological Research* LXXIX: 332–356.
Malmgren, A.-S. (2011) "Rationalism and the content of intuitive judgments," *Mind* 120: 263–327.
Norton, J. (1991) "Thought experiments in Einstein's work," in *Thought Experiments in Science and Philosophy*, edited by T. Horowitz and G. Massey, New York: Rowman and Littlefield.
Norton, J. D. (1996) "Are thought experiments just what you thought?" *Canadian Journal of Philosophy* 26: 333–366.
Norton, J. D. (2004a) "Why thought experiments do not transcend empiricism," in *Contemporary Debates in Philosophy of Science*, edited by C. Hitchcock, Malden: Blackwell.
Norton, J. D. (2004b) "On thought experiments: Is there more to the argument?" *Philosophy of Science* 71: 1139–1151.
Sorensen, R. A. (1992) *Thought Experiments*, Oxford: Oxford University Press.
Thomson, J. J. (1985) "The trolley problem," *The Yale Law Journal* 94: 1395–1415
Weinberg, J. (2007) "How to challenge intuitions empirically without risking skepticism," *Midwest Studies in Philosophy* 30: 318–343.
Weinberg, J., Nichols, S. and Stich, S. (2001) "Normativity and epistemic intuitions," *Philosophical Topics* 29: 429–460.
Williamson, T. (2005) "Armchair philosophy, metaphysical modality and counterfactual thinking," *Proceedings of the Aristotelian Society* 105: 1–23.
Williamson, T. (2007) *The Philosophy of Philosophy*, Malden: Blackwell.
Williamson, T. (2009) "Replies to Ichikawa, Martin and Weinberg," *Philosophical Studies* 145: 465–476.
Williamson, T. (2013) "How deep is the distinction between a priori and a posteriori knowledge?," in *The A Priori in Philosophy*, edited by A. Casullo and J. Thurow, Oxford: Oxford University Press.
Williamson, T. (2014) "Logic, metalogic, and neutrality," *Erkenntnis* 79: 211–231.
Yablo, S. (1993) "Is conceivability a guide to possibility," *Philosophy and Phenomenological Research* 53: 1–42.

23
HISTORICISM AND CROSS-CULTURE COMPARISON

James W. McAllister

1 Thought experiment: what, where, how

This chapter looks at three issues. It investigates the identity conditions of thought experiment: under which conditions does a methodological device count as thought experiment and when should we regard a device as something else, even if it resembles thought experiment? Second, it inquires where and when thought experiment is practised: in which philosophical and scientific discourses does the practice of thought experiment occur? Third, it considers the conditions under which thought experiment carries weight: in which contexts and on which presuppositions does thought experiment acquire evidential significance, and where is it evidentially inert? The aim is to problematize the category of thought experiment and its application in different historical and cultural contexts.

Let us start with the third issue. Evidential significance is the power of a methodological device to decide – conclusively or tentatively, on its own or with other factors – controversies in evidence-based discourses, such as philosophy and science. When a controversy arises in such a discourse, members attempt to resolve it by adducing factors that have evidential significance. This works straightforwardly when the same factors have evidential significance for all participants; in other cases, participants will differ about the evidential significance of factors as well as about the resolution of the controversy.

Which factors have evidential significance in philosophy and science, and how do they come to have it? There are two main ways of tackling this question. On a logicist approach, factors have or lack evidential significance intrinsically. This means that a factor – whether this is divination, intuition, mathematical proof or experiment – has or lacks evidential significance as a matter of objective, timeless fact, irrespective of intellectual and cultural context. If some participant does not accept the persuasiveness of a factor that has evidential significance, on this view, the sole possible explanation is that he or she is mistaken.

On a historicist approach, by contrast, evidential significance is a historical attainment: a factor has or lacks evidential significance not intrinsically, but only by virtue of certain assumptions and in certain contexts. A particular factor acquires evidential significance at a historical time by the efforts of members of a discourse: members of other discourses, who do not subscribe to the relevant assumptions, may legitimately deny it evidential significance.

2 Learning from experiment

To illustrate the logicist and historicist approaches to evidential significance, let us consider concrete experiment in science. Many writers take the logicist approach, portraying experiment as having evidential significance intrinsically. For example, Allan Franklin and Slobodan Perović (2015) write, "Physics, and natural science in general, ... provides us with knowledge of the physical world, and it is experiment that provides the evidence that grounds this knowledge." This simple statement encapsulates the view that experiment has evidential significance self-evidently, in all contexts and historical periods, and irrespective of background assumptions.

The historicist approach, by contrast, holds that experiment has evidential significance only under assumptions such as the following: the object of scientific knowledge is regularities that underlie appearances, rather than nature in its full variety, and occurrences produced by human intervention in the unnatural and isolated setting of the laboratory are a trustworthy guide to these regularities. These assumptions are neither self-evidently true nor universally endorsed. This means that experiment has evidential significance only in certain contexts and historical periods.

History and social studies of science provide support for this view. First, science in different disciplines and historical periods has been practised in different epistemic genres or regimes, sometimes called "styles" or "ways of knowing" (Crombie 1994; Pickstone 2000; Kwa 2011). In some of these, such as John V. Pickstone's "natural history," experiment has carried no weight. More specifically, experiment gained evidential significance in European natural philosophy in the late sixteenth and early seventeenth centuries thanks to the persuasive efforts of some practitioners and against the objections of others (Shapin and Schaffer 1985, 3–21; Dear 2009, 127–44; Anstey 2014). Indeed, some seventeenth-century English writers called their new science "experimental philosophy" to distinguish it from earlier practices, which did not rely on experiment (Anstey 2005).

The logicist and historicist views have implications also for two further questions: what counts as experiment, and where and when is experiment practised? Because logicists believe that experiment has evidential significance irrespective of context, they expect all inquirers to use it, and they are quick to categorize empirical trials throughout history as instances of experiment.

On the historicist view, by contrast, experiment is a particular form of empirical trial, underpinned by assumptions that attribute evidential significance to it. If an empirical trial in history does not belong to a discourse that endorses these assumptions, it does not count as an instance of experiment, even if it resembles experiment in involving manipulation or control. This means that we will find experiment only in specific cultural contexts, historical periods, and branches of science.

For an illustration, let us look at the debate on ancient Greek science. Most historians have accepted the logicist assumption that experiment had evidential significance as much for ancient Greeks as for present-day natural scientists. They have argued only about whether the ancient Greeks used experiment a lot, in which case their science was good, or a little, in which case it was poor (Lloyd 1991, 70).

A historicist view offers, I believe, a more sensitive reconstruction. The ancient Greeks did not share the systematic and elaborate epistemological and methodological assumptions that, from the sixteenth and seventeenth centuries onwards, have attributed evidential significance to what we call "experiment." It is implausible that the ancient Greeks engaged in a practice that lacked evidential significance for them. We should therefore conclude that, whereas the ancient Greeks carried out empirical trials sporadically, these did not amount to a practice and culture of experimentation. In short, the ancient Greeks did not do experiment. This finding does not disqualify their science, of course: they may still have practised good science in a distinct style, attributing evidential significance to empirical procedures other than experiment.

As Edward Grant has concluded, "Science in the late ancient and medieval periods was ... radically different from modern science. Although some interesting experiments were carried out, they were relatively rare occurrences and certainly did not constitute a recognized aspect of scientific activity ... The experimental method did not yet exist" (Grant 2004, 24) – though a more generic term than "experiments," such as "empirical trials," in the second sentence might have better served his point.

3 How thought experiment gained evidential significance

I have advocated extending the historicist view of evidential significance to thought experiment. On this view, thought experiment has evidential significance not intrinsically, but only by virtue of certain metaphysical and epistemological assumptions. This opens new questions about the practice of thought experiment. The first is, when and how did thought experiment acquire evidential significance?

I have suggested that thought experiment acquired evidential significance in European philosophy and science in the sixteenth and seventeenth centuries in the same historical process that attributed evidential significance to concrete experiment (see McAllister 1996, 2004, 2005 for details and references). Let us follow this development in the work of Galileo Galilei, one of the pioneers of thought experiment.

Aristotelian natural philosophy was largely a programme to gain knowledge about nature as it naturally manifested itself – in its full variety and without human intervention. Its preferred source of empirical evidence was, correspondingly, observation of natural occurrences. Inspired by Pythagoreanism and Platonism, by contrast, Galileo came to believe that nature partly revealed – and partly masked – structures that characterized the world more deeply than natural occurrences did and that scientific knowledge was knowledge of these underlying structures rather than of natural occurrences.

Galileo conjectured that every natural occurrence was the resultant of one or more phenomena and a great number of accidents. Phenomena were universal and stable modes in which physical reality was articulated and accounted for the underlying uniformities of the world. Accidents, by contrast, were local, variable, and irreproducible, and were responsible for the great variability of natural occurrences. Mechanics, for Galileo, aimed to identify phenomena and describe them in laws of nature: no scientific knowledge of accidents was possible in his view.

What sources of evidence could Galileo use? Since natural occurrences reflected to a large degree the influence of accidents, they failed to support Galileo's laws. Galileo therefore proposed to withdraw evidential significance in mechanics from observations of natural occurrences, and to vest it in new sources of evidence that, he believed, better revealed phenomena. These were occurrences in which the influence of accidents was kept as small as possible, allowing the underlying phenomenon to show through more clearly. Any such occurrence, of course, would have to be produced artificially, by reducing the magnitude of irregularities and perturbations in the apparatus used. Galileo called such a contrived occurrence "experiment."

In some cases, this strategy yielded the desired result. As Galileo would have said, his experiments produced occurrences that were determined to only a small degree by accidents, and therefore displayed the properties of a phenomenon. In other cases, however, it proved impossible to reduce the influence of accidents sufficiently to exhibit a phenomenon clearly. Distinct performances of an experiment in these cases yielded different outcomes, indicating that accidents had substantially determined the occurrences. Galileo was aware that, in these cases, no concrete experiment that he could perform would convincingly establish a law of nature.

Galileo devised thought experiment, I have suggested, as a source of evidence about phenomena where all feasible concrete experiment exhibited this shortcoming. Thought experiment represented a continuation of the process of reducing accidents until the entire, imperfect physical apparatus had been eliminated. With the abstract experimental apparatus that remained, Galileo could at last be certain that accidents no longer masked the phenomenon. This explains why Galileo, in the case of some phenomena, withdrew from the sphere of sense data and sought knowledge about the world in thought experiment rather than in concrete experiment.

In summary, I have claimed that thought experiment gained evidential significance in Galileo's work by virtue of the following assumptions: science aims at identifying and describing "phenomena," or universal and stable modes in which the world is articulated; natural occurrences – and in some cases even concrete experiments – display phenomena only imperfectly; and pure thought can grasp phenomena where concrete experiment fails. In domains and styles of science that take these assumptions to hold, thought experiment acquires evidential significance: it makes sense to seek to establish and undermine claims by thought experiment. Where these assumptions are not endorsed, thought experiment is evidentially inert.

4 Logicist view of thought experiment

Most writers about thought experiment, by contrast, take a logicist view of evidential significance: they think that thought experiment has evidential significance intrinsically. They think that everyone in the history of science was bound to recognize thought experiment as persuasive.

For example, James Robert Brown, who holds that thought experiment yields a priori knowledge of laws of nature, has written that Galileo's thought experiment on free fall self-evidently discredited Aristotle's account and established that the rate of fall of bodies was independent of their weight (J. R. Brown 2011, 99–100). John D. Norton, who thinks that thought experiment is argument with picturesque premises, has agreed that Aristotelian natural philosophers must have accepted Galileo's thought experiment as a source of evidence, especially since, he has claimed, "Thought experiments appear throughout Aristotle's corpus" (Norton 2004, 1149).

Historical evidence casts doubt on this view, however. Galileo's Aristotelian interlocutors did not share Galileo's assumptions about the aims and methods of science. They saw the aim of science as knowledge about nature in its natural state, and, correspondingly, they vested evidential significance in observations of natural occurrences. Since they did not attribute evidential significance to it, they found thought experiment pointless.

This is why, when Galileo advanced a thought experiment, his Aristotelian interlocutors responded mostly not with an alternative thought experiment, but with observations of natural occurrences. For example, in his argument for Copernicanism, Galileo presented a thought experiment in which an object dropped from the crow's nest of a moving ship landed at the foot of the mast (Galilei [1632] 1953, 141–5). Aristotelian natural philosophers countered with actual observations of objects dropped from ship's masts under natural circumstances. In treatises of 1631 and 1634, Libert Froidmont, a professor at the University of Louvain, described the observations of Jean Gallé, a military engineer: "On the Adriatic Sea, Gallé let fall, from the top of the main mast of a Venetian galley, a lead mass: the mass did not fall at the foot of the mast, but deviated towards the stern, thus providing for Ptolemy's followers the appearance of a verification of their doctrine" (De Waard 1937, 74). Scipione Chiaramonti and Giovanni Barenghi, in treatises of 1633 and 1638, respectively, and Bonaventura Belluto and Bartolomeo Mastri, in their 1640 commentary on Aristotle's *De caelo*, cited the testimony of Ioannis Kottounios, a professor at the University of Padua, that a rock had fallen aft of the mast (Finocchiaro 2010, 96; Grant 1984, 41).

Logicists, for whom thought experiment has evidential significance intrinsically, would say that these writers refused to face the evidence that Galileo presented. A better explanation, I think, is that thought experiment lacked force for them because they rejected the assumptions of Galilean science that attributed evidential significance to it.

The historicist view raises also the questions, what counts as thought experiment and where do we find it? Logicists expect thinkers in all contexts and historical periods to make use of thought experiment. They therefore identify as thought experiment many methodological devices found in antiquity and the Middle Ages.

For example, Deborah Levine Gera (2000) has suggested that the *Dissoi Logoi* (fifth–early fourth centuries BCE), a compilation of sophist writings, used thought experiment to investigate the acquisition of knowledge and moral values, and that ancient Greek thinkers may have turned to mental experiment because they had no propensity for concrete experiment. Katerina Ierodiakonou has credited Archytas of Tarentum (fourth century BCE) with "the first recorded thought experiment, the ancient thought experiment of the man who stands at the edge of the universe extending his hand or his stick" (Ierodiakonou 2011, 37). Ierodiakonou (2005) has described the "ship of Theseus" example, first recorded by Plutarch (first century CE), as a further thought experiment. G. E. R. Lloyd (2013, 441) has listed thought experiment among the forms of reasoning and argument most frequently found in both ancient Greece and China.

Scholars have been similarly quick to identify thought experiment in medieval philosophy. Mikko Yrjönsuuri (1996) has interpreted *obligatio* – a disputation format used in the thirteenth and fourteenth centuries to analyse propositions – as thought experiment. Thomas Dewender (2006) has identified arguments *secundum imaginationem*, some of which were attempts to gauge what God, in his infinite power, could achieve, with thought experiment. Lastly, Carla Rita Palmerino has written that many medieval thinkers, such as Nicole Oresme (fourteenth century), used the device. To establish that the four elements were not intrinsically heavy or light, for example,

> Oresme makes use of an interesting thought experiment. He argues that if a pipe extending from the centre of the earth to the heavens were filled with fire except for a very small amount of air at the top, the air would descend; if instead the pipe were filled with water except for some air near the centre of the earth, the air would mount up to the heavens.
>
> (Palmerino 2011, 114)

Such examples, according to Palmerino, showed that thought experiment pre-dated Galileo.

The claim that writers in a wide variety of contexts over 2,500 years have used what we now call "thought experiment" is implausible, I suggest, especially if thought experiment derived from an experimental tradition that arose 400 years ago. None of these cases formed part of the project of apprehending fundamental structures that underlay – and were partly masked by – appearances. In short, none was an instance of the device of thought experiment for which Galileo provided the theoretical underpinning. The cited cases, from the *Dissoi Logoi* to Oresme, are better regarded as inferences from hypothetical or counterfactual premises, familiar to Aristotelian logic and dialectics.

Just as the category of experiment is narrower than that of empirical trial, and it is preferable to reserve it for the practice that arose in European natural philosophy in the sixteenth and seventeenth centuries, so the category of thought experiment is more specific than that of imaginative inference, and it is prudent to reserve it for the practice that Galileo and others developed in the same period.

5 Limits of thought experiment: an example

Even today, thought experiment has evidential significance in some settings and lacks it elsewhere. Let us take the discipline of history as an example.

Historians practise their discipline in two different forms: as a nomothetic and as an idiographic discipline (Malewski and Topolski 2011). Historians who take the nomothetic approach presuppose that causal regularities, which may be partly confounded by contingent circumstances, underlie historical events. History proceeds largely by identifying and explaining these causal regularities, in some cases by means of lawlike relations. In short, nomothetic history endorses something akin to the Galilean doctrine of phenomena. Much economic, demographic, strategic, and military history takes this form.

Thought experiment has evidential significance in nomothetic history. The assumption of underlying regularities allows the historian to hypothesize the alternate development that would have ensued from non-actual starting points – often called "what if?" scenarios. The historian may thereby gauge the causal contribution or historical significance of actual events.

An early example was the investigation by Robert W. Fogel (1964) of the impact of railways on US economic development. Fogel supposed that, even if the railway had not been invented, economic regularities – the law of supply and demand, say – would have continued to hold. This allowed Fogel to conjecture how the US economy would have grown in the absence of railways, concluding that their effect was surprisingly modest. All other commonly discussed examples of thought experiment or, more broadly, of counterfactual reasoning in history lie similarly in economic, demographic, strategic or military history (Tetlock, Lebow, and Parker 2006).

Historians who take the idiographic approach, by contrast, regard human acts as creative and as irreducible to patterns: as a consequence, they conceive history as a sequence of unique and contingent events. Idiographic history, thus, does not endorse anything resembling the Galilean doctrine of phenomena, or of universal invariances that underlie occurrences. Most cultural and intellectual history, including literary and art history, takes this form.

Thought experiment has no force in idiographic history. Imagining, say, how twentieth-century art would have developed if impressionism had not arisen would not yield any informative conclusions for an art historian: the question has no determinate answer in an idiographic discipline. This is because the idiographic approach posits no underlying historical regularities that operate in all alternate scenarios: the sequence of contingent actual events is all that there is. This explains why historians of literature and of art do not use thought experiment to justify claims about their object of study.

Because most recent philosophical discussions of thought experiment in history (De Mey and Weber 2003; Reiss 2009) have neglected the idiographic form of the discipline, they have inadvertently lent credence to the logicist view that thought experiment occurs and has evidential significance everywhere.

6 Responses to thought experiment across cultures: experimental studies

We may pose the questions that motivate this chapter also in an intercultural connection: do all cultures have thought experiment, or is thought experiment evidentially inert in some cultures? One approach is to investigate how people raised in different cultures respond to typical instances of thought experiment (this section). Another is to consider whether we should classify appeals to imaginative scenarios made in various cultures as thought experiment (next section).

Richard E. Nisbett (2003) suggested that culture partly shaped cognition: East Asians tended to think holistically, dialectically, and on the basis of their experience, whereas Westerners thought analytically, logically, and abstractly. For example, Nisbett claimed, Easterners dealt with contradiction dialectically, trying to reconcile opposites, whereas Westerners chose one side over the other. Ara Norenzayan, Edward E. Smith, Beom Jun Kim, and Nisbett (2002) reported that Chinese and Korean students at the University of Michigan relied on intuitive cognitive strategies more than European Americans, who preferred formal reasoning. Such findings suggested that there existed specifically Chinese thinking styles (Ji, Lee, and Guo 2010): if so, Western thought experiments, which often turn on abstraction, intuition, and contradiction, might lead Chinese thinkers to different conclusions, or to no conclusion at all.

This work has attracted criticism on both methodological and empirical grounds. Lloyd (2007, 160–4) has objected to stereotyping diverse populations as "Asians" and "Westerners." Adam B. Cohen (2009) has criticized cultural psychology for considering only cultures on the continental scale. Several writers have presented data suggesting that Easterners and Westerners showed no systematic cognitive differences and that both could use holistic or analytic thinking as context demanded (Lee and Johnson-Laird 2006; Mercier 2011). More specifically, Sara J. Unsworth and Douglas L. Medin (2005) found no cultural difference in preferences for intuitive versus formal reasoning, and Hugo Mercier et al. (2015) none in dealing with contradiction.

Writers in experimental philosophy have pursued similar lines. Some have presented empirical findings that people raised in different cultures had differing philosophical intuitions. They have argued that these findings cast doubt on traditional or "armchair" analytic philosophy, since this relied on intuitions as evidence. Other writers have denied that these findings troubled traditional analytic philosophy, either because intuitions have never served as evidence in analytic philosophy (Deutsch 2015) or because the empirical findings failed to show that intuitions were unreliable evidence (Boyd and Nagel 2014).

In at least three cases, the discussion has focused on thought experiments that analytic philosophers have used to elicit intuitions. First, epistemologists since Edmund L. Gettier (1963) have relied on thought experiment to ground a distinction between knowledge and accidentally true belief. Citing as inspiration Nisbett's early work on East–West differences in thinking, Jonathan M. Weinberg, Shaun Nichols, and Stephen Stich surveyed Rutgers University students. They reported that, while a large majority of students of European ancestry made the orthodox distinction in Gettier cases, a majority of students of East and South Asian descent accepted accidental true belief as knowledge: "If these results are robust, then it seems that what counts as knowledge on the banks of the Ganges does not count as knowledge on the banks of the Mississippi!" (Weinberg, Nichols, and Stich 2001, 444). The authors concluded that the thought experiments on which epistemologists since Gettier have depended in these cases were an unreliable source of evidence. More recently, however, other researchers have found that East and South Asian and Western subjects were equally likely to make the orthodox distinction in Gettier cases (Nagel, San Juan, and Mar 2013; Turri 2013; Seyedsayamdost 2015; Kim and Yuan 2015; Machery et al. 2015). If anything, therefore, experimental philosophy seems to have delivered empirical evidence that epistemic intuitions are culturally invariant.

Second, philosophers of language since the 1970s have used thought experiment to probe intuitions about reference. Edouard Machery, Ron Mallon, Nichols, and Stich (2004) reported that East Asian speakers of Cantonese tended to have descriptivist intuitions about the referents of proper names, while Western speakers of English tended to have causal-historical intuitions. Again, though, there has been methodological criticism (Ludwig 2007) and replication attempts have yielded mixed results (Lam 2010; Sytsma, Livengood, Sato, and Oguchi 2015).

Third, moral philosophers since the 1960s have cited "trolley dilemma" thought experiments as evidence that there was a morally significant difference between causing and allowing harm. Patricia O'Neill and Lewis Petrinovich (1998) found no difference in the responses of Taiwanese and US students to these thought experiments. Other researchers have reported that the responses of Russian, American, and British subjects were more utilitarian than those of Chinese subjects (Ahlenius and Tännsjö 2012; Gold, Colman, and Pulford 2014).

If the findings of earlier sections of this chapter are correct, then thought experiment, even in Western culture, has force in some discourses but not in others. In this light, rather than compare the responses of Western and Asian subjects to a given thought experiment, it would seem more productive for experimental philosophy to inquire in which specific discourses in both Western and Asian cultures thought experiment has evidential significance and on what presuppositions it acquired that significance.

7 Does thought experiment occur in Indian and Chinese culture?

There is a long tradition of hypothetical and imaginative reasoning in both Indian and Chinese culture. Several writers in Anglo-American philosophy have used the category of thought experiment to classify such reasoning. The question, however, is whether the identification of these forms of reasoning with thought experiment is warranted or a misleading representation of a discourse in terms taken from a radically different tradition.

Let us start with treatments of knowledge in traditional Indian texts. Sriharsa (twelfth century) discussed the case of a person who mistook fog for smoke and then inferred the presence of fire, where there really was fire. Sriharsa concluded that "true awareness" was not sufficient for knowledge and that a further condition, "produced by a faithful cause," was required. Gaṅgeśa, the founder of the Nyaya school (twelfth–thirteenth century), discussed the case of a mistaken liar who, while trying to deceive a listener, uttered the truth. Gaṅgeśa suggested that, as long as the listener had no indication that the speaker was a habitual liar, he or she would gain knowledge from the utterance. Other members of the Nyaya school disagreed, holding that the mistaken liar was not a reliable testifier. In their histories of Indian philosophy, Bimal Krishna Matilal (1986, 135–40; 1990, 70) and Jonardon Ganeri (1999, 70, 77–78; 2007, 133–40) have interpreted these passages as Gettier cases *avant la lettre*. Stephen H. Phillips (2012, 12–13) has treated several further texts of the Nyaya school as Gettier cases.

Joseph Shieber has classified Gaṅgeśa's discussion of the mistaken liar as thought experiment. He cited the disagreement within the Nyaya school in his critique of experimental philosophy: "Interestingly, this suggests that one needn't have appealed to experimental philosophy to discover that there is disagreement – even among communities of sophisticated, highly trained philosophers – as to the interpretation of thought experiments." He concluded on a positive note, however: "the example of Gangesa suggests that disagreement – even about such core cases – does not in fact invalidate the use of thought experiment in philosophy" (Shieber 2010, 560).

But is it legitimate to regard these passages as thought experiment? Just as Jonathan Stoltz (2007) has cautioned against assuming that Gettier addressed the same issues as earlier Indian writers, so we should beware lest superficial similarities between Indian and Anglo-American forms of philosophical reasoning lead us too quickly to interpret Indian writers as engaging in thought experiment.

The same holds for Chinese culture. Several authors writing in English have applied the category of thought experiment to describe various passages in traditional Chinese moral thinking.

For example, commentators have described as thought experiment several passages in the *Mozi*, the compilation of the doctrines of Mozi (Mo Tzu, fifth century BCE), an early critic of Confucianism. Loy Hui-chieh (2006) has interpreted as thought experiment the passage "Exalting Unity" (*Shang Tong*, chapters 11–13), which opened with a hypothetical scenario in which people lacked any form of social and political authority. Mozi inferred that people in that scenario would hold to a variety of conflicting moralities and, consequently, would live in a state of anarchy (Johnston 2010, 91). Bryan W. Van Norden has characterized the passage "Impartial Caring" (*Jian Ai*, chapters 14–16) as "probably the first use of 'thought experiments' in Chinese philosophy, and perhaps their first use in the world" (Van Norden 2007, 179). Mozi argued there that even a person more concerned for self than for others had reason to value impartial care: such a person, departing on a long journey, would prefer to put his or her family in the care of someone committed to impartial care rather than of a partialist (Johnston 2010, 153). Carine Defoort (2006, 132) has also analysed this passage in terms of thought experiment.

Mengzi (Mencius, fourth century BCE), a Confucian, argued that all humans innately possessed dispositions toward virtuous feelings, including a disposition towards benevolence: "Suppose someone suddenly saw a child about to fall into a well: anyone in such a situation would have a feeling of alarm and compassion – not because one sought to get in good with the child's parents, not because one wanted fame among one's neighbors and friends, and not because one would dislike the sound of the child's cries." (Van Norden 2008, 46). Philip J. Ivanhoe (2000, 19) and Van Norden (2007, 215–18) interpreted this passage as a thought experiment, and one now commonly finds it called a thought experiment in English-language philosophical discussions (Schmidt 2011, 272; Wang and Solum 2013, 117–18; Stępień 2014, 82).

But is it legitimate to say that Mozi and Mengzi used thought experiment? Identifying these passages as thought experiment might be an example of the tendency to appropriate elements of Chinese culture and thought for Western intellectual purposes, against which many writers, such as David L. Hall and Roger T. Ames (1995, 111–79) have warned. We might do more justice to these texts, and preserve their cultural specificity, by refraining from applying to them a category that was first put forward in a very different setting, Galileo's reform of mechanics in seventeenth-century Florence. Even within Western discourses, the category of thought experiment cannot be applied to all instances of imaginative reasoning, or so I have argued above. Of course, if present-day Chinese writers use imaginative and counterfactual reasoning to probe traditional Chinese moral doctrines, this may well count as thought experiment: an example is Yiu-ming Fung (2001, 258–65), who consciously draws on the methodology of Western analytic philosophy.

In sum, I advocate learning from interpretations of the dream accounts that are widespread in Chinese culture (C. T. Brown 1988; Strassberg 2008, 1–47). Zhuangzi's "Dream of the Butterfly" (fourth century BCE; Ziporyn 2009, 21) is a good example. Many translators and commentators have enrolled this dream account in modern Western philosophical concerns, presenting it as an argument for a certain metaphysical or epistemological claim. For example, Han Xiaoqiang has interpreted it as "a skeptical response to Descartes' refutation of skepticism based on his *Cogito, ergo sum* proof" (Han 2009, 1), put forward nearly 2,000 years later. A more sensitive approach, I think, is to regard this dream account as *sui generis*, investigating its nature and place in Chinese thinking without reducing it to

Western philosophical genres and standpoints (Moeller 2004, 44–55; Kohn 2014, 39–43). Adopting the same caution would mean interpreting the passages of Mozi and Mengzi not as thought experiment but as a distinct form of imaginative reasoning.

8 Conclusions

The aim of this chapter was to problematize the category of thought experiment and its application in different historical and cultural contexts. Writers in both history of science and comparative philosophy have been liberal in their use of the category, as we have seen, identifying many forms of reasoning in diverse contexts as instances of thought experiment. I believe that this usage presupposes a logicist view of evidential significance: if thought experiment has evidential significance intrinsically, it is reasonable to suppose that all writers in all settings will find it persuasive, and thus will use the device throughout intellectual history.

In this chapter, I have presented arguments and evidence for an alternative, historicist view of the evidential significance of thought experiment. On this view, thought experiment has evidential significance not intrinsically or everywhere, but only where particular metaphysical and epistemological assumptions have attributed evidential significance to it. Galileo was, I have suggested, the first person to have carried out this attribution of evidential significance: Galileo, we may say, invented thought experiment. Discourses that have descended from Galilean natural philosophy – including much present-day natural science and areas of Anglo-American philosophy that take natural science as their model – have inherited thought experiment as an evidence-bearing factor. In other discourses, by contrast, thought experiment is evidentially inert and is thus not used. These discourses include Western natural philosophy before Galileo, idiographic disciplines, and intellectual traditions distinct from Western philosophy and science. In these discourses, even if a methodological device or argument form resembles thought experiment, we should resist the temptation to call it thought experiment.

The outcome is that the domain of application of the category "thought experiment" is much narrower that we might have expected. I suggest, however, that the historical and cultural specificity and sensitivity that this approach brings more than make up for the loss of apparent breadth.

References

Ahlenius, H. and Tännsjö, T. (2012) "Chinese and Westerners respond differently to the trolley dilemmas," *Journal of Cognition and Culture* 12: 195–201.

Anstey, P. R. (2005) "Experimental versus speculative natural philosophy," in *The Science of Nature in the Seventeenth Century: Patterns of Change in Early Modern Natural Philosophy*, edited by P. R. Anstey and J. A. Schuster, Berlin: Springer.

Anstey, P. R. (2014) "Philosophy of experiment in early modern England: The case of Bacon, Boyle and Hooke," *Early Science and Medicine* 19: 103–132.

Boyd, K. and Nagel, J. (2014) "The reliability of epistemic intuitions," in *Current Controversies in Experimental Philosophy*, edited by E. Machery and E. O'Neill, New York: Routledge.

Brown, C. T. (ed.) (1988) *Psycho-Sinology: The Universe of Dreams in Chinese Culture*, Washington: Woodrow Wilson International Center for Scholars.

Brown, J. R. (2011) *The Laboratory of the Mind: Thought Experiments in the Natural Sciences*, 2nd ed., New York: Routledge.
Cohen, A. B. (2009) "Many forms of culture," *American Psychologist* 64: 194–204.
Crombie, A. C. (1994) *Styles of Scientific Thinking in the European Tradition: The History of Argument and Explanation Especially in the Mathematical and Biomedical Sciences and Arts*, London: Duckworth.
Dear, P. (2009) *Revolutionizing the Sciences: European Knowledge and Its Ambitions, 1500–1700*, 2nd ed., Princeton: Princeton University Press.
Defoort, C. (2006) "The growing scope of *Jian*: Differences between chapters 14, 15 and 16 of the *Mozi*," *Oriens Extremus* 45: 119–140.
De Mey, T. and Weber, E. (2003) "Explanation and thought experiments in history," *History and Theory* 42: 28–38.
Deutsch, M. (2015) *The Myth of the Intuitive: Experimental Philosophy and Philosophical Method*, Cambridge: MIT Press.
De Waard, C. (ed.) (1937) *Correspondance du P. Marin Mersenne. II. 1628–1630*, Paris: Gabriel Beauchesne.
Dewender, T. (2006) "Imaginary experiments (*procedere secundum imaginationem*) in later medieval natural philosophy," in *Intellect et imagination dans la philosophie médiévale*, edited by M. C. Pacheco and J. F. Meirinhos, Turnhout: Brepols.
Finocchiaro, M. A. (2010) "Defending Copernicus and Galileo: Critical reasoning and the ship experiment argument," *Review of Metaphysics* 64: 75–103.
Fogel, R. W. (1964) *Railroads and American Economic Growth: Essays in Econometric History*, Baltimore: Johns Hopkins University Press.
Franklin, A. and Perović, S. (2015) "Experiment in physics," in *Stanford Encyclopedia of Philosophy*, edited by E. N. Zalta, http://plato.stanford.edu/archives/sum2015/entries/physics-experiment (accessed 15 November 2016).
Fung, Y. (2001) "Three dogmas of new Confucianism: A perspective of analytic philosophy," in *Two Roads to Wisdom? Chinese and Analytic Philosophical Traditions*, edited by B. Mou, Chicago: Open Court.
Galilei, G. (1632 [1953]) *Dialogue Concerning the Two Chief World Systems – Ptolemaic and Copernican*, translated by S. Drake, Berkeley: University of California Press.
Ganeri, J. (1999) *Semantic Powers: Meaning and the Means of Knowing in Classical Indian Philosophy*, Oxford: Clarendon Press.
Ganeri, J. (2007) *The Concealed Art of the Soul: Theories of Self and Practices of Truth in Indian Ethics and Epistemology*, Oxford: Oxford University Press.
Gera, D. L. (2000) "Two thought experiments in the *Dissoi Logoi*," *American Journal of Philology* 121: 21–45.
Gettier, E. L. (1963) "Is justified true belief knowledge?" *Analysis* 23: 121–123.
Gold, N., Colman, A. M. and Pulford, B. D. (2014) "Cultural differences in responses to real-life and hypothetical trolley problems," *Judgment and Decision Making* 9: 65–76.
Grant, E. (1984) "In defense of the Earth's centrality and immobility: Scholastic reaction to Copernicanism in the seventeenth century," *Transactions of the American Philosophical Society* 74, Part 4.
Grant, E. (2004) *Science and Religion, 400 B.C. to A.D. 1550: From Aristotle to Copernicus*, Westport, CT: Greenwood Press.
Hall, D. L. and Ames, R. T. (1995) *Anticipating China: Thinking Through the Narratives of Chinese and Western Culture*, Albany: SUNY Press.
Han, X. (2009) "Interpreting the butterfly dream," *Asian Philosophy* 19: 1–9.
Ierodiakonou, K. (2005) "Ancient thought experiments: A first approach," *Ancient Philosophy* 25: 125–140.
Ierodiakonou, K. (2011) "Remarks on the history of an ancient thought experiment," in *Thought Experiments in Methodological and Historical Contexts*, edited by K. Ierodiakonou and S. Roux, Leiden: Brill.
Ivanhoe, P. J. (2000) *Confucian Moral Self Cultivation*, 2nd ed., Indianapolis: Hackett.
Ji, L.-J., Lee, A. and Guo, T. (2010) "The thinking styles of Chinese people," in *The Oxford Handbook of Chinese Psychology*, edited by M. H. Bond, Oxford: Oxford University Press.

Johnston, I. (ed.) (2010) *The Mozi: A Complete Translation*, Hong Kong: Chinese University Press.
Kim, M. and Yuan, Y. (2015) "No cross-cultural differences in the Gettier car case intuition: A replication study of Weinberg et al. 2001," *Episteme* 12: 355–361.
Kohn, L. (2014) *Zhuangzi: Text and Context*, St. Petersburg, FL: Three Pines Press.
Kwa, C. (2011) *Styles of Knowing: A New History of Science from Ancient Times to the Present*, translated by D. McKay, Pittsburgh: University of Pittsburgh Press.
Lam, B. (2010) "Are Cantonese-speakers really descriptivists? Revisiting cross-cultural semantics," *Cognition* 115: 320–329.
Lee, N. Y. L. and Johnson-Laird, P. N. (2006) "Are there cross-cultural differences in reasoning?" in *Proceedings of the 28th Annual Meeting of the Cognitive Science Society*, edited by R. Sun and N. Miyake, Mahwah, NJ: Lawrence Erlbaum.
Lloyd, G. E. R. (1991) *Methods and Problems in Greek Science*, Cambridge: Cambridge University Press.
Lloyd, G. E. R. (2007) *Cognitive Variations: Reflections on the Unity and Diversity of the Human Mind*, Oxford: Clarendon Press.
Lloyd, G. E. R. (2013) "Reasoning and culture in a historical perspective," *Journal of Cognition and Culture* 13: 437–457.
Loy, H. (2006) "On a *Gedankenexperiment* in the *Mozi* core chapters," *Oriens Extremus* 45: 141–158.
Ludwig, K. (2007) "The epistemology of thought experiments: First person versus third person approaches," *Midwest Studies in Philosophy* 31: 128–159.
Machery, E., Mallon, R., Nichols, S. and Stich, S. P. (2004) "Semantics, cross-cultural style," *Cognition* 92: B1–B12.
Machery, E., Stich, S., Rose, D., Chatterjee, A., Karasawa, K., Struchiner, N., Sirker, S., Usui, N. and Hashimoto, T. (2015) "Gettier across cultures," *Noûs*.
Malewski, A. and Topolski, J. (2011) "The nomothetic versus the idiographic approach to history," in *Idealization XIII: Modeling in History*, edited by K. Brzechczyn, Amsterdam: Rodopi.
Matilal, B. K. (1986) *Perception: An Essay on Classical Indian Theories of Knowledge*, Oxford: Clarendon Press.
Matilal, B. K. (1990) *The Word and the World: India's Contribution to the Study of Language*, Delhi: Oxford University Press.
McAllister, J. W. (1996) "The evidential significance of thought experiment in science," *Studies in History and Philosophy of Science* 27: 233–250.
McAllister, J. W. (2004) "Thought experiments and the belief in phenomena," *Philosophy of Science* 71: 1164–1175.
McAllister, J. W. (2005) "The virtual laboratory: Thought experiments in seventeenth-century mechanics," in *Collection, Laboratory, Theater: Scenes of Knowledge in the 17th Century*, edited by H. Schramm, L. Schwarte, and J. Lazardzig, New York: De Gruyter.
Mercier, H. (2011) "On the universality of argumentative reasoning," *Journal of Cognition and Culture* 11: 85–113.
Mercier, H., Zhang, J., Qu, Y., Peng, L. and Van Der Henst, J.-P. (2015) "Do Easterners and Westerners treat contradiction differently?" *Journal of Cognition and Culture* 15: 45–63.
Moeller, H.-G. (2004) *Daoism Explained: From the Dream of the Butterfly to the Fishnet Allegory*, Chicago: Open Court.
Nagel, J., San Juan, V. and Mar, R. A. (2013) "Lay denial of knowledge for justified true beliefs," *Cognition* 129: 652–661.
Nisbett, R. E. (2003) *The Geography of Thought: How Asians and Westerners Think Differently… and Why*, New York: Free Press.
Norenzayan, A., Smith, E. E., Kim, B. J. and Nisbett, R. E. (2002) "Cultural preferences for formal versus intuitive reasoning," *Cognitive Science* 26: 653–684.
Norton, J. D. (2004) "On thought experiments: Is there more to the argument?" *Philosophy of Science* 71: 1139–1151.
O'Neill, P. and Petrinovich, L. (1998) "A preliminary cross-cultural study of moral intuitions," *Evolution and Human Behavior* 19: 349–367.
Palmerino, C. R. (2011) "Galileo's use of medieval thought experiments," in *Thought Experiments in Methodological and Historical Contexts*, edited by K. Ierodiakonou and S. Roux, Leiden: Brill.

Phillips, S. H. (2012) *Epistemology in Classical India: The Knowledge Sources of the Nyaya School*, New York: Routledge.
Pickstone, J. V. (2000) *Ways of Knowing: A New History of Science, Technology and Medicine*, Manchester: Manchester University Press.
Reiss, J. (2009) "Counterfactuals, thought experiments, and singular causal analysis in history," *Philosophy of Science* 76: 712–723.
Schmidt, S. (2011) "Mou Zongsan, Hegel, and Kant: The quest for Confucian modernity," *Philosophy East and West* 61: 260–302.
Seyedsayamdost, H. (2015) "On normativity and epistemic intuitions: Failure of replication," *Episteme* 12: 95–116.
Shapin, S. and Schaffer, S. (1985) *Leviathan and the Air-Pump: Hobbes, Boyle, and the Experimental Life*, Princeton: Princeton University Press.
Shieber, J. (2010) "On the nature of thought experiments and a core motivation of experimental philosophy," *Philosophical Psychology* 23: 547–564.
Stępień, M. (2014) "The relationship between human nature and human rights: The Confucian example," in *Human Rights and Human Nature*, edited by M. Albers, T. Hoffmann, and J. Reinhardt, Dordrecht: Springer.
Stoltz, J. (2007) "Gettier and factivity in Indo-Tibetan epistemology," *Philosophical Quarterly* 57: 394–415.
Strassberg, R. E. (ed.) (2008) *Wandering Spirits: Chen Shiyuan's Encyclopedia of Dreams*, Berkeley: University of California Press.
Sytsma, J., Livengood, J., Sato, R. and Oguchi, M. (2015) "Reference in the land of the rising sun: A cross-cultural study on the reference of proper names," *Review of Philosophy and Psychology* 6: 213–230.
Tetlock, P. E., Lebow, R. N. and Parker, G. (eds) (2006) *Unmaking the West: "What-if?" Scenarios that Rewrite World History*, Ann Arbor: University of Michigan Press.
Turri, J. (2013) "A conspicuous art: Putting Gettier to the test," *Philosophers' Imprint* 13, no. 10: 1–16.
Unsworth, S. J. and Medin, D. L. (2005) "Cultural differences in belief bias associated with deductive reasoning?" *Cognitive Science* 29: 525–530.
Van Norden, B. W. (2007) *Virtue Ethics and Consequentialism in Early Chinese Philosophy*, Cambridge: Cambridge University Press.
Van Norden, B. W. (ed.) (2008) *Mengzi: With Selections from Traditional Commentaries*, Indianapolis: Hackett.
Wang, L. and Solum, L. B. (2013) "Confucian virtue jurisprudence," in *Law, Virtue and Justice*, edited by A. Amaya and H. H. Lai, Oxford: Hart.
Weinberg, J. M., Nichols, S. and Stich, S. (2001) "Normativity and epistemic intuitions," *Philosophical Topics* 29: 429–460.
Yrjönsuuri, M. (1996) "Obligations as thought experiments," in *Studies on the History of Logic*, edited by I. Angelelli and M. Cerezo, Berlin: De Gruyter.
Ziporyn, B. (ed.) (2009) *Zhuangzi: The Essential Writings, with Selections from Traditional Commentaries*, Indianapolis: Hackett.

24
A DIALECTICAL ACCOUNT OF THOUGHT EXPERIMENTS

Jean-Yves Goffi and Sophie Roux

One of the many questions that have been asked about thought experiments is the ontological question concerning what thought experiments are, and more specifically, if they are some sort of experiments – perhaps experiments with specific characteristics, but experiments nonetheless (Mach 1905/1926 149; Sorensen 1992; Buzzoni 2013; Bokulich and Frappier, this volume). After all, if they were not experiments, how could they bring us new genuine knowledge about the world? But, on the other hand, since they are just counterfactual scenarios, how could it make sense to say that they are experiments? Thus, the ontological question of what thought experiments are is entangled with the epistemological question of understanding where the knowledge that they bring may come from and what kind of knowledge exactly they can bring. Without dissociating the ontological question and the epistemological question, we will defend in this chapter a dialectical account of thought experiments.

In order to defend this dialectical account of thought experiments, we will proceed in the following way:

First, starting from a fairly broad characterization of what thought experiments are in general, we will focus on a tension between two of their characteristics, a tension that puts thought experiments in what we will describe as an ontological state of unstable equilibrium.

Second, having interpreted the epistemological debate between James Robert Brown and John Norton in terms of this ontological unstable equilibrium, we will clarify our position in this debate. To put it bluntly, we agree with Norton when he argues against Brown's Platonist positions, but we do not agree with him when he maintains that thought experiments are only arguments in the sense of valid arguments. According to us, scenarios that thought experiments involve always including some kind of opacity that cannot be immediately reduced, thought experiments cannot be assimilated to arguments.

Third, we will argue that, to account for the acquisition of knowledge that is at stake in thought experimenting, one should propose a dialectical account of argumentation.

Finally, we will answer some possible objections.

1 A tension in thought experiments

All thought experiments involve exploring the outcomes of counterfactual scenarios in a cognitive context. Without giving a too strict definition of what a thought experiment is, one should note that thought experiments imply three characteristics (Gendler 2004, 1155; Roux 2011, 19–26):

(i) First, they involve what we just called a scenario. Such scenarios do not concern entire complete possible worlds; they are rather localized variations, most features of the real world being preserved (Hintikka and Hintikka 1989, 75; Häggqvist 1996, 146–7). They involve concrete particulars that are usually weaved in short narratives. Some of these particulars are parts of the argument, but some of them are only a psychological crutch for our imagination. For example, if Gyges' ring thought experiment (see Becker, this volume) can make us think about our motivations when we respect moral norms, it is because there is a device making humans and their actions invisible; whatever this device is, it constitutes so to speak the very bones of this thought experiment, what structures it, and in that sense it is a particular which is essential to the thought experiment. But when Plato tells us that Gyges was a shepherd, who was feeding his flock, when there was a storm, which obliged him to find a shelter in a cave, etc., such particulars do not fundamentally change the thought experiment, they only help us to imagine how it might be that a shepherd comes to possess a magic ring, and in that sense they are inessential, although they help us to consider a story that is not true as relevant and give us reasons to continue with the thought experiment. The distinction between these two kinds of particulars is not always easy to make in practice – to take another example in ethics, many variations were introduced in the Trolley thought experiment initially proposed by Philippa Foot (see Brun, this volume), the outcome of these variations being that what at first sight may have appeared to be inessential particulars turned out to be relevant for our moral judgements. But scenarios are crucial for thought experiments. As we will argue in the second section of this chapter, scenarios involve some kind of opacity and this is the reason why thoughts experiments cannot be reduced to arguments.

(ii) The second characteristic is that the scenarios at stake in thought experiments are counterfactual. As opposed to a real experiment, a thought experiment does not have to take place in reality; rather, it seems that we reach its result merely by thinking, a thought experiment being literally an experiment that happens in thought. Here again, some distinctions can be introduced, because there are different degrees of counterfactuality between zero counterfactuality, which corresponds exactly to reality, and maximal counterfactuality, which deals with metaphysical and logical impossibilities. A weaker counterfactuality might concern thought experiments that are physically possible and that could have been produced in reality considering human ability and technical means available at the time they were proposed. However, they were not carried out for whatever reason: this is, for example, what we see in Galileo's two strapped bodies, the negative part of which can be described as a reductio ad absurdum of the Aristotelian thesis that two bodies of the same material descend in the same medium with speeds proportional to their weights. A stronger counterfactuality involves scenarios which not only did not happen, but which, given our human capacity to intervene in the world and the technical means available at the time they were proposed, could not happen. This was, for example, the case of the EPR thought experiment, at least when it was first proposed in 1935. A stronger counterfactuality still is at stake with Dawkins's thought experiment of rewinding time and playing back history to see if evolution would produce the same results, because it does not depend from technical means (that keep evolving) but make intervene our very concept of time. In the present chapter, we are not interested in the counterfactual aspect of thought experiments.

(iii) Third and last, the scenario is framed with a well-defined cognitive intention in a determined cognitive context. If considered independently of their context, Gyges' adventures could belong to a storybook, to a science-fiction novel or to fantasy literature. But they do not, and this is because Plato had a well-determined cognitive intention concerning ethics in view. He wanted his readers to ask themselves how they would behave if they could perform immoral actions without being discovered and, consequently, without being punished. In a word, Gyges' ring thought experiment plays the role of an argument for Plato, an argument being here, quite generally, what intervenes in a determined cognitive context to make an interlocutor change her mind. Again, distinctions could be introduced. In the case of Gyges' ring thought experiment, Plato made the reader test her capacity to act according to ethical norms even if her bad behaviour would not be punished. But intervening as an argument can amount to other moves: it can, for example, amount to introducing a conceptual distinction, to refuting a usually admitted thesis, to testing a declaration by highlighting a paradox, or even proving a previously unknown result (Sorensen 1992, 135–52). In this chapter, we do not want to dwell on these distinctions, but we are definitively concerned with the notion of an argument. We would like to clarify which notion of an argument is at stake when it is said that a thought experiment intervenes as an argument.

That thought experiments present these three characteristics (involving a scenario, being counterfactual, playing the role of an argument) is in general fairly broadly accepted, at least in the recent philosophical literature (see Bokulich and Frappier, this volume, for more on the identify conditions of thought experiments). But, perhaps because of the stress that was put on the counterfactual aspect of thought experiments, it has not been noticed that the first characteristic and the last one imply that thought experiments are, so to speak, in a state of unstable equilibrium between non-propositional knowledge and propositional knowledge:

On the one hand, thought experiments rely on scenarios in which non-propositional knowledge intervenes. In a former paper, we were led to minimize the importance of the scenario (Goffi and Roux 2011). The point we would like to make in this chapter is that even those particulars that are essential to the scenario are not sufficient to make explicit all the propositions that would be necessary to make a complete argument from a logical point of view. Unlike logical arguments, thought experiments involve scenarios in which non-propositional knowledge intervenes, whether it is called implicit knowledge, tacit knowledge or background knowledge (Gendler 1998, 404–8; Atkinson and Peijnenburg 2004, 121–5).

But, on the other hand, thought experiments are framed with well-determined cognitive intentions and they are used in determined cognitive contexts in which propositional knowledge is important. If the inventor of a thought experiment did not specify why she introduced this or that thought experiment, we could take her thought experiment for a pleasant story to be read before sleeping. Thus, thought experiments are connected to propositional knowledge; the implicit knowledge, tacit knowledge or background knowledge that intervene in the scenarios that they propose is supposed to play the role of premises with regard to a conclusion.

In other words, there is some tension between the non-propositional scenario that a thought experiment involves and the propositional knowledge of the determined cognitive context in which the thought experiment operates. To gain a better grasp of this idea, we can bring experiments and thought experiments closer together. An experiment may intervene in an argumentative context, but is not an argument, simply because it happens that we do experiments without arguing; similarly, a thought experiment intervenes in an argumentative context, but is not an argument for the same reason: it is rather a process that supplies premises for an argument or that consists in unfolding an initial scenario (Sorensen 1992, 214, 230–40; Häggqvist 1996, 87; Bishop 1999; Häggqvist 2009, 61; El Skaf and Imbert 2013). However, the difference between the experiment and the argument that this experiment supports is manifest when one is dealing with a real experiment – even if the experiment is presented in an article or in a book, one assumes that, at some point, a real experiment was actually performed out there and that its outcome could have been something other than what we expected. But the difference between the "experiment" and the argument may be blurred in the case of a thought experiment, because the scenario that the thought experiment describes is not something that happens in reality, but something that unfolds so to speak at the same level as the argument.

To sum up, in the case of a real experiment that intervenes and in the case of a thought experiment, there are two elements, on the one hand a non-propositional element, on the other hand a propositional element. But, while the difference between the two is manifest in the case of a real experiment, it tends to be blurred in the case of thought experiments. This is why thought experiments are, to say it metaphorically, in a state of unstable equilibrium: it is as if a thought experiment was always on the verge of tilting to one side or the other. What we would like to argue next is that this state of unstable equilibrium may throw some light on the epistemological debate between Brown and Norton. To put it in a nutshell, both of them insist on one characteristic of thought experiments to the detriment of the other, and this, because of their background epistemologies.

2 The unstable epistemological equilibrium of thought experiments

As it often happens in contemporary philosophy, the epistemological debate about thought experiments took the form of a choice between two contradictory positions, one of these positions being taken by Brown in his book *The Laboratory of the Mind: Thought Experiments in the Natural Sciences* (1991b [2011]) as well as in a number of other papers where he confronted his views to Norton's, and the other position being taken by Norton, who contributed a paper on Einstein's thought experiments to a volume *Thought Experiments in Science and Philosophy* that was published the same year as Brown's book (1991a; Norton

1991), and then published a number of papers where he contrasted his views to Brown's (2004a, 2004b). The debate between them is prima facie not a debate on what thought experiments are: Brown and Norton rely on the same set of thought experiments and they would probably agree on a working definition of thought experiments. They rather view their dispute as an epistemological debate concerning the source of the epistemic authority of thought experiments.

For Brown, thought experiments consist literally in observing the outcome of a scenario. In this, thought experiments tilt on the side of non-propositional knowledge; but since this non-propositional knowledge does not build on real experiments concerning the actual world perceived with our ordinary faculties, it has to involve another kind of world, perceived with another kind of faculty. As Brown sees it, in "Platonic" thought experiments we are simply "seeing" the universals or "grasping" the relevant law of nature (Brown 1986, 12–13). One would think that we have only metaphors here but, true to Plato, Brown actually thinks that, in contrast with regular experiences where we learn laws empirically, thought experiments give us an intuition of a law of nature, laws being defined as relations among properties (Brown 2004b, 33). Häggqvist has nicely summarized: the magic of Brown's Platonic thought experiments consists in their granting "epistemic progress in the absence of new empirical data" (Häggqvist 2007, 50; for a critical appraisal of Brown's view, see Grundmann in this volume).

Norton denies this kind of epistemic magic. Being an empiricist, he thinks that thought experiments being in thought, they are not real experiments; and that, being not real experiments, they cannot bring us by themselves any kind of new genuine knowledge about the world. Thus, thought experiments have nothing epistemologically remarkable: "thought experiments draw upon what we already know of it, either explicitly or tacitly; they then transform that knowledge by disguised argumentation" (Norton 2004a, 45). In that case, thought experiments tilt on the side of propositional knowledge and standard empiricism is preserved. Norton proposed another justification of his position which he takes to be independent from empiricism: if thought experiments can be used reliably, then they must be arguments that justify their outcomes or reconstructible as such arguments (Norton 2004b, 1143). We are not convinced that this justification is independent from Norton's empiricism; it still presupposes the division of labour between experiments, which give us knowledge, and logic, which transforms this knowledge. But, without discussing further, suffice it to refer to the aphorism that Norton himself introduced to summarize his position: "A good thought experiment is a good argument; a bad thought experiment is a bad argument" (Norton 1991, 131).

We seem to face a dilemma, where a choice is to be made between two positions on thought experiments:

1 Either we consider with Brown that there are at least some thought experiments that give us a kind of exceptionally privileged non-propositional knowledge, and we say that their epistemic authority comes from another source of knowledge than our usual sources of knowledge,
2 Or we assert with Norton that thought experiments having no special epistemic authority, they provide only standard propositional knowledge that comes from our usual sources of knowledge, even if, in their case, this standard propositional knowledge appears in a disguised form.

Being completely satisfied neither with Brown's nor with Norton's view, we would like to consider a new option, one that is not associated to any specific epistemological agenda, whether Platonist or empiricist.

In a previous paper, we followed a suggestion of Nicholas Rescher (Rescher 2005) to try to pinpoint the difference between a thought experiment that fails and a thought experiment that succeeds. We described thought experiments as devices aimed at testing the consistency of a set of beliefs when a new belief is introduced as a consequence of the counterfactual situation pictured in the scenario. In a successful thought experience, the "experimenter" and her audience are able to reach an agreement on the weakest belief and to eliminate it; a thought experiment fails when it cannot do this (Goffi and Roux 2011, 165–91). Such an analysis amounts to considering that thought experimenters proceed by adjusting beliefs and not by "seeing" with the "mind's eye" laws of nature, or moral norms and values (Brown 2004b, 32). In that sense, we are ready to claim with Norton that thought experiments are better reconstructed as arguments. We prefer such a constructivism that conforms to the principle of parsimony to Brown's recourse to Platonic intuitions.

In the present chapter, however, we would like to explain why, contrary to Norton, we do not believe that thought experiments are only arguments in disguise. To claim that thought experiments are not arguments in disguise amounts in a way to stating the obvious: if all that is needed to make a complete argument was already given in a thought experiment, this would no longer be a thought experiment but a logical argument. One can moreover wonder what being an argument in disguise could exactly mean: an argument is explicitly formulated or it is no argument at all. Last, but not least, if thought experiments were disguised arguments, because of what we call the opacity of the scenarios on which they rely, they would be doomed to be poorer than regular arguments.

The notion of "opacity," which is essential to our account, can be introduced with a quote from Sören Häggqvist. Having claimed that the connection between experiments and arguments is that the former supply premises for the latter, Häggqvist explains the differences between regular experiments and thought experiments in the following way:

> In the case of laboratory experiments, this [the supplying of premises] is done by causing observers to hold relevant observation statements true (or false) where the causes are the actual physical goings-on in the laboratory. In the case of thought experiments, it is done by causing thought experimenters – whether inventors or audience – to hold relevant non-observational statements true (or false) where the causes are the actual psychological goings-on in the thought experimenter's heads.
>
> (Häggqvist 1996, 87)

Without going into details about Häggqvist's causal theory of belief, we note that he clearly distinguishes two cognitive contexts: in the first context, experimenters deal with actual observations resulting from publicly accepted procedures; in the second context, experimenters deal with actual psychological goings-on triggered by a scenario. In the first case, one has to deal with an observer and observations; in the second case, one encounters a speaker and its audience. The consequences of the distinction between these two contexts are sweeping: in a thought experiment, much more depends on the narrative than in a regular experiment; more precisely, much more depends on the interpretations that the inventor of the thought experiment and her interlocutors give of a scenario. If a scenario is opaque in general, it is precisely because it allows for different interpretations by different interlocutors. It remains to say how (see Lenhard, this volume, for a different discussion of opacity).

In the first place, there can be different interpretations of the relevance of the scenario with respect to the question asked. In the case of Thomson's violinist, some may believe that the relation between a pregnant woman and her foetus is not adequately captured by the scenario of someone finding herself back to back in bed with an unconscious violinist whose circulatory system has been plugged into hers. According to those dissenters, such a scenario would not have paid enough attention to what is really important in the situation it aimed at describing.

But there can also be different interpretations of the relevance of the scenario with respect to the conclusion that it is supposed to lead to. In the case of Mary the scientist, some may believe that the scenario fails from the start to distinguish between discovering new abilities (knowledge how) and gaining new factual knowledge (knowledge that). According to those, although this scenario clearly points to what is relevant in the situation that it describes, it would lack relevance for the conclusion that is drawn from it.

Finally, a scenario can also be said "opaque" in the sense that some details might be relevant according to the interlocutors, which were not evaluated in the way intended by the inventor of the thought experiment. Bohr famously answered to Einstein's clock-in-the-box that, according to the very theory of relativity discovered by Einstein himself some years earlier, the time as measured by the clock in the box should admit of a minimum level of uncertainty because of the clock's changing position in the gravitational field of the Earth (for more details on the evolution of this thought experiment, see Bokulich and Frappier, this volume). Thus, although Bohr considered the clock-in-the-box as relevant both for the question and the conclusion at stake, he judged that Einstein ignored a relevant detail in the scenario, namely the uncertainty of time implied by his general theory of relativity.

This is not to say that a scenario can never be rescued from being opaque. "Opacity" here is not a kind of mystical obscurity that must remain shrouded in darkness. Something opaque is rather something that calls for a process of clarification, a process that in the case of thought experiments will happen, not through "mental reasoning" or "seeing with the mind's eye," but through actual discussions between interlocutors who disagree. Discussing the possible interpretations and implications of a scenario is thus an important part of the work that the interlocutors perform when they deal with a thought experiment. Sometimes, they will succeed in rescuing the scenario from its initial opacity. But such rescue missions cannot end as long as the thought experiment is a thought experiment; when it is ended, the thought experiment may indeed boil down to a "mere" argument – but then, it is not anymore a thought experiment.

But if, as we argued, the scenarios of thought experiments are opaque, how can we describe the acquisition of knowledge that is at stake in them, without hypothesizing some exceptional faculties as Brown does, and without claiming that thought experiments boil down to arguments, as Norton does? This is the question that we would like to answer in the next section.

3 Steadying the equilibrium: a dialectical account of thought experiments

We think that, in order to describe the acquisition of knowledge that is at stake in thought experiments, a strict epistemological view of argumentation is not sufficient. Rather, we will argue that an enlarged view of argumentation should be adopted. We will dub this enlarged view of argumentation "dialectical." As we will explain in some detail, "dialectics" refers here to the domain that Aristotle wanted to establish between rhetoric and science. But speaking of dialectics is also consonant with another idea that we would like to insist on: from an historical point of view, thought experiments never appeared on the private mental scenes of individuals, but in controversial contexts, where a choice between competing theories was to be made. In such contexts, thought experiments were supposed to help the interlocutors make a choice. But the interpretation of thought experiments was rarely straightforward, both because of the opacity of their scenarios, which is something we explored in the previous section, and because of another kind of opacity that we will explore now: the opacity of the background assumptions involved in the scenarios.

To introduce this new kind of opacity, let us come back to Brown and Norton for a last time. It is to be noted that both of them begin by assuming that there are some thought experiments that are good thought experiments *per se*, independently of the epistemic situations of the thought experimenters. It is only when they want to understand what makes a thought experiment a good thought experiment that some disagreement between them emerges, Brown claims that its epistemic authority comes from a vision of natural laws, Norton says that it comes from the disguised argument that it contains, whether this argument is valid in the case of a deductive argument (if one accepts the premises, one is logically bound to accept the conclusion) or it is at least good enough in the case of an inductive argument (if one accepts the premises, one is logically bound to regard the conclusion as probable).

Our suggestion is rather that we should take into account the epistemic situations of the interlocutors and say that a thought experiment is good when it is successful in rightly convincing one's interlocutor. Even when the opacity of a thought experiment has been reduced, a thought experiment may work or not work. It works when the interlocutors are in such an epistemic situation that they share the same background assumptions and a certain hierarchy of beliefs, so that, when confronted with a putative inconsistency in their beliefs, they will agree to abandon one belief rather than another. On the other hand, if they do not share the same background assumptions or if they disagree on the hierarchy of beliefs, the thought experiment will not work. In our previous paper, we insisted on two such situations:

First, it can happen that thought experiments fail to hit on a set of shared assumptions (Goffi and Roux 2011, 184). This is especially striking in what Norton aptly called thought experiment/anti-thought experiments pairs (Norton 2004a, 45–9). As already noted by others, this is, for example, the case of the two Marys, brilliant scientists who, from birth, were confined to a laboratory, where they had only black and white experiences, but learned everything about colours and colour perception. Mary Jackson experiences something new when she leaves her laboratory and sees red for the first time. Mary Dennett, however, when she leaves her lab, just exclaims: "Ah! Colour perception is just as I thought it would be! This banana should have been yellow, not blue!" But a similar situation might have been the case also for what has usually been considered as successful thought experiments. Galileo's two strapped bodies might have been an unsuccessful thought experiment if Salviati had conversed with an Aristotelian who would have refused the assumption that natural speed is mediative or yet with a physicist who would have been able to take into account the variation of speed with respect to the distance of the earth or the actual medium in which the bodies fall (Atkinson and Peijnenburg 2004). Thomson's violinist might have been an unsuccessful thought experiment if Thomson's interlocutors had disagreed with her from the start, dispensing with the language of rights and arguing instead that life is a gift from God and that one cannot define a proper stance towards foetal life without being responsive to this property and the personal relationship analogies behind the metaphor. In these cases, Salviati and his opponents, as Thomson and her interlocutors, would have failed to find common ground, exactly as did Jackson and Dennett.

Second, it may happen that two speakers agree on a set of background assumptions but do not agree on which proposition should be dropped. In the same paper, we gave the example of a kind of counterfactual argument that is to be found in Aristotle's *Politics* (Goffi and Roux 2011, 185–6). Aristotle began asking the question "what would happen if every tool could perform its own work," but, then, the thought experiment aborts and there is no clear conclusion. We argued that such a failure comes from the fact that Aristotle was dealing with beliefs that were so closely united for him (and probably for his contemporaries) that he could not identify the weakest belief that had to be eliminated, so that all the beliefs had either to stand or to fall together.

Because the same thought experiment may work or not work depending on the background assumptions of the interlocutors and on their hierarchy of beliefs, we think that the epistemic situations of the interlocutors should be taken into account when a thought experiment is evaluated. Of course, this is true not only of thought experiments but also of every argument. But, considering the initial opacity of the scenarios and the role played by background assumptions and the hierarchy of beliefs, thought experiments are more sensitive to this context-dependence. In that respect, if we are ready to say that a thought experiment can intervene as an argument in a determined cognitive context to make an interlocutor change her mind, we are not ready to share Norton's notion of an argument, which erases the opacity of the scenario and what could be called the opacity of the background assumptions and of the hierarchy of beliefs. Obviously, the price to pay is to renounce the idea that thought experiments can pretend to a kind of justification that would be as strong as the justification of a valid deductive or cogent inductive argument. But are there positive references that could substantiate our enlarged view of argumentation?

We think that the tradition of dialectics provides exactly these kinds of references. First of all, we must say that we do not claim here to be part of the Marxist or Hegelian tradition, where "dialectics" refers to the process by which internal contradictions are transcended, rationally or otherwise. Neither do we think that a dialectical argument contains special logical constants, logical proofs or logical laws different from the usual ones. Referring to the Aristotelian tradition, we consider instead that what sets apart a dialectical argument, above all, is its context. Dialectical arguments have their rightful place in controversial contexts, where the issue is not settled in advance: because the issues at stake are opaque and difficult to clarify, each case will allow for different and initially equally plausible answers. As was aptly shown by Marta Spranzi (2011, 161–72), Aristotle's dialectical tradition inspired several developments in the field of argumentation theory in the twentieth century. Without pretending to be exhaustive, we would like to examine three of these developments in order to decide which of them is the fittest to make clear our case about thought experiments.

In their *New Rhetoric*, first published in 1958, Chaïm Perelman and Lucie Olbrechts-Tyteca insisted that their aim was to break with the conception of reason and reasoning that was introduced in the seventeenth century and to rehabilitate the domain that Aristotle used to characterize as the domain of "dialectical argumentation," that is the domain of verisimilar, likely, plausible and probable arguments. From a strictly logical point of view, such arguments are not valid since they are not constraining proofs that rely on necessity and truth. But, still, they are much more than the expression of subjective points of view that would imply affects, feelings and instincts (Perelman and Olbrechts-Tyteca 1971, 1–10). However, in practice, the distinction between dialectics and rhetoric tends to be blurred in the *New Rhetoric*. Perelman and Olbrechts-Tyteca rightly point out that dialectical arguments are submitted to an audience and they rightly distinguish between particular audiences (made of *de facto* publics whom the speaker actually addresses in specific situations) and the universal audience (made of a *de jure* public who, in an ideal situation, would rely on logical proofs only, or who, from a God's eye point of view, would be identical to the output of the totality of beings capable of reason). Still, they waver between two interpretations of the notion of universal audience: on the one hand, they consider that scientists addressing their peers rightly think that they address a universal audience (Perelman and Olbrechts-Tyteca 1971, 30–1); but, on the other hand, they bluntly assert that "each individual, each culture has its own conception of the universal audience" (Perelman and Olbrechts-Tyteca 1971, 33). This amounts to subscribing to an individual or cultural relativism, according to which there would be as many universal audiences as speakers or as cultures. Even if the notion of universal audience is better understood as a regulative notion, in as much as actual parties in an dialogue are "floating incarnations of this universal audience" (Perelman and Olbrechts-Tyteca 1971, 31), since the genuine aim of argumentation is securing an efficient action on minds to aid in discourse (Perelman and Olbrechts-Tyteca 1971, 19), it seems that this characterization of dialectics falls under rhetoric.

That there is more than this in dialectics has been nicely captured by Frans H. Van Eemeren and Rob Grootendorst. They advocate what they call "pragma-dialectics," where argumentation is understood as an element in a critical discussion aimed at "resolving a difference of opinion" (Van Eemeren and Grootendorst 2004, 52). They insist that resolving a difference of opinion is not the same as settling a dispute: a dispute is settled when the initial difference of opinion has been ended by some external procedure (a vote, a judgment or whatever) even if the various protagonists in the dispute may very well, in *foro interno*, stick to their initial opinion. On the contrary, a difference of opinion is resolved "if a joint conclusion is reached on the acceptability of the standpoints at issue on the basis of a regulated and unimpaired exchange of arguments and criticism." Sometimes, a party just surrenders to the other party's argument, throwing in the towel, so to speak and retracting her standpoint (Van Eemeren and Grootendorst 2004, 58; for a similar distinction between resolving, closing and abandoning a controversy, see for example McMullin

1987, 77–82). More interestingly, it may happen that both standpoints are accepted as various possible opinions about the issue. But Van Eemeren and Grootendorst also miss something: they do not say anything about the possibility that a new standpoint emerges thanks to the efforts of each party to show the weaknesses of the other party's standpoint and the strength of its own standpoint. In other words, they seem to take the opposing views as ultimate views that are not susceptible of evolving, while genuine controversies are sometimes resolved when a new standpoint or conceptual system that supersedes the old standpoints of conceptual systems emerges (Freudenthal 2002).

Thus, to Perelman's and Olbrechts-Tyteca's or to Van Eemeren's and Grootendorst's attempts, we prefer Nicholas Rescher's attempt to understand dialectics in the context of a controversy-oriented approach to the theory of knowledge, where a dialectical argument appears as a process for examining claims to knowledge (Rescher 1977). Rescher considers formal disputation as practiced in the universities during the Middle Ages and since as a model for rational controversy. Indeed, in medieval disputations, Aristotle and Thomas Aquinas were supposed to be the material rule of truth. Still, what is interesting here is the formal process through which claims to knowledge were authenticated. A contender would have to defend a thesis against counterarguments presented by his opponents, arguments and counterarguments being parts of a "process that probes ever more deeply into the grounding of the proponent's thesis, developing in subtle and comprehensive detail the structure or rational support which he envisages for his focal contention" (1977, 5). In other words, in such a disputation, opposing views are not to be taken as *ultimate* (in contrast to what happens in the pragma-dialectics model) but as various *knowledge claims* about a controversial issue (in contrast to what happens in the new rhetoric model). In such dialectical argumentation, knowledge claims may be plausible, but not yet secure. They are plausible in the sense that they have prima facie credentials that have to be examined. After a careful analysis of these credentials, they may be deemed relevant or irrelevant; but often the verdict will be a verdict of partial relevance: a reasonable doubt remains, because a pertinent objection has been raised. In that case, the analysis will go on. In any event, claims to knowledge are carefully tested, and we say that a powerful tool for carrying out such tests is thought experimenting. Dialectically understood, a thought experiment is thus an argument in a process through which knowledge claims are tested: Do they involve a contradiction? Are they as obvious or commonsensical as they seemed at first sight? Are they based on an ambiguity in their formulation? If this is the case, the party who made the assumption must, at least provisionally, bear the burden of proof and put forward a new argument, a new piece of evidence or a more sophisticated interpretation of her thesis.

Let us come back to Thomson's violinist. This thought experiment intends to show that the right to life cannot be understood in such a way that it would give a person the right to use another person's body against her will, even if it were a matter of life and death. As we noted earlier, the experiment does not work if the opponents view life as a gift from God, so that, according to them, the language of rights is not appropriate to settle the issue. But from a dialectical point of view, there is still something to learn even if the experiment does not work. The proponent of the thought experiment will, for example, remind her opponent that she will encounter many problems if she really intends to defend the idea that life is a gift from God (see, for example, Pabst Battin 1995, 26–74). Unsuccessful as it was in convincing the opponent, Thomson's thought experiment would have helped to show where the disagreement lies exactly. Thus, the initial opacity will have been reduced: even if the protagonists fail to reach common ground, they will see the issue more clearly than was the case before. Maybe a definitive answer will forever remain out of reach, but the proposed answers of the opponents will rest on firmer ground.

4 Preventing disequilibrium: an answer to some objections

We would like to end our chapter by briefly answering three objections that might be addressed to our thesis that thought experiments are dialectical arguments.

(i) The first objection is the following. If thought experiments are only dialectic arguments, how is it that Norton is able to reconstruct them as logically valid arguments or that we were able to present them as a way to test the consistency of a set of beliefs? Or still, how is it that Sorensen and Häggqvist are able to regiment them in logical models? Let us discuss these questions in the case of Häggqvist, who quite convincingly shows that an important class of thought experiments that refute theories can be enrolled in the following logical model (Häggqvist 1996, 97–102; Häggqvist 2009, 63–68):

> C (C being the counterfactual situation described in the scenario) is possible.
>
> T (T being the target theory) implies that C necessarily implies W (W being a statement that, considering T, should be the case in the situation described by C).
>
> However C necessarily implies ¬W.
>
> Hence, the target theory T is falsified.

This model is elegant, because it is simple from a logical point of view: it uses only four lines in modal propositional logic. It is fecund as well, because of the consequences that might be drawn from the fact that it is a modalized version of the hypothetico-deductive model. This is not a surprising fact, since it is restricted to thought experiments that test theories (Häggqvist 2009, 63). But this allows Häggqvist to show that such thought experiments are threatened by holism for the same reasons as crucial experiments are (Häggqvist 1996, 107–17). There are namely three ways to escape the conclusion that ¬T: by denying that C is possible, by denying that T implies that C implies necessarily W, or, by denying that C necessarily implies ¬W (Häggqvist 2009, 65–9).

If we admit that a good number of thought experiments are to be enrolled in such a logical model, how can we pretend that thought experiments are dialectical? At stake is the interpretation of what a logical model means. We think that the regimentation of thought experiments in such a logical model does not imply that everything is constraining in thought experiments. On the contrary, as Häggqvist himself notes, such a model helps us to see many reasons why thought experiments may be unsuccessful in certain contexts and to illuminate the disagreement that they can inspire. In the case of real experiments that intervene according to the hypothetico-deductive model, one has controlled and public observations that provide "intersubjectively accessible checkpoints"; in the case of thought experiments, neither the statement describing the counterfactual scenario nor the statement describing its outcome (C necessarily implies ¬W) is such an "intersubjectively accessible checkpoint" (Häggqvist 1996, 118). In a word, the regimentation of thought experiments in a logical model does not eliminate dialectics, it only helps us in seeing where dialectics intervenes.

(ii) The second objection comes from the idea that thought experiments would be more reliable in the sciences than in philosophy. There were indeed philosophers, for example, Kathleen Wilkes in her book *Real People*, who defended the idea that an essential distinction between scientific and philosophical thought experiments should be introduced. According to Wilkes, scientific thought experiments describe adequately their background, deal with natural kinds, and introduce impossible assumptions only if they are not relevant for the conclusion, while philosophical thought experiments give an inadequate description of their background, deal with indeterminate terms of ordinary language, and rely on assumptions that are both impossible and directly relevant for the conclusion (Wilkes 1988, 13–47; see also Thagard 2013). In these circumstances, the second objection is the following: when we enlarge the notion of argument, are we not trying to save philosophical thought experiments to the detriment of scientific thought experiments? In other words, are we not downgrading sound scientific arguments to dialectical tricks and throwing the baby out with the bathwater?

Our answer to this objection relies on our position about the relationship between scientific and philosophical thought experiments. To put it in a nutshell, we do not see why there would be an essential difference between thought experiments in the sciences and in the other fields of knowledge (Cooper 2005; Sorensen 1992, 11–15; Atkinson and Peijnenburg 2003, 317–18). But we nevertheless think that there is a de facto distinction, which is due to the fact that thought experiments have a different cognitive environment of the sciences than the cognitive environment that they have, for example, in philosophy. Without attempting to describe in detail the cognitive environment of the sciences, we would like to note that, in the sciences, real experiments are not the only "intersubjectively accessible checkpoints"; there are also the controlled extrapolations that are made from these experiments, laws and principles that often trump all other propositions, mathematical formalisms that help us to avoid incoherence, and even general theories. All these devices form the cognitive environment of thought experiments in the sciences, and they guide our modal intuitions in the context of performing a thought experiment. Thus, it is not necessary to suppose that there is an essential difference between thought experiments in the sciences and in philosophy to explain that they yield different results. Suffice it to say that they are inserted in different cognitive environments. In that respect, claiming that thought experiments are dialectical is only being realistic about thought experiments: per se, thought experiments are not reliable and do not provide us with indefeasible justified true belief; if it happens that a thought experiment contributes to prove something, it is because of its cognitive environment.

(iii) We will be quite brief on the third and last objection, because it is only a consequence of the second objection. Does not the thesis that thought experiments should be conceived as dialectical arguments open the way to relativism? Speaking of "shared beliefs" and of "common background assumptions" may evoke certain relativistic theses.

The answer to this objection is simple: we defend a local contextualism as to thought experiences that does not necessarily lead to relativism. First, relativism does not consist in saying that there are shared beliefs in certain contexts, and beliefs that are not shared in others; it is the thesis that shared beliefs, because and only because they are shared, are good beliefs – in other words, the thesis that a shared belief is per se a good belief – and that there is no epistemological criterion for choosing among opposing and competing shared beliefs. Second, even if we would be relativists with respect to thought experiments, such a local relativism would not necessarily imply a general relativism that could be extended to the sciences in general – precisely because, as we said before, there are in the sciences other devices than thought experiments, devices that all together contribute to the fecundity and stability of the sciences.

In this chapter, we first characterized thought experiments and insisted on the heterogeneity between propositional and non-propositional knowledge that such a characterization implies. This helped us to throw some light on the debate between Brown and Norton, the former insisting on non-propositional knowledge, the latter privileging propositional knowledge. More importantly, we argued that, in order to escape the dilemma that Brown's and Norton's position constitute, we should renounce the question that was common to them both, namely the question of what justifies the knowledge that would be provided by thought experiments, and rather conceive of thought experiments as dialectical arguments that provide defeasible knowledge. Thus, if we are ready to say with Norton that thought experiments are arguments, we have contrary to him a dialectical understanding of what an argument is. And this is what was meant by our broad characterization of an argument as "what intervenes in a cognitive context to make an interlocutor change her mind." By stating "change her mind," we wanted to underscore the pragmatic dimension of our interpretation; by stating "cognitive context," we wanted to stress that a thought experiment will not necessarily be successful in any context whatsoever.

Acknowledgements

We thank the editors of this volume for their valuable comments on an early version and for their careful editing of the final version of our chapter.

References

Atkinson, D. and Peijnenburg, J. (2003) "When are thought experiments poor ones?" *Journal for General Philosophy of Science* 34: 305–322.
Atkinson, D. and Peijnenburg, J. (2004) "Galileo and prior philosophy," *Studies in History and Philosophy of Science* 35: 115–136.
Bishop, M. (1999) "Why thought experiments are not arguments," *Philosophy of Science* 66: 534–551.
Brown, J. R. (1986) "Thought experiments since the scientific revolution," *International Studies in the Philosophy of Science* 1: 1–15.
Brown, J. R. (1991a) "Thought experiments: A Platonic account," in *Thought Experiments in Science and Philosophy*, edited by T. Horowitz and G. Massey, New York: Rowman and Littlefield.
Brown, J. R. (1991b/2011) *The Laboratory of the Mind: Thought Experiments in the Natural Sciences*, London: Routledge.
Brown, J. R. (2004a) "Peeking into Plato's heaven," *Philosophy of Science* 71: 1126–1138.
Brown, J. R. (2004b) "Do thought experiments transcend empiricism?" in *Contemporary Debates in Philosophy of Science*, edited by C. Hitchcock, Malden: Blackwell.
Buzzoni, M. (2013) "Thought experiments from a Kantian point of view," in *Thought Experiments in Philosophy, Science, and the Arts*, edited by M. Frappier, L. Meynell and J. Brown. New York: Routledge.

Cooper, R. (2005) "Thought experiments," *Metaphilosophy* 36: 328–347.
El Skaf, R. and Imbert, C. (2013) "Unfolding in the empirical sciences: Experiments, thought experiments and computer simulations," *Synthese* 190: 3451–3474.
Freudenthal, G. (2002) "Perpetuum mobile: The Leibniz-Papin controversy," *Studies in History and Philosophy of Science Part A* 33: 573–637.
Gendler, T. S. (1998) "Galileo and the indispensability of scientific thought experiment," *The British Journal for the Philosophy of Science* 49: 397–424.
Gendler, T. S. (2004) "Thought experiments rethought—and reperceived," *The British Journal for the Philosophy of Science* 71: 1152–1163.
Goffi, J-Y. and Roux, S. (2011) "On the very idea of a thought experiment," in *Thought Experiments in Methodological and Historical Contexts*, edited by K. Ierodiakonou and S. Roux, Leiden: Brill.
Häggqvist, S. (1996) *Thought Experiments in Philosophy*, Stockholm: Almqvist and Wiksell International.
Häggqvist, S. (2007) "The a priori thesis: A critical assessment," *Croatian Journal of Philosophy* 19: 47–61.
Häggqvist, S. (2009) "A model for thought experiments," *Canadian Journal of Philosophy* 39: 55–76.
Hintikka, J. and Hintikka, M. (1989) *The Logic of Epistemology and the Epistemology of Logic*, Dordrecht: Kluwer Academic Publishers.
Mach, E. ([1905] 1926) *Erkenntnis und Irrtum*. 5th edition. Leipzig: Barth. Translated by T. J. McCormack as *Knowledge and Error*, Dordrecht and Boston: Reidel.
McMullin, E. (1987) "Scientific controversy and its termination," in *Scientific Controversies: Case Studies in the Resolution and Closure of Disputes in Science and Technology*, edited by H. T. Engelhardt Jr. and A. L. Caplan, Cambridge: Cambridge University Press.
Norton, J. D. (1991) "Thought experiments in Einstein's work," in *Thought Experiments in Science and Philosophy*, edited by T. Horowitz and G. Massey, Savage: Rowman and Littlefield.
Norton, J. D. (2004a) "Why thought experiments do not transcend empiricism," in *Contemporary Debates in the Philosophy of Science*, edited by C. Hitchcock, Oxford: Blackwell.
Norton, J. D. (2004b) "On thought experiments: Is there more to the argument?" *Philosophy of Science* 71: 1139–1151.
Pabst Battin, M. (1995) *Ethical Issues in Suicide*, Englewood Cliffs: Prentice-Hall.
Perelman, C. and Olbrechts-Tyteca, L. (1971) *The New Rhetoric: A Treatise on Argumentation*, translated by J. Wilkinson and P. Weaver, London: University of Notre Dame Press.
Rescher, N. (1977) *Dialectics: A Controversy-Oriented Approach to the Theory of Knowledge*, Albany: SUNY Press.
Rescher, N. (2005) *What If? Thought Experimentation in Philosophy*, London: Transaction Publishers.
Roux, S. (2011) "Introduction," in *Thought Experiments in Methodological and Historical Contexts*, edited by K. Ierodiakonou and S. Roux, Leiden: Brill.
Sorensen, R. (1992) *Thought Experiments*, Oxford: Oxford University Press.
Spranzi, M. (2011) *The Art of Dialectic between Dialogue and Rhetoric: The Aristotelian Tradition*, Philadelphia: John Benjamins.
Thagard, P. (2013) "Thought experiments considered harmful," *Perspectives on Science* 22: 288–305.
Van Eemeren, F. H. and Grootendorst, R. (2004) *A Systematic Theory of Argumentation*, Cambridge: Cambridge University Press.
Wilkes, K. (1988) *Real People: Personal Identity Without Thought Experiments*, Oxford: Clarendon Press.

25
THE WORST THOUGHT EXPERIMENT

John D. Norton

1 Introduction

When the great nineteenth-century physicist James Clerk Maxwell imagined (1871, 308) "a being whose faculties are so sharpened that he can follow every molecule in its course," he could not have foreseen the unlikely career his thought creation would have. A little over 50 years later, in a thought experiment devised by Leo Szilard and published in 1929, the demon was manipulating a single molecule and providing the grounding for a connection between information gathering or information processing and thermodynamic entropy. That 1929 thought experiment and its subsequent reception will be the principal subject of this chapter.

Part I will recount a standard narrative of the path to Szilard's thought experiment and its subsequent development. Sections 2 and 3 below sketch how Maxwell's original concerns evolved into Szilard's thought experiment. The thought experiment and its subsequent development will be described in Sections 4–7.

The narrative thus far will recapitulate, mostly, the standard, celebratory view of the thought experiment. In Part II, starting in Section 8, I will give a dissenting, less celebratory view of the thought experiment. It is, I will argue, a failed thought experiment and the locus and origin of enduring confusions in the subsequent literature. In Section 9, I will try to account for how a thought experiment like this can fail so badly. The failure, I will argue, derives from routinely accepted narrative conventions in thought experimenting. We give the thought experimenter extensive latitude in introducing idealizations, so that inessential distractions can be set aside. To avoid the clutter of needless generality, we grant the thought experimenter the presumption that the specific case developed is typical, so its behavior can stand in for a general result. The failure of the Szilard thought experiment results from misuse of both conventions.

PART I: RISE

2 Maxwell and his demon

Maxwell's overall project was to understand how large collections of molecules could manifest as familiar thermal systems, like gases. The natural approach was to devise a dynamical theory that would track the courses of individual molecules, just as Newton's celestial mechanics tracked planets, moons and comet in their courses. Maxwell realized that there are too many molecules in a gas, all interacting in unimaginably complicated ways, for this dynamical approach to work. Instead, he must use statistical methods, such as employed in the study of mass populations. He could then arrive at a serviceable theory of molecular gases. The molecules are treated en masse only, through suitable probability distributions and statistical parameters.

An interesting consequence, Maxwell realized, is that the second law of thermodynamics depends essentially on the restriction to this statistical treatment of molecules. The law would be violated, he noted, if somehow we could manipulate molecules individually. To make his point, he imagined the being with sharpened faculties mentioned above. Such a being could, without the expenditure of work, cause a gas at uniform temperature to separate out into a hotter portion of faster moving molecules and a colder portion of slower moving molecules, in violation of the second law of thermodynamics. All that was needed was to confine the gas to a vessel with a dividing wall. The being would open and close a hole in the wall, when molecules approached it, so as to allow the faster molecules to accumulate on one side and the slower ones on the other.

Maxwell saw no special problem when he conceived his demon. He envisaged no threat to the second law in this thought experiment. The point was precisely that *we* do not have the powers of his imaginary being. We must treat molecules en masse, so we cannot overturn the second law.

3 Thermal fluctuations

Circumstances changed in the early twentieth century with the observation and analysis of thermal fluctuations. Einstein showed in 1905 that the jiggling motion of microscopically visible particles – "Brownian motion" – was due to the accumulated effect of many collisions of the particles with water molecules. Each time a microscopically visible particle was raised by these motions, we were seeing the full conversion of the heat energy of the water into work, in the form of the potential energy of height. This full conversion of heat into work is precisely a process prohibited by a standard statement of the law. It is a microscopic violation of the second law of thermodynamics.

The pressing question then was whether these microscopic violations could be accumulated into a macroscopic violation of the law. At that moment, Maxwell's demon had ceased to be a benign illustration of the statistical character of the second law. It had become a mortal threat to it. The threat was soon parried, decisively. The most thorough analysis came from Marian Smoluchowski (1912, 1914). He considered numerous mechanisms, each designed to accumulate these thermal fluctuations into a macroscopic violation of the second law. In each case, he showed that further fluctuations within the mechanisms themselves would on average defeat the intended accumulation. The demon must fail since the demon is itself a thermal system, rife with the very thermal fluctuations it sought to exploit. Momentary violations were possible, but they could not be accumulated. The second law was safe, as far as the average behavior of systems was concerned.

In the best known of many examples, Smoluchowski replaced Maxwell's cleverly opened hole in the gas chamber dividing wall with a simple, one-way flapper value, which later came to be known as the Smoluchowski trapdoor. The flapper or trapdoor is lightly spring-loaded to keep it shut and is hinged so that it can open in one direction only. Collisions with molecules seeking to pass in that direction open it and they pass. Molecules seeking to pass in the reverse direction slam it shut. Over time, one part of the gas chamber becomes spontaneously pressurized, without any compensating process elsewhere, in violation of the second law.

This is a simple and apparently secure mechanical realization of Maxwell's imaginary being. It will fail in its purpose, Smoluchowski argued, since the trapdoor will have its own thermal energy. Since the trapdoor must be very light and lightly spring-loaded if a collision with a molecule can open it, that thermal energy will lead it to flap about wildly, allowing molecules to pass freely in both directions.

4 Intelligent intervention

A loophole remained. What if the mechanism that accumulated the fluctuations were operated intelligently by an animate being? The operation of that being would, in virtue of its vitality, lie outside the normal constraints of physics. This was the question put to Smoluchowski by Kaufmann at the conclusion of his lecture at the 84th *Naturforscherversammlung* (Meeting of Natural Scientists) in Münster in 1912. It would, Kaufmann suggested be (Smoluchowski 1912, 1018):

> a conclusion that one possibly could regard as proof, in the sense of the neo-vitalistic conception, that the physico-chemical laws alone are not sufficient for the explanation of biological and psychic occurrences.

Smoluchowski, taken somewhat aback by the question, granted the neo-vitalist presumption in his reply:

> What was said in the lecture certainly pertains only to automatic devices, and there is certainly no doubt that an intelligent being, for whom physical phenomena are transparent, could bring about processes that contradict the second law. Indeed Maxwell has already proven this with his demon.

He then recovered and proceeded to suggest that perhaps even an intelligent being is constrained by normal physics, so that some neglected physical process would still protect the second law. Two years later, with the publication of a follow-up lecture, Smoluchowski was more certain that even an intelligent demon could not escape the confines of physics. He wrote then (1914, 397) of the demon:

> For the production of any physical effect through the operation of its sensory and also its motor nervous system is always connected with an energy cost, leaving aside the fact that its entire existence is bound up with continuing dissipation.

Smoluchowski concluded that successful operation even of an intelligent demon was thus "very doubtful, even though our ignorance of living processes precludes a definite answer."

5 Szilard and his one-molecule engine

The question of intervention by an intelligent demon languished until it was taken up by Leo Szilard in the next decade. His 1929 "On the decrease of entropy in a thermodynamic system by the intervention of intelligent beings" became the founding paper of a new literature. Szilard explained his limited ambitions in the introductory section. He had just completed his doctoral dissertation on the topic of thermal fluctuations. Citing this work, he announced as established that no automatic machine or no strictly periodic intervention is able to exploit thermal fluctuations to produce a violation of second law. His goal was limited (Szilard 1929, 302): "[We] intend here only to consider the difficulties that occur when intelligent beings intervene in a system."

In pursuit of this goal, Szilard devised the simplest possible manifestation of thermal fluctuations, one that proved especially well-suited to easy analysis. For an ideal gas of many, say n, molecules, the probability that the gas fluctuates isothermally from the full vessel volume V to some smaller, lower entropy, volume $(V-\Delta V)$ is negligible, unless the fluctuation in volume ΔV is small with respect to V/n.[1] Since n is of the order of 10^{24} for ordinary samples of gases, volume fluctuations in them are minuscule – of the order of one part in 10^{24}. They become more prominent as n becomes smaller. The extreme case is $n = 1$. It is a gas of a single molecule whose density fluctuates wildly as the molecule bounces rapidly to and fro inside the confining chamber.

Described macroscopically, when the molecule has moved to one side of the chamber, its volume has fluctuated into that side and had momentarily, spontaneously compressed in volume. Szilard's ingenious idea was a mechanism that could lock in this spontaneous fluctuation to a lower entropy state: simply insert a partition into the chamber, dividing it into two parts. The molecule will be trapped on one side and, with it, we have locked in a volume fluctuation to a lower entropy state.

In the simplest case, we divide the chamber volume in half. Then inserting the partition halves the volume of space occupied by the one-molecule gas. It has been compressed from its initial volume V to $V/2$. Since the thermodynamic entropy varies with volume for an ideal, one-molecule gas according to $k \log$ (volume), where k is Boltzmann's constant, the process has reduced the thermodynamic entropy of the gas by:

$$\Delta S = k \log (V/2) - k \log V = - k \log 2$$

We assume some apparently benign idealizations: the partition can be inserted without friction and is massless so no work is done in moving it. Thus the sole effect of this step is to reduce the thermodynamic entropy of the gas, without compensating changes elsewhere, in violation of the second law.

What remains is to accumulate this molecular-scale violation of the second law by incorporating the uncompensated compression into a cycle that can be repeated indefinitely. Szilard devised a process that would accumulate these repeated entropy reductions in the entropy of an environmental heat bath that maintains the one-molecule gas at a constant temperature T.

To do this, the partition becomes a piston against which the confined one-molecule gas exerts a pressure, due to repeated impacts. The piston is coupled to a weight in such a way that, when the one-molecule gas expands isothermally, the work done by the gas on the piston raises the weight. As the gas expands, it cools slightly due to the loss of energy transmitted as work to the raised weight. This lost energy is replaced by heat conducted to the one-molecule gas from the heat bath. Since the pressure exerted by the one-molecule gas is $P = kT/V$, the work W done by the gas in the expansion and the heat passed to the gas Q are given by[2]

$$Q = W = \int_{V/2}^{V} P dV = \int_{V/2}^{V} \frac{kT}{V} dV = kT \log \frac{V}{V/2} = kT \log 2$$

An essential condition on the cycle is that all processes be carried out in a thermodynamically reversible manner, else there will be unwanted thermodynamic entropy created in the process, undermining the goal. If heat $Q = kT \log 2$, passes reversibly from the heat bath, then its thermodynamic entropy is reduced by

$$\Delta S = -Q/T = -k \log 2$$

At the end of the cycle, the gas is restored to its initial state and the thermodynamic entropy of the heat bath has been reduced by $k \log 2$. This is a net reduction in the thermodynamic entropy of the universe, in violation of the second law. Merely repeating the cycle at will yields an arbitrarily large violation. It is a one-molecule heat engine that fully converts heat drawn from the heat sink into the work energy stored in the raised weight.

6 Szilard's principle: the entropy cost of measurement

A violation of the second law seems all but assured by this simple mechanism. How could it fail? Szilard had an answer. The account above neglects the presence of the agent operating the one-molecule engine. Successful operation requires that, upon insertion of the partition, the agent must discern on which side – left or right – the molecule is trapped. For that measurement is needed in determining which coupling to use for the pressure-driven raising of the weight. Does the gas expand to the left or the right?

Szilard's escape was to assume that this measurement requires the creation of entropy (1929, 303):

> We shall realize that the Second Law is not threatened as much by this entropy decrease as one would think, as soon as we see that the entropy decrease resulting from the intervention would be compensated completely in any event if the execution of such a measurement were, for instance, always accompanied by production of $k \log 2$ units of entropy.

The direct way of arriving at this entropy cost of measurement is simply to work backwards from the assumption that the second law is not violated, as Szilard notes (302):

> At first we calculate this production of entropy quite generally from the postulate that full compensation is made in the sense of the Second Law ...

This is an awkward moment. The demonstration of the necessary failure of the demon begins with the *assumption* of its failure? To escape the obvious circularity, Szilard devoted an extended part of his analysis to a specific, independent scheme for carrying out the measurements. The details of that scheme have proven to be opaque to later commentators and it has played no role in subsequent developments.[3] See Leff and Rex (2003, §1.3).

What survived in the subsequent literature was a much simpler version of Szilard's escape. John von Neumann, Szilard's fellow student in Berlin and Hungarian compatriot, included the simplified version in his authoritative and much admired text, *Mathematical Foundations of Quantum Mechanics* (1932). Having recounted the operation of Szilard's one-molecule engine, he stressed the importance of knowing the location of the trapped molecule for the cycle to be completed. He concluded (400): "That is, we have exchanged our knowledge for the entropy decrease $\kappa \ln 2$ [here, $k \log 2$]." To this sentence, von Neumann appended the footnote:

> L. Szilard has [reference] shown that one cannot get this "knowledge" without a compensating entropy increase $\kappa \ln 2$. In general, $\kappa \ln 2$ is the "thermodynamic value" of the knowledge, which consists of an alternative of two cases. All attempts to carry out the process described above without the knowledge of the half of the container in which the molecule is located, can be proved to be invalid, although they may occasionally lead to very complicated automatic mechanisms.

Modern readers will see in this talk of "alternative of two cases" and the thermodynamic value of knowledge an immediate connection to Shannon and Weaver's mathematical theory of communication. There, information in a communication channel is quantified as information entropy, using the same formula in the probability calculus as can be used to compute the thermodynamic entropy of a thermal system. Shannon's theory, however, comes well after Szilard's work. Its founding paper was published in 1948 and, in a more popular introductory discussion to the canonical *The Mathematical Theory of Communication*, Weaver (1964, 3) cites both Szilard's and von Neumann's earlier work as precursors.

In the 1950s and 1960s, the idea of a connection between thermodynamic entropy and information entropy drew energetic attention.[4] The leading idea of this literature was subsequently labeled "Szilard's Principle": the gaining of information that allows us to discern among n equally likely states is associated with the creation of a minimum of $k \log n$ of thermodynamic entropy (Earman and Norton 1999, 5).

This was an era of many thought experiments illustrating how an entropy cost in information acquisition leads to the failure of a Maxwell's demon. A simple and popular example was provided by Leon Brillouin (1950), one of the founders of modern, solid state physics, in the Brillouin torch. It supplied the missing details in a quantum mechanical account of how the demon could locate a molecule: the demon would bounce a photon – a quantum of light – off it. The photon, however, must be sufficiently energetic for it to be visible above the thermal background. This condition forced so much entropy creation that it precluded the demon exploiting the information gained to violate the second law.

A celebratory headnote to the 1964 translation of Szilard's (1929) article in the journal *Behavioral Science* affirmed Szilard's priority:

This is one of the earliest, if not the earliest paper, in which the relations of physical entropy to information (in the sense of modern mathematical theory of communication) were rigorously demonstrated and in which Maxwell's famous demon was successfully exorcised: a milestone in the integration of physical and cognitive concepts.

7 Landauer's principle: the entropy cost of erasure

This last explanation of the necessary failure of Maxwell's demon was short-lived. Within a few decades, it had been eclipsed by another exorcism. Bennett (1987, 108) reported this unexpected turn in a popular article in *Scientific American*:

> To protect the second law, physicists have proposed various reasons the demon cannot function as Maxwell described. Surprisingly, nearly all these proposals have been flawed. Often flaws arose because workers had been misled by advances in other fields of physics; many of them thought (incorrectly, as it turns out) that various limitations imposed by quantum theory invalidated Maxwell's demon.
>
> The correct answer – the real reason Maxwell's demon cannot violate the second law – has been uncovered only recently. It is the unexpected result of a very different line of research: research on the energy requirements of computers.

The new exorcism was founded on an idea proposed by Rolf Landauer (1961). When a computer memory is erased, heat is generated; and the heat generated creates entropy in the environment to which it passes. The amount created can be quantified under the rubric of "Landauer's principle": erasing a memory device with n states leads to the creation of $k \log n$ of thermodynamic entropy in the environment.

In the new exorcism, as elaborated in Bennett (1982, §V; 1987), the key fact was that the demon must record or remember the location of the molecule in operating a machine like the Szilard one-molecule engine. Left or right? One of the two states must recorded. Then the record must be erased if the demon is to complete the cycle and return to its initial state. That erasure, according to Landauer's principle, will create $k \log 2$ of thermodynamic entropy in the environment, cancelling precisely the $k \log 2$ entropy reduction of the earlier steps of the cycle.

The new exorcism moves the locus of creation of the compensating entropy from information acquisition to information erasure. Hence its cogency depends essentially on the possibility of processes that could acquire information without creating thermodynamic entropy. Szilard, von Neumann, Brillouin and others who worked in the earlier tradition gave powerful affirmations that this was impossible. Yet Bennett (1982, §V; 1987) now described several measurement devices that purportedly required no entropy creation. (Awkwardly, it was obvious to anyone who had absorbed the import of Smoluchowski's original analysis, that none of these devices could carry out dissipationless measurement. As noted in Earman and Norton (1999, 13–14), their delicate internal mechanisms would be fatally disrupted by thermal fluctuations.)

In any case, as the survey in Leff and Rex (2003) records, the new erasure-based exorcism now dominates a flourishing literature. In 2012, Bérut et al. (2012), in a letter to the prestigious journal *Nature*, announced experimental confirmation of Landauer's principle and summarized its importance as:[5]

> Landauer's principle hence seems to be a central result that not only exorcizes Maxwell's demon, but also represents the fundamental physical limit of irreversible computation.

PART II: FALL

8 The worst thought experiment

The narrative so far has replicated the celebratory tone of standard accounts of the Szilard thought experiment. I do not share in the celebration. Rather I believe that this thought experiment is fatally flawed. It is the origin and an enduring stimulus for long-lived confusions in the subsequent literature. We have already seen a clue to the serious problems to be recounted below: the tradition of exorcism based on Szilard's principle simply collapsed when a new contender emerged. There was no new experimental result. There was merely an imperfectly supported pronouncement that decades of pronouncements by earlier, leading thinkers were wrong.

In its capacity to engender mischief and confusion, Szilard's thought experiment is unmatched.[6] It is the worst thought experiment I know in science. Let me count the ways it has misled us.

8.1 A worse solution to the Maxwell demon problem

The stated goal of Szilard's thought experiment was to treat the case not of an automated Maxwell's demon, but of an intelligent demon. We saw above that Smoluchowski had already dealt with that case quite effectively. If the intelligent demon has neo-vitalist powers that put it outside normal physics, then what it can do lies beyond what physical theory can determine. It can break physical laws since it is outside them. If however it is naturalized as a physical system,[7] then its proper functioning requires thermodynamic dissipation; and, if its mechanism is delicately balanced, thermal fluctuations will disrupt it. This basic idea is essentially correct. It can be developed into a much stronger exorcism, as shown in Subsections 8.2 and 8.5.

In its place, Szilard created a vague notion of an information gathering or measuring system, whose behavior will be all but impossible to quantify outside oversimplified and contrived cases like the one-molecule engine.

Almost immediately, this new approach became the only mode of exorcism in the literature. Information processing was the key, supposedly, to explaining why all Maxwell's demon must fail. Yet there are many proposals for Maxwell's demons to which this analysis cannot be applied. How can it explain the failure of the Smoluchowski trapdoor? How much information does the trapdoor gather? Where does this simple trapdoor mechanism store the information whose erasure is key to its failure? The information-based exorcism fails where Smoluchowski's simple observation of the disruptive effect of fluctuations succeeds.

8.2 Inadmissible idealizations that selectively neglect fluctuations

In the transition from the exorcism based on Szilard's principle to one based on Landauer's principle, the governing question was just which process is *the* ineliminable locus of dissipation. Measurement or erasure? The common assumption was that all the other processes could, in principle, be carried out without creating thermodynamic entropy and thus could be idealized as dissipationless processes.

This assumption is the most egregious of all assumptions in this literature. It is fatally and disastrously wrong. Thermal fluctuations are present in the systems of every step of the thought experiment; and dissipative, thermodynamic entropy creating processes are needed to suppress them and allow the step to complete. Since Szilard's one-molecule engine is driven by thermal fluctuations, to ignore them in some places but to depend on their presence in others is to render the whole analysis an inconsistent use of thermal physics.

We will see the need for dissipative processes to suppress fluctuations throughout the operation of the engine, first in an example and then in a quite general result. Consider the partition that is slid into the chamber to divide it. The partition is routinely assumed massless and to slide frictionlessly, so that no work is needed to move it. However it is just as much a component in the thermal system as is the molecule of the gas. Like the Smoluchowski trapdoor, it will have its own thermal energy as result of its thermal interactions with the environment. If it slides in one dimension, the equipartition theorem of classical statistical mechanics assigns it a mean thermal energy of $kT/2$. That will manifest as a jiggling motion, akin to Brownian motion. The partition can be slid into place and locked only by overcoming these motions, which requires the application of an unbalanced, dissipative force whose work energy is degraded into heat. Rendering the partition massless will make the operation more difficult. For its mean thermal energy $kT/2$ will equal its mean kinetic energy $mv^2/2$, where m is the partition mass and v its root mean square velocity. As we make the mass m small without limit, then the velocity v increases without limit, if the mean kinetic energy is to remain constant. That is, a near massless partition would be moving with near infinite speed!

This analysis could be continued for each step of the Szilard's cycle: the detection of the molecule; the coupling of the weight to the partition-piston; the expansion of the one-molecule gas and the raising of the weight; and the decoupling and the removal of the partition-piston.[8] In each case we would find that dissipative forces are needed to overcome fluctuations.

Fortunately, we do not need to labor through every case. There is a general result that covers them all. See Norton (2013, §9). On molecular scales, thermal fluctuations prevent assured completion of any process. There is always a chance that some fluctuation will undo the process. However a dissipative process that creates entropy ΔS can enhance the probability P_{fin} that the system will be in its desired final state, as compared to the probability P_{init} that the system has fluctuated back to its initial state. The three quantities are related by

$$\Delta S = k \log(P_{fin}/P_{init})$$

The quantities of entropy that this formula requires are large on molecular scales. If we ask only for a meager ratio favoring success of $P_{fin}/P_{init} = 20$, then the theorem tells us that, at minimum, we must create $k \log 20 = 3k$ of thermodynamic entropy. This minimum quantity exceeds the $k \log 2 = 0.69k$ tracked in the Szilard's and Landauer's principle literature. This minimum quantity must be created not just once, but once for each of the many completing steps in the cycle.

8.3 The exorcisms rely on tendentious principles

Smoluchowski was right: fluctuations in the demon's mechanism will defeat it. Suppressing them will require creation of quantities of entropy that far exceed those tracked by Szilard's and Landauer's principle. This simple fact renders the principles insignificant in the analysis of Maxwell's demon, even if they are correct principles.

There are good reasons, however, to doubt their correctness. The most common derivation of Szilard's principle is to work backwards to arrive at the precise quantitative measure of entropy creation, $k \log n$, when discerning among n outcomes (see Earman and Norton 1999, §2.1). One assumes that the second law prevails in systems like the Szilard one-molecule engine and works backwards to the entropy that must be created in the measurement to protect the law. It is assumed – crucially – that measurement is the only step that must create entropy. Since this last crucial assumption fails, so does the derivation. Other, less precise demonstrations, such as the Brillouin torch, in effect exploit the general fact of Section 8.2 that any process on molecular scales that completes must be dissipative. That the process is a measurement is incidental to the dissipation inferred.

Landauer's principle, when it was first suggested in 1961, was an interesting speculation, founded on a loose plausibility argument, but in need of precise grounding. Over half a century later, in spite of considerable efforts, the principle remains at best loose speculation, grounded in many repetitions of the same misapplications of thermal physics. The details are too complex to be elaborated here. Discussion of these difficulties and an entrance in the broader literature, can be found in Norton (2011, 2013, §3.5).

8.4 The thought experiment legitimated a bad exemplar

Szilard's 1929 thought experiment introduced into the literature an exemplar for how thermodynamic analysis can be carried out on systems at molecular scales. It legitimated the idea that many processes can be effected reversibly, that is, dissipationlessly, including the insertion and removal of partitions into a one-molecule gas chamber and the reversible compression and expansion of the one-molecule gas. The literature, especially on Landauer's principle, is replete with manipulations of this type. A single molecule trapped in one or other side of a chamber has become the canonical example of a molecular-scale memory device; and it is manipulated by all the above processes. For a recent example, see Ladyman, Presnell, Short, and Groisman (2007); Ladyman, Presnell, and Short (2008); and for my critique, see Norton (2011).

The difficulty is that none of these processes can be carried out without dissipation. Hence the entire analytic regime is flawed, as is any result derived within it. The harm caused by Szilard's exemplar is not limited to the analysis of a one-molecule gas. The thermal properties of a one-molecule gas are analogous to those of other single component systems that may be used as memory or detection devices, such as a molecular-scale magnetic dipole in a thermal environment. The position of the molecule is analogous to the direction of the dipole moment; and the compression of the one-molecule gas by a piston is analogous to the restriction of the direction of the dipole by an external magnetic field. The restriction is a compression in an abstract state space. It is routine to assume that the analogous operations on the dipole can be carried out dissipationlessly (see, for example, Bennett 1982, §5). These operations are, of course, equally disrupted by thermal fluctuations. No molecular-scale processes can be completed on them without dissipation.

8.5 Distraction from a far simpler exorcism: Liouville's theorem

The idea that information processing in some guise is the key to demonstrating the failure of Maxwell's demon has great popular appeal. It has, as a result, come to dominate virtually all writing on Maxwell's demon and has been responsible for an explosion of feckless analysis. It is only now becoming clear how thoroughly this seductive idea has misdirected us. Had we maintained Smoluchowski's focus on the mundane statistical physics, we might much earlier have hit upon a remarkably simple and quite general exorcism of Maxwell's demon. It requires nothing more than elementary notions in statistical physics and can be developed without even mentioning the sometimes troublesome notion of entropy. It turns out that a simple description of what a Maxwell's demon is required to do is incompatible with the Liouville theorem of Hamiltonian dynamics. Since this theorem is fundamental to classical statistical physics, it assures us that no Maxwell demon is possible. See Norton (2013, §4); and for a quantum theoretic version of the same exorcism, Norton (forthcoming).

9 How a thought experiment can fail

Were they not delivered through the medium of a thought experiment, I like to think that Szilard's misleading and troublesome speculations of 1929 would not have received assent. For his paper has no cogent demonstration that, as a general matter, an intelligent demon must fail because of entropy costs associated quite specifically with measurement, as quantified in his formulae. There is something about the medium of a thought experiment that induced this assent.

That something derives from the special narrative role that thought experiments play in science and especially physics. Results there are often quite complicated and hard to grasp, if displayed in precise terms and full generality. Here thought experiments have traditionally played a pedagogical role. They give us just the essentials in a form that is easy to visualize and easy to grasp. In return, we are willing to grant the thought experimenter considerable latitude. The failures of Szilard's thought experiment can be traced to a misuse of this latitude. It comes it two forms.

9.1 Hasty acceptance of idealizations

First, we allow many processes to be idealized away as nuisance distractions, so that we may focus just on the one that matters. Einstein (1952, Ch. XX; Peacock, this volume) asks us to image a large chest in a remote part of space with an observer inside. It is accelerated, he says, by "a 'being' (what kind is immaterial to us)," who pulls with constant force on a rope attached to the lid, uniformly accelerating the chest. We suspend scepticism over whether such an idealized being really is possible. We accept Einstein's assurance that questioning this detail is an unhelpful distraction.

Szilard misuses this liberty in his thought experiment. It is simply assumed that most of the operations of his one-molecule engine can be carried out without dissipation. He briefly addresses the fluctuations ("agitations") that must be present when a piston, light enough to be raised by a collision with a single molecule, is repeatedly struck by one. He writes (1929, 304–5):

> It is best to imagine the mass of the piston as large and its speed sufficiently great, so that the thermal agitation of the piston at the temperature in question can be neglected.

This scheme would suppress the manifestation of molecular fluctuations only because a fast-moving, massive piston is in a state far from the equilibrium that non-dissipative processes demand.[9] Since thermal fluctuations are the primary subject, we should expect a more cogent defense of an idealization that eventually proves to be fatal. We are prompted by the narrative conventions of a thought experiment, however, not to press when the thought experimenter assures us that the idealization is benign.[10]

9.2 Hasty generalization

Instead of proving a result in all generality, a thought experiment may merely display typical behaviour. To enable a simple narrative, we accept that it is typical – a simplified surrogate for a complicated general statement.

The observer in Einstein's chest finds bodies inside it to fall just as if they are in a gravitational field. It is a striking coincidence and we are led immediately to connect acceleration and gravitation. The point of the thought experiment is that this is no mere coincidence, but a manifestation of a broader generality: all processes in a gravitational field proceed just as they do in the chest. Einstein immediately uses this generalization to infer that clocks deeper in a gravitational field are slowed, because clocks lower in the chest are slowed; and that light is bent by a gravitational field, since its propagation is bent inside the chest.

Without the thought experiment, we might well be reluctant to admit the generalization. Surely we should be more circumspect in jumping from the fall of ordinary bodies to the rates of clocks and the bending of light. However, we are carried along by the fictions in the narrative. Imagining ourselves with the observer in the chest, we agree that things are just as if we are in a gravitational field, as far as the motion of bodies is concerned. We have no means to know otherwise. How could we know that things are any different for other processes? Even if doubts linger, we conform with the narrative convention and grant that the thought experimenter knows which results are typical and thus support generalization.

Szilard's thought experiment misuses this latitude. The bare operation of the one-molecule engine leads to a reduction in thermodynamic entropy of $k \log 2$. We notice immediately, with von Neumann, that the two in the formula matches the count of alternatives of left and right available to the operating demon. Then, Shannon attaches $k \log 2$

of information entropy to a choice between two equally likely signals. Remarkably, the quantities of thermodynamic entropy and information entropy match.

This is a striking coincidence and seeing it is a memorable moment, when one first encounters the thought experiment. It is so striking that we readily accept the thought experimenter's suggestion that it is no mere coincidence. It is, we are to believe, a manifestation of a deeper generality. The entropy reduction produced by the machinations of Maxwell's demon will, in general, be compensated by entropy created in manipulating information, either acquiring it or erasing it. We readily assent because we presume that the thought experimenter is simplifying a deeper analysis, whose full details are suppressed by a narrative convention in the interests of preserving the simplicity of the thought experiment.

Alas, the latitude we accord to the thought experimenter in this case is misplaced. Aside from a few variant forms of the thought experiment with slight elaborations, there is no cogent general theory whose details are being suppressed for simplicity. We have been induced to make a faulty generalization.

10 Conclusion

In the standard view, Szilard's thought experiment was the initiating stimulus for a new tradition in physics. Until it drew attention to the role of information, we are supposed to believe, it was impossible to understand the necessity of failure of Maxwell's demon. The thought experiment illustrated how a quantitative relation is possible between information acquired or, later, erased and thermodynamic entropy. The principle that governs this relation, whichever it might be, forms the foundation of a new science of the thermodynamics of information or computation, with the exorcism of Maxwell's demon its signal achievement.

Alas, this standard view is a mirage and illusion. Szilard's novel response to Maxwell's demon added nothing useful to the superior analysis already given by Smoluchowski over a decade before. Instead, that older, better analysis was preempted by the popular appeal of the apparently paradoxical connection of information and thermodynamic entropy. What followed were expanding efforts to make precise ideas that are, at their heart, sufficiently vague and flawed as to admit no cogent development. The core of Szilard's thought experiment, his one-molecule engine, was an inconsistent muddle of improper idealizations. Yet it became the workhorse of new theorizing, ensuring that new ideas derived with its help, such as Landauer's principle, inherited its flaws.

The power of a thought experiment in physics lies in its capacity to focus on just the most essential. It can do that since the experiment is conducted purely in thought, where inessential distractions can be eradicated under the guise of idealizations; and one representative example can speak simply for the generality. For the activity to succeed, we must give the thought experimenter considerable latitude in deciding just which processes are the instructive, representative examples and just which can be idealized away as inessential. When that latitude is exercised well, we gain wonderful illumination. However that latitude can be misused. Through it, we may be induced to accept assumptions, hidden in the picturesque scenario, that we would never accept were they made explicit in a less picturesque environment. Szilard's thought experiment is a powerful example of how this latitude can be misused. It is, in my view, unparalleled in science in the mischief it has caused. It is the worst thought experiment in science.

Notes

1. This follows since the probability of the fluctuation is $[(V-\Delta V)/V]^n \approx [1 - \Delta V/(V/n)]$ for large n and small $\Delta V/V$.
2. This equality $Q=W$ follows since the internal energy of the one-molecule gas remains unchanged in the isothermal process; it is a function of temperature only.
3. Similarly, Szilard concluded that the $k \log 2$ of entropy produced is an average only, so that the second law is preserved only in the averaging of many cycles.
4. For a convenient survey and compilation of papers, see the two editions Leff and Rex (1990 and 2003). Note that the earlier edition contains more material pertinent to this period than the later edition.
5. The claim of experimental confirmation is mistaken. See Norton (2013, §3.7).
6. Thought experiments in science are generally illuminating or, at the least, benign. It is not so with thought experiments in philosophy. They are a locus of misdirection and deception. We are supposed to derive important conclusions about fundamental matters from bizarre imaginings of zombies, who behave exactly like conscious humans, but are not conscious; or of substances that share exactly all the physical properties of water, but are not water. The narrative conventions of a thought experiment authorize us to contemplate hokum that would otherwise never survive scrutiny.
7. Szilard explicitly adopts this case, writing (1929, 302): "We may be sure that intelligent living beings – insofar as we are dealing with their intervention in a thermodynamic system – can be replaced by non-living devices whose 'biological phenomena' one could follow ..."
8. For detailed computation of these effects for the gas expansion, see Norton (2017).
9. For more discussion, see Norton (2013, §7).
10. This analysis conforms with El Skaf's (2016, ch. 6) account of how thought experiments can evolve. Tacit possibility claims in the background of the scenario are subsequently identified and brought to the foreground, where they are challenged.

References

Bennett, C. H. (1982) "The thermodynamics of computation – a review," *International Journal of Theoretical Physics* 21: 905–940.
Bennett, C. H. (1987) "Demons, engines and the second law," *Scientific American* 257: 108–116.
Bérut, A., Arakelyan, A., Petrosyan, A., Ciliberto, S., Dillenschneider, R. and Lutz, E. (2012) "Experimental verification of Landauer's principle linking information and thermodynamics," *Nature* 48: 187–190.
Brillouin, L. (1950) "Maxwell's demon cannot operate: Information and entropy I," in *Maxwell's Demon 2: Entropy, Classical and Quantum Information, Computing*, edited by H. S. Leff and A. Rex (pp. 120–123), Philadelphia: Institute of Physics Publishing.
Earman, J. and Norton, J. D. (1998, 1999) "Exorcist XIV: The wrath of Maxwell's demon," *Studies in the History and Philosophy of Modern Physics*, Part I "From Maxwell to Szilard," 29 (1998), 435–471; Part II: "From Szilard to Landauer and beyond," 30 (1999), 1–40.
Einstein, A. (1952) *Relativity: The Special and the General Theory*, New York: Bonanza.
El Skaf, R. (2016) *La Structure des Expériences de Pensée Scientifiques*, Ph.D. thesis, Université Paris I Panthéon-Sorbonne.
Ladyman, J., Presnell, S. and Short, A. J. (2008) "The use of the information-theoretic entropy in thermodynamics," *Studies in History and Philosophy of Modern Physics* 39: 315–324.
Ladyman, J., Presnell, S., Short, A. J. and Groisman, B. (2007) "The connection between logical and thermodynamic irreversibility," *Studies in the History and Philosophy of Modern Physics* 38: 58–79.

Landauer, R. (1961) "Irreversibility and heat generation in the computing process," *IBM Journal of Research and Development* 5: 183–191.

Leff, H. S. and Rex, A. (eds) (1990) *Maxwell's Demon: Entropy, Classical and Quantum Information, Computing*, Bristol: Adam Hilger.

Leff, H. S. and Rex, A. (eds) (2003) *Maxwell's Demon 2: Entropy, Classical and Quantum Information, Computing*, Philadelphia: Institute of Physics Publishing.

Maxwell, J. C. (1871) *A Theory of Heat*, London: Longmans, Green and Co.

Norton, J. D. (2011) "Waiting for Landauer," *Studies in History and Philosophy of Modern Physics* 42: 184–198.

Norton, J. D. (2013) "All shook up: Fluctuations, Maxwell's demon and the thermodynamics of computation," *Entropy* 15: 4432–4483.

Norton, J. D. (2017) "Thermodynamically reversible processes in statistical physics," *American Journal of Physics* 85: 135–145.

Norton, J. D. (forthcoming) "Maxwell's demon does not compute," in *Physical Perspectives on Computation, Computational Perspectives on Physics*, edited by M. E. Cuffaro and S. C. Fletcher, Cambridge: Cambridge University Press.

Shannon, C. E. and Weaver, W. (1964) *The Mathematical Theory of Communication*, Urbana, IL: University of Illinois Press.

Smoluchowski, M. (1912) "Experimentell nachweisbare, der üblichen Thermodynamik widersprechende Molekularphänomene," *Physikalische Zeitschrift* 13: 1069–1080.

Smoluchowski, M. (1914) "Gültigkeitsgrenzen des Zweiten Hauptsatzes der Warmetheorie," in *Vorträge über die Kinetische Theorie der Materie und der Elektrizität*, Berlin: B. G. Teubner; reprinted in *Oeuvres de Marie Smoluchowski*, Cracow: Jagellonian University Press (1927).

Szilard, L. (1929) "Über die Entropieverminderung in einem thermodynamischen System bei Eingriffen intelligenter Wesen," *Zeitschrift für Physik* 53: 840–56; translated as "On the decrease of entropy in a thermodynamic system by the intervention of intelligent beings," *Behavioral Science* 9: 301–310, and *The Collected Works of Leo Szilard: Scientific Papers*, Cambridge: MIT Press (1972).

von Neumann, J. (1932) *Mathematische Grundlagen der Quantenmechanik*, Berlin: Julius Springer; translated by R. T. Beyer as *Mathematical Foundations of Quantum Mechanics*, Princeton: Princeton University Press.

26
THOUGHT EXPERIMENTS AND IDEALIZATIONS

Julian Reiss

1 Introduction

Scientists rarely experiment on "nature" herself. Instead, they devise systems that are simplified, shielded from outside influences, arranged deliberately in ways that differ significantly from their naturally found analogues, made manageable and that stand in for natural systems before performing an experiment and making an inference to a principle that is hoped to extend beyond the experimental set up.

The deliberate distortions of nature that aim to address questions more effectively than asking nature directly would achieve are referred to as idealizations. They can occur in physical space, as when a glass tube is evacuated in order to prevent a cathode ray from ionizing gas molecules. But they can, and very frequently do, also occur in hypothetical space, when they are performed not on a chunk of nature but on a *representation* of it.

Scientific models idealize, often in order to make a problem mathematically tractable. This chapter considers idealizations in a context about which much less has been written, thought experiments. In what follows, I shall first introduce a small number of examples of idealizing thought experiments from physics, economics and biology. I will then distinguish a number of different kinds of idealizations one finds in these thought experiments and argue that they are all made for essentially the same purpose. The main discussion of this chapter occurs in Section 4, which asks how and under what conditions idealizations in thought experiments can be justified. Section 5 concludes by drawing some consequences of the discussion of the chapter's main argument for estimations of the chances of finding successful thought experiments in different scientific domains.

2 Thought experiments in physics, economics, and biology: some examples

Thought experiments are, like concrete experiments, manipulations on very special systems – except that they obtain in thought rather than in reality. Consider Galileo's

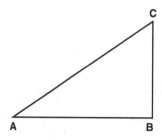

Figure 26.1

famous thought experiment of the inclined plane (Galilei 1967). In the thought experiment, Galileo constructs a system of two planes, one vertical (CB in Figure 26.1) and the other slanted (CA).

Along CA Galileo imagines a ball rolling, and along CB, a ball falling freely. As Salviati, Galileo's spokesman, says (Galilei 1967: 23),

> Now the line CA is meant to be an inclined plane, exquisitely polished and hard, upon which descends a perfectly round ball of some very hard substance. Suppose another ball, quite similar, to fall freely along the perpendicular CB.

The main point of the thought experiment is made when Salviati leads Sagredo, one of his interlocutors, into a contradiction by asking him about the speed of the balls. On the one hand, Sagredo agrees that both balls will have the same impetus (speed) when reaching points A and B, respectively – the speed required to take them back up to the same height. But on the other hand, it seems that the ball sliding down CA will have a lower speed than the falling ball. After all, CB is much shorter than CA, and the falling ball reaches B before the sliding ball reaches A. According to Thomas Kuhn, the chief lesson of this thought experiment is conceptual change (Kuhn 1981 [1963]). This is because the only way to resolve the tension of competing claims about the speeds of the balls is to distinguish different concepts of speed. There is, first, a concept of *instantaneous* velocity that measures a body's speed at a single point in time. And there is, second, a concept of speed that measures the time a body needs to traverse a given distance. As a body can be faster in one sense but not in the other, there is no contradiction.

Now consider a famous thought experiment from economics. In a seminal paper, George Akerlof seeks to explain the large price differential between new cars and cars that have just left the showroom (Akerlof 1970). Though Akerlof observes that there is a widely accepted explanation – people simply have a preference for new cars – he thinks that there is a better alternative. An important step in his argument that establishes his alternative explanation is the following thought experiment (489):

> Suppose (for the sake of clarity rather than reality) that there are just four kinds of cars. There are new cars and used cars. There are good cars and bad cars (which in America are known as "lemons"). A new car may be a good car or a lemon, and of course the same is true of used cars.

> The individuals in this market buy a new automobile without knowing whether the car they buy will be good or a lemon. But they do know that with probability q it is a good car and with probability (1 − q) it is a lemon; by assumption, q is the proportion of good cars produced and (1 − q) is the proportion of lemons.
>
> After owning a specific car, however, for a length of time, the car owner can form a good idea of the quality of this machine; i.e., the owner assigns a new probability to the event that his car is a lemon. This estimate is more accurate than the original estimate. An asymmetry in available information has developed: for the sellers now have more knowledge about the quality of a car than the buyers. But good cars and bad cars must still sell at the same price – since it is impossible for a buyer to tell the difference between a good car and a bad car. It is apparent that a used car cannot have the same valuation as a new car – if it did have the same valuation, it would clearly be advantageous to trade a lemon at the price of new car, and buy another new car, at a higher probability q of being good and a lower probability of being bad. Thus the owner of a good machine must be locked in. Not only is it true that he cannot receive the true value of his car, but he cannot even obtain the expected value of a new car.

It is the asymmetry in the information distribution that explains the price differential between new and used cars. This explanation is better than the original one because it does without an assumption about a specific preference individuals might or might not have. A structural explanation is preferable to one that requires an assumption about how individuals value certain goods. Moreover, as Akerlof indicates in an "applications" section of the paper, the new explanation can be reused in a variety of different contexts – insurance markets, labour markets, businesses where honesty matters, and credit markets in developing countries. His explanation is thus more unifying than positing a specific preference for new cars.

For a final example, let us turn to biology. Biology is rarely discussed in the literature on thought experiments. James Brown and Yiftach Fehige's otherwise comprehensive *Stanford Encyclopedia of Philosophy* entry, for example, leaves out biology completely (Brown and Fehige 2016). And yet, one can find thought experiments in evolutionary biology, population genetics, molecular biology, and artificial life and computational modelling in biology (Lennox 1991; Schlaepfer and Weber, this volume). Here is a famous one from Darwin's *Origin of the Species* (quoted from Lennox 1991, 228–9):

> Let us take the case of a wolf, which preys on various animals, securing some by craft, some by strength, and some by fleetness; and let us suppose that the fleetest prey, a deer for instance, had from any change in the country increased in numbers, or that other prey had decreased in numbers, during that season of the year when the wolf is hardest pressed for food. I can under such circumstances see no reason to doubt that the swiftest and slimmest wolves would have the best chance of surviving, and so be preserved or selected.
>
> Now, if any slight innate change of habit or of structure benefited an individual wolf, it would have the best chance of surviving and of leaving offspring. Some of its young would probably inherit the same habits or structure, and by the repetition of this process, a new variety might be formed which would either supplant or coexist with the parent-form of wolf.

According to James Lennox, thought experiments such as this do not play an evidential role; instead, they help to explore the explanatory potential of a theory, in this case the theory of natural selection.

3 Idealizations

Idealizations are ubiquitous in science and play a variety of roles. The models one finds in mathematical sciences such as theoretical physics, theoretical economics and theoretical biology often idealize in order to make problems mathematically tractable. For around 30 years, computer simulations have become more popular in these sciences, and computer simulations require different kinds of idealizations. They are, on the one hand, not constrained by the need to find closed-form solutions to a mathematical problem. But on the other, the more complex a problem becomes, the more computing time is needed, and computational resources are scarce. Thus different kinds of idealizations are introduced in order to save computing time. These kinds of "mathematical idealization" will not be considered further here, however, as thought experiments achieve their results without mathematization or computation.

Ernan McMullin considers what he calls "Galilean idealizations" and, among them, distinguishes "construct idealizations" and "causal idealizations." Both are "Galilean" in that they simplify the envisaged situation relative to the reality it stands for. However, the former changes the conceptual representation of an object whereas the latter changes the problem situation itself (McMullin 1985, 255). An example of a construct idealization is Galileo's assumption that two weights suspended from a balance make right angles with the balance. The assumption is false since both weights are directed to the centre of the Earth. Among construct idealizations, McMullin further distinguishes between *formal* and *material* idealizations. Formal idealizations are false assumptions about features that are known to make a difference to the kind of explanation offered, but that are required in order to derive a result (258). Material idealizations concern features that are left unspecified in the envisaged situation because they are deemed irrelevant to the inquiry at hand (*ibid.*). This kind of idealization is also variously referred to as "Aristotelian" (Brown 2012; Frigg and Hartmann 2012) and "abstraction" (as opposed to idealization, see Cartwright 1989; Jones 2005).

Thought experiments are full of both formal and material construct idealizations. Galileo's thought experiment of the inclined plane, for instance, assumes "perfectly round" balls of "some very hard" substance (Galilei 1967, 23). There is no doubt that a less than perfectly round or soft ball would roll down the slope in a different manner (and so this is a formal idealization Galileo makes in order to derive his result). Given it is perfectly round and hard, it does not matter which colour the ball is or what it is made of. So Galileo specifies only that the substance is very hard and idealizes away all other properties it might have.

In Akerlof's thought experiment, there are only two categories of cars, "good" and "bad." Clearly, cars have more relevant properties than quality, quality is itself a vector rather than a scalar, and each dimension has more than just two values. Unlike in Galileo's physical inquiry, in an economic inquiry the colour of the object might matter a great deal. On the other hand, there are certainly some properties of cars that are not relevant to their tradability – the number of molecules they are made of, or whether they were made by a German or a Korean robot (assuming that that does not affect their quality!).

McMullin describes the reason for making causal idealizations as follows (264):

> The unordered world of Nature is a tangle of causal lines; there is no hope of a "firm science" unless one can somehow simplify the tangle by eliminating, or otherwise neutralizing, the causal lines which impede, or complicate, the action of the factors one is trying to sort out.

Causal idealization too comes in two forms: experimental and subjunctive. Experimental idealization is the contrivance of a simplified physical (or biological, social, etc.) system, designed to answer specific scientific questions or problems (265ff.). Subjunctive idealization contrives such a system in the imagination: it answers "what would happen if ... ?" questions (268ff.).

All thought experiments involve causal idealizations of the subjunctive kind. Galileo assumes away air resistance and, implicitly, all other forces that might influence the speed of the balls. Akerlof, again, implicitly, keeps constant all factors that might influence individuals' propensities to buy and sell cars such as incomes, preferences, expectations and so on. Darwin's perhaps appears as the least idealized thought experiment, and it does not make any explicitly idealizing assumptions. However, it too has to assume that the relative increase of fleeting prey is the only cause of the change in the wolf's genetic pool. After all, if the reason for the decimation of the non-fleeting prey was, say, a virus that also befell swift and slim (but not other) wolves, we would not expect the formation of a new variety of wolf, or at least not of the same new variety Darwin imagines.

Among the subjunctive idealizations, McMullin further distinguishes between merely hypothetical and counterfactual ones, depending on whether or not the hypothesized idealized system could, in principle, be physically (biologically, socially, etc.) realized. It is certainly conceivable that a wolf territory can be controlled in such a way that an increase in fleeting prey is the only possible cause of changes in swift and slim wolves' fitness. On the other hand, perfect vacuums, spheres and perfectly smooth planes can, at best, be approximated.

4 Justifying idealizations

4.1 Weisberg on idealizations

Michael Weisberg argues that there are three different kinds of idealization in scientific practice, each coming with its own goals, rationale and justification (Weisberg 2007). The Galilean type, called "minimalist" by Weisberg, is only one among others. The other two I will refer to as Pythagorean and perspectivist, respectively.[1] Pythagorean assumptions aim to make a problem mathematically or computationally tractable. They are, according to Weisberg, justified pragmatically: "We simplify to more computationally tractable theories in order to get traction on the problem. If the theorist had not idealized, she would have been in a worse situation, stuck with an intractable theory" (641). This type is sensitive to developments in computational power and mathematical techniques; advances in the latter should bring about a degree of de-idealization. At any rate, different kinds of mathematics and computation techniques require different kinds of idealizing assumptions. In the ideal limit, Pythagorean idealizations are unnecessary. If the language of mathematics becomes infinitely flexible and computers infinitely powerful, there is no need to make false assumptions for the sake of mathematical or computational tractability.

Perspectival idealizations aim to represent an aspect of a phenomenon accurately. One and the same phenomenon can be regarded from different angles and different representations can bring out different aspects of a phenomenon. Different representations focus on different causal processes and provide different accounts of phenomena. No one explanation is the uniquely correct one. One reason for this is that researchers pursue different goals with their representations: explanatory power, accuracy, precision and so on. There are inherent trade-offs between these goals and so no representation can maximize all of them at the same time. Different idealizations help to achieve different goals (646).

In my view, there are no Pythagorean or perspectival idealizations in thought experiments. As intuitions and not mathematical deduction or computer-aided calculation drive the derivation of the result, no Pythagorean idealizations are needed, and I am not aware of any set of competing thought experiments that examine the same phenomenon.[2]

4.2 Analysis and synthesis

Typical idealizations in thought experiments are thus all of the "Galilean" type considered in Section 3. They all serve one and the same purpose: to apply the first (analytic) stage of the method of analysis and synthesis. A complex problem such as that of calculating the speed of a falling body in, as Carl Menger would call it, "full empirical reality" (Menger 1963 [1887]) is addressed by first translating it into a related but simpler problem that considers only one or a small number of main causes of the phenomenon of interest; then a principle is established that allows the explanation and prediction of the simplified phenomenon; a prediction or explanation of the original phenomenon is finally reached by adding in corrections for the omitted causes. The analytic stage of the method proceeds by separating individual causal lines from each other and establishing a principle for each one. The synthetic stage combines the different principles to make a prediction or explanation of a complex phenomenon.

The fruitfulness of the method of analysis and synthesis, and of using thought experiments to implement its first stage, depends on whether or not two conditions are met: an epistemic and an empirical condition. The epistemic condition is that there are reliable methods for finding out what a single causal line does in isolation. In the present context, the question is whether thought experimentation can be justified as such a method. The empirical condition is that single causal lines make a systematic contribution to the outcome of interest that persists when "accidents" or disturbing causes are present. This is independent of whatever method is used, but information about whether the second condition is met or not will help to explain where certain methods work, why they fail and why we find a preponderance (or dearth) of certain methods in certain domains.

4.3 Thought experiments and the epistemology of idealizations

The success of experiments often turns on researchers' ability to make effective experimental idealizations. Peter Achinstein discusses Heinrich Hertz's attempts to determine whether cathode rays are electrically charged (Achinstein 2001). In one experiment, he introduced oppositely electrified plates into the cathode tube and reasoned that if cathode rays were electrically charged they should be deflected by these plates. The deflection did not occur and Hertz inferred that cathode rays are electrically neutral. The reason for the absence of a visible deflection was not, however, that the rays were not charged, as J. J. Thomson found out fourteen years later. He reasoned that if they were charged, they would ionize the gas molecules in the cathode tube, producing positive and negative charges that will neutralize the charge on the metal plates between which the cathode rays travel. Indeed, repeating Hertz's experiment with a properly evacuated tube, Thomson could observe the deflection of the rays. Thus, the failure of an experimental idealization can be responsible for the misinterpretation of the result of the experiment. If the idealizations work, however, there is not much uncertainty about the results as it is produced by nature.

A thought experiment has opposite characteristics. There can be little doubt about the success of a subjunctive idealization – we cannot fail to assume away air resistance or to make a plane perfectly smooth. We might fail to think of every possible cause of an outcome of interest, but even in this case the catchall assumption, "No other causes affect the outcome," will do the trick. On the other hand, since it is reached by intuition, there can be considerable uncertainty about the accuracy of the result. Who is to guarantee that nature, if asked the same question in a well-designed and executed experiment, would give the same answer? And how do we know how nature would answer in the first place?

Richard Laymon argues that idealizing assumptions in a thought experiment can be defended in either of two ways (Laymon 1991): there exists a series of (real/material) experiments such that the idealized situation is asymptotically approachable or there exist experiments and good theories of the disturbing causes so that their influence on the result can be calculated. Theories of disturbing forces are not normally available in the contexts where thought experiments play important roles. An early theory of air resistance is due to Newton who published it about a century after Galileo's *Dialogue*. In economics there are no quantitative theories of disturbing causes that I can think of. Series of experiments that asymptotically approach idealized set-ups, on the other hand, are plentiful. Half a century before Galileo published his *Dialogue*, Simon Stevin, the Flemish physicist and mathematician, refuted Aristotle's theory of falling bodies empirically (quoted from Kühne 2005, 32):

> The experience against Aristotle is the following: Let us take (as the very learned Mr. Jan Cornets de Groot, most industrious investigator of the secrets of Nature, and myself have done) two spheres of lead, the one ten times larger and heavier than the other, and drop them together from a height of 30 feet on to a board or something on which they give a perceptible sound [*merckelick gheluyt*]. Then it will be found that the lighter will not be ten times longer on its way than the heavier, but that they fall together on to the board so simultaneously that their two sounds seem to be one and the same rap. The same is found also to happen in practice with two equally large bodies whose gravities are in the ratio of one to ten; therefore Aristotle's aforesaid proportion is incorrect.

Galileo's *Dialogue* contains similar experimental results (in addition to his famous thought experiments). It is also at least conceivable that he experimented with slopes of an increasing degree of smoothness. Akerlof's argument is based on the idea that people do not leave massive arbitrage opportunities unexploited. This again is something for which a good deal of empirical evidence existed at the time Akerlof published his thought experiment.

Margaret Schabas has an interesting theory of thought experiments in economics, a discussion of which will bring out another aspect of the epistemology of idealizations (Schabas 2008, this volume). According to her, bona fide thought experiments usually have two characteristics that set them apart from related techniques such as mathematical demonstration, modelling or narration. First, they involve a genuinely experimental moment such as a manipulation or intervention. Second, they begin with a jarring counterfactual "that transports the mind to a different and distant world, as opposed to a proximate alternative world" (Schabas 2008, 162). One of Hume's famous monetary thought experiments is a case in point (quoted from Schabas 2008, 161):

> For suppose, that, by miracle, every man in GREAT BRITAIN should have five pounds slipt into his pocket in one night; this would much more than double the whole money that is at present in the kingdom; yet there would not next day, nor for some time, be any more lenders, nor any variation in the interest [rate].

Schabas argues that Hume used this thought experiment to make the "in principle" neutrality of money and its "in practice" non-neutrality compatible with each other. Milton Friedman's present-day analogy achieves something similar (Friedman 1969, 4–5):

> Let us suppose now that one day a helicopter flies over this community and drops an additional $1,000 in bills from the sky, which is, of course, hastily collected by members of the community. Let us suppose further that everyone is convinced that this is a unique event which will never be repeated.

Both are clearly thought experiments according to Schabas's criteria as there is a quasi-experimental manipulation and the initial counterfactual is one which is jarring: neither overnight miraculous doublings of the money stock nor helicopter drops of large quantities of money occur in real economies, not even approximately. In my view, these thought experiments aim to achieve the same as those we have considered so far by making one dramatic idealization instead of a number of less conspicuous ones: they isolate a single causal line. In Hume's and Friedman's thought experiments, this happens by artificially increasing the size of the causal factor of interest; whatever other factors then might contribute to the outcome, it will be negligible relative to the main factor. To use Marcel Boumans's apt terminology, whereas the thought experiments from Section 2 require "*ceteris absentibus*" assumptions, due to the causal effect size of the idealization in Hume's and Friedman's thought experiments, only a "*ceteris neglectis*" assumption concerning the other factors has to be made (Boumans 2005, 118–19; see also Musgrave 1981 on assumptions in economic models and Morgan 2013 on "swamping" causes that help the analysis of natural experiments).

Historians often use counterfactuals in order to establish singular causal explanations. In order to establish, say, whether the assassination of Archduke Franz Ferdinand played a causal role in the outbreak of World War I or the Greeks' victory in the battle of Salamis in the development of the hegemony of Western values, they ask if the war had broken out if Franz Ferdinand had not been assassinated or if Western values had still risen to dominance if the Greeks had lost (Hanson 2006; Lebow 2014). In order to assess these counterfactuals, historians use a "historical consistency" criterion (Tetlock and Belkin 1996; Reiss 2009, 2012). Not too much history is supposed to be rewritten in order to make the counterfactual antecedent true. Importantly, historians ask whether the counterfactual antecedent is "co-tenable" with what else is known about history: the counterfactual antecedent A is co-tenable with a proposition S if it is not the case that S would be false if A were true (Goodman 1954, 15). So to assess whether an antecedent is historically consistent, they test whether making the antecedent true would violate firmly held beliefs about historical events and patterns. Hume's counterfactual is, arguably, not historically consistent in this sense. For miracles to occur, many beliefs about history would have to be different.

The rationale behind this aside on historiographic methodology was to draw attention to one of the historians' reasons for not rewriting history too much when making counterfactual thought experiments, which is an epistemic reason (Lebow 2010, 55, original emphasis):[3]

> Max Weber insisted that plausible counterfactuals should make as [minimal] historical changes as possible on the grounds that the more we disturb the values, goals, and contexts in which actors operate, the less predictable their behavior becomes. Counterfactual arguments make a credible case for a dramatically different future on the basis of one small change in reality are very powerful and the plausible rewrite rule should be followed whenever possible. The *nature* of the changes made by the experiment are nevertheless more important than the *number* of changes. A plausible rewrite that makes only one alteration in reality may not qualify as a plausible world counterfactual if the counterfactual is unrealistic or if numerous subsequent counterfactual steps are necessary to reach the hypothesized consequent. A counterfactual based on several small changes, all of them appearing plausible, may be more plausible, especially if they lead more directly to the consequent.

We do not know how people would react if their wealth suddenly doubles overnight. Hence, according to historians in the Weber tradition, we should not ask what would happen if it were to double. The historians' criterion is not exactly the same as Laymon's. A historically consistent counterfactual might be one for which there is no series of asymptotically approaching experiments. And even if we have such a series of experiments, the counterfactual might still be historically inconsistent because it is an alteration of the course of history that is, even though generally possible, implausible in a given historical context.[4] Both criteria can help us to determine whether a given idealization meets the epistemic condition.

4.4 Idealization and causality

The second condition for the method of analysis and synthesis to be used fruitfully is empirical: causes have to combine additively, at least approximately. If, say, the linear air resistance hypothesis is true, according to which the force due to air resistance is proportional to speed and acts in the direction opposite to motion, the total force acting on a falling body is given by:

$$F_{tot} = F_{grav} + F_{air} = mg - ks(t),$$

where F_{tot} is the total force, F_{grav} the force due to the Earth's gravitational field, F_{air} air resistance, m the body's mass, g the gravitational acceleration, k a constant and $s(t)$ the body's speed at t. In this case, both forces make simple, additive contributions to the total force. Ronald Laymon describes the advantages of this type of behaviour as follows (Laymon 1995, 361):

> In summary, additivity has two significant virtues. First, it allows ignored causes to be treated as if they had value zero. Second, it allows for the easy transfer of causal information from one situation to another because the effects of a variation in cause remain the same regardless of what combination of other causes is present.

To see this, suppose, by contrast, that the force due to gravity interacts with air resistance. What I mean by "interaction" is that the functional form of the relation between speed and the Earth's gravity and thus the size of the contribution gravity makes to the total force, is itself dependent on the value of force due to air resistance. The amount of air resistance an object experiences depends on its speed, its cross-sectional area, its shape and the density of the air. In the extreme, we could have not one law of falling bodies but many: one law for slim and swift bodies, one for large and laggard, one for the English wet summer (as humidity and temperature affect the density of the air; and of course there would be different English wet summer laws for swift/slim bodies and for large/laggard ones), one for the dry Californian winter and so on and so forth. This is clearly not how falling bodies behave. That they do not behave this way is something we learn from empirical evidence, and Galileo was well aware of the empirical facts before presenting his thought experiment.

Not all things are as regularly behaved as falling bodies. To give one example from social science, the causes of economic growth are manifold. There was a time when many policy makers and economists subscribed to the "Washington consensus" – a set of economic policy prescriptions made to help crisis-ridden developing countries trigger and sustain growth. The original list was the following (Rodrik 2007, 17):

A   Fiscal discipline
B   Reorientation of public expenditures
C   Tax reform
D   Interest rate liberalization
E   Unified and competitive exchange rates
F   Trade liberalization
G   Openness to foreign direct investment
H   Privatization
I   Deregulation
J   Secure property rights

It would be a mistake to assume that each of these recommendations corresponds to a factor that has an independent additive effect on growth. In fact, looking at recent empirical evidence, it looks as though there is no correlation or a negative correlation between a developing country's success at implementing these policies and its economic success – "best practice" countries (such as some Latin American countries) have done fairly poorly, and countries that have a poor record in at least some of these dimensions have done very well (such as China).

After a look at the data from a large set of developing countries, Dani Rodrik assesses the situation as follows (Rodrik 2007, 39): "No country has experienced rapid growth without minimal adherence to what I have termed higher-order principles of sound economic governance – property rights, market-oriented incentives, sound money, fiscal solvency. But ... , these principles have often been implemented via policy arrangements that are quite unconventional." Thus, some of the items of the Washington consensus seem to be necessary conditions for growth. However, what matters is that a country gets the specific mix right, and what that means is very different from country to country. If Rodrik is correct about this, the causes of economic growth are such that the contribution a factor makes to the outcome depends on the background constellation of other factors within which it operates.

4.5 Causality, metaphysics and semantics

Is what I called the "empirical condition" in fact a metaphysical condition? Does it tell us anything about the nature of causality? It is certainly true that the most prominent attempts to make sense of this aspect of scientific methodology is often underwritten with a form of Aristotelian realism about causal powers or capacities (see in particular Cartwright 1999, especially ch. 4, and Mumford and Anjum 2011). Aristotelian realism is particularly popular among social scientists (see, for instance, Pawson 2006 and Groff 2008, part III). But as I have argued in previous work, the idea that complex situations can be analyzed by examining the laws that describe what individual factors do in isolation and then to predict what happens on the basis of these laws plus a law of composition is in fact metaphysically neutral. For one thing, apart from Aristotelian realist, there are also Kantian (Watkins 2005) and fictionalist (Vaihinger 1924) interpretations of causal contributions available. For another, what matters is *whether* the method of analysis and synthesis works, not *why* it works when it does. That factors have powers or capacities that make stable causal contributions is at best a sufficient condition for the method to work, but it is not necessary. For the method to work it would be entirely sufficient if the factors behaved *as though* they had causal powers/capacities.

In my view, the question is more one of semantics. Whether or not a causal factor makes stable contributions (or behaves as though it does) makes an enormous difference to scientists' inferential practices and abilities. On the one hand, it makes a difference to the methods with which causal claims are established – in particular to the kinds of idealizations these methods can properly make. Galilean idealizations work best when factors (behave as though they) make stable causal contributions. On the other hand, it makes a difference to the inferences that the acceptance of the causal claim entitles scientists to make. A claim that ascribes to a factor the power/capacity to make stable causal contributions allows inferences about situations that differ significantly from the (thought) experimental situation, whereas a contextualist causal claim does not license such inferences. To the extent that the meaning of causal claims is related to these inferential practices and abilities, the applicability of the Galilean method has therefore conceptual consequences (for a defence of such an inferentialist interpretation of causal claims, see Reiss 2015).

It certainly did so for John Stuart Mill. Mill would only call factors causes if they had the property of additivity (Laymon 1995, 360):

> Mill wanted more: that something not be a cause unless it had this property. In a nutshell, Mill's idea was that being a cause requires an independence of potency that can only exist if the efficacy of the cause does not depend on the values of other descriptive or causal parameters.

Laymon endorses Mill's view in the end (371), but it seems overly strong. Causes are difference makers. Their presence should make a difference to the outcome in the context in which the outcome obtains. Whether or not it continues to be a difference maker in other contexts, and in particular, whether the size of the difference it makes is stable across contexts should not affect our conceptualization of a factor as a cause (though it can of course affect our conceptualization of a factor as a particular kind of cause). All difference-making accounts of cause such as regularity accounts (e.g., Mackie 1980), counterfactual accounts (e.g., Lewis 1973) and interventionist accounts (e.g., Woodward 2003) agree with this reading.

5 Conclusions: thought experiments and their proper domain

Even though above I have described an example from physics where causes are additive and one from economics where they are not, it is not the case that one can generally assume that physics causes are additive and causes in the special sciences are not. Forces are additive, but many other causes in physics are not (for a detailed discussion of additivity in physics and its relation to idealization, see Laymon 1995). There is evidence that at least some economics causes have this property (Reiss forthcoming).

Nevertheless it is true that the method of analysis and synthesis appears to work much better in some domains than in others. In the natural sciences, it has been popular and successful since its Galilean origins. In the social and behavioural sciences, it is popular and being used, but often not very successfully. As McMullin remarks (McMullin 1985, 267–8):

> We have become accustomed in recent decades to the charge that this sort of ... idealization can, in the context of the behavioral sciences, distort the behavior one is trying to understand. Ethologists have urged that the "Galilean methods" advocated by behaviorists and others in biology and psychology inevitably alter the behavior to be studied in ways that undermine the value of these methods as guides to genuine scientific truth. The technique of isolating causal lines does not seem to work so well when the object under study is a complex organism or a social group. The "impediments" cannot be defined and eliminated as they can in the case of a ball on an inclined plane.

Perhaps this explains why we find thought experiments more frequently in some sciences rather than others. All thought experiments make Galilean idealizations, and these will be successful only to the extent that the two conditions discussed in Section 4 are met. As McMullin argues, the second condition is unlikely to be met in the social and behavioural sciences, and there are reasons to believe that the same is true for the epistemic condition. Schabas suggests that thought experiments are rare in economics. If what I have been argued in this chapter is correct, she may well be right.[5]

Notes

1 Weisberg calls them "Galilean" and "multiple model idealizations." The former I find rather misleading, as Galileo himself clearly aimed at providing accounts of single causal lines, which, according to Weisberg, is the main purpose of what he calls "minimalist" idealizations. That some of the principles that describe the behaviour of single causal lines can be described in mathematical terms is true, but the reason for the idealization is to get to the single causes. Mathematical description is a by-product. This is entirely different, for instance, in contemporary mathematical economics where idealizations are frequently introduced in order to make a problem mathematically tractable whether or not the outcome is a representation of a single cause. If a production function is assumed to be Cobb-Douglas, this assumption is made for mathematical convenience, not in order to focus on an isolated cause and at the expense of what Galileo called accidents. Because of their goal to make a problem mathematically (or computationally) tractable, I call these non-Galilean idealizations "Pythagorean."
2 John Norton examines what he calls "thought experiment – anti-thought experiment pairs" (Norton 2004). But his purpose is to show that it is possible to find convincing pairs of narratives so that one demonstrates the truth of a claim and the other its falsehood. The different thought experiments thus have the *same* goal but *opposite* results rather than different goals.
3 I substituted a "minimal" for the original "few" because it is more consistent with what Lebow says later on in the quote. I also omitted a footnote that provides a reference to Max Weber's (1905).
4 An example for such a historically inconsistent albeit possible counterfactual might be, "Had Chamberlain confronted Germany about the Sudetenland ..." There are certainly situations in history in which an aggressor state was confronted by a large imperial power. And yet, given what we know about Chamberlain, it is most unlikely that *he* would ever have done so. See Khong (1996) for a discussion.
5 Having a more liberal understanding of the term I do not think that thought experiments are quite as rare as Schabas suggests. However, I entirely agree that *successful* thought experiments in economics are rare, for the reasons given.

References

Achinstein, P. (2001) *The Book of Evidence*, Oxford: Oxford University Press.
Akerlof, G. (1970) "The market for 'lemons': Quality uncertainty and the market mechanism," *Quarterly Journal of Economics* 84: 488–500.
Boumans, M. (2005) *How Economists Model the World Into Numbers*, London: Routledge.
Brown, J. R. (2012) "What do we see in a thought experiment?" in *Thought Experiments in Science, Philosophy, and the Arts*, edited by M. Frappier, L. Meynell, and J. R. Brown, London: Routledge.
Brown, J. R. and Fehige, Y. (2016) "Thought experiments," *Stanford Encyclopedia of Philosophy*. Available here: http://plato.stanford.edu/archives/spr2016/entries/thought-experiment/ (accessed 15 November 2016).
Cartwright, N. (1989) *Nature's Capacities and Their Measurement*, Oxford: Clarendon.
Cartwright, N. (1999) *The Dappled World*, Cambridge: Cambridge University Press.
Friedman, M. (1969) *The Optimum Quantity of Money and Other Essays*, Chicago: Aldine Publishers.

Frigg, R. and Hartmann, S. (2012) "Models in science," *The Stanford Encyclopedia of Philosophy*. Available here: http://plato.stanford.edu/entries/models-science/ (accessed 15 November 2016).

Galilei, G. (1967) *Dialogue Concerning the Two Chief World Systems – Ptolemaic and Copernican*, translated by S. Drake, Berkeley: University of California Press.

Goodman, N. (1954) *Fact, Fiction and Forecast*, Atlantic Highlands: Athlone Press.

Groff, R. (2008) *Revitalizing Causality: Realism about Causality in Philosophy and Social Science*, London: Routledge.

Hanson, V. D. (2006) "A stillborn west? Themistocles at Salamis, 480 BC," in *Unmaking the West: "What-if?" Scenarios that Rewrite World History*, edited by P. Tetlock, R. N. Lebow, and G. Parker, Ann Arbor: University of Michigan Press.

Jones, M. (2005) "Idealization and abstraction: A framework," in *Idealization XII: Correcting the Model – Idealization and Abstraction in the Sciences*, edited by M. Jones and N. Cartwright, Amsterdam: Rodopi.

Khong, Y. F. (1996) "Confronting Hitler and its consequences," in *Counterfactual Thought Experiments in World Politics*, edited by P. Tetlock and A. Belkin, Princeton: Princeton University Press.

Kuhn, T. (1981 [1963]) "A function for thought experiments," in *The Structure of Scientific Revolutions*, Oxford: Oxford University Press.

Kühne, U. (2005) *Die Methode des Gedankenexperiments*, Frankfurt: Suhrkamp.

Laymon, R. (1991) "Thought experiments by Stevin, Mach and Gouy: Thought experiments as ideal limits and as semantic domains," in *Thought Experiments in Science and Philosophy*, edited by T. Horowitz and G. Massey, Savage: Rowman & Littlefield.

Laymon, R. (1995) "Experimentation and the legitimacy of idealization," *Philosophical Studies* 77: 353–375.

Lebow, R. N. (2010) *Forbidden Fruit: Counterfactuals and International Relations*, Princeton: Princeton University Press.

Lebow, R. N. (2014) *Archduke Franz Ferdinand Lives!: A World Without World War I*, New York: Palgrave Macmillan.

Lennox, J. (1991) "Darwinian thought experiments: A function for just-so stories," in *Thought Experiments in Science and Philosophy*, edited by T. Horowitz and G. Massey, Savage: Rowman & Littlefield.

Lewis, D. (1973) "Causation," *Journal of Philosophy* 70: 556–567.

Mackie, J. (1980) *The Cement of the Universe: A Study of Causation*, 2nd ed., Oxford: Oxford University Press.

McMullin, E. (1985) "Galilean idealization," *Studies in the History and Philosophy of Science* 16: 247–273.

Menger, C. (1963 [1887]) *Problems of Economics and Sociology*, translated by F. J. Nock, Urbana: University of Illinois Press.

Morgan, M. (2013) "Nature's experiments and natural experiments in the social sciences," *Philosophy of the Social Sciences* 43: 341–357.

Mumford, S. and Anjum, R. L. (2011) *Getting Causes from Powers*, Oxford: Oxford University Press.

Musgrave, A. (1981) "'Unreal assumptions' in economic theory: The F-twist untwisted," *Kyklos* 34: 377–387.

Norton, J. (2004) "Why thought experiments do not transcend empiricism," in *Contemporary Debates in the Philosophy of Science*, edited by C. Hitchcock, Oxford: Blackwell.

Pawson, R. (2006) *Evidence-Based Policy: A Realist Perspective*, London: Sage.

Reiss, J. (2009) "Counterfactuals, thought experiments and singular causal analysis in history," *Philosophy of Science* 76: 712–723.

Reiss, J. (2012) "Counterfactuals," in *The Oxford Handbook of the Philosophy of Social Science*, edited by H. Kincaid, Oxford: Oxford University Press.

Reiss, J. (2015) *Causation, Evidence, and Inference*, New York: Routledge.

Reiss, J. (forthcoming) "Are there social scientific laws?," in *The Routledge Companion to Philosophy of Social Science*, edited by L. McIntyre and A. Rosenberg, London: Routledge.

Rodrik, D. (2007) *One Economics, Many Recipes: Globalization, Institutions, and Economic Growth*, Princeton: Princeton University Press.

Schabas, M. (2008) "Hume's monetary thought experiments," *Studies in History and Philosophy of Science Part A* 29: 161–169.
Tetlock, P. and Belkin, A. (eds) (1996) *Counterfactual Thought Experiments in World Politics: Logical, Methodological and Psychological Perspectives*, Princeton: Princeton University Press.
Vaihinger, H. (1924) *The Philosophy of 'As If': A System of the Theoretical, Practical and Religious Fictions of Mankind*, London: Routledge and Keagan Paul.
Watkins, E. (2005) *Kant and the Metaphysics of Causality*, Cambridge: Cambridge University Press.
Weber, M. (1905 [1949]) "Objective possibility and adequate causation in historical explanation," in *The Methodology of the Social Sciences*, edited by M. Weber, E. Shils, and H. Finch, Glencoe: Free Press.
Weisberg, M. (2007) "Three kinds of idealization," *Journal of Philosophy* 104: 639–659.
Woodward, J. (2003) *Making Things Happen*, Oxford: Oxford University Press.

27
THOUGHT EXPERIMENTS AND SIMULATION EXPERIMENTS
Exploring hypothetical worlds

Johannes Lenhard

1 Introduction

Both thought experiments and simulation experiments apparently belong to the family of experiments, though they are somewhat special members because they work without intervention into the natural world. Instead they explore hypothetical worlds. For this reason many have wondered whether referring to them as "experiments" is justified at all. While most authors are concerned with only one type of "imagined" experiment – either simulation or thought experiment – this chapter hopes to gain new insight by considering what the two types of experiment share, and what they do not. A close look reveals at least one fundamental methodological difference between thought and simulation experiments: while thought experiments are a cognitive process that employs intuition, simulation experiments rest on automated iterations of formal algorithms. It will be argued that this difference has important epistemological ramifications.

Section 2 will review positions in the literature that are concerned with the relationship between these types of experiment. The relatively few contributions vary greatly, and the matter is complicated by the fact that neither thought experiments nor simulation experiments have agreed upon definitions. This results in contributions that highlight different similarities and dissimilarities. After this overview, Section 3 will undertake to combine the various insights about similarities and dissimilarities between the two types of experiment. Both thought and simulation experiments explore hypothetical worlds, but via different means – and the main claim is that this matters for epistemology. While thought experiments are – in a sense to be explained later – "epistemically transparent," simulation experiments can be called "epistemically opaque." Consequently, surprises play a more significant role in the latter. If this claim is correct, an immediate question arises: in what sense do simulation experiments create opacity, and how they deal with it? This question will be addressed in Section 4, where a number of examples are analyzed from the perspective of this question. Section 5 puts forward a consideration about the common ancestral line of thought experiments and simulation experiments, and considers what this says about scientific rationality.

2 Debates about taxonomy

In this section we will try to gain some insight by comparing thought experiments and simulation experiments. This task is complicated by the fact that the status (and closeness) of both as family members is controversial. Let us start therefore with a brief consideration of thought experiments, the older sibling, not with a general discussion, but one oriented at facilitating a comparison to simulation experiments.

2.1 Thought experiments

Obviously thought experiments are extremely economical experiments – intricate conditions can be represented cheaply in thought. It is controversial, however, whether this is an epistemological advantage or disadvantage. Do they play a merely heuristic role, or do they generate trustworthy knowledge? Empirical experiments bring scientific hypotheses and the natural world into contact, which is to say, they integrate them as independent witnesses. Is not this contact an essential part of the notion of experiment? If so it would be highly problematic to speak of thought "experimentation."[1]

Ian Hacking (1982) is responsible for a famous argument according to which experimental interventions justify a realistic conception of scientific objects. Experiments lead an incorruptible "life of their own." This is what Hacking denies for thought experiments (Hacking 1992). What then characterizes thought experiments in a positive way?

One important facet is that they make certain intuitions accessible. Thought experiments have to meet high standards of intelligibility, because the whole process takes place in cognition. If it is ever unclear what happens next, that is, if one cannot comprehend why a certain outcome should happen, the thought experiment fails. It does not fail because of an unwanted outcome, but because it does not work *as a thought experiment*. In this sense, the perceived transparency is a precondition for the feasibility of experimenting in thought.

Is this precondition a strength or a weakness? Jim Brown, among others, advocates the former (see, e.g., Brown 1992) and takes intuitive accessibility as indicating credibility, or truth. Brown favours a Platonic account according to which thought experiments allow humans to peek into Plato's heaven. He focuses on the methods and results of mathematics which are arguably a special case of thought experimentation because of its completely hypothetical form. The context in this case is fixed by definition. Take as an example the often-cited checker board problem: First cut out two squares from diagonal corners of a checkerboard. Is it still possible to arrange the board into rectangular pieces, each consisting of one white and one black square? Here, the question defines the problem so that asking whether the problem is adequately posed is missing the point.

In contrast to logico-mathematical puzzle solving, the question of adequate formulation matters in cases that are related to applications. The wonderful thought experiment with a light-clock in a spaceship might serve as an example. This clock consists of two perfect mirrors between which a light pulse "ticks." The spaceship starts from the earth, perpendicular to the clock's light pulse, and the clock is viewed from two different perspectives: an observer on earth and an astronaut in the ship. Because of the constancy of the speed of light, the clock ticks with the same speed for both observers. Seen from the earthling's perspective, however, the ship moves, hence the light pulse has to travel a slightly longer way from one mirror to the other. Since it has the same speed but a longer way to travel, time itself has to be stretched accordingly. Now, the formula for time dilatation follows elegantly from the theorem of Pythagoras.[2] The full derivation does not matter here, because my point is a different one.

The thought experiment happens in a setting or scenario that might be misleading. There is no guarantee that this experiment, as elegant as it might be, will lead to the correct formula for time dilatation. Perhaps it is not that the result is justified by the premises, but the other way around. The somewhat exotic setting of the experiment is first accepted, because it gives the right (already known) formula. Afterwards, the argument has sedimented and became a thought experiment. The result of relativity theory, time dilatation, is not questioned at any time, rather it is ennobled when we show that it is accessible even from a thought experiment.

This role for thought experiments (to only *seem* to establish) is well known in the literature. For instance, Humphreys assumes it when he highlights the exploratory function of thought experiments that makes clear which assumptions are necessary to obtain a given conclusion (Humphreys 1993, 218). Once an experiment has been worked out – like in the example above – it changes into a rhetorical instrument, targeted rather at an already-known formula than establishing something unknown. Ian Hacking also directs attention to the state when a thought experiment has been worked out. At this point, the outcome is no longer at stake. For this reason Hacking describes such experiments as "fixed, rather immutable" (Hacking 1992, 307). Finally, Ulrich Kühne, in his monograph on thought experiments (2005), sees their main function in cementing knowledge rather than creating it. However, he urges us to consider more carefully the *evolution* of thought experiments. Only by analyzing the development from exploration toward an accepted, fixed form can we understand their main characteristics.

There is a reason why the activity of performing a thought experiment might lead to further development of the same experiment, and also to its eventual convergence on an "immutable" state. Thought experiments, whatever their aim or function, explore imaginary scenarios that provide a certain setting or context. During the exploratory phase, such a context might be useful, especially in cases when that context is not fully explicated and contains a surplus of possibly relevant material that can be exploited for creating and framing the thought experiment. In situations where complex actions are modelled, such a context might include a rich but implicit reservoir of additional aspects and facts that are also relevant. Nancy Nersessian (1992) stresses this potential when she counts thought experiments as a class of model-based reasoning. Experimenters take the model for granted and let it lead the way.

Certainly the course of the experiment has to fulfil high standards of transparency. Gaps in the argumentation like "the reader might calculate easily" have to be ruled out. Instead, all phases of the experiment have to flow more or less continuously and without creating any gap in the mind. Of course, this need not happen on the first attempt; it might require a couple of iterations. Such iterations, if successful, efface any initial opacity and hopefully make possible free access to a clear intuitive judgement.

It might require some effort to satisfy this condition. Galileo, for example, reckoned it necessary to spend 20 pages in the *Discorsi* for making plausible what happens in the famous thought experiment with two falling and (un-)connected bodies (for more on this thought experiment, see Palmieri, this volume). There is regular dispute about whether certain thought experiments are indeed feasible or have gaps. Bohr and Einstein are a case in point for duels of this kind (see Bishop 1999). Hence thought experiments, or proposals for thought experiments, might be changed or even overthrown during the exploratory phase. Initial opacity about what follows in a given model or scenario requires iteration and critical discussion. One condition, again, is crucial: If the proposal shall eventually be accepted as a thought experiment, iteration has to efface opacity. Only an epistemically transparent process is able to sediment into a thought experiment – maybe with the qualification that a consensus among a group of educated people (and educated intuitions) is sufficient.

2.2 Simulation experiments

Simulation experiments are a newborn sibling in the family of experiments. Their epistemic status is arguably the most debated topic in the growing literature on computer simulation. The general strategy is to discuss the status of simulation experiments by locating them in an established coordinate system, i.e., by stressing certain similarities and dissimilarities to other methods. A most striking feature is that these experiments do not intervene in the natural world. This makes them similar to thought experiments, and inspires the hope that a comparative epistemological study will bear fruit.

Simulation experiments seem to be a special kind of experiment. They investigate the behaviour of simulation models by computer methods and have been analyzed as experiments with models, virtual experiments, or experiments without materiality (respectively by Deborah Dowling 1999, Eric Winsberg 2003, and Mary Morgan 2003, to name just a small sample of the growing philosophical literature). Although simulation experiments appear to be at least partially experimental, it is controversial in the philosophical literature whether this justifies speaking of them as experiments. Depending on what we take to be essential for being an "experiment," simulation experiments are advocated as a new kind of experiment, or not as experiments at all. To different degrees, Francesco Guala (2002), Morgan (2003, 2005), and Anouk Barberousse, Sara Franceschelli, and Cyrille Imbert (2009) argue for the latter standpoint, while Winsberg (2003, 2009) and Wendy Parker (2009) want to include simulation experiments into the esteemed family of experiments. I do not intend to enter the taxonomical debate on the status of simulations, rather I will focus on the comparison between simulation experiments and thought experiments.

Only a relatively small number of contributions exist that tackle the relationship between these two types of experiments. Some of them come from researchers working with simulation experiments, notably in the field of social simulations. While many or most scientific fields with well-established experimental traditions, like physics or mechanical engineering, have added simulation experiments to their repertoires, the problem of categorizing the experimental practices comes up in social simulation in a particular way. The whole field came into existence with simulation methods, so there is no methodological tradition of manipulating models or doing experiments *apart* from simulation. Thus it seems plausible that the question for scientists who reflect about their own practice is especially pressing. It seems, at least, that there is no direct interrelationship possible between simulation experiments and experiments that would intervene into the natural world to check whether the former got it right. Hence scientists like Ezequiel di Paolo, Jason Noble, and Seth Bullock (2000) take thought experiments as a point of comparison, exactly because thought experiments have an independent history as a method and also do not intervene.[3]

Di Paolo, Noble, and Bullock (2000) categorize simulation experiments as "opaque thought experiments," meaning that they explore the interplay of hypothetical assumptions, but in a computational way that human beings could not follow. Di Paolo and his colleagues touch upon a most important point when they bring opacity into play. This notion will play a major role in the following discussion. However, from a logical point of view, it seems a bit misleading to subsume simulation experiments under thought experiments. It has been argued above that epistemic transparency is an essential precondition for thought experiments; hence, speaking of opaque thought experiments seems questionable or even inconsistent.

Aside from social scientists, there are also philosophers of science who have asked whether simulation experiments should be counted as a sort of thought experiment. The fact that interventions are missing from both is the genus proximum, but then opinions diverge. Claus Beisbart and John D. Norton (2012) argue that thought and simulation experiments only logically analyze some set of starting assumptions. Hence they both do not belong to the family of experiments, but to that of arguments – a position that Norton has earlier advocated with regard to thought experiments.

Sanjay Chandrasekharan, Nersessian, and Vrishali Subramanian (2012) also analyze the way both experiment types deal with their assumptions, but arrive at a different conclusion. They stress that a thought experiment starts rather with a mental model than with a set of logical assumptions, and proceeds by analyzing this model in intuition – also a standpoint earlier advocated by the co-authoring Nersessian (see Nersessian, this volume). Simulation experiments are similar to thought experiments, since both are a sort of model-based reasoning. However, simulation experiments, unlike thought experiments, are not tied to intuition, but can utilize a range of algorithmic procedures. Therefore, Chandrasekharan and colleagues conclude that simulations will likely outpace (and eventually *replace*) thought experiments.

Finally, Rawad El Skaf and Cyrille Imbert (2013) take an ecumenic stance and reconceptualize the genus proximum. They underline that thought experiments as well as simulation experiments proceed by allowing us to see how a scenario unfolds. According to this view, the initial assumptions or hypotheses from which one starts somehow entail what will happen in the experiment and hence determine its outcome. The outcome is not initially known. Instead, it takes the unfolding as part of an experimental process that brings to light what was actually included already in the hypotheses. This viewpoint seems to be compatible with Nersessian's as well as with Norton's, at the cost of accepting a broad spectrum of what "unfolding a scenario" means.

There is of course a counterpart in the literature that also stresses the dissimilarities between thought and simulation experiments, especially with respect to their "unfolding" processes. Humphreys (1993), for instance, rightly points out that algorithmic processes are very different from the processes of intuition. From this perspective, thought and simulation experiments take place in very different realms. Let us turn therefore to the compatibility of the two kinds of experiment in more detail.

3 Experimenting, iteration, and opacity

A most important difference between thought and simulation experiments is that normally, simulations are epistemically opaque. This opacity deserves further attention. At first sight, it appears paradoxical since compiled computer programs are arguably the most explicit of all descriptions in scientific use. Executable software cannot tolerate any vagueness because at each step of the program the next step has to be specified precisely, else the compiler would not accept it. However, this condition does not guarantee transparency. Simulations are not opaque because it would be unclear how one step follows from its predecessors. On the contrary, it is the multitude of interrelated steps that can render the overall process opaque. Humphreys characterizes this problem in the following way:

> This opacity can result in a loss of understanding because in most traditional static models our understanding is based upon the ability to decompose the process between model inputs and outputs into modular steps, each of which is methodologically acceptable both individually and in combination with the others.
> (2004, 148)

Of course, there can be simulation models that are not opaque at all. Opacity is a feature of complex models, though the use of such models is widespread. Even if interactions in a simple target system were modelled in a simple way, a great number of them could lead to very complex model dynamics; especially when the simple events of the target system are highly related. The analysis of such real-world systems is therefore too complicated for analytical mathematical treatment and so testing the dynamics of the system has to proceed via simulation experiments. In brief, *algorithmic* transparency is a condition for executable programs, which however is consistent with the creation of epistemic opacity.

Despite the important separation in terms of epistemic transparency and opacity, there is an important methodological similarity: the use of iteration. It will be useful to discern two types of iteration for the following discussion. Iteration is not a standard topic in philosophy and there are only few recent attempts to give iteration a standing in the epistemology of science (see Hasok Chang 2007, who examines "epistemic iteration" in the development of scientific concepts).

I would like to discern two types of iterations pragmatically, namely, the "convergence" and the "atlas" type. The first is involved in cases like exploring a new pathway that eventually becomes your routine way. At the beginning, there is much uncertainty and back-and-forth, but after a couple of repetitions the pathway begins to stabilize. After many iterations, it sediments to become a routine path that you inattentively take. Repeating exercises in music or sports is often of this kind. A violinist uses her bow intuitively, as does an archer. In this way, iterations create "convergence," which can influence and educate intuition. Such iteration can generate high levels of certainty, but is usually bound to a fixed context. If the violinist plays a piano, or the archer uses a pistol, the question of how to maintain intuitive mastership becomes legitimate.

The second type of iteration works rather by exhausting the possibilities and thereby creating a compendium, or atlas. It functions on a more abstract level. Iteration here is used for exploring a set of options under controlled variations, gathering the results and thus obtaining an overview. Such iterations, again, are very common in science as well as in everyday life. My children, for instance, are quick in scanning each piece of a cake to find out which one is the biggest (and most attractive) one. If the number of possibilities is high, however, one will have to resort to automated iterations, which is exactly what computers are good at.

Thought experiments are tied to the convergence type of iteration. When you perform a thought experiment, repeated execution eliminates initial intransparency or ambiguity. Simulation experiments, on the other hand, involve the atlas type of iteration. Repeated, and slightly varied, model runs do not eliminate opacity, but rather explore the space of possible model behaviour. Thus the dynamics can be understood like an atlas that compiles many single maps. In sum, thought experiments have to conform to a condition of epistemic transparency, which accords to the convergence type of iteration. Simulation experiments, in contrast, are part of simulation modelling because epistemic transparency about model behaviour is not attainable. The computer as an instrument, in particular one with an ability to automate iterations, offers an instrumental compensation for lack of transparency. The set of gathered results then substitutes for intuitive certainty.

While thought experiments and simulation experiments are similar in that they exploit the facts contained in assumptions or modelled situations, they are dissimilar regarding the types of methods they use. Processing in intuition requires transparency, which computer-automated iterations often cannot provide. However, the insights simulations gain from collecting many results are something thought experiments do not provide.

4 Dealing with opacity

How can one work with epistemically opaque systems? And how can epistemically opaque models play an epistemically fruitful role? This section will briefly discuss a number of typical examples with increasing degrees of complication that illustrate how simulation experiments deal with opacity.

4.1 Social segregation

The first example is the well-known model for urban social segregation introduced by economist Thomas Schelling (1978). An idealized simple town map is represented by a grid of neighbouring cells, like a checkerboard. Each cell has inhabitants of a certain type (like skin colour) and with certain preferences, for instance, not having a majority of neighbours of type different from their own. Inhabitants will move to an available cell so that their preference is satisfied.

It is obvious that such preferences, if strong enough, will lead to segregation. In the extreme case, when everybody would insist on a homogeneous neighbourhood, segregation happens immediately. The model gets interesting with weaker preferences. The surprising result of Schelling's is that even under conditions of great tolerance, i.e., when inhabitants welcome a mixed neighbourhood, but not one too dominated by the other type, complete segregation obtains. What does "too dominated" mean? Reasoning does not help here, one needs to try out and actually perform a great number of iterations. In the model, one cell is inspected after the other and it is determined whether inhabitants want to move. After all cells have been checked, the process starts over. After many iterations, an equilibrium will occur and then one can see whether segregation has happened or not. The intriguing question is how weak preferences have to be to prevent segregation. This question can be answered only by exploratory trials with varying parameter values.

The simulation looks like a thought experiment, but the role of iteration is importantly different. There is no way to determine the segregating behaviour of the simulated inhabitants under varying parameter values, except by iterated trials. Schelling started with a checkerboard and some coins and attempted to find a feasible specification of the model. The decisive point is how robust the phenomenon of segregation is. That segregation can occur in particular models is trivial. A model that shows how weak assumptions can be that nevertheless lead to segregation is an interesting model since it indicates how generic the phenomenon is. Therefore, everything depends on the actual range of parameters that generate segregation. This range can be determined only by a great number of iterations. Consequently, Schelling had to give up the checkerboard and employ a computer, i.e., run a simulation experiment, to process a sufficient number of iterations. This experiment produced a great number of single results that allowed him to compile a sort of atlas of model behaviour. If instead he had dispensed with simulation experiments he could not have gained insight about the likelihood of segregation via various degrees of bias; no thought experiment could possibly sediment from the simulation runs to produce an epistemically transparent intuition of comparable import.

4.2 Phase transition

The next example, the Ising-model of physics, predates the computer and its architecture which served as the blueprint for Schelling's model. It works again on a regular grid. Each grid point (or cell) can take on one of two states (spin up – spin down) and neighbouring cells influence each other, for example by the tendency to take on the state of their neighbour. There is also a thermic parameter that controls the strength of influence. The higher the temperature, the higher the tendency to flip to an arbitrary state, i.e., the lower the influence of neighbouring states. The Ising-model is famous because it can exhibit phase transitions. In other words, there is a critical value of the thermic parameter above which sudden dramatic fluctuations occur, and below which widely mixed states grow into homogeneous clusters. This behaviour makes it a model for magnetization, a similar phenomenon.

Today one can conveniently simulate and experiment with the Ising-model on a computer screen, and again, this model presents great difficulties for a mathematical-analytical treatment. By analytical I mean that one can hardly show more than the existence of phase transitions, i.e., the critical parameters. This has made the model famous among philosophers for combining conceptual simplicity with computational complexity. The latter arises from the high level of interdependence, i.e., from the fact that the state at one grid point depends on that of its neighbours, which in turn depend on others, etc.

An iterative algorithm can simulate the model in a straightforward way, much like in the first example. Then, in a second layer of iterations, the temperature can be varied to sound out what the critical value is and how clusters form near this value. These iterations are not compressible, i.e., they have to be actually performed – which is feasible only by using a machine. However, this strategy brings even modern computers quickly to their limits. The number of necessary computational steps increases exponentially with the number of cells, and in cases of computational complexity like this, brute force strategies regularly fail.

At this point the Ising-model ceases to be parallel to the social segregation model. Only a second layer of simulation experiments has led to a methodological breakthrough, namely the use of so-called Monte-Carlo Markov-chains. The trick is to replace the unfeasibly large iteration problem by iterations on a different layer, namely by iterations of a random process.[4] This process is locally defined, i.e., for each state of the process the transition probabilities to other states are given. Iteration of this random process approximates the long-term behaviour of the process. In a sense, the simulated Markov-chain explores the territory that is otherwise unknown. By compiling the results of the much-iterated simulation experiments (runs of the random process) one eventually gets the desired atlas of the space that was originally "too big."

4.3 Chaos

The third example is iconic of complexity theory, as it connects to computational models. It illustrates how simulation experiments are employed to circumvent opacity. A famous instance of a complex system was identified early on by the meteorologist Edward Lorenz. Using partial differential equations, he investigated a dynamic meteorological system, and found it to display some alarming behaviour. A marginal change in the initial conditions could lead to a severe alteration of the overall behaviour. This system property has been aptly named "deterministic chaos" (cf. Lorenz 1967, 1993). In deterministic systems, the initial conditions completely determine the future development. At the same time, this system is unpredictable in the sense that even the slightest uncertainty about initial conditions, which is unavoidable in any practical application, could potentially change the long-term behaviour entirely. Such systems are called "chaotic." The term "nonlinear behaviour" refers to more or less the same thing: the long-term behaviour of the model does not depend in any linear way on the initial conditions; in other words, closely neighboured initial conditions can lead to widely differing final states.

Lorenz's example is famous, and has become a paradigm of chaos theory, or the theory of complex dynamical systems. His model, however, was not deliberately constructed for its mathematical properties, but emerged from his work in meteorology. And the results were relevant for that subject. The so-called "butterfly-effect" conceptualizes nonlinearity in a picture: Even small events can have great effects; a butterfly can change the weather – at least in principle. All these considerations concern dynamical systems theory, a field expressed in the mathematical language of differential equations. The point is that analytical methods could discover how strange the behaviour can be, but they are not sufficient to give insight into what happens in these systems. How should one conceptualize a system that would be attracted to very different states depending on an initial waggle?

The mysteriousness vanished only when the computer-generated image of the Lorenz attractor displayed the intricate trajectories of the system, making sense of their strange behaviour. Such visualizations were based on simulation experiments that were iterated many times. For each grid point (or pixel), the system's behaviour is computed. In a way, the computer scans or sounds out the system for systematically varying initial conditions, and afterwards the isolated results are put together into one image. Only then a picture of the overall dynamics emerges that suggests continuity and gives a vivid impression, though it is based on a great number of single results, comparable to pointillism in art. In this way, visualizations can provide insights into complex dynamics, although it is often not well understood how the assumptions that are used interact with each other in detail while bringing about the dynamics. The enormous computational capacity of computers renders possible the exploration of phase space and, inversely, visualizations render complex behaviour cognitively graspable. In this way, the epistemic opacity due to computational and target system complexity gets circumvented.

4.4 Electron density

The fourth and final example comes from the interface of computational chemistry and computational physics. The Schrödinger equation of quantum theory describes the electronic structure of atoms and molecules. This is true only in principle, however, since even the simplest cases involving molecules are already at the limit of mathematical tractability. For all application-oriented problems, the Schrödinger equation is too complex to be solvable. Again, this complexity arises from interdependence, namely the interdependence of the energy potentials of interacting electrons. The so-called "density functional theory" (DFT) offered a ground-breaking simplification. It is based on the fact that the many interacting energy potentials can be replaced by one single density function. The fundamental work was done by Walter Kohn and his co-workers Pierre Hohenberg and Liu Sham in the mid-1960s. This work on DFT won Kohn the Noble Prize in chemistry in 1998. He shared the prize with John Pople who received it for his development of computational methods. Today, DFT is widely used in computational quantum chemistry, at least partially because it is included in software packages that are convenient to use, for instance the package "Gaussian," that Pople helped to create.[5]

A Noble Prize for computer methods is remarkable; it makes plain the growing role of computational methods in supporting scientific theory. Again, the success of DFT in chemistry depended on the availability of the software. From a theoretical perspective, DFT is implemented in a computer program. And DFT does not just exist in *one* program; there are dozens of programs and packages, many of them available online, that feature the theory. Typically, such software comes with a blurb indicating the sets of situations, materials, and mixtures with which it performs well. Hence DFT is not simply implemented, but splits into many different variants. Why is this a significant observation?

The answer is closely related to the iterative character of simulation modelling. The step from a theoretical model to a computer model involves a separate, partly autonomous construction task. This task must bridge the gap between the continuous formalism of traditional mathematics in which theories are formulated, and the discrete operations digital machines can perform. Of course, one can reason with limiting cases, for instance the limit of an infinitely fine-grained grid, but one must always compute in finite steps. Therefore, theoretical laws and models, like Schrödinger's wave-equation, have to be fit into a Procrustean bed. Discretization, the name for this step, inevitably distorts. Each simulation model therefore requires some way to compensate for the distortions in the simulation model so that it remains relevant to the theoretical model or target system. Normally it is hard to discern whether such measures really re-establish the quality of the original theoretical model, or whether they merely compensate for some of its imperfection.

These compensation measures are a regular part of simulation models that we expect to increase their theoretical impact. Whether and how they do this can be guided by mathematical formalism only to a very rudimentary degree. Therefore simulation experiments are necessary to check and balance the compensating measures, and to adapt the simulation model accordingly.[6]

Given these considerations, the multitude of DFT methods looks less surprising. They differ essentially in the compensating strategies they implement. Since these are based on instrumental reasons rather than theoretical ones, they have to be judged according to the net-effect they produce on the dynamics of the model system. In other words, assessing and modifying DFT methods depends heavily on our knowledge of the applications for which they will be used. Over the course of such modifications, which take the form of stepwise iterated software developments, a particular instantiation of DFT will be formed by the applications for which it has been prepared, and in view of which it will be developed.

Experiments therefore take a central position in simulation modelling and help to make usable simulations as an instrument, especially at first. Instead of eliminating opacity, however, they work around it, replacing epistemic transparency with stepwise exploration. For this, a single simulation experiment does not suffice. Rather, one needs a whole series of experiments for charting model behaviour. A series of experiments like this utilizes iterations which we have called atlas type. To sum up: simulation modelling regularly resorts to artificial (compensating) measures that are motivated by the performance of a simulation model, not by theoretical reasoning. Such measures have to be coordinated according to their interactions in the embedding model. They have to be tried out in an iterative and exploratory mode; hence the atlas type of iteration is part-and-parcel of simulation modelling.

5 Conclusion: the common root of thought experiments and simulations

Thought experiments and simulation experiments are similar in that both make use of iterations. However, they differ fundamentally in the types of iterations they use, and in the functions those iterations fulfil. In thought experiments, the iterations of the convergence type eventually produce a cognitive tool that is sufficiently transparent to run in human intuition. Simulation experiments, on the other hand, do not remove, but rather circumvent or compensate opacity with the help of atlas type iterations. Iterative algorithms utilize computational power and can work where thought experiments cannot.

In particular, if iterations are incompressible, there is hardly a chance to render the results epistemically transparent.

Thought experiments entail the possibility of an aha-effect that is arguably tied to epistemic transparency. Converging iterations then can bring about new aha-effects. In contrast to this, simulation experiments result in an instrument-based collection of single calculations. Such collection lacks the intimacy of intuition, and therefore creates a certain cognitive distance, even if visualizations occasionally help to negate this distance.

Hence the essential difference is: The iterative mode in thought experiments eventually makes iterations superfluous by crystalizing the most intuitive approach. In simulation experiments, in contrast, the iterations remain structurally necessary. They do not crystalize a cognitive pathway to an intuition; instead, the extensive set of iterations are preserved. Of course, there must be some way to make the output of the set of iterations comprehensible, as the atlas type of iteration is suitable only under this condition. But this is not at all the same thing.

Let me conclude by presenting a perspective that puts thought and simulation experiments under the same historical framework. Here is some uncontroversial common ground shared by the different viewpoints discussed in this chapter: The thought-experimenter immerses himself or herself into a hypothetical world, a world explored in intuition. This exercise of creating and exploring hypothetical worlds has been part of the arsenal of modern science since its inception. This indicates how closely related the (philosophical) formation of human epistemological subjects and the emergence of modern science are. Kant's classic formulation of this relationship can be found in his *Critique of Pure Reason*: that human epistemology depends on the constructive activity of epistemic subjects. He was motivated by Newton, whose theory of gravity can be seen as the paradigm of a mathematized science. From an epistemological viewpoint, it intertwined the construction of a mathematical model with scientific – or more generally, *human* – rationality and epistemology. The way simulation experiments differ from thought experiments tells us something about the evolution of mathematical modelling, and our relationship to it.

Mathematization proved to be an essential element of what are now called the "hard" sciences. Ongoing formalization and, in particular, algebraization since the seventeenth century went hand in hand with ever more elaborate algorithms and mathematical constructions. However, human tractability has been a limitation that prevented constructions from becoming too complicated or lengthy. There were several phases in history at which the development of mathematics was thought to be at an end, because it reached the limits of tractability and transparency. Generalization proved to be the way forward for mathematization in the attempt to provide or re-establish epistemic transparency, arguably culminating in twentieth-century axiomatic thinking.

The pivotal impact of constructive activity for human culture reached a new level with the industrial revolution. Automation was an integral part of this revolution, and it has continued to gain importance in ever more areas of society and culture. This is the point where we re-enter our discussion. Simulation experiments, like thought experiments, are a method of exploring hypothetical models. Simulation experiments, however, make this possible using automated iterations.[7] In this sense, simulation experiments can be seen as transformed thought experiments. They present a new and surprising methodological twist to find out or determine the conclusions that follow from our assumptions. The surprising fact is that we have to encounter our own epistemological inventions as complex and foreign objects and employ machines to help us deal with them. This is hardly compatible with the classical paradigm of mathematical construction and epistemology.

Thought experiments are meant to help us gain insight into a complicated world. Simulation experiments explore new possibilities that automated calculations open up. The intricate relationship between thought and simulation experiments is a product of, and perhaps the key to understanding, the position of human subjects in a culture increasingly suffused with computer models and algorithms.

Acknowledgements

I would like to thank Mike Stuart for his insightful comments and also for his invaluable help with the English language.

Notes

1 Since the literature on thought experiments is extensively discussed in this volume, I will only reference the contributions on this issue by Jim Brown, David Gooding, Nancy Nersessian, and Ian Hacking (all 1992) to a symposium at *PSA 1992*. These provide a good entry point into the recent discussions in philosophy of science. Hacking as well as Paul Humphreys (1992) favour a more critical approach to the epistemic virtues of thought experiments.
2 See Schwinger (2002, ch. 2) for a detailed version of this experiment.
3 In general, it is a widely held opinion in the field of social simulation and artificial societies that thought experiments are the adequate benchmark for simulation experiments. Michael Weisberg (2013) analyzes how thought experiments and simulations both represent target systems, though he admittedly does not discuss further aspects of their relationship.
4 This does not seem to be an advantage, because the random process takes place in a logical space that is too big to analyze. The advantage lies in the mathematical fact that Markov processes converge surprisingly quickly. A Markov process in stationary distribution indicates the typical territory, so the reasoning goes, even if much is left out. In this way, the complexity barrier is circumvented by the random process approach – with the caveat that there are no results concerning the actual speed of convergence of the Markov process. The high speed of convergence, though often observed, remains a kind of mystery, hence the adequate number of iterations depends on the feeling of the simulation modellers. R.I.G. Hughes (1999) discusses Ising model simulations, and the mathematician Persi Diaconis (2009) appreciates the revolutionary character of Markov-chain Monte-Carlo methods.
5 For more details on density functional theory in the context of quantum chemistry and computer methods, see Lenhard (2014).
6 For a discussion of particular cases, cf. Winsberg (2003) about "artificial viscosity," and Lenhard (2007) about the "Arakawa-Operator," a feat of atmospheric modeling.
7 This perspective is in line with Humphreys' concluding verdict that humans are driven out of the center of epistemology (2004).

References

Barberousse, A., Franceschelli, S. and Imbert, C. (2009) "Computer simulations as experiments," *Synthese* 169: 557–574.
Beisbart, C. and Norton, J. D. (2012) "Why Monte Carlo simulations are inferences and not experiments," *International Studies in the Philosophy of Science* 26: 403–422.
Bishop, M. (1999) "Why thought experiments are not arguments," *Philosophy of Science* 66: 534–541.

Brown, J. R. (1992) "Why empiricism won't work," *PSA 1992*, vol. 2: 271–279.
Chandrasekharan, S., Nersessian, N. and Subramanian, V. (2012) "Computational modeling: Is this the end of thought experiments in science?" in *Thought Experiments in Philosophy, Science and the Arts*, edited by M. Frappier, L. Meynell, and J. R. Brown, London: Routledge.
Chang, H. (2007) *Inventing Temperature: Measurement and Scientific Progress*, Oxford: Oxford University Press.
Diaconis, P. (2009) "The Markov chain Monte Carlo revolution," *Bulletin of the American Mathematical Society* 46: 179–205.
Di Paolo, A., Ezequiel A., Noble, J. and Bullock, S. (2000) "Simulation models as opaque thought experiments," in *Artificial Life VII: Proceedings of the Seventh International Conference on Artificial Life*, edited by M. Bedau, J. S. McCaskill, N. H. Packard, and S. Rasmussen, Cambridge: MIT Press.
Dowling, D. (1999) "Experimenting on theories," *Science in Context* 12: 261–273.
El Skaf, R. and Imbert, C. (2013) "Unfolding in the empirical sciences: Experiments, thought experiments, and computer simulations," *Synthese* 190: 3451–3474.
Gooding, D. (1992) "What is experimental about thought experiments?" *Philosophy of Science Association 1992* 2: 280–290.
Guala, F. (2002) "Models, simulations, and experiments," in *Model-Based Reasoning: Science, Technology, Values*, edited by L. Magnani and N. Nersessian, New York: Kluwer.
Hacking, I. (1983) *Representing and Intervening: Introductory Topics in the Philosophy of Natural Science*, Cambridge: Cambridge University Press.
Hacking, I. (1992) "Do thought experiments have a life of their own? Comments on James Brown, Nancy Nersessian and David Gooding," *PSA 1992*, vol. 2: 302–308.
Hughes, R. I. G. (1999) "The Ising model, computer simulation, and universal physics," in *Models as Mediators*, edited by M. Morgan and M. Morrison, Cambridge: Cambridge University Press.
Humphreys, P. (1993) "Seven theses on thought experiments," in *Philosophical Problems of the Internal and External Worlds: Essays on the Philosophy of Adolf Grünbaum*, edited by J. Earman, Pittsburgh: Pittsburgh University Press.
Humphreys, P. (2004) *Extending ourselves. Computational science, empiricism, and scientific method*, Oxford: Oxford University Press.
Kühne, U. (2005) *Die Methode des Gedankenexperiments*, Frankfurt: Suhrkamp.
Lenhard, J. (2007) "Computer simulation: The cooperation between experimenting and modeling," *Philosophy of Science* 74: 176–194.
Lenhard, J. (2014) "Disciplines, models, and computers: The path to computational quantum chemistry," *Studies in History and Philosophy of Science Part* 48: 89–96.
Lorenz, E. (1967) "The nature of the theory of the general circulation of the atmosphere," *Technical Paper 218*, pp. 115–161, Geneva: World Meteorological Organization.
Lorenz, E. (1993) *The Essence of Chaos*, Seattle: University of Washington Press.
Morgan, M. S. (2003) "Experiments without material intervention: Model experiments, virtual experiments, and virtually experiments," in *The Philosophy of Scientific Experimentation*, edited by H. Radder, Pittsburgh: University of Pittsburgh Press.
Morgan, M. S. (2005) "Experiments versus models: New phenomena, inference, and surprise," *Journal of Economic Methodology* 12: 317–329.
Nersessian, N. J. (1992). "In the theoretician's laboratory: Thought experimenting as mental modeling" *Proceedings of the Philosophy of Science Association* 2: 291–301.
Parker, W. (2009) "Does matter really matter? Computer simulations, experiments, and materiality," *Synthese* 169: 483–496.
Schelling, T. (1978) *Micromotives and Macrobehavior*, New York: Norton.
Schwinger, J. (2002) *Einstein's Legacy: The Unity of Space and Time*, Mineola, NY: Dover Publications.
Weisberg, M. (2013) *Simulation and Similarity*, New York: Oxford University Press.
Winsberg, E. (2003) "Simulated experiments: Methodology for a virtual world," *Philosophy of Science* 70: 105–125.
Winsberg, E. (2009) "A tale of two methods," *Synthese* 169: 575–592.

28
IMAGES AND IMAGINATION IN THOUGHT EXPERIMENTS

Letitia Meynell

1 Introduction

Hardly any discussion about thought experiments (TEs) takes place without mention of the imagination. Whether conceived of as a colourful addendum to an underlying argument (Norton 1991; see Brendel this volume), the faculty of perception of a Platonic realm (Brown 2011), or the location of design for real experiments (Buzzoni 2013), the imagination is understood to be a characteristic component in the practice of thought experimenting. What is less obvious is what is meant by "the imagination." If one surveys the now sizable literature on the philosophy of TEs one could be forgiven for suspecting that in fact many of these authors mean quite different things, despite all employing the same term. In striking contrast to the ubiquitously acknowledged and yet mysterious relationship between TEs and the imagination, the relationship between TEs and images (specifically the visual representations that frequently accompany TEs) is both rarely mentioned and considerably less mysterious. With this in mind I will attempt to gain some insight into the imaginative character of TEs through investigating how images can play a role in thought experimenting.

It must immediately be conceded that not all imaginings are visual. We can imagine anything that could be perceived through our five senses and a good deal more, including feelings and possible truths (and, perhaps, some impossible falsehoods, too). Nothing about my discussion denies the importance of various non-visual sensory modes of imagining or that some TEs may deploy these modes. However, there is something to be learned by interrogating the interplay between TEs and the visual images that sometimes accompany them that directly addresses visual aspects of the imagination.

Given this proviso, it will surprise some readers that this chapter has little to say about mental imagery or the related concept of mental modelling. There are, after all, a number of accounts of TEs that rely heavily on mental images of some sort. James R. Brown's intuitionism suggests that we "see" those truths that are revealed by these processes in the mind's eye. Nancy Nersessian maintains that TEs are types of mental models which we imaginatively manipulate (1993) that are non-propositional in character (see also Nersessian, this volume), with Nenad Miščević taking an explicitly visual approach to the same idea (1992). However, Nersessian also identifies the basic problem with her own approach by acknowledging the diversity of views and controversy that surrounds scientific investigations of mental content. The sciences of mind and cognitive science in particular are not only young but highly contentious (Nersessian 2007, 130 ff.). Given that there is disagreement about whether the idea of visual mental content is plausible, let alone scientifically tractable (due to its apparent privacy), philosophical theories about visual or spatial mental content are likely to be at best speculative.[1] Moreover, even if we allow that there is a well-evidenced, tractable theory of mental imagery or mental models that advances a distinction between sensory and cognitive imagination (roughly imagining seeing x versus imagining believing that p) (e.g., Arcangeli 2010), it is not at all clear that this will ultimately prove especially useful. It could hardly be diagnostic of thought experimenting, as a number of TEs do not seem to be particularly visual or spatial (consider Thomson's violinist). More troubling yet, disagreements over whether the imaginative content of a given TE is properly visuo-sensory or logico-propositional seem wholly undecidable and unproductive. Happily, there is a good deal we can say without this currently unpromising detour, by following the example of linguistic analysis and assessing explicit, intersubjectively accessible content – in our case, images rendered on a surface (typically pictures on a page) and the texts that they accompany.

With this in mind, in Section 2 I make a few remarks comparing the ways in which visual images and texts present their content with a view to identifying when images are likely to be particularly important or useful for certain types of thought experimentation. In Section 3, I turn my attention to an account of TEs that takes their common association with images to be a theoretically important feature. Happily, this approach is centrally organized around Kendall Walton's account of representation from *Mimesis as Make-Believe* (1990), which is also thought to offer, if not a general theory of the imagination, crucial philosophical insights into its nature. I then in Section 4 employ this account to elucidate an example – Einstein's famous train TE, showing the relativity of simultaneity (and ultimately other results of special relativity). This classic TE is typically presented with an accompanying picture; indeed, Einstein's version from *Relativity: The Special and the General Theory* (1921) is so intimately tied to the figure that accompanies it that it would be difficult to make sense of the text of the TE without it. In Section 5 I turn back to the imagination to see what insights might be gleaned from the preceding discussion.

2 The limitations of text and image

There are several different means by which we may express[2] states of affairs in the name of extending or clarifying our own beliefs and ideas or to communicate some of them to others. Philosophers in the twentieth century have tended to focus on the capacity of language to do this, though it can hardly be denied that we use various other means of expression to characterize, clarify, and communicate our ideas. (Consider the safety card in the seat pocket in front of you next time you take a commercial flight). As with other means of expression, images have particular strengths and weaknesses, they express some things well and others badly. When it comes to thought experimenting, or indeed any other type of expressive or communicative context, which medium (or combination of media) should be employed is a question of the relative strengths and weaknesses of the medium, the content to be expressed, the capacities of the expected audience, and the technical constraints and available resources.

So, what is it that images do that language cannot do, or at least, does not do so well? One of the most obvious distinctions between images (pictorial and non-pictorial) and language is the one-dimensional (or sequential) character of language when compared with the two-dimensional character of images (see Perini 2005, 263–4). There is only one way to read a paragraph properly and that is to start at the beginning and read each sentence until you get to the end. While a written passage may contain a set of interrelated ideas, the author orders the content for the reader. Readers cannot reorder the content themselves, retaining all relevant truth values, unless they have clearly understood and can remember the content, which often takes significant effort. In contrast, images present their content all at once. Thus the viewer's understanding or acceptance of them is not based on some logical order of presentation as it is with sentences. In fact, with only a few exceptions, viewers order the content of images. Edward Tufte comments that good scientific representations both allow their viewers to take a panoptic view of the content as a whole and also to zoom in on specific points of interest to the viewer. Images are particularly good at inviting comparison of aspects of the content, encouraging viewers to appreciate a part in relation to the whole or the whole in terms of its parts (1990, esp. 37–52). Thus images allow their viewers a kind of freedom regarding the ways in which they order, interrogate and ultimately master the represented content that is unavailable to readers of texts.[3]

This freedom of approach and content organization does not affect the content itself but only how the viewer makes cognitive use of it. It is shared by both highly abstract visual displays of data as well as naturalistic depictions of scenes – what we might refer to as visual languages and pictures respectively.[4] Visual languages have characters with particular referents and rules for putting them together. Though visual languages are ubiquitous in the sciences (consider visual displays of quantitative data; see, e.g., Tufte 2001), it is rarely this kind of image that accompanies TEs. Pictures show states of affairs by displaying scenes that in some sense resemble the spatial characteristics of the objects, properties and relations that they express. In "The Truth in Pictures," Laura Perini explicates the referential role of spatial relations in images in contrast to language by comparing the following two expressions:

The square is on the right of the diamond

◆■

(264)

Perini's point is that, unlike natural language, for which the spatial relations of the components in an expression are arbitrary with respect to the content expressed, for an image the specific spatial characteristics of the component parts and their spatial relations to each other determine its content (a point that applies to both visual languages and pictures). However, the same case can also be used as an example of the minimally pictorial. In order to be pictorial at all, images must retain some of the spatial relations from the scene they depict and these spatial relations must determine the content. As John Willats deftly explains, for those pictures that employ projection systems (i.e., orthogonal, oblique or perspective projection), the projection system itself determines how the visual characteristics of the scene are transferred to the page. But pictures need not employ a projection system. Young children's pictures, for instance, transfer only the most basic and general spatial information from the depicted state of affairs onto the page, such as spatial order, enclosure, and contiguity (or lack thereof).[5] Perini's example implicitly suggests that the sentence and the image express the same content. However, if the images were an expression in a visual language there would be no principled reason to expect that the spatial relations of the components would in any way resemble the ideas it expresses. The character "◆" might denote "cat," the character "■" might denote "dog," and the their ordering from left to right might denote a temporal ordering. (We can even imagine a context where this kind of visual language might be useful – e.g., a vet's office.) However, in Perini's example the spatial relations comprising the expression resemble its referent – a diamond is expressed by the shape of a diamond, a square by the shape of a square, and so forth, despite being highly abstract. Thus, the expression above is fundamentally pictorial because the spatial characteristics (including relational characteristics) of the objects in the scene resemble the spatial characteristics of the objects themselves.[6]

This feature of pictures can, however, be importantly limiting. After all, we cannot express in a picture the idea of being to the right of something else without also drawing and thus specifying two objects (or perhaps one object in a specified space). In Perini's example we have a square and a diamond. Whatever forms we might introduce to express the idea of "being to the right of" in pictorial form will themselves have some shape or other and properties that go along with shape, such as area or colour. Suppose, rather than a diamond and a square we use the pictures of a dog and a cat. Such images will necessarily introduce a set of other characteristics. Even the most abstract picture of a cat or dog will have them in some posture or other (perhaps sitting, or lying down, or running, etc.). Moreover, they will be presented as if seen from some position or other (perhaps from above, or from below, or more typically, face on at their level, etc.). Thus not only are objects in the scene spatially related with respect to each other, but they are also spatially related with respect to the viewer, who is implicitly given a certain location in the broader world of which the scene is a part. Indeed, there are various techniques by which artists can emphasize this effect as when a *trompe l'oeil* landscape employs perspective projection and includes a window frame, clearly locating the viewer with respect to the scene. For philosophers of science a famous example would be Mach's drawing of himself on a sofa as seen by his left eye (Figure 28.1, from Mach 1914, 19).

These "viewer-centered descriptions" bring the viewer into the scene, just as "object-centered descriptions," where artists depict the shapes and spatial relations of objects independent of any particular view, and suggest an impersonal and nonspecific God's eye view (Willats 1997, 151 ff.). Use of projection systems other than perspective and idealization or abstraction of the content are techniques that can contribute to this effect. Nonetheless, by virtue of their visual resemblance to visually perceived states of affairs, all pictures introduce at least some spatial details (both within the depicted scene and with respect to a viewer) that can easily be left out of verbal descriptions.

We do not only see spatial relationships in pictures, but also the causal relationships implicit in the depicted situation. We are guided by our knowledge of how relevantly similar states of affairs in the world tend to progress from one moment to the next[7]; when

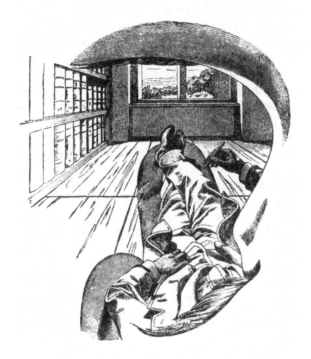

Figure 28.1

objects of the pictured kind are in their pictured state we can imagine what is going to happen next. Insofar as causes are complex, such that mutually constraining interrelated systems evolve from one set of states into another, pictures are extremely effective means for expressing them. When this kind of content is expressed in words, the linearity of language enforces an ordering that is at best arbitrary and may be misleading, whereas the spatial ordering of affairs in an image is neither arbitrary nor misleading. Moreover, because it is viewers who, through scanning and focussing on parts of the image, cognitively organize the content, each viewer can focus on different relations and connections, interrogating the picture in their own way in order to make sense of it. Thus we find that pictorial images are particularly effective at representing spatial and causal relations, especially complex interrelations, and are conducive to allowing their viewers to organize and interrogate this content in their own way.

It is this causal component that makes pictures such effective companions to certain TEs. From the considerations above, we can expect that certain types of thought experimental content will be poorly expressed linguistically and simply better displayed pictorially. Presumably, this will be the case for TEs that are thought experientially visual, inherently spatial, relational and causal. It is then hardly surprising that although pictorial accompaniment of philosophical TEs is fairly rare it is relatively common with TEs in physics. We have, moreover, reason to think that pictorial accompaniment *should* be fairly rare in philosophical TEs. When spatial and spatially causal (i.e., mechanistic) relationships are irrelevant, we have reason to expect pictorial accompaniments may not be very useful. If there are pictorial accompaniments they will often be purely decorative, failing to inform or enhance the content of the TE at all. Worse yet, a picture might detract from the effectiveness of a TE or distract from its point. For instance, a picture accompanying Thompson's violinist TE would impose specificity that would undermine the importantly subjective first personal character of this TE. Of course, not all extraneous TE images are so destructive. Indeed, when TEs are particularly esoteric, pictures done in a familiar and accessible style can serve to reassure the thought experimenter that they are in fact imagining the right thing. Illustrations of various versions of Lucretius'[8] attempts to send something through the edge of the universe are cases in point (see, for example, Brown 2004, fig. 1.2; Norton 2004, fig. 2.1). Although the content here is spatial the relationship between components is not complex so the images do not so much clarify as reassure. This is an effect that can be bracketed off as purely heuristic and not of any real epistemological interest.

3 Thought experiments and the images that accompany them

Armed with some sense of the comparative strengths of pictures we are ready to tackle their role in TEs. Elsewhere (2014) I have made a case for treating TEs as representational devices that are best understood through the lens of aesthetics and I summarize that approach here. Following Kendall Walton's account of representation, I argue that TEs are props for the imagination, through which we engage in games of make-believe. "TEs are narratives that are created to prompt their readers to imagine specific fictional worlds, as kinds of situational set-ups that, when you 'run,' 'perform' or simply imagine them, lead to specific results" (4164–5). Of course, TEs are more than this. Through imagining these fictional worlds we are able to make inferences about the actual world. However, this is necessarily a second step, any account of which must be constrained by proper consideration of the imaginative character of TEs. Happily, Walton's theory also offers a powerful analysis of pictures and this shared theoretical basis promises to bring together TEs and the pictures that sometimes accompany them seamlessly.

One of the virtues of a Waltonian approach is that it explains how TEs and, indeed, other types of representation, can have both an intersubjectively accessible, clearly articulated content and an experiential, even personal, character. He distinguishes between the work world of a representation and the game world of a representation, the first being the intersubjectively accessible content of the representation and the second being the content that a particular appreciator imagines through the representation. Both are, in Walton's terms, "fictional worlds," which can be thought of as a set of fictional truths (Walton 1990, 213 ff.).[9] The text of a TE alone is not enough to generate the content of either the work world or the game world. One needs to apply a set of principles of generation (PGs). These are, in effect, a set of imaginative resources – a dispositional well upon which the occurrent imagination not only can but must draw in its construction of a game world if it is to imagine the correct content (Walton 1990, 110–12). While each reader will have a somewhat different imaginative experience (necessarily so, if they are required by the TE to imagine themselves in the described scenario), thus generating somewhat different sets of fictional truths, there will be a subset of fictional truths that all these different game worlds and the work world share. It is in this important sense that they imagine the same TE.

So, what are PGs? They are the cognitive capacities, habits of mind, and background beliefs that are required, in concert with the text, to produce the appropriate imaginings. Although this sounds dangerously circular, PGs often exist entirely independently of a given representation that employs them. Many PGs are a result of inculcation; we are trained by the cultures and subcultures (including, for instance, academic disciplines) in which we live to interpret various narrative styles and engage in kinds of deliberative thinking. Moreover, we are inculcated with conceptual schemas and background beliefs that inform how we think about the world around us and how we imagine it might be. Walton points out that our imaginings are in an important sense quite conservative. Unless the imaginative context dictates otherwise we tend to fill in the details of our fictional worlds with background beliefs about the actual world (Walton 1990, 144–61). This is clearly true for artworks but equally true of TEs. Presumably, this is why narratives and images from cultures very different from our own can seem rather odd, perhaps so odd as to be incomprehensible. Along with culturally specific PGs there are also many cognitive capacities that are shared across cultures and subcultures, albeit not necessarily by all members. Thus the sighted among us have a set of visual capacities that are given by their physiology that are as much PGs for visual representations as the various conventions, beliefs and habits of mind that also go into understanding pictorial content.[10] Each of these PGs is trained through practice and application and though some are explicitly stipulated, many are tacitly developed. When authors write TEs they assume various PGs and when readers read TEs they employ them.

Even with the determining factors of the text and PGs, many of the details of a given fictional world are left unspecified and can even produce points of ambiguity. Ambiguity, however, can provide imaginative freedom that can be productive in various artistic representations and is particularly important in TEs. The idea of directed play, varying a specific feature in a thought experimental world, is widely recognized as an epistemically valuable component in TEs (Kujundzic 1998). Thus, a vividly imagined and thoroughly explored TE may take its imaginer through various subtly different game worlds – perhaps she as an observer inhabits a different perspective in each one as she imagines the different ways the same event would appear from various positions – all of which are consistent with the work world that is given and shared among thought experimenters.

A Waltonian approach to TEs renders the role of accompanying images entirely unmysterious. A picture is simply an additional prop for imagining the fictional world of the TE. When chosen well it will work seamlessly with the text to clarify the content or make it easier to grasp. It will not add distracting detail that draws attention away from the key parts of the TE that provide insight. Nor will it require for gleaning its content PGs that the anticipated viewer/readers are unlikely to possess. In brief, image and TE should work together to prompt the imaginings required to produce the appropriate thought experimental results, allowing the reader/viewer to infer the appropriate insights.

4 Train of thought

With a Waltonian approach to TEs and our reflections on the strengths and limitations of images in hand, we are in a position to work through our example. In the first few chapters of *Relativity: The Special and the General Theory* (1921), Einstein sets up the train travelling along an embankment as a kind of thought experimental apparatus that is deployed in a set of iterated TEs. Just as with a real experimental apparatus, we start with fairly easy experiments in order to gain both familiarity with the working apparatus and confidence in our ability to use it. In Waltonian terms, these earlier, simpler experiments serve to present a fictional world with which readers become familiarized by imagining what they are directed to imagine. This is also a method that introduces and shores up crucial PGs. A fascinating interplay takes place in these passages between the fictional world, ordinary beliefs and observations, the technical vocabulary and conceptual framework of physics, and requisite idealizations. Through these iterated TEs Einstein methodically provides his reader with a sufficiently detailed fictional world so that when he gets to the rather challenging simultaneity experiment the reader can both follow the TE and understand its significance.

In early chapters we are provided with the PGs that attach coordinate systems to moving bodies producing measureable and tractable frames of reference. In the first visit into the fictional train world we discover that Galilean relativity holds, and we learn that we can (and probably should) ignore the effects of air resistance. In navigating this fictional world we discover principles of empiricism are central. Emphasis is always given to what observers, stationed on the train and on the embankment, can actually observe (Norton 1991, 135ff) with, for instance, the passage of time being operationalized with clocks.

Now, lightning strikes the rails at two points, A and B, at either end of the train and equidistant from the observers on the train and the embankment. The strikes happen *simultaneously*. No sooner has Einstein introduced this fictional truth than he draws it into question, pushing his reader to identify what observations could determine whether the lightning strikes at A and B were actually simultaneous or not:

> Up to now our considerations have been referred to a particular body of reference, which we have styled a "railway embankment." We suppose a very long train travelling along the rails with the constant velocity v and in the direction indicated in Fig. [28.2]. People travelling in this train will with advantage use the train as a rigid reference-body (co-ordinate system); they regard all events in reference to

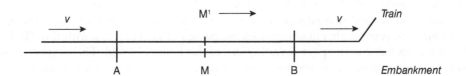

Figure 28.2

> the train. Then every event which takes place along the line also takes place at a particular point of the train. Also the definition of simultaneity can be given relative to the train in exactly the same way as with respect to the embankment. As a natural consequence, however, the following question arises:
>
> Are two events (*e.g.* the two strokes of lightening A and B) which are simultaneous *with reference to the railway embankment* also simultaneous *relatively to the train*? We shall show directly that the answer must be in the negative.

When we say that the lightening strokes A and B are simultaneous with respect to the embankment, we mean: the rays of light emitted at the places A and B, where the lightening occurs, meet each other at the mid-point M of the length $A \to B$ of the embankment. But the events A and B also correspond to positions A and B on the train. Let M' be the mid-point of the distance $A \to B$ on the travelling train. Just when the flashes [as judged from the embankment] of lightening occur, this point M' naturally coincides with the point M, but it moves towards the right in the diagram with the velocity v of the train. If an observer sitting in the position M' in the train did not possess this velocity, then he would remain permanently at M, and the light rays emitted by the flashes of lightening at A and B would reach him simultaneously, *i.e.* they would meet just where he is situated. Now in reality (considered with reference to the railway embankment) he is hastening towards the beam of light coming from B, whilst he is riding on ahead of the beam of light coming from A. Hence the observer will see the beam of light emitted from B earlier than he will see that emitted from A. Observers who take the railway train as their reference-body must therefore come to the conclusion that the lightening flash B took place earlier than the lightening flash A. We thus arrive at the important result:

Events which are simultaneous with reference to the embankment are not simultaneous with respect to the train, and vice versa (relativity of simultaneity). Every reference-body (co-ordinate system) has its own particular time; unless we are told the reference-body to which the statement of time refers, there is no meaning in a statement of the time of an event.

(29–31, italics his)

As was suggested above, the image in this TE clearly functions as an extra prop for imagining. The interplay between image and text is particularly obvious in this example as Einstein explicitly directs us to imagine the state of affairs described in the text through the image. In the narrative the lightning strikes on the train *are* the points on the figure. We might wonder why, given the reader's familiarity with the work world, derived from previous experience with the train, Einstein would introduce an image at this point. However, when we consider both the particular challenges of this TE, its importance to what follows, and the capacities and strengths of pictorial expressions, the answer is obvious. Thought experimenters, particularly physics novices, are going to face a problem with this TE that they have not faced in the prior investigations of this fictional world. The imaginings are counterintuitive from a common sense perspective, which assumes that it is meaningful to identify two events as simultaneous simpliciter, that is, without reference to something else. Many thought experimenters will have to work against their own habits of mind and quite probably implicit beliefs in order to imagine as they are directed. (Notice, expert readers, because they have trained habits of mind and different beliefs may not feel the same imaginative resistance. To them the image may seem and be superfluous). The image not only prompts the right imaginings but helps to reassure thought experimenters that they are imagining what they are supposed to.

The image also helps to direct attention indicating which of the PGs are particularly salient. We have at this point a very rich fictional world, but the image foregrounds the key components of the current TE and invites game world investigations of how this set-up might relate to insights and assumptions gleaned from previous events on the train. The image stabilizes imaginings and directs attention. Nonetheless, it remains generic, helping the viewer generalize and use the TE as a model for thinking about events in the real world. This genericizing has the crucial side effect of showing that the particulars of the train are thought experimental assumptions that may be discharged when applying the insight in the world.[11]

Finally, this picture does what pictures generally do well: it reveals a set of multiply, mutually related components. Despite the image being static, we can imagine the relevant motions through it – M′ moving to the right and the light coming from A and B to the middle – and see how the components should move forward in time. Because the image presents its content all at once it allows viewers to find their own paths through understanding the multiple mutual relationships. This freedom of ordering the game world is difficult to enact within a linear, non-pictorial language but it allows a viewer/reader to try multiple ways of thinking through the content as they imagine the counterintuitive processes and results of the TE.

5 Imagining

The preceding discussion neither assumes nor produces an exhaustive account of the role of the imagination in TEs. We are, however, in a position to make some remarks on the topic. The Waltonian approach treats TEs as props in deliberate, occurrent, social imaginings. TEs join their readers not only by bringing them to the same results but also through imagining a shared fictional world. (This gets us some way to figuring out what counts as "the same" TE, though clearly there is much more to be said on the topic see Bokulich and Frappier, this volume). Though TEs and their content are intersubjectively accessible, thought experimenters enjoy considerable freedom within work worlds and different thought experimenters may have quite different experiences, varying in detail and vividness, while still employing the correct PGs, performing the requisite procedures, and achieving the appropriate outcomes and insights. Thought experimenters also practice and hone the PGs that produce a given TE as they imagine it, thus readers come to share various background beliefs, habits of mind and thought experimental conventions. In this way TEs have looping effects, as the TEs we have imagined in the past influence how we come to imagine TEs (and arguably other states of affairs) in the future.

These looping effects may offer insight into some of the findings of experimental philosophy, which suggest that some of so-called philosophical intuitions (which often appear obvious, perhaps even self-evident, to professional philosophers) only emerge after considerable philosophical training (see Ludwig, this volume; Stich and Tobia, this volume). In a Waltonian approach we have no need of brute intuitions (what we might call extramentalist intuitions; Stich and Tobia, this volume, 370 ff.) that are imbued with some kind of distinctive epistemic status. PGs with their various sources – biological and cultural, credible and problematic – do the job of determining the content of the set-up of a TE, how to run it and thus its result. This not only draws into question intuitionist accounts of TEs, like Brown's, but it also supports those views that take the dialectical context to be particularly important for determining the content and epistemic efficacy of TEs (see Cohnitz and Häggqvist, this volume). Moreover, it deflates a central controversy in experimental philosophy, which rests on the status of the intuitions that supposedly result from various TEs.

Even though we have set aside the exact character of the mental content and the question of whether TEs prompt inherently visual imaginings, the role of pictures in some TEs does give some insight into the visual imagination. Because many of the pictures that enhance TEs do so because they retain some of the relevant spatial information that would be found in the depicted state of affairs were it to exist in reality, this suggests that the visual imagination shares something important with perception. Whatever the character of the content of knowledge of immediately perceived states of affairs, the content of visual imagination seems to share this character. It is important, however, not to infer too much from this. We must remember that pictures can clearly locate the viewer in the scene – as with Mach's view from the sofa, mentioned above – but they can also offer a kind of view from nowhere, a generic display of a state of affairs. This is something no real observer ever actually observes. For both narratives and pictures, the PGs will typically indicate the extent to which a viewer is to imagine themselves in the scene, although these may well be implicitly packed into the conventions of the genre or the representation itself.

James McAllister (2013b) has noted that there is no consensus on the proper role of the imagination in the sciences and it seems his remarks might be applied to the role of the imagination in epistemological endeavours generally. McAllister identifies four views. The first sees imagination as a kind of extension of observation, postulating what might be the case when it cannot (yet) be clearly observed or decisively determined; thus it is associated with the hypothetico-deductive method, model-building and, indeed, TEs (2013b, 12–13). The second view is critical of the first, condemning the imagination's creativity as insufficiently constrained by reality, unruly, and tending to be arbitrary (13–14). The third view is similarly distrustful of the imagination but for contrary reasons, seeing it as inherently conservative – tending too much toward the familiar and incapable of genuinely novel insight (14–15). The fourth view places imagination right as the heart of interpretation, demanding that whenever we make sense of a visual stimulus we employ the imagination (16).

There seems to be a kernel of truth in all of these attitudes and Walton's account helps to show how they may be consistent. The idea that the imagination fuels observation, suggested by the fourth view, fits comfortably with the idea that pictures can fuel the visual imagination because of their spatial similarity to the depicted states of affairs themselves. We see here a complex feedback loop with belief, imagination, and representation informing each other. When imagination is prompted only by what is already believed within a discipline it is likely that the criticism we find in the third view will be well deserved – such imaginings will be incapable of genuinely novel insight. Of course, beliefs are only one type of PG; suppositions, hypotheses, flights of fancy, habits of mind, and conventions from quite disparate areas, including the fine arts and cultures other than our own, may also inform the imagination. Thus some imaginative constructions may fall prey to the criticisms of the second view, veering towards the absurd and arbitrary, particularly when diverse PGs are *randomly* drawn upon and those appropriate to different genres and subject matters are *carelessly* mixed. However, even if the imagination sometimes tends toward unreflective conservativism and at other times tends toward flights of fancy, certain lines of counterfactual thought that are carefully constructed and doggedly followed can lead to extraordinary innovation, as so many of Einstein's TEs exemplify. Moreover, we can train our own creativity by engaging art works, TEs, and other representational devices that stretch our imaginative capacities and challenge us to draw on and develop new PGs. It seems, then, that we can expect that imaginings will be as robust, well-grounded, and epistemically interesting as the principles that generate them.

Finally, it remains to be noted that different media are better or worse at prompting different types of imagining. TEs are narratives but sometimes the imaginings they produce are importantly visual, identifying spatially and causally specific states of affairs and relations unfolding as if to be observed by the mind's eye. When these events are sufficiently complex, surprising or unfamiliar, a picture offers our actual eyes something to work with to help us imagine running the TE. Thus narrative and image work together prompting us to imagine one fictional world.

6 Conclusion

I have made the case for an important interaction between images and TEs that rests on their crucially sharing a certain imaginative character, understood through Walton's theory of representation. Whether we identify the TE as the imagining itself (which happens to be produced by reading some text) or as the text that produces the imagining, it must be recognized that text because of its form can be better or worse at conveying what is to be imagined. Pictures are often used in concert with the text of TEs, particularly in the physical sciences, because they can more efficiently and effectively evoke certain types of imagining.

Acknowledgements

I would like to thank Mike Stuart, Tyler Brunet, Ford Doolittle, Carlos Mariscal, Gordon McOuat, a Dalhousie Philosophy Department colloquium audience, and especially Mélanie Frappier for their feedback and advice on various versions of this chapter.

Notes

1 This impasse is exemplified by the imagery debates in cognitive science (associated with Zenon Pylyshyn and Stephen Kosslyn), nicely summarized by Thomas (2014, §4.4). The significance and intractability of the debate is also mentioned in Nersessian (2007, 231–3). Nonetheless, for my own part, I find the evidence for the existence of mental imagery and models of the kind that ground Nersessian's account highly plausible (see her chapter in this volume), even as the problems of privacy strike me as insurmountable for an account of TEs that has any analytical power or normative force for intersubjective assessment. I expect that in large part the mental modelling account is complementary to the one that I offer here, if we understand a Waltonian fictional (and purely internal) game world to be a Nersessian-style mental model. If one rejects the mental modelling account, however, a Waltonian account remains available because it does not presuppose any specific account of the character of mental content. Indeed, I suspect that a Waltonian account of TEs would be equally consistent with a phenomenological account of the imagination (see Wiltsche, this volume).
2 "Represent" might be a more natural word to use here, but as it is employed with quite different intentions by Walton (who explicitly coins his own definition to suit his purposes) I have used "express," "communicate" and "characterize" instead. None of these terms are ideal as they

are burdened with theoretical baggage inherited from any number of competing philosophical programs. "Denotation" and "reference" might also be used were it not for the ontological implications that typically travel with them, suggesting the existence of that which is denoted (see, for example, Goodman's theory of representation (1968).

3 It is worth noting that mathematical expressions can share some of this flexibility of content organization, though one perhaps needs more facility with mathematics in order to make the most of it. James McAllister makes this point in "Reasoning with Visual Metaphors," where he maintains that reasoning with mathematical laws, particularly in physics, is non-linear, sharing something with the free play of metaphorical connections and requiring a kind of dialectical rather than deductive approach (2013a).
4 I explore this distinction more thoroughly in Meynell (2013 and 2015).
5 For a more thorough treatment see Willats' discussion of topological transformations in (1997, especially 13, 70–6). Those who are familiar with contemporary physics will recognize this idea as the basic spatial information that is retained through transformations from one geometry, such as Euclidean geometry, to another, say Reimanian, geometry. Subway maps provide a useful example of the less technical transformations from state of affairs to representation that Willats has in mind (1997, fig. 1.11).
6 There are two different ways of reading this image. One is self-referentially, so that the diamond and the square refer to themselves. The other is representationally in the way that is to be defined below. Though the self-referential reading is possible, it is a distraction in the current discussion.
7 There are many different ways of cashing out this idea in the philosophical cannon and, for my purposes, I do not think it is helpful to wed the rudimentary account that I offer here to any particular theory or philosophical tradition. That being said, those readers with phenomenological sympathies may find Harald Wiltsche's discussion of anticipation and background knowledge in perception useful for fleshing out the ways in which immediate perceptual experiences and representations of fictional experiences are replete with causal capacities anticipating future possibilities (Wiltsche, this volume).
8 Although often this TE has been associated with Lucretius, increasingly people are attributing its first formulation to Archytas (see Ierodiakonou, this volume).
9 It is important to note that Walton does not mean to adopt any metaphysical, logical or linguistic thesis by employing the term "truth" (1990, 41–2). It is simply a convenient way of articulating components of the content, whatever its form or means of expression might be. Even though mental imagery is implied, the theory is neutral as to whether the mental content is truly visual in character or fundamentally propositional at base, thus avoiding the imagery debates, mentioned above.
10 Indeed, despite the limitations of cognitive science, there is neuroscientific evidence that some of the areas of the brain responsible for visual perception are also responsible for visual imaginings (see Thomas 2014, §4.42; Nersessian this volume, §2.2).
11 See Sorensen (2013) for a useful discussion of this idea.

References

Arcangeli, M. (2010) "Imagination in thought experimentation: Sketching a cognitive approach to thought experiments," in *Model-Based Reasoning in Science and Technology: Abduction, Logic, and Computational Discovery*, edited by L. Magnani, W. Carnielli, and C. Pizzi, Berlin: Springer.

Brown, J. R. (2004) "Why thought experiments transcend empiricism," in *Contemporary Debates in the Philosophy of Science*, edited by C. Hitchcock, Madden: Blackwell.

Brown, J. R. (2011) *The Laboratory of the Mind*, 2nd ed., London: Routledge.

Buzzoni, M. (2013) "Thought experiments from a Kantian point of view," in *Thought Experiments in Philosophy, Science and the Arts*, edited by M. Frappier, L. Meynell, and J. R. Brown, London: Routledge.

Einstein, A. (1921) *Relativity: The Special and the General Theory*, translated by R. W. Lawson, New York: Henry Holt and Company.

Goodman, N. (1968) *Languages of Art: An Approach to a Theory of Symbols*, New York: Bobbs-Merrill.

Kujundzic, N. (1998) "The role of variation in thought experiments," *International Studies in the Philosophy of Science* 12: 239–243.

Mach, E. (1914) *The Analysis of Sensations and the Relation of the Physical to the Psychical*, translated by C. M. Williams, Chicago: Open Court.

McAllister, J. (2013a) "Reasoning with visual metaphors," *Knowledge Engineering Review* 28: 367–379.

McAllister, J. (2013b) "Thought experiment and the exercise of imagination in science," in *Thought Experiments in Philosophy, Science and the Arts*, edited by M. Frappier, L. Meynell, and J. R. Brown, London: Routledge.

Meynell, L. (2013) "Parsing pictures: On analyzing the content of images in science," *Knowledge Engineering Review* 28: 327–345.

Meynell, L. (2014) "Imagination and insight: A new account of the content of thought experiments," *Synthese* 191: 4149–4168.

Meynell, L. (2015) "See what I mean? On developing norms for the production and publication of scientific images," in *Narratives of Science and Nature*, edited by J. Kanjirakkat, G. McOuat, and S. Sarukkai, London: Routledge.

Miščević, N. (1992) "Mental models and thought experiments," *International Studies in the Philosophy of Science* 6: 215–226.

Nersessian, N. (1992) "In the theoretician's laboratory: Thought experimenting as mental modeling," *Proceedings of the Philosophy of Science Association* 2: 291–301.

Nersessian, N. (2007) "Thought experiments as mental modelling: Empiricism without logic," *Croatian Journal of Philosophy* VII: 125–161.

Norton, J. (1991) "Thought experiments in Einstein's work," in *Thought Experiments in Science and Philosophy*, edited by T. Horowitz and G. Massey, Lanham: Rowman and Littlefield.

Norton, J. (2004) "On thought experiments: Is there more to the argument?" *Proceedings of the 2002 Biennial Meeting of the Philosophy of Science Association, Philosophy of Science* 71: 1139–1151.

Perini, L. (2005) "The truth in pictures," *Philosophy of Science* 72: 262–285.

Sorensen, R. (2013) "Veridical idealizations," in *Thought Experiments in Philosophy, Science and the Arts*, edited by M. Frappier, L. Meynell, and J. R. Brown, London: Routledge.

Thomas, N. (2014) "Mental imagery," *The Stanford Encyclopedia of Philosophy*. Available here: http://plato.stanford.edu/archives/fall2014/entries/mental-imagery/ (accessed on 15 November 2016).

Tufte, E. (1990) *Envisioning Information*, Cheshire: The Graphics Press.

Tufte, E. (2001) *The Visual Display of Quantitative Data*, 2nd ed., Cheshire: The Graphics Press.

Walton, K. (1990) *Mimesis as Make-Believe: On the Foundations of the Representational Arts*, Cambridge: Harvard University Press.

Willats, J. (1997) *Art and Representation: New Principles in the Analysis of Pictures*, Princeton: Princeton University Press.

29
ART AND THOUGHT EXPERIMENTS
David Davies

1 Thought experiments in the arts: an overview

Philosophers of literature and philosophers of film have appealed to thought experiments (TEs) in attempting to answer a much-voiced objection to the claim that the fictional narratives articulated in works of literary and cinematic fiction can further our understanding of the extra-fictional world and thereby have cognitive value. The charge against "cognitivist" claims concerning such works is that their fictional narratives can provide at best interesting *hypotheses* whose credibility requires independent empirical support. In responding to this charge, some supporters of artistic cognitivism have reasoned as follows:

(1) TEs are accorded a cognitive value in science and philosophy.
(2) Such TEs are themselves short fictional narratives.
(3) There is no principled reason why the lengthier fictional narratives presented in works of literature and cinema cannot also serve as thought experiments and have a similar cognitive value.

In following sections, I shall elaborate first upon the kinds of claims that have been made by cognitivists about literary artworks, and the kinds of objections levied against cognitivism. I shall then show why an appeal to TEs might be thought an effective response to such objections. To evaluate such an appeal, I shall consider debates about the cognitive value of TEs in science and in philosophy more generally. I shall also examine the claim that *cinematic* narratives can operate as TEs and can be ways whereby films can "do philosophy." Finally, I shall briefly comment on the use of TEs as a resource in the *philosophy* of Art.

2 Literary cognitivism: claims and counter-claims

What is valuable about reading literature? What explains the place of literary works in the educational curriculum, and their importance in the lives of so many people? For many, the right answer to these questions is some form of what James Young (2001) terms "literary cognitivism." Literature, the cognitivist maintains, is valuable because it is a source of *knowledge*, or at least of *warranted belief*, concerning the extra-fictional world.

There are at least four ways in which fictional narratives might be thought to possess cognitive value (see, e.g., Novitz 1987, ch. 6): First, they might be a source of *factual information about the world*. Authors of fictions may incorporate true statements into their narratives in providing their fiction with a real setting. Second, literary fictions might provide readers with an *understanding of general principles* – moral, metaphysical, or psychological, for example – which govern the unfolding of events in the real world. Such principles may be explicitly or (more usually) implicitly exemplified in the fiction, and thereby made salient to readers. Third, some writers (e.g., Goodman 1976, 1978; Elgin 2007) have claimed that literary fictions are a source of *categorial understanding*, furnishing the reader with new categories or kinds, natural or psychological, whose application to the real world illuminates certain matters of fact. Finally, literary fictions might be a source of *affective knowledge* – knowledge of "what it would be like" to be in a particular set of circumstances. This may be an ethically valuable feature of fictions, bearing upon our ability to comprehend, and respond appropriately to, morally complex situations that we encounter in the actual world (see, e.g., Putnam 1976).

It might be questioned, however, whether literature can provide *knowledge*, or even *warranted belief*, of any of these kinds, if the latter requires true beliefs or right classifications to which we are in some way epistemically *entitled*. In physical science and history – paradigm examples of knowledge-yielding practices – we can usually obtain consensus by appeal to shared epistemic norms as to the truth or warranted acceptability of assertions made about the world, or can engage in reasoned debate, by appeal to such norms. But literary works do not seem to have cognitive value through making explicit assertions about the real world assessable in such ways. Even when a literary work contains sentences expressing factual truths, the fiction does not work through asserting these sentences, but rather by inviting the reader to make-believe what is fictively true in the story.

Some critics, generalizing from these concerns, argue that reading fictions yields at best *hypotheses* about the general ordering of things in the world or the affective dimensions of situations, *beliefs* about specific aspects of the world, or *potentially insightful* ways of categorizing things. Talk of "learning" from fiction, it is said, is justified only if what we derive from our reading is subjected to further testing. These reservations are developed in a systematic and forthright manner by Jerome Stolnitz, who argues (1992) for the "cognitive triviality" of literature. Stolnitz presents what Noel Carroll (2002) terms the "no evidence" argument against cognitivism: even if there are truths, particular or general, contained in literary fictions, the fictions themselves provide us with no good reasons to accept those truths. Art, Stolnitz maintains, never "confirms" its "truths." While general principles might be extracted, as "thematic meanings" from the fictional narratives of literary works, the supposed "evidence" for the reality of these principles is flawed in three ways: (a) the work cites no actual cases, (b) it relies on a single example, and (c) it is gerrymandered to support such principles, having been carefully designed to exemplify them.

Some defenders of literary cognitivism seem to grant this objection without seeing how serious it is for their views. Novitz, for example, argues that we can validate the conceptual and cognitive resources that we derive from literary works, and the beliefs about the non-fictional world that are generated in our reading, by "projecting" what is gleaned from a literary work onto the world: "Readers can only acquire conceptual or cognitive skills from fiction by tentatively projecting the factual beliefs gleaned from the work on to the world about them. They try to see specific objects, events, and relationships in terms of these new beliefs, and they attempt to rethink, perhaps to explain, what was previously baffling or bewildering" (1987, 138). Literature and science, Novitz maintains, are analogous enterprises. Each provides us with hypotheses that must be tested against the experienced world before any claims to knowledge can be justified.

But the comparison with science, which might seem to respond to the epistemological challenge to literary cognitivism, in fact concedes the very point at issue. The cognitive credentials of science rest upon its being a practice encompassing both the formulation of hypotheses and their assessment in light of experimental testing. But Novitz seems to grant that literature merely furnishes us with hypotheses, and is thus a valid source of knowledge only if taken together with an *independent* practice of subjecting such hypotheses to empirical scrutiny.

The full significance of the "no-evidence" objection to cognitivism emerges when it is combined with what Carroll terms the "no argument" objection. Considering the cognitivist claim that literary works may have (usually) implicit "thematic meanings" that express valuable insights into reality, Peter Lamarque and Stein Olsen (1994) object that it is not part of the ordinary activity of readers or critics to inquire into the truth or falsity of such "insights," and that determining their truth or falsity is not a proper part of literary appreciation. General thematic statements in literary fictions, according to Lamarque and Olsen, are not properly viewed as conclusions whose truth we are invited to endorse as a result of reading the work, but are devices for organizing and producing aesthetically interesting structure in the story's narrative content.

The projective testing of the content of fictional works to which Novitz appeals fall foul of this objection. The work of the theoretical scientist bears upon the acquisition of scientific knowledge only because it is complemented by the work of her experimental colleagues. Only in virtue of their collective endeavors is *science* properly viewed as a source of knowledge of the world. In the literary case, however, insofar as we can identify "hypotheses" somehow embodied in literary fictions, the empirical "testing" of these hypotheses against the world is arguably not part of our *literary* practice. The "no-argument" objection against cognitivism explicitly denies that "testing" the thematic contents of literary fictions plays any legitimate part in that practice. If so, then this seems to undermine any talk of distinctively *artistic* knowledge parallel to our talk of scientific knowledge. "Projecting" the thematic meanings of literary works onto the world is quite extraneous to the proper engagement with literary works *as literature*, it will be claimed.

3 The idea of literary works as thought experiments

In response to these kinds of arguments, some philosophers (e.g., Carroll 2002; Elgin 2007) have appealed to an analogy between literary narratives and TEs in science and/or philosophy. While Carroll's and Elgin's approaches are in other respects different, neither, I shall suggest, fully comes to terms with the arguments against literary cognitivism. This also applies to Young's more detailed defense of cognitivism. While he does not draw an explicit analogy between literary fictions and TEs, his account closely resembles Elgin's in certain key respects and, I argue, is open to the same objections.

Carroll takes as his model the use of TEs in philosophy. He notes that the very philosophers who bring anti-cognitivist arguments against literature seem perfectly happy to employ fictional narratives for cognitive purposes in their philosophical use of TEs. Philosophical TEs, for Carroll, function as arguments by "excavating conceptual refinements and relationships." The imaginary situations canvassed in the narratives are designed to mobilize conceptual knowledge we already possess and elicit from us intuitions grounded in that knowledge. Philosophical TEs are not open to the "no-evidence" argument directed at literary fictions since, being aimed at unearthing conceptual knowledge, they do not require empirical evidence. Nor are they vulnerable to the "no-argument" objection since they function as arguments in virtue of the reflective processes that go on in the reader when she entertains the TE. Carroll talks here of the mobilization of "implicit knowledge" of concepts which provides the necessary dialectical supplementation to the philosophical text in our reflective reading of it At least some literary fictions, according to Carroll, function in the same way as philosophical TEs. In support of this claim, he cites the philosophical use of some literary fictions (e.g., Borges's short story cited below) as TEs. He also cites literary works such as Graham Greene's *The Third Man* and E. M. Forster's *Howards End* which, he maintains, were intended to work as extended TEs in the interests of conceptual refinement. Literary fictions, he further maintains, are particularly adept at helping to clarify, and refine our capacity to apply, moral concepts.

There are clearly literary fictions of the sort that Carroll describes, although Lamarque and Olsen might argue that, when intended or made to serve as devices for conceptual clarification, they are no longer functioning as literary works. We may also agree that the kinds of philosophical TEs cited by Carroll play a legitimate cognitive role, although some might view this as less a matter of unearthing conceptual knowledge already possessed and more a matter of providing resources for arriving at a rational equilibrium between our concepts and the practices they are intended to serve. But such a defense of the cognitive virtues of literature hardly seems to do justice to the claims of the literary cognitivist. The latter standardly maintains that literary fictions can help us to better understand the world, and not merely that they help to tune up our conceptual apparatus. Also, while Carroll explicitly addresses the "no-argument" argument, his response to the "no-evidence" argument only applies if the cognitivist's claims are restricted to conceptual knowledge.

Kuhn (1964), in a seminal article on scientific TEs, rejects the idea that the role of TEs in science is simply to clarify our concepts. TEs, he maintains, are like real experiments in that they also change our beliefs about the world by revealing that the world does not comport with certain assumptions built into our concepts. We find a more "Kuhnian" view of the way in which literary fictions can function cognitively as TEs in Elgin's approach. She argues that the idea that we can make cognitive progress through reading fictions is puzzling only if we operate with what she terms the "information transfer" view of cognitive progress, the view that we progress by amassing information about the world. She claims, to the contrary, that the main obstacle to cognitive progress is a lack of "right" ways of organizing, classifying, and properly orienting ourselves towards the information we already possess. Cognitive progress, for Elgin, involves creative "reconfiguration" which allows us to arrive at new and valuable ways of configuring our experience and thereby the world. Both real experiments and TEs in science are ways of doing this. In each case, we set up a constrained situation and determine the consequences of particular ways of configuring things in those circumstances. If the choice of constraints in setting up the situation is felicitous, then a TE functions as a "laboratory of the mind" in which we can not only control, elaborate, and test various ways of configuring things in the fiction, but also expect that the configurations that work in the fiction will also work in the world: "An experiment or a TE brings it about that certain features are exemplified and manifests why they matter in the (artificial, carefully contrived) experimental setting. It thereby affords reason to suspect that they matter elsewhere. So it indicates that we would do well to consider such factors salient in related real-life situations."

Literary fictions, she argues, perform the same cognitive functions as scientific TEs so conceived. A fiction advances understanding by presenting us with a fictional world that exemplifies certain of its features. It draws out consequences in this world of those features, and thereby affords us reason to think that these same features are a fruitful way of configuring things outside the fiction. Literary fictions, as TEs, differ from TEs in philosophy in being much more detailed, and from TEs in science in lacking an established background theory that provides a thick context within which agreement is achieved on their import. The narratives of literary fictions, she claims, have certain of Goodman's proclaimed "symptoms of the aesthetic" in symbolic functioning (Goodman 1976, 1978) – they are replete and semantically dense. For this reason, the appropriate determiner of the import of a literary fiction is what she terms the widely read, aesthetically sensitive reader whose experience "equips her to know what to look for, what to focus on, what characters are important. Approaching fiction thoughtfully and sensitively, she reflects on a work and her reactions to it. She reads a work in light of her understanding of the world and understands the world in light of the works she has read." Such a reader "tests her insights to see whether they make sense of the text and whether they ring true when projected beyond the text, thus heightening her awareness of patterns, perspectives, and possibilities both in the work and the world."

There is much to admire in Elgin's account – not least its attempt to provide a systematic defense of both literary fictions and TEs in science in terms of the cognitive value of "reconfiguration." But the real teeth of the anti-cognitivist challenge have not been drawn. For, while the widely read, aesthetically sensitive reader may be more adept at extracting thematic content from the dense and replete literary symbol, it is not clear why this also makes her a good judge of the cognitive value of this content. Indeed, the test of truth or correctness of the cognitive content of a literary fiction seems to be, as with Novitz, the result of projecting what we extract from the fiction onto the world. Thus, in spite of the sophistication of Elgin's analysis, it might be thought that she has not really moved us much beyond the skeptical views of Stolnitz which, as we shall see in the next section, mirror the extreme deflationism of Pierre Duhem vis à vis TEs in science. While testing through "projection" may indeed provide evidence for the thematic claims of a literary work, it is not clear why such testing is properly viewed as integral to our engagement with literary fictions as literature, and thus why we are entitled to view literature as a source of knowledge rather than as merely a source of hypotheses.

Similar remarks apply to Young's (2001) defense of literary cognitivism. Young neither draws a comparison between literary fictions and TEs, nor provides the richer contextualization that Elgin offers in her account of "reconfiguration." But the notion of "illustrative demonstration" central to his account seems closely analogous to Elgin's notion of "exemplification." He claims that works of fiction can represent reality even though they contain fictional narratives, because what they characteristically represent are not concrete individuals or situations, but, rather, *types* of individuals or situations. Fictions function as what he terms "illustrative representations," which represent in virtue of various kinds of resemblance between the experience elicited by the work and the experience elicited by the thing it represents. Illustrative representations, he claims, provide knowledge through providing "illustrative demonstrations" which place the receiver in a position where she can acquire a new way of interpreting – a new "perspective" on – the type of object or situation represented. We can determine the *rightness* of a perspective if we bring to our engagement with a literary work other knowledge we possess, and apply that perspective in our attempts to acquire further knowledge of the object, and to make sense of other features of our experience.

As with Elgin, the cognitive claims of literary fictions are defended in terms of two factors: (a) knowledge that the reader brings to her encounter with the literary work; and (b) the "projection" of the thematic content of the literary work onto the real world, as a "test" of its rightness. Again, as with Elgin, this does not seem to address the "no-argument" objection. For, while the knowledge that a reader brings to her encounter with a literary work can plausibly be claimed to enter into the activity of reading itself, and thus to be intrinsic to a proper literary engagement with the work, the "projection" that seems to act as the test of the literary work's claims to furnish us with knowledge, and thus to answer the "no-evidence" argument, might be thought to be extrinsic to such an engagement. To counter this sort of anti-cognitivist move, we need to bring the two "factors" together, to show how the process of "testing" can rightly be viewed as intrinsic to the activity of reading, where, as we read, we bring to bear in novel ways knowledge we already possess.

4 A "moderate inflationist" defense of literary cognitivism

To see how the appeal to the role of TEs in science and/or philosophy might aid the cause of literary cognitivism, we need to address debates over the cognitive credentials of the former. As other papers in this Companion spell out more fully, TEs in science take the form of short narratives in which various experimental procedures are described. The competent reader understands that these procedures have not been, and usually could not (for some appropriate modality) be, enacted. She is invited, however, to imagine or make believe that these procedures *are* enacted and to conclude that certain consequences would ensue, where this is taken to bear upon a more general question which is the topic of the TE. As Carroll observes, TEs so construed also play a substantial cognitive role in philosophy, especially within the analytic tradition.

As many writers have pointed out (e.g., Sorensen 1992; Nersessian 1992; McAllister 1996), scientific and philosophical TEs take the form of short *fictional* narratives. While there is an extensive (and contested! – see Matravers 2014) literature on the nature of fiction, I have elsewhere argued for two plausible necessary and sufficient conditions for the fictionality of a narrative (Davies 2007a ch. 2, 2015a). First, fictional narratives must be products of acts of "fiction-making," where the maker's intention is that we make-believe, rather than believe, the fictional content of the story narrated. Second, the primary constraint on the construction of a fictional narrative must not be what I term the "fidelity constraint" ("include only events you believe to have occurred, narrated as occurring in the order in which you believe them to have occurred"), but, rather, some more general purpose in story-telling. The second condition elaborates upon the first by placing a constraint on what can count as a legitimate act of fiction-making. TEs, whether scientific or philosophical, clearly seem to involve the construction of fictional narratives so construed. First, they present the reader with a hypothetical situation in which an event or process is taken to occur. The reader is intended to make-believe, rather than believe, that the hypothetical situation obtains and the described sequence of events occurs. Second, the author of a TE does not think that the envisaged situation and sequence of events actually occurred, and is therefore not guided by the fidelity constraint

Defenders of literary cognitivism who appeal to TEs do not, of course, claim that *all* literary fictions are TEs. They claim only that because some paradigm works of literary fiction function as TEs they can share in the cognitive value that the latter possess elsewhere. But the import of the connection between fictions and TEs for those whose primary interest is in TEs differs in one striking respect from its import for those defending literary cognitivism. The claim that TEs are fictional narratives is generally taken to *problematize* the cognitive credentials of TEs. James McAllister, for example, sets up the "epistemological problem" for TEs in science as follows: how can we make genuine cognitive progress through engaging with TEs if they are *merely* fictional narratives? On the other hand, the claim that at least some literary fictions are TEs has been taken to *un*problematize the cognitive credentials of such fictions. Literary fictions, it is claimed, can have genuine cognitive value *because* they are elaborate TEs and (it is assumed) the latter possess such cognitive virtue. Thus, rather paradoxically, that TEs are fictions has been taken (by some) to call into question the very thing that is supposed to be established (for others) by the fact that fictions are TEs!

What unites those who reflect on the fictional nature of TEs and those who claim the status of TEs for some literary fictions is an epistemological concern with the claim to cognitive status of certain narratives. In the case of scientific TEs, the focus of this concern is a puzzle clearly posed by Thomas Kuhn (1964). There is an apparent tension between the following three claims:

C1. Scientific TEs do not rely on or provide any new empirical data concerning the state of the world. Any empirical data upon which we draw must have been known and generally accepted before the TE was conceived.
C2. TEs provide us with new information about the physical world.
C3. TEs, while they involve reasoning, cannot be reduced without epistemic loss to inferences of any standard kind (deductive, inductive, or abductive).

We need C3 to get a genuine puzzle because we routinely learn new things about the world by *constructing inferences* based on existing knowledge.

This "puzzle" admits of broadly "deflationary" and "inflationary responses" (see Davies 2007b, 2010):

1 A *deflationary* response denies that there is a genuine puzzle, either by denying C2, or by denying C3. (We may take C1 to be true by definition, if "new empirical data" means new evidence about the world derived directly or indirectly from sense experience).

2   An *inflationary* response accepts C2 and C3, thereby takes TEs to have a distinctive cognitive value, and offers an explanation of how TEs are able to possess that value.

There are extreme and moderate versions of each kind of response. An extreme deflationist simply denies C2. A moderate deflationist retains C2 but casts doubt on the distinctive epistemic virtues of TEs by denying C3. A moderate inflationist supplements C1 by arguing that prior empirical knowledge can be mobilized in a new way by TEs. And an extreme inflationist argues that TEs involve non-empirical modes of intuition.

For extreme deflationists such as Pierre Duhem (1954) and Carl Hempel (1965), scientific TEs are of at best heuristic value. A TE may *suggest* that physical reality has a certain feature, and may even provide the idea for a concrete experiment, but TEs cannot themselves teach us anything about the world. Moderate deflationism is exemplified in the writings of John Norton (1991, 1996). He maintains that, insofar as TEs can tell us about the world, they are epistemically unremarkable, merely colorful uses of our standard epistemic resources – ordinary experiences and the inferences that are to be drawn from them. TEs simply reorganize and make explicit what we already know about the physical world. According to Norton's "reconstruction thesis," all TEs can be reconstructed as arguments once we fill in the tacit or explicit assumptions. Belief in the conclusion of a TE is justified only insofar as that conclusion is justified by the reconstructed argument.

Neither of these ways of conceiving of TEs in science can assist the defender of literary cognitivism, since they are effectively arguments against a cognitivist view of TEs! This is readily apparent in the case of extreme deflationism. The extreme deflationist claims that TEs have the very properties that the skeptic about literary cognitivism ascribes to literary fictions: they are merely useful "heuristic" devices and furnish us with no knowledge of the world unless their conclusions are put to independent empirical test. And for the moderate deflationist, the locus of cognitive value in TEs is the underlying dialectical structure. The narrative detail is merely a distraction. The more detailed and elaborate narratives in works of literary fiction can only serve a negative purpose for cognition, since they make it much more difficult to reconstruct the underlying dialectical structure that, for the moderate deflationist, does all of the cognitive work.

James Brown (1991, 1992), promoting the extreme inflationist response, offers an account of what he terms "Platonic TEs." He maintains that we find such TEs in mathematics, where "we can sometimes prove things with pictures." In such cases, "we grasp an abstract pattern" via a kind of "intellectual perception." TEs in the natural sciences can also function platonically, according to Brown. In Galileo's "tower" TE, the move to the final conclusion is "immediate," involving an exercise of intellectual intuition which reveals a law of nature. Such laws, for Brown, are relations between universals, and sometimes a TE can lead us to grasp such laws.

A defense of literary cognitivism that parallels the extreme inflationist account of scientific TEs might be the "Romantic" view of the literary artist as one whose words transmit to others her intuitive insight into the inner nature of things. But extreme inflationism seems unpromising as a defense of the epistemic virtues of scientific TEs, for it cannot prevail over moderate inflationism if the principal arguments offered in its favor are intended to show that it is preferable to some form of deflationism. And this indeed seems to be an objection to Brown's form of extreme inflationism, which is defended largely by pointing to aspects of the functioning of TEs for which the moderate deflationist cannot provide a plausible account. Miščević (1992) argues that the "mental modelling" account offered by moderate inflationists (see below) can explain all of these aspects of the functioning of TEs. If so, the greater explanatory burden that must be shouldered by the extreme inflationist – who must tell a convincing story about our capacity to grasp relations between universals in our engagement with TEs – tells in favor of the moderate position. I think analogous difficulties would plague an "extreme inflationist" defense of literary cognitivism.

The approach to the cognitive value of scientific TEs most favorable to the cause of literary cognitivism is moderate inflationism. Indeed, as will be apparent, Carroll's defense of literary cognitivism tacitly appeals to considerations central to the latter. The moderate inflationist claims that TEs allow the scientist to mobilize cognitive resources not available in the kinds of scientific reasoning celebrated by moderate deflationism. TEs, she maintains, are epistemically singular and cannot be reconstructed as deductive or inductive arguments without epistemic loss, because of *the way in which* they mobilize prior cognitive resources. Ernst Mach (1905), the progenitor of this approach, argued that we have "instinctive knowledge," derived from experience but never articulated and perhaps even incapable of being made explicit. This knowledge is activated when we imagine ourselves in a hypothetical experimental situation. It is only through the mobilization of such instinctive knowledge that we can "immediately" draw the required conclusion from the TE narrative.

More recent commentators have echoed Mach's strategy. Tamar Gendler (1998, 2002), for example, argues that Norton's attempts to reconstruct Galileo's "tower" TE as a deductive argument fail to capture how the way the phenomena are represented in the TE invokes experientially grounded "tacit knowledge." The demonstrative force of Galileo's TE, she argues, depends crucially upon such knowledge. And David Gooding (1992) argues that the narratives whereby both real and thought experiments are presented are persuasive only if they manage to convey the "relevant experimental know-how," much of it what Gooding terms "an experimenter's embodied familiarity with the world," upon which she necessarily draws in her experimental practice.

Nancy Nersessian (1992) and Nenad Miščević (1992) also pursue this kind of moderate inflationist strategy, drawing on work in cognitive science on the construction and manipulation of mental models in narrative comprehension (e.g., Johnson-Laird 1983). Receivers of TE narratives, it is claimed, use the narrative to construct a quasi-spatial "mental model" of the hypothetical situation. In running the TE, the receiver operates directly upon the model, deriving the experimental conclusion by manipulating the latter rather than operating upon the linguistic representations comprised by the TE narrative. Crucially, in constructing and manipulating the model, the receiver mobilizes a number of other cognitive resources. These include her everyday understandings of the world, based on practical experience; other forms of tacit knowledge, such as individual expertise, practical know-how, and the "embodied familiarity" with the world discussed by Gooding; and geometrical intuitions. It is in virtue of the role played by these unarticulated cognitive resources in the mental modeling of TEs that the latter yield determinate conclusions and have a bearing on the real world. Miščević sets out clearly (1992, 24) how this approach solves the Kuhnian puzzle about TEs. TEs enable us to produce new data by manipulating old data through the generation of a manipulable representation of a problem. In constructing and manipulating this model, we mobilize prior cognitive resources in ways not possible if we were to work directly on a regimented propositional account of that problem. Thus we cannot reconstruct a TE as an argument without epistemic loss.

A moderate inflationist view of scientific TEs might fund a more comprehensive response to the arguments against literary cognitivism. The "no evidence" objection, we may recall, is that the most we can get from reading literary fictions are hypotheses about the general ordering of things in the world, beliefs about specific aspects of the world including affect, or potentially insightful ways of categorizing things in our experience. Only if those hypotheses or beliefs pass further tests can they qualify as knowledge, it is claimed. To evade the "no-argument" objection, any "tests" to which the cognitivist points in attempting to answer the "no-evidence" objection must be intrinsic to a proper engagement with literary works *as literature*. The "moderate inflationist" suggestion is that our responses to some literary fictions mobilize unarticulated cognitive resources. The narrative makes us aware of patterns that seem to underlie the complexity of prior and present actual experience, and this response is to be trusted because it reflects the operation of unarticulated cognitive resources in our reading. This answers the "no-argument" objection because it makes the process of "empirical testing" *internal* to the process of reading, rather than something we have to do through projection after we have read the fiction.

5 Assessing "moderate inflationism"

5.1 The scope of the defense

Caution is needed in a number of respects if we are to endorse such a defense of literary cognitivism. In the first place, an account that appeals to the mobilization of unarticulated cognitive resources can justify only some of the different kinds of knowledge claims made on behalf of literary cognitivism. In the case of knowledge of particular matters of fact, justified belief would seem to require that the fictional narrative be, or be rightly believed to be, a reliable source of knowledge of facts of this kind. Similarly, claims about affective knowledge derivable from fictions are plausible only if the author is, or is rightly believed to be, a reliable source of knowledge as to the affective nature of such an experienced situation.

The moderate inflationist account of scientific TEs bears most obviously on the claim that literary fictions can yield knowledge of general principles operative in real events, and, perhaps, the claim that, in our reading of such fictions, we can acquire new and illuminating ways of classifying real entities or events. Even here, the claim that such cognitive benefits can accrue in the act of reading a fictional narrative, without the need to carry out some additional empirical verification requires that we clarify what is to be included in "the act of reading." What must be excluded, if we are to answer the anti-cognitivist arguments, is any recourse to empirical further investigation or a process of "projecting" the thematic or categorical content of the novel onto the world.

5.2 The problem of detail

In assessing arguments for according to at least some literary fictions the same kind of cognitive value accorded to TEs in science and philosophy, we must consider certain significant differences between the fictional narratives involved. Most obviously, the cognitivist needs to demonstrate that such cognitive values are not compromised by the much greater narrative detail to be found in standard literary works. Some have maintained that such detail dictates a distinct kind of imaginative engagement on the part of the reader – "dramatic" rather than "hypothetical" imagining (Moran 1994) – and that the cognitive value of philosophical TEs rests on their ability to prompt hypothetical imagining. Our immersion as readers in the narrative detail of standard fictional narratives, however, and the intricate complexity of those narratives, prevents or hinders us from engaging in the kind of hypothetical imagining upon which the cognitive value of scientific and philosophical TEs depends. To the extent that, as readers of literary fictions, we try to abstract from the detail in order to extract some propositionally characterizable "thematic meaning," we cease to treat the narratives as works of literary fiction (see, e.g., Livingston 2006; Smith 2006).

To answer this objection, one would need to look first at the role of dramatic imagining in the running of TEs. One would then need to inquire more generally into the ways in which such imagining can serve our cognitive interests. TEs whose working seems to require some kind of dramatic imagining can be termed "dramatized" TEs, in that they require that the person mentally running the TE not merely entertains hypothetically the kind of situation propositionally characterized in a narrative but also imagines being in that very situation and responding to it affectively in certain ways. A salient question is whether even some scientific and philosophical TEs call for dramatic imagining, and whether the need for dramatic imagining undermines the cognitive claims of such TEs. It is also worth asking whether there can be distinctive cognitive benefits of dramatized TEs, and, if so, what kinds of cognitive advances they can yield (see Davies 2015b).

5.3 *The limits of moderate inflationism*

It is also important to clarify what a moderate inflationist defense of literary cognitivism can establish. The claim is not that, because our sense, in reading a work of fiction, that we are learning something about the real world draws upon unarticulated cognitive resources, we can trust this sense and rest content, without further exploration or reflection, that we are indeed learning what we believe ourselves to be. For our sense that we are learning is trustworthy only in proportion to the adequacy of the unarticulated cognitive resources upon which we draw. Any reasons to question whether what we bring to bear is unarticulated *knowledge* (as opposed to unarticulated *ignorance*) are reasons to question the moderate inflationist defense of the cognitive virtues of a particular TE or class of TEs. This is no different from the situation in respect of scientific TEs. The claim, therefore, is not that a reader's sense of having learned from fiction itself justifies her belief that she has so learned. The claim is only that, when the sense of having learned from a fiction is *in fact* grounded in the right kind of unarticulated knowledge, the reader can indeed be said to have learned what she believes herself to have learned. The claim is, in this respect, an externalist rather than an internalist one, depending upon how the agent in fact stands in relation to the knowledge claim, rather than how she sees herself as standing in relation to it.

6 Can thought experiments be screened?

Some authors have maintained that, even if the fictional narratives in literary works can function as TEs that advance our philosophical understanding, this cognitive role cannot be extended to fictional narratives presented cinematically, if we require that the philosophical content supposedly articulated through these narratives relies upon exclusively cinematic resources. This does not, of course, prevent a literary narrative that itself has cognitive content being filmed, as in the case of the film version of *The Third Man*. But, it is argued, exclusively cinematic resources are those that relate to the visual properties of cinema, and any putative philosophical insight conveyed visually must be extracted from a film in a verbally articulate form in order to be located in a pre-existing philosophical problematic before any philosophical work can be done with this exported content (Livingston 2006; for the claim that films can function as philosophical TEs, see Wartenberg 2007).

To assess this argument, we must investigate more carefully a number of the ideas upon which it draws (see Davies 2012). First, we must ask whether the notion of "exclusively cinematic resources" is properly understood as encompassing only visual means. Secondly, we must ask whether this argument, even if it demonstrates that film cannot itself be a medium in which we "do philosophy," establishes a parallel conclusion for the more general cognitive claims of fictional narrative cinema. Finally, we need to ask whether, even in the case of advances in philosophical understanding, these necessarily require the kind of verbal mediation claimed by the proponent of the foregoing argument. We might return here to our earlier discussion of the cognitive possibilities of dramatized TEs (see again Davies 2015b).

7 Thought experiments in the philosophy of art

Appeals to our moral intuitions in ethics frequently involve the use of TEs as "intuition pumps" designed to mobilize our practically based understanding of our concepts. By presenting us with hypothetical "purified" cases that are less cluttered than the kinds of cases that we encounter in ordinary life, TEs like the "trolley problem" are designed to elicit from us conclusions about the scope of those concepts that we apply in everyday situations, and thereby to provide us with a theoretically refined moral understanding that can be brought to bear on particular moral issues. In philosophy of art, however, a much stronger role is played by appeals to actual artistic practice than by appeal to hypothetical cases. This is not to say that TEs have played no role in philosophy of art, but they have figured most prominently in philosophical contexts where the appeal to actual cases is practically difficult, or where the intended conclusion relates to what is possible or conceivable. For example, they have been a principal resource upon which philosophers have drawn in arguing for the idea that artworks are partly constituted by the art-historical and art-theoretical contexts in which an artist produces something that serves as the focus of our appreciative attention. Arthur Danto's "gallery of perceptually indistinguishable red rectangles" instancing different works of visual art (Danto 1981), Jerrold Levinson's sonically indistinguishable yet distinct musical works (Levinson 1980), and Gregory Currie's textually indistinguishable literary works (Currie 1991), compensate for the limitations of our artistic practices by positing distinct works whose distinctness can be explained only by reference to differences in artistic context. Many of these writers explicitly refer to a short fictional story by the Argentinian writer Jorge Luis Borges (1970), which is taken to illustrate the possibility of such works by describing a modern author who deliberately, but without simply copying, produces a work which is textually identical to part of Cervantes' *Don Quixote*. But, save for cases like this where actual artistic practice is mute, it is from actual practice that philosophers of art tend to draw the examples upon which they exercise their theoretical powers.

References

Borges, J. L. (1970) "Pierre Menard, author of the Quixote," in *Labyrinths*, translated by J. E. Irby, Harmondsworth: Penguin.
Brown, J. R. (1991) *The Laboratory of the Mind: Thought Experiments in the Natural Sciences*, London: Routledge.
Brown, J. R. (1992) "Why empiricism won't work," in *Philosophy of Science Association 1992*, edited by D. Hull, M. Forbes, and K. Okruhlik, vol. 2, pp. 271–279, East Lansing, MI: Philosophy of Science Association.
Carroll, N. (2002) "The wheel of virtue: Art, literature, and moral knowledge," *Journal of Aesthetics and Art Criticism* 60: 3–26.
Currie, G. (1991) "Work and text," *Mind* New Series 100: 325–340.
Danto, A. (1981) *The Transfiguration of the Commonplace*, Cambridge: Harvard University Press.
Davies, D. (2007a) *Aesthetics and Literature*, London: Continuum.
Davies, D. (2007b) "Thought experiments and fictional narratives," *Croatian Journal of Philosophy* 7: 29–46.
Davies, D. (2010) "Learning through fictional narratives in art and science," in *Beyond Mimesis and Convention: Representation in Art and Science*, edited by R. Frigg and M. Hunter, Dordrecht: Springer.
Davies, D. (2012) "Can philosophical thought experiments be 'screened'?" in *Thought Experiments in Philosophy, Science, and the Arts*, edited by M. Frappier, L. Meynell, and J. R. Brown, London: Routledge.
Davies, D. (2015a) "Fictive utterance and the fictionality of narratives and works," *British Journal of Aesthetics* 55: 39–55.
Davies, D. (2015b) "*Blade Runner* and the cognitive values of cinema," in *Blade Runner*, edited by A. Coplan and D. Davies, London: Routledge.
Duhem, P. (1954) *The Aim and Structure of Physical Theory*, translated by P. Weiner, Princeton: Princeton University Press.
Elgin, C. Z. (2007) "The laboratory of the mind," in *A Sense of the World: Essays on Fiction, Narrative, and Knowledge*, edited by W. Huerner, J. Gibson, and L. Pocci, London: Routledge.
Gendler, T. (1998) "Galileo and the indispensability of thought experiments," *British Journal for the Philosophy of Science* 49: 397–424.
Gendler, T. (2002) "Thought experiments," in *The Encyclopedia of Cognitive Science*, London: Routledge.
Gooding, D. (1992) "What is Experimental about thought experiments?" in *Philosophy of Science Association*, vol. 2, pp. 280–290, East Lansing, MI: Philosophy of Science Association.
Goodman, N. (1976) *Languages of Art*, 2nd ed., Indianapolis: Hackett.
Goodman, N. (1978) *Ways of Worldmaking*, Indianapolis: Hackett.
Hempel, C. (1965) *Aspects of Scientific Explanation*, New York: Free Press.
Johnson-Laird, P. N. (1983) *Mental Models*, Cambridge: Harvard University Press.
Kuhn, T. (1964) "A function for thought experiments," in *The Essential Tension* (1977), Chicago: University of Chicago Press.

Lamarque, P. and Olsen, S. H. (1994) *Truth, Fiction, and Literature*, Oxford: Clarendon Press.
Levinson, J. (1980) "What a musical work is," *Journal of Philosophy* 77: 5–28.
Livingston, P. (2006) "Theses on cinema as philosophy," *Journal of Aesthetics and Art Criticism* 64: 11–18.
Mach, E. (1975 [1905]) "On thought experiments," reprinted in *Knowledge and Error*, Dordrecht: Reidel.
Matravers, D. (2014) *Fiction and Narrative*, Oxford: Oxford University Press.
McAllister, J. (1996) "The evidential significance of thought experiments in science," *Studies in History and Philosophy of Science* 27: 233–250.
Miščević, N. (1992) "Mental models and thought experiments," *International Studies in the Philosophy of Science* 6: 215–226.
Moran, R. (1994) "The expression of feeling in imagination," *The Philosophical Review* 103: 75–106.
Nersessian, N. (1992) "In the theoretician's laboratory: Thought experimenting as mental modeling," *Proceedings of the Philosophy of Science Association* 2: 291–301.
Norton, J. D. (1991) "Thought experiments in Einstein's work," in *Thought Experiments in Science and Philosophy*, edited by T. Horowitz and G. Massey, Lanham: Rowman & Littlefield.
Norton, J. D. (1996) "Are thought experiments just what you thought?" *Canadian Journal of Philosophy* 26: 333–366.
Novitz, D. (1987) *Knowledge, Fiction, and Imagination*, Philadelphia: Temple University Press.
Putnam, H. (1976) "Literature, science, and reflection," in *Meaning and the Moral Sciences*, London: Routledge and Kegan Paul.
Smith, M. (2006) "Film art, argument, and ambiguity," *Journal of Aesthetics and Art Criticism* 64: 33–42.
Sorensen, R. (1992) *Thought Experiments*, Oxford: Oxford University Press.
Stolnitz, J. (1992) "On the cognitive triviality of art," *British Journal of Aesthetics* 32: 191–200.
Wartenberg, T. (2007) *Thinking on Screen: Film as Philosophy*, London: Routledge.
Young, J. (2001) *Art and Knowledge*, London: Routledge.

30
HOW THOUGHT EXPERIMENTS INCREASE UNDERSTANDING

Michael T. Stuart

Thought experiments can and do increase our understanding. In this chapter, I use resources from mainstream epistemology to help explain this feat. I present three main kinds of understanding identified in mainstream epistemology, and show how each of these may be created by thought experiments in different ways. I close with some epistemological discussion of those ways, and the cognitive activities that underpin them. While everything I say is meant to hold for the relation between thought experiments and understanding in general, my examples will come from the scientific domain.

1 Why talk about thought experiments in the context of understanding?

It can be tempting to see the entire epistemological literature on thought experiments as focused on a single issue: whether the facts about thought experiments support rationalism, empiricism, or whether some naturalist middle ground is to be preferred. Rationalism, empiricism, and naturalism are views about the source of knowledge. Taken as an issue concerning knowledge, the epistemological question about thought experiments is: how do thought experiments produce new empirical knowledge without new experience? And indeed, many authors frame their accounts explicitly in answer to this question (e.g., Kuhn 1977, 241; Brown 2004, 34; Gendler 2004, 1152; Norton 2004, 44; Häggqvist 2009; Thagard 2010, 251; Davies, this volume; Goffi and Roux, this volume). But knowledge is not the only or even necessarily the most interesting epistemological desideratum. I think *understanding* gives it a run for its money, and many others do too (Kvanvig 2003, 2009; Elgin 2006; Pritchard 2009, 2010; Grimm 2012; Dellsén 2016).

To motivate the point, here are a few uses of thought experiments that seem to aim at understanding: thought experiments can illustrate a theory or theoretical claim (Brown 1991, 32; Peacock, this volume; Schabas, this volume), they can control extraneous variables and "invert ideals of natural order" (Sorensen 1992, 11–16), they can "exemplify" properties and relations (Elgin 2014), they can provide "hypothetical explanations" (Schlaepfer and Weber, this volume), they can help us to see how rival theories lead to different results (Brun, this volume), and they can make certain intuitions accessible (Lenhard, this volume).

Thought experiments that play the above roles can improve the quality of our epistemological relationships with the world without necessarily (or merely) increasing our stock of justified true beliefs. For instance, illustrating a claim is not the same as justifying that claim or suggesting that it is true, since we can illustrate false claims. The same goes for attention-drawing. I do not deny that new knowledge can result from such thought experiments (e.g., we can always gain knowledge that we have just performed a thought experiment). I merely claim that there is more to the epistemological power of thought experiments than knowledge production.[1] We must not restrict our epistemologies of thought experiments therefore to whatever is reconstructible as a set of true propositions.[2]

Before we explore how thought experiments increase our understanding, we need to say something about understanding itself.

2 Kinds of understanding

Having recovered from philosophical banishment by the positivists (see De Regt 2009, 22–4) and behaviorists (see Barsalou 1999), understanding is again a respectable notion in epistemology. And there are many characterizations of what it could be. Wesley Salmon portrayed understanding as whatever a good explanation provides (Salmon 1984). According to Michael Friedman, understanding is what we get when we reduce the number of fundamental entities that we have to admit in a theory (1974). Phillip Kitcher modified this idea by portraying understanding as what happens when we find a way to explain different phenomena using the same patterns of argument (1981). Henk De Regt characterizes understanding in terms of intelligibility, which is "the value that scientists attribute to the cluster of virtues (of a theory in one or more of its representations) that facilitate the use of the theory for the construction of models" (2009, 31). Hasok Chang argues that understanding "is knowing how to perform an epistemic activity" (2009, 75). Catherine Elgin claims that

> We understand rules and reasons, actions and passions, objectives and obstacles, techniques and tools, forms and functions and fictions as well as facts. We also understand pictures, words, equations, and diagrams ... Understanding need not be couched in sentences. It might equally be located in apt terminology, insightful questions, effective nonverbal symbols ... Even a scientist's understanding of her subject typically outstrips her words. It is realized in her framing of problems, her design and execution of experiments, her response to research failures and successes, and so on.
>
> (1993, 14–15)

It is implicit in this passage that we should not limit the objects of understanding to propositions: we can also understand e.g., actions, passions, etc. And Elgin points out that not all understanding is linguistically expressible, which further distances it from propositional knowledge. Finally, Elgin hints where to find understanding: it is in the way we speak, work, wonder, and interact with the world. It is a matter of knowing where something fits in with our existing commitments and abilities.

The literature on understanding accommodates the above insights in classic analytic fashion by breaking up the concept of understanding into sub-types, each of which captures a different set of the properties we intuitively want to ascribe to understanding. Philosophers have therefore distinguished transitive from intransitive understanding; propositional from non-propositional understanding; interrogative (understanding what, where, and how) from non-interrogative understanding (see Baumberger 2011, 68–71; Carter and Gordon 2014, 3; and Baumberger, Beisbart, and Brun 2016); understanding as a *faculty* from understanding as a *process* from understanding as a *result* (Baumberger 2011, 69); and among moral, aesthetic, scientific, mathematical, and philosophical understandings (Hills 2015). Any distinction is as good as any other in principle: what matters is the philosophical work it allows us to do. In this chapter, I will focus primarily on a distinction found in the literature between three types of understanding, as follows.

The first type is *explanatory* understanding, which is discussed by, e.g., Duncan Pritchard (2010, 74), Carl Hempel (1965, 334), Philip Kitcher (1989, 419), Stephen Grimm (2008), De Regt (2009, 588), Kareem Khalifa (2012), Michael Strevens (2013), Alison Hills (2015), Michael Hannon (forthcoming), and many others. The second is *objectual* understanding, discussed by, e.g., Christoph Baumberger (2011), Baumberger and Georg Brun (2016), Elgin (2007), Jonathan Kvanvig (2003), Khalifa (2013), Daniel Wilkenfeld (2014), and Christoph Kelp (2015). Finally, there is *practical* understanding, which is mentioned by many but discussed in depth by few, at least in the main debate in epistemology. Let us look more closely at these types of understanding.

Explanatory understanding (EU) is having an explanation for why something is the case (De Regt 2009, 25; Khalifa 2011, 108). It can be propositional, though it need not be. For instance, Grimm (2006) and Hazlett (forthcoming) argue that explanations can be ostensive, as when my mechanic explains why my car won't start by pointing to the burnt-out ignition switches (Grimm 2006, 531).

Objectual understanding (OU) is understanding a thing, set of related things, or a subject matter. One popular way of characterizing this sort of understanding is as grasping the "coherence-making relationships" in a comprehensive body of information (Kvanvig 2003, 192), or as grasping and committing to a theory of something (Baumberger 2011, forthcoming). It relates to Elgin's claim (1993, 14–15) that "understanding a particular fact or finding, concept or value, technique or law is largely a matter of knowing where it fits and how it functions in the matrix of commitments that constitute the science." Here is an example of OU from Baumberger,

> Understanding global warming involves, for instance, understanding what effects (on natural and social systems) it will have, how it is linked to human activities (such as burning fossil fuels and deforestation) and related phenomena (such as the destruction of stratospheric ozone and global dimming), how far greenhouse gas emissions and, as a result, temperatures are likely to rise in the future, and how the changes will vary over the globe.
>
> (Baumberger 2011, 77–8)

Finally, there is practical understanding (PU), as in, "Jimi understands how to play guitar," which is "clearly not explanatory" (Khalifa 2013, 123). Elgin captures it this way:

> Understanding physics is not merely or mainly a matter of knowing physical truths. It involves a feel for the subject, a capacity to operate successfully within the constraints the discipline dictates or to challenge those constraints effectively. And it involves an ability to profit from cognitive labors, to draw out the implications of findings, to integrate them into theory, to utilize them in practice.
>
> (1993, 14–15)

PU may be phrased as knowledge-how or tacit knowledge, but in any case it is not standard propositional knowledge. For example, it does not appear to be susceptible to Gettier-style defeaters. Furthermore, it is not OU, as having that sort of understanding of guitars or playing guitars would not imply that Jimi could actually play the guitar, which is something that is necessary for PU. Likewise it is not EU, since Jimi arguably does not need to possess or be able to provide any explanations concerning guitar playing in order to play.

There is an on-going discussion in the literature about whether we can reduce some of the types of understanding mentioned to one or some of the others. For example, Khalifa (2013) tries to reduce OU to EU. Baumberger (2011) and Kvanvig (2009) argue that EU and OU cannot be reduced to one another. In my opinion, the most plausible scenario concerns the reduction of EU and OU to PU. Chang (2009), Hills (2010, 2015), Baumberger (2011) and Wilkenfeld (2013) make claims that are at least partially in line with this suggestion. Having PU is having certain abilities, one of which might be the ability to provide, grasp or assess explanations. Having EU could then be explicated in terms of having a specific sort of PU. We also have the ability to grasp and express the relations among events, objects, domains, etc. So having OU could again be explicable in terms of having a particular sort of PU.

However, even if EU and OU were reducible to PU (and much more would need to be said), the abilities to give and assess explanations, as well as to grasp and express internal relations among members of a set, are so important that they merit their own discussions anyway. For example, a lack of EU will be diagnosed and remedied in particular ways that we would not necessarily use to diagnose and remedy a lack of PU. For instance, we can lack PU of x because we have not had any practice with x, or because we cannot see how to apply x to a new case. But we usually lack the ability to give an explanation of x because we lack some relevant knowledge of x (whether causal or otherwise).

In other words, even if EU, OU and PU were mutually reducible, we would still want to keep them apart since there are different ways of obtaining each type of understanding and different ways of determining when each has been achieved. This is particularly clear in the scientific context (Stuart 2016). In any case, *until OU and PU are reduced to EU*, the current overwhelming focus in mainstream epistemology on EU is misplaced. Epistemologists should take OU and PU into account, especially if they want their accounts of understanding to include scientific understanding.

Now that we can talk about understanding more precisely, we can begin to see how thought experiments might produce it. The question: "How might a thought experiment increase S's understanding of x (where S is an individual or community)?" must first be split into three questions.

First, if we mean S's EU of x, then we can increase this with a thought experiment that contributes to a (good) explanation of x.

If we mean S's OU of x, this is more complicated. OU consists in grasping relations between objects, events, and domains on the one hand, and other objects, experiences, background knowledge, and so on, on the other. What sorts of relations are there between say, the uncertainty principle and the rest of quantum mechanics? Or between chemistry and our experience of chemical substances? One important kind of relation that we might grasp between these elements is a *semantic* relation. With respect to the notion of a semantic relation, I want to be inclusive: it could be (a) the pairing or mapping of propositions, terms, concepts, variables, etc., to their referents; (b) the intensions or psychological "senses" of propositions, terms, concepts, variables, etc. (which might take the form of prototypes, proxytypes, theories, exemplars, definitions, etc.); (c) the location of a proposition, concept, etc., in a system of knowledge; (d) truth conditions; or (e) something else. In any case, building semantic connections or grasping semantic content is not the same thing as increasing knowledge since an increase in semantic understanding is either a *process* of establishing/grasping semantic connections, which cannot be identified with a set of justified true propositional beliefs because processes are not propositions. Or it will be a cognitive state which results from having established new semantic connections. This state could be reconstructed propositionally, but the proposition "S has grasped 'unmarried adult male' as the semantic content of 'bachelor'" is no more S's actual cognitive state than the proposition "I have eaten" is my being full. I conclude therefore that *one* interesting way to increase S's OU of x is by grasping the semantic content of x.

Finally, if we mean S's PU of x, we have to increase (the quality of) S's abilities that are relevant to x.

My task in the next section is to examine whether thought experiments can increase EU, OU and PU in these ways.[3]

3 Thought experiments increase understanding

3.1 *Thought experiments can contribute to explanations*

First, if you simply ask people what their "favourite deep elegant or beautiful explanation" is, they sometimes answer with a thought experiment. In 2012 the website edge.org did exactly this, putting the above question to 192 people, including Daniel Dennett, Lawrence Kraus, Tania Lombrozo, Richard Nisbett, and Stephen Pinker.[4] Twenty-one of the replies were well-known thought experiments, and another 8 were imagination-based inferences that any broad-minded characterization of thought experiments should include. Almost a sixth of the participants therefore gave a thought experiment as their *favourite* example of a deep, elegant or beautiful explanation, which shows that at least some people naturally think that thought experiments can be (very) good explanations.

Second, a study of thought experiments in textbooks revealed that many thought experiments survive even when "superseded at the cutting edge of science" because they "may still be in use to explain particular phenomena economically" (Gilbert and Reiner 2000, 268). In other words, we continue to educate using outdated thought experiments because they explain a given phenomenon particularly well. In another study, high school students, undergraduates and doctoral students were given hard problems in mechanics and dynamics and then observed to see what thought experiments they invented and why. The authors found that "the most frequently observed purpose of using a thought experiment is for 'explanation'" (Kösem and Özdemir 2014, 882).

Finally, if we consider the main characterizations of explanation in the literature, we can find examples of thought experiments that fit into each of them. Perhaps the most famous account of explanation is Carl Hempel's, according to which an explanation is the subsumption of a phenomenon under covering laws, that is, "exhibiting the phenomenon to be explained as a special case of some general regularity" (Hempel 1965, 257). Darwin's eye thought experiment (described on page 532) helps us to explain the vertebrate eye since it provides a series of steps that show how the eye could be subsumed under the framework of evolution by natural selection.

For others, an explanation is what we get when we unify various disparate phenomena (see Friedman 1974; Kitcher 1989; Bangu 2016), for example, by subsuming such phenomena under a common vocabulary, a common cause, a common mechanism, or a common formalism. Isaac Newton unified projectile motion (such as throwing a ball on Earth) and orbital motion (such as the moon orbiting the Earth) in a "paradigmatic" case of unification (Woodward 2014). And Newton's achievement at least partially relies on his use of a thought experiment, what we now call Newton's cannonball.

Another account portrays explanation as whatever answers a why-question given a contrast class (e.g., van Fraassen 1980). That is, why does x happen as opposed to y? Many thought experiments fit into this account, including perhaps the most famous thought experiment in the literature, Galileo's falling bodies thought experiment (see Brown 1991; McAllister 1996; Norton 1996; Gendler 1998; Palmieri 2003, this volume; Buzzoni 2008, 106–7), which tells us that bodies of different weights fall at the same speed *as opposed* to speeds that are proportional to their weights. It goes part of the way towards explaining why bodies fall this way (and not another way) by suggesting that there could be no other way for them to fall.

Finally, there are accounts of explanation that focus on the identification of causal chains, causal counterfactuals, or causal networks (see Salmon 1984, Woodward 2003, and Strevens 2009, 2013, respectively). Thought experiments will be important here since they are one of our main methods for investigating counterfactual dependence claims and answering "what if" questions. Häggqvist (2009) explicitly characterizes an important class of thought experiments as playing this role, and many others (including e.g., Williamson 2004) agree that thought experiments are needed to validate counterfactuals (see also Cohnitz and Häggqvist, this volume).

In sum, if any of these accounts of explanation are on the right track, thought experiments can play an important role in explanations.

According to the recent literature on understanding, this means that thought experiments can help to increase understanding since coming to possess a good explanation is either identical to or very strongly correlated with increased EU (see Hempel 1965; Friedman 1974; Achinstein 1983; Kim 1994, 1996; De Regt and Dieks 2005; Keil 2006; Lombrozo 2006, 2011; De Regt 2009; Riggs 2009; Khalifa 2011, 2012; Strevens 2013; Greco 2014; Kelp 2014; Wilkenfeld 2014; Hills 2015; Hannon forthcoming).

To conclude, while there might be good reasons to be skeptical about inter-defining understanding and explanation *in general* (Lipton 2009; Gijsbers 2013), it is nevertheless the case that since having an explanation provides EU, then, since thought experiments can play an important role in generating explanations, they can help to provide EU.

3.2 Thought experiments increase meaningfulness

Existing pedagogical methods test for the semantic form of OU. To see this we need only consider written tests of any kind. The sort of question that asks a test-taker to put something into his or her own words, define a term, or fill in a blank, are testing precisely for OU (Stuart 2016). When we pass this sort of test, it is only because at some previous point in time we made semantic connections between the idea in question and our other beliefs, concepts or abilities in a way that made it meaningful for us. Can thought experiments aid us in this regard?

In Stuart (2016) I gave three examples of thought experiments that seem to have been designed explicitly for this purpose. I will quickly mention two.

The first is Darwin's vertebrate eye. By the time we get to this thought experiment in Chapter 5 of the *Origin*, Darwin has already introduced and argued for natural selection. Now he wants to forestall some possible objections. Perhaps the most famous is the eye, which appears too complicated to have been the result of chance mutations. Darwin answers with a thought experiment that takes us through a possible course of evolution from a single nerve sensitive to light, to a patch of nerves, the addition of muscles to focus the light, to the organ you are using right now to read this. The eye thought experiment helps us understand what it *means* for an organ like the eye to be a product of evolution. We do not learn how eyes actually evolved; that is something fossil evidence is unlikely ever to reveal. Instead, on completing the thought experiment, we come to appreciate what it means for eyes to have evolved.

Another example is Maxwell's demon. Briefly, Maxwell found himself in the following situation by the end of *A Theory of Heat*: He knew his version of the second law of thermodynamics could be violated in principle, but not in practice. And he knew that it would not be quite clear what this meant. That is, if we could violate the second law in principle, why can't we violate it in practice? And if we could *never* violate it in practice, there must be some reason for this which would make our inability to violate the second law a matter of principle. Maxwell answers with the demon thought experiment (see Peacock, this volume, 212–15). By performing it we come to appreciate why we will not witness any actual violations of the law in nature but *that* such violations are not forbidden. We do this by seeing that if we were the demon, we could violate the second law. Meanwhile we recognize that there is probably nothing in nature that could actually do what the demon does on a time scale relevant to human interests. This way, we come to understand the meaning or semantic content (including modal strength) of Maxwell's statistical second law.

The idea that thought experiments can increase the meaningfulness of a scientific idea, concept, event, etc., crops up again and again in the history of science, especially in the history of physics (Beller 1999, 107; Norton, unpublished, ch. 29). Alexander Koyré noted that thought experiments take a concept and make it meaningful by connecting it to our experience. In his words, thought experiments "help scientists to bridge the gap between empirical facts and theoretical concepts" (Koyré 1968). In other words, they provide empirical semantic content for parts of theory. Athanasios Velentzas and Krystallia Halkia argue that thought experiments are used "both for clarifying the consequences of physics theories and for bridging the gap between the abstract concepts inherent in the theories and everyday life experiences" (Velentzas and Halkia 2013a, 3027). And in a similar vein, Lynn Stephens and John Clement argue that thought experiments "appear to have considerable value as a sense-making strategy" (Stephens and Clement 2006).

Thought experiments have therefore been recognized as helping us to create semantic connections between new ideas, concepts, models, etc., on the one hand, and experiences that we have already had, experiences we might have, existing knowledge, abilities, concepts, etc., on the other. In other words, through them we can schematize difficult theoretical entities (in Kant's sense; see Buzzoni, this volume, 336; Stuart 2017).[5]

But is this the same as increasing OU? Many philosophers argue that learning what something means is an instance of increased understanding (e.g., Davies 1981; Elgin 2000; Pettit 2002; Longworth 2008). And as with explanations and EU, we can be quite hesitant to identify meaning-making with understanding *in general*, and still happy to identify it as a means to or type of OU, since semantic relations do seem to be one sort of "coherence-making" relation that we can grasp. Thus, since we can increase meaningfulness using thought experiments, we can increase OU using thought experiments.

3.3 Thought experiments increase fruitfulness

Again focusing on pedagogical orthodoxy, we already test for fruitfulness when we have test-takers derive, explain, extrapolate, or otherwise evince that they can *use* an idea to do something they could not before. And we take this to be evidence that a test-taker understands that idea. This can be applied to the case of thought experiments in the following way: a thought experiment increases S's understanding of *x* if after performing the thought experiment S can do something that S could not before, for example, manipulate a model, make a successful prediction, produce a good explanation for a phenomenon, derive a particular conclusion, etc. Even if the new abilities are accompanied by an increase in our stock of justified true beliefs, we would still want to deny that they just *are* justified true beliefs.

There are reasons to think that thought experiments can increase fruitfulness. Consider thought experiments that are used in therapy to give participants power over themselves to, for example, overcome a fear of heights or face an abusive partner (see Gendler 2004). Examples can be found in the scientific context as well. Velentzas and Halkia (2013b) took a group of high school students who could not make correct inferences about the relation between orbital and projectile motion. They presented the students with Newton's cannonball thought experiment and the students could then pass their tests, even with questions that required a good deal of extrapolation. They repeated this study using Einstein's elevator and train with the same results (2013a).

The case can also be made historically. After performing Darwin's eye thought experiment the scientific community gained (and continues to profit from) the ability to investigate complicated traits by imagining a string of possible mutations, each of which is adaptive given its environment for the organism that possesses it. This has been a useful strategy in addressing objections to evolution as well as providing new hypotheses for traits and organs of interest.

To summarize the last few sections: thought experiments can increase EU of x by helping to explain x, OU of x by increasing the meaningfulness of x, and PU of x by increasing the fruitfulness of x.[6] Now, let's see what the literature on understanding can contribute to the epistemology of thought experiments.

4 How do thought experiments increase understanding?

4.1 How thought experiments increase explanatory understanding (EU)

To say precisely how thought experiments contribute to EU, we would first need to choose or defend a characterization of explanation (or if we are pluralists, several). Given a particular characterization, we can then ask what sorts of explanations thought experiments take part in and how, whether thought experiment-based explanations have special qualities that make them better or worse than other kinds of explanations (for example, their experimental, narrative, or dialogical features), whether thought experiment-based explanations work by testimony, and how thought experiments justify modal claims (when that is their role in an explanation). It would require more space than I have to enter into the long-standing debates surrounding these questions. Instead, I will focus on OU and PU.

4.2 How thought experiments increase objectual understanding (OU)

There is no direct discussion of OU in the literature on thought experiments, but there are a number of resources in epistemology (not to mention aesthetics, hermeneutics, phenomenology, and philosophy of language) that can be brought to bear. In the space I have, I will highlight the work of Elizabeth Camp (2003, 2006, 2007, 2008, 2009, unpublished), which turns on the notions of *perspectives*, *characterizations*, and *frames*. The basic idea of a perspective is that when we read a narrative from a certain point of view, we learn to see the world *as if it were* the way the narrative presents it. We pay attention to different features of the world, and we are directed to experience those features as having specific relevance and intensities. We may evaluate these features differently, too, making moral, aesthetic or other value judgments in a way we would not otherwise. While watching a Saturday morning cartoon, we think it is morally acceptable for characters to smash one another over the head with mallets. And we feel uncomfortable reading *Lolita* because we are supposed to take up Humbert's perspective, and we don't want to.

When we *apply* a perspective (even our own) to something particular, we have a *characterization*. Because we are taking up Humbert's perspective when we read *Lolita*, we (are supposed to) characterize Dolores as an object of sexual desire. And on Saturday mornings we (are supposed to) characterize Daffy Duck as occasionally deserving a good mallet-smashing.

More recently, Camp has introduced the notion of a *frame*. A frame is a representational vehicle that crystalizes a perspective by suggesting a characterization. For example, Romeo regards ("characterizes") Juliet as so much "above" everyone else that you cannot even look at her without being "blinded" by her charm. Romeo encourages us to share in this characterization with the utterance (frame): "Juliet is the sun." Likewise, I might want you to enter into a characterization that portrays our friend Jane as someone who always expects everything to go wrong, thinks everything is her fault, and demurs to any authority. To do this I present the frame: "It's as if Jane had a puppy who died when she was little and she's still convinced it was her fault" (Camp 2009, 110). It is easy to see how models in science may serve as frames. For example, Bohr's model of the atom is a frame which prompts us to characterize features of atoms in certain ways.

Perspectives, characterizations and frames are non-propositional. They are not thoughts but tools for thinking. We can express frames and characterizations using propositions, but these expressions are not the frames or characterizations themselves. This is because any characterization or perspective will outstrip its propositional reconstruction since the characterization can always be applied to new situations which were not included in the propositional reconstruction. To actually have a characterization, one must have the appropriate dispositions to evaluate, focus on, interpret, and relate together the features of a subject in a certain way.

OU-oriented thought experiments can be understood as frames which are meant to snap us into certain characterizations.[7] Some of Darwin's opponents characterized the eye as a watch. Even if we saw a watch on a deserted island, we would nevertheless assume the watch was created because of its complexity and obvious purposefulness. This frame suggests a characterization of the eye as being like a watch, which is complex, purposeful and the product of intentional creation. That is how the frame casts doubt on the idea that eyes are the result of a series of chance mutations. Darwin, on the other hand, presents a competing characterization using his thought experiment, which narrates a series of mutations that could plausibly result in a fully functioning eye beginning with a single nerve. This characterization makes it easy to see the eye as having evolved.

Darwin's frame succeeded because it allowed us to associate with the eye (and other complicated organs) a whole new set of semantic and explanatory relationships, possible causal histories, relations to other organs, evaluations, and so on, in a way that accords with the values of science (explanatory power, simplicity, predictive accuracy, etc.). Since possessing such a characterization is not possessing any specific propositions but rather certain dispositions, it is clear how the right frame could enable someone to pass the relevant tests of meaningfulness mentioned above.

How exactly do we gain OU by using frames? Camp writes "I might, for instance, gain a more intimate appreciation for the anguish of orphanhood, or for the attractions of gambling or being a bully, by empathizing with characters who undergo those emotions" (2009, 116). Such imaginative exercises help us understand orphanhood, gambling addiction or bullying by grasping what these mean from a first-person perspective. And, as Elgin (2014) argues, thought experiments can exemplify properties. That is, they can provide (perceptual or cognitive) access to an instance of a property, while also referring to that property, allowing us to make new inferences about the class of things that possess that property. This extends our semantic reach; not only do we grasp the meaning of, e.g., a specific gambling addiction by imagining ourselves as a specific gambling addict, we now begin to understand gambling addicts of all sorts, and even perhaps addicts in general. This is how thought experiments increase semantic OU in an epistemologically interesting way: they give us direct access to properties and indirect (inferential) access to the class of objects that possess those properties (by exemplification) *while also* providing new tools for thinking about those objects (by the characterization).[8]

Furthermore, thought experiments will be particularly helpful as frames since they do not simply suggest a characterization; they prompt us to experiment with that characterization, filling it in ourselves as we go. More on this below.

I conclude that one way for an OU-oriented thought experiment to be successful is to be a good frame. That is, a good OU-oriented thought experiment will prompt in an efficient manner an epistemically and semantically valuable characterization or perspective. This allows us to appeal to a normative theory of perspectives in order to work out a normative theory of thought experiments, which I think is an attractive prospect.

4.3 How thought experiments increase practical understanding (PU)

Portraying thought experiments as frames allows us to explain some of their potential to create PU. For example, Camp notes that in Shakespeare's sonnet 73, Shakespeare likens his own dying to fall becoming winter, twilight becoming night, and fire becoming ash. These frames help us characterize DEATH. But they also provide a way to *cope* with death. We realize that death is "a natural and inevitable moment following on from more abundant, energetic ones." We may not like the cold and lonely images of winter and night, but we may be comforted by "acceptance and awareness of what lies ahead" (2009, 118). Likewise, it is only because we can see Newton's cannonball *as* the projectile which fills the gap between projectile and orbital motion that we can learn to apply our knowledge of one context to the other.

Besides this plausible option, there are other ways to explain the ability of thought experiments to increase PU. Again, space constrains me to consider only one. In this case, I will look briefly at the work of Alison Hills (2010, 2015).

Hills discusses understanding in terms of "grasp," which she explicates as an increase of "cognitive control."

> The best way of thinking of [understanding] is by an analogy with grasping a ball or cup of tea or similar. If you grasp a ball, you have it under your control. You can manipulate it, move it, turn it round, and so on, that is you (normally) have a set of practical abilities or practical know how, which you can exercise if you choose.
>
> (2015, 3)

More formally, you understand p when you can follow an explanation for why p, explain why p in your own words, draw the conclusion that p from q, make analogical inferences from q' to the relevantly similar p', use p to explain other related propositions, and finally, use p' analogically to explain related propositions, q'.

Those are Hills's conditions, which she uses to explicate understanding-why (the sort of understanding we have when we understand that q is why p). This might seem like a departure from PU, but it is only a particular case. Hills claims that "guidance from an expert can certainly help, but that help does not necessarily take the form of assertions passing on standard propositional knowledge; or even if it does, that only works if it is combined with practice," and, "I don't think that it is very plausible to identify cognitive control with extra propositional knowledge. For no particular extra number of pieces of propositional knowledge guarantees that you have the grasp required of understanding, the ability to draw conclusions yourself in a new case" (2015, 11).

Having cognitive control is a matter of having a certain set of abilities concerning propositions, for Hills, and that set of abilities, though often expressible in propositions, is not propositional itself. Hills's account can be extended to PU by removing the requirement that the object of understanding be a proposition. Jimi understands how to play the guitar because he has a set of abilities towards a musical instrument instead of a proposition. Likewise, a student may be said to understand a signalling pathway in biochemistry when she can create a computer simulation that captures its behaviour accurately and robustly.

With Hills's notion of understanding extended to PU, we can focus on how thought experiments might produce it. I will be drawing on some recent remarks made by Hills, concerning how understanding comes from analogies and questions.[9]

First, consider knowledge, which can be gained through the testimony of others. A trusted expert asserts a true proposition, and we justifiably believe it and thereby gain knowledge. However, this will not work for PU, which requires the development of a set of abilities and not merely believing the right propositions. Instead, when we gain understanding with the help of others we are like Meno's slave boy, who is led to understanding by a series of actions that he performs in response to leading questions. Besides leading questions, we can also use analogies. Hills provides the example of treating light as a wave to understand the interference pattern in a double slit experiment. Since knowing requires believing true propositions, questions and analogies will not typically be able to transmit knowledge by testimony because questions do not assert propositions, and analogies are (often) literally false. What is common to understanding gained through questioning and analogy is that questions and analogies require us to *work on our own*. We are not given the answer to the question nor the key to interpreting the analogy, though we are encouraged to try to find them. And this exercise helps us develop new abilities or link existing abilities to new situations, until we can properly be said to have the relevant PU. For example, a computer scientist might ask a student, "Why do you think you are getting this error message?" as a way of helping her understand where she has gone wrong, and thereby increase her PU of a particular computer model. A driving instructor might tell a student to think of driving as a video game to increase the student's PU of driving. If you have a fear of airline travel, a therapist might ask you to visualize getting on a plane, flying, and landing, over and over, until you have the ability to fly and are no longer afraid (Gendler 2004).

The key is the open-endedness of the prompt, which forces the agent to work things out for herself. In so doing, she lays the groundwork for the new abilities which constitute PU. A good PU-oriented thought experiment must therefore present a problem, along with enough information to work it out, without being prohibitively difficult. There will be enough information to set the agent on the right track, but not so much that the information can be accepted without developing any of the desired cognitive control.

Of course it is not just questions, metaphors and analogies that spur us into (cognitive) action. A thought experiment could be open-ended in this sense by employing a diagram, as these can be approached in many different ways (see Meynell 2014, this volume). There are also riddles and puzzles, which are regularly employed by logicians to get logic students to learn certain styles of reasoning.[10] A well-timed exclamation can also do the job.

Thought experiments can be exemplary prompts. First, they can combine several of the above prompt-types in one. Einstein and Galileo's thought experiments were often presented in the form of a paradox or puzzle and accompanied by a diagram. Second, their (at least semi-) experimental nature ensures their open-endedness. Thought experiments begin with a scenario or the statement of a problem, which causes us to create an imaginary world to explore the scenario or problem. We "set up" or "design" a thought experiment in this imaginary world, which we then "run" and "observe." John Gilbert and Miriam Reiner (2000) argue that thought experiments in science textbooks are typically suboptimal precisely because they do not require students to run the thought experiment and then observe what happens in their own minds. In too many cases, the conclusion of the thought experiment is given first, and then the imagined scenario is introduced, which is supposed to lend credence to the conclusion. In this case, students do not vary variables in their minds; they simply follow along a text. This is better than simply reading the conclusion, but is not as good as having the student work through the problem on their own. The most successful thought experiments require our mental effort.[11] Einstein asks, "What would light look like if you were riding on a lightwave?" and Maxwell asks, "Could a demon in a closed system decrease the system's entropy?" To answer these questions, the scientific community required time and effort, which is exactly what was needed to increase the relevant PU.

5 Concluding thoughts

Much more needs to be said about how thought experiments increase understanding. For instance, we need to identify how thought experiments can mislead us, and if there are any kinds of understanding that thought experiments cannot provide. Relevant to the discussion of EU, Brown (2014) points out that thought experiments seem to provide "top-down" (or formal) explanations more easily or more often than "bottom-up" or mechanistic explanations. Is this necessarily the case, and if so, why?

And there are many more ways the literature on understanding can interact with the literature on thought experiments. There is agreement in the epistemological literature that understanding comes in grades (Kvanvig 2003; Elgin 2007; Baumberger 2011, forthcoming; Grimm 2014; Hills 2015; Hannon forthcoming). We will therefore have grades of EU, OU and PU. The tests we give to others and to ourselves in academic contexts are graded, and so, as graders of tests, we already have an idea of what counts as less than perfect understanding, and how much a thought experiment can help to increase the degree of someone's understanding. Perhaps one way epistemologists can therefore investigate degrees of EU, OU and PU is to look at the tests we give our students (and ourselves) and ask how thought experiments aid us in passing them.

Also, grades can be measures of breadth or depth (Elgin 2007; Strevens 2013; Greco 2014). This is helpful for increasing the precision with which we classify good understanding-oriented thought experiments. Can thought experiments provide both broad and deep EU, OU and PU? If not, why not?

Finally, understanding is a success term (Baumberger 2011). This is clearly true in science, where a student is judged to understand a model, system, method, or concept only when she or he can pass certain tests of understanding, which will be contextual (depending on the domain and problem type) and conventional (like the 5-sigma confidence level in physics). These tests can amount to operationalizations of the success conditions for understanding (Stuart 2016). But much more needs to be said about the aptness of any given test as a means for evaluating the state of someone's understanding relative to the success conditions and also about the success conditions themselves, e.g., must they track whether our understanding "latches on" to the world? If so, how can they do this? How "objective" can the tests be?

***

In this chapter, I drew attention to the potential for mutual illumination between the literature on thought experiments and the literature on understanding. We saw that thought experiments can increase explanatory, objectual and practical understanding, and also that what counts as a good understanding-oriented thought experiment will depend on the sort of understanding we want. A good explanatory thought experiment will participate in a good explanation. One way to be a good objectual thought experiment is to create a good frame to get us into the right characterization or perspective. And one way to be a good practical thought experiment is to be an open-ended, goal-directed prompt that entreats us to perform certain cognitive actions, which can then be repeated and reinforced to build new abilities.

Acknowledgments

I'd like to thank Michael Hannon, Christoph Baumberger, Marco Buzzoni, Catherine Elgin, Jim Brown, Nancy Nersessian, John Norton, Guillaume Schlaepfer, Elizabeth Camp, Alison Hills, the organizers of the Summer Seminar on Understanding (part of the Varieties of the Understanding project), as well as the audience of that seminar, and an audience at the University of Macerata. The work in this chapter was made possible by funding from the University of Pittsburgh's Center for Philosophy of Science, and the Social Sciences and Humanities Research Council of Canada.

Notes

1 The suggestion that thought experiments increase understanding is not new. Brown made a similar point much earlier (1992, 274), although principally as a criticism of Norton. He has recently turned back to the issue, looking at thought experiments and understanding more directly (Brown 2014). Other philosophers of science have focused on understanding in thought experiments as well (e.g., Nersessian 1992, 2007; Humphreys 1993; Gooding 1992, 1994; Gendler 1998, 2000; Arthur 1999; Lipton 2009; Camilleri 2014), but none (save Catherine Elgin) have taken advantage of the recent work on understanding in mainstream epistemology. That is my aim in this chapter.
2 Whether all forms of understanding can be reconstructed exclusively in terms of knowledge is the subject of a large debate (see, e.g., Hetherington 2001; Zagzebski 2001; Kvanvig 2003; Grimm 2006; Pritchard 2009; Hills 2015; Riaz 2015; Hannon forthcoming). I do not want to commit myself to a position here. Perhaps some forms of understanding can be reduced to ordinary propositional knowledge, and others to non-propositional knowledge (such as knowledge-how). I claim below that several forms of understanding are not reducible to propositional knowledge, and this is sufficient to distance these forms of understanding from knowledge, standardly conceived.

3 One reason I chose this tripartite distinction is because it subsumes most of the ways thought experiments lead to understanding that were mentioned at the beginning. For example, to illustrate a theory or idea is often to explain it (EU) or help us grasp its coherence-making relations (OU). Controlling for extraneous variables and inverting ideals of natural order enable us to do things we could not do before, which is a way of increasing PU. To exemplify a property is to provide direct access to that property (which is a way of drawing new semantic or explanatory relations to it) and also to refer to the property, which allows us to make inferences about all items with that property, which is to increase its PU. And so on.
4 www.edge.org/responses/what-is-your-favorite-deep-elegant-or-beautiful-explanation.
5 This is not a trivial accomplishment. Determining the semantic content of theoretical entities is the general case of a solution to what Bas van Fraassen has called the "problem of coordination" (van Fraassen 2008). I discuss the idea that thought experiments are used in science to solve it in Stuart (2017).
6 The same thought experiment might do more than one of these, even at the same time; see (Stuart 2016) for examples.
7 Portraying thought experiments as frames would make them tools to increase understanding rather than knowledge, not just for me, but for Camp as well. She writes,

> Insofar as philosophy seeks understanding, we need to do more than just identify a set of justified true propositions. We need to know which propositions we should pay attention to, what explanatory structures to impose upon them, and (in the moral case at least) even how we should feel about them.
>
> (2009, 128)

I am merely emphasizing the power that frames and characterizations have for exploring and evaluating the semantic content of entities, terms, events or domains, and showing how this can lead specifically to OU.
8 Camp hints at thought experiments having such dual powers herself when she writes,

> Philosophers also use thought experiments ... to present a supposedly common phenomenon in especially stark and vivid terms, thereby helping us to focus our attention on its structurally relevant features ... But such thought experiments can also operate ... by describing counterfactual situations in concrete detail, they can trigger a kind of experiential acquaintance that an abstract description misses.
>
> (2009, 124)

9 This discussion draws on a presentation given by Hills at Fordham University, New York, June 20, 2016.
10 Philosophical discussions of riddles, and riddles *as* metaphors, can be found at least as far back as William of Conches (c. 1090 – 1154 CE), who (to some extent) equated the two. William believed that riddles and metaphors were important for appealing to our cognition, which was a faculty of the soul, using speech (a faculty of the body). According to William, riddles, metaphors, allegories, and fables were "labyrinths of imagery" that enclosed truth in darkness. Peter Dronke summarizes "The initiate can enter that darkness and there find the truth. Yet it is not only a dark place, but a passage in which [s/]he must walk: what [s/]he finds in the labyrinth, we might say to paraphrase, is not a truth ready-made, but a challenge ... " (1974, 49–50). Another interesting anticipation of this discussion is in pseudo-Dionysius, who says that "incongruous symbols" (*per dissimilia symbola*) are sometimes best for teaching people about difficult subjects, because they are not so similar to their targets that they could be confused for the object of study itself (Roques, Heil, and de Gandillac 1970, 74ff.). Thanks to Maximilian Wick for discussion and references on this point.
11 This will be true for laboratory experiments as well. As regards PU, being told the conclusion of an experiment is less helpful than watching that experiment performed, which is less helpful than being guided through the experiment step-by-step, which is less helpful than running the experiment yourself.

References

Achinstein, P. (1983) *The Nature of Explanation*, New York: Oxford University Press.
Arthur, R. (1999) "On thought experiments as a priori science," *International Studies in the Philosophy of Science* 13: 215–229.
Bangu, S. (2016) "Scientific explanation and understanding: Unificationism reconsidered," *European Journal of Philosophy of Science*, DOI: 10.1007/s13194-016-0148-y.
Barsalou, L. (1999) "Perceptual symbol systems," *Behavioral and Brain Sciences* 22: 577–660.
Baumberger, C. (2011) "Types of understanding: Their nature and their relation to knowledge," *Conceptus* 40: 67–88.
Baumberger, C. (forthcoming) "Explicating objectual understanding taking degrees seriously", *Journal for General Philosophy of Science*.
Baumberger, C. and Brun, G. (2016) "Dimensions of objectual understanding," in *Explaining Understanding: New Essays in Epistemology and the Philosophy of Science*, edited by S. Grimm, C. Baumberger, and S. Ammon, London: Routledge.
Baumberger, C., Beisbart, C. and Brun, G. (2016) "What is understanding? An overview of recent debates in epistemology and philosophy of science," in *Explaining Understanding: New Essays in Epistemology and the Philosophy of Science*, edited by S. Grimm, C. Baumberger, and S. Ammon, London: Routledge.
Beller, M. (1999) *Quantum Dialogue*, Chicago: University of Chicago Press.
Brown, J. (1992) "Why empiricism won't work," *Proc Philos Sci Assoc* 2: 271–279.
Brown, J. R. (2004) "Why thought experiments do transcend empiricism," in *Contemporary Debates in the Philosophy of Science*, edited by Christopher Hitchcock, Malden: Blackwell.
Brown, J. R. (2011 [1991]) *The Laboratory of the Mind: Thought Experiments in the Natural Sciences*, London: Routledge.
Brown, J. R. (2014) "Explaining, seeing, and understanding in thought experiments," *Perspectives on Science* 22: 357–376.
Buzzoni, M. (2008) *Thought Experiment in the Natural Sciences*, Würzburg: Königshausen and Neumann.
Camilleri, K. (2014) "Towards a constructivist epistemology of thought experiments," *Synthese* 191: 1697–1716.
Camp, E. (2003) *Saying and Seeing-As: The Linguistic Uses and Cognitive Effects of Metaphor*, Ph.D. thesis, University of California, Berkeley.
Camp, E. (2006) "Metaphor and that certain 'je ne sais quoi,'" *Philosophical Studies* 129: 1–25.
Camp, E. (2007) "Thinking with maps," in *Philosophical Perspectives 21: Philosophy of Mind*, edited by J. Hawthorne, Oxford: Wiley-Blackwell.
Camp, E. (2008) "Showing, telling, and seeing: Metaphor and 'poetic' language," *The Baltic International Yearbook of Cognition, Logic and Communication, vol. 3: A Figure of Speech*, edited by E. Camp, Manhattan, KS: Prairie Press.
Camp, E. (2009) "Two varieties of literary imagination: Metaphor, fiction, and thought experiments," *Midwest Studies in Philosophy* XXXIII: 107–130.
Camp, E. (Unpublished manuscript) "Perspectives in imaginative engagement with fiction."
Carter, A. J. and Gordon, E. C. (2014) "Objectual understanding and the value problem," *American Philosophical Quarterly* 51: 1–14.
Chang, H. (2009) "Ontological principles and the intelligibility of epistemic activities," in *Scientific Understanding*, edited by H. De Regt, S. Leonelli, and K. Eigner, Pittsburgh: University of Pittsburgh Press.
Davies, M. (1981) "Meaning, structure and understanding," *Synthese* 48: 135–161.
De Regt, H. (2009) "Understanding and scientific explanation," in *Scientific Understanding*, edited by H. De Regt, S. Leonelli, and K. Eigner, Pittsburgh: University of Pittsburgh Press.
De Regt, H. and Dieks, D. (2005) "A contextual approach to scientific understanding," *Synthese* 144: 137–170.
Dellsén, F. (2016) "Scientific progress: Knowledge versus understanding," *Studies in History and Philosophy of Science* 56: 72–83.
Dronke, P. (1974) *Fabula: Explorations into the Uses of Myth in Medieval Platonism*, Leiden: Brill.

Elgin, C. Z. (1993) "Understanding art and science," *Synthese* 95, 13–28.
Elgin, C. Z. (2000) "Interpretation and understanding," *Erkenntnis* 52: 175–183.
Elgin, C. Z. (2006) "From knowledge to understanding," in *Epistemology Futures*, edited by S. Hetherington, Oxford: Oxford University Press.
Elgin, C. Z. (2007) "Understanding and the facts," *Philosophical Studies* 132: 33–42.
Elgin, C. Z. (2014) "Fiction as thought experiment," *Perspectives on Science* 22: 221–241.
Friedman, M. (1974) "Explanation and scientific understanding," *Journal of Philosophy* 71: 5–19.
Gendler, T. S. (1998) "Galileo and the indispensability of scientific thought experiments," *British Journal for the Philosophy of Science* 49: 397–424.
Gendler, T. S. (2000) *Thought Experiment: On the Powers and Limits of Imaginary Cases*, New York: Garland Press.
Gendler, T. (2004) "Thought experiments rethought—and reperceived," *Philosophy of Science* 71: 1152–1163.
Gijsbers, V. (2013) "Understanding, explanation and unification," *Studies in the History and Philosophy of Science* 44: 516–522.
Gilbert, J. and Reiner, M. (2000) "Thought experiments in science education: Potential and current realization," *International Journal of Science Education* 22: 265–283.
Gooding, D. (1992) "What is experimental about thought experiments?" *Philosophy of Science Association 1992* 2: 280–290.
Gooding, D. (1994) "Imaginary science," *British Journal for the Philosophy of Science* 45: 1029–1045.
Greco, J. (2014) "Episteme: Knowledge and understanding," in *Virtues and Their Vices*, edited by K. Timpe and C. Boyd, Oxford: Oxford University Press.
Grimm, S. (2006) "Is understanding a species of knowledge?" *British Journal for the Philosophy of Science* 57: 515–535.
Grimm, S. (2008) "Epistemic goals and epistemic values," *Philosophy and Phenomenological Research* 77: 725–744.
Grimm, S. (2012) "The value of understanding," *Philosophy Compass* 7: 103–117.
Grimm, S. (2014) "Understanding as knowledge of causes," in *Virtue Epistemology Naturalized: Bridges Between Virtue Epistemology and Philosophy of Science*, edited by A. Fairweather, Synthese Library, Switzerland: Springer.
Häggqvist, S. (2009) "A model for thought experiments," *Canadian Journal of Philosophy* 39: 55–76.
Hannon, M. (forthcoming) "What's the point of understanding?"
Hazlett, A. (forthcoming) "Testimony, understanding, and art criticism," in *Philosophy and Art: New Essays at the Intersection*, edited by C. Mag Uidhir, Oxford: Oxford University Press.
Hempel, C. G. (1965) *Aspects of Scientific Explanation and Other Essays in the Philosophy of Science*, New York: The Free Press.
Hetherington, S. (2001) *Good Knowledge, Bad Knowledge: On Two Dogmas of Epistemology*, Oxford: Oxford University Press.
Hills, A. (2010) *The Beloved Self: Morality and the Challenge from Egoism*, Oxford: Oxford University Press.
Hills, A. (2015) "Understanding why," *Nous*, DOI: 10.1111/nous.12092.
Humphreys, P. (1993) "Seven theses on thought experiments," in *Philosophical Problems of the Internal and External World: Essays on the Philosophy of Adolf Grünbaum*, edited by J. Earman, Pittsburgh: University of Pittsburgh Press.
Keil, F. C. (2006) "Explanation and understanding," *Annual Review of Psychology* 57: 227–254.
Kelp, C. (2014) "Knowledge, understanding, and virtue," in *Virtue Epistemology Naturalized: Bridges Between Virtue Epistemology and Philosophy of Science*, edited by A. Fairweather and Synthese Library, Switzerland: Springer.
Kelp, C. (2015) "Understanding phenomena," *Synthese* 192: 3799–3816.
Khalifa, K. (2011) "Understanding, knowledge, and scientific antirealism," *Grazer Philosophische Studien* 83: 93–112.
Khalifa, K. (2012) "Inaugurating understanding or repackaging explanation?" *Philosophy of Science* 79: 15–37.
Khalifa, K. (2013) "Is understanding explanatory or objectual?" *Synthese* 190: 1153–1171.
Kim, J. (1994) "Explanatory knowledge and metaphysical dependence," *Philosophical Issues* 5: 51–69.

Kim, J. (1996) *Philosophy of Mind*, New York: Westview Press.
Kitcher, P. (1981) "Explanatory unification," *Philosophy of Science* 48, 507–531.
Kitcher, P. (1989) "Explanatory unification and the causal structure of the world," in *Scientific Explanation*, edited by P. Kitcher and W. Salmon, Minneapolis: University of Minnesota Press.
Kösem, Ş. D. and Özdemir, Ö. F. (2014) "The nature and function of thought experiments in solving conceptual problems," *Science and Education* 23: 865–895.
Koyré, A. (1968) *Metaphysics and Measurement*, Harvard: Harvard University Press.
Kuhn, T. S. (1977) "A function for thought experiments," in *The Essential Tension*, Chicago: University of Chicago Press.
Kvanvig, J. (2003) *The Value of Knowledge and the Pursuit of Understanding*, Cambridge: Cambridge University Press.
Kvanvig, J. (2009) "The value of understanding," in *Epistemic Value*, edited by A. Haddock, A. Millar, and D. Pritchard, Oxford: Oxford University Press.
Lipton, P. (2009) "Understanding without explanation," in *Scientific Understanding*, edited by H. De Regt, S. Leonelli, and K. Eigner, Pittsburgh: University of Pittsburgh Press.
Lombrozo, T. (2006) "The structure and function of explanations," *Trends in Cognitive Sciences* 10: 464–470.
Lombrozo, T. (2011) "The instrumental value of explanations," *Philosophy Compass* 6: 539–551.
Longworth, G. (2008) "Linguistic understanding and knowledge," *Nous* 42: 50–79.
McAllister, J. W. (1996) "The evidential significance of thought experiment in science," *Studies in the History of the Philosophy of Science* 27: 233–250.
Meynell, L. (2014) "Imagination and insight: A new account of the content of thought experiments," *Synthese* 191: 4149–4168.
Nersessian, N. (1992) "How do scientists think? Capturing the dynamics of conceptual change in science," in *Cognitive Models of Science*, edited by R. N. Giere, Minneapolis: University of Minnesota Press.
Nersessian, N. (2007) "Thought experiments as mental modelling: Empiricism without logic," *Croatian Journal of Philosophy* VII: 125–161.
Norton, J. (1996) "Are thought experiments just what you thought?" *Canadian Journal of Philosophy* 26: 333–366.
Norton, J. (2004) "Why thought experiments do not transcend empiricism," in *Contemporary Debates in the Philosophy of Science*, edited by C. Hitchcock, Somerset: Wiley-Blackwell.
Norton, J. (Unpublished manuscript) *Einstein for Everyone*. Available here: www.pitt.edu/~jdnorton/teaching/HPS_0410/chapters_2013_Jan_1/index.html (accessed 15 November 2016).
Palmieri, P. (2003) "Mental models in Galileo's early mathematization of nature," *Studies in History and Philosophy of Science* 34: 229–264.
Pettit, D. (2002) "Why knowledge is unnecessary for understanding language," *Mind* 111: 519–550.
Pritchard, D. (2009) "Knowledge, understanding, and epistemic value," in *Epistemology*, edited by A. O'Hear, Cambridge: Cambridge University Press.
Pritchard, D. (2010) "Knowledge and understanding," in *The Nature and Value of Knowledge: Three Investigations*, edited by A. Haddock, A. Millar, and D. Pritchard, Oxford: Oxford University Press.
Riaz, A. (2015) "Moral understanding and knowledge," *Philosophical Studies* 172: 113–128.
Riggs, W. (2009) "Understanding, knowledge, and the Meno requirement," in *Epistemic Value*, edited by A. Haddock, A. Millar, and D. Pritchard, Oxford University Press.
Roques, R., Heil, G. and de Gandillac, M. (1970) *Denys l'Aréopagite, La Hiérarchie Céleste*, 2nd ed., Paris: Sources Chrétiennes.
Salmon, W. (1984) *Scientific Explanation and the Causal Structure of the World*, Princeton: Princeton University Press.
Sorensen, R. (1992) *Thought Experiments*, Oxford: Oxford University Press.
Stephens, L. A. and Clement, J. J. (2006) "Designing classroom thought experiments: What we can learn from imagery indicators and expert protocols," *Proceedings of the 2006 Annual Meeting of the National Association for Research in Science Teaching*, April 3–6, 2006, San Francisco, CA.
Strevens, M. (2009) *Depth: An Account of Scientific Explanation*, Cambridge: Harvard University Press.
Strevens, M. (2013) "No understanding without explanation," *Studies in History and Philosophy of Science* 44: 510–515.

Stuart, M. T. (2016) "Taming theory with thought experiments: Understanding and scientific progress," *Studies in the History and Philosophy of Science* 58: 24–33.
Stuart, M. T. (2017) "Imagination: A sine qua non of science," *Croatian Journal of Philosophy*.
Thagard, P. (2010) *The Brain and the Meaning of Life*, Princeton: Princeton University Press.
van Fraassen, B. (1980) *The Scientific Image*, Oxford: Clarendon.
van Fraassen, B. (2008) *Scientific representation: Paradoxes of perspective*, Oxford: Oxford University Press.
Velentzas, A. and Halkia, K. (2013a) "The use of thought experiments in teaching physics to upper secondary-level students: Two examples from the theory of relativity," *International Journal of Science Education* 35: 3026–3049.
Velentzas, A. and Halkia, K. (2013b) "From Earth to Heaven: Using 'Newton's cannon' thought experiment for teaching satellite physics," *Science and Education* 22: 2621–2640.
Wilkenfeld, D. A. (2013) "Understanding as representation manipulability," *Synthese* 190: 997–1016.
Wilkenfeld, D. (2014) "Functional explaining: A new approach to the philosophy of explanation," *Synthese* 191: 3367–3391.
Williamson, T. (2004) "Philosophical 'intuitions' and scepticism about judgement," *Dialectica* 58: 109–153.
Woodward, J. (2003) *Making Things Happen: A Theory of Causal Explanation*, Oxford: Oxford University Press.
Woodward, J. (2014) "Scientific explanation," *Stanford Online Encyclopedia of Philosophy*. Available here: http://plato.stanford.edu/entries/scientific-explanation/ (accessed on 15 November 2016).
Zagzebski, L. (2001) "Recovering understanding," in *Knowledge, Truth, and Duty: Essays on Epistemic Justification, Responsibility, and Virtue*, edited by M. Steup, Oxford: Oxford University Press.

31
ON THE IDENTITY OF THOUGHT EXPERIMENTS
Thought experiments rethought

Alisa Bokulich and Mélanie Frappier

1 Introduction

From Lucretius' spear modification of Archytas' fourth century BC thought experiment about the size of the universe to David Bohm's modification of the EPR Gedankenexperiment about the completeness of quantum mechanics, historical research has revealed that, similarly to physical experiments, thought experiments can be replicated, reworked, and even retooled for very different ends by different thinkers at different times.[1] This historical insight raises the philosophical question of what is to count as the *same* thought experiment. Can one identify identity conditions for thought experiments? How similar do two narratives need to be in order to count as the same thought experiment? Can two thinkers perform the same thought experiment, and yet reach different conclusions?

One of the challenges in trying to answer such questions is that there is no consensus on what exactly thought experiments are. Are thought experiments *experiments* (Mach 1926; Brown 1991; Sorensen 1992a; Rowbottom 2014), *arguments* (Norton 1996; 2004a; 2004b; see Brendel, this volume), *cognitive models* (Nersessian 1992; 2008, this volume), mere *intuition pumps* (Dennett 1984, 1995), *props* for the imagination (Meynell 2014, this volume), or something else? As we shall see, what position one adopts on the nature of thought experiments has implications for one's view on the identity question. Second, as Roy Sörensen (1992a, 163) has noted, as with any discussion about identity, which aspects one identifies as being the most salient often depends on the purpose of one's inquiry: hence, for some projects historical continuity might be the most important, whereas for others it might be propositional content. Rather than trying to determine one set of identity conditions for thought experiments, a more fruitful approach, perhaps, is to explore how different ways of delimiting the identity of thought experiments enable different sorts of inquiries to unfold and different insights into the nature and use of thought experiments to be gained.

Some scholars, such as Ian Hacking, have outright denied that thought experiments can evolve and be retooled:

> I think of [physical] experiments as having a life: maturing, evolving, adapting, being not only recycled but also, quite literally retooled. But thought experiments are rather fixed, largely immutable.
>
> (Hacking 1992, 307)

Other scholars, when confronted with prima facie evidence about the historical evolution of a particular thought experiment, argue that this plasticity is only an illusion, and that thought experiments, when *properly construed*, are immutable. John Norton (1996, 2004a, 2004b), for example, has repeatedly argued that thought experiments are nothing but arguments; hence, if the premises and conclusions of two instances of a thought experiment are not identical, then they are not in fact the same thought experiment. Similarly, Roy Sorensen (1992a) sets out a set-theoretic conception of thought experiments that also imposes stringent identity conditions on thoughts experiments.

On the other hand, scholars such as Alisa Bokulich (2001) and Darrell Rowbottom (2014) have adopted a lenient construal of the identity of two thought experiments, appealing to criteria such as a resemblance of the hypothetical or counterfactual states of affairs and continuity through historical connection. Bokulich argues *pace* Hacking that thought experiments do have a life of their own and that they can be rethought from the perspective of different and even incompatible theories (Bokulich 2001, 286). In order to better understand these debates between those who think thought experiments can evolve and those who think they cannot, it is helpful to begin by briefly reviewing some historical examples.

2 The historical evolution of thought experiments: some examples

When examining the history of various thought experiments, one can find a wide spectrum of variation: some thought experiments are relatively stable over time, such as Galileo's falling bodies thought experiment; others have undergone a series of minor modifications, such as Lucretius' spear modification of Archytas' hand at the edge of the universe; and some thought experiments have been given radically different interpretations by different thinkers even during the same period of time. At this latter extreme we find what have come to be known as "thought experiment–anti-thought experiment pairs."[2] These are defined as any two thought experiments that lead to opposite conclusions.

A particularly interesting subclass of these for our discussion here is thought experiment pairs involving the *same* scenario and yet having analyses that lead to opposite conclusions.[3] A classic example of such a case is Newton's (1999 [1687], 412–13) bucket thought experiment, which invites us to imagine a bucket full of water hanging from a rope that has been twisted tight. When the bucket is released and the rope begins to unwind, the water in the spinning bucket will initially be flat, even though there is a relative motion between the bucket and water. Eventually as the spinning motion is communicated to the water, it will begin to climb the sides of the bucket, forming a concave surface even though the water is now stationary relative to the bucket (as it was initially before it began to unwind). On one reading, Newton can be seen as arguing that this establishes that the water's spinning motion is absolute, that it is motion in reference to absolute space, and that such motions have observable effects that are distinguishable from mere relative motion. Ernst

Mach, in his *Science of Mechanics* (1883), reanalyzes this same thought experiment and argues that it does not establish the existence of absolute space or absolute motion, only that motion relative to the Earth or fixed stars produces such effects (whereas the water's motion relative to the bucket does not).[4] Here we seem to have the same thought experiment narrative, and yet the conclusions drawn from this thought experiment are diametrically opposed.

Another sort of case involves thought experiments with the same central narrative and that reach the *same* conclusion, but do so by appealing to different underlying theories and analyses. An example of a thought experiment of this sort is the rockets-and-thread thought experiment, discussed by Bokulich (2001). The scenario involves two rockets initially at rest in frame S, 100 meters apart and connected by a thread of the same length; both rockets fire simultaneously in this frame and accelerate to 4/5ths the speed of light, stop accelerating, and are moving with a uniform velocity relative to S. Will the thread break? Dewan and Beran (1959) use special relativity to show that according to an observer in S, the thread is Lorentz contracted to a length of 60 meters and so can no longer span the 100 meters between the rockets. Dewan and Beran show how this breaking thread is in fact a consistent result for an observer that is at rest in the rockets final inertial frame, S', because from this frame of reference the accelerations were not in tandem and the distance between the rockets grew, hence also leading to the thread breaking. Dewan and Beran's aim is to use this thought experiment to show that, despite intuitions of many to the contrary, Lorentz contraction can cause measurable stresses on moving bodies. Almost 20 years later, John S. Bell (1993/1976) rethinks this same thought experiment scenario from the perspective of Lorentz's aether theory, arguing that one can arrive at this same conclusion by means of this very different, though arguably more intuitive, theory.

Yet a third example of the ways in which thought experiments can be rethought is Albert Einstein's and Niels Bohr's development and analyses of the clock-in-the-box thought experiment to test the completeness of quantum mechanics. Bohr (1949) recounts the evolution of this thought experiment in his discussions with Einstein, beginning at the 1927 Solvay conference, undergoing modifications in their discussions at the 1930 Solvay conference, and yet further changes during their meeting in Princeton shortly after the 1933 Solvay conference. When Einstein first proposed this thought experiment, it consisted simply of a particle passing through a narrow slit in a diaphragm that was placed some distance before a photographic plate. Bohr recounts how the first modification involved inserting another diaphragm with two slits, in between the single-slit diaphragm and photographic plate. Bohr then makes what he describes as his "pseudo-realistic" modifications to the thought experiment, first imagining the two diaphragms firmly bolted to the table, then with the diaphragm suspended by springs and allowed to move up and down as the particle passes through (representations which he uses to underscore the incompatibility of various experimental arrangements and their role in the production of the phenomenon). On the next iteration of the thought experiment, Einstein replaces the slit with a shutter in a box that could be opened or closed, allowing a particle to escape, and then attaches that shutter to a clock. Once again, Bohr presents a "pseudorealistic" diagram of Einstein's clock-shutter device, with the support bolted to the table and the box suspended from the support by a spring allowing the box to move up and down. As Bohr recounts, this thought experiment appeared to show a violation of the energy-time uncertainty relations:

> [A] single photon was released through the hole at a moment known with as great accuracy as desired. Moreover, it would apparently also be possible, by weighing the whole box before and after this event, to measure the energy of the photon with any accuracy wanted, in definite contradiction to the reciprocal indeterminacy of time and energy quantities in quantum mechanics.
> (Bohr 1949, 225–6)

Bohr recounts his initial surprise over this result and then reanalysis of the thought experiment leading to the opposite conclusion: according to general relativity, the rate of the clock would change as the box shifted its position in the Earth's gravitational field, introducing an indeterminacy on the time measurement that would satisfy the uncertainty principle.

The first thing to notice about this brief history of the clock-in-the-box thought experiment is that this thought experiment underwent a long evolution through a series of stepwise modifications. Each of these steps helped to refine the thought experimenters' thinking and bring to light different aspects of the phenomenon. Although the final version of the thought experiment looks quite different from the initial set up, the intervening steps show a strong pairwise similarity, and moreover there is a clear intention on the part of the thought experimenters to be discussing and modifying the *same* thought experiment. The situation here seems to be quite analogous to two experimenters making several runs of the same physical experiment, while tinkering with and swapping out components of their table-top apparatus as they try to refine their setup.

The second feature to note about this history of the clock-in-the-box thought experiment is how Bohr and Einstein were led to differing conclusions regarding the validity of the uncertainty relations, illustrating a thought experiment–anti-thought experiment pair, analogous to the Newton's bucket case. As will be discussed in more detail in Section 4, Michael Bishop uses this fact that the same thought experiment can be used to reach opposing conclusions, to challenge Norton's (1996) claim that thought experiments are nothing but arguments. Conversely Bishop argues that while Bohr and Einstein were discussing the same thought experiment, each was drawing a different argument from the scenario (Bishop 1999, 535). It is only if we admit that thought experiments can be analyzed through different arguments that we can, Bishop concludes, make sense of such historical episodes (see Brendel, this volume, for a thorough discussion of this debate).

Further historical research suggests that Bohr and Einstein did not just disagree about the conclusion of the clock-in-the-box thought experiment, rather they more fundamentally disagreed about what this thought experiment was supposed to show. Citing a letter from Ehrenfest to Bohr, Don Howard, for example, has cogently argued that Einstein did not in fact intend the clock-in-the-box thought experiment as an argument against the limits of the uncertainty relations:

> He [Einstein] said to me that, for a very long time already, he absolutely no longer doubted the uncertainty relations, and that he thus, e.g., had BY NO MEANS invented the "weighable light-flash box" (let us call it simply L-F-box) "contra uncertainty relation," but for a totally different purpose.
> (Ehrenfest to Bohr, 9 July 1931, Bohr Scientific Correspondence, Archive for History of Quantum Physics; quoted in Howard 2007)

Howard argues that Einstein instead intended the clock-in-the-box experiment as a proto-EPR thought experiment to show the incompleteness of quantum mechanics: the photon is allowed to leave the box and is later reflected back, say, half a light-year away; we then choose either to weigh the box or check the clock, hence ascribing a different physical state to the photon depending on which distant measurement we choose to perform, even though no signal from our measurement could reach the photon and alter its state. If this historical reading is right, then Bohr and Einstein were not simply disagreeing about the conclusion of the clock-in-the box thought experiment, rather they were disagreeing about what phenomenon the thought experiment was supposed to explore.[5]

In the three examples briefly reviewed here, we can recognize a strong historical continuity in these thought experiments and there is at least the intention on the part of these thought experimenters to be discussing the *same* thought experiment. On the other hand, the details of the scenarios, the underlying theories and analyses, and even the purposes and conclusions drawn can change. Hence these examples bring out the opposing intuitions that such cases both do and do not involve the same thought experiment. Moreover, these examples are by no means anomalous; many more examples of the evolution of thought experiments can be found, such as in Carla Palmerino's (2011) work identifying medieval precursors to many of Galileo's thought experiments, the different version of the chain-around-a-double-incline-plane thought experiments attributed to Stevin (Rowbottom 2014) and other examples discussed in the historical entries of this handbook (e.g., Ierodiakonou, this volume; for important qualifications on the various epistemological roles a given thought experimental scenario can play in different contexts, see McAllister, this volume also).

As noted earlier, one's intuitions about whether thought experiments can evolve and be retooled are strongly shaped by one's views on what thought experiments are. Hence, let us turn to four key competing views of the nature of thought experiments and see what implications they have for the question of whether thought experiments can be rethought.

3 Thought experiments on the intuitionist approaches

Many intuition-based accounts of thought experiments underscore the continuity between physical experiments and thought experiments, but argue that the latter work by harnessing physical or modal intuitions to give us new insights into nature. There are two broad classes of intuitionist approaches: "a priori" intuitionist approaches, such as Brown's (1991) that argue thought experiments give us a priori access to the laws of nature and "naturalist" intuitionist approaches, such as Sorensen's (1992a, 1992b), that argue thought experiments allow us to harness intuitions of laws, intuitions which are refined through natural selection. Intuitionist approaches are fallibilist, though they assume our intuitions are sufficiently reliable to explain the successful uses of thought experiments (Rowbottom 2014).

A key question for this approach, then, is whether one needs to harness the same intuitions in a thought experiment in order for it to count as the same thought experiment. One worry is that there is growing empirical evidence that people's intuitions can vary greatly depending on their culture, training, socioeconomic status, etc. (Reiss 2002; Weinberg, Nichols, and Stich 2008; Stich and Buckwalter 2011; Stich and Tobia, this volume).

Hence on this construal thought experiments might only be replicable for similar members of a social group. If, on the other hand, the intuitions invoked in a thought experiment are not essential to the type identity of the thought experiment, then on intuitionist approaches thought experiments can be replicated by different people at different times. This latter approach is adopted by Brown (1991), who seems to identify a continuity in the central narrative as all that is required to replicate a thought experiment.

As we saw earlier, this is not the case on Sorensen's intuitionist approach, which imposes stringent conditions on the identity of thought experiments. For Sorensen a thought experiment is defined by a set of propositions, and any modification of a thought experiment amounts to changing at least one proposition in the set. He writes, "since a set is defined in terms of its members, you no longer have the same set. Therefore we are forced to say that any alteration of a thought experiment yields a new thought experiment" (Sorensen 1992a, 160). He justifies this more stringent approach based, first, on the fact the context of theoretical classification demands maximally fine-grained criteria, and, second, on the fact that our ability to compare two versions of a thought experiment leads us to conclude, when pressed, that they are not really identical.[6]

4 Thought experiments as arguments

Like Sorensen, Norton thinks that a modified thought experiment constitutes a new thought experiment; hence thought experiments cannot be rethought and evolve. According to Norton, thought experiments are nothing but arguments disguised in picturesque or narrative form (e.g., Norton 2004a). Norton defends what he calls the Reconstruction Thesis:

> All thought experiments can be reconstructed as arguments based on tacit or explicit assumptions. Belief in the outcome-conclusion of the thought experiment is justified only insofar as the reconstructed argument can justify the conclusion.
> (Norton 1996, 339)

More specifically, Norton takes the Reconstruction Thesis to be true precisely because thought experiments just are arguments.[7] Hence, if any of the premises or conclusion of a thought experiment changes, then it is not the same thought experiment.

Strictly speaking, Norton's criteria for the identity of a thought experiment are slightly less stringent than Sorensen's set-theoretic criterion in that they allow for inconsequential modifications – i.e., those that do not affect the premises or conclusion of the argument. For example, Norton would presumably allow that one could change the colors of the balls that Galileo is dropping off his tower, since this would not affect the corresponding "t-argument" (which Bishop 1999 defines as the argument reconstructed from a thought experiment). Whereas for Sorensen, asserting that the ball being dropped is purple, rather than red, for example, would presumably change the propositional content of the thought experiment, and hence be a different thought experiment, even if it does not change the corresponding argument.

Norton's conditions for the identity of thought experiments, namely, that they must involve the same premises and conclusion, can be clearly seen in the Norton-Bishop debate about whether Einstein and Bohr were discussing the same clock-in-the-box thought experiment. According to Norton (2004b), the fact that they reached different conclusions regarding the validity of the uncertainty principle shows that they were executing different thought experiments, that is, different t-arguments: Einstein had an implicit premise assuming a non-relativistic space-time, whereas Bohr had an explicit premise assuming a relativistic space-time: non-identical premises therefore non-identical thought experiments.

A challenge for Norton's account is that it is not always clear how precisely to reconstruct the argument associated with a thought experiment. As we saw earlier, for example, this common reconstruction of Einstein's thought experiment has been disputed by Howard (2007). Often thought experiments are underspecified in such a way that their corresponding arguments are underdetermined. Rather than seeing this as a liability or weakness, however, one might argue that it is precisely their constrained-but-still-underdetermined status that makes them such fruitful tools in scientific investigation (an aspect that is captured by a dialectical approach to thought experiments like that of Goffi and Roux, this volume).

5 Thought experiments as simulative model-based reasoning

Nancy Nersessian (1992, this volume) has argued that this conception of thought experiments as being nothing but arguments is impoverished and that it fails to appreciate both the non-algorithmic forms of reasoning that take place in a thought experiment and the broader role that thought experiments play in helping scientists to change their conceptual structures (Nersessian 1992, 291). According to Nersessian, thought experiments are a form of what she calls simulative model-based reasoning. On this view, to perform a thought experiment is to construct a mental model and then simulate what would happen in that model under various manipulations.

Nersessian allows that the thought experiment narrative will underspecify the corresponding mental model, and thus the mental models in the minds of various thought experimenters will likely be different. As long as the mental models constructed by the various thought experimenters were generated by the relevant narrative and embody the same constraints with respect to the target phenomenon, then they should be treated as replications of the same thought experiment. She writes,

> On a mental modeling account, then, a thought-experimental model is a conceptual system representing the physical system that is being reasoned about. More than one instantiation or realization of a situation described in the narrative is possible. The constructed model need only be of *the same kind* with respect to salient dimensions of target phenomena.
>
> (Nersessian 2008, 179; original emphasis)

Thus, despite worries over the potentially private and unique nature of mental-model simulations, on Nersessian's view thought experiments can be rethought. Moreover, in the process of constructing and manipulating these models, thought experimenters can observe how various constraints interact with one another and how neglected constraints can perhaps become salient. There are, as she explains, "cycles of construction, simulation, evaluation, and adaptation of [the] models" (Nersessian 2008, 184). Hence it is a central feature of this approach that thought experiments can be replicated, evolve, and be retooled.

6 Thought experiments as props for the imagination

Some, however, have questioned whether such mental modeling accounts can provide adequate identity conditions for thought experiments. Letitia Meynell, for example, writes,

> given the explicit internalism of mental modeling accounts we inevitably come up against the problem of other minds in the guise of the problem of decisively identifying private mental content. If two thought experimenters report that they have run GFTE [Galileo's falling bodies thought experiment] and they report the same result how can we authoritatively assess whether they have actually experienced the same mental process or even a relevantly similar one?
>
> (Meynell 2014, 4157)

By contrast, Meynell seeks to provide an account of the content of thought experiments that is objective and intersubjectively accessible (Mcynell 2014, this volume also). Her account draws on Kendall Walton's (1990) work *Mimesis as Make-Believe* and treats thought experiments as props for imagining fictional worlds.

On this Waltonian approach, the written or spoken text of the thought experiment (along with any diagrams, etc.) functions as a "prop," which along with "principles of generation" (which include things such as explicit stipulations, implicit cultural conventions, or background knowledge) tell the thought experimenter what to imagine and generate the "fictional truths" within that imagining. The set of fictional truths that the work (e.g., the painting, novel, or thought experiment) generates is called the "work world." According to Walton, there is an objectivity to work worlds in so far as they are "out there" to be investigated and explored (Walton 1990, 42). An individual's subjective imaginings, based on the props and principles of generation, are called the "game world." So there is one set of fictional truths in the "work world" and another presumably overlapping set of fictional truths in the "game world." Walton notes that we can think of the game world as a subjective expansion of the objective work world (216).

Meynell uses this Waltonian framework to provide an account of thought experiments and their identity conditions. The work world, which is fixed by the props of the thought experiment (i.e., the text narrative and diagrams) along with the appropriate principles of generation, is objective and intersubjectively accessible. When a person performs a thought experiment, he or she generates a game world expansion that shares certain fictional truths with the work world. This distinction, she argues, can then explain how it is that two people can perform the same thought experiment:

> We perform the same TE [thought experiment] when we imagine two game worlds which share the same fictional truths as the work world of a TE. The fictional truths of the work world are what confer identity, which allows that rather different descriptions of a TE ... are still importantly the same TE.
>
> (Meynell 2014, 4166)

She goes on to note that this framework can also explain what is happening when two thought experimenters reach different conclusions: they have generated two different game worlds on the basis of the same work world. The question then becomes one of determining whether one of the thought experimenters used the wrong principle(s) of generation, whether the principles of generation are unclear, or whether they are controversial, etc.

In some cases, the disagreement between two thought experimenters might just reflect that fact that one of them incorrectly applied the relevant principle of generation, such as in the rockets-and-thread thought experiment where Bell reports that the majority of physicists in the Theory Division at CERN answered incorrectly that the thread would *not* break (Bell 1993/1976, 68). Such cases can easily be dismissed as mistakes on the part of those thought experimenters.

In other cases of disagreement, the two thought experimenters may arrive at importantly different game worlds because there is an underdetermination of the generating principles; that is, more than one set of generating principles can be legitimately applied to the same narrative, leading to divergent results. So, for example, when Newton and Mach performed the rotating bucket thought experiment, they shared the same "work world" – they both imagined a bucket hanging from a rope, the bucket rotating as the rope unwound, and the water rising up the sides of the bucket – but they used different principles of generation in the creation of their respective "game worlds." The thought experiment allowed two different principles of generation: one related to Newton's absolute space and the other to Mach's relationist account.

At first sight, Meynell's account seems to readily explain how thought experiments are rethought. When first presented with the clock-in-the-box experiment, Bohr wrongly concluded that it offered a counterexample to the uncertainty principle because he imagined the device in a Newtonian spacetime. Once he changed his generating principles to include a relativistic setting, he reached the opposite conclusion. Similarly, Bell reconceptualized the rockets-and-thread experiment by abandoning special relativity in favor of a Lorentzian theory of motion.

The challenge, however, for a Waltonian account of thought experiments is to articulate exactly how the narrative and generating principles work together to determine the content of the thought experiment. Thinking back to the one-slit thought experiment that started the Bohr-Einstein debate, it seems that the original one-slit thought experiment was an invitation from Einstein to Bohr to attempt to develop an imaginary experimental setup that would point to quantum mechanics' incompleteness. In their exploration of the completeness problem, Einstein and Bohr freely tinkered with the experiment, adding a shutter, adding a clock, getting rid of the photographic plate, suspending the diaphragm, etc. On this reading, the Einstein-Bohr conversation offers a great example of the evolution of a thought experiment.

On a Waltonian approach, however, it seems we should instead conclude that Bohr is simply offering a series of distinct thought experiments, insofar as a thought experiment is completely determined by its narrative, images, and allowable generating principles. The images and corresponding narratives in each permutation of this thought experiment have changed: hence, the work world of the one-slit experiment is limited to Einstein's initial scenario and the simple diagram that accompanied it; the subsequent iterations where a shutter is added, the photographic plate is removed, or the diaphragm is transformed into a box would be different work worlds, and hence different thought experiments. In other words, Meynell's Waltonian demand that the content be objectively determined by its scenario, pictures, and generating principles may mean that, ultimately, on her account, thought experiments do not organically evolve. Instead – in a fashion reminiscent to Norton's argument – they would lead to similar, yet strictly speaking, different thought experiments. More work is needed to show that such an account does allow for a tinkering and evolution of thought experiments, as Meynell describes.

7 Replicating physical experiments and replicating thought experiments

On many accounts, thought experiments are viewed as being on a continuum with ordinary physical experiments (see for example, Palmieri or Buzzoni, this volume), with the key difference that they are carried out in the "laboratory of the mind," to use James Robert Brown's (1991) phrase. If this is right, one might hope that some insight into the identity of thought experiments can be gleaned by thinking about the replicability of physical experiments. It is widely accepted that physical experiments can be replicated and that in replicating an experiment there will inevitably be some differences, though presumably inconsequential ones (Mulkay and Gilbert 1986). Hacking for example writes: "[experiments] develop, change, and yet retain a certain long-term development which makes us talk about repeating and replicating experiments" (Hacking 1992, 307).

As Hans Radder (1993) and Jutta Schickore (2011) have pointed out, however, there are different things that can be meant by "replicating an experiment," and these have changed over time. For example, one can talk of replicating the "material realization" of an experiment, replicating it from a given theoretical point of view, or replicating the outcome of an experiment by a different theoretical or material means (Radder 1993, 64–5). Hence, what is to count as a replication of a physical experiment is itself also likely to depend on the context and purpose of the inquiry. Radder defines material realization as the whole of the experimental actions carried out, and which can be described as a set of actions in ordinary language. This is then contrasted with the theoretical interpretation of those actions. Radder illustrates this dual description of an experiment with the following example:

> Suppose we want to determine experimentally the mass of an object that is at rest in relation to the measurement equipment. Two scientists each carry out such an experiment in the same way. Nevertheless, one interprets the actions performed as a measurement of the Newtonian mass; and the other, as a determination of the Einsteinian mass. But both performed "the same" actions and thus – in a certain sense – the same experiment ... [yet] concrete experimental action is always action on the basis of certain theoretical ideas: without theoretical ideas there can be no experiments.
>
> (Radder 1996, 13)

Hence, although both the material realization and the theoretical interpretation are instantiated in an experiment, they are conceptually distinct. In other words, there is a kind of underdetermination of the theoretical interpretation of an experiment by the material realization (Radder 1996, 20). One can reproduce the material realization of an experiment without reproducing a particular theoretical interpretation of that material realization.

Tim De Mey (2003) and Letitia Meynell (see above) have extended Radder's approach to the case of thought experiments, arguing that they too have a dual structure. In the case of thought experiments, De Mey describes as the counterpart to "material realization" the actions to be performed by the thought experimenter, as phrased in everyday language. In his discussion of the clock-in-the-box thought experiment (on the standard interpretation as being about the uncertainty relations), De Mey writes,

> Thought experiments like that of the clock-in-the-box have a dual structure: they involve (1) the description of an imaginary situation and (2) the description of its settlement or winding up ... [O]n the experiment view of thought experiments [e.g., Bishop's], sameness of or difference between thought experiments is identified on the basis of (1). On the argument view of thought experiments [e.g., Norton's], by contrast, sameness or difference between thought experiments is identified on the basis of (2).
>
> (De Mey 2003, 71)

While this dual structure approach helps to clarify some of these debates, it still leaves open the identity question. There are three obvious possibilities: To be the same thought experiment it must be the case that one has (1) only the same material realization, (2) only the same theoretical interpretation, or (3) both the same material realization and the same theoretical interpretation. Prompted by some prominent historical examples, one might conclude that either condition (1) or condition (2) is sufficient for counting as the same thought experiment. It is still not clear, however, that cases such as the evolution of the clock-in-the-box thought experiment, as described here, can be adequately handled on either approach, in that it involved both changes in the material realization of the thought experiment and changes in its theoretical interpretation. But as those who emphasize the continuity between thought experiments and physical experiments will be quick to point out, these sorts of challenges are not unique to thought experiments (see Miščević, this volume).

Notes

1 For the history of Lucretius' spear thought experiment see Ierodiakonou (2011) and for Bohm's modification of EPR see Bohm (1951, 610–23) and references therein.
2 Norton (2004a, b) defines a thought experiment–anti-thought experiment pair as any two thought experiments that reach opposite conclusions (one of his examples is Aristotle's thought experiment involving a rotating pointer to show that space is finite and Archytas' thought experiment involving going to the edge of the universe and sticking out your arm to show space is infinite).
3 As James Robert Brown notes, this can occur for a variety of reasons: even if they accept the same premises, thought experimenter can fail to reach the same conclusion either because they disagree about what phenomenon will be observed, or they agree on the outcome, but disagree on the proper lessons to draw from that outcome (2007, 158).
4 This brief summary glosses over some historical interpretive issues that are, for example, more fully dealt with in Huggett and Hoefer (2009) and Laymon (1978).

5 Arthur's (2013) analysis of the *Rota Aristotelica* and Brown's (2013) study of the Terrell effect offer further examples of cases where thought experimenters disagree about which phenomenon is being explored in the thought experiment.
6 As we saw before, Sorensen allows that in other contexts, such as in establishing the priority of historical authorship, more lenient standards for identity may apply.
7 Note that one can endorse the Reconstruction Thesis, without further maintaining that thought experiments are *identical* to these arguments.

References

Arthur, R. T. W. (2013) "Can thought experiments be resolved by experiments? The case of Aristotle's wheel," in *Thought Experiments in Science, Philosophy and the Arts*, edited by M. Frappier, L. Meynell, and J. R. Brown, London: Routledge.
Bell, J. S. (1993 [1976]) "How to teach special relativity," in *Speakable and Unspeakable in Quantum Mechanics*, Cambridge: Cambridge University Press.
Bishop, M. (1999) "Why thought experiments are not arguments," *Philosophy of Science* 66: 534–541.
Bohm, D. (1951) *Quantum Theory*, Englewood Cliffs: Prentice Hall.
Bohr, N. (1949) "Discussion with Einstein on epistemological problems in atomic physics," in *Albert Einstein: Philosopher-Scientist*, edited by P. Schilpp, Evanston: The Library of Living Philosophers.
Bokulich, A. (2001) "Rethinking thought experiments," *Perspectives on Science* 9: 285–307.
Brown, J. R. (2007) "Counter thought experiments," *Royal Institute of Philosophy Supplement* 61: 155–177.
Brown, J. R. (2011 [1991]) *The Laboratory of the Mind: Thought Experiments in the Natural Sciences*, 2nd ed., London: Routledge.
Brown, J. R. (2013) "What do we see in a thought experiment?" in *Thought Experiments in Science, Philosophy and the Arts*, edited by M. Frappier, L. Meynell, and J. R. Brown, London: Routledge.
De Mey, T. (2003) "The dual nature view of thought experiments," *Philosophica* 72: 61–78.
Dennett, D. C. (1984) *Elbow Room: The Varieties of Free Will Worth Wanting*, Cambridge: MIT Press.
Dennett, D. C. (1995) "Intuition pumps," in *The Third Culture: Beyond the Scientific Revolution*, edited by J. Brockman, New York: Simon and Schuster.
Dewan, E. and Beran, M. (1959) "Note on stress effects due to relativistic contraction," *American Journal of Physics* 27: 517–518.
Hacking, I. (1992) "Do thought experiments have a life of their own? Comments on James Brown, Nancy Nersessian, and David Gooding," in *Philosophy of Science Association 1992*, vol. 2, pp. 302–308, edited by D. Hull, M. Forbes, and K. Okruhlik, East Lansing, MI: Philosophy of Science Association.
Howard, D. (2007) "Revisiting the Einstein-Bohr dialogue," *Iyyun: The Jerusalem Philosophical Quarterly* 56: 57–90.
Huggett, N. and Hoefer, C. (2009) "Absolute and relational theories of space and motion," *The Stanford Encyclopedia of Philosophy*. Available here: http://plato.stanford.edu/archives/fall2009/entries/spacetime-theories/ (accessed 15 November 2016).
Ierodiakonou, K. (2011) "Remarks on the history of an ancient thought experiment," in *Thought Experiments in Methodological and Historical Contexts*, edited by K. Ierodiakonou and S. Roux, Leiden: Brill.
Laymon, R. (1978) "Newton's bucket experiment," *Journal of the History of Philosophy* 16: 399–413.
Mach, E. (1919 [1883]) *The Science of Mechanics: A Critical and Historical Account of its Development*, translated by T. J. McCourmack, Chicago: Open Court Publishing.
Mach, E. (1976 [1926]) *Knowledge and Error: Sketches on the Psychology of Enquiry*, Dordrecht: D. Reidel Publishing Company.
Meynell, L. (2014) "Imagination and insight: A new account of the content of thought experiments," *Synthese* 191: 4149–4168.
Mulkay, M. and Gilbert, G. N. (1986) "Replication and mere replication," *Philosophy of the Social Sciences* 16: 21–37.
Nersessian, N. (1992) "In the theoretician's laboratory: Thought experimenting as mental modeling," in *Philosophy of Science Association 1992*, vol. 2, edited by D. Hull, M. Forbes, and K. Okruhlik, East Lansing, MI: Philosophy of Science Association.

Nersessian, N. (2008) *Creating Scientific Concepts*, Cambridge: MIT Press.
Newton, I. (1999 [1687]) *The Principia: Mathematical Principles of Natural Philosophy*, translated by I. B. Cohen and A. Whitman, Berkeley: University of California Press.
Norton, J. (1996) "Are thought experiments just what you thought?" *Canadian Journal of Philosophy* 26: 333–366.
Norton, J. (2004a) "On thought experiments: Is there more to the argument?" *Proceedings of the 2002 Biennial Meeting of the Philosophy of Science Association, Philosophy of Science* 71: 1139–1151.
Norton, J. (2004b) "Why thought experiments do not transcend empiricism," in *Contemporary Debates in the Philosophy of Science*, edited by C. Hitchcock, Oxford: Blackwell.
Palmerino, C. R. (2011) "Galileo's use of Medieval thought experiments," in *Thought Experiments in Methodological and Historical Contexts*, edited by K. Ierodiakonou and S. Roux, Leiden: Brill.
Radder, H. (1993) "Experimental reproducibility and the experimenters' regress," *PSA: Proceedings of the Biennial Meeting of the Philosophy of Science Association*, vol. 1, Contributed Papers: 63–73.
Radder, H. (1996) *In and About the World: Philosophical Studies of Science and Technology*, Albany: SUNY Press.
Reiss, J. (2002) *Causal Inference in the Abstract or Seven Myths about Thought Experiments*, Technical report (CPNSS Research Project), CTR 03/03. Centre for Philosophy of Natural and Social Sciences, London School of Economics and Political Science, London. Available here: www.lse.ac.uk/CPNSS/pdf/DP_withCover_Causality/CTR03-02-3.pdf (accessed 15 November 2016).
Rowbottom, D. P. (2014) "Intuitions in science: Thought experiments as argument pumps," in *Intuitions*, edited by A. Booth and D. Rowbottom, Oxford: Oxford University Press.
Schickore, J. (2011) "The significance of re-doing experiments: A contribution to historically informed methodology," *Erkenntnis* 75: 325–347.
Sorensen, R. (1992a) *Thought Experiments*, Oxford: Oxford University Press.
Sorensen, R. (1992b) "Thought experiments and the epistemology of laws," *Canadian Journal of Philosophy* 22: 15–44.
Stich, S. and Buckwalter, W. (2011) "Gender and the philosophy club," *The Philosophers' Magazine* 52: 60–65.
Walton, K. (1990) *Mimesis as Make-Believe*, Cambridge: Harvard University Press.
Weinberg, J. M., Nichols, S. and Stich, S. P. (2008) "Normativity and epistemic intuitions," in *Experimental Philosophy*, edited by J. M. Knobe and S. Nichols, Oxford: Oxford University Press.

though
INDEX OF THOUGHT EXPERIMENTS DISCUSSED, MENTIONED OR INVENTED IN THIS COMPANION

Note to the Reader: Entries are organized into *Pre-modern* and *Modern*. Within the modern section, thought experiments are divided roughly into fields of study. Within a field, thought experiments are given in chronological order (where possible). We include cases brought up by authors who end up denying that what we have is really a thought experiment.

Pre-modern

a community lacking moral and social authority (Mozi) 434
comparing partial to impartial caring (Mozi) 434
throwing a spear at the edge of the universe (Archytas of Tarentum, also Lucretius) 21n3, 31–2, 35, 41n1, 55n1, 429, 503, 545–6, 555n1–2
a child falling into a well (Mengzi) 434
Zhuangzi's "Dream of the Butterfly" 434
Zeno's paradoxes 287
Plato's allegory of the cave 46–7, 50–1, 407
Plato's model city 5, 45–6, 52–4, 153, 156, 159
Plato's myth of Er 50
Plato's noble lie 51–2, 159
Plato's *Republic* 54, 156, 159–60, 164
Plato's ring of Gyges 32, 35–6, 39–40, 48–50, 441; two ring variant 41n3
Plato's Muse's tale 45
the *Phaedo* 56n15
Sextus Empiricus's thought experiment contra atomism 32, 41n5
the ship of Theseus 33, 35–7, 429
people shipwrecked at sea and only one can be saved (Stoics and Skeptics) 37, 40, 42n13
the Skeptic's evil demon 38, 42n14–15
indistinguishable entities (eggs, twins) (Skeptics) 37–8
"If all things were colours" (Aristotle) 64–5
"If white were the only perceptible" (Aristotle) 66; variants using sound and figure 75n13
the "Stripping argument" (Aristotle) 62–3
Aristotle's wheel (Rota Aristotelica) 556n5

Aristotle's cave thought experiment 61
if there were a second Sun (Aristotle) 63
Aristotle's thought experiments concerning motion 67–8
the organ of touch (Aristotle) 65–6
Atlas spinning the cosmos (Aristotle) 69–71
Deon and Theon (Chrysippus) 36–7, 42n11–12
Ibn al-Haytham's refracting spheres 87–8
Ibn Sīnā's "flying man" 4, 80–1
the infinitely large and small (Ibn Sīnā's) 81
removing matter from form (Ibn Sīnā) 81–2
the impossibility of motion in a void (Ibn Sīnā) 82–3
sphere on a wheel (Ibn Sīnā) 85–6
choosing among indiscernibles (al-Ghazālī) 83–4
inferring something true (that there is fire) from a false assumption (the "smoke" you see is only fog) (Sriharsa) 433
a liar who accidentally tells the truth (Gaṅgeśa) 433
Ṭūsī couple 87
Ṭūsī couple as a counterexample to Aristotle's medial rest (Shīrāzī) 87
how the four elements would act in a pipe that traverses the centre of the earth (Oresme) 430

Modern

Arts and humanities

Howards End 515
The Third Man 515
Borges's "Pierre Menard, author of the Quixote" 524

INDEX OF THOUGHT EXPERIMENTS

Danto's perceptually indistinguishable red rectangles 523
Currie's textually indistinguishable literary works 523–4
Levinson's sonically indistinguishable yet distinct musical works 523
if Franz Ferdinand hadn't been assassinated 476–7
if the Greeks had lost at Salamis 476–7

Biology

Darwin's eye 531–5
Darwin's wolf 244–6, 471–3
Darwin's bees and flowers 254n2
Jenkin's thought experiments against Darwinian evolution 244, 254n1
Crick's infinite enzyme regress 250–3
Levinthal's paradox 251–3
a Darwinian demon 248–9, 253
rewinding and playing back the tape of evolution (Gould, Kaufmann, Dawkins) 441
artificial life 252–3
a biological version of Maxwell's demon *see* Maxwell's demon

Chemistry

Kekulé's dream 222

Mathematics

tiling a checkerboard (e.g., with dominoes) 485
Freiling's "refutation" of the Continuum hypothesis 287
solving algebraic (polynomial) equations 257
untying knots in knot theory 259–61
colouring the trefoil knot 263
measuring the diameter of a circle graph 264–6
the regularity of Cayley graphs 269
vertex transitivity of Cayley graphs 269–72
zooming out from infinite Cayley graphs 273–5
counting vertices of polyhedra 276
determining the Euler characteristic of Platonic solids 276

Philosophy

Descartes's evil demon 129
Descartes's wax thought experiment 113; Newton's counter thought experiment 113
Locke's day-man and night-man 123
Leibniz's mill 124–5
Leibniz's two spheres 123–4
the *Critique of Pure Reason* 329

Kant's "transcendental chaos" 140–2
Kant's universalizability test 155
Hegel's reductio ad absurdum of naïve realism 137–40
if the properties of objects fluctuated drastically (Wittgenstein) 143–4
the Gettier case 16, 132, 198, 284–5, 294–5, 305, 371, 374, 390, 411–16, 432
the trolley problem 21n2, 195–6, 200–1, 203, 206–7, 208n2, 370–2, 374, 387, 407–8, 432, 440, 523; footbridge variant 374, 387, 407–8; variant with millions of people (J. J. C. Smart) 197, 201
if "extremely general facts of nature" ceased to hold (Wittgenstein) 143–4
Singer's pond (drowning child) 7, 195, 200,
Thomson's violinist 7, 195, 199, 204, 207, 208n2, 445, 447, 449, 499, 503
Putnam's Twin Earth 198
fake barn cases 362n9
Shue's ticking bomb 7, 195, 199, 207–8,
Mary the colour scientist 408, 422, 445–7
Searle's Chinese room 21n2, 125, 200
Parfit's teletransportation cases 205
if x-phi were the dominant philosophical methodology (Ludwig) 402n14

Physics

Galileo's sinking wood chips 102
Stevin's prism 295, 299, 354, 358, 549
Galileo's dropping objects from the top of a ship's mast 429
Galileo's ship cabin relativity thought experiment 354
Galileo's falling bodies 10, 21, 93, 100–105, 107, 158, 172, 175, 186, 212, 282–3, 286, 288, 295–296, 299, 320–1, 337–8, 359, 362n11, 422, 428, 440, 447, 475, 487, 519–20, 531, 546, 550, 552
Galileo's inclined planes 97–99, 105, 358, 470, 472
Galileo's pendulum 95–97, 105
Hobbes's "feigning the world to be annihilated" 125n3
Leibniz shift thought experiments 115–120, 126n10; space shift 117–18; time shift 118–19; rotation shift 119; velocity shift 119–20; gauge shift 126n10
Leibniz's two squares 114–15
a collision considered from different perspectives (Leibniz) 114
Newton's corporeal space 112
Newton's bucket 111, 120–2, 172, 180n4, 354, 546, 548, 553
Newton's cannonball 531, 533, 536
Newton's two spheres 122

INDEX OF THOUGHT EXPERIMENTS

Maxwell's demon 7, 17, 21n3, 212–15, 246, 249, 454–6, 459–66, 532, 538; biological version 214–15, 237n4
Mach's bucket 212, 547, 553
Einstein's chasing a light beam 7, 34, 77, 215–217
Plank's resonators 223
a moving light clock (special relativity) 485–6
Einstein's mirror 7, 223–4
the Smoluchowski trapdoor 455–6, 461–2
the effect on Earth's orbit if the sun suddenly exploded 407
Einstein's "hole" argument 7, 220–1
Einstein's elevator 7, 34, 218–19, 335, 359, 465
Einstein's observer falling off a roof 7, 217–18, 222
Einstein's train 7, 9, 18, 34, 77, 291, 504–7
Einstein's rotating disk 7, 219
Einstein's boxes 238n15
Heisenberg's microscope 7, 9, 21n3, 224–6, 354
Szilard's one molecule engine 457–66
the clock in the box (Einstein/Bohr) 189–90, 285, 338, 445, 487, 547–51, 553–4, 555
Einstein–Podolsky–Rosen thought experiment 7, 212, 226–34, 238n16, 354, 441, 545, 555n1
Schrödinger's cat 7, 21n3, 231–2
rockets connected by a piece of thread 547, 553
car and garage thought experiment in special relativity (ladder paradox) 354, 356–60, 362n9, 556n5
Wheeler's grand interferometer 235–6
quantum computation 7, 235–6

Politics

Plato's *Republic* see Pre-Modern
Rousseau's social contract 153, 161, 168n8, 169n12
Orwell's *Animal Farm* 168n10
Rawl's original position 21n2, 161–2, 195–6, 202
Rawl's veil of ignorance 6, 153–4, 167, 195, 396–7
Le Guin's *The Dispossessed* 168n10
Dworkin's shipwrecked society 153–4
Kukathas's liberal archipelago 154, 162
Cohen's camping trip 166, 167n2

Social science

Hume's monetary thought experiment 174, 180n1, 476–7
Malthas's population growth and agrarian output 177
Ricardo's leap forward in machine labour 176–7
von Mises's evenly rotating economy 175
the Ellsberg paradox 178
cliometrics (e.g., if the railway hadn't been invented) 175–6, 431
Friedman's helicopter drop thought experiment 174–5, 476
the market value of used cars (Akerlof) 179, 470–3, 476
future economies in a world of climate change 177
severe bank runs during a crash 179
the "Washington consensus" on economic growth 478–9
the promise of a future inheritance 179
cigarettes as currency in WWII POW camps 180n1
economics of a babysitting co-op 180n1
mischievous gnomes crashing the market 180n1
a society with perfect economic equality 179

Theology

a stone too heavy for God to lift 191
transubstantiation 191–3, 193n3
a mouse eating consecrated hosts 192–3
Nazi's knocking on your door: conflicting divine commands 184
Hick's two travellers 190–1
heaven 187–8

Misc.

mentally counting the windows in your house 309
moving furniture through a doorway 261, 320–1, 352
new furniture "going with" existing furniture 261
number of adults comfortably fitting into your car 261
preparing a meal given certain ingredients 261

AUTHOR–SUBJECT INDEX

a priori 306n7–9; and alethic refuters 411; capacity of mind 333, 336; concepts 140; as conviction 102; functional vs. material readings of 327, 330, 332–3, 337; justification 39, 132, 246, 296; in Kant 15, 218, 327–39; knowledge 249, 282, 294–306, 329, 336, 410, 413–15, 420–1, 428; and logic 290; and mathematics 276; and M. Friedman 336–8; and philosophical method 132, 289; reasoning 23n10, 140–1, 289, 302, 327, 331, 549; as relativized 142, 337; and schemata 336; and scientific method 331, 339, 411; truth 378
absolute space 117–22, 126n9, 126n11, 328, 359, 546–7, 553
abstraction: cultural relativity of 431; and epistemic access 322; and estimative faculty 87, *see also* estimative faculty; vs. idealization 165, 169n10, 472; level of 174; in mathematics 86; and models 171, 174; and perceptual symbols 318; vs. real things 126n9
Abū Ḥāmid al-Ghazālī 4, 77, 83–4
Abū l-Barakāt 89
action at a distance 217, 230, 234
adaptationism 245–6, 249
Akerlof, G. 179, 470–3, 476
alethic refuters 406, 409–15, 418, 421
Al-Farabi 159
algebra 257
al-Ghazālī *see* Abū Ḥāmid al-Ghazālī
Alhazen *see* Ibn al-Haytham
analogy 13, 34, 123–4, 173, 204–5, 207–8, 286–7, 289, 311, 407, 536–7
Aristotle 4, 31, 57–76, 78, 82, 85, 89n4, 102–3, 159, 164, 282–3, 295–6, 429, 446–9, 475, 555n2; Atlas theory 67–72; esoteric vs. exoteric writings 60–1; on experiment 57–9; external supporting point principle 67–72; forms of reasoning 73; gods in 61; notion of thought experiment 58; Platonic Ideas 63–4; pole-theory 68–9, 75n17; substance 62
Arthur, R. T. W. 4–5, 12, 21n2–3, 238n14, 539, 556n5
artificial life 252–3, 471
Austin, J. L. 129, 144–5

Averroes *see* Ibn Rushd
Avicenna *see* Ibn Sīnā

Becker, A. 3–4, 5, 21n2, 41n4, 78, 440
Bell, J. S. 228–9, 233–5, 238n22–4, 547, 553
Benacerraf, P. 303
Bird, A. 301
Bishop, M. 190, 284–5, 441, 487, 548, 550, 555
Bohm, D. 232–3, 238n20–1, 545, 555n1
Bohr, N. 187, 189–90, 226–9, 238n16, 285, 445, 487, 547–51, 553
Bokulich, A. 3, 12, 20, 22n6, 22n10, 439, 441, 445, 507, 546–7
Brendel, E. 11, 22n6, 22n8, 281, 363n11, 498, 545, 548
Brillouin, L. 459–60, 463
Brown, J. R. 9–11, 13–14, 21–2, 92–3, 108n1, 155, 168n4, 189, 198–9, 244, 255n7, 282–3, 286–91, 294–306, 332–4, 344, 355, 362n9, 363n14, 410–11, 428–9, 439, 442–6, 452, 471, 485, 496n1, 498, 503, 507, 519, 526, 531, 538, 539n1, 545, 549–50, 554, 555n3, 556n5
Brun, G. 6–7, 21n2, 168n5, 197, 203, 209n4, 440, 527–8
Buzzoni, M. 14–15, 21n3, 22n6, 22n10, 277n13, 327–39, 439, 498, 531, 533, 554

Camp, E. 2, 20, 534–6, 539, 540n7–8
Cappelen, H. 208n2, 378–9, 387, 390n9, 409, 418–19, 421, 422n1, 423n8
Carnap, R. 130–3, 136
Carroll, N. 2, 513–15, 517, 520
Cayley graphs 266–75, 278n19–20
Chalmers, D. 409, 418, 420–1, 423n11
chaos 492–3; transcendental chaos *see* Kant
characterizations 534–6, 539
Chomsky, N. 369, 379n2
Chrysippus 3, 36–7, 41n8, 42n11–12, 42n15
Clark, S. 111, 114, 117–21, 120, 126n8–9
cliometrics 175–6
cognitive control 536–8
Cohnitz, D. 16, 20, 22n10, 168n5, 331, 380n9, 387n2, 387n5, 406, 409, 417–18, 421–2, 507, 531

computer simulations 18, 186, 252, 254, 255n6, 407, 472, 474, 484–97, 537; opacity of 18, 445, 484, 487–90, 492–4; relation to thought experiments 254, 484–97
conceivability 16, 129, 131; as guide to modal truth 302, 406, 419–21, 423n12
conceptual analysis 23n11, 128, 131–2, 136, 145, 198, 304, 370–1, 375, 387, 389, 401n4, 412, 414
Condorcet Jury Theorem 391, 393, 397
constraint: on being a (good) thought experiment 48–9, 422; on fictional narrative 518; on imagination 351–5; in mental models 13, 311–14, 319, 322, 551; revealed by thought experiment 248–50, 253–4; in thought experiments 254, 500, 516
contextualism about thought experiments 15, 22n10, 425–38, 451
Continuum Hypothesis 286–7
Cooper, R. 22n6, 22n10, 451
Counterfactual Thought Experiments in World Politics 6, 168n3
counterfactuals: and causation 303, 480; in cliometrics 176, 431; degrees of 440–1, 477; as descriptions of scenarios 34, 67, 140, 143, 154–5, 157, 161, 173–80, 251, 253, 284, 439–41, 444, 450, 540n8, 546; as descriptions of worlds 174, 301, 477; and estimative faculty 80, see also estimative faculty; to evaluate truth of a modal claim 16, 72, 412, 420, 531; evaluation of 294, 299, 415, 421, 477; and explanation 531; facility with 166, 420, 508; in history 476–7, 481n4; and idealization 473; knowledge of 293–4, 305, 413; and laws of nature 297–8; in models 174–80; as premises 79–80, 158, 162, 430, 476–7; as propositions 178; reasoning with 197–8, 201, 208n1, 306, 333, 336, 434, 508, 531; truth of 304, 402n8
Craik, K. 310–12
Crick, F. 250–3
cultural relativity: and experimental philosophy 401n1; of identify conditions of thought experiments 16–17, 425–6, 431–5; of intuitions 372, 374; of knowledge 416; of mathematical knowledge 391; of mental models 312; of outcomes of thought experiments 205, 391, 395, 415–16; of principles of generation 504, 507, 552; of stereotypes 204; of theories of reference 372
cycle graphs 264–5, 277n12

Dancy, J. 8, 199, 201, 205, 207
Darwin, Charles 7, 215, 243–9, 253, 254n1, 471, 473, 532–3, 535
Davidson, D. 128, 132, 135
Davies, D. 6, 19, 358, 362n10, 517, 522, 523

De Mey, T. 11, 20, 431, 555
deflationism about thought experiments see empiricist accounts of thought experiments
Dennett, D. 8–9, 21n2, 22n10, 200, 252, 254, 290, 363n13, 447, 530, 545
Density Functional Theory 493–4, 496n5
Descartes, R. 5, 100, 113, 121, 129, 131, 135, 138, 156, 434
Deutsch, M. 388, 418–19, 432
Devitt, M. 377, 379n1, 380n5–6, 416–17
dialectic: accounts of reasoning 17, 430, 510n3, 515; account of thought experiments 439–50, 551; argument 439, 446, 449–52, 519; context of thought experiments 16–17, 431, 450, 507; justification 422; pragma see pragma-dialectics
discourse models 313–14
divine command theory 183–5
Dretske, F. 132–3, 145n6, 297–8
Dretske–Tooley–Armstrong account of the laws of nature 11, 297–301, 307n14
Dual view of thought experiments 12, 20, 555
Duhem, P. 8, 22n10, 332, 516, 519
dystopia see utopia

Einstein 34, 77, 122, 212, 215–38, 285, 291, 505, 547–51, 553
Einstein's principle of equivalence 126n12, 218–20, 237n5
electron density 493–4
Elgin, C. 6, 12, 133, 188, 198, 209n4, 321–2, 513–17, 527–9, 535, 539n1
Ellis, B. 301
Ellsberg paradox 178–9
emotion 289, 322n2, 389, 535
empiricist accounts of thought experiments 8, 89, 158, 281–91, 337, 344, 443–4, 526
epistemic magic 9–10, 443
estimative faculty 79–89; see also Ibn Sīnā, *wahm*
evidence: accessibility of 6; concept of 346; in conceptual analysis 371; empirical 7–8, 10–11, 40, 186, 276, 296–7, 299, 427, 515; for extra-mentalist theories 16, 371–5; in fiction 513–21; in the head 11, 19, 297, 371; history as a source of 3; intuitions as 369–80, 387, 398, 416–17, 432; in mathematics 8, 262–3, 276; modal 11, 35; nature of 2, 17, 421; produced by the imagination 351; produced by a thought experiment 5–8, 16, 23n10, 35, 39, 99, 183, 185–6, 207, 244–5, 262–3, 272, 428–9, 435; textual 53–4, 216; of understanding 533; visual 262–3, 286
evidential significance 425–35; see also cultural relativity
exemplification 321–2, 334, 508, 513, 516–17, 526–7, 535–6, 540n3

experimental philosophy 16, 22n4, 205, 371–80, 385–402, 432–3, 507–8
expertise defense 16, 376–7, 416–18
explanation 58, 76n27, 531–8; evolutionary 248; hypothetical 244, 527; kinds of 531; thought experiments as evaluators of 243; thought experiments as steps in 470–1, 474, 476, 527–38; and truth 125n6; and understanding 527–38
explication 131–2, 136, 199
extra-mentalism *see* mentalism

fables 540n10
factivity 78
Fehige, Y. 6, 14, 23n10, 199, 328–39, 363n16, 471
film as thought experiment 2, 19, 512, 523
Fisher, R. 7, 246–9, 254n4
frames 534–6, 539
Franklin, A. 426
Frappier, M. 3, 20, 22n10, 441, 445, 507
free will 114, 193n1, 302, 305, 372–4
Friedman, Michael 328, 333, 336–8, 527, 531
Friedman, Milton 174–5, 476
fulfillment (phenomenology) 345–6, 343–4, 349–51, 361n, 4362n8

Galileo, G. 3–4, 10, 17, 21n2, 92–110, 131, 158, 172, 175, 186, 212, 216, 218, 251, 282–3, 286, 288, 295–6, 298–9, 320–1, 337–8, 354, 359, 362n11, 422, 427–30, 434–5, 440, 447, 469–70, 472–3, 475, 478, 481n1, 487, 538, 546, 549, 550, 552; inclined planes 1, 7, 93–4, 97–9, 104–5, 470, 472, 480; paradoxes and 4, 93, 99–107, 109n9, 109n13; pendulums and 1, 95–7, 99, 104–5, 108n5
Gaṅgeśa 433
Geach, P. 183–5, 193n1
Gendler, T. S. 2, 9, 12–14, 16, 21, 22n7, 108n1, 155–6, 197–8, 202, 205, 283, 287–90, 299, 322n1, 337, 359–60, 422, 440–1, 520, 526, 531, 533, 537, 539n1
geometric group theory 7, 272–5
Giaquinto, M. 7, 22n3
global perceptual skepticism 128–9, 131, 135, 139–40, 145
Gödel, K. 300
Goffi, J.-Y. 14, 16–17, 441, 444, 446–7, 526, 551
Goldman, A. 303, 370–1, 380n3, 388
Goodman, N. 321, 323, 380n7, 477, 510n2, 513, 516
graph theory 7, 264–72
Growing Argument, the 36, 41n8
Grozdanoff, B. 291
Grundmann, T. 11, 296, 304, 305, 306n8, 307n17, 380n5, 380n8, 401n6, 443

Hacking, I. 3, 174, 408, 485–6, 545–6, 554
Häggqvist, S. 11, 16–17, 20, 22n8, 22n10, 154, 168n5, 196–7, 207, 284, 303, 306n3, 307n16, 380n9, 387n2, 387n5, 406, 411, 421, 440, 442–4, 450, 507, 526, 531
Hegel, G. W. F. 5, 137–40, 146n13, 159, 332, 447
Heisenberg, W. 225–8, 238n14
Hills, A. 20, 201, 528–9, 531, 536–8, 539n2
Hintikka, J. 156, 369, 440
historicism 3, 16–17, 57–8, 425–38
Hobbes, T. 5, 74n7, 125n3, 160
Hopp, W. 15, 342, 346, 355, 362n8, 362n10
horizon (phenomenology) 346–8
horizontal givenness 15, 349, 353, 357
Howard, D. 227, 229, 238n16, 238n18, 338, 548–9, 551
Hume, D. 6, 139–40, 144, 146n12, 159, 172, 174–5, 180, 249, 476–7
Husserl, E. 15, 21, 94, 95, 107–8, 337, 342–3, 347–51, 355, 358, 361n1–5
Huygens, C. 117, 172

Ibn al-Haytham 4, 77, 87–9
Ibn Rushd 84
Ibn Sīnā 77, 79–83, 85–9; void 81–3; *wahm* 4, 79
Ichikawa, J. 19, 305, 411–17, 420–1, 423n4, 423n12
ideal vs. non-ideal theory 6, 165
idealization 17–18, 77, 80, 87, 165, 173–4, 177, 273, 321, 457, 462–6, 472–81; causal idealization 18, 472–3; Galilean idealization 18, 472–4, 479–81; material idealization 18, 472; mechanical idealization 77, 83, 87
Ierodiakonou, K. 4, 21n3, 32, 41n2, 42n10, 48, 55n1, 78, 429, 510n8, 549, 555n1
imagination: aesthetic 18, 498–509; as cognitive process 288; in Einstein 212; epistemological concerns about 4, 79, 263, 335, 351–3; to evaluate counterfactual claims 293, 297, 299, 420; as faculty 4, 12, 18, 79–80; and fiction 249; in Galileo 105–6; in Hume 139; indispensability of 155–6, 336; justification of use of 18, 237, 261–2, 266, 276, 297, 299, 306n8, 336, 351–5, 358, 498–509; nature of 2, 155–6, 244, 361n3; non-propositionality of 193; offline processing 297; props for the 20, 498–509, 552–4; psychology of 78–80; relation to perception 349–55, 362n8; in Rousseau 168n8–9; and semantics 336; sensory 7–8, 257, 259, 261–3, 266, 269, 271–6, 314–15, 498–509; in thought experiments 7, 155–6, 168n10, 243–4, 253–4, 498–509; training of 254n4; and utopia 160
inference to the best explanation 11, 74, 198, 255n5, 286

intuition 16, 156, 197, 203–4, 289, 369–81, 386–7, 398–400; demarcating 53; as evidence 16, 35–6, 39–40, 49–59, 156–8, 167, 199, 204–6, 369–81, 386–90, 398–400, 402n7, 412, 414–19, 425, 432, 515, 520, 549–50; and experimental philosophy 15–16, 20, 369–81, 386–90, 398–400, 431–2, 507–8, 549; indispensability of 208n2, 409, 418–19, 422n1, 488, 507; linguistic 369; mathematical 331, 371; and modality 414–21, 451, 549; as output of thought experiment 12; 15–16, 18, 20, 35–6, 40, 49–50, 154, 156–7, 159, 173, 177–8, 197, 200, 203, 205, 289–90, 330, 369–81, 386–90, 413, 432, 474–5, 484, 485, 489–91, 494–5, 527, 549–50; phenomenological 358; philosophical 284, 307n17, 344–5, 369–381, 402n7, 414–17, 422, 507, 523; rational 294, 296, 299, 302, 306n1–2, 337, 443–4, 498, 519, 549–50; scientific 222, 224, 237, 253, 547
intuition pump 8, 20, 22n10, 77, 88, 200, 290, 363n13, 523, 545
Ising-model 18, 491–2, 496n4
iteration: computational 18, 484, 487, 489–95, 496n4; epistemic 489; in thought experiment 309, 320, 547, 553

Jackson, F. 371, 388, 402n9, 408, 420, 422, 423n10, 447
Jarvis, B. 19, 305, 411–17, 420–1, 423n12
Johnson-Laird, N. 288, 311–13, 520

Kalin, M. 329
Kant 5, 8, 14, 22n10, 74n2, 128–31, 136–42, 145, 155, 159, 169n12, 296, 327–39, 343, 495; categorical imperative 202; transcendental chaos 142
Kantian accounts of thought experiments 8, 14–16, 327–39, 533
Knobe, J. 373, 385–6, 401n1, 401n4
knot theory 7, 258–63
Kripke, S. 301
Kuhn, T. S. 8–9, 12, 22n5, 72, 245, 470, 515
Kühne, U. 2, 8, 329–31, 422, 475, 486
Kukkonen, T. 75n24, 78–9, 81, 84, 89n1

Lakatos, I. 8, 22n3, 235
Landauer's principle 460–3, 466
Langkau, J. 380n9, 419
laws of nature 10–11, 86, 217, 283, 289, 293–4, 297–302, 306, 334, 344, 362n10, 423n6, 427–8, 444, 549
Leibniz, G. W. 4–5, 111–26, 139–40
Lenhard, J. 18, 254, 255n6, 445, 496n5, 527
Lennox, J. 7, 76n27, 244–6, 254n1, 471–2
Levinthal paradox 250–4

Lewis, C. I. 129–30, 142, 337
Lewis, D. 174, 380n7, 480
Lichtenberg, G. C. 8, 12, 330–2
life history theory 248
Liouville's Theorem 214, 464
literary cognitivism 512–24
Locke, J. 5, 32, 113–14, 123–5, 159–60, 167, 169n14
logicism 428–30
Ludwig, K. 16, 22n4, 168n5, 201, 203, 205, 294, 378, 380n5, 380n7, 388–9, 391, 398, 401n6, 402n9, 432, 507

McAllister, J. W. 3, 16–17, 21, 22n10, 108n1, 186, 210n3, 286, 337, 362n11, 427, 508, 517, 518, 531, 549
McGinnis, J. 4, 81, 85, 86, 89
Mach, E. 8–9, 12, 22n10, 58, 74n8, 122, 155, 161, 212, 235, 293, 327, 331–2, 334, 406, 439, 501, 508, 520, 545, 553
Machery, E. 206, 372–3, 377, 380n4, 386, 389, 391, 395, 415, 417, 432
McMullin, E. 18, 448–9, 472–3, 480–1
make believe 128, 503, 513, 517–18
Malmgren, A.-S. 34–5, 42n16, 294, 305, 409–14
Malthus, T. R. 171, 177
Maxwell, J. C. 212–17, 222, 249, 454–6, 460, 532, 538
Maxwell's equations 215–17
Meinong, A. 8, 23n10
memory 12, 79, 123–4, 289, 303, 310–13, 317–18, 369
Mengzi 434–5
mental models 12–14, 309–22, 488, 498–9, 509n1, 520, 551–2
mentalism vs. extra-mentalism 16, 23n1, 370–2, 374–7, 379, 380n3
metaphor 510n3, 537, 540n10
Meynell, L. 6, 18, 20, 21n3, 510n4, 537, 545, 552–5
Miščević, N. 5–6, 12–13, 21n2, 55n5, 56n11, 108n1, 158, 168n6, 169n13, 254, 288, 309, 344, 499, 520, 555
modality *see* possibility
moderate inflationism 519–22
molecular biology 250–2
Mozi 434–5

narrative 13, 19, 45–6, 156–7, 168n10, 174–5, 188–9, 281, 287–9, 312–14, 319–20, 335, 356–60, 440, 444–5, 465–6, 467n6, 503–4, 508–9, 512–24, 534, 545, 547, 550–3
Naṣīr al-Dīn al-Ṭūsī 87
natural selection 214–15, 244–9, 254n1, 472, 531–2
naturalist accounts of thought experiments 8, 12–14, 23n10, 302, 307n17, 363n16, 526, 549

naturalized epistemology 132–3
Nersessian, N. J. 2, 5, 12–13, 18, 172, 180n2, 254, 255n6, 288–9, 309–10, 313, 317, 319, 344, 486, 488, 496n1, 498–9, 509n1, 510n10, 517, 520, 539n1, 545, 551–2
Newton, I. 4, 32, 111–26, 172, 180n4, 217, 237n8–9, 332, 475, 495, 531, 533, 536, 546, 548, 553
Nichols, S. 307n17, 372–3, 380n4, 380n7, 386, 388–9, 391, 394–5, 401n1, 415–16, 432, 549
Norton, J. D. 9–14, 17, 21, 22n6–8, 22n10, 108n1, 158, 189, 213–14, 216–17, 220, 237n3–6, 238n12, 261, 281–91, 293, 299, 320–1, 333, 344, 363n11, 410–11, 428–9, 439, 442–7, 450, 452, 459, 460, 462–4, 467n5, 467n8–9, 481n2, 488, 496n1, 498, 503, 505, 519–20, 526, 531–2, 539n1, 545–6, 548, 550–1, 554–5; Elimination thesis 283, 285, 287–8, 291; Epistemic thesis 283, 289–91; Reconstruction thesis 11, 17, 283, 285–8, 290–1, 519, 550–1, 556n8; Reliability thesis 283, 286, 291
Novalis 8, 330–2
novelty 9–14, 61, 253, 309–10, 508, 517
Novitz, D. 513–14, 516

opacity: dialectical 444–7, 450; epistemic 18, 445, 484, 487–90, 492–4
Oresme, N. 31, 430
Ørsted, H.-C. 1, 8, 34, 327–32, 337
Orwell, G.: *1984* 2, 168n10; *Animal Farm* 168n10

Palmerino, C. R. 2, 430, 549
Palmieri, P. 4, 10, 21, 105, 108n1, 108n3, 108n5, 108n7, 108n9, 251, 362n11, 487, 531, 554
paradeigma(ta) 3, 33, 73
paradigm 9–10, 172, 190, 222, 337–8
paradox of thought experiments 9–11, 16, 344, 349, 351
Peacock, K. A. 7, 21n3, 224, 238n17, 246, 249, 464, 526, 532
Peirce, C. S. 252, 255n5
Perović, S. 426
personal identity 123, 205
perspectives 534–6, 539
phantasia 37, 79
phase transitions 491–2
phenomenological accounts of thought experiments 8, 15, 342–63, 509n1, 510n7
Pickstone, J. 426
Plank, M. 222–5, 238n12
Plato 3–4, 21n2, 32–3, 41n3, 44–56, 75n17, 82, 89n3, 153, 159–61, 164, 167, 303, 330, 440–1; dialogue form 44, 47, 54; kinds of fiction in 45–7; lies 46; model city/state 4, 45, 51–4, 156, 159; myth in 4, 32, 45–6, 48–52, 55n2–3; noble lie 51–2, 159; *Republic* 3–4, 32–3, 36, 39–40, 42n13, 44–8, 50, 52–5, 153, 156, 159–60, 164, 169n12; simile in 46–7, 50–1, 55n4
Platonism about thought experiments 8, 11, 54, 189, 255n7, 282, 286–91, 293–307, 337, 344, 355, 362n10, 439, 443–4, 485, 498, 519
pluralism about thought experiments 15, 16, 22n10
Plutarch 33–6, 38, 42n9, 94, 429
population genetics 246–9, 471
Positive Bias Assumption 393–6, 400
possibility 71–2, 163–4; biological 245, 253; of global perceptual skepticism 142; of growth and diminution 36; inference from conceivability to 16, 85, 129–32, 136, 199, 302; institutional 163; of a just state 53; kinds of 71–2, 253; logical 129, 136, 191, 253, 332; mathematical 262; metaphysical 71–2, 164, 412–15; of motion 32; motivational 163; in other worlds vs. in our world 163–4; physical 70–2, 86, 262; of physical entities being otherwise than they are 71; of practical realization of a thought experiment 335, 467n10; production 178; psychological 163; of self-locomotive change 67, 78, 84; theoretical 253; thought experiments as tools of exploring 251, 253; transcendental 8, 14, 142, 333; of a void 82–3
pragma-dialectics 448–9
predication 62–3, 134, 138
prediction 87, 304, 322, 474, 533
Principle of Individuation (Leibniz) 114–15, 119
Principle of Sufficient Reason 83, 117, 126n11
Principle of the Identify of Indiscernibles 114, 116–17, 123, 126n9
principles of generation 20, 503–9, 552–3
proof: burden of 288, 423n8; in logic 388, 447–9; in mathematics 172, 272, 276–7, 286–7, 397, 425; in philosophy 41n3, 49–50, 78, 81–2, 84, 88–9, 131, 136, 144, 173, 434; in science 100, 103, 245, 251
props for the imagination *see* thought experiments and imagination
protein folding 251–2
protein synthesis 250–1
psychologism 133
Pust, J. 304, 370–1, 379n2
Putnam, H. 198, 387, 513
puzzles 537, 540n10

quantum computing 235–6
quantum information theory 235–6
quantum mechanics 107, 187–8, 190, 212, 217, 219, 222–38, 285, 301, 332, 336, 354, 459, 460, 464, 493, 530, 545, 547, 548–9, 553

Quine, W. V. O. 128, 133, 135, 145n8, 145n10, 387, 415
Quṭb al-Dīn Shīrāzī 87

Rawls, J. 6–7, 153, 159–67, 196, 202, 209n4: *A Theory of Justice* 153, 156, 159, 162, 164; original position 7, 21n2, 161, 195–6, 202; reflective equilibrium *see* reflective equilibrium; veil of ignorance 6, 153–4, 167, 195, 397
reductio ad absurdum 35, 73, 103, 138–9, 440
reflective equilibrium 156–7, 196, 202–4, 207, 209n4, 399
Reidemeister moves 261–3, 277n6
Reidemeister's Theorem 262
Reiss, J. 6, 17–18, 171, 175, 431, 477, 480, 549
Relativity theory: general 122, 237n5, 237n7, 445, 548; special 225, 302, 354, 362n9, 486, 499, 504–6, 547, 553
Rescher, N. 17, 197, 205–8, 444, 449
revealed theology 6, 183, 191–3
Ricardo, D. 176–7
riddles 537, 540n10
Rorty, R. 128, 135–6, 146n12
Rousseau, J. J. 153, 156, 159, 161, 167n1, 168n9: social contract 153, 161, 168n8, 169n12
Roux, S. 14, 16–17, 34, 440–1, 444, 446–7, 526, 551

Schabas, M. 6–7, 176, 476, 481, 526
Schelling's model of social segregation 18, 490–1
Schlaepfer, G. 7, 471, 527
Schrödinger, E. 224–7, 229, 231–2, 234
second law of thermodynamics 213–14, 249, 455–60, 463, 467n3, 532
Sextus Empiricus 32–4, 38, 41n5, 41n7
situation models 313–14
skeptical modes 38–9
skepticism about thought experiments 15, 22n10, 184–6, 193n1, 201, 206–7, 352, 371, 379, 390, 516
Smoluchowski, M. 213–14, 455–6, 460–4, 466
Sober, E. 249
social segregation 490–1
somatic markers 289
Sorensen, R. 9, 12–13, 172, 173, 284, 545, 549–550
Sosa, E. 375, 378, 387, 388, 391, 401n6
spacetime 111, 216, 219–21, 285, 553
Sriharsa 433
Starikova, I. 7, 22n3, 275, 278n20
Stich, S. 16–17, 20, 22n10, 23n11, 168n5, 197, 201, 205, 307n17, 371–4, 380n4, 380n7, 386, 388–9, 391, 394, 398–9, 401n1, 402n7, 415–16, 432, 507, 549

Strawon, P. F. 136, 146n16, 294
Stuart, M. 8, 11–12, 19–20, 21n3, 22n7, 23n10, 186, 286–7, 307, 329–31, 336–7, 339, 529, 532, 533, 539, 540n5–6
Stump, E. 188–90
subjunctive mood 245, 331, 473, 475
supposition 78, 80, 83, 103, 157, 177–2, 244, 508
suspension of judgment 3, 31, 36, 38–40
Swan, L. S. 252, 254
synthetic a priori 333, 337
Szilard, L. 17, 213–14, 454–67

tame knots 258, 262
Thagard, P. 22n10, 185–6, 451, 526
thought experiment–anti-thought experiment pairs 446, 481n2, 546, 548, 555n2
thought experiments: aesthetic properties of 6, 19, 188–90, 236–7, 498–509, 514–17, 521–2, 534–8; as arguments 8–9, 14, 20, 217, 281–92, 320, 409, 444, 515, 519, 550–1; characterization of 2–3, 16–17, 20, 32–4, 48, 57–9, 77–8, 93, 154–7, 173–4, 196, 211–12, 243–4, 257, 277n1, 281, 283, 293–5, 309, 327–8, 425–35, 440–2, 469–70, 485, 498–9, 514–15, 545–56; vs. computer simulations 18, 186, 252–3, 255n6, 472, 484–95; and conditionals 4, 33–4, 78, 88, 412–13, 420; constructive 73, 199, 202, 282, 286, 294–5, 305; core vs. extended 196–207; counter 189–90, 244; as counterexamples 16, 35, 64–5, 199, 272, 406, 408–15, 421–2; destructive 199, 203–4, 282, 294–5, 305; examples of *see* special index on thought experiments; as (parts of) explanations 530–2, 534, 538; and fictions 19, 44, 190, 197, 249, 290, 414, 417, 430, 441, 465, 503–9, 512–22, 552; formal reconstructions of 16, 410–14; function of 1–14, 19, 31–2, 34–5, 37–40, 48, 54, 57–60, 73–4, 77–8, 156, 175, 190–1, 198–202, 212, 243–4, 254, 257, 275–7, 281, 294–5, 322, 406–9, 441–2, 466, 473, 485–7, 515–16, 526–7, 530–4, 545–56; heuristic 54, 74, 75n22, 76n27, 167, 200–1, 203, 206, 209n3, 217, 293, 408, 418, 485, 503, 519; illustrative 4, 7, 34–5, 47–8, 60, 67, 158, 166, 189, 196–7, 200–1, 212, 215, 217–18, 228, 244–9, 258, 281, 387, 407–9, 420, 459, 466, 517, 524, 526–7, 540n3; indispensability of 6, 73, 78, 154, 157–8, 166–7, 249, 287; kinds of possibility in *see* possibility; life of their own 3, 20, 174, 408, 485–6, 546–549, 554; as mental models 6, 8, 12–14, 19–20, 172, 254, 288–90, 309–26, 344, 488, 498–9, 509n1, 520, 551–2; vs. models 173–6, 476, 486–96; as props for the imagination 18, 20, 503, 552–554; as

propositional vs. non-propositional 14, 17, 189–90, 198, 288, 314–15, 320, 362n5, 363n16, 441–3, 452, 499, 510n9, 520–2, 528, 535–7, 545, 550; as puzzles 41n8, 54, 154, 387–8, 388n6, 407–9, 418, 422n1, 485, 537–8, 540n10; realizability of 77, 163–4, 197, 334–5; relation to other kinds of experiment 6, 10, 41n6, 49, 57, 156, 277n13, 293, 327–8, 332–6, 439, 554–5; replication of 551, 554–5; rhetorical 103, 200, 208, 289, 418, 486; in textbooks 1, 34, 200, 211–12, 356, 407, 409, 530–1, 538; theory-internal (clarificatory) 13, 70, 196, 201–2, 220, 228, 254, 282, 387, 515, 516, 533; wide vs. narrow conception of 155–6, 171, 196–7, 244, 310; *see also* core vs. extended

Tierra (a-life) 252–3

Tobia, K. 16–17, 20, 22n10, 23n11, 168n5, 197, 201, 205, 372–4, 398–9, 402n7, 507, 549

trefoil knot 263, 275

understanding 11–12, 19–20, 201, 281, 322, 336, 397, 500, 513, 516, 520, 526–40; degrees of 538; explanatory 528–34, 538–9, 540n3; kinds of 527–9; objectual 528–30, 532–6, 538–9, 540n3, 540n7; practical 529–30, 534, 536–9, 540n3, 540n11; as a success term 538–9; thought experiments and 526–40

unknot 259, 261, 263, 275

Urbaniak, R. 288

Ursula K. LeGuin 168n10

utopia 153, 159–60, 162–3, 165, 167, 168n10

van Fraassen, B. 301, 531, 540n5

vera causa 245

vertex transitivity 269–72

visualization 2, 13, 222, 236–7, 289, 310, 314–19, 334, 356, 464, 493, 495, 537; in mathematics 7–8, 259–66, 270–1, 274, 276

wahm see Ibn Sīnā

Walton, K. 18, 499, 503–4, 507–9, 510n9, 552–4

Weber, Marcel 7, 251, 471, 527

Weinberg, J. 307n17, 372–3, 378–9, 380n7, 386–9, 391, 394, 401n1, 401n6, 415–16, 432, 549

Weisberg, M. 247, 473–4, 481n1, 496n3

Westphal, K. 5, 21, 136, 138–9, 142, 145n1–2, 145n7–8, 145n10, 146n13–15, 329–30

wild knots *see* tame knots

Wilkes, K. 205, 451

Will, F. L. 129, 145

Williamson, T. 11–12, 156, 161, 285, 293, 297, 299, 377, 380n5, 388, 401n6, 409–15, 420–1, 423n2–3, 423n5, 423n13, 531

Wiltsche, H. 15, 342, 509n1, 510n7

Winsberg, E. 252, 487, 496n6

Wittgenstein, L. 1, 3, 5, 142–5, 337, 362n7

Young, J. 512, 514, 516